American Indian Medicine

The Civilization of the American Indian Series

American Indian Medicine

by VIRGIL J. VOGEL

University of Oklahoma Press
Norman and London

To Louise, Johnny, Carol, and Eugene

by Virgil J. Vogel

Indian Place Names in Illinois (Springfield, Illinois, 1963)
American Indian Medicine (Norman, 1970)
This Country Was Ours: A Documentary History of the American Indian (New York, 1972)
Iowa Place Names of Indian Origin (Iowa City, 1983)
Indian Place Names in Michigan (Ann Arbor, 1986)

Library of Congress Catalog Card Number: 69–10626
ISBN: 0–8061–2293–5

American Indian Medicine is Volume 95 in The Civilization of the American Indian Series.

10   11   12   13   14   15   16   17   18   19   20   21   22

Preface to the Paperback Edition

When *American Indian Medicine* was first published twenty years ago, it had few rivals in its field. Often the material available in obscure places had a narrow focus, dealing with particular tribes or regions or the treatment of specific ills. For a long time the prevailing view was that Indian medicine was a branch of folklore and had little scientific interest.

There were some notable exceptions. Among the earliest was Dr. Jacob M. Toner, whose "Address to the Rocky Mountain Medical Association, 1877" (*Virginia Medical Monthly*, August, 1877) praised Indian medical practitioners for, among other things, their use of syringes, sutures, and the enema, their knowledge of anatomy, and their childbirth practices. Dr. Aleš

Hrdlička treated Indian healing practices with considerable respect in his *Physiological and Medical Observations among the Indians of Southwestern United States and Northern Mexico* (1908) and, a generation later, in his article, "Disease, Medicine and Surgery among the American Aborigines" (*Journal of the American Medical Association*, November 12, 1932). Dr. Harlow Brooks, who was intimately acquainted with Ojibwa and Navajo medicine, left no doubt of his favorable opinions in his two articles, both entitled "The Medicine of the American Indian," in *Bulletin of the New York Academy of Medicine*, June, 1929, and *Journal of Laboratory and Clinical Medicine*, October, 1933. Contemporary with Hrdlička and Brooks, Dr. Eric Stone brought forth his little book, *Medicine among the American Indians* (1932; reprint, 1962), which listed many medicinal herbs and their uses among Indians and praised Indian practices in childbirth, wounds, and fractures. He pointed out that fifty-nine drugs then listed in the *U.S. Pharmacopeia* were borrowed from the Indians.

The activities of Indian medicine men drew the favorable attention of William T. Corlett in *The Medicine Man of the American Indian and His Cultural Background* (1935). Rounding out this decade of rediscovery was Wilton Krogman's article, "Medical Practices and Diseases of the Aboriginal American Indians" (*Ciba Symposia*, April, 1939).

Still, the majority of the medical profession kept its distance from what was regarded as little more than bizarre superstition. Most writing in the field was done by anthropologists, ethnobotanists, folklorists, and pharmacists. My own interest in the subject was first attracted by Margaret Kreig's *Green Medicine* (1964), which dealt with the search for new botanical drugs. I knew of claims that some Indian medicinal substances were effective in treating certain ills, not to mention their psychological effect. As one without medical training, I felt unqualified to make a scientific study of Indian medicine, but believed I might trace the history of Indian drugs and medical practice and their influence on conventional medicine.

As earlier noted, this study was accepted for a Ph.D. dissertation in the University of Chicago history department. The work was mainly done in libraries and archives. Although I had briefly visited about sixty Indian reservations and communities, I was not trained in anthropological fieldwork, and, in any case, the tyranny of time dictated that a field study would have a narrow focus. The libraries were already crowded with forgotten tomes containing the results of narrow studies. I am grateful that my mentors, Professor Daniel Boorstin, Dr. Lester King, and Professor Fred Eggan, tolerated a survey of the curative methods and the medicinal drugs of the Indians of the entire United States. Such a project required, among other things, an examination of the journals, letters, and accounts (published or unpublished) of dozens of explorers, missionaries, traders, and military personnel. The resulting manuscript was accepted for my degree in 1967, and, after some revision and expansion, it was accepted for publication by Savoie Lottinville at the University of Oklahoma Press. It was published in 1970, and a paperback edition appeared in 1973, by arrangement with Ballantine. Though the paperback edition sold out quickly, the cloth edition remained in print through five printings, ending in 1990. Presently the University of Oklahoma Press is issuing the first paperback edition under its own banner, and for this I was invited to write a new preface, which affords an opportunity to deal with certain questions that have arisen.

According to reports, this book was in demand among young people captivated by the drug culture. They were probably disappointed, because the number of psychoactive drugs used by American Indians was small. Some popular drugs, such as the adventive marijuana, were not used at all by early American Indians. The American hemp plant (*Apocynum cannabinum*) was used by Indians mainly for cordage. Some hallucinogenic fungi and the peyote cactus were used in Mexico, and the latter spread slowly into the United States, but did not become important here until after 1890.

In western South America, coca leaves were widely used, and their derivative, cocaine, a local anesthetic, was eventually adopted in conventional medicine. W. E. Safford first listed the native American drugs of this class in his forgotten article, "Narcotic Plants and Stimulants of the Ancient Americans," published in the *Annual Report of the Smithsonian Institution* for 1916.

From letters I received, it appeared that some readers wanted a guide to self-treatment. I declared in my original preface that I had no medical training and could give no judgment on remedies or treatments described, and I certainly had no quarrel with scientific medicine. To discourage use of my book for self-treatment, I avoided details of dosage or methods of preparation. Since some plant medicines can have toxic or even fatal consequences, it is hazardous for inexpert persons to use them.

Following publication of this book there was an efflorescence of books dealing with Indian and natural remedies, including reprints of several forgotten works of years past. There were also first-time studies of the medicines of some tribes and regions and a few that plagiarized my work. Whether this sudden spurt was a reflection of the times or whether it was partly inspired by my book, I do not know. My book was well received, however, and was widely reviewed.

While most reviews were favorable, a few were not. The book was criticized by Dr. Erwin Ackerknecht, a reputable medical historian, in the *Bulletin of the History of Medicine*, Spring, 1972. My reply to Dr. Ackerknecht was not published by the *Bulletin*. I will send a copy of his review and my unpublished reply to anyone who sends a request with a stamped, self-addressed envelope to me at 1819 Maple Street, Northbrook, Illinois 60062.

There were also a few reviews that tried to make a joke of Indian medicine, comparing it to irrational superstition or the conjurations of old-time medicine shows. The last-named fraudulent enterprises were white, not Indian. As for religious rituals, they were and are frequently a central part of the native healing process, and many observers believe that these features have valuable psychotherapeutic effects. Whatever our judgment about their spiritual context, the curative agents used deserve a fair evaluation.

The native American medicine man (or woman), long hounded by the government as an alleged barrier to civilization, still continues as a healer in many places. At least a dozen books about medicine people have appeared in the last decade. The Cree healer Russell Willier, of northern Alberta, is the subject of the most recent one, *Cry of the Eagle*, by David Young et al. (1989). Willier participated with researchers from the University of Alberta in a psoriasis treatment project. Indian healers enjoy much esteem among southwestern tribes, especially the Navajo. The Indian Health Service often uses them as consultants.

There is sufficient interest in the practical and mystical aspects of Indian medicine to induce impostors, both red and white, to proclaim themselves the possessors of ancient secrets and to charge fat fees for performance of sweat baths, purification rites, and so forth. Such practitioners have been condemned by legitimate Indian groups.

Some people mistakenly believe that synthetic drugs have eliminated Indian and natural remedies. The first *U.S. Pharmacopeia* (1820) listed 296 substances, of which 130 were drugs used by Indians. Some were dropped and others were added at the decennial (now quinquennial) revisions, but altogether about 220 substances used by the Indians were listed in the *USP* and *National Formulary* between 1820 and 1965. The number of herbal medicines, of which Indian drugs formed such a large part, indeed declined after 1890. Still it is significant that 41 new substances of American Indian usage became official after 1890.

USAN and the USP Dictionary of Drug Names through June, 1981, lists thirty-two substances or derivatives from substances used medicinally by American Indians. This figure excludes numerous compounds that are partially based on such native drugs as the antimalarial *quinine*, from *cinchona*. Among others are *atropine*, derived from *datura* (jimson weed), used as a parasympatholytic; *cascara*, the notable cathartic; *cocaine*; *tubocurarine chloride*, incorporating elements of *curare* (arrow poison), a muscle relaxant; *ipecac*, the famous emetic, from the rain forest; *podophyllum* and its resin, from May apple root, in powdered form once a cathartic, now a caustic; *kaolin*, an adsorbent; *papain*, from *papaya*, an enzyme; *Peruvian balsam*, a rubefacient; and *balsam of Tolu*, an expectorant.

As it is my purpose to do no more than present a factual account of the history and present status of Indian medicine, I make no predictions about its future. I wish only to illuminate a little-understood aspect of American cultural and scientific history. All else can be evaluated by others.

VIRGIL J. VOGEL

Northbrook, Illinois
February 5, 1990

Preface to the
First Edition

Most of the general works dealing with American Indian medicine dwell upon its shamanistic aspects. While ritual played an important part in Indian curing procedure, there was also extensive use of what has been called rational therapy. In the latter, indigenous botanical drugs played an extraordinary part, and they receive major attention in this book. The author is a historian without medical expertise and can therefore render no judgment on the efficacy of the remedies and treatments described.

To American Indians the term medicine embraced much more than the cure of disease and the healing of injuries, but the focus here is on these aspects, and particularly those that we have borrowed. For the sake of clarity, a definition of terms is in order. This book follows the definition of medicine given in *Dorland's Medical Dictionary*: "the art or science of healing diseases," but with the addition of "treatment of external injuries and other conditions involving human physical welfare." Pharmacology, which is a central theme here, signifies knowledge regarding drugs, and drugs are defined as "any medicinal substance."

Botanical nomenclature, both common and scientific, changes frequently. In listing herein the plant drugs which were official in *The Pharmacopeia of the United States* or *National Formulary*, the nomenclature used in those compendia is followed. When authors are cited or quoted, their own nomenclature, however archaic, must be used. In other cases, the principal authority for the names of nonarboreal plants mentioned in this book is Fernald's revision of *Gray's Manual of Botany*.[1] For the nomenclature of trees, Sargent's *Manual of the Trees of North America*[2] has been relied upon. Synonyms, both common and Latin, are provided in some cases, but in a work of this sort, an exhaustive synonymy cannot be attempted.

This work began as a doctoral dissertation in the Department of History at the University of Chicago, but in preparation for publication it was amended and expanded at some length. I am deeply indebted to the members of my dissertation committee who were so helpful during the original work. Dr. Lester S. King, medical historian, pathologist, member of the medical faculty of the university, and senior editor of the *Journal of the American Medical Association*, served as chairman. Professor Daniel J. Boorstin, of the Department of History, and Professor Fred Eggan of the Department of Anthropology, both distinguished men in their fields, were the other committee members

[1] *Gray's Manual of Botany*, rewritten and expanded by Merritt Lyndon Fernald (8th [centennial] ed.; New York, American Book Co., 1950).

[2] Charles Sprague Sargent, *Manual of the Trees of North America* (2 vols.; New York, Dover Publications, 1961).

who undertook the onerous task of guiding my efforts. The advice and encouragement of Dr. Boorstin, my principal mentor in advanced graduate work, is beyond repayment. All of my advisers guided and assisted but left me free to write what I wished, and I am to blame for any shortcomings in the final result.

Valuable help and advice were given to me by Dr. Glenn Sonnedecker, of the University of Wisconsin School of Pharmacy and the American Institute of the History of Pharmacy. Among those who gave other assistance, such as providing source material or answering inquiries by mail, were Mrs. Katherine Carlson of Abbott Laboratories, Donald Chaput of the Michigan Historical Commission, Frances Lee Harper of Chapel Hill, North Carolina, Gertrude Hess, associate librarian of the American Philosophical Society, John R. Leitz, associate director of research for the Hires Company, Dolores Nemec, librarian of the Power Pharmaceutical Library of Madison, Mary Frances Rhymer of the Chicago Historical Society, Robert Rosenthal and Helen Smith of the University of Chicago Libraries, Dr. William C. Sturtevant of the Smithsonian Institution, and John Warning, R.Ph. Mrs. Goldie Gillespie typed the bibliography, and my wife, Louise Vogel, drew two illustrations and helped in other ways too numerous to describe.

St. Louis University lent Edward Francis Maguire's master's thesis on "Frequent Diseases and Intended Remedies of the Frontier," and the University of Pennsylvania furnished a reproduction of Anna Katherine Stimson's master's thesis on "Contributions toward a Bibliography of the Medicinal Use of Plants by the Indians of the United States." Other institutions which aided me are the Chicago Historical Society, the John Crerar Library, the Field Museum of Natural History, the library of the Medical School of the University of Illinois, the Indiana Historical Society, the Lloyd Library and Museum of Cincinnati, the Midwest Inter-Library Center, the National Research Council, the Newberry Library of Chicago, the Searle Library of the

Medical School of Northwestern University, and the University of Chicago Libraries. To many people in these institutions I am deeply grateful.

VIRGIL J. VOGEL

Chicago, Illinois

Contents

Illustrations

"Jimson weed"
Witch hazel
Sweet gum
Flowering dogwood
May apple
Sassafras

American Indian Medicine

I.

What the
Red Men
Gave Us

During the bitter cold winter of 1535–36, the three ships of Jacques Cartier were frozen fast in the fathom-deep ice of the St. Lawrence River near the site of Montreal. Isolated by four feet of snow, the company of 110 men subsisted on the fare stored in the holds of their ships. Soon scurvy was so rampant among them that by mid-March, 25 men had died and the others, "only three or foure excepted," were so ill that hope for their recovery was abandoned. As the crisis deepened, Cartier had the good fortune to encounter once again the local Indian chief, Domagaia, who had cured himself of the same disease with "the juice and sappe of a certain Tree." The Indian women gathered branches of the magical tree, "boiling the bark and leaves for a decoction, and placing the dregs upon the legs." All those so treated rapidly recovered their health, and the Frenchmen marveled at the curative skill of the natives.

These Indians had never heard of vitamin C, and there was no value in the external application of their remedy. Through trial and error since prehistoric times, however, they had stumbled upon an effective internal remedy for the deficiency disease known as scurvy, which most Europeans believed to be caused by bad air. More than two hundred years after Cartier's experience, James Lind, a British naval surgeon, having read of this incident, launched the experiments which proved the dietary basis of scurvy.

For a long time our ethnic arrogance foreclosed any serious attention to the medical knowledge which the "savages" might have. Our ancestors were repelled by the "superstitious rites" which often accompanied the native curing procedures, and shrank from the notion that an "uncivilized" race might have something to teach them. Consequently, "Indian medicine" long remained the last resort of the explorer and frontiersman, and was later the adopted child of "folk medicine." Only after it had gone through these stages, in the course of centuries, did some of the Indian discoveries attract the attention of scientific medicine. Much was found to be worthless, but an astonishing number of Indian drugs and treatments were found to be of enormous value. Even in comparatively recent times, Indian discoveries have helped to open new frontiers in medical history. Peruvian Indians knew the narcotic effects of coca leaves for hundreds of years, but not until 1884 did Carl Koller ascertain the value of cocaine as a local anesthetic.[1] In this century, practical applications have been found for curare, the arrow poison of the Amazon tribes. Dr. Frederick Banting, discoverer of insulin, credited Indian healers with the "pharmaceutical spadework" which led to it. Prior to his untimely death, he had planned to write a book on Indian and Eskimo medical practice. Indian drugs which were

[1] Chauncey D. Leake, "Historical Notes on the Pharmacology of Anesthesia," *Journal of the History of Medicine*, Vol. I, No. 4 (October, 1946), 576–79.

used to suppress ovulation and control the menstrual cycle started researchers on the road which led to "the pill." Some Indians even stumbled upon the working principle of modern antibiotics, although of course they were unaware of how and why certain molds and fungi produced desired results.

Clearly there is a vast untold story here. When Frederick Jackson Turner set forth his thesis on the frontier influence in American history, near the end of the last century, he pointed out that the pioneer, at first, was compelled by the environment to live like an Indian. "The wilderness masters the colonist," he wrote, and "the frontier environment is at first too strong for the man. He must accept the conditions which it furnishes, or perish."[2] We know he dressed like an Indian, hunted like an Indian, and planted Indian corn. He also accepted native remedies and treatments for his illnesses. "In the days of our sickness," wrote Hector St. John de Crèvecoeur in the eighteenth century, "we shall have recourse to their [the Indians'] medical knowledge, which is well calculated for the simple diseases to which they are subject."[3] Such words were inspired by necessity rather than by any Rousseauvian concept of the noble savage. Circumstances compelled the adoption of Indian medicine on the frontier, but its influence did not stop there, or even at the seacoast; nor did it end with the passing of the frontier.

Acculturation, as the anthropologists indicate, proceeds in more than one direction, although the drama of the conquest and settlement of America has tended to obscure this reality. We have seen so much of the visible aspects of American Indian culture diminish or disappear and have lost sight of the origin of so much that we have borrowed that there is little wonder that awareness is lacking in some circles concerning the extent of "counter-acculturation" upon the numerically and politically dominant race. It is here sought to bring to light something that has been ignored or forgotten, and to provide some small basis for a new appraisal of the acculturation process in America.

[2] *The Frontier in American History* (New York, Henry Holt & Co., 1958), 4.
[3] *Letters from an American Farmer*, 218.

The most important evidence of Indian influence on American medicine is seen in the fact that more than two hundred indigenous drugs which were used by one or more Indian tribes have been official in *The Pharmacopeia of the United States of America* for varying periods since the first edition appeared in 1820, or in the *National Formulary* since it began in 1888.[4] So complete, in fact, was the aboriginal knowledge of their native flora that Indian usage can be demonstrated for all but a bare half dozen, at most, of our indigenous vegetable drugs. In a surprising number of instances, moreover, the aboriginal uses of these drugs corresponded with those approved in the *Dispensatory of the United States*. There is in addition a list of several hundred aboriginal remedies which have been used in domestic medicine as well as by physicians, although they have not won official acceptance.

Dr. Erwin Ackerknecht has declared that "there are no good modern monographs on Indian medicine."[5] What is especially lacking is a study of the extent to which American Indian remedies and therapeutic practices have been adopted by white society. A few comments which have been made by some medical historians will serve to illustrate this need. Colonel P. M. Ashburn, of the United States Army Medical Corps, has declared that "the savage Indians and the Negroes contributed little or nothing of value to any branch of medicine, and from them we received a mass of superstition and ignorance that reinforced and strengthened what we had brought from Europe, a heritage that still plagues us." Not even the Aztecs or the Incas, in Ashburn's view,

4 This number includes about four dozen drugs which are native to Latin America. It is difficult to give an exact number for several reasons. Several derivatives and by-products are sometimes listed as separate drugs. Different varieties and species are sometimes listed separately, and at other times under one pharmaceutical name. Various parts of a plant (fruit, flowers, seeds, leaves, stems, trunk bark, root bark) are sometimes official at different times. Pharmaceutical names are sometimes changed, and there has been occasional confusion over the identity of species. There is also some disagreement concerning the place of origin of some plant species. We have here given a minimal number. See further comment on p. 404.

5 *A Short History of Medicine*, 230.

contributed anything valuable to the sum of European medicine.[6] Yet the Aztecs, whose herbal knowledge is revealed in the *Badianus Manuscript*,[7] knew and used cochineal, liquidambar, cotton, tobacco, passion flowers, *datura*, and other drugs which have been adopted into European and American pharmacopeias. South American Indians contributed such well-known drugs as coca, cinchona, curare, and ipecac to world medicine. The Mayas used capsicum, chenopodium, guaiacum, and vanilla, along with many other drugs which were later adopted by Europeans.[8]

While there is no doubt that Indian medicine, from Bering Strait to the Strait of Magellan, was nowhere a science, there are perhaps grounds for comparing it in that respect with European medicine of the same period, which was still under the sway of the doctrine of signatures and the Galenic humors. While the Aztecs used such substances as decomposed corpse, excrement, and menstrual blood, along with their useful simples, the *Pharmacopoeia Londinensis* of 1618 included mummy dust, human and pigeon excrement, and stag's penis. As late as the eighteenth century, the materia medica of Herman Boerhaave included dragon's blood, oil of scorpions, troches of vipers, crab's eyes, and chalk.[9]

In retrospect, one who is cognizant of all the miracles of modern scientific medicine may find little to admire in American primitive medicine, but physicians contemporary with the early exploratory period sometimes took a more favorable view. Nicholas Monardes, "a physician of Seville" (1493–1588), extolled the virtues of such products of the American native materia medica as tobacco, sassafras, guaiacum, sarsaparilla, and balsams,

---

[6] *The Ranks of Death: A Medical History of the Conquest of America*, 51.

[7] Emily Walcott Emmart (ed.), *Badianus Manuscript . . . by Martin de la Cruz and Juannes Badianus*. This was probably the first herbal written in America after the Conquest, and was composed and illustrated in the year 1552 by two Aztec apothecaries who had been educated by the Spanish priests.

[8] Ralph L. Roys, *The Ethno-Botany of the Maya.*

[9] *Herman Boerhaave's Materia Medica: or, a Series of Prescriptions Adapted to the Sections of his Practical Aphorisms Concerning the Knowledge and Cure of Diseases*, 96, 108, 121, 185.

7

wherewith thei doe cure and make whole many infirmities, which if wee did lacke them, thei were incurable, and without any remedie . . . for which cause I did pretend to treate, and to write, of all thynges that thei bryng from out Indias, whiche serveth for the arte and use of Medicine.[10]

The American Indian contribution to medicine is minimized by John Duffy,[11] who takes issue with the claim of Charles Gayarré that the Natchez Indians discovered over three hundred medicinal plants, of which a collection was sent to France by the King's commissary, La Chaise, together with a memoir on the subject by Le Page du Pratz.[12] In reply, Duffy cites Dr. Eric Stone's report that the Indians added fifty-nine drugs to the "modern pharmacopeia,"[13] and charges that Gayarré was led astray by his enthusiasm, stemming from the fact that he "belonged to the generation of James Fenimore Cooper and the noble savage." Stone, however, merely totaled the number of Indian medicinals which were official at the time he wrote. Moreover, many Indian drugs which have been used in medicine have never been included in the pharmacopeia.

Dr. Johann David Schöpf, a German physician, published in 1787 a list of 335 vegetable remedies indigenous to the eastern United States,[14] many of which were reputedly learned from the Indians. The Reverend Manasseh Cutler in 1785 gave credit to the Indians for many of the 379 indigenous medical plants which he described.[15] The first *United States Pharmacopeia*, in 1820, listed only 225 vegetable remedies, foreign and domestic. Heber W. Youngken, a pharmaceutical historian, in 1924–25 culled from the work of various investigators a list of 450 plant remedies

10 *Joyfull Newes out of the Newe Founde Worlde*, I, 10.

11 *The Rudolph Matas History of Medicine in Louisiana*, I, 42.

12 *History of Louisiana* (4 vols., 3d ed.; New Orleans, Armand Hawkins, 1885), I, 348.

13 *Medicine Among the American Indians*, 121.

14 *Materia Medica Americana, Potissimum Regni Vegetabilis.*

15 *An Account of Some of the Vegetable Productions Naturally Growing in this Part of America.*

used by the Indians.[16] In the present work, confined to remedies used by both Indians and whites, more than 500 botanical drugs have been listed. Huron H. Smith listed more than 200 botanical remedies used by the Meskwaki tribe alone, of which very few are adventive plants.[17]

Some ethnologists have understated the extent of Indian medical discoveries. Ruth Underhill listed only two medicinal plants, cinchona and ipecac, as native to nuclear America.[18] Walter James Hoffman, who was initiated into the *Midewiwin* or Grand Medicine Society in both the Ojibwa and Menominee tribes, was convinced that the efficacious Indian remedies had been learned from whites:

> When there is an administration of a remedy for a given complaint, based upon true scientific principles, it is only in consequence of such practice having been acquired from the whites, as it has usually been the custom of the Catholic Fathers to utilize all ordinary and available remedies for the treatment of the common disorders of life.

After listing fifty-six drugs used by the Ojibwas, many of which he found to be, from a scientific and medical standpoint, specific remedies for the complaints for which they were recommended, he remarked that "It is probable that long continued intercourse between the Ojibwa and the Catholic Fathers, who were tolerably well versed in the ruder forms of medication, had much to do with improving an older and purely aboriginal form of practicing medical magic."[19] Even a cursory examination of the *Jesuit Relations*, however, indicates that the French priests were more disposed to rely on prayer and European drugs in sickness, and

16 "Drugs of the North American Indians," *American Journal of Pharmacy*, Vol. XCVI, No. 96 (July, 1924), 485–502; Vol. XCVII, No. 97 (March, 1925), 158–185, Vol. XCVII, No. 98 (April, 1925), 257–71.

17 *Ethnobotany of the Meskwaki Indians*, 175–326. Hereafter cited as *Meskwaki Ethnobotany*.

18 *Red Man's America*, 17.

19 "The Mide'wiwin or 'Grand Medicine Society' of the Ojibwa," *Seventh Annual Report of the Bureau of American Ethnology, 1885–86*, 159, 197.

that occasionally the Indian tried to teach them something of indigenous remedies. Among the Hurons in 1637, Father François Joseph Le Mercier wrote that a sorcerer proposed sweat, prayers, and certain roots to cure fevers among the French, and that the Indian "named to us two roots,—very efficacious, he said against fevers,—and instructed us in the method of using them." The priest replied that sweating and prayers to the devil were of no use, but "as far as natural remedies were concerned, we would willingly employ them, and that he would oblige us by teaching us some of them."[20]

Dr. Robert Carlisle Major has declared that the medicine of the Indians was "as good as could be expected, and, freed of its grosser superstitions, would not have been so far inferior, in its practical results, to that of their conquerors," but concluded that "we look in vain for any outstanding contribution and that is natural in the very order of things."[21] In contrast, Melvin R. Gilmore, in his study of the medicine of the Plains tribes, held that the Indians, because of their dependence upon nature, were especially observant of their natural environment and reported that his informants "generally showed keen powers of perception of the structure, habits, and local distribution of plants throughout a wide range of observation, thus manifesting the incipiency of phytogeography, plant ecology, and morphology."[22] Among the pharmaceutical contributions of Indians north of the Río Grande, Dr. Stone has singled out cascara sagrada, lobelia, puccoon, and cohosh as worthy of note.[23] Dr. Harlow Brooks praised the Indians for their knowledge of laxative, diuretic, emetic, and febrifuge drugs, and added that the American variety of foxglove was correctly used by them for its cardiac stimulant properties for hundreds of years before Withering discovered digitalis in

20 Reuben Gold Thwaites (ed.), *The Jesuit Relations and Allied Documents*, XIII, 103–105.

21 "Aboriginal American Medicine North of Mexico," *Annals of Medical History*, N.S., Vol. X, No. 6 (November, 1938), 547.

22 "Uses of Plants by Indians of the Missouri River Region," *Thirty-third Annual Report of the Bureau of American Ethnology, 1911–12*, 137.

23 Stone, *Medicine Among the American Indians*, 121.

England.[24] Captain John G. Bourke, an army officer with experience on the Indian frontier late in the last century, was convinced that "the world owes a large debt to the medicine-men of America, who first discovered the virtues of coca, sarsaparilla, jalap, cinchona, and guiacum." Bourke called attention to their knowledge of enemata, for which they used a syringe made of an animal bladder and a hollow leg bone.[25] Several writers have credited the Indians with the independent invention of this useful device. According to Clark Wissler, South American Indians used a rubber syringe in pre-Columbian times,[26] and Gilmore claims that the animal bladder and bone syringe was in use by Indians of the United States prior to contact with Europeans.[27] Charlevoix noted the use of such an instrument by Canadian Indians in 1721,[28] and later writers reported its use in widely scattered places.[29] Syringes were also used to medicate wounds.[30]

In a plea for abandonment of the prevalent bias against folk science, the anthropologist Weston La Barre has called attention to the extraordinary contributions of South American Indians to medicine, and declared:

As scientists we cannot afford the luxury of an ethnocentric snobbery which assumes *a priori* that primitive cultures have nothing whatsoever to contribute to civilization. Our civilization is in fact a compendium of such borrowings, and it is a demonstrable error to believe that contacts of "higher"

[24] "The Medicine of the American Indian," *Journal of Laboratory and Clinical Medicine*, Vol. XIX, No. 1 (October, 1933), 2, 17–19.

[25] "The Medicine-Men of the Apache," *Ninth Annual Report of the Bureau of American Ethnology, 1887–88*, 471.

[26] *Indians of the United States*, 295.

[27] Gilmore, "Uses of Plants by Indians of the Missouri River Region," *Thirty-third Annual Report of the Bureau of American Ethnology, 1911–12*, 90.

[28] *Journal of a Voyage to North America*, ed. Louise Phelps Kellogg, I, 162.

[29] A. I. Hallowell, "The Bulbed Enema Syringe in North America," *American Anthropologist*, N.S., Vol. XXXVII (1935), 708–10.

[30] Zina Pitcher in Henry Rowe Schoolcraft, *Historical and Statistical Information Respecting the History, Condition and Prospects of the Indian Tribes of the United States*, IV, 513.

and "lower" cultures show benefits flowing exclusively in one direction. Indeed, a good case could probably be made that in the long run it is the "higher" culture which benefits the more through being enriched, while the "lower" culture not uncommonly disappears entirely as a result of the contact.[31]

31 "Folk Medicine and Folk Science," *Journal of American Folk-Lore*, Vol. LV (October–December, 1942), 199–200.

II.

Indian Theories
of Disease,
and
Shamanistic
Practices

It is not here contended that American Indians used scientific methods of experiment and reasoning in adopting remedies and methods of treatment. Indian medicine was not more rational than that of Europe at the time of the discovery, with the possible exception of obstetric practices; whether it was less so is a debatable question. The number of worthless simples used by Indians is perhaps not greater than that found in early European works on materia medica. Although sixteenth-century European medicine was on the threshold of a tremendous forward movement, it was still filled with superstition and untested theories.

Indian treatment of externally caused injuries, in which the origin of the ailment was perfectly obvious, was usually rational and often effective. In such a category were fractures, dislocations, wounds of all kinds, including snake and insect bites, skin irritations, bruises, and the like. In cases of persistent internal disease, where the cause was not apparent, the usual Indian custom was to attribute the disease to supernatural agency. If ordinary medicines did not soon bring relief, they resorted to shamanistic methods, such as incantations, charms, prayers, dances, the shaking of rattles, and the beating of drums.

Much has been written on these irrational features of Indian medicine; the literature on them is so extensive and readily available that there is no need here to do more than give a brief description. The disproportionate attention that they have received has tended to obscure much that is potentially useful in aboriginal medicine.

The beliefs of mankind in general, W. H. R. Rivers has indicated, attribute all diseases to one of three causes: human agency, supernatural agency, and natural causes.[1] Among the supernatural causes of disease avowed by American Indians, Forrest Clements listed sorcery, taboo violation, disease-object intrusion, spirit intrusion, and soul loss.[2] In certain tribes and areas, some of these causes are more important than others. An additional disease cause, prevalent among Iroquoian tribes, is unfulfilled dreams or desires.[3]

William T. Corlett's summary of disease-origin beliefs held by Indians of the southeastern Woodland area includes much that is applicable to other parts of the United States:

> Of the supernatural causes of disease, the most important probably are the spirits of the animals, who thus gain revenge for slights and abuses. Disrespect toward fire, such as urinating on the ashes, or throwing offal on it, or spitting on it, will

[1] *Medicine, Magic and Religion*, 7.

[2] "Primitive Concepts of Disease," *University of California Publications in American Archaeology and Ethnology*, Vol. XXXII (1932), 186–90.

[3] Anthony F. C. Wallace, "Dreams and Wishes of the Soul: A Type of Psychoanalytic Theory among the Seventeenth Century Iroquois," *American Anthropologist*, N.S., Vol. LX, No. 2 (April, 1958), 234–48.

bring disaster. Insults of like nature to the river have their penalty. Human ghosts who naturally feel lonesome for their friends and relatives cause a disease, so as to provide congenial company, while an animal ghost will cause trouble if respect has not been shown to its body after it has been killed. A powerful disease-bringer is the magic used by witches to cause sickness. Other causes of disease are dreams, omens, neglected taboos, and the evil influence attributed to woman during her catamenial period.[4]

Belief in witchcraft as a cause of disease is especially prevalent in Southwestern tribes. Among the Zuñis, Aleš Hrdlička reported, "when an epidemic or persistent ill fortune visits the tribe, and even in individual cases, a suspicion arises that the affliction is due to witchcraft. The offender is then sought, and:

the blame may fall upon some old, friendless man or woman or even upon a young person, who is pressed to confess the witchcraft. If he does so, it is said that he is simply exiled. . . . If the individual does not confess, he is severely tortured and maltreated, and may be hanged or otherwise killed.[5]

The principle of taboo violation is illustrated among the Senecas by Arthur C. Parker: "When one is ungrateful to the water-animals, as a wasteful fisherman, or a hunter who kills muskrats or beaver without asking permission or offering tobacco to their spirits, he becomes strangely ill, so it is believed."[6] It is then the task of the Otter society, one of their many medicine societies, to seek a cure by sprinkling the patient with spring water. An Indian who hunted animals or gathered herbs must always sing the necessary songs or prayers, or offer gifts of tobacco to the spirits of the animals or plants, as failure to do so might

[4] *The Medicine Man of the American Indian and His Cultural Background*, 146.

[5] *Physiological and Medical Observations among the Indians of Southwestern United States and Northern Mexico, Bulletin 34*, Bureau of American Ethnology, 169.

[6] "Secret Medicine Societies of the Seneca," *American Anthropologist*, N.S., Vol. XI, No. 2 (April–June, 1909), 161–85.

lead to bad luck or illness. Among the Creeks nearly every disease has the name of an animal which is supposed to have caused it.[7]

Disease-object intrusion means that a worm, snake, insect, or small animal has entered the body and caused illness. The disease-causing object is eliminated by drumming and singing, sucking, and sometimes by bitter medicines which were supposed to make the patient's body an uncomfortable place for the invader to reside. John Tanner, a white Indian captive for thirty years, has given a report of the extraction of disease objects by a Cree medicine man in Canada in the early nineteenth century:

> Old Mukkwah . . . imitated, as well as he could, various sounds, and endeavoured to make those standing by believe they proceeded from the breast of the sick man. At length he said he heard the sound of bad fire in the breast of the Naudoway, and putting one hand to his breast, the other and his mouth to the back, he continued for some time blowing and rubbing, when he, as if by accident, dropped a little ball on the ground. . . . he at length threw it into the fire, where it burned, with a little whizzing noise, like damp powder. This did not surprise me at all, as I saw he had taken the precaution to sprinkle a little powder on that part of the floor of the lodge where the ball fell. . . . he pretended that there was a snake in the breast of the sick man which he could not remove till the following day, when with similar preparations, and similar mummeries, he seemed to draw out of the body of the sick man, a small snake.[8]

Tanner added that the treatment, for which the shaman was paid in advance nine beaver skins and a piece of cloth, "had no perceptible effect upon the sick man."

Sucking was commonly employed in removing alleged foreign

[7] John R. Swanton, "Religious Beliefs and Medical Practices of the Creek Indians," *Forty-second Annual Report of the Bureau of American Ethnology,* *1924–25,* 636–70.

[8] *A Narrative of the Captivity and Adventures of John Tanner during Thirty Years Residence among the Indians* . . . , ed. Edwin James (Minneapolis, Ross & Haines, Inc., 1956), 74.

objects from the body, and was usually done with the assistance of a hollow tube, often a bone. The object extracted was not always animate; sometimes a stone or stick was held up by the doctor as the alleged offender. At other times, as in the treatment of wounds or snakebite, the sucking served a really therapeutic purpose, when the doctor drew out pus or venom and spit it into a bowl. As John Lee Maddox has pointed out, these primitive procedures, originally intended to draw out evil spirits, grew into the cupping procedures which have scientific value today.[9] Shamanistic sucking to remove disease, still practiced by some Indians, has been described in detail by Robert Ritzenthaler.[10]

Recounting a Minitaree medicine dance in 1833, Maximilian, Prince of Wied, related: "Almost all these people pretended that they had some animal in their stomach. . . . [one] pretended that he had three live lizards in his inside, [complaining] that these animals gave him pain."[11] Belief in the intrusion of extraneous objects as a disease cause existed also among whites. Fortescue Cuming (*Tour of the West*, 1807–1809), described this alleged incident at a spring near Bedford, Pennsylvania:

> It is perhaps worth while for the sake of a curious and important fact, to mention the extraordinary effects of the water on a gentleman who had visited this spring in the summer of 1809, and who before he left it, discharged from his bowels a *living monster*, described by some who saw it, as *a lizard*, by others as a *crab*, with legs, claws, &c. and of considerable size.—The unhappy man had been ill for several years, without being able to get any relief by the aid of skilful physicians. Immediately after this, he began to recover, and is now in a fair way of regaining his health.[12]

9 *The Medicine Man: A Sociological Study of the Character and Evolution of Shamanism*, 192.

10 *Chippewa Preoccupation with Health*, Milwaukee Public Museum Bulletin, Vol. XIX, No. 4 (1953), 193–94, 204–207.

11 *Travels in the Interior of North America, 1832–1834* (Part III), Vol. XXIV in Reuben Gold Thwaites (ed.), *Early Western Travels*, 34.

12 *Sketches of a Tour of the Western Country . . . Concluded in 1809*, Vol. IV in Thwaites (ed.), *Early Western Travels*, 65.

Spirit intrusion, like so many aboriginal concepts, was an idea widely held in Europe during the Middle Ages, and even in America in colonial days.[13] The numerous references in the Bible to persons being "possessed by devils" and to "casting out devils" provided a respectable background for such survivals of primitive lore. Dr. Walter C. Alvarez saw survivals of spirit-intrusion beliefs among white people in such figures of speech as "I wonder what possessed me to do that," and "I wonder what can have gotten into that child." He saw a similar signification in our calling apoplexy a "stroke," and the custom of "rapping on wood" to ward off evil,[14] which appears to be no different in principle than the Indian custom of beating on drums and shaking rattles.

The Cherokees recognized several dozen disease-causing spirits, animal and human. The medicine man's task was to determine which spirit was causing the trouble, as a different curative agent was prescribed for each of them.[15] Their linguistic relatives, the Iroquois, likewise held that pestilence and disease were often the work of evil spirits. Witches and enchanters, as well as poisonous roots and plants, were possessed of such spirits. At religious festivals, the aid of *Ha-wen-ne-yu* (great spirit) and his entourage was invoked to shield them from the designs of bad spirits.[16] When "the Quack comes to visit the Patient," Baron de Lahontan wrote of the Algonquins, "he examines him very carefully; *If the Evil Spirit be here,* says he, *we shall quickly dislodge him.*"[17] According-ing to Louis Hennepin, whose acquaintance was principally with the Illinois and Miamis, the "juggler" examined the patient's body and then announced "there's a Charm or Spell in such a part, in the Head, Leg, or Stomach, or where he thinks fit;

---

[13] Thomas Jefferson Wertenbaker, *The First Americans,* 169–70.

[14] "The Emergence of Modern Medicine from Ancient Folkways," *Annual Report of the Board of Regents of the Smithsonian Institution . . . June 30, 1938,* 417–20.

[15] James Mooney and Frans M. Olbrechts, *Swimmer Manuscript—Cherokee Sacred Formulas and Medicinal Prescriptions,* Bulletin 99, Bureau of American Ethnology, 42–50.

[16] Lewis H. Morgan, *League of the Ho-de-no-sau-nee or Iroquois,* I, 155.

[17] *New Voyages to North-America,* ed. Reuben Gold Thwaites, II, 467–68.

he adds, that he must remove this same Charm, and that it can't be done but with a great deal of difficulty."[18]

Another kind of spirit intrusion is the return of the souls of the dead to live in the bodies of their living relatives. Corlett reports that an Eskimo father, for three months after the death of a son, may not drink from an uncovered cup for fear of swallowing some ghost impurity, which would cause certain death. The Cayapas of Colombia believe that the soul of a dead person returns to his house to infect or hurt in some way the people living there, and the shaman seeks to force these spirits away with a wand.[19]

The Kootenais "believe that some evil spirit has caused the sickness, and that the evil spirit must be driven out."[20] The Hurons did not fear the souls of friends and relatives or enemies killed in battle, but the souls of tortured captives had to be expelled from their lodges by making "a horrible and universal noise."[21] The Alabamas believed that persons who had been near a grave would attract ghosts which could cause fits in those with whom they came into contact.[22]

Soul-loss illness occurred when the soul, during a dream, left the body and traveled about. Unless the soul could be brought back by some means, the patient would surely die.[23] Sometimes the soul was stolen by malignant shamans, witches, evil spirits, or earth dwarfs.[24] Some of the Hurons believed that souls were

---

[18] *A New Discovery of a Vast Country in America*, ed. Reuben Gold Thwaites, II, 485.

[19] Corlett, *Medicine Man of the American Indian*, 72, 200.

[20] Alexander F. Chamberlain, "Kootenay Medicine Men," *Journal of American Folk-Lore*, Vol. XIV (1901), 97.

[21] Elizabeth Tooker, *Ethnography of the Huron Indians, 1615-1649*, Bulletin 190, Bureau of American Ethnology, 39.

[22] Swanton, "Religious Beliefs and Medical Practices of the Creek Indians . . . ," *Forty-second Annual Report of the Bureau of American Ethnology, 1924-25*, 653.

[23] Hrdlička, *Physiological and Medical Observations*, 155.

[24] William W. Elmendorf, "Soul Loss Illness in Western North America," in Sol Tax (ed.), *Indian Tribes of Aboriginal America: Selected Papers of XXIXth International Congress of Americanists*, II, 108-10.

stolen by the Jesuit priests; Father Paul Le Jeune's relation of 1656–57 records that among this tribe a "calumny" was

> instigated by the Devil against the Father who started last Winter from Onnontaghe to come for us; his journey gave rise to the belief, that the great mortality which prevailed in the country was due to his search for souls, a box full of which he wished to take along with him. Although their traditional belief that Souls issue forth from their bodies from time to time, especially a short while before death, seemed to favor that delusion, this rumor, nevertheless, soon disappeared of its own accord.[25]

Some tribes which held the soul-loss belief did not believe that the soul once lost could be recovered; in others, such as the Kwakiutls, it was the function of the medicine man to recover the soul by appropriate rituals.[26]

The theory of disease causation from unfulfilled dreams or desires was most highly developed among the Iroquoian tribes. "They believe there are two main causes of disease," wrote the Jesuit priest Joseph Jouvency:

> One of these is in the mind of the patient himself, which desires something, and will vex the body of the sick man until it possesses the thing required. For they think that there are in every man certain inborn desires, often unknown to themselves, upon which the happiness of individuals depends. For the purpose of ascertaining desires and innate appetites of this character, they summon soothsayers, who, as they think, have a divinely imparted power to look into the inmost recesses of the mind.[27]

Such unfulfilled desires were sometimes revealed in dreams, and it was the function of the medicine man to ascertain them

---

[25] Thwaites (ed.), *Jesuit Relations*, XLIII, 292–93.

[26] Elmendorf, "Soul Loss Illness in Western North American," in Tax (ed.), *Indian Tribes*, 112; Franz Boas, "Current Beliefs of the Kwakiutl Indians," *Journal of American Folk-Lore*, Vol. XLV, No. 176 (April–June, 1932), 181.

[27] Thwaites (ed.), *Jesuit Relations*, I, 259.

by adroit questioning. Dreams therefore occupied an important place in the disease theory of these tribes. Of the Hurons, Father Jean de Brebeuf related:

> The dream is the oracle that all these poor Peoples consult and listen to, the Prophet which predicts to them future events, the Cassandra which warns them of misfortunes that threaten them, the usual Physician in their sicknesses, the Esculapius and Galen of the whole Country,—the most absolute master they have. If a Captain speaks one way and a dream another, the Captain might shout his head off in vain,—the dream is first obeyed. It is their Mercury in their journeys, their domestic Economy in families. The dream often presides in their councils; traffic, fishing, and hunting are undertaken usually under its sanction, and almost as if only to satisfy it. They hold nothing so precious that they would not readily deprive themselves of it for the sake of a dream. . . . It prescribes their feasts, their dances, their songs, their games,—in a word, the dream does everything and is in truth the principal God of the Hurons.[28]

It was firmly believed that whatever a person saw in a dream revealed desires which must be fulfilled in order to cure sickness. The *Jesuit Relations* contain several descriptions of the acting out of demands imposed by dreams. In a report from the Onondaga country in 1676, we are told that medicine men persuaded the parents of a sick girl that she had seen nine feasts in dreams, and that if they gave these feasts she would be cured. Thus followed days of revelry, which seemed diabolical to the fathers.[29]

Dreams also played a role in Cherokee medicine. Mooney reported that when the Cherokee medicine man is called in, he generally begins by asking the sick man about his dreams, to get at the cause of the trouble. If the man has dreamed of fish, the doctor asserts that the ghosts of some of the fish he has taken have entered into his body to trouble him. He therefore recites a

[28] *Ibid.*, X, 169–71.
[29] Jean de Lamberville, in Thwaites (ed.), *Jesuit Relations*, LX, 189–93.

prayer calling upon some larger fish, or perhaps a fishhawk, to come and banish the disease-causing fish.[30]

The Medicine Man, or Shaman

The central figure in Indian healing is the medicine man, often called, by ethnologists, by the Asian term *shaman*, and by the early observers, juggler, conjurer, sorcerer, quack, priest, and even physician. Ackerknecht took sharp issue with the last designation, arguing that medicine men and modern physicians are antagonists and not colleagues; all they have in common is that both treat diseases. The medicine man, he wrote, "is rather the ancestor of the priest, the antagonist of the physician for centuries. If there is any ancestor or colleague of the physician in primitive society, it is the lay healer, usually a woman, the midwife."[31]

The medicine man is indeed many things. He is, wrote Roland Dixon, "in the lower stages of culture, at once healer, sorcerer, seer, educator, and priest; but while often the single shaman sums up in himself thus all or most of these functions, there is frequently specialization, as a result of which each of these activities is exercised by a different person."[32] In some tribes, several classes of medical practitioners are distinguished. Among the Ojibwas, Hoffman described four: highest in rank were the priests of the *Midewiwin*, or medicine society, to which membership was gained by initiation and the payment of gifts. Next in rank were the *Wabenos*, "dawn men," practicers of medical magic, hunting medicine, love powders, etc.; third were the *Jessakid*, seers and prophets, revealers of hidden truths, possessors of a gift of clairvoyance received from the thunder god. Last were those whom most modern opinions have held to be the most useful of the lot, *Mashki-kike-winini*, or herbalists, who were generally denominated medicine men, as their name implied.

[30] "Indian Doctors," *Am ur-Quell, Monatschrift Für Volkkunde*, IV:B, 38.

[31] "Problems of Primitive Medicine," *Bulletin of the History of Medicine*, Vol. XI, No. 5 (May, 1942), 508–509.

[32] "Some Aspects of the American Shaman," *Journal of American Folk-Lore*, Vol. XXI (1908), 7.

Their calling [wrote Hoffman] is a simple one, and consists in knowing the mysterious properties of a variety of plants, herbs, roots and berries, which are revealed upon application for a fee. . . . Although these herbalists are aware that certain plants or roots will produce a specified effect upon the human system, they attribute the benefit to the fact that such remedies are distasteful and injurious to the demons who are present in the system and to whom the disease is attributed. Many of these herbalists are found among women, also; and these, too, are generally members of the Midē'-wiwin.[33]

Hoffman also noted that the Mide societies were the main opposition to the introduction of Christianity, due to the fact that "the traditions of Indian genesis and cosmogony and the ritual of initiation into the Society of the Mide constitutes what is to them a religion, even more powerful and impressive than the Christian religion is to the average civilized man." He saw the purpose of the society as the preservation of Indian traditions and as giving "a certain class of ambitious men and women sufficient influence through their acknowledged power of exorcism and necromancy to lead a comfortable life at the expense of the credulous."[34]

Hoffman's view that the medicine men were insincere exploiters of their people was not shared by all who studied them. Hrdlička believed that many of them, at least, were sincere,[35] while Dr. Brooks declared that:

. . . the removal of the foreign body on the part of the priest has precisely the same significance as the very similar ceremonies practiced by our shamen. The attempt to deceive and willful faking is not in the mind of the respectable practitioner any more than it is in the mind of our psychiatrists when they do practically the same thing in their practice.[36]

[33] Hoffman, "The Midē'wiwin or 'Grand Medicine Society' of the Ojibwa," *Seventh Annual Report, Bureau of American Ethnology, 1885–86,* 159.

[34] *Ibid.*

[35] Hrdlička, *Physiological and Medical Observations,* 223.

[36] "The Medicine of the American Indian," *Journal of Laboratory and Clinical Medicine,* Vol. XIX, No. 1 (October, 1933), 16.

Dr. Stone relates the impression of Washington Mathews that the performers of the Navaho mountain chant (a curing ritual) so thoroughly believed in "the supernatural powers of their own deceptions that even during the practice before the performance he has seen the men trembling with fear and awe and looking as pale as an Indian could look, from sheer emotion."[37]

Medicine societies are found in a number of tribes besides the Ojibwas and Menominees as reported by Hoffman. Arthur C. Parker described thirteen such organizations still functioning among the Senecas early in the present century,[38] and in recent years the well-known writer Edmund Wilson described the "Little water ceremony" of the Senecas, (also mentioned earlier by Parker), which he was privileged to attend.[39] Some of the rituals of Seneca medicine societies, such as the sprinkling of water to banish disease, and the chanting in unison of certain songs in language unintelligible even to the participants,[40] are suggestive of certain practices of some of the Christian churches.

Leslie White described in detail the functioning of thirteen medicine fraternities among the Zuñis, each of which was charged with the treatment of a different disease or complex of diseases, or conjuring exercises, such as prayers for rain.[41] Ralph Linton has told of a number of medicine societies that once existed among the Pawnees.[42]

Indian Definition of Medicine

The meaning of the term *medicine* to an Indian was quite different from that which is ordinarily held in white society. To most Indians, medicine signified an array of ideas and concepts

[37] Stone, *Medicine Among the American Indians*, 92.

[38] "Secret Medicine Societies of the Seneca," *American Anthropologist*, N.S., Vol. XI, No. 2 (April–June, 1909), 161–85.

[39] *Apologies to the Iroquois*, Chap. IX.

[40] Parker, "Secret Medicine Societies of the Seneca," *American Anthropologist*, N.S., Vol. XI, No. 2 (April-June, 1909), 161–85.

[41] "Medicine Societies of the Southwest" (unpublished Ph.D. dissertation, Dept. of Anthropology, University of Chicago, 1927).

[42] *Annual Ceremony of the Pawnee Medicine Men.*

rather than remedies and treatment alone. George Bird Grinnell, who was intimately associated with northern Plains tribes, has written:

> All these things which we speak of as medicine the Indian calls mysterious, and when he calls them mysterious this only means that they are beyond his power to account for. . . . We say that the Indian calls whisky "medicine water." He really calls it mysterious water—that is, water which acts in a way that he cannot understand. . . . In the same way some tribes call the horse "medicine dog," and gun "medicine iron," meaning mysterious dog and mysterious iron. He whom we call a medicine man may be a doctor, a healer of diseases; or if he is a juggler, a worker of magic, he is a mystery man. All Indian languages have words which are the equivalent of our word medicine, sometimes with curative properties; but the Indian's translation of "medicine," used in the sense of magical or supernatural, would be mysterious, inexplicable, unaccountable.[43]

John James Audubon, the painter, thought it notable that Missouri valley Indians called the steamboat "great medicine."[44] Even a glance at the map reveals the varied applications of the term "medicine" by the Indians: Medicine Bow, Wyoming; Medicine Hat, Alberta; Medicine Lake, Montana; Medicine Lodge, Kansas; Medicine Mound, Texas; and Medicine Park, Oklahoma. There are also, in Indian parlance, such things as medicine stick, big medicine, bad medicine, good medicine, medicine dance, medicine pipe, medicine drum, and war medicine. "Whereas we think in terms of drugs, ointments, or cathartics which will benefit the body in a predictable fashion," wrote Robert F. Greenlee, "the Seminole thinks of benefits which one can produce only through the office of the medicine man." This functionary believes that he can surely cure if he can recite the prescribed medicinal formulas, perform the necessary rites, and

---

[43] *The Story of the Indian*, 180–81.
[44] *Audubon and His Journals*, ed. Maria R. Audubon, II, 19.

blow on the brewed medicine in a certain way. His medical theory arises from the reasoning that "he can control the forces of nature and hence make disease yield to his personal efforts."[45] Consequently, curative agents are indeed "medicine," but only one kind of medicine, and that only in association with prescribed rites. Greenlee further remarked that the Seminole concept of medicine covers diagnosis, the curing of bodily ills, and mysterious mental ailments. The medicine man is entrusted with ceremonies connected with birth and death, magical ceremonies, and the perpetuation of tribal lore. He further served as the spokesman of the group in Indian-white relations.

Maddox has stated that savage medicine includes "clairvoyance, ecstaism, spiritism, divination, demonology, prophesy, necromancy, and all things incomprehensible. Hence the medicine man is not only the primitive doctor, but he is the diviner, the rain-maker, the soothsayer, the prophet, the priest, and in some instances, the chief or king."[46] Indeed, some of the better-known Indian "chiefs" were in fact medicine men: Corn Planter, Gall, Sitting Bull, Joseph, Geronimo, Cochise, and others.[47]

Medicine power is often attributed to a fetish or charm adopted to typify a tutelary demon, or mystery guardian, and the superior performance of one "juggler" over another is often attributed to the fact that his "medicine" is the stronger. Medicine is also associated with magic numbers, as it sometimes is among whites ("lucky seven," "unlucky thirteen"). The usual sacred number among Indians is four, signifying the cardinal directions, but sometimes six, adding the up and down directions. Medical prescriptions will sometimes specify, for this reason, a certain number of remedies, or the administration of the remedies for so many days, or that they be gathered in so many places.

Omens were watched for by Indian doctors to determine the probable results of treatment, or to foretell future events. This

[45] "Medicine and Curing Practices of the Modern Florida Seminoles," *American Anthropologist*, N.S., Vol. XLVI, No. 3 (July–September, 1944), 317–19.

[46] Maddox, *The Medicine Man*, 25.

[47] A. Hyatt Verrill, *The American Indian: North, South and Central America* (New York, The New Home Library, 1943), 124.

practice was well developed in Middle and South America[48] but also persists among North American tribes, as it does among white people. Ruth Landes reported that when her Kansas Potawatomi informant left the reservation for war industry and marriage, "he found that his white associates also observed omens everywhere, divined by cards, ghosts, and dreams, and solicited Indian shamans for love medicine."[49]

Equipment of the Medicine Man

The medicine man was equipped with paraphernalia and equipment appropriate to his calling. These might include special costume, such as animal skins as shown in George Catlin's famous painting of the Mandan medicine man, a medicine bundle that contains charms and fetishes, medicine sticks serving as an offering, a warning, or an invitation,[50] and sometimes a bag of herbs. The function of providing the herbs was sometimes relegated to an assistant, or "apothecary." The medicine man might also have a drum, rattle, a scarification instrument—in former times made of flint, obsidian, or snake fangs—a hollow bone for sucking, a mortar and pestle for mixing medicines, and, in many places, a syringe for injecting medicine into wounds or administering an enema.

From the religious viewpoint, which was uppermost to the Indian, the medicine bundle was perhaps the most important. In the thirties the medicine bundle cult still survived among the Kansas Potawatomis, along with the more recent "religion" or drum dance, and the peyote religion, as one of the three curing cults still extant.[51] The medicine bundle was usually made of an animal skin, often from a totemic animal, and included such fetishes as deer tails, dried fingers, and often the maw stone of a

---

[48] Daniel G. Brinton, *The Myths of the New World*, 106, 297.

[49] "Potawatomi Medicine," *Transactions Kansas Academy of Science*, Vol. LXVI, No. 4 (Winter, 1963), 572.

[50] Verrill, *The American Indian*, 125.

[51] Landes, "Potawatomi Medicine," *Transactions Kansas Academy of Science*, Vol. LXVI, No. 4 (Winter, 1963), 588.

27

buffalo.[52] These bags were handed down from father to son, or to newly initiated medicine men by the instructor. La Potherie has described a seventeenth-century Miami medicine bag:

> In the cabin of the great chief of the Miamis an altar had been erected, on which he had caused to be placed a Pindiko-san. This is a warrior's pouch, filled with medicinal herbs wrapped in the skins of animals, the rarest that they can find; it usually contains all that inspires their dreams.[53]

The charms in the medicine bag, to ward off evil, were often more important than the curative agents, which they might or might not contain. Benjamin Hawkins reported that the Creeks carried in their shot bags "a charm, a protection against all ills, called the war physic, composed of . . . bones of the snake and lion."[54]

The use of charms or fetishes is old in human history. While the French Jesuits ridiculed the Indian charms, they soberly wrote of miraculous cures performed by swallowing in water or in broth a little dust from the tomb of Kateri Tekakwitha, the saintly Iroquois Christian girl who died in 1680.[55] Several cures attributed to baptism are recounted in the *Jesuit Relations*, including "instant" recovery of an Indian child so ill with "consumptive fever" that he was "reduced to a mere skeleton."[56] One account from Virginia related the cure of an Indian boy through baptism performed according to the liturgy of the Church of England.[57] Cure by relics is claimed in an account written in Illinois in 1700 by Father Jacques Gravier:

> I have found an excellent remedy for curing our French of their fever. I promised God, jointly with Pierre de bonne,—

[52] Linton, *Annual Ceremony of the Pawnee Medicine Men*, 4.

[53] Louise Phelps Kellogg (ed.), *Early Narratives of the Northwest*, 87.

[54] *A Sketch of the Creek Country in the Years 1798 and 1799*, Vol. III, Pt. I of *Collections of the Georgia Historical Society*, 79.

[55] Thwaites (ed.), *Jesuit Relations*, LXV, 31.

[56] *Ibid.*, XLII, 145–47.

[57] Peter Force, *Tracts and Other Papers, Relating Principally to the Origin, Settlement, and Progress of the Colonies in North America* . . . , I, 9.

who had a violent tertian fever for a long time,—to recite for 9 days some prayers in honor of Father François Regis, whose relics I have. These I applied to him at his Strongest paroxysm, which suddenly ceased, and he has had none since.[58]

Father Gravier reported four other cures accomplished in the same way. "A small piece of Father François Regis's hat, which one of his servants gave me," he wrote, "is the most infallible remedy that I know of for curing all kinds of fever." In an earlier instance, Pierre Biard in 1612 cautiously suggested that he may have cured the son of an Indian chief of a dangerous illness, after the French apothecary had failed, by "putting upon the sufferer a bone taken from the precious relics of the glorified Saint Lawrence . . . at the same time offering our vows to him, and then he improved."[59]

According to John G. Bourke, the South Texas Mexicans put a string of coral beads around the neck to stop nosebleed,[60] a practice similar to the Penobscot custom of preventing bleeding by wearing a necklace made of bloodroot.[61] Bernard Romans, who would have no truck with Indian "superstitions," reported that Spaniards in the Gulf region wore "the nest of the great travelling spider sowed in a rag about their neck as a sure way to assuage a hecktick fever, and I think with great success."[62]

Charm remedies and sympathetic magic are reported among the Pennsylvania Germans and numerous other American subcultures. In eighteenth-century Pennsylvania, Joseph Doddridge relates, "charms and incantations were in use for the cure of many diseases. I learned, when young, the incantation in German, for the cure of burns, stopping blood, for the toothache, and the charm against bullets in battle."[63] These parallels in the

---

[58] Thwaites (ed.), *Jesuit Relations*, LXV, 107–109.

[59] *Ibid.*, II, 19.

[60] "Popular Medicine, Customs, and Superstitions of the Rio Grande," *Journal of American Folk-Lore*, Vol. VII, No. 25 (April–June, 1894), 137.

[61] Frank G. Speck, "Medicine Practices of the Northeastern Algonquians," *Proceedings, XIXth International Congress of Americanists*, 311.

[62] *A Concise Natural History of East and West Florida*, 168.

[63] *Notes on the Settlement and Indian Wars of the Western Parts of Virginia and Pennsylvania*, 172.

practices of the two races are cited as examples of their universality and do not indicate that either race learned them from the other.

Indian Methods of Treatment

There were variations in healing procedure from tribe to tribe, and in different culture areas. However, there were some methods which were nearly universal. A survey of all of them is quite outside the scope of this study, but much of the procedure common to eastern Woodland tribes can be seen in the description provided by Pierre de Liette for the Illinois-Miami tribes of the late seventeenth century. He reported that most of the old men were healers, and that when a person was sick, his relatives would hang in the cabin certain gifts for the medicine man, such as a kettle, guns, or blankets. The healer was summoned, and would question the patient about the nature and extent of his illness. The healer would then leave, and return with his bag of medicines, and his *chichicoya*, or gourd rattle. The rattle was shaken, while the healer intoned in a loud voice that certain animal spirits had revealed to him the proper remedies, which were certain to cure. He next called for warm water, and, taking some of it in his *micoine* (spoon), he mixed his remedies, and the medicine was swallowed by the patient. The healer would also take some of the medicine in his own mouth, spout it upon the seat of pain, and bandage it. He returned twice a day and sang incantations, followed by violent sucking of the ailing parts of the body. He then revealed an object said to have been drawn from the body, such as an eagle claw or cougar's hair, which was called the cause of the ailment. Then in a long song:

> he thanks his manitou with his *chichicoya* for making it possible for him frequently to obtain merchandise through his favor. He takes his patient out for a bath, or washes him in the cabin, according to the season. He takes what had been hung up for him in the cabin and carries it off without saying anything. The relatives rise and pass their hands over his head and his legs, a sign of profound gratitude. Generally

they do not cure the sick, although assuredly they have excellent drugs, because they are ignorant of internal maladies.[64]

While De Liette believed that their treatment of internal diseases was ineffective, he praised their treatment of wounds and thought that the sucking process was a good device to remove infection.

Indian medical treatment is here seen as a combination of rational and religious practices, differing from the usual white practice in that *both are performed by the same functionary* among the Indians. In our own society there are some religious sects which combine treatment with supernatural appeals and some which eschew medical treatment altogether. Comparing the two, Dr. Harlow Brooks commented: "I fail to find in the service of our modern faiths anything more dignified, beautiful, and worshipful than some of the chants or 'dances' of the red man, conducted for the benefit of the sick, or for the purpose of imploring the assistance of their divine being in the welfare of their people."[65]

Tribal differences, however, should not be overlooked. It was one scholar's opinion that "the New England Indians apparently had nothing like those formal, elaborately organized priesthoods of the West and South which dominate most discussions of Indian cults and superstitions."[66] Similar claims to a separation of medical practice from ritual have been made for the Catawbas.[67] Some classes of practitioners, such as midwives and herbalists, minimized or dispensed with ritual, and it was not commonly employed in the treatment of external injuries for which the cause was obvious.

Among the Winnebagos, the medicine man scattered tobacco,

[64] Milo M. Quaife (ed.), *The Western Country in the Seventeenth Century*, 144–45.

[65] "The Medicine of the American Indian," *Journal of Laboratory and Clinical Medicine*, Vol. XIX, No. 1 (October, 1933), 13.

[66] Will T. Bradley, "Medical Practices of the New England Aborigines," *Journal of the American Pharmaceutical Association*, Vol. XXV, No. 2 (February, 1936), 142.

[67] Frank Speck, "Catawba Herbals and Curing Practices," *Journal of American Folk-Lore*, Vol. LVII, No. 223 (January–March, 1944), 38–39.

feathers, or some such substance to exorcise the spirit causing the disease, meanwhile repeating prayers, often in ancient, unintelligible dialect. Sometimes a dog was sacrificed to prevent an illness from attacking other members of the family.[68] Tobacco is also used among the Seminoles,[69] and other tribes to ward off evil influences, not only of disease, but of such natural phenomena as storms and lightning. It was used by the Virginia Indians, wrote John Smith, to "offer the water in passing in fowle weather."[70]

The use of rattles or drums seems to to be universal. "To cure the sick," Smith wrote, "a man, with a Rattle, and extreame howling, showting, singing and such violent gestures and Anticke actions over the patient, will sucke out blood and flegme from the patient, out of the unable stomacke, or any diseased place."[71] Maximilian reported among the Blackfeet: "In all cases they have recourse to the drum and rattle, and have great confidence in the intolerable noise caused by those instruments."[72]

Herbs employed by the medicine men were believed to derive their strength from ceremonies performed to make them powerful. Among the Onondagas, wrote the Jesuit priest Jean de Quen, "all the village Sorcerers and Jugglers, the Physicians of the Country, assemble, to give strength to their drugs, and by the ceremony performed, to impart to them a virtue entirely distinct from that derived from the soil."[73] The same procedure is reported among the Miamis by Charlevoix:

> The whole town being assembled, one of these quacks declares he is going to communicate to the roots and plants, of which he takes care to provide good store, the virtue of healing all sorts of wounds, and even of restoring the dead to life.

[68] Fanny D. Bergen, "Some Customs and Beliefs of the Winnebago Indians," *ibid.*, Vol. IX, No. 33 (January–March, 1896), 53–55.

[69] Greenlee, "Medicine and Curing Practices of the Modern Florida Seminoles," *American Anthropologist*, N.S., Vol. XLVI, No. 3 (July–September, 1944), 323.

[70] Lyon G. Tyler (ed.), *Narratives of Early Virginia, 1606–1625*, 51.

[71] *Ibid.*

[72] *Travels in the Interior of North America, 1832–1834* (Part II), Vol. XXIII in Thwaites (ed.), *Early Western Travels*, 120.

[73] Thwaites (ed.), *Jesuit Relations*, XLII, 173.

He falls immediately to singing; the other quacks make responses to him, and it is believed that during the concert, which would not appear to your ear very melodious, and which is accompanied with many grimaces on the part of the actors, the medicinal quality is communicated to the plants.[74]

The doctrine of signatures played an important role in Indian medicine, as it once did in European medicine. "Like cures like" was the essence of this belief; thus, yellow plants were good for jaundice; red ones were good for the blood. Some part of the plant might resemble the organ of the body it was designed to cure, according to this belief. Reminders of the former prevalence of such conceptions among Europeans are indicated by plant names such as hepatica, formerly believed to be useful in liver complaints, and lungwort, once believed valuable in pulmonary infections.[75] Speck called this belief "sympathetic influence" and gave several examples of it among Indians. The form and the Indian name of ginseng (*Panax quinquefolius* L.), a noted panacea, indicated its value to the Penobscots for promoting female fertility. The use of wormroot (*Apocynum cannabinum*) for worms, and snakeroot (*Aristolochia serpentaria*) for fits or "contortions" was determined from their appearance. Elm bark was used in this tribe for bleeding lungs because of its slippery quality, and bloodroot was used to prevent bleeding because of the red juice contained in it.[76]

The Indians also commonly believed that certain roots or plants were beneficial to the system because they were distasteful and injurious to the demons present in the body which were causing the disease.[77] Consequently, foul-tasting medicines, emetics, and purges were often used.

[74] Charlevoix, *Journal of a Voyage*, I, 316–17.

[75] Rodney H. True, "Folk Materia Medica," *Journal of American Folk-Lore*, Vol. XIV (1901), 106.

[76] "Medicine Practices of the Northeastern Algonquians," *Proceedings XIXth Congress of Americanists*, 306.

[77] Hoffman, "The Mide'wiwin or 'Grand Medicine Society' of the Ojibwa," *Seventh Annual Report of the Bureau of American Ethnology, 1885–86*, 159.

33

The Results of Shamanistic Treatment

The shaman was often successful, not only in the treatment of Indians, but also whites. Most writers have attributed this success at least in part to psychological factors not recognized in earlier times but given much attention today. Many curative measures, Rivers has indicated, "owe their success to the faith they inspire, or to the more mysterious property we call suggestion."[78] James Mooney recognized this when he wrote that:

> The faith of the patient has much to do with his recovery, for the Indian has the same implicit confidence in the shaman that a child has in a more intelligent physician. The ceremonies and prayers are well calculated to inspire this feeling, and the effect thus produced upon the mind of the sick man undoubtedly reacts favorably upon his physical organization.[79]

Josiah Gregg, writing of the Comanches in the 1830s, remarked that "they have great faith in their 'medicine men,' who pretend to cure the sick with conjurations and charms; and the Comanche and many others often keep up an irksome, monotonous singing over the diseased person, to frighten away the evil spirit which is supposed to torment him; all of which, from its effect upon the imagination, often tends, no doubt, to hasten recovery."[80] Such views have been finding increasing corroboration among modern anthropologists, physicians, and others. Dr. Ackerknecht has written that "the participation of the community in the healing rites, and the strong connection between these rites and the whole religion and tradition of the tribe, produce certain psychotherapeutic advantages for the medicine man which the modern physician lacks."[81]

[78] Rivers, *Medicine, Magic, and Religion*, 122.

[79] "Sacred Formulas of the Cherokees," *Seventh Annual Report of the Bureau of American Ethnology, 1885–86*, 323.

[80] *Commerce of the Prairies, Or the Journal of a Santa Fe Trader*, Vol. XX in Thwaites (ed.), *Early Western Travels*, 334–35.

[81] "Primitive Medicine: A Contrast with Modern Practice," *The Merck Report*, 8.

The Medicine Man and White Society

The Indian medicine man, being also a priest and highly respected tribal leader, was long recognized by the whites as a principal barrier to the eradication of Indian culture. John Bourke saw in the medicine man "an influence antagonistic to the rapid absorption of new ideas and the adoption of new customs." He believed that only "after we have thoroughly routed the medicine men from their intrenchments and made them an object of ridicule" could whites "hope to bend and train the mind of our Indian wards in the direction of civilization."[82] More recently, Huron H. Smith reported that "the government takes cognizance of the Indian medicine man and is trying to wean the Indians away from his dominance."[83]

The hostility of the Christian missionaries to the medicine men is revealed in many of their accounts. Thus, all of the principal forces of European erosion of Indian society have been brought to bear in the assault against the medicine man. To the extent that his influence was weakened, white influence was able to penetrate. The campaign has made great headway, and yet the old ways, sometimes driven underground, continue to flourish in many ways. Even though Indians are coming to depend more upon white doctors and hospitals, provided to them free if they are on reservations, they sometimes resort to their medicine men if a quick cure is not forthcoming.[84] If the Indian medicine man eventually disappears, he will nevertheless have left to mankind an important store of remedies and curing methods, which, however irrational his notions about them, have often proved useful to the conquerors and will stand as his enduring monument.

[82] "The Medicine-Men of the Apache," *Ninth Annual Report, Bureau of American Ethnology, 1887–88*, 451, 594.

[83] *Ethnobotany of the Menomini Indians*, Bulletin of the Public Museum of the City of Milwaukee, Vol. IV, No. 1 (December 10, 1923), 20; hereafter cited as *Menomini Ethnobotany*.

[84] Ritzenthaler, *Chippewa Preoccupation with Health*, 202.

III.

Early Observations
of White Men
on
Indian Medicine

The English Colonies

Virginia

A prominent feature of nearly all the early accounts of America is a description of the strange new plants and animals and other natural phenomena. The Indian usages of medicinal plants often occupy a prominent place in these descriptions, beginning with reports of Raleigh's settlement on Roanoke Island in 1585. Thomas Hariot boasted of the availability of *"Sweet Gummes* of divers kindes and many other apothecary drugges of which wee will make speciall mention." He described the native use of *uppówoc* (tobacco), "which purgeth superfluous steam and other grosse humors," and to which he ascribed the Indians' freedom from "many greevous diseases wherewithal we from England are oftentimes afflicted." Of no less importance was an aromatic wood, *winauk*, or sassafras, which was "of most rare vertues in phisick for the cure of many diseases."[1]

Indian methods of treating the sick also attracted the interest, if not always the approval, of the earliest settlers. To Captain John Smith we are indebted for the earliest description for this region of the Indian use of emetics, sweat baths, cauterization, sucking, and scarification as therapeutic devices:

> Every spring they make themselves sicke with drinking the juice of a root they call *wighsacan*, and water, whereof they powre so great a quantity, that it purgeth them in a very violent manner; so that in 3 or 4 daies after, they scarce recover their former health. Sometimes they are troubled with dropsies, swellings, aches, and such like diseases; for cure whereof they build a stove in the form of a dovehouse with mats, so close that a few coales therein covered with a pot, will make the patient sweate extremely. For swellings also they use smal peeces of touchwood, in the forme of cloves, which pricking on the griefe, they burne close to the flesh, and from thence draw the corruption with their mouth. With this root *wighsacan* they ordinarily heal greene wounds: but to scarrifie a swelling or make incision, their best instruments are some splinted stone. Old ulcers or putrified hurtes are seldome seene cured amongst them. They have many professed Phisitions, who with their charmes and Rattels, with an infernall rowt of words and actions, will seeme to sucke their inwarde griefe from their navels or their grieved places; but of our Chirurgeons they were so concepted, that they beleeved any Plaister would heale any hurt.[2]

It is noteworthy that two plant products used by the Indians, sassafras and tobacco, soon became the basis of the early Virginia

[1] *A Briefe and True Report of the New Found Land of Virginia*, n.p.
[2] Tyler (ed.), *Narratives of Early Virginia*, 108.

economy.[3] The first physician at Jamestown, Dr. Lawrence Bohun, occupied himself during his brief stay (1610–11) with an investigation of the medicinal properties of sassafras and wild rhubarb.[4]

In the next century (1736), Dr. John Tennent published at Williamsburg an "Essay on Pleurisy," which was one of the earliest medical works written in America. It was concerned with the virtues of a plant obtained from the Indians, the Seneca snakeroot (*Polygala senega*), which Tennent extolled as a sovereign remedy for pulmonary ailments. For his services the Virginia Assembly voted him a reward of one hundred pounds.[5]

The early Virginia physicians and apothecaries, in infrequent communication with Europe, were often dependent upon Indian remedies. While the apprentice apothecaries served under physicians, Blanton informs us, "their masters sent them into the woods in search of such popular Indian medicines as Indian hemp, papoose root, Indian tobacco, blood root, and mandrake."[6]

Even more dependent on native remedies were the planters, of whom William Byrd serves as an extraordinary example. Not only his rural situation, but his conviction that "Priests, Lawyers, and Physicians" were the "3 great Scourges of Mankind" prepared him for what the native woods and fields might offer in the way of simples.[7] His partisanship for such Indian roots, barks, and herbs as dogwood, ginseng, wild ipecac, and the several varieties of snakeroot is exhibited throughout his writings.[8]

Perhaps no writer on the Virginia aborigines had a more favorable opinion of their curative methods than Robert Beverley. Their priest-physicians, he wrote, were "very knowing in the hidden qualities of Plants, and other Natural things." He ob-

---

[3] Conway Robinson (ed.), *Abstract of Proceedings of the Virginia Company of London*, II, 20–21, 31–32, 100.

[4] Blanton P. Seward, "Pioneer Medicine in Virginia," Pt. I, *Annals of Medical History*, N.S., Vol. X, No. 1 (January, 1930), 62.

[5] Wyndham P. Blanton, *Medicine in Virginia in the Eighteenth Century*, 214.

[6] *Ibid.*, 33.

[7] *History of the Dividing Line and Other Tracts*, ed. Thomas H. Wynne, I, 12.

[8] *E.g., ibid.*, 82.

served that "they take great delight in Sweating, and therefore in every Town they have a Sweating-House, and a Doctor is paid by the Publick to attend it." The Indians were found to be reluctant to reveal their medical secrets for fear of offending the spirits, "so they suffer only the Rattle Snake Root to be known, and such other Antidotes, as must be immediately apply'd." He mentioned an ointment they devised by crushing the roots of puccoon and wild angelica, which was mixed with bear's oil and rubbed on the skin to "conserve the substance of the Body." This mixture also kept away "Lice, Fleas, and other troublesome Vermine from coming near them."[9]

New England

Eighteen years before the shivering Pilgrims set foot on the grim New England coast, London "adventurers" sent Captain Gosnold to those shores, where the Indians "bearing us company everyday into the woods, and helpt us to cut and carie out Sassafras." This valuable cargo caused a fall in the price of sassafras on the London market, which brought forth a complaint from Sir Walter Raleigh that his rights as patentee were infringed. The next year, nevertheless, Martin Pring returned with two ships which were loaded with "Sassafras a plant of sovereigne vertue for the French Poxe, and as some of late have learnedly written good against the Plage and many other Maladies."[10]

Perhaps this celebrated Indian remedy was more honored abroad than by whites in its land of origin. One looks in vain for mention of it in accounts of the settlements of Plymouth and Massachusetts Bay. The early reports of these colonies are likewise nearly barren of any reference to Indian medical practices. Perhaps the gulf separating the Pilgrim and Puritan saints from the "Salvage Hounds"[11] who inhabited the forests was too wide

9 *The History and Present State of Virginia*, ed. Louis B. Wright, 217–20.

10 Henry S. Burrage (ed.), *Early English and French Voyages*, 325, 334–35, 338–40, 349–51.

11 Cotton Mather, "Decennium Luctuosum" (1699), in Charles H. Lincoln (ed.), *Narratives of the Indian Wars 1675–1699*, 232.

to permit interest in any aspect of their culture. A people who equated the natives with the wild animals, as indicated by William Bradford's description of the New Zion as "a hidious & desolate wilderness, full of wild beasts & willd men,"[12] could hardly be expected to learn much from such natural enemies. They could only give thanks to God that an epidemic of smallpox brought by English fishermen or slave-catchers had wiped out most of the coastal Indians about four years before their arrival.[13]

The theocrats of New England were, however, eminently practical folk, despite their devout belief in the power of witches and the satanic origin of Indians and Quakers. In their early weakness, some accommodation with the local fauna, both biped and quadruped, was indisputably necessary, as perhaps Squanto's lessons in maize culture demonstrated to them. One of the few recorded instances of English gratitude, however it may have been motivated by self-interest, strangely enough involves medical aid to Massasoit, chief of the Wampanoags:

> . . . the Governor and people hear had notice that Massasoyte ther freind was sick and near unto death. They sent to vissete him, and withall sente him such comfortable things as gave him great contente, and was a means of his recovery; upon which occasion he discovers the conspiracie of these Indeans, how they were resolved to cutt of Mr. Westons peo-

12 *Of Plymouth Plantation*, ed. Harvey Wish, 60. Earlier, Bradford had written of "the vast & unpeopled countries of America, which are frutfull & fitt for habitation, being devoyd of all civill inhabitants, wher ther are only salvage & brutish men, which range up and downe, litle otherwise than the wild beasts of the same." *Ibid.*, 40.

13 On March 16, 1621, the Pilgrims received their first Indian visitor, Samoset, who informed them that "about foure yeares agoe, all the Inhabitants dyed of an extraordinary plague, and there is neither man, woman, nor childe remaining, as indeed we haue found none, so as there is none to hinder our possession, or to lay claime unto it . . . ." George B. Cheever (ed.), *The Journal of the Pilgrims at Plymouth in New England, in 1620: Reprinted from the Original Volume* (New York, John Wiley, 1849), 58.

English ships had been landing on the New England coast since early in the century, and one of them in 1616 took Samoset and Squanto to England, from which they later returned with enough knowledge of the language to speak with the Pilgrims.

ple, for the continuall injuries they did them, & would now take opportunitie of their weaknes to doe it."[14]

This succor was thus amply repaid by the prevention of a massacre. Fortune continued to smile upon Plymouth, and later upon the colony of Massachusetts Bay, as the remaining Indians were decimated by renewed scourges of smallpox. In November of 1633, Governor Winthrop reported the death of the sagamore of Naponsett (Neponset) and many of his people. The following month the disease spread to other Indian villages, wiping out all but one or two at Pacataquack. In January, 1634, an indentured servant, John Seales, "who ran from his master to the Indians, came home again," reporting that four of seven Indians with whom he had taken refuge had died of the pestilence. At the same time, a party which had gone to Connecticut in November returned with the report that "the small pox was gone as far as any Indian plantation was known to the west, and much people dead of it, by reason whereof they could have no trade." Seven hundred were reported dead at Narragansett alone.[15]

The helplessness of the Indians before this introduced malady could hardly promote their reputation for medical prowess. A half century elapsed before the first learned disquisition on the medicinal resources of New England appeared, under the name of John Josselyn, Gent.[16] It was an account of vegetable, animal, and mineral substances native to the region composed by a reasonably competent herbalist who was prone to notice things left unobserved by other chroniclers, and who never allowed European bias to restrain him from learning what the Indians might have to teach. Josselyn made it clear that he obtained much of his information about remedies from the Indians, but it also appears that many of his conclusions were the result of European training. His writings give the impression that there was nothing

[14] Bradford, *Of Plymouth Plantation*, 87.

[15] John Winthrop, *Winthrop's Journal, History of New England 1630–1649*, I, 111, 114–15, 118–19.

[16] *New-England's Rarities Discovered, in Birds, Beasts, Fishes, Serpents, and Plants of that Country*, 105–238.

in New England which grew, flew, swam, or crawled that did not possess marvelous medicinal properties. Such excessive enthusiasm should not blind us, however, to the useful parts of his exposition, for many of the remedies he described eventually achieved official recognition in pharmacopeias, formularies, and dispensatories. He was perhaps the first to describe the virtues of the green hellebore (*Veratrum viride* Ait.), which he called white hellebore. Of its native uses, he wrote:

> The Indians cure their wounds with it; annointing the wound first with raccoon's greese or wildcat's greese, and strewing upon it the powder of the roots: and, for aches, they scarify the grieved part, and annoint it with one of the foresaid oyls; then strew upon it the powder. The powder of the root, put into a hollow tooth, is good for the toothach. The root, sliced thin and boyled in vineagar, is very good against *herpes milliaris*.[17]

Josselyn proclaimed the merits of the bearberry (*Arctostaphylus uva ursi* L.), which became official in the American pharmacopeia and all British pharmacopeias. He pronounced the bearberries "excellent against the scurvy" and "also good to allay the fervour of hot diseases." They were also used as food by the Indians and the English.

Among the numerous remedies described by Josselyn were the ubiquitous sassafras, drunk as a decoction in fevers and made into an ointment for bruises; acorn oil, made into an ointment to "annoint their naked limbs," and spermaceti, taken from whales cast upon the beach, which was "admirable for bruises and aches."[18]

Four years after Josselyn published *New-England's Rarities*, Metacomet, or King Philip, unleashed his warriors against the Englishmen who had been tolerated for half a century by his patient father, Massasoit. A "Drug List" for the use of physicians attending the militia in this campaign was prepared by William Locke, "Chirurgeon of the Massachusetts forces in the Mount

[17] *Ibid.*, 173–74.   [18] *Ibid.*, 166, 182, 202.

Hope campaign." This ancestor of our pharmacopeia is notable for the fact that it contains no medicinal products of American origin. As Dr. Edward Kremers declared in an editorial introduction to the published document:

> The items demanded are, with few exceptions, contained in the London Pharmacopeia of 1650. In all probability, therefore, the articles were not compounded in the colonies, but imported from England.[19]

The refusal of New Englanders to recognize things at their own doorstep because of the savage taint may be illustrated by the comment of Dr. Henry R. Viets that although "many new drugs were introduced from the western hemisphere," and although the earliest settlers who came to Massachusetts "were constantly on the lookout for drugs to take back to England," they were unfortunately able to find none "on the barren shores of New England."[20]

There is evidence that the materia medica on those barren shores was as varied as that of England. Will T. Bradley, of the Massachusetts College of Pharmacy, listed thirty drugs used by New England Indians which were still official in the *U.S. Pharmacopeia* or *National Formulary* in 1920.[21] Many of the seventy-five Mohegan vegetable remedies listed by Gladys Tantaquidgeon have been used in domestic medicine and by physicians.[22] Some idea of the herbal knowledge and medical practices of seventeenth-century Algonquian tribes of the New England region can be gained from a reading of Frank Speck's study of the remedies used by some of these tribes in the present century.[23]

Toward the remedies of more distant "salvages" some of the New Englanders were more receptive. If the aging Cotton Mather

[19] William Locke, "A Drug List of King Philip's War," *Badger Pharmacist*, No. 25 (February, 1939), 4.

[20] *A Brief History of Medicine in Massachusetts*, 5.

[21] "Medical Practices of the New England Aborigines," *Journal of the American Pharmaceutical Association*, Vol. XXV, No. 2 (February, 1936), 138–147.

[22] "Mohegan Medicinal Practices, Weather-Lore and Superstition," *Forty-Third Annual Report of the Bureau of American Ethnology*, 1925–26, 264–279.

[23] "Medicine Practices of the Northeastern Algonquians," *Proceedings XIXth International Congress of Americanists*, 303–321.

was unable to find any redeeming virtue in the "Rapacious Wolves" still lurking in the backwoods at a safe distance from their ancient village of Shawmut, now called Boston, he found it possible to extol the ingenuity of South American Indians, not to mention African Negroes, from one of whom he learned of smallpox inoculation, which he introduced at Boston in 1721.[24] In *The Christian Philosopher* he granted that tobacco had many virtues and called an ointment made of it "one of the best in the dispensatory," though he deplored the smoking habit. The varied uses of the cocoa tree (*Theobroma cacao* L.) by the natives of Spanish America excited his wonder:

> The cocoa-tree supplies the Indians with bread, water, wine, vinegar, brandy, milk, oil, honey, sugar, needles, thread, linen, clothes, caps, spoons, besoms, baskets, paper, and nails; timber, coverings for their houses; masts, sails, cordage for their vessels; and medicines for their diseases; and what can be desired more?[25]

Two years later, in *The Angel of Bethesda*, said to be the earliest medical treatise written in this country, Mather spoke of *ipecacuanha*, an emetic discovered by Brazilian natives, as "the most fashionable vomit," and cited Sir John Colbatch's opinion that "Tis the safest, and perhaps the best Vomit, to cleanse the stomach." (It still enjoys a high reputation.) He recommended decoctions or infusions of sassafras, sarsaparilla, "guajacum," "China-roots" (ginseng?), or coltsfoot, for "sweetening the Blood." He claimed that "Our Indians cure Consumptions with a Mullein-Tea," and held that the tea made from the root bark of sassafras (an old aboriginal remedy) "has marvelously cured coughs wherein a Consumption has been threatned, if not actually entred."[26] Except for ipecac, none of these remedies is now held to possess the virtues once ascribed to them, but it must

24 Henry R. Viets, "Some Features of the History of Medicine in Massachusetts during the Colonial Period," *Isis*, Vol. XXIII (1935), 397.

25 *The Christian Philosopher*, 142, 145–46.

26 Otho T. Beall, Jr., and Richard H. Shryock, *Cotton Mather: First Significant Figure in American Medicine*, 208–209, 223.

be said that Mather showed an uncommon openmindedness, for his time, in his willingness to credit the remedies of the "tawney serpents." Paradoxically, he was ahead of, as well as behind, his age.

The reason for the nearly total rejection of everything connected with the Indians by the New England colonists (except in Rhode Island, where the benevolent Roger Williams made his mark) seems to be rooted in their Old Testament conviction that they were the chosen people, destined to exterminate the Philistines who occupied the Promised Land. Here there was no union with a savage "princess" like that of John Rolfe, and the aboriginal place names came as near to obliteration as the people who gave them. It is in this context that their rejection of Indian remedies must be viewed.

Long before American independence, the aboriginal tribes of southern New England had nearly disappeared, save for a few bands of "praying Indians" safely corralled on tiny reservations, where they soon lost their own culture. Only in those areas where at least a part of the white population established rapport with the natives, as in Pennsylvania and Georgia, was there general acceptance of Indian remedies. Not only the European unwillingness to learn, but also an aboriginal refusal to teach, marks those areas which seethed with racial antagonism. Under the best conditions, Indians were reluctant to reveal their medical knowledge, such as it was, and only traders and missionaries who won their friendship were able to pry it from them.

New York

Small Algonquian tribes, bands, or subtribes, sometimes collectively known as "river Indians," occupied the banks of the lower Hudson River. It was members of these groups who climbed aboard Henry Hudson's *Half Moon* in 1609, bearing "Indian Corne, Pompions [Pumpkins], and Tabacco," for which they received "trifles" in return.[27] The herbal knowledge of these peaceful farmers was noticed by Nicolaes van Wassenaer, who

[27] Robert Juet, "The Third Voyage of Master Henry Hudson," in J. Franklin Jameson (ed.), *Narratives of New Netherland, 1609–1664*, 21.

wrote in 1624: "In some places they have abundant means, with herbs and leaves or roots, to cure their ailments. There is not an ailment they have not a remedy for."[28] Their familiarity with both poisonous and emetic herbs and roots was remarked upon by Isaack de Rasieres, who reported that the initiation ordeal of a young Indian required that:

> he must go into the forest to seek wild herbs and roots, which they know to be the most poisonous and bitter; these they bruise in water and press the juice out of them, which he must drink, and immediately have ready such herbs as will preserve him from death or vomiting.[29]

Johan de Laet remarked on the "great variety of herbaceous plants, some of which bear splendid flowers, and others are considered valuable for their medicinal properties."[30] In "Representation of New Netherland," believed to have been written principally by Adriaen van der Donck in 1650, about three dozen indigenous medical plants are listed, with the observation:

> ... yet it is not to be doubted that experts would be able to find many simples of great and different virtues, in which we have confidence, principally because the Indians know how to cure very dangerous and perilous wounds and sores by roots, leaves and other little things.

The same document remarked on the dangers of rattlesnake bite, for which, fortunately, an Indian cure was available, for "there grows spontaneously in the country the true snakeroot, which is very highly esteemed by the Indians as an unfailing cure."[31]

To the Dutchman David de Vries we are also indebted for one of our early descriptions of the aboriginal sweat bath:

> When they wish to cleanse themselves of their foulness, they go in the autumn, when it begins to grow cold, to make, away

28 "Historisch Verhael," in Jameson, *Narratives of New Netherland*, 72.
29 Jameson, *Narratives of New Netherland*, 114.
30 *Ibid.*, 55–56.   31 *Ibid.*, 298–99.

off, near a running brook, a small oven, large enough for three or four men to lie in it. In making it they first take twigs of trees, and then cover them tight with clay, so that smoke cannot escape. This being done, they take a parcel of stones, which they heat in a fire, and then put in the oven, and when they think it is sufficiently hot, take the stones out again, and go and lie in it, men and women, boys and girls, and come out perspiring, that every hair has a drop of sweat on it. In this state they plunge into the cold water; saying that it is healthy, but I let its healthfulness pass; they then become entirely clean, and are more attractive than before.[32]

Western Europeans, to whom in that period any kind of bathing was an abomination, understandably had doubts about the hygienic practice of the Indians. The sweat bath, however, was known to Asiatic peoples, and it may have been brought from Asia by the first Indians, for this ubiquitous custom has been mentioned by nearly every early commentator on the Indians.

The most numerous and powerful group of Indians in New York were the Iroquois or Five Nations (later the Six Nations), whose towns stretched across the Mohawk valley from Albany to Niagara. The French missionaries were active among them, and it is from their accounts that the most extensive descriptions of Iroquois herbalism and medical practices are to be found. Jean François Lafitau commented that they had some good remedies, but often gave them in doses strong enough to kill a horse:

> En general, leurs remedes topiques sont trèsbons. Il n'en est pas de même de leurs vomitifs & de leurs purgatifs. Ils sont obligés de les doser fortement pour qu'ils puissent produire quelque effet. Ce sont comme des décoctions de lavemens très-dégoûtantes, & qui noyent un estomach. D'ailleurs ils ne se croyent pas purgés suffisament, s'ils ne prennent des médecines tres-fortes, qui les vuident avec excès, & qui pourroient tuer un cheval.[33]

---

[32] *Ibid.*, 217–18.

[33] *Moeurs des Sauvages Ameriquains Comparees aux Moeurs des Premiers Temps*, II, 368.

In 1656 the Jesuit priest Paul Le Jeune was favorably impressed by the virtues of the sassafras tree, here growing near the northern limit of its range:

> . . . the most common and wonderful plant in those countries is that which we call the universal plant, because its leaves, when pounded, heal in a short time wounds of all kinds; these leaves, which are as broad as one's hand, have the shape of a lily as depicted in heraldry; and its roots have the smell of the laurel.[34]

William Beauchamp has shown that the Iroquois had names and uses for a large number of plants.[35] Outstanding among them for its fame is the Seneca, or Senega, snakeroot (*Polygala senega* L.), which was official in the American pharmacopeia for over a century. It was used by the Seneca as a snakebite remedy, though whites used it also for a stimulant and expectorant in pulmonary ailments.[36] Among the numerous drugs used by the Iroquois were the maidenhair fern (*Adiantum pedatum* L.) and the notable ginseng, (*Panax quinquefolium* L.). Ginseng was discovered in China, where it was regarded as a panacea, and from there its reputation spread to Europe. William N. Fenton has told how Lafitau found this plant growing in Iroquois territory in 1716, following which it became an important article of commerce.[37]

One of the greatest reputations among Iroquois medicinals was enjoyed by blue lobelia (*Lobelia syphilitica* L.), one of the many varieties of lobelia, or Indian tobacco. As the Latin name suggests, it was considered a remedy for syphilis and was purchased from the Indians for that purpose by Sir William Johnson,

34 Thwaites (ed.), *Jesuit Relations*, XLIII, 259.

35 "Onondaga Plant Names," *Journal of American Folk-Lore*, Vol. XV, No. 17 (April–June, 1902), 91–103.

36 Charles Whitebread, "The Indian Medical Exhibit of the Division of Medicine of the United States National Museum," *Proceedings of the United States National Museum*, LXVII, 23.

37 "Contacts Between Iroquois Herbalism and Colonial Medicine," *Annual Report of the Board of Regents of the Smithsonian Institution for 1941*, 517–20.

official agent of the British government to the northern Indians.[38] It was adopted in white medicine also as an expectorant, emetic, and diuretic and became a major remedy of the Thomsonian empirics.

One of the best friends of the Iroquois was Cadwallader Colden (1688–1776), a physician, botanist, and statesman of note, who served for a time as lieutenant governor of colonial New York. His *History of the Five Indian Nations* unfortunately contains no information about their medicine, but his correspondence is more fruitful. The Mohawks told him of a root which they chewed when they were "quite faint with travel & fasting," by which they found "their spirits restored wonderfully."[39] The Indian pokeroot (*Phytolacca decandra* L.), according to reports he received from John Bartram and others, was a cure for "cancer." Colden was sufficiently convinced to communicate his views on the subject to Benjamin Franklin. He further claimed that pokeroot would banish corns within twenty-four hours. He shared in the general faith in the antivenereal powers of blue lobelia.[40] Colden had no confidence, however, in the celebrated Seneca root as a snakebite remedy, insisting that hog's lard was the most effective application for the bites of venomous reptiles.[41]

The missionaries of the United Brethren, or Moravian church. were active among the Onondagas, and from their reports we are informed of the Iroquois knowledge of the poisonous properties of the may-apple root (*Podophyllum peltatum* L.). From them we also have accounts of the medicinal use of petroleum by the Seneca Indians, who gathered it from pools in western New York and Pennsylvania. It acquired a reputation among the whites as a remedy for rheumatism and muscular aches and pains and became an important article of trade.[42]

---

[38] Benjamin S. Barton, *Collections for an Essay Towards a Materia Medica of the United States*, I, 36–37.

[39] *The Letters and Papers of Cadwallader Colden*, Vols. I–VII, in *Collections of the New–York Historical Society*, Vols. L–LVI, III, 90.

[40] *Ibid.*, II, 274–75; III, 121, 123–24, 128–29; IV, 317, 323, 328; V, 64–65, 262.

[41] *Ibid.*, III, 89.

[42] William M. Beauchamp (ed.), *Moravian Journals Relating to Central New York, 1745–1766*, 38, 72, 109.

Benjamin F. Barton was favorably impressed by the medical knowledge of the "northern Indians," and his *Essay* is strewn with references to them. He called the Seneca snakeroot a valuable drug and reported that the Indians used a decoction of it for syphilis and malignant sore throat. He mentioned their use of a mineral remedy, sulphate of iron, as an emetic.[43]

A modern writer, Dr. Eric Stone, has praised the Iroquois for their advanced knowledge in the treatment of wounds, fractures, fevers, and the difficulties of childbirth. In fevers, he has written:

> the Iroquois recognized the syndrome of a dry hot skin, chills, thirst, prostration and muscular pains. Their management of the case seems quite modern as it included rest, sweating, purgation, diuresis and a restriction of the diet to liquids. Copious infusions of elderberries (*Sambucus canadensis*), either the fruit or the inner bark, were given to cause sweating and diuresis, which properties the medicine actually possesses. When the thirst had subsided and the skin had become moist, elimination was further promoted by sweat baths. Boneset (*Eupatorium perfoliatum*) was used as a hot decoction or the bush bean (*Phaseolus vulgaris*) was chewed in this or in other conditions where purgation was desired. They also practiced phlebotomy in fevers.[44]

Dr. Stone also mentioned the efficacy of Iroquois emetics, rheumatism therapy, and obstetrical practice. "Crede's method of expulsion," he declared, "was universally applied by the American Indian generations before it was described by the eminent French obstetrician." Their treatment of gunshot wounds "sounds like a leaf from the medical history of the World War," and these Indians "developed a splint for legs, which, in their time, was superior to those used by the whites."[45]

---

[43] Barton, *Essay Towards a Materia Medica*, Pt. II, 56–58, appendix, xiii–xiv.

[44] "Medicine Among the Iroquois," *Annals of Medical History*, N.S., Vol. VI, No. 6 (November, 1934), 531–32.

[45] *Ibid.*, 532–34. Dr. Credé was actually a native of Leipzig, Germany.

The Carolinas

"No doubt the settler expected to find among the Indians drugs and methods which would be new to him," wrote Dr. Joseph I. Waring, medical historian of South Carolina, "and he did encounter among the natives of the area a considerable system of treatment with roots, herbs and vegetable concoctions which was probably about as effective as his own."[46] We are fortunate in having extensive accounts of Indian medicine in the Carolinas through the writings of John Lawson and John Brickell and the scattered comments of Thomas Ashe, Mark Catesby, and Alexander Garden.

Of indigenous medicinal herbs, wrote Ashe in 1682, the "knowing Planters" had "Variety of such whose Medicinal Vertues were rare and admirable. The China[47] grows plentifully there, whose Root infus'd, yields us that pleasant Drink, which we know by the Name of China Ale in England; in Medicinal Uses it's far more excellent. . . . It mundifies and sweetens the Blood: It's good in Fevers, Scurvy, Gonorrhoea, and the Lues Venerea."[48]

Ashe mentioned three varieties of Snakeroot,

all Sovereign against the Mortal Bites of that Snake, too frequent in the West Indies: In all Pestilential Distempers, as Plague, Small Pox, and Malignant Fevers, it's a Noble Specifick; when stung, they eat the Root, applying it to the Venemous Wound; or they boyl the Roots in Water; which drunk, fortifies and corroborates the Heart, exciteing strong and generous Sweate: by which endangered Nature is relieved, and the Poyson carried off, and expelled.[49]

In Ashe's opinion, some of the Indians had an "exquisite Knowledge" in medicine and the nature of simples "and in the Cure of Scorbutick, Venereal, and Malignant Distempers are

[46] *A History of Medicine in South Carolina, 1670–1825,* 5.
[47] China-root (*Smilax tamnoides* L.) or China brier (*Smilax Bòna-nóx*).
[48] Thomas Ashe, "Carolina, or a Description of the Present State of that Country," in A. S. Salley, Jr. (ed.), *Narratives of Early Carolina, 1650–1708,* 144–45.
[49] *Ibid.,* 145.

admirable: In all External Diseases they suck the part affected with many Incantations." He found them reluctant, however, to reveal their medical secrets, "which by long Experience are religiously transmitted and conveyed in a continued Line from one Generation to another, for which those skill'd in this Faculty are held in great Veneration and Esteem."[50]

John Lawson, whose *History of North Carolina* was first published in 1714, provides one of the earliest accounts of the Indians of that colony,[51] and he devotes ample space to their medical practices. Along with descriptions of much shamanistic ritual, Lawson mentions other practices which he thought rational enough for whites to imitate:

> . . . they drink the Juices of Plants to free Nature of her Burdens, and not out of Foppery and Fashion as other Nations are oftentimes found to do. Amongst all the Discoveries of America by the Missionaries of the French and Spaniards I wonder none of them was so kind to the World as to have kept a Catalogue of the Distempers they found the Savages capable of curing, and their Method of Cure, which might have been of some advantage to our *Materia Medica* at home, when delivered by Men of Learning and other Qualifications, as most of them are. Authors generally tell us that the Savages are well enough acquainted with those Plants which their Climate affords, and that some of them effect great Cures, but by what Means and in what Form, we are left in the dark.

With the "Spontaneous Plants of America" he found that "the Savages are well acquainted withal, and a Flux of Blood never follows any of their Operations." Their materia medica, he informs us, included no minerals and few animal substances, since they relied chiefly on vegetable medicines. They made much use of the bark of the sassafras tree, and he reported their method of using it:

[50] *Ibid.*, 156.
[51] We except, of course, the accounts of the earlier Roanoke Island settlement.

They generally torrefy it in the Embers, so strip off the Bark from the Root, beating it to a Consistence fit to spread, so lay it on the grieved Part, which both cleanses a fowl Ulcer, and after Scarification being applied to a Contusion or Swelling, draws forth the Pain and reduces the Part to its pristine State of Health, as I have often seen effected.[52]

The only purge or emetic he found in use among the Carolina Indians was Yaupon tea (from the leaves of *Ilex cassine* or *Ilex vomitoria*), which they drank in vast quantities, "vomiting it up again as clear as they drink it." This was, he declared, a custom among all those tribes which could procure it, a statement corroborated by all writers on the southern Indians. "Besides their great Diuretick Quality," observed Lawson, "their Tea carries off a great deal that perhaps might prejudice their Health by Agues and Fevers."

"The Cures I have seen performed by the Indians," Lawson declared, "are too many to repeat here," but he cited their success in curing scalds, burns, and wounds. A drunken man who had fallen into a fire was:

> burnt in such a manner . . . that I did not think he could recover; yet they cured him in ten Days, so that he went about. I knew another blown up with Powder, that was cured to Admiration. I never saw an Indian have an Ulcer, or foul Wound in my life; neither is there any such thing to be found among them.[53]

One of their important remedies in the treatment of all these injuries was acorn oil. They had several remedies for toothache and used the juice of the tulip tree in treatment of "the pox" (venereal disease).

Although the Indians were, in Lawson's view, reckless about their health, he found them remarkably healthy and maintained that their worst scourges, smallpox and venereal diseases, had

[52] *History of North Carolina*, 235–36.
[53] *Ibid.*, 231.

53

been brought to them from without. They were also well formed; among the Tuscaroras he was surprised to see a humpbacked Indian, "which was the only crooked one I ever met withal." While Lawson was born too early to be affected by Cooper's (or even Rousseau's) view of the "noble savage," to which some writers ascribe contemporary admiration of anything aboriginal, he took such a favorable view of the Indians that he strongly advocated European intermarriage with them. Not the least of the benefits to be derived from such admixture, he pointed out, was that "by this Method, also, we should have a true Knowledge of all the Indian's Skill in Medicine and Surgery."[54]

John Brickell, reputedly a physician, published his *Natural History of North-Carolina* in 1737. Critics have correctly complained that he plagiarized large portions of it from Lawson, yet the work also contains notices of many floral, and especially faunal, remedies which are not found in Lawson. Presumably also, Brickell was qualified by his background to evaluate the efficacy of these substances in the light of the medical knowledge of his day, such as it was. Brickell does not always indicate whether he obtained his information concerning indigenous remedies from the Indians, just as he never credited Lawson for those parts of his work which were obviously copied from him. His expressed praise for Indian medical skill, however, suggests that he learned a good deal from them:

> As there are in this Country many poysonous Herbs and Creatures, so the *Indian* People have excellent Skill in applying effectual Antidotes to them; for Medicinal Herbs are here found in great Plenty, the *Woods* and *Savannas* being their *Apothecary's* Shops, from whence they fetch *Herbs, Leaves, Barks of Trees*, with which they make all their Medicines, and perform notable Cures; of which it may not be amiss to give some Instances, because they seem strange, if compared with our Method of curing Distempers.[55]

54 *Ibid.*, 258.
55 *The Natural History of North-Carolina, With an Account of the Trade, Manners, and Customs of the Christian and Indian Inhabitants*, 394.

The Indians, he further reported, cultivated herb gardens to guarantee a ready supply of plant remedies; such gardens were often seen at the sites of their abandoned towns. Of the uses of the plants found there, the Indians were said to be well acquainted, and Brickell was "persuaded that the reason why they took all these pains in planting these Simples was owing to their Doctor's Care, that upon all Occasions they might be provided with these Vegetables that were proper for the Indian Distempers, or any other use they might have occasion to make of them."

Like Josselyn, Brickell was prone to see remedial virtues in all living things, if we may judge by his extensive descriptions. He was the first to attribute medicinal properties to the "scarlet root," a plant obtained at the foot of the mountains, which had been mentioned earlier by Lawson as the source of a red pigment which the Indians mixed with bear's oil to anoint their bodies.[56] This plant, said Brickell, "has the Virtues to kill *Lice*, and suffer none to abide in their Heads." The leaves, which were likened to spearmint, were "used with good Success for Thrushes and sore Mouths."[57]

A renowned observer and illustrator of the flora and fauna of the Carolinas in the eighteenth century was Mark Catesby (1679–1749), whose *Natural History of Carolina, Florida, and the Bahama Islands* was published in 1754. In two oversize volumes, filled with hand-colored plates, Catesby depicted much of the plant, bird, animal, reptile, and insect life of this region. Al-

[56] Lawson, *History of North Carolina*, 181.

[57] Brickell, *Natural History* 22, 279. The identity of this plant is uncertain, because several plants have been called "red root" or "scarlet root," including New Jersey tea, or *Ceanothus americanus*, which has been used both as a beverage and as a remedy for numerous ailments by both Indians and whites. Dr. A. Clapp in 1852 gave the name "red root" to *Lachnanthes tinctoria* Ell., while Frank G. Speck in 1937 identified "red root" as *Cyrotheca capitata*, which was used by the Catawba Indians as a horse tonic. At the same time, he said that *Salix tristis* was called "red root" by the Catawbas, and he believed that this might be the red root of Lawson and Brickell. The Catawbas were using it to make a lotion for washing sore nipples on women's breasts, and sore mouths in children. Frank G. Speck, "Catawba Medicines and Curative Practices," *Publications of the Philadelphia Anthropological Society*, ed. D. S. Davidson, I, 188–90.

though he was a naturalist rather than a physician, he frequently expressed opinions about Indian medicine:

> Indians [he wrote] are wholly ignorant in Anatomy, and their Knowledge in surgery very superficial; amputation & phlebotomy they are strangers to; yet they know many good vulnerary plants of virtue, which they apply with good success: the cure of ulcers and dangerous wounds is facilitated by severe abstinence, which they endure with a resolution and patience peculiar to themselves. They knew not the pox [venereal disease, probably syphilis] in North *America*, till it was introduced by the *Europeans*.[58]

Contrary to the opinions expressed by Catesby, both amputation and phlebotomy have been reported as practiced among the Indians.[59] His other views, however, are in agreement with those of most observers. He freely praised Indian herbal remedies, being among the first to extol the vermifuge properties of the pinkroot (*Spigelia marilandica* L.). He called sassafras "a great sweetner of the blood," and reported that a decoction of it was sometimes given with much success in Virginia for intermittent fever (malaria). Of the celebrated "Casena" or Yaupon tea, he wrote:

> They say it restores lost appetite, strengthens the stomach, giving them agility and courage in war &c. . . . In South-Carolina it is called *Cassena*. In Virginia and North Carolina it is known by the name of *Yapon*; in the latter of which places it is as much in use among the white people as among the Indians, at least among those who inhabit the seacoasts.[60]

All of the foregoing writers mentioned several varieties of snakeroot in the Carolinas. Some species of snakeroot were used

58 *Natural History of Carolina, Florida, and the Bahama Islands.*

59 For a report of Indian amputation technique, see Lawson, *History of North Carolina*, 210. Several writers have reported phlebotomy among the Indians, *e.g.*, Benjamin Rush, *An Inquiry into the Natural History of Medicine among the Indians of North America . . .* , 123.

60 Catesby, *Natural History*, II, 57.

in medical practice at Charleston, although accounts do not identify the kind used. In 1711 snakeroot was used in treating patients during a "pleurisy" epidemic, which Waring believes was actually a form of influenza.[61] In the summer and fall of 1728 the palmetto metropolis was visited by "a sort of pestilential pleuritick fever," the third time in five years, and the reported treatment included phlebotomy and the administration of snakeroot, "with unknown results."[62] The Virginia snakeroot (*Aristolochia serpentaria* L.) was reported in use in 1760 "to expel morbific matter from the blood."[63]

Perhaps the most celebrated plant remedy to reach the world by way of the Carolinas was the Indian pinkroot (*Spigelia marilandica* L.), a Cherokee remedy for worms, which was adopted into the London, Dublin, and Edinburgh pharmacopeias, and was official in the American pharmacopeia from 1820 to 1926. Its properties were first called to the attention of the medical profession by Dr. John Lining (1708–60), of Charleston, South Carolina, who extolled its virtues as a vermifuge, and noted its toxic effects, reporting its use by both planters and physicians.[64] While Lining's paper on pinkroot was the first published notice of it, priority in its discovery has been accorded also to Dr. Alexander Garden, who sent specimens to an English correspondent as early as 1752. Garden observed the use of the plant while on an expedition to the Cherokee country in the company of the royal governor.[65]

In 1849, Dr. Francis P. Porcher of Charleston prepared for the American Medical Association a report on the indigenous medical plants of South Carolina.[66] The total number of plants catalogued by Dr. Porcher was 464, of which 55 were cultivated exotics or nonmedical. Dr. Porcher was a physician, not an eth-

---

[61] Waring, *Medicine in South Carolina*, 20.

[62] *Ibid.*, 35.

[63] *Ibid.*, 83, citing David Ramsay, *History of South Carolina*, II, 116–20.

[64] *Ibid.*, 259.

[65] *Ibid.*, 70.

[66] "Report on the Indigenous Medical Plants of South Carolina," *Transactions of the American Medical Association*, II, 677–862.

nologist or historian, and made no effort to determine which plants had been used by the Indians. Nevertheless, he made incidental reference to Indian usage of 35 of these plants, while overlooking the Indian medicinal use of such well-known botanicals as blue flag, pokeroot, sassafras, and Spigelia. By the most conservative count, at least 129 other plants on his list are known, from published evidence, to have been used by Indians, either in the Carolinas or elsewhere. A thorough search of sources might add many more to the 164 plants in Porcher's list which were used by Indians.

The Middle Colonies
Pennsylvania, New Jersey, Delaware, and Maryland

A half century before the first English settlements in Pennsylvania, a passenger on a Dutch ship ascending the Delaware reported that the land gave off a sweet smell:

> The 2d, threw the lead in fourteen fathoms, sandy bottom, and smelt the land, which gave off a sweet perfume, as the wind comes from the northwest, which blew off the land, and caused these sweet odors. This comes from the Indians setting fire, at this time of year, to the woods and thickets, in order to hunt; and the land is full of sweet-smelling herbs, as sassafras, which has a sweet smell. When the wind blows out of the northwest, and the smoke is driven to the sea, it happens that the land is smelt before it is seen.[67]

In such a manner did the universal remedy of the Indian tribes announce its presence in Pennsylvania. It seems appropriate that the *winachk*, or good tree, of the Delawares should be the first thing to attract the attention of these early visitors. Fifty years later William Penn listed this tree among those "of most note" and went on to list other curative plants:

> There are diverse Plants that not only the Indians tell us, but we have had occasion to prove by Swellings, Burnings, Cuts,

[67] "David DeVries Notes" (1632), in A. C. Myers (ed.), *Narratives of Early Pennsylvania, West New Jersey and Delaware, 1630–1707*, 16.

etc., that they are of great Vertue, suddenly curing the Patient: and for smell, I have observed several, especially one, the wild Mirtle; the other I know not what to call, but are most fragrant.[68]

The Indian knowledge of the uses of native flora, wrote Gabriel Thomas in 1698, compared favorably with that of European physicians:

There are many curious and excellent Physical Wild Herbs, Roots, and Drugs of great Vertue, and very sanative, as the Sassafras, and Sarsaparilla, so much us'd in Diet-Drinks for the Cure of the Venereal Disease, which makes the Indians by a right application of them, as able Doctors and Surgeons as any in Europe, performing celebrated Cures therewith, and by the use of some particular Plants only, find Remedy in all Swellings, Burnings, Cuts, etc. There grows also in great plenty the Black Snake-Root, (fam'd for its sometimes preserving, but often curing the Plague, being infused only in Wine, Brandy, or Rumm) Rattle-Snake-Root, Poke-Root, called in England Jallop, with several other beneficial Herbs, Plants and Roots, which Physicians have approved of, far exceeding in Nature and Vertue, those of other Countries.[69]

Thomas called attention to the prevalence of pennyroyal, mint, mustard, sage, rue, and tansy, "with diverse others, which there is great store of."

Eighteenth-century accounts of medical practices among the Delawares, the principal Indian tribe of this area, have been bequeathed to posterity by the United Brethren missionaries John Heckewelder, David Zeisberger, and George Henry Loskiel. Their reports, like those of the Catholic Jesuits, are not always favorable, for the Indian medical practice was frequently joined with religious exercises which the missionaries classed as devil worship. Nevertheless, these observers did not allow their aver-

---

[68] "Letter to the Committee of the Free Society of Traders" (1683), in Myers (ed), *Narratives*, 227–29.

[69] "An Historical and Geographical Account of Pensilvania and of West–New-Jersey" (1698), in Myers, (ed.), *Narratives*, 323.

sion to "heathen" incantations to blind them to the possible utility of some Indian medicines. Of these Heckewelder wrote:

The *Materia Medica* of the Indians consist of various roots and plants known to themselves, the properties of which they are not fond of disclosing to strangers. They make considerable use of the barks of trees, such as the white and black oak, the white walnut, of which they make pills, the cherry, dogwood, maple, birch, and several others. They prepare and compound these medicines in different ways, which they keep a profound secret. Those preparations are frequently mixed with superstitious practices, calculated to guard against the powers of witchcraft, in which, unfortunately, they have a strong fixed belief.[70]

Heckewelder mentioned their use of emetics, bleeding, and the sweat bath. He gave a detailed description of the last and cited the case of a white man from Detroit who was cured of an undisclosed infirmity after taking the Indian sweat treatment.[71] David Zeisberger called the Indians reckless of their health, and poor nurses for the sick:

Care and attention for the sick amount to but little, the Indians being poor nurses. So long as they can go out they lie on the hard bed of boards; no longer able to do this they are laid on the ground near the fire, possibly upon grass or hay, a small hole in the ground under the patient serving as a bed-pan. In time of sickness their diet consists of thin soup of pounded corn, without either butter, fat or salt. Not until a patient is convalescent is he allowed any meat.[72]

Such a dietary regimen has been considered correct for certain ailments; its equivalent among the Iroquois was approved by Dr. Eric Stone. Zeisberger further believed that the Indians

---

70 *History Manners and Customs of the Indian Nations Who Once Inhabited Pennsylvania, and the Neighbouring States,* 224.

71 *Ibid.,* 224–27.

72 "History of the North American Indians," Parts I–II, ed. Archer B. Hulbert and William N. Schwarze, *Ohio Archaeological and Historical Quarterly,* Vol. XIX, Nos. 1–2 (January and April, 1910), Pt. I, 24.

lacked both knowledge and skill for the treatment of internal ills, but, he continued, "wounds and external injuries they treat very successfully, knowing what applications to make. In the curing of those suffering from snake-bite, they are particularly capable. For the bite of every variety of snake they have a special *Beson*." He acknowledged that some Indians had "considerable knowledge of the virtue of roots and herbs, learned from their fathers, and who bring about relief." For this they were well paid and kept their knowledge to themselves until approaching death induced them to communicate it to a child or friend. Their doctors, who were often aging men too infirm to hunt longer, were "charlatans" who resorted to dreams for their diagnosis and prescriptions, who engaged in "howling" and deceptive practices and drained the patients, their families, and friends of their worldly goods in payment for "useless doctoring."[73]

George Henry Loskiel shared some of these critical views and further complained that the Indian doctors did not give proper doses of their medicines, being inclined to overdo it. After scoring the supernatural elements in their therapy, he went on to praise their treatment of external injuries, and called them "especially well skilled in healing bruises and wounds." Moreover:

They also extract splinters, pieces of iron, and balls so carefully that the wound is not enlarged by the operation. They are perfect masters in the treatment of fractures and dislocations. . . .

In burnings and chilblains they use a decoction of beech leaves, as a speedy and successful remedy. A warm poultice, made of the flour of Indian corn, is laid upon all boils and impostumes, till they are ripe, when they are opened with a lancet. In letting blood, a small piece of flint or glass is fastened to a wooden handle, and placed upon the vein; which they strike, till the blood gushes out. Teeth are drawn with a common pair of pincers.[74]

[73] *Ibid.*, 24–27.
[74] *History of the Mission of the United Brethren among the Indians in North America, in Three Parts*, tr. Christian Ignatius Latrobe, Pt. I, 112–13.

Loskiel included a substantial list of remedies employed by the Indians for various ills, including the prickly ash, tulip tree, flowering dogwood, laurel, sassafras, elder, poison ash, wintergreen, liverwort, pokeweed, wild jalap, wild ipecac, wild sarsaparilla, Canadian sanicle, bloodroot, "Cuckow-pint" (*Arum maculatum*), Virginia snakeroot, ginseng, and "fossil-oil."[75]

The Medical Botanists of Philadelphia

Philadelphia was the capital of medical botany in the United States in the last half of the eighteenth century and well into the nineteenth. From the Quaker City sallied forth into the woods such eminent investigators as John and William Bartram, Benjamin S. Barton and his nephew William P. C. Barton, Caspar Wistar, G. H. E. Muhlenberg, the Turkish-born French-Italian genius Constantine Samuel Rafinesque, and such distinguished foreign visitors as Peter Kalm, André Michaux, Frederick Pursh, Johann David Schöpf, and Thomas Nuttall. No one who was anyone in science could afford to bypass this intellectual center or fail to call upon its giants. Numerous studies of the medicinal properties of American flora found their way into the *Transactions of the American Philosophical Society* and the published "inaugural dissertations" of candidates for medical degrees at the University of Pennsylvania. Many of these men found some merit in Indian botanical remedies, and their writings abound with discussions of them. In this way the Indian influence on early American science came to be of some weight.

Although not a botanist, Dr. Benjamin Rush deserves some consideration here as one of the most distinguished American physicians of his time. He was constantly seeking information about Indian health and medical practices from travelers and from occasional Indians who came to Philadelphia. Some of the information obtained in this manner formed the basis of his "oration" on Indian medicine delivered before the American Philosophical Society on February 4, 1774. It is a mixture of

[75] *Ibid.*, 115–17.

approval and scorn and bestowed the most favor on those Indian practices which accorded with his own conceptions. Thus
he viewed the Indian practice of phlebotomy with some favor:

> To know that opening a vein in the arm, or foot, would re-
> lieve a pain in the head or side, supposes some knowledge
> of the animal economy, and therefore marks an advanced
> period in the history of medicine.[76]

Among natural treatments of the Indians, he had some favorable impression of their drinking cold water, sweating, purging,
and vomiting. He knew of their astringent medicines, their
emetics and cathartics, and declared "if they are simple, they are
like their eloquence, full of strength; if they are few in number,
they are accomodated, as their languages are, to their ideas, to the
whole of their diseases." The only disease among them, he held,
was "fevers."

He had heard of cauterization among the Indians:

> We have an account of the Indians using something like a
> POTENTIAL CAUSTIC, in obstinate pains. It consists of
> a piece of rotten wood, called *punk*, which they place upon
> the part affected, & afterwards set it on fire: the fire gradually
> consumes the wood, & its ashes burn a hole in the flesh.[77]

Regarding Indian specifics other than the few he mentioned,
he said that he had "taken pains to inquire into the success of
some of these Indian specifics, & have never heard of one well
attested case of their efficacy."[78] He added that "we have no discoveries in the materia medica to hope for from the Indians of
North America," because "it would be a reproach to our schools
of physic if modern physicians were not more successful than the
Indians even in the treatment of their own diseases."[79]

Nevertheless, Rush evidenced a continuing interest in Indian
health and physiology. When Chief Alexander McGillivray of

[76] *An Inquiry into the Natural History of Medicine among the Indians of
North America,* 123.

[77] *Ibid.*   [78] *Ibid.,* 129.   [79] *Ibid.,* 152.

the Creeks went to New York in 1790 for a conference with George Washington, he stopped briefly in Philadelphia, whereupon Rush took advantage of the opportunity for a personal interview and asked the chief to reply to a list of questions to be submitted later in writing. With the questions, Rush sent McGillivray a copy of his oration on Indian medicine. His queries dealt with the diseases common among the Indians, whether Indian women ever died in childbirth, the mortality among Indian children, the prevalence of suicide, the effects of aging upon mental facility, and the strength of "passion for the female sex" among the Indians.[80] It is notable that Rush failed to ask about Indian remedies, of which a great many were known to the Creeks.

The following year, when Timothy Pickering was about to undertake a mission to the Seneca Indians of western New York, Rush sent him a list of eighteen questions to be asked of the Indians. The questions previously put to McGillivray were repeated, in addition to new ones asking about Indian means of obviating fatigue or hunger, whether they ate during the day on long marches, whether they slept more than "civilized" people, and whether they dreamed much; there were inquiries about the prevalence of female disorders and the age of beginning and cessation of menstruation, the age of weaning children, the age of menopause, whether Indians lost their teeth in old age, the prevalence of gray hair in old people, the regularity of stool excretions, whether they were affected by the recent influenza epidemic, and the prevalence of venereal disease.[81] It is again notable that only one of these questions ("obviating fatigue and hunger") evidenced any interest in Indian drugs.

In 1803, reportedly at the suggestion of President Jefferson, Dr. Rush submitted a list of questions to be asked of western Indians by Meriwether Lewis on his projected expedition up the

[80] *The Autobiography of Benjamin Rush*, 189.

[81] Rush to Pickering, May 2, 1791, from MS, Pickering Papers, Massachusetts Historical Society, in Rush, *Autobiography*, 580–81.

[82] *Autobiography*, 265–66.

Missouri River. This time he asked about longevity, the state of the pulse at various ages, the practice of bleeding, whether the Indians practiced sweating and fasting, the time of bathing, their diet and methods of food preservation, and, a new departure: "What are their remedies?"[82]

In his diary for December 15, 1812, Rush recorded having tea with the French botanist François André Michaux, who had just returned from a trip to northern parts of Quebec. Among the plants he found there was Labrador tea (*Ledum latifolium* Ait.), a popular beverage substance among the Indians of that region.[83] Apparently it was less popular with the French, for he found them, from their diet of salt meat and seals, as he put it, suffering from scorbutic complaints. The Indians, he reported to Rush, "who eat wild fruits plentifully escape the scurvy."[84]

Without mentioning the Indians, Dr. Rush paid indirect tribute to them when he advocated the use of one of their native products, maple sugar, instead of cane sugar. The latter product, then obtained principally from the West Indies, he held to be too often unclean, besides being morally tainted as a product of slave labor. He quoted Baron Lahontan's remark that there was "no better remedy for fortifying the stomach" than maple sugar. Rush believed that sugar in the diet would have medicinal value in preventing worms, malignant fevers, disorders of the breast, and "weakness and acrid defluxions upon other parts of the body." He placed no credence in reports that sugar was harmful to the teeth.[85]

One of the foreign visitors at Philadelphia in the late eight-

---

[83] Frank Speck reported *Ledum* tea in use by the Montagnais to "purify the blood," and for chills. "Medicine Practices of the Northeastern Algonquians," *Proceedings XIXth International Congress of Americanists*, 313. Henry David Thoreau reported its use, as well as hemlock leaves, by the Penobscots of Maine, in *The Maine Woods*, 125. *Ledum* may have helped to fortify the northern Indians against scurvy in winter; *Ledum palustre* L., according to the 1950 *Dispensatory of the United States*, contains the glycoside ericolin, tannin, valeric acid, and other substances.

[84] Rush, *Autobiography*, 303.

[85] "An Account of the Sugar Maple-Tree of the United States . . . in a Letter to Thomas Jefferson, Esq., Secretary of State . . . ," *Transactions of the American Philosophical Society*, III, 64–81.

eenth century was Dr. Johann David Schöpf, who had come to America as a physician with German troops in the British service during the Revolutionary War. He remained to make an extensive tour of the United States during which he catalogued more than four hundred medicinal plants and other therapeutic substances. His work was published in Latin at Erlangen, Germany, in 1787 and has been regarded as a pioneer work in American medical botany. The *Materia Medica Americana* is in large part an *aboriginal* materia medica, although he did not call it that, nor report how he came by his information. Constantine Rafinesque flatly states that Schöpf collected his materials from the Indians,[86] and there seems no reason to doubt that this is so. In some instances, Dr. Schöpf mentioned the Indian uses of plants,[87] although, considering the extent of the Indian contribution, the recognition given is sparing. Whether this parsimony is due to the extraordinary brevity of his treatment of each plant listed or to racial arrogance, it is not possible to say. In his *Travels*, Dr. Schöpf maintained that the medical reputation of the Indians was exaggerated:

> Of the medical knowledge of the Indians the opinion here and there in America is still very high. The greater number, but not the well-informed, are convinced that the Indians, mysteriously skilled in many excellent remedies, carefully and jealously conceal them from the white Europeans. As always so here, people are deceived by the fancy that behind a veil of mystery there lie hidden great and powerful things. I see no reason to expect anything extraordinary or important, and I am almost certain that with the passage of time nothing will be brought to light, if as is the case, outright specifics are looked for and presumably infallible remedies.

[86] *American Medical Flora, or Manual of the Medical Botany of the United States of America*, I, ii.

[87] E.g., *Cornus Amomum*, or Swamp dogwood, *Angelica atropurpurea, Cassine, Trillium cernuum, Sophora tinctoria, Arbutus uva ursi, Prunus sylvestris*, and *Arum sagittaefolium*. Some of these names are no longer current.

He did not wish to deny, however, "that we must thank the northern half of America for sundry medicaments of value," and that "every new remedy must be to the patriotic American physician a treasured contribution to his domestic medical store." Showing the influence of Rush, to whose oration on Indian medicine he called attention, he held that the diseases of the Indians, for the healing of which their skill was especially praised, were simple ones consisting chiefly of "fevers and superficial injuries." Moreover:

The observers and panegyrists of the so much belauded Indian methods of therapy are commonly ignorant people who find things and circumstances wonderful because they cannot offer explanations from general principles. The bodily constitution of an Indian, hardened from youth by vehement exercise and by many difficult feats, demands and bears stronger medical excitants; and endowed originally with more elasticity, the physical system of an Indian often rids itself of a malady more promptly than that of a European, weaker and softer, is able to do. . . . The medicines of which they make use are few and simple, potent naturally or through the heaviness of the dose. . . . The most of their praised specifics are purgatives, perspiratives, or urine-stimulants, which they use not sparingly at the first approach of disease, and in this way often check the process of the malady.

Dr. Schöpf argued that Indians often failed to cure diseases, particularly those brought to them by Europeans. He praised them, however, for "their generous readiness to produce without reward their manifold roots, barks, and herbs for the behoof of those needing aid, even if they do not indicate where they got them. They show at least no selfish and mercenary views, which are the commonest motives among the no less numerous mystery-usurers of more civilized and enlightened nations."[88]

Despite Dr. Schöpf's critical evaluation of Indian herbalism, he paid them unexpressed tribute by including hundreds of their

[88] *Travels in the Confederation (1783–1784)*, ed. Alfred J. Morrison, I, 284–87.

curative agents in his book. Moreover, he urged American physicians, as a patriotic duty, to make greater use of their indigenous materia medica.

A much more favorable attitude toward Indian medicine was held by Dr. Benjamin S. Barton, a botanist and member of the medical faculty at the University of Pennsylvania. With due regard for his faults, and with awareness of his borrowings from the researches of William Bartram and David Schöpf,[89] it can be said that Barton was free of the kind of ethnocentric arrogance which prevented some of the giants from giving the Indians their due.

For one class of Indian remedies, the snakebite specifics, Barton had only scorn. In an article written in 1793, he listed some three dozen herbal remedies used by Indians and whites for snakebite and pronounced them as mainly useless save for the rubefacient properties of some of them. To the extent that cures were reported through the use of these, he claimed that it was due to sucking out the poison and the application of a ligature to prevent its spread.[90]

Toward many other aboriginal drugs he was disposed to acknowledge considerable utility. In an address delivered before the Philadelphia Medical Society on February 21, 1798, and later published in several editions,[91] he stated that, with the exception of the snakebite simples, the Indian materia medica:

> . . . contains but few substances as inert as many of those which have a place in our books on this science, and on other parts of medicine. The astringents and tonics, which they

[89] Francis Lee Harper, of Chapel Hill, N.C., in a personal communication to this writer, February 3, 1966, makes these points and several others unfavorable to Barton. Mr. Harper declares that Barton "was constantly endeavoring to gain the knowledge and experience of others and converting them to his own use, with little or no acknowledgement." Mr. Harper edited *The Travels of William Bartram*.

[90] "An Account of the most effectual means of preventing the deleterious consequences of the bite of the Crotalus Horridus, or Rattle-Snake," *Transactions of the American Philosophical Society*, III, 100–14.

[91] *Idem, Collections for an Essay Towards a Materia Medica of the United States.*

employ in the treatment of intermittent fevers, are the barks of some species of Cornus, or Dogwood . . . which are found to possess properties very nearly allied to those of Cinchona, or Peruvian bark; their purgatives are different species of Iris, or Flag, the root of Podophyllum peltatum, or May-apple; the bark of the Juglans cinerea, or Butternut, and some others: their emetics are the Spiraea trifoliata, or Indian Physic; the Euphorbia Ipecacuanha, Sulphat of Iron, or Copperas, and many others; their sudorifics are the active Polygala Senega, or Seneca snake-root, the Eupatorium perfoliatum, or Thorough-wort, the Lobelia syphilitica, &c: their anthelmintics are the Spigelia Marilandica, or Carolina Pink-root, the Lobelia Cardinalis, or Cardinal-Flower, &c.[92]

Barton listed in this work sixty indigenous and one foreign remedy, and their supposed properties. He believed that the number could easily be extended, and asserted that it was "obvious, that the Indians of North-America are in possession of a number of active and important remedies." He conceded that the Indians did not always apply their remedies with "judgement and discernment," but added: "What treasures of medicine may not be expected from a people, who although destitute of the lights of science, have discovered the properties of some of the most inestimable medicines with which we are acquainted?"[93]

In 1793, Dr. Nicholas Collin called to the attention of the American Philosophical Society that "above an hundred" native plants were known to be in use among the "inhabitants," but that the qualities of few of them were well known and a very small number had yet been adopted by apothecaries and physicians. He invited more attention to the native plants in order to free the medical profession from dependence upon foreign products, which were expensive, often adulterated, and subject to depreciation from age. Such an inquiry on native plants would necessarily begin with the Indians, who:

[92] *Ibid.*, Pt. II, xiii–xiv.
[93] *Ibid.*, xiv.

have several remedies against the diseases and accidents aris-
ing from the climate, and their savage mode of life; as fevers,
rheumatism, wounds, bruises, scalding, chillblains, bite of
venomous serpents; besides emetics, cathartics, sudorifics,
and dietics. These have the sanction of time and simplicity.
It is also generally believed, that they possess very important
secrets, of which only a few extraordinary specimens are related with plausible authenticity.[94]

In the two decades between 1790 and 1810, the influence of the
medical botanists in Philadelphia, and especially those on the
faculty of the University of Pennsylvania, seems to have inspired
a number of candidates for the degree of doctor of medicine to
devote their "inaugural dissertations" to the study of indigenous
medicines. Dr. Barton in his *Essay* called attention to several of
these which were the work of his students and which he drew
upon in his discussion of indigenous drugs. Among them we find
studies by James Woodhouse on the properties of the persimmon
tree, by Henry Wilkins on emetics, Benjamin Shultz on the Indian pokeweed, John Willis on the vegetable astringents, Samuel
Cooper on the Jimson weed, Isaac Winston on the Seneca snakeroot, Edward Brailsford on tobacco, Patrick K. Rogers on the
tulip tree, Thomas D. Price on the *Magnolia glauca*, or sweet
bay, William Downey on the puccoon, or bloodroot, John S.
Mitchell on the bearberry and wintergreen, Daniel Legare on
the use of tobacco smoke in drowning cases, John Floyd on two
species of magnolia, and Jacob De La Motta on the Indian
physic.[95]

[94] "An Essay on Those Inquiries in Natural Philosophy, Which at Present are
Most Beneficial to the United States of North America," *Transactions of the American Philosophical Society*, III, iii–xxvii.

[95] The works are listed here in chronological order. The publication data and
locations are listed after authors' names in Robert B. Austin, *Early American Medical Imprints, A Guide to Works Printed in the United States, 1668–1820* (Washington, D.C., U.S. Department of Health, Education, and Welfare, 1961). About 1807
the university no longer required publication of medical dissertations. *The Philadelphia Medical and Physical Journal*, Vol. III (1808), of which Barton was editor,
listed sixty unpublished medical dissertations accepted at the university for 1808
alone. Several of these dealt with native drugs.

This extraordinary scientific interest in native medicines should not be viewed simply as a romantic interest in the achievements of the "noble savage." More likely it reflected an awakening of nationalistic spirit born of the troubled state of the world during the period of the French Revolution and the Napoleonic Wars. Cut off by the warring giants from the normal avenues of world trade, hampered even by such midget annoyances as the Barbary pirates, harried by blockades and counterblockades, the people of the infant nation were brought to a fresh realization of the ideological gulf which separated them from Europe more completely than the oceans. They were determined to make the United States independent not only in government and diplomacy, but also in science, medicine, and economics. It was an early form of isolationism created by conditions from without as well as from within.

This explanation seems more plausible when one reflects that these Americans had already lived in proximity to the "savages," in many instances for more than a century and a half, and yet their humble herbalism had, with a few exceptions, won the respect only of hunters and backwoods farmers who scratched a precarious living from the wilderness. Only at the close of the eighteenth century, when the full meaning of American separation from Europe dawned in the minds of thinking men, did they turn toward inquiries into the virtues of native medicines. This was the meaning of Jacob Bigelow's remarks, in his *American Medical Botany*, that Americans should develop their native plants in order to "diminish tribute to foreigners," and avoid the "embarrassments occasioned by the chances of war and commercial restrictions."[96] But in turning its back upon Europe, America had to face the red man—this time not as a conqueror, but as a pupil.

Georgia

The last of the English colonies to be established within the territory now occupied by the United States came into existence at least partly because of the search for new drugs which might

[96] *American Medical Botany*, I, preface, viii.

make Great Britain independent of sources in Spanish America. A document which enumerates the aims of the philanthropic trustees declares:

> The Colony of *Georgia* lying about the same latitude with part of *China, Persia, Palestine,* and the *Madeiras,* it is highly probable that when hereafter it shall be well-peopled and rightly cultivated, ENGLAND may be supplied from thence with raw Silk, Wine, Oil, Dyes, Drugs, and many other materials for manufactures, which she is obliged to purchase from Southern countries.[97]

Of particular interest to those interested in the colony was the determination whether the land might contain, in the wild state, such drugs as cinchona, ipecac, jalap, coca, and the cochineal insect, and if such were not the case, they intended to discover whether these commodities might be cultivated there. In 1730–31, an Apothecaries Company of England, encouraged by the trustees of Georgia, was formed to investigate these matters, and further to find drugs which might be used for those of the Spanish territories.[98] The trustees, acting in cooperation with the apothecaries, engaged Dr. William Houstoun, a botanist, to set up headquarters in Jamaica to search the Caribbean for medicinal or other plants which might be grown in Georgia. His instructions provided:

> At all these places you are to use your utmost Diligence to procure Seeds, Roots of all useful Plants, such as Ipecac, Jalap, Contrayerva, Sarsaparilla, and Jesuits Bark, the Trees which yield Peruvian and Capivi Balsam, the Gum Elemi, etc., the Cockineal Plant with the Animals upon it, and all other things you shall judge may be of use to the Colony of Georgia.[99]

[97] "Some Account of the Designs of the Trustees for Establishing the Colony of Georgia in America," in Peter Force (ed.), *Tracts and Other Papers*, 5–6.

[98] Robert Cuming Wilson, *Drugs and Pharmacy in the Life of Georgia, 1733–1959*, 6.

[99] *Ibid.*, 11–12; Trustees minutes of Oct. 3, 1733, in Allen D. Candler (ed.), *The Colonial Records of the State of Georgia*, II, 5.

72

Dr. Houstoun died after six months and was succeeded by Robert Miller, who asked for and was denied permission by the Spanish authorities to investigate the medicinal plants of Florida. What the eventual outcome of these efforts was is not clear, but they signify the envy the English must have felt to be divorced from access to the pharmaceutical products with which the natives of the West Indies and Central and South America had endowed their Spanish conquerors.

Years before the first English settlement was established at Savannah in 1733, the Spanish and English had been exporting sassafras from the unoccupied territory. Not long after settlement, ships filled their holds with cargoes of "Bear's Oyl, Snakeroot, Rattlesnake-root, Sea-rod, China Root, Sassafras, and Shumack."[100] Proprietor James Edward Oglethorpe wrote to the trustees in 1739 that there was under cultivation in the colony cotton, indigo, cochineal, aloes, sassafras, snakeroot, sumach, myrtle, "and many other drugs that will not grow in England."[101]

When, in 1740, the administration and possibilities of the colony were being called into question both among the settlers and in England, Benjamin Martyn argued that the colony, in addition to the numerous drugs it was producing, was also rich in timber resources, and was possessed of the source of the treasured red dye of the Spanish provinces:

The prickly Pear Shrubs (upon which the Fly feeds, from which is taken the Cochineal,) are in Abundance upon the Islands in the Southern Part of the Province; and the Fly has been taken upon them, which, being squeezed by some Persons between their Fingers, has dyed them with the fine red Colour which the Cochineal gives.[102]

100 R. C. Wilson, *Drugs and Pha⸱ ⸱acy,* 14, citing Chandler (ed.), *Colonial Records of Georgia,* III, 97.

101 *Ibid.,* 15, citing Egmont MSS, Phillips Collection, Vol. 14204, 32–36.

102 *An Impartial Inquiry into the State and Utility of the Province of Georgia,* 21. Cochineal dye was used by Mexican and South American Indians. It was official in the *U. S. Pharmacopeia,* 1831–1955, and *National Formulary* since 1955, being used principally as a coloring agent. Formerly it was used in domestic medicine for whooping cough and neuralgic ailments.

As the settlers advanced farther from the seacoast, their means of contact with the Old World diminished, and, situated far from physicians and apothecaries, they came to depend upon the native remedies they could obtain from the Indians. Many simples used by the Creeks and Cherokees found their way into the white man's folk medicine and were later admitted to the pharmacopeia. Of the four-hundred-odd drugs reported by Youngken as being used by American Indians, Robert C. Wilson found that seventy were indigenous to Georgia.[103]

A well-known figure who was as interested in the medical secrets of primitive peoples as he was in the folk medicine of the Old World was the evangelist John Wesley (1703–91), who preached in Georgia from 1735 to 1737. He was favorably impressed with the rugged health of the Indians and praised their health and medical practices in his book, *Primitive Physic*, which was first published at London in 1747.[104] It enjoyed phenomenal popularity, going through forty-odd editions in the next hundred years. In it he speculates that the knowledge of "physic," like religion, was at first traditional, and that information about the most efficacious medicines proper to the diseases of each season and climate were handed down from fathers to sons. "It is certain," he continued,

> that this is the method wherein the art of healing is preserved among the Americans [Indians] to this day. Their diseases, indeed, are exceeding few; nor do they often occur, by reason of their continual exercise, and (till of late, universal) temperance. But if any are sick, or bit by a serpent, or torn by a wild beast, the fathers immediately tell their children what remedy to apply. And it is rare that the patient suffers long; those medicines being quick, as well as generally infallible.[105]

Simple medical knowledge, he believed, was once the property of people everywhere until "men of learning began to set experi-

103 R. C. Wilson, *Drugs and Pharmacy*, 428.
104 *Primitive Physic; or, an Easy and Natural Method of Curing Most Diseases.*
105 *Ibid.*, 5–6.

ence aside, to build physic on hypotheses, to form theories of diseases and their cure, and to substitute these in place of experiments." He held that the physicians had estranged the practice of medicine from the people for their own advantage and maintained that lovers of mankind labored to reduce physic to its ancient standard, "to explode out of it all hypotheses and finespun theories, and to make it a plain intelligible thing, as it was in the beginning." No strange chemicals, exotics, or compound medicines were necessary, said he, "but a single plant or fruit duly applied."

Most of the simples prescribed by Wesley are of European origin, only a few, such as nettle and tobacco, being used by the Indians. It appears that Wesley learned little of their remedies, although he may have seen in them the embodiment of his idea that medical practice could be "empirical" and that no special education was necessary for the art. In many Indian tribes, however, medicine was a rather exclusive profession, closely linked with priestly functions. Some herbal knowledge, however, was possessed by almost everyone, although it was often believed that these herbs required the proper ritual to be effective.

The Spanish Colonies

There is much that can be learned of the medical knowledge of the Indians of the West Indies, Mexico, Central America, and South America in the writings of Sahagún, Oviedo, Garcilaso de la Vega, Monardes, Von Humboldt, the *Badianus Manuscript*, and other sources. A surprising number of the more spectacular drugs, such as cinchona (source of quinine) and coca (source of cocaine), guaiacum, once a celebrated remedy for syphilis, and jalap, the famous purgative, were used by natives of Spanish or Portuguese America. The limits of this study, however, will not permit that interesting excursion,[106] and so is confined to some brief notice of Florida, the Southwest, and California.

[106] See the Appendix for a brief discussion of Latin-American Indian medicine and ethnobotany and a list of official drugs derived from that region.

Florida

The Spanish physician Nicholas Monardes, in *Joyfull Newes out of the Newe Founde Worlde*, has given a quaintly delightful account of several dozen medicinal products of the New World, and he was not at all conservative in enumerating the virtues of such later-to-be-celebrated remedies as sarsaparilla, guaiacum, mechoacan, tacamahaca, copal, jalap, and, of special interest here, the ubiquitous sassafras. It was in Florida, Monardes relates, that this panacea-to-be was first found by French Huguenot settlers, who learned of its uses from the Indians. So wonderful were its virtues as he proclaimed them that it is no wonder trading ships from England were crossing the ocean to get it long before any settlement was made:

> From the Florida . . . thei bryng a woodd and roote of a tree that groweth in those partes, of great vertues, and great excellencies, that thei heale there with grievous and variable deseases.
>
> [A Frenchman] tolde me that the Frenchemen, which had been in Florida at that tyme, when thei came into those partes, thei had been sicke the moste of theim, of greevous and variable diseases, and that the Indians did showe them this Tree, and the maner how thei should use it, and so thei did, and thei healed of many evilles, which surely it doeth bryng admiration, that one onely remedy should doe so variable, and so merveilous effectes.[107]

Following this, the Spaniards, who "did beginne to waxe sicke" were shown the use of this remedy by the surviving French, whereupon "Our Spaniardes did begin to cure theim selves with the water of this Tree, and it did in theim greate effects, that it is almoste incredible."

The root was best, Monardes advised, of all the parts of the tree, and a decoction of it would cure agues (malaria), "opilations" (dropsy), stomach and liver ailments, headaches, kidney stones, and several other malfunctions.

107 *Joyfull Newes*, I, 99–101.

"The Medicine Man," by Cyrus Dallin (1861–1944). This statue was erected in Fairmount Park, Philadelphia, in 1903. The sculptor spent his early life in intimate contact with the Ute Indians.

Navaho sacred masks used in healing ceremonies, an exhibit in the Field Museum

Sacred masks of the False Face Healing Society, Iroquois Indians, an exhibit in the Field Museum of Natural History, Chicago. The masks were used to frighten away disease-causing spirits.

SACRED MASKS
OF THE FALSE FACE HEALING SOCIETY
IROQUOIS INDIANS OF THE EASTERN WOODLANDS

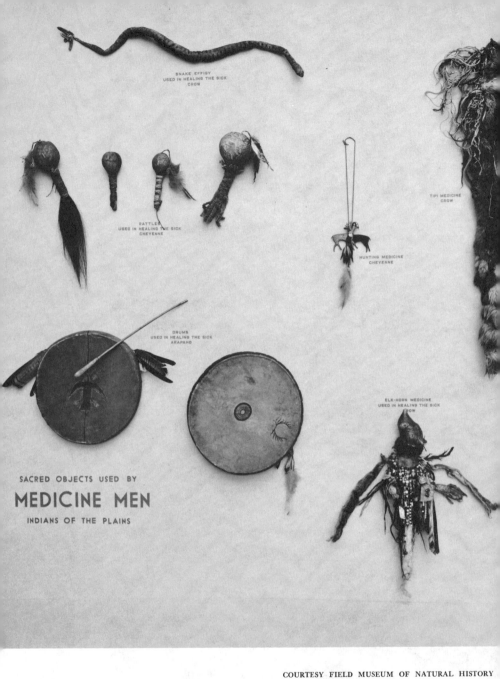

Labels within image:

SNAKE EFFIGY
USED IN HEALING THE SICK
CROW

RATTLES
USED IN HEALING THE SICK
CHEYENNE

TIPI MEDICINE
CROW

HUNTING MEDICINE
CHEYENNE

DRUMS
USED IN HEALING THE SICK
ARAPAHO

ELK-HORN MEDICINE
USED IN HEALING THE SICK
CROW

SACRED OBJECTS USED BY
MEDICINE MEN
INDIANS OF THE PLAINS

Sacred objects used by medicine men, Indians of the Plains, an exhibit case at the Field Museum of Natural History. *Left side of case*: Snake effigy used in healing the sick, Crow; rattles used in healing the sick, Cheyenne; drums used in healing the sick, Arapaho; hunting medicine, Cheyenne; tipi medicine, Crow; elk-horn medicine used in healing the sick, Crow.

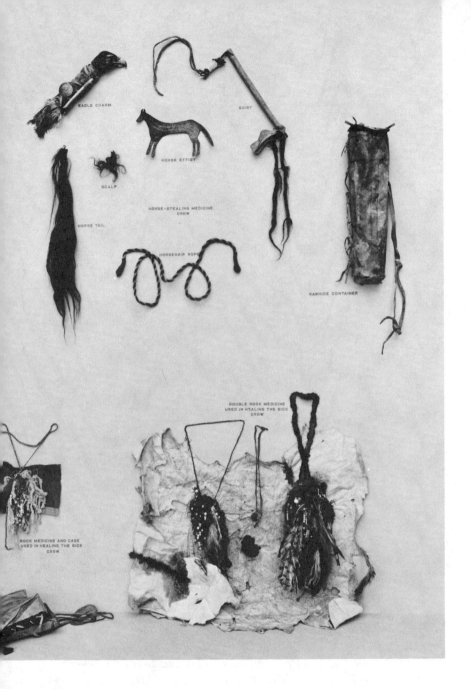

EAGLE CHARM

QUIRT

HORSE EFFIGY

SCALP

HORSE-STEALING MEDICINE
CROW

HORSE TAIL

HORSEHAIR ROPE

RAWHIDE CONTAINER

DOUBLE ROCK MEDICINE
USED IN HEALING THE SICK
CROW

ROCK MEDICINE AND CASE
USED IN HEALING THE SICK
CROW

Right side of case: Horse-stealing medicine, Crow—eagle charm, horse effigy, quirt, horse tail, scalp, horsehair rope, rawhide container; rock medicine and case used in healing the sick, Crow; double rock medicine used in healing the sick, Crow. As the objects indicate, "medicine" involved not only curing the sick, but bringing good luck in hunting, war, or horse-stealing.

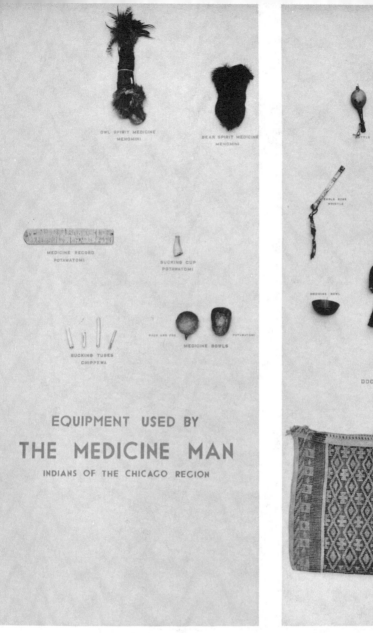

Equipment used by the medicine man, Indians of the Chicago region, an exhibit in the Field Museum of Natural History. *Left*: Owl spirit medicine, Menomini; bear spirit medicine, Menomini; medicine record, Potawatomi; sucking cup, Potawatomi; sucking tubes, Chippewa; medicine bowls, Sauk and Fox, Potawatomi; doctor's outfit, Winnebago—rattle, eagle spirit medicine, eagle bone whistle, sucking cup, tally stick of bone, medicine bowl, spirit doll, bows and arrows, doctor's bag.

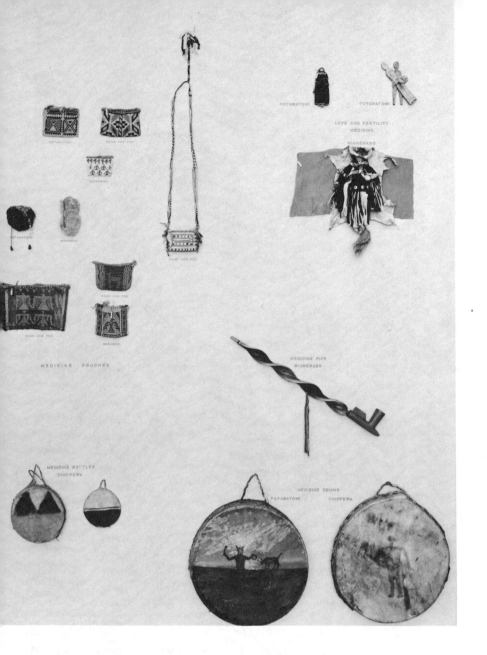

Right, top: Medicine pouches, Potawatomi, Sauk and Fox, Menomini; love and fertility medicine, Potawatomi, Winnebago. *Bottom*: Medicine pipe, Winnebago; medicine rattles, Chippewa; medicine drums, Potawatomi, Chippewa.

Yellow Nose, Cheyenne medicine man about sixty years old, *circa* 1890. Crayon drawing by Wuxpais (Daniel Littlechief). A splinter of wood covered with beads has been inserted into a twist of hair. A golden eagle feather rises above the head. The face is painted in different colors—red, blue, yellow. The blue line surrounding the face probably signifies the earth. A crescent and star are visible on the cheek. A red mark on the chest shows where the heart is. Little packages tied to the buckskin string around the neck contain curative medicines. A tobacco pipe leans toward the uplifted right hand. (Descriptive information based on notes by Albert Gatschet from explanation supplied him by the artist.)

Medicine man administering to a patient. Notice the bowl and pestle for mixing medicines. The medicine man is shaking a gourd rattle and may be singing a medicine song. From Schoolcraft's *History, Condition and Prospects of the Indian Tribes . . . .*

"The Manner of Curing the Sick in California" (*top*); "Sorcerers of California" (*bottom*). The Indians shown are probably of the Cochimi tribe. Notice the tube-like instrument used for sucking out the supposed disease-causing object. From Venegas' *A Natural and Civil History of California*.

Top: Unknown artist's impression of smallpox epidemic among Massachusetts Indians. *Bottom*: Treatment of Massasoit, Wampanoag chief, by Mr. Winslow of Plymouth. According to William Bradford, the grateful chief repaid the favor by warning of a planned attack of hostile Indians. From an engraving, source unknown.

Indian conjurer, or medicine man, North Carolina, *circa* 1586. Inscribed "The Flyer," by Thomas Hariot. Watercolor by John White, of the Roanoke colony. Original in the British Museum. The bag attached to the man's waist may have contained medicines.

MEDICINE. LODGE.

"Medicine Lodge." The patient lies in a Plains tipi. The Indian at left shakes a gourd rattle. The central figure, apparently the medicine man, holds a pipe in his right hand and the patient's wrist in the other, as if taking the pulse. A drummer sits at right. From "Life of an Indian," in *Harper's Illustrated Weekly*, June 20, 1868.

Cherokee love charm formula. Facsimile of Gatigwanasti manuscript (nineteenth century) written in the Cherokee syllabary invented by Sequoyah. From Mooney's "Sacred Formulas of the Cherokees," in *Seventh Annual Report, Bureau of American Ethnology*.

New-Englands
RARITIES
Difcovered:
IN
Birds, Beafts, Fifhes, Serpents,
and *Plants* of that Country.
Together with
The *Phyfical* and *Chyrurgical* REME-
DIES wherewith the *Natives* con-
ftantly ufe to Cure their DISTEM-
PERS, WOUNDS, and SORES.
ALSO
A perfeét *Defcription* of an *Indian*
SQUA, in all her Bravery ; with a
POEM not improperly conferr'd
upon her.
LASTLY
A CHRONOLOGICAL TABLE
of the moft remarkable Paffages in that
Country amongft the ENGLISH.

Illuftrated with CUTS.

By *JOHN JOSSELYN*, Gent.

London, Printed for *G. Widdowes* at the
Green Dragon in St. *Pauls* Church yard, 1672.

Facsimile of title page of John Josselyn's *New-England's Rarities Discovered*, first published in 1672. This was the earliest extensive dis-
course on American Indian remedies north of Mexico.

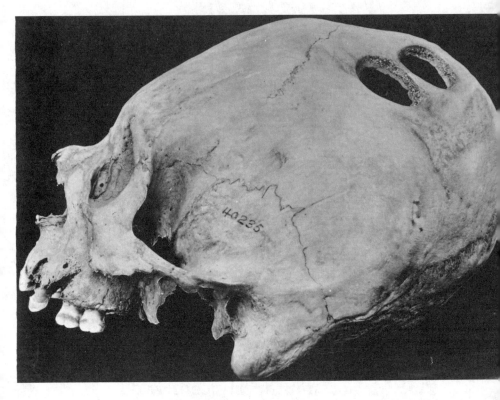

Skull of adult showing three scars from trephining. One of them is almost healed. Huaracando, Peru.

The sixteenth-century panacea for syphilis, guaiacum wood, also grows in Florida, although the source of it in those days was the West Indies. According to Oviedo, whose *Natural History* was published in Spain in 1526,[108] large forests of the "holy wood" grew on Hispaniola and adjacent islands, although he was unaware that it grew on the mainland. "The Indians of the islands cure themselves very easily with this wood," he asserted, and "in Tierra Firme they use in addition other herbs that they know, for they are expert herbalists." Oviedo in this account also makes the controversial statement, much disputed later by such medical scholars as Aleš Hrdlička,[109] R. C. Holcomb,[110] and R. S. Munger,[111] that the disease originated in the New World, and was carried back to Spain by the sailors of Columbus.[112]

Mindful of Oviedo's comment that mainland Indians had other herbal remedies for the venereal scourge, it is pertinent to note a letter written from Pensacola, Florida, on January 7, 1769, by Dr. J. Lorimer, to his friend Hugh Williamson of Philadelphia. There was in Florida, Dr. Lorimer wrote, "a plant of the pea kind, said to be used by the Indians as a universal remedy in venereal cases."[113]

[108] *Natural History of the West Indies*, ed. Sterling Aubrey Stoudemire, 88–90.

[109] "Notwithstanding some claims to the contrary, there is as yet not a single instance of thoroughly authenticated precolumbian syphilis." Aleš Hrdlička, "Disease, Medicine, and Surgery among the American Aborigines," *Journal of the American Medical Association*, Vol. XCIX, No. 20 (November 12, 1932), 1662.

[110] "The Antiquity of Congenital Syphilis," *Bulletin of the History of Medicine*, Vol. X, No. 2 (July, 1941), 148–177. Holcomb claims that the word "syphilis" did not come into vogue until around 1530, but that the disease was present in Europe during the Middle Ages, under a variety of names, especially "leprosy."

[111] "Guaiacum, the Holy Wood from the New World," *Journal of the History of Medicine*, Vol. IV, No. 2 (Spring, 1949), 196–229. Munger claims that "the earliest Spanish physicians who wrote about syphilis *per se* . . . had no notion that it came from America or even that it existed in America."

[112] Oviedo, *Natural History*, 89. For arguments in support of the hypothesis of pre-Columbian syphilis in America, see Wilton M. Krogman, "Medical Practices and Diseases of the Aboriginal American Indians," *Ciba Symposia*, Vol. I, No. 1 (April, 1939), 14, and his bibliography. Krogman maintained that lesions on pre-Columbian skulls indicate the existence of syphilis.

[113] J. Lorimer, Letter to Hugh Williamson. *Transactions of the American Philosophical Society*, I (2d ed. corrected; Philadelphia, 1789), 320–21.

Apparently the Caloosas and other aboriginal inhabitants of Florida, who long preceded the Seminoles, were as devoted to the "black drink" (yaupon, *Ilex cassine*) as their brethren in other parts of the South. Disturbed over the hostility of the natives toward the Spanish, the naval officer Pedro Menendez in 1573 sent a pilot as emissary to the cacique (chief) of Ays, bearing "a certain herb whereof the Indians make a certain water as a drink, because it is not found in that region, and is the greatest gift that can be made to them."[114] Lawson reported that the Indian beverage was equally popular with the Spanish:

> The Spaniards in New Spain have this Plant very plentifully on the Coast of Florida, and hold it in great Esteem. Sometimes they cure it as the Indians do, or else beat it to a Powder, so mix it as Coffee; yet before they drink it, they filter the same. They prefer it to all Liquids to drink with Physic, to carry the same safely and speedily through the Passages for which it is admirable, as I myself have experienced.[115]

Yaupon, as the Catawbas styled the black drink, was reputedly a popular drink among the white settlers in Florida, Georgia, and the Carolinas.[116] Porcher wrote in 1849 that the inhabitants of North Carolina purified brackish water by boiling it with *cassine* leaves.[117] Catesby called it an "emetick Broth" which "restores the Appetite and strengthens the Stomach."[118] It was also mentioned by Adair, Ashe, Bartram, Bossu, Brickell, and Romans. To this day it is an important element in the training of Seminole medicine men and in their treatments.[119]

---

[114] Jeanette Thurber Connor (tr. and ed.), *Colonial Records of Spanish Florida* (Deland, Florida, Florida State Historical Society, 1925–30), I, 55.

[115] Lawson, *History of North Carolina*, 93.

[116] W. E. Stafford, "Narcotic Plants and Stimulants of the Ancient Americans," *Annual Report of the Board of Regents of the Smithsonian Institution for 1916*, 418.

[117] "Report on the Indigenous Medical Plants of South Carolina," in *Transactions of the American Medical Association*, II (1849), 782–83.

[118] *Natural History*, II, 57.

[119] Greenlee, "Medicine and Curing Practices of the Modern Florida Sem-

It is a curious fact that the accounts of the early Spanish explorers in Florida and elsewhere have little to say of the native medicines. One looks in vain for references to these in the accounts of Cabeza de Vaca and the expedition of De Soto by the gentleman of Elvas. In fact, according to De Vaca's account, some sick Indians were cured when Alonzo del Castillo made the sign of the cross over them, whereupon other Indians, hearing of the miracle, came to the Spanish seeking this easy cure.[120] We learn of the Indians bringing gifts of prickly pear (*Opuntia*) as frequently as more northern tribes brought corn and tobacco to white visitors. We are told only of its use as food, though its medicinal applications by several southeastern and southwestern tribes is a matter of record.[121]

The English freebooter, John Hawkins, who visited Florida in 1565, remarked that the natives "have for apothecary herbs, trees, roots and gummes great store, as Storax liquids, Turpintine, Gumme, Myrrhe, and Frankinscence, with many others, whereof I know not the names."[122]

The Southwest (Exclusive of California)

Among the chief sources of pharmaceutical products growing wild or cultivated in this region which passed from Indian usage to official acceptance are cotton, creosote, gourds, hemp, mesquite, peyote, and pumpkin seed. The ethnobotany and aboriginal medical practice of the region have been well described by Aleš Hrdlička, Leslie A. White, John G. Bourke, Leland Wyman and S. K. Harris, Edward Palmer, Matilda Coxe Stevenson,

inoles," *American Anthropologist*, N.S., Vol. XLVI, No. 3 (July–September, 1944), 318.

120 Frederick Webb Hodge (ed.), *The Spanish Explorers in the Southern United States, 1528–1543*, 74–76. This incident occurred after the expedition reached Texas.

121 *E.g.*, Gilmore, "Uses of Plants by Indians of the Missouri River Region," *Thirty-Third Annual Report of the Bureau of American Ethnology*, 104; Hrdlička, *Physiological and Medical Observations*, 234, 244; see also Brickell, *Natural History*, 96–98; Oviedo, *Natural History*, 99–100; Emmart (ed.), *Badianus Manuscript*, 301, 316.

122 Burrage (ed.), *Early English and French Voyages*, 126.

L. S. M. Curtin, and Wilford W. Robbins and John P. Harrington. However, most of this information was gathered within the past century.

The accounts of early Spanish explorers in the American Southwest shed almost no light on Indian medical practice. Perhaps men who were so intent on finding gold could not be expected to probe into lesser matters, and their propensity for roasting alive the recalcitrant natives hardly encouraged the release of medical secrets. Pedro Castañeda's account of Coronado's expedition (1540–42) yields only a few fragments of relevant information. We are told of a dry sweat bath, or fumigant shelter, among the Zuñis:

> They have a hearth made like the binnacle of a compass box of a ship, in which they burn a handful of thyme at a time to keep up the heat, and they can stay in there just as in a bath. . . . Some were large enough for a game of ball.

Sanitary practices of the Zuñis were also noticed: "The villages are free from nuisances, because they go outside to excrete, and they pass their water into clay vessels, which they empty at a distance from the village."

The cultivation of cotton was observed and also the use of "very good salt in crystals, which they bring from a lake a day's journey from here."[123] Eastern Indians generally abhorred salt, but in the Southwest, Don Juan de Oñate observed in 1598, "Salt is the universal article of traffic of all these barbarians, and their regular food, for they even eat or suck it alone as we do sugar."

Oñate, Antonio de Espejo, and Juan de Mendoza all mentioned the use of prickly pear (*Opuntia*) and "mescale" (maguey) as food, but none was aware of any medical uses. Espejo wrote (1583) that Indians of the Río Grande valley brought gifts of "*mesquital*, which is made of a fruit like the carob bean." There was no indication of the medical applications of mesquite, which later studies show was widely used in a wash for sore eyes, as well as a

___

[123] Pedro Castañeda, *The Journey of Coronado*, ed. by G. P. Winship, 98–100, 176.

remedy for stomach troubles and other ills. Espejo did reveal, however, that "the people of all those provinces are large and more vigorous than the Mexicans, are healthy, for no illness was heard of among them."

In "Pimeria" (southern Arizona) Father Eusebio Kino recorded that the country yielded "much bezoar, and the efficacious *contrayerba*, and in many parts the important medicinal fruit called the *jojoba*" (*Phaseolus* sp., beans).[124] Kino's contrayerba was not the same plant which was used in Maya medicine (*Dorstenia contrayerva*, USP 1820–64), and which passed to white medicine as a stimulant, sudorific, tonic, and febrifuge.[125] The local variety was, however, used in white domestic medicine.[126]

In this historical-geographical survey the continent has not been divided according to aboriginal culture areas, as an anthropologist might do, but instead follows the course of political history and white settlement patterns. It is significant, however, that Alfred L. Kroeber divided the subcultures of the lower Great Basin area into two zones based on the range of two plants, the creosote bush (*Covillea tridentata*) and sagebrush or wormwood (*Artemisia tridentata*).[127] Both of these plants were used in Indian medicine.

Mrs. L. S. M. Curtin's recent book, *Healing Herbs of the Upper Rio Grande*, reveals that the folk medicine of that region is a mixture of American Indian, Spanish, and Moorish practices. "From Mexico, too," she wrote, "have come names and uses learned from the Aztec, and not a little knowledge has accrued from a long and friendly intercourse with the local Pueblo Indians. Such are the exigencies of sickness in a land without doctors that the memories of the people must be stored with the harvest of centuries."[128]

[124] Herbert E. Bolton (ed.), *Spanish Exploration in the Southwest, 1542–1706*, 175, 220, 243, 459.
[125] Roys, *Ethno-Botany of the Maya*, 222; Jacob Bigelow, *A Treatise on the Materia Medica*, 144; Charles F. Millspaugh, *American Medicinal Plants*, I, 293.
[126] L. S. M. Curtin, *Healing Herbs of the Upper Rio Grande*, 67.
[127] *Cultural and Natural Areas of Native North America*, 34.
[128] Curtin, *Healing Herbs*, 12.

California

As in Florida and the Southwest, accounts of Spanish California are nearly barren of information on Indian medical practice. What little there is mainly concerns the Indians of the peninsula of Baja California, now a part of Mexico. Father Jakob Baegert (1717–72) believed that "their medical art is very limited." He mentioned, however, the natives' resort to bleeding to relieve inflammation, and the sensible treatment of snakebite by application of a tight binding between the wound and the heart. He also described their use of a litter for transporting the sick.[129]

The Jesuit priest Miguel Venegas published in 1757 a *History of California* in which he devoted some attention to the natural products of the land, observing that "there is scarce a herb or root which they do not apply to some use." Some of the vegetable foods are named, but no remedial herb is mentioned except wild tobacco. There is, however, a description of the practice of sorcerers among the Cochimis, who were,

> the only physicians from whom they could hope to be relieved of their pains and distempers: and whatever was the medicine, it was always administered with great ostentation and solemnity. One was very remarkable, and the good effect it sometimes produced, heightened the reputation of the physician. They applied to the suffering part of the patient's body the chacuaco, or a tube formed out of a very hard black stone, and through this they sometimes sucked, and other times blew, but both as hard as they were able, supposing that thus the disease was either exhaled or dispersed. Sometimes the tube was filled with cimarron or wild tobacco lighted, and here they either sucked in, or blew down the smoke, according to the physician's direction; and this powerful caustic sometimes, without any other remedy, has been known entirely to remove the disorder.[130]

129 "An Account of the Aboriginal Inhabitants of the Californian Peninsula," *Annual Report of the Smithsonian Institution, 1863–64*, 386–87.
130 *A Natural and Civil History of California*, I, 97.

It was not until recent times, when much of the knowledge of the past had been lost, that some investigation of the herbal knowledge of California Indians was attempted. One of these studies was made in 1954 by Mrs. L. S. M. Curtin, who recorded the plant uses of the remnant of Yuki Indians of Round Valley, in northern California. Sixteen medical plants were listed, half of which belonged to species or genera which were admitted to the official drug compendia.[131]

John Culley has listed among the therapeutically useful remedies employed by the California Indians more than forty different substances and yet concluded that "the California Indians evidently did not contribute anything of value to modern surgical, dental, medical and pharmaceutical practice, nor did they introduce anything of very great value to modern materia medica."[132] However, at least three of the remedies listed by Culley as used by California Indians were admitted to the *U. S. Pharmacopeia*: *Eriodictyon californicum* (yerba santa, or holy plant), used in bronchitis; the *Rhamnus purshiana* (cascara sagrada, or sacred bark), a well-known cathartic, and *Grindelia robusta*, "used internally for lung troubles and externally for skin diseases."[133]

California Indians also made wide use of a species of *Datura*, similar to that known in the East as "Jimson weed" (*D. stramonium* L.). The latter was also used by Indians and has been an official drug since 1820. Its action has been described as similar to belladonna, and it is classed as a "parasympatholytic, a narcotic, an anodyne, and a mydriatic."[134] The Indian uses of *Datura* as reported by Culley tally with the preceding: the pounded root was used as an application to cuts, wounds, and bruises; a

[131] *Some Plants Used by the Yuki Indians of Round Valley, Northern California, passim.*

[132] "The California Indians: Their Medical Practices and their Drugs," *Journal of the American Pharmaceutical Association,* Vol. XXV, No. 4 (April, 1936), 339.

[133] John W. Shuman, "Southern California Medicine, Part I," *Annals of Medical History,* N.S., Vol. X, No. 3 (1938), 221. See also V. K. Chesnut, *Plants Used by the Indians of Mendocino County, California.* Later writers have made liberal use of this excellent study.

[134] Edward P. Claus, *Gathercoal and Wirth Pharmacognosy,* 450–51.

decoction of the blossoms and root was given for a narcotic effect; it was employed for "paralysis and general debility," and was given as an anesthetic to patients during the setting of fractures, and it was used as an aphrodisiac."[135]

Dr. John W. Shuman not only called attention to those drugs of the California Indians which have been officially recognized, but praised their dietary habits, their hygienic customs, their obstetric care, and their frequent bathing of infants. He credited them with being the first to use the hot springs which later became popular spas for white tourists.[136]

Edward Palmer cited an interesting personal experience with *Euphorbia polycarpa*, a snakebite remedy used by Indians of Arizona and southern California in the nineteenth century. While wading in salt water at San Diego he was injured by a stingray which "plunged the bony projection at the base of its tail into my left foot and soon the swelling and pain became excessive; a Mexican woman made several gallons of a very strong decoction from this plant and plunged my leg up to the knee into it while hot, and in a few hours relief came."[137]

The French Colonies

Canada

Near the site of Montreal in the year 1535 occurred the first recorded cure performed by Indians in this continent north of Mexico, and it was so notable that it has found its way into numerous accounts. In the journal of Cartier's second voyage up the St. Lawrence, it is reported that his ships were frozen in the ice from mid-November until mid-March, during which time scurvy caused the death of "five and twentie of our best and chiefest men, and all the rest were so sicke, that wee thought they

[135] "The California Indians: Their Medical Practices and Their Drugs," *Journal of the American Pharmaceutical Association*, Vol. XXV, No. 4 (April, 1936), 337.

[136] "Southern California Medicine, Part I," *Annals of Medical History*, N.S. Vol. X, No. 3 (1938), 221–22.

[137] "Plants Used by the Indians of the United States," *American Naturalist*, Vol. XII (September and October, 1878), 651.

should never recover againe, only three or foure excepted. Then it pleased God to cast his pitiful eye upon us, and sent us the knowledge of remedie of our healthes and recoverie."[138]

The messengers which it "pleased God" to send with the remedy proved to be the humble aborigines. While Cartier was walking upon the ice, he saw a group of Indians,

> among which was Domagaia, who not passing ten or twelve days afore, had bene very sicke with that disease, and had his knee swolne as bigge as a childe of two yeres old, all his sinews shrunke together, his teeth spoyled, his gummes rotten, and stinking. Our Captaine seeing him whole and sound, was thereat marvellous glad, hoping to understand and know of him how he had healed himselfe, to the end he might ease and help his men. So soone as they were come neere him, he asked Domagaia how he had done to heale himselfe: he answered, that he had taken the juice and sappe of the leaves of a certain Tree, and therewith had healed himselfe: For it is a singular remedy against that disease.

Cartier asked to be shown the healing tree, pretending that he wished to cure a servant, "because he would not shew the number of his sicke men." Domagaia sent two women to gather branches of it and showed the French how to use it, boiling the bark and leaves for a decoction and placing the dregs upon the legs. The Indians declared "that the vertue of this tree was, to heale any other disease: the tree is in their language called Ameda or Hanneda, this is thought to be the Sassafras tree."[139]

---

138 Burrage, *Early English and French Voyages*, 75.

139 *Ibid.*, 75–77. Since Monardes, who is believed to be the first to describe the supposed virtues of sassafras, did not publish his book until forty years later, it is probable that some translator of later times inserted "Sassafras" in this account. It is known, and was pointed out by Peter Kalm, who visited Canada in 1749, that sassafras does not grow as far north as the region of Montreal. Peter Kalm, *Peter Kalm's Travels in North America*, ed. Adolph B. Benson, II, 509. Moreover, sassafras is not an evergreen, and it would have had no leaves during the season mentioned.

Burrage, editor of the Cartier account, pointed out in a note that "the bark of the white pine is an antiscorbutic," thus suggesting that this was the remedy used.

The French at first had some difficulty in overcoming their reluctance to drink the strange medicine, but once having done so, they were soon cured. It was further claimed that the same medicine was used successfully to cure several of the men of the "French Pockes." The account concluded that if all the physicians of Montpelier and Louvain had been there with all the drugs of Alexandria, "they would not have done so much in one yere, as that tree did in sixe days, for it did so prevaile, that as many as used of it, by the grace of God recovered their health."

Logan Clendening reports that the Cartier account was noticed by James Lind of Edinburgh (1716–94), a British naval surgeon whose experiments with scurvy patients led to the conclusions that lemon juice was the best preventative.[140]

Since the French made no settlements in America until seventy-three years after Cartier's notable experience, there are no further accounts of Canadian aboriginal medicine until the seventeenth century. The *Jesuit Relations*, unfortunately, gave few details on the specific remedies used among the Indians, although they contain considerable information on the beliefs of the Hurons and Iroquois concerning the cause of disease. Among the Hurons, if the normal remedies such as potions, emetics, poultices, or scarification should fail, the medicine man concluded that "it is a disease caused by desires of the soul that trouble it." The satisfaction of these desires was considered a prerequisite to the cure, and the whole village was mobilized to fulfill them.[141] The follow-up was a succession of dances, feasts, games, and sometimes so much gift-giving that a man "becomes wealthy in a day," as Father Ragueneau reported. "After that," the priest continued, "the patient never fails to say that he is cured, although he some-

---

William Fenton believed that the tree used was either hemlock or white pine. Fenton, "Contacts between Iroquois Herbalism and Colonial Medicine," *Annual Report, Smithsonian Institution, 1941*, 506. Both of these trees are still used by tribes of the area. John Josselyn wrote (1672) that "the tops of green spruce-boughs, boiled in bear [beer?] and drunk, is assuredly one of the best remedies for the scurvy; restoring the infected party in a short time." *New-England's Rarities*, 200.

140 *Source Book of Medical History*, 464.

141 Thwaites (ed.), *Jesuit Relations*, XXXIII, 199–209.

times dies a day after the solemnity. But, as these illnesses are usually mere shams or slight passing ailments, the sick man is often really cured; and that is what gives those remedies so great a reputation."[142] It did not occur to the missionary that the combination of faith in the method, the probing of the "doctor," and the community concern for the patient could contribute to his recovery, though contemporary writers have placed much weight on these factors. "It may not be unreasonable to conclude," Spencer Rogers has written, "that the shaman has stumbled upon techniques which gave him success in psychotherapy."[143]

The French priests, though scorning the shamanistic practices of the Indians, did not always reject their herbal remedies; in fact, they occasionally showed more faith in them than was justified. When Father Jacques Marquette was journeying up the Fox River of Wisconsin in 1673, he wrote:

I also took time to look for a medicinal plant which a savage, who knows its secret, showed to Father Alloues with many ceremonies. Its root is employed to Counteract snake-bites, God having been pleased to give this antidote against a poison which is very common in these countries. It is very pungent, & tastes like powder when crushed with the teeth; it must be masticated & placed upon the bite inflicted by the snake. . . . The plant bears several stalks, a foot high, with rather long leaves; a white flower, which greatly resembles the wallflower.[144]

Marquette was even carried away by Indian reports that "the reptile has so great a horror of it that it even flees from a Person who has rubbed himself with it."

Father Louis Hennepin, the Recollect priest who accompanied La Salle, was acquainted with the Illinois and Miami tribes, and remarked on their ability to cure "Tertian or Quartan Agues"

142 *Ibid.*, 209.
143 "The Methods, Results, and Values of Shamanistic Therapy," *Ciba Symposia*, Vol. IV, No. 1 (April, 1942), 1224.
144 Thwaites (ed.), *Jesuit Relations*, LIX, 101.

with a decoction of an unidentified bark. "They have some knowledge of Herbs and Roots," he continued, "with which they cure several Distempers. They have infallible Remedies against the Poison of Toads [sic], Rattlesnakes, and other dangerous Animals; but none against the Small-Pox, as we have."[145]

Baron de Lahontan described Algonquin medical practices which seem quite rational today and were perhaps in advance of those in Europe at that time. "When sick," he reported, "they only drink Broth, and eat sparingly." They rejected emetics and phlebotomy, thus differing not only from the whites but also from more southerly tribes:

> They cannot conceive how we come to be such Fools as to make use of Vomits; for when ever they see a *French*-man take down such a violent Remedy, they cannot forbear saying that he swallows an *Iroquese*. They plead, that this sort of Remedy shakes the whole Machine, and makes terrible Efforts upon all the inward Parts. But they are yet more astonish'd at our custom of Bleeding; For, say they, *the Blood being the Taper of Life, we have more occasion to pour it in than to take it out, considering that Life sinks when its Principal Cause is mov'd off; from whence 'tis a Natural Consequence, that after loss of Blood Nature acts but feebly and heavily, the Intrails are over-heated, and the Parts are dry'd, which gives rise to all the Diseases that afflict the Europeans.*[146]

Lahontan further remarked that "they cannot be persuaded to drink Ice-water, for they alledge that it infeebles the Stomach, and retards Digestion." Perhaps with tongue in cheek, Lahontan concluded; "Such, Sir, are their fantastical Opinions of things, which proceed from their Prepossession and Bigotry with reference to their own Customs and ways of Living."

The curative herbs of the Indians won the respect of most of the French. "Necessity has forced these Indians to find many

145 *A New Discovery*, II, 484–85.
146 *New Voyages to North-America*, I, 469.

good simples for healing their wounds and other accidents,"
wrote Diron d'Artaguiette of the Illinois tribes, in 1723.[147] The
Huron medicine men, wrote Father Gabriel Sagard, "always
carry with them a bag full of herbs and drugs, to doctor the sick."
These dignitaries were assisted by "an apothecary, cheap enough,
who trails after them with his drugs." He mentioned their use of
a highly esteemed drug, "called Oscar, which does wonders in
healing all kinds of wounds, ulcers, and other sores."[148] To
Sagard we are indebted for an early description of the isolation
of Indian patients who were suffering from diseases believed to
be communicable:

> Sometimes the medicine-man orders one of the sick people
> to leave the town and encamp in the woods or in some other
> place apart, so that he may practice upon him there during
> the night his devilish contrivances. I do not know any other
> reason that he could have for removing the sick person, since
> usually this is only done for those who are infected with some
> unclean or dangerous disease, and such persons only, and no
> others, do they force to isolate themselves from the com-
> munity until they are completely cured. This is a laudable
> and most excellent custom and ordinance, which indeed
> ought to be adopted in every country.[149]

Pierre Charlevoix was certain that the Indians were "in possession of secrets and remedies which are admirable." A broken
bone was immediately set and was "perfectly solid in eight days
time." He spoke of a French soldier cured of epilepsy by an
Indian woman who administered a pulverized root. "These
people have also," he reported, "speedy and sovereign remedies
against the palsy, dropsy, and venereal complaints." Of especial
importance is his observation in 1721 of the use of enema
syringes:

[147] Newton D. Mereness (ed.), *Travels in the American Colonies, 1690–1783*, 74.
[148] *The Long Journey to the Country of the Hurons*, ed. George M. Wrong,
193, 195.
[149] *Ibid.*, 198.

In the northern parts they made much use of glisters, a bladder was their instrument for this purpose. They have a remedy for the bloody-flux which seldom or never fails; this is a juice expressed from the extremities of cedar branches after they have been well boiled.[150]

Although laymen and members of other orders often praised Indian medical practice, most of the Jesuits rather consistently campaigned against placing trust in Indian medicine. The savage medicine men, declared Father Pierre Biard in 1616, were "sorcerers... Jugglers, liars, and cheats." Moreover, "all their science consists in a knowledge of a few simple laxatives, or astringents, hot or cold applications, lenitives or irritants for the liver or kidneys, leaving the rest to luck, nothing more. But they are well versed in tricks and impositions."[151] Father Joseph Jouvency complained that "since the race is altogether ignorant of the art of medicine, they readily despair of the sick, and neither provide them with food or care for them in any way."[152] Among the Illinois, in 1699, Father Julien Binneteau wrote:

God continues to be served here, in spite of the opposition of the devil, who raises up people bitterly hostile to Christianity. We call them Jugglers here. In public they perform a hundred mummeries full of impiety; and talk to the skins of animals, and to dead birds, as divinities. They claim that medicinal herbs are gods, from whom they have life, and that no others must be worshipped. Every day they sing songs in honor of their little manitous, as they call them. They inveigh against our religion and against the missionaries.[153]

150 *Journal of a Voyage to North America*, ed. Louise Phelps Kellogg, I, 162. Miss Kellogg, in a note, states that the French word was "lavement," meaning a clyster or enema. This is apparently the first notice of the use of such an instrument by North American Indians. Charlevoix did not identify the tribe, though the mention of "northern parts" suggests Canada north of the Great Lakes. At the time of writing, he was among the Miami at Fort St. Joseph, in southwest Michigan.

151 Thwaites (ed.), *Jesuit Relations*, III, 117.

152 *Ibid.*, I, 211.

153 *Ibid.*, LXV, 65.

Here again appears the intimate association of Indian healing with religion, which seems to have been the irritant which incurred the displeasure of the Catholic priests against both. A continued dependence upon European medicines is indicated by an invoice of goods requested for the Illinois missions in 1702:

One Syringe; one livre of Theriac; ointment, plasters, alum, vitriol, aniseed, medicines, and pastils.[154]

A more extensive list of medicines requested in 1665 by the Ursuline nuns for their hospital in Quebec consisted almost entirely of Old World drugs. It included senna, rhubarb, jalap (used by Mexican Indians), myrrh, aloes, scammony, opium, litharge, camomile, vitriol, corrosive sublimate, diapalam, diachylon, divinum, betonica, balm, ointments, "mundificative," althea, burgundy pitch, suppurative, and almonds.[155]

The laymen, however, especially in remote places, were willing to borrow whatever useful drugs they could obtain from the Indians. We are told that at Detroit Madame Cadillac, whose duty it was to treat the sick at that frontier outpost, had no aversion to adopting the red man's herbals along with imported European remedies.[156]

Lower Louisiana

Jean-Bernard Bossu (1720–92) reported in the middle of the eighteenth century that "many plants of medicinal value grow in Louisiana, among them gensing, whose root makes an excellent cough syrup, jalap, rhubarb, smilax, snakeroot, sarsaparilla, and St. John's-wort, from which an excellent oil for healing wounds is made." There were plants which acted as antidotes to poisons, "but recognizing them and knowing how to use them are rare and precious gifts which the Creator has not granted to

[154] Edna Kenton (ed.), *Black Gown and Redskins, Adventures and Travels of the Jesuit Missionaries in North America, 1610–1791*, 393.

[155] *Ibid.*, 169–70.

[156] Fanny J. Anderson, "Medicine at Fort Detroit in the Colony of New France, 1701–1760," *Journal of the History of Medicine*, Vol. I, No. 2 (April, 1946), 217.

everyone." He soberly claimed that "the Indians know a thousand medicinal plants good for purifying the blood." Bossu contended that "the Americans value their medicinal herbs more than they do all the gold of Mexico or Peru."[157]

The fruit of the persimmon tree, Bossu reported, was used by the Indians to make a bread for use on long trips. He maintained that the fruit was "an excellent astringent and a superb remedy for dysentery and the bloody flux." A decoction of the powdered seeds was held to be a sure cure for kidney stones.

The medicine men of the Choctaws, Bossu believed, were familiar with several plants which were excellent for the "common diseases of the country" and knew a sure cure for the bite of the rattlesnake and other "venomous animals." He related one experience in which his interpreter was saved from the effects of snakebite by an unknown powder applied by a medicine man. He reported that the natives used rattlesnake grease for rheumatism and that Indian women swallowed a decoction of powdered rattles from the rattlesnake in the belief that this would help them through childbirth without pain.[158]

Le Page du Pratz, in his *Histoire de la Louisiane*, enthusiastically described "*quelques Droques propres a la Médecine & à la Teinture.*" Among them were such well-known native simples as bear's oil, chinaroot, copal or sweet gum, sarsaparilla, sassafras, and ground ivy. Sassafras was called well known to the botanists for its medicinal qualities. The sweet gum, or "copalm," as he called it, was a common tree having "*un baume dont les vertus son infinies; son e'corse est dure & noire.*" He considered it an excellent febrifuge and a cure for numerous other ailments including wounds, ulcers, consumption, and obstructions.[159]

---

[157] *Travels in the Interior of North America, 1751–1762*, ed. Seymour Feiler, 196.

[158] *Ibid.*, 200. Exactly the same remedy was used to expedite and ease parturition by Sacajawea, the Shoshoni woman who guided the Lewis and Clark expedition in 1804–1805. Drake W. Will, "The Medical and Surgical Practice of the Lewis and Clark Expedition," *Journal of the History of Medicine*, Vol. XIV, No. 3 (July, 1959), 288.

[159] *Histoire de la Louisiane*, II, 27–29.

Du Pratz described a rattlesnake herb which had a tuberous root like an onion and which was *"la reméde specifique contre les morsures de ce dangereux Reptile."*[160] On two occasions Du Pratz was successfully treated for his ailments by Indian doctors, and he had an especially high opinion of the healing skill of the Natchez.[161]

It should not be supposed, however, that Indian medicines and treatments were at once generally accepted in Louisiana. Louisiana was, as Duffy has pointed out, better supplied with doctors than the English colonies because physicians were attached to the military units which accompanied all French colonial ventures. These physicians and surgeons had European training, relied on European books, and were conditioned by European ideas and practice.[162] The medical supplies sent to the Dauphine Island colony near Mobile in 1717 included ipecac, theriac, cinchona, emetics, Guiller's remedy, purgative pastilles, and brandy.[163] It is notable that two South American medicines, ipecac and cinchona, had won acceptance by this time, but the other drugs were of the Old World. Diron d'Artaguiette, inspector-general of Louisiana, reported that the Indians knew large numbers of medicinal plants for all sorts of maladies, but few Frenchmen knew about them, because the "Savages who know their properties use them with success, but zealously guard the secret from the French."[164]

The Trans-Allegheny Frontier:
English and Early American Period

The Treaty of Paris in 1763 brought the western Indians a new set of masters. The change was not accomplished without some resistance, as the recalcitrant Pontiac and his allies delayed

160 *Ibid.*, II, 60–61.
161 *Ibid.*, I, 135–36, 207–209; III, 37.
162 Duffy, *History of Medicine in Louisiana*, I, 44–45.
163 *Ibid.*, 18.
164 *Ibid.*, 43, citing Heloise H. Cruzat, "Sidelights on Louisiana," *Louisiana Historical Quarterly*, Vol. I, No. 3 (January 8, 1918), 98.

for two years the British occupation of the surrendered posts in the Great Lakes region. Once the transfer was accomplished, British agents began to penetrate the area and report on what they found. One of these was Jonathan Carver.

Carver has been reproached as a liar, and some deny that he ever lived among the Sioux in the valley of the St. Peter's (Minnesota) River, as he claimed. There seems to be no doubt, however, that he did explore Wisconsin, and his account of the medical treatments and remedies of the Indians of that region seems credible enough.

Carver describes the prevalent diseases and observed that the infectious European maladies, including venereal complaints (which he believed to be of Old World origin) had not yet reached the northwest Indians. Dropsy and paralytic ailments were rare; for these and fevers, he reported that "they make use of lotions and decoctions, composed of herbs, which the physicians know perfectly well how to compound and apply." Medicines alone were not regarded as sufficient, but were always accompanied by "superstitious ceremonies." He praised the judgment of the Indians in the use of simples for wounds, fractures, and bruises; through them they were able to extract, without incision, "splinters, iron, or any sort of matter by which the wound is caused. In cures of this kind they are extremely dextrous, and complete them in much less time than might be expected from their mode of proceeding." Pains in the limbs or joints were treated by scarification, performed with a sharp flint by those having no trade with Europeans. "It is surprizing," he wrote, "to see to how fine a point they have the dexterity to bring them; a lancet can scarcely exceed in sharpness the instruments they make of this unmalleable substance."

No one was considered ill while he had an appetite; once nourishment was rejected, the patient received great attention, and while the disorder continued, "the physician refuses his patient no sort of food that he is desirous of." Notwithstanding the use of the *"chichicoue"* (rattle) for the divination of the nature of ailments and the necessary remedies, Carver believed

94

that "they exercise their art by principles which are founded on the knowledge of simples, and on experience which they acquire by an indefatigable attention to their operations."[165]

Other claims made by Carver are less believable. One of them is his report of the cure of gonorrhea in a white man by a Winnebago doctor who used prickly ash. Another is the alleged cure of venomous snakebites by "rattlesnake plantain." This herb,

> being chewed and applied immediately to the wound, and some of the juice swallowed, seldom fails of averting every dangerous symptom. So convinced are the Indians of the power of this infallible antidote, that for a trifling bribe of spirituous liquor, they will at any time permit a rattle snake to drive his fangs into their flesh. It is to be remarked that during these months in which the bite of these creatures is most venomous, that this remedy for it is in greatest perfection, and most luxuriant in its growth.[166]

Indians of the northern forests made much use of trees in their medicine, and particularly of the barks, leaves, gums and resins obtained from pine, spruce, hemlock, and birch; they made use of such common herbs of the region as the wintergreen, rich in salicin, and the *Sarracenia purpurea*, or pitcher plant. The latter is found in the materia medica of all tribes of the northern forests and was used as a smallpox remedy by some Canadian Indians, with good results according to one British surgeon.[167]

The properties of birch oil, an officially recognized source of methyl salicylate, were known to the Indians. All writers on the materia medica of the northern tribes mention the use of various parts of this tree by the Indians, and we have an interesting anecdote from the diary of J. W. Phelps, an army officer stationed at Mackinac in 1840–41. While exploring an island with a group which included the Ojibwa wife of Henry R. Schoolcraft, he related that Mrs. Schoolcraft "stripped off the bark from a birch

[165] *Travels Through the Interior Parts of North America*, 365–72.

[166] *Ibid.*, 482–83. The identity of this plant has never been established, though half a dozen different species have been mentioned as "rattlesnake plantain."

[167] Charles F. Millspaugh, *American Medicinal Plants*, I, 19ff.

tree and scraped from the trunk a milky substance which is said to be a good remedy for consumptives."[168]

Dr. Zina Pitcher, a founder of the Michigan Medical Association, described the Indian skill in treatment of gunshot and other wounds, and particularly wounds affecting the body cavities. He mentioned their use of a litter, or stretcher, and a syringe to introduce medicine into wounds. Their use of powdered puffball as a hemostatic was considered effective. Pitcher listed fifty-nine herbal remedies used by the Indians, and their uses, and concluded:

> There is no denying the fact, that either by their discernment, or the force of an unerring instinct, they have been guided to a knowledge of a good proportion of the medicinal plants indigenous to their respective sections of the country.[169]

In the first years of the nineteenth century the Delaware Indians, formerly residents of Pennsylvania, were established on the White River of Indiana. Again the missionaries of the United Brethren are an important source of information about them. In the diary of the White River mission for 1802, it is told that a Delaware woman convert, Sister Louisa, "knows of many medicinal plants which she hunted at once and gave them to the sick Sr. Catherine. They had the desired effect at once and in a few days she was out of danger and soon recovered nicely."[170] Two years later the same diary records the curing of a horse bitten by a rattlesnake through the application of certain crushed roots collected by a Cherokee Indian.[171]

The diary entry for January 23, 1805, reports that a Christian Indian named Joshua, and his wife, "went to another Indian

---

[168] "Diary, Kept While at Mackinac, Chicago, and Western Posts," MS, 1840–41, University of Chicago Library, microfilm, n.p.

[169] "Medical Knowledge of the Indians," in Schoolcraft, *Indian Tribes of the United States*, IV, 518.

[170] Lawrence Henry Gipson (ed.), *The Moravian Indian Mission on White River, Diaries and Letters, May 5, 1799 to November 12, 1806*, 200.

[171] *Ibid.*, 290–91.

town to purchase corn with the proceeds derived from a salve which they make for the healing of wounds." The same Joshua had apparently some reputation among the whites, for the diary of August 28 records that:

A French trader brought his brother here,—an old Frenchman who has suffered for a number of years from an open sore on his leg. He wanted Joshua to cure him because Joshua had told him that he had very good roots and plants with which he had cured more than one person and which would also help this man. The trader was very happy to hear this and promised him $50 if he would cure his brother. Should he be unable to heal his brother, he would give him $20 for his trouble.

The next day the trader gave Joshua a horse with which to look for the necessary plants and roots forty miles away, and on the 31st, the diary continues:

Joshua returned and brought with him about half a bushel of snakeroot and other herbs with which he at once began the treatment. Joshua's wife, who is also acquainted with good curative herbs, brought hers together and the beginning looked very promising, because the herbs and roots began to have a good effect.[172]

In neighboring Illinois, the English traveler William Faux reported in 1819 that "the woods abound with medical herbs. The Ching Sang [ginseng] and Ipecacuanha are found, for emetics. . . . the trees are full of gum. The Dogwood Bark is also found as efficient as the Peruvian, and the Sassafras tea is in general use for two or three months." Faux may not have known that these were all aboriginal remedies, but his observation that "a doctor, of little or no skill, lives twelve miles distant," might account for their popularity with the settlers.[173]

172 Ibid., 330, 376.
173 Memorable Days in America, Vol. XI in Thwaites (ed.), Early Western Travels, 228–229.

Two years later another Englishman, John Woods, one of the founders of the colony of English expatriates at Albion, Illinois, reported that "the following trees and herbs are used in medicine —snake-root, gentian, genseng, Columbia-root, and sumach, and sassafras trees."[174] Since no Indians remained in that part of the state, and the last Illinois natives were to be removed within the next fifteen years, this report indicates that the Indian plant remedies had become a part of the frontier materia medica.

One of the earliest and best-known physicians to practice in the Ohio valley was Dr. Daniel Drake of Cincinnati. His first book, *Natural and Statistical View*, published in 1815, contains perhaps the earliest catalogue of western medical plants. It was a short list, containing about three dozen remedies in a few pages, but it indicated acceptance by a physician of old aboriginal simples.[175]

Dr. Drake, in his advanced years, published a "treatise" on the "principal diseases of the interior valley," in which he paid particular attention to malaria, which frequently raged in the Ohio and Mississippi valleys. He believed that such a vast country would "forever remain subject to intermittent fever" and called it a "duty of patriotism and humanity to test, by exhibition and analysis, such of our indigenous plants as in their sensible qualities bear any resemblance to the cinchona. He who should discover, in our country, a substitute for the bark, out of which the quinine is manufactured, would be regarded as a benefactor." He mentioned several remedies which had the reputation of being useful in treating the disease, and among them were the familiar aboriginal febrifuges: *Cornus florida*, or dogwood, *Liriodendron tulipifera*, the yellow poplar or tulip tree, *Prunus virginiana*, or wild cherry, *Eupatorium perfoliatum*, or boneset, and the barks of oak, or *Quercus*.[176]

174 *Two Years Residence . . . in the Illinois Country . . . June 5, 1820–July 3, 1821*, in Vol. X in Thwaites (ed.), *Early Western Travels*, 303.
175 *Natural and Statistical View, or Picture of Cincinnati and the Miami Country*.
176 Daniel Drake, *A Systematic Treatise, Historical, Etiological, and Practical, on the Principal Diseases of the Interior Valley of North America . . . , 750.*

In 1808, an English physician, Fortescue Cuming, while staying at a private home near Marietta, Ohio, prescribed for the malaria of his host's son a combination of the old European remedy, calomel, with Peruvian bark, and the North American Indian's snakeroot and ginseng, "during all the intermissions."[177] When the English botanist Thomas Nuttall was ill with "intermittent fever" in Arkansas in 1819, he reported:

> No medicines being at hand . . . I took in the evening about a pint of a strong and very bitter decoction, of the *Eupatorium cuneifolium*, the *E. perfoliatum* or Bone-set, not being to be found in the neighbourhood. This dose, though very nauseous, did not prove sufficient to operate as an emetic, but acted as a diaphoretic and gentle laxative, and prevented the proximate return of the disease.[178]

The various species of *Eupatoria* are likewise old Indian fever remedies, although Nuttall gave no indication that he was aware of that.[179]

The most qualified person in the early Ohio valley who was pre-eminently interested in Indian medicine was Constantine Samuel Rafinesque (1783–1840), the immigrant botanist who, after spending some time in Philadelphia, was for seven years on the faculty of Transylvania University, Lexington, Kentucky. More honored since his death than he was in life, Rafinesque fully recognized the debt of medical botany to the aborigines:

> When America was settled [he wrote], the native tribes were in possession of many valuable vegetable remedies discovered by long experience, the knowledge of which they gradually imparted to their neighbours.
>
> This knowledge partly adopted even as far as Europe, and partly rejected by medical skepticks, became scattered

[177] *Sketches of a Tour*, Vol. IV in Thwaites (ed.), *Early Western Travels*, 123.

[178] *A Journal of Travels into the Arkansa Territory During the Year 1819 . . .*, Vol. XIII in Thwaites (ed.), *Early Western Travels*, 244.

[179] See *Boneset* and *Joe Pye Weed* in the chapter on Indian remedies. The Indian associations of the *Eupatoria* species is partly indicated by the application to them of the common names "Indian sage" and "Indian gravel root."

99

through our country in the hands of country practitioners, Herbalists, Empirics, and Botanists.

Schoepf collected his materials from them, and noticed about three hundred and sixty plants as medical; but he did not go everywhere, nor exhaust the subject, since nearly double that number are actually in common use in different States of the Union.[180]

All of the numerous works on materia medica, he maintained, had but scratched the surface, none of them mentioning one tenth of the plants in actual use. In his own *Medical Flora* he selected only 105 to be figured and described, chosen from the "most active and efficient medical types." What sets his work apart from others dealing with native medical flora are the facts he sets forth concerning Indian usage of botanical remedies. Subsequently he was widely quoted by other writers on indigenous materia medica, such as Francis Porcher, Stephen Williams, and A. Clapp.

Unfortunately for the historical record, the coastal Indian tribes were nearly exterminated, and their culture extinguished, before an adequate survey of their materia medica had been made. The folk medicine of their surviving remnants may have been influenced by white practice. In the interior the case is more fortunate, for tribal groups remained physically and culturally intact for a much longer time. Some reasonably literate individuals have reported something of the medical practice of the Creeks, Choctaws, Chickasaws, and Cherokees, which were the principal tribes of the southern frontier until the 1830's.

James Adair, an educated trader among the southern Indians in the third quarter of the eighteenth century, was obsessed with the belief that Indians were of Hebrew origin, and was inclined to hold that they were therefore endowed with special gifts, including medical skill. Concerning the Cherokees, he wrote:

. . . they, as well as all other Indian nations, have a great knowledge of specific virtues in simples; applying herbs and

180 Rafinesque, *Medical Flora*, I, ii.

plants, on the most dangerous occasions, and seldom if ever, fail to effect a thorough cure, from the natural bush. . . .

. . . .

. . . the Indians, instigated by nature, and quickened by experience, have discovered the peculiar properties of vegetables, as far as needful in their situation of life. For my own part, I would prefer an old Indian before any chirurgeon whatsoever, in curing green wounds by bullets, arrows, &c. both for the certainty, ease, and speediness of cure; for if those parts of the body are not hurt, which are essential to the preservation of life, they cure the wounded in a trice. They bring the patient into a good temperament of body, by a decoction of proper herbs and roots: and always enjoin a most abstemious life: they forbid them women, salt, and every kind of fresh meat, applying mountain-allum, as the chief ingredient.[181]

He remarked that they were, however, unable to cure introduced diseases, such as smallpox, but rather increased the fatality rate by first taking a sweat bath, then plunging into cold streams. In treating indigenous maladies, such as snakebite, they were held to be infallible:

I do not remember to have seen or heard of any Indian dying by the bite of a snake . . . although they are often bitten by the most dangerous snakes—every one carries in his shot-pouch, a piece of the best snake-root, such as the Seneeka, or fern-snake-root, or the wild hore-hound, wild plantain, St. Andrew's cross, and a variety of other herbs and roots, which are plenty, and well known to those who range the American woods, and are exposed to such dangers, and will effect a thorough and speedy cure if timely applied.[182]

A substantial group of Cherokees escaped removal to Oklahoma in the 1830's and remains today in the Great Smoky moun-

[181] *The History of the American Indians, Particularly Those Nations Adjoining to the Mississippi* . . . , 234.
[182] *Ibid.*, 235–36.

tains of western North Carolina. A compendium of their medical formulas was obtained in the 1880's by James Mooney, of which a portion was published in 1891,[183] and the remainder in 1932.[184] Mooney's complete *Swimmer Manuscript* contains 115 herbal remedies, many of them used in combinations. In "The Sacred Formulas of the Cherokees," Mooney compared the Cherokee uses of twenty selected remedies with those recommended in the 14th edition of the *United States Dispensatory* (1880), and concluded that 25 per cent, or at most 35 per cent, were correctly used.[185] He found that five of the species from his selected list, which were included in the *Dispensatory*, "have generally pronounced medicinal qualities, and are used by the Cherokees for the very purposes for which, according to the Dispensatory, they are best adapted; so we must admit that so much of their practice is correct, however false the reasoning by which they have arrived at this result."

Mooney assumed that at least five of the plants not listed in the *Dispensatory* were of no value, "unless we are disposed to believe that Indians are better informed in this regard than the

183 James Mooney, "The Sacred Formulas of the Cherokees," *Seventh Annual Report of the Bureau of American Ethnology, 1885–86*, 301–97.

184 Mooney and Olbrechts, *Swimmer Manuscript*.

185 Mooney, "The Sacred Formulas of the Cherokees," *Seventh Annual Report of the Bureau of American Ethnology, 1885–86*, 328–29. Seven of the plants were not listed in the Dispensatory. The list of plants compared follows, with * after those he found were correctly used in whole or in part; and # after those not listed; + follows those belonging to "genera which seem to have some of the properties ascribed by the Indians to the species."

1. *Aristolochia serpentaria* (Virginia snakeroot) 2. *Cynoglossum morrisoni* (Beggar lice)#+ 3. *Cassia marilandica* (Wild senna) 4. *Gnaphalium decurrens* (Life everlasting)#+ 5. *Vicia caroliniana* (Vetch)# 6. *Tephrosia virginiana* (Catgut) 7. *Euphorbia hypericifolia* (Milkweed)* 8. *Scutellaria lateriflora* (Skullcap) 9. *Adiantum pedatum* (Maidenhair fern) 10. *Geranium maculatum* (Cranesbill)* 11. *Gillenia trifoliata* (Indian physic) 12. *Hepatica acutiloba* (Liverwort)* 13. *Cacalia atrilicifolia* (Tassel flower)# 14. *Aralia quinquefolia* (Ginseng) 15. *Thalictrum anemonoides* (Meadow rue)# 16. *Cypripedium parviflorum* (Lady slipper) 17. *Rudbeckia fulgida* (Cone flower)# 18. *Polygonatum multiflorum latifolium* (Solomon's Seal)* 19. *Eupatorium purpureum* (Queen of the meadow [Joe Pye Weed])* 20. *Aspidium acrostichoides* (Shield Fern)#.

best educated white physicians in the country." He further remarked that they may "probably be set down as worthless, inasmuch as they are not named in the Dispensatory," and "it is absurd to suppose that the savage, a child in intelligence, has reached a higher development in any branch of science than has been attained by civilized man, the product of long ages of intellectual growth."[186]

Unfortunately, Mooney overlooked certain factors: (1) the white man had not lived in this continent for long ages, though the Indian had, and not all potentially valuable plants had been investigated at the time he wrote, or even since; (2) the mere fact that a plant is not listed in the *Dispensatory*, or the *Pharmacopeia*, or the *Formulary*, does not necessarily signify that the plant is without medical value; neither coca or cocaine was listed in the *Dispensatory* used by Mooney; (3) Mooney's list included only a small portion of the Cherokee materia medica and omitted some of their most famous remedies which were official until recently, such as spigelia, lobelia, eryngium, stillingia, sanguinaria, etc.; (4) at the time Mooney wrote, about twenty-five North American Indian botanical remedies which were later listed in the *U. S. Pharmacopeia* or *National Formulary* had not yet been officially accepted; by Mooney's standard, they would have to be considered worthless because white scientists in 1885 had not yet discovered their properties.[187]

[186] Mooney, "The Sacred Formulas of the Cherokees," *Seventh Annual Report of the Bureau of American Ethnology, 1885–86*, 328–29.

[187] Drugs used by American Indians which first became official in 1890 or later are: *Cascara Sagrada* (USP 1894), *Aralia Racemosa*, or Spikenard (NF 1916), *Dioscorea villosa* (wild yam root, NF 1916), *Chionanthus* or Fringe Tree bark (NF 1916), *Helonias* (Blazing Star, NF 1916), *Trillium* or Beth root (NF 1916), *Populus alba* (poplar bark, USP 1895), Poplar buds (NF 1916), *Viburnum Opulus* (High bush cranberry bark, USP 1894), White Ash bark (NF 1916), *Hydrangea* (NF 1916), Witch Hazel bark (USP 1906), *Mitchella* (Squaw vine, NF 1926), Sweet birch oil (USP 1894), Saw Palmetto berries (USP 1906), Yerba Santa (USP 1894), *Euphorbia pilulifera* (NF 1916), *Zanthoxylum* (Prickly Ash berries, NF 1916), Bayberry or Wax Myrtle bark (NF 1916), White Pine bark (NF 1916), Horse Nettle (NF 1916), *Corydalis* (NF 1916), Oregon Grape root (USP 1905), *Senecio* root (NF 1916), *Passiflora* (NF 1916), and Corn and Corn silk (NF 1894). This list does not include

There is no intention here to overrate Cherokee wisdom. No one can quarrel with Mooney's statement that some plants were rightly used for the wrong reasons, or Frans Olbrechts' *caveat* that "if a simple used by the Cherokee in the treatment of a particular disease happens to be incorporated in a Dispensatory, or listed in a Handbook of Pharmacy, this mere fact in no way confirms the efficacy of the Cherokee mode of using it."[188]

The early medicine of the Creeks found an interested commentator in William Bartram. The Quaker botanist from Philadelphia toured the South in 1788 and reported several observations on the ethnobotany of this tribe. He described "a tall species of Silphium," the stem of which was often cracked or split from the weight of its flowers, "from whence exudes a gummy or resinous substance, which the sun and air harden into semi-pellucid drops or tears of a pale amber colour; this resin possesses a very agreeable fragrance and bitterish taste . . . is chewed by the Indians and traders, to cleanse their teeth and mouth, and sweeten their breath."[189]

Bartram found that the Creeks had one of their favorite floral remedies under cultivation. At the Indian town of Attasse he found the natives fasting, praying, and taking medicine to avert some calamity of sickness, during which they ate only a gruel of corn-flour and water,

> . . . taking at the same time by way of medicine or physic, a strong decoction of the roots of the Iris versicolor, which is a powerful cathartic; they hold this root in high estimation, every town cultivates a little plantation of it, having a large artificial pond, just without the town, planted and almost overgrown with it, where they usually dig clay for pottery,

---

a number of drugs used by aborigines of Latin America which became official later than 1890.

Two of the above drugs, poplar bark and Hydrangea, were used by the Cherokees. Thirty-five other botanical medicines mentioned in the *Swimmer Manuscript* as part of the Cherokee materia medica were official drugs before 1890.

188 *Swimmer Manuscript*, 81–82.
189 *Travels*, 252–53.

and mortar and plaster for their buildings, and I observed where they had lately been digging up this root.[190]

The rhizome of this plant was an official medicine in the American pharmacopeia for seventy-five years, and in the formulary for twenty-six years. Cathartic, emetic, and diuretic powers have been ascribed to it.[191]

Reports of Southern aboriginal medicine were not always favorable. The accounts of Bernard Romans, first published in 1775, attribute little virtue to Indian healing procedure. While he was among the Choctaws, the principal tribe in what is now Mississippi, he related:

> ... I had the misfortune to be afflicted with a violent fever which ended in a flux; my own skill being baffled, I applied to my guide, who had the reputation of being a knowing Physician well acquainted with the simples used among them. I submitted to his prescription; he got some herbs and roots, and made a decoction of them; I drank it; while the effect was expected, he alternately burnt some of the simples and sat down by me blowing upon me to drive away the disorder; I found no benefit by it; and on my refusing an other trial he said I was a fool, the next time the physic would be stronger, but he was not affronted.[192]

Romans believed, however, in the efficacy of the Indian pinkroot (*Spigelia marilandica*) for expelling worms, reporting that an infusion of the entire plant, as a tea, was employed. He reported the same remedy was used by whites for "intermittent fever," but advised that it be used with caution because of a strong narcotic quality.[193]

During the 1830's, under the relentless pressure of the Indianophobe chief executive, Andrew Jackson, the bulk of the population of the southern Indian tribes was forcibly exiled to

---

190 *Ibid.*, 288.
191 Claus, *Pharmacognosy*, 383.
192 *Natural History of East and West Florida*, 52.
193 *Ibid.*, 156, 160.

Oklahoma, leaving only a few remnants in their ancient home-
land. The effect upon their culture was catastrophic; so far as
their medicine was concerned, many of its necessary remedies
could not be found in their new home. That portion of their
healing customs and materia medica which survived into the
present century, however, has been studied by anthropologists,
and especially John R. Swanton.[194] All of it is, of course, associated intimately with legend, religion, and ritual, but it also reveals some notions of the properties of herbs which have been
found valid by white men.

The collection of wild medicinal plants for the drug market
was for some time a source of supplementary income for many
southern rural folk, especially the Negroes. The abandonment
of some exhausted lands formerly devoted to cotton culture
brought a resurgence of some of these plants which had become
scarce because of crop cultivation and overcollecting. Thirty
years ago, W. W. Barkley of the Kansas City College of Pharmacy
wrote an article on "Drug Collecting and Cultivation in Mississippi," in which he listed ninety-eight drug plants growing in
Mississippi for which there was some commercial demand.[195]
According to my own study, no less than ninety-six of these were
used medicinally by one or more Indian tribes. Their mark upon
the land they left was clearly something more than place names.

The Trans-Mississippi West

The materia medica of the Quapaws, Osages, and some exiled
Eastern and Northern tribes, such as the Shawnees and the Sauks,
in the area of Arkansas territory (which then included the present
state of Oklahoma), Missouri, and parts of Kansas, was recorded
in 1823 by John D. Hunter, who was a captive for about twenty

194 "Social and Religious Beliefs and Practices of the Chickasaw Indians,"
Forty-fourth Annual Report of the Bureau of American Ethnology, 1926–27, 169–
274; *Idem,* "Religious Beliefs and Medical Practices of the Creek Indians," *Forty-
second Annual Report of the Bureau of American Ethnology, 1924–25,* 473–672.

195 "Drug Collecting and Cultivation in Mississippi," *Journal of the American
Pharmaceutical Association,* Vol. XXV, No. 12 (December, 1936), 1156–59.

years.[196] He states that the Indians in this region used the inner bark of black locust as an emetic, wild gentian for stomach ailments, hazel-bark poultice for ulcers, Indian turnip, in combinations, as a decoction, for coughs and intermittent fevers, may apple as a cathartic, milkweed in decoction for dysentery, dropsy, and asthma, moss from shellbark walnut (hickory?) in infusion for catarrhs and asthmas, and a decoction of inner bark of the "mountain birch" as a remedy in coughs, colds, and pulmonary diseases. Other remedies used among them included oak bark, pipsissewa, prickly ash, puccoon, rushes, "sap pine," "sarvas tree," sassafras, Seneca snakeroot, slippery elm bark, spikenard, starflower, sumac, tobacco, tulip tree root bark, turkey pea, Virginia snakeroot, white plantain, wild cucumber, wild ginger, "wood soot," and "yellow root."[197]

Hunter's chapter on "the Indian practice of surgery and medicine" indicates that, for the most part, these tribes performed in ways similar to those of their eastern brethren. They practiced bleeding, but sparingly, as well as sucking, scarification, and cauterization. "They sometimes relieve inward pains," he wrote, "by setting a piece of touch-wood on fire, and permitting it to produce a blister over the pained part. They say 'that such treatment draws the enemy from his lurking place, and exposes him to direct attack.'" The Indians commenced "the cure of most of their acute diseases by an emetic, by bleeding, purging and sweating, the last of which is by far the most common." Rheumatism was a common ailment for which they used many methods of treatment. Hunter found them "generally successful in relieving acute cases, and even the cronic [sic] ones sometimes yield to their remedies, but they are very liable to return."[198]

Thomas Jefferson and Benjamin Rush were interested in learning something of the medical practice and herbal knowledge of the western tribes. Lewis and Clark, in accordance with instruc-

---

[196] *Manners and Customs of the Several Indian Tribes Located West of the Mississippi*, Chaps. XV, XVI.

[197] *Ibid.*, 368–95.

[198] *Ibid.*, 396–402.

tions, sent back from Fort Mandan 128 plant specimens, including an unidentified one having roots which were "highly prized by the natives as an efficatious remidy in cases of the bite of the rattle Snake or Mad Dog."[199]

Dr. Edwin James, physician with Stephen Long's expedition to the Rocky mountains (1819–20), described some of the diseases and practices of the Omaha Indians. "We did not learn," he wrote, "that they possessed any knowledge of cathartic or emetic medicines. But as a substitute for the latter, a feather is thrust down the throat, until its irritating effect produces vomiting."[200] This is a curious statement, since Gilmore's study indicated that the types of medicines which Dr. Edwin James "could not learn" about made up a substantial portion of the remedies of Missouri valley tribes.[201]

James further declared that:

> The medical and surgical knowledge of the Omawhaws is very inconsiderable, and what there is, is so much blended with ceremonies, which to us appear superstitious, inert, and absurd, that it would seem, that, with the exception of a few instances, they have no reasonable mode of practice.

He found them "very successful in the cure of gunshot wounds," but less so in mending fractures and dislocations, claiming that in the one case "the member usually remains more or less bent or crooked," and in the latter "the limb [frequently] remains permanently disjointed."

Catastrophe struck Long's expedition when three hundred of his men were afflicted with scurvy, resulting in the deaths of one hundred of them. Dr. James could only comment that "the causes which have been productive of this disease, are not dis-

---

199 Bernard DeVoto (ed.), *The Journals of Lewis and Clark*, 494. Dr. Edwin James (*infra*) saw no evidence of rabies among Indian dogs in this region.

200 *Account of an Expedition, from Pittsburgh to the Rocky Mountains*, Vol. XV in Thwaites (ed.), *Early Western Travels*, 47.

201 Gilmore, "Uses of Plants by Indians of the Missouri River Region," *Thirty-third Annual Report, Bureau of American Ethnology, 1911–12*, 43–154.

tinctly known, although there are many supposed ones to which it has been imputed. But it was generally remarked, that the hunters, who were much employed in their avocation, and almost constantly absent from Camp Missouri, escaped the malady."[202] It is not from Dr. James, but from the account of Maximilian, Prince of Wied, more than ten years later, that we learn that some of the men in Major Long's command were cured of scurvy with the green herbs and bulbs of *Allium reticulatum*, or wild garlic, a plant used by the Indians. When the prince was so severely ill with scurvy at Fort Clark in 1834 that he was given up as hopeless, a Negro cook who had been with Major Long remembered this remedy and had the Indian children gather it for the prince, who ate the cut up bulbs and recovered.[203]

At Astoria on the Columbia River (1811–14), Gabriel Franchère commented that the country contained an abundance of cranberries and a great variety of nutritive roots, the natives making "great use of those which have the virtue of curing or preventing the scurvy."[204] In British Columbia, in April of 1835, Dr. William F. Tolmie was unable to cure scurvy which afflicted several of the men there until he visited an Indian village and "brought home a quantity of Nettles & the herbaceous plant so much eaten by the natives."[205]

Some physicians were unaware of the Indian origin of their remedies. In Oregon in 1832–34, Dr. John K. Townsend cured an Indian girl of intermittent fever by the use of cathartics and quinine, but upon being asked to treat two other girls, he found his supply of quinine exhausted, so that he had to substitute an extract boiled from the bark of a species of dogwood which he called *Cornus Nuttali*, and effected a cure. He remarked that he "often thought it strange that the sagacity of the Indians should

---

[202] *Account of an Expedition*, Vol. XIV in Thwaites (ed.), *Early Western Travels*, 283.

[203] *Travels in the Interior of North America, 1832–1834* (Part III), Vol. XXIV in Thwaites (ed.), *Early Western Travels*, 82.

[204] *Narrative of a Voyage to the Northwest Coast*, Vol. VI in Thwaites (ed.), *Early Western Travels*, 321.

[205] *The Journals of William Fraser Tolmie*, 307.

not long ago have made them acquainted with this remedy."[206] Dogwood was, however, long used as a remedy for the "ague" among eastern Indians; perhaps the northwest Indians knew no remedy for this disease because it was new to them.

The northwest Indians contributed to the white man's pharmacopeia the Oregon grape root (*Berberis aquifolium*), which was used as a bitter tonic. [207] Tribes of this region, like those of northern California, also used the famous cathartic, *Cascara sagrada.*

[206] *Wyeth's Oregon and Townsend's Narrative*, Vol. XXI in Thwaites (ed.), *Early Western Travels*, 342–44.

[207] Franz Boas, "Current Beliefs of the Kwakiutl Indians," *Journal of American Folk-Lore*, Vol. XLV, No. 176 (April–June, 1932), 186; Alice Henkel, *American Root Drugs*, 37; Claus, *Pharmacognosy*, 484.

IV.

Services of
Indian Doctors
to Whites

"One of the powerful influences brought to bear on the colonists engaged in the practice of medicine," wrote Maurice Bear Gordon, "was wrought by the Indians. Friend or foe, the medical practice of the red man could not help but seep into the therapeutics of the pioneers of the New World." The reasons for this, he indicated, are that the colonial medical practitioners (not always physicians), especially the native-born ones, were poorly trained and equipped and were ready to receive useful information from any source. Being also in a new world and strangers to its medical flora, it was not unnatural to accept the native as a tutor.[1]

[1] *Aesculapius Comes to the Colonies*, 7.

Even in the coastal settlements, doctors were for a long time scarce, and on the frontier this remained true as long as there was a frontier; even today there are complaints of inadequate physician and hospital service in rural parts of the United States. "There was no eminent physician in New England before 1720," wrote Dr. Henry R. Viets, "and no scientific work of importance was accomplished during this era. The few physicians who came to America were forced by the environment to serve as bedside doctors in a hard-bitten country without any of the European refinements."[2] The Old World distinction between physicians who theorized and surgeons who did the hard work was broken in the wilderness. Moreover, because of the scarcity of trained medical men of any kind, the healing art was in those days largely the work of ministers "and the lowest class of medical men, the barber-surgeons." Dr. Viets saw at least one advantage in this, for the colonists were spared much that was bad in English and Continental medicine, and "American medicine, thus, became distinctive almost from the start and independence became its chief characteristic."[3]

Only twenty-six persons who graduated from Harvard before 1700 are known to have practiced medicine in New England, Viets declared, and only two of these had medical degrees. Of a total of 134 individuals known to have practiced medicine in Massachusetts before 1692, Viets reported that perhaps twelve or more practiced surgery, three were barber-surgeons, six or seven were ministers as well as physicians (though O. W. Holmes believed that more were not recorded), one practitioner was listed as a doctor, a schoolmaster, and a poet (in Savage's *Genealogical Dictionary*); another kept a tavern, and one was female.[4] Under these conditions, the division between medicine and pharmacy also broke down, for doctors often made their own medicines. As Dr. William Douglas of Boston wrote to Dr. Cadwallader Colden of New York in 1721:

[2] "Some Features of the History of Medicine in Massachusetts During the Colonial Period, 1620–1770," *Isis*, Vol. XXIII (1935), 389.

[3] *A Brief History of Medicine in Massachusetts*, 1.

[4] *Ibid.*, 42, 50.

You complain of the Practice of Physic being undervalued in your parts and with reason, we are not much better in that respect in this place; we abound with Practitioners tho no other graduate than myself, we have 14 Apothecary shops in Boston, all our Practitioners dispense their own medicines, my self excepted being the first who has lived here by Practice without the advantage of advance on Medicines.[5]

The situation was no better in South Carolina. If a Carolina colonist had a doctor, wrote Waring, "he had a doctor of doubtful efficacy, one who might deplete him with drastic measures or, less likely, one who, like Sydenham, might be willing to depend more conservatively on the often more effective virtues of the *vis medicatrix naturae*."[6]

Conditions which prevailed on the eastern seaboard in the early period were repeated in the West during later years. In the 1830's, reported Josiah Gregg, there was no physician in New Mexico, "although a great multitude of singular cures are daily performed with indigenous roots and herbs that grow in abundance all over the country." He cautioned against a migration of doctors to that region however, pointing out that it was not the want of patients but the poverty of the people which accounted for their absence.[7]

It is not to be wondered that a people poorly supplied with trained physicians would resort to lay healers and even Indian shamans. Neither poverty nor the scarcity of doctors, however, can fully explain the resort to nonprofessional practitioners. There was prevalent in many circles, well into the nineteenth century, a distrust, even hostility toward the medical profession. This was manifested in Virginia by the passage, as early as 1639, of bills regulating doctors, in which physicians were described as "avaritious and gripeing practitioners of phisick and chirurgery" who exacted "excessive and immoderate prices" for their serv-

---

[5] *Letters and Papers*, I, 114.

[6] *History of Medicine in South Carolina*, 5.

[7] *Commerce of the Prairies, Or the Journal of a Santa Fe Trader*, Vol. XIX in Thwaites (ed.), *Early Western Travels*, 332–33.

ices.[8] An early chronicler of Pennsylvania, Gabriel Thomas, declared:

> Of Lawyers and Physicians I shall say nothing, because this Countrey is very Peaceable and Healthy; long may it so continue and never have occasion for the Tongue of the one, nor the Pen of the other, both equally destructive to Mens Estates and Lives; besides forsooth, they, Hang-Man like, have a license to Murder and make Mischief.[9]

Thomas Jefferson probably voiced a wide sentiment when, in a letter to Dr. Caspar Wistar, professor of anatomy and surgery at the University of Pennsylvania, he deplored the changing fashions in medical doctrines, alleging that medical theorists "succeed one another like the shifting figures of a magic lantern." He scoffed at most medicines and in most instances favored letting nature take its unimpeded course:

> I believe we may safely affirm [Jefferson continued] that the inexperienced and presumptious band of medical tyros let loose upon the world, destroys more of human life in one year, than all the Robinhoods, Cartouches, and Macheaths do in a century. It is in this part of medicine that I wish to see reform, an abandonment of hypothesis for sober facts, the first degree of value set on clinical observation, and the lowest on visionary theories.[10]

In the nineteenth century, wrote Thomas Neville Bonner, "the stubborn addiction of most physicians to mercury, bleeding, and calomel was responsible for widespread fear of medical men and their medicines."[11] The American medical mind, wrote Dr. Oliver Wendell Holmes, schooled and given direction by Ben-

<hr />

8 Seward, "Pioneer Medicine in Virginia," *Annals of Medical History*, N.S., Vol. X, No. 2 (March, 1938), 182.

9 Myers (ed.), *Narratives*, 328.

10 Adrienne Koch and William Peden (eds.), *The Life and Selected Writings of Thomas Jefferson*, 584–85.

11 *Medicine in Chicago, 1850–1950*, 204.

jamin Rush, "has clearly tended to extravagance in remedies, as in everything else." Like Jefferson, Holmes rebuked the medical profession for overmedication, holding that "nature heals most diseases without help from the pharmaceutic art." In language scarcely equaled by nonmedical critics, Dr. Holmes alleged that:

> The disgrace of medicine has been that colossal system of self-deception, in obedience to which mines have been emptied of their cankering minerals, the vegetable kingdom robbed of all its noxious growths, the entrails of animals taxed for their impurities, the poison-bags of reptiles drained of their venom, and all the inconceivable abominations thus obtained thrust down the throats of human beings suffering from some fault of organization, nourishment, or vital stimulation.[12]

Dr. Benjamin Rush believed that tetanus could be contracted by lying on a damp brick pavement in hot weather,[13] and that the cutting of trees contributed to malaria, because standing trees helped to purify the air.[14] Dr. Paul Aliot, an early nineteenth-century doctor in New Orleans, excoriated the profession for its "ignorance," and charged that "skilled physicians who have travelled to Louisiana have always considered those who practice that profession (there) as men who have no understanding of that art so useful for the preservation of human life."[15]

Dr. Edwin James refused to believe that "milk sickness" was caused by any vegetation eaten by cows, as the Missouri farmers maintained, but insisted that milk was a naturally "unwholesome article of diet." He argued that "in some of the sickliest parts of the valley of the Mississippi, where bilious and typhoid fevers

[12] *Medical Essays, 1842–1882*, in *Collected Works*, IX, 193, 257, 265.

[13] Benjamin Rush, "Observations on the Cause and Cure of Tetanus," *Transactions of the American Philosophical Society*, II (Philadelphia, Robert Aitken, 1786), 226.

[14] *Idem*, "An Enquiry into the Cause of the Increase of Bilious and intermitting Fevers in Pennsylvania . . . ," *Transactions of the American Philosophical Society*, II, 206–207.

[15] James A. Robertson, *Louisiana under the Rule of Spain, France, and the United States, 1785–1807*, I, 63.

prevail, through summer and autumn, the most unrestrained use is made of butter, milk, eggs, and similar articles of diet." He further held the prevailing view of his time that malaria arose from "impure and offensive atmosphere."[16]

Many persons were understandably unenthusiastic about entrusting themselves to the care of doctors whose remedies and treatment were often as ill-founded as their theories of the causes of disease. While folk medicine did not originate on this continent, it was doubtless encouraged by the foregoing circumstances combined with New World conditions. Every household had its stock of native remedies, and in many communities a lay healer, resident or itinerant, enjoyed a considerable practice. A unique phenomenon of the American frontier was the white "Indian doctor," claiming to have been tutored by the red men, whose role will be discussed in the next chapter. In the preceding chapter, white observations of the treatment of Indians by their own medicine men have been cited. The treatment of whites by aboriginal Indian doctors is another story altogether, for it places the white man in the subordinate role of patient and learner.

The Indian "doctor" is mentioned most often as a skillful healer in the accounts of explorers who, traveling far from any settlement, could have no recourse to any other treatment except their own. "For a century," Pickard and Buley have written,

French *voyageurs* and *coureurs du bois* had preferred the Indian treatment of wounds and chronic sores with poultices and herbs to that of the whites. Native medicine men also doctored many other ills with concoctions of herbs, drinks, sweatings, and rubbings, usually accompanied with ceremonials, incantations, ghost shooting in the night, and similar aids. They even sucked out manitous, or evil spirits. In some western communities in the earlier years there were Indian doctors who were held in quite as high repute as regular white doctors.[17]

16 *Account of an Expedition*, in Thwaites (ed.), *Early Western Travels*, XIV, 141–42; XVII, 82–85.
17 *The Midwest Pioneer, His Ills, Cures and Doctors*, 36.

Dr. Harlow Brooks declared that "in frontier medicine much, one may even say most, of the settlers' knowledge in regard to the treatment of traumata has been bodily copied from the Indians."[18]

An early account of Indian healing by a white man in the role of patient is given by the German surgeon, John Lederer. On August 26, 1670, while on an exploring expedition in the Blue Ridge mountains of Virginia, he reported:

> Here was I stung in my sleep by a Mountain-spider; and had not an Indian suckt out the poyson, I had died: for receiving the hurt at the tip of one of my fingers, the venome shot up immediately into my shoulder, and so inflamed my side, that it is not possible to express my torment. The means used by my Physician, was first a small dose of Snakeroot-powder, which I took in a little water; and then making a kinde of Plaister of the same, applied it neer to the part affected: when he had done so, he swallowed some by way of Antidote himselfe, and suckt my fingers end so violently, that I felt the venome retire back from my side into my shoulder, and from thence down my arm: having thus sucked half a score time, and spit as often, I was eased of all my pain, and perfectly recovered.[19]

Lederer, in a letter to Governor John Winthrop of Connecticut, November 17, 1674, mentioned an "Old Indian Doctor, whow cured many sore eyes of a long standing in 3. or four days time, of wich I have many seen and admired, and especially such as doth procede from a salt and sharp deflucion." The remedy used was the chewed inner bark of red oak soaked in water.[20]

The Indian sweat bath was adopted by some white men, not only as a treatment for specific ills, but for its supposed value in promoting general health and hygiene. "I have seen some of our

---

[18] "The Medicine of the American Indian," *Bulletin of the New York Academy of Medicine*, 2d ser., Vol. V, No. 6 (June, 1929), 519.

[19] John Lederer, *The Discoveries of John Lederer*, ed. William P. Cumming, 36–37.

[20] *Ibid.*, 54–55.

Frenchmen," reported Gabriel Sagard, "in these sweat-baths along with the savages, and I was astonished that they wished and were able to endure it, and that a sense of propriety did not lead them to hold aloof from it."[21]

John Brickell reported that Indian doctors were unwilling to divulge their medical secrets to white men, but would treat white people who were afflicted with disorders familiar to the Indians, although declining to test their skill on European maladies of which they had no knowledge. He gave a detailed account of the treatment of a North Carolina planter by an Indian:

> There was a Planter in *North Carolina* who had a grievous *Ulcer* in his Leg for many Years, which was deemed incurable by all those that beheld it; and many attempts were made by the best *Christian* artists in that Country to perfect the Cure, but all to no purpose, for his Leg still grew worse and worse; at last he was prevailed upon to apply himself to one of those *Indian* Doctors, who performed the Cure in a very short time for the value of three Shillings *Sterling*, though it had cost him above one hundred Pounds before to little or no Purpose.
>
> The *Indian* Doctor performed this Cure after the following manner; first he made a strong Decoction of the Bark of the Root of *Sassafras*, in which he bathed the Patients Leg very well, then he took the rotten Grains of the *Maiz*, or *Indian Corn*, well dried and beaten to Powder, and the soft Down that grows upon the Turkeys Rump, with this he quickly dried up the filthy *Ulcer*, and made a perfect Cure, of what was thought incurable, to the great Joy and satisfaction of the Planter, who had so long laboured under it. This I had affirmed to me by the Planter himself, and several others that were Eye-witnesses to the whole Affair.[22]

In Louisiana, Le Page du Pratz related that he was relieved of pains in the thigh by an Indian doctor who made incisions and sucked the blood, then applied poultices. In another instance an

[21] *Long Journey*, 198.   [22] *Natural History of North–Carolina*, 344, 395–96.

Indian cured him of a "fistula" in the eye by daily bathing with a decoction of boiled herbs.[23]

Several medical writers have briefly mentioned Joe Pye, a New England Indian healer whose name is perpetuated by Joe Pye (or Jopi) weed (*Eupatorium purpureum* L.). It is reported that he used this plant to produce profuse sweating in the treatment of typhus fever.[24] The rhizome and roots of this plant, which is also known as purple boneset, gravel root, and queen of the meadow, were an official drug in the *U. S. Pharmacopeia* from 1820–42. With other members of the eupatoria family, it has been used as a diaphoretic, diuretic, stimulant, astringent, emetic, and cathartic.[25]

Henry David Thoreau, while on a canoe trip in the Maine woods, reported that "our Indian said that he was a doctor, and could tell me some medicinal use for every plant I could show him. I immediately tried him. He said that the inner bark of the aspen (*Populus tremuloides*) was good for sore eyes; and so with various other plants, proving himself as good as his word. According to his account, he had acquired such knowledge in his youth from a wise old Indian with whom he was associated, and he lamented that the present generation of Indians 'had lost a great deal.' "[26]

Dr. Stephen W. Williams, who in 1849 compiled for the American Medical Association a report on the medical flora of his home state of Massachusetts, mentioned Louis Watso, a Canadian Indian doctor who, with a party of Indians, visited Deerfield in 1837. He provided Dr. Williams with an account of the principal medical plants used in Indian practice. Williams was told that a plaster made by boiling the narrow-leaved laurel plant (*Kalmia angustifolia*) would cure rheumatism. The Indian reported the use of the creeping checkerberry (*Mitchella repens*) in combination with a species of hardhack (*Spiraea alba*) for the

23 *Historie de la Louisiane*, I, 135–36, 207–209.
24 Stephen W. Williams, "Report on the Indigenous Medical Botany of Massachusetts," *Transactions of the American Medical Association*, II, 894.
25 Jacob Bigelow, *A Treatise*, 176; Claus, *Pharmacognosy*, 217.
26 *The Maine Woods*, 159.

cure of salt rheum. Dr. Williams himself recommended the former plant as a valuable diuretic, which was extensively used in dropsy, and said that the mildly astringent berries were useful in the cure of diarrhea.[27] Hardhack was then listed in the pharmacopeia, but the checkerberry, or squaw vine, did not become an official drug until 1926, when it was admitted to the *National Formulary*.

Dr. Stone names several Indians who served as doctors to white communities and reports the remarkable trust placed by whites in an old Sioux doctor named Baptiste, who was a shaman at the Winnebago agency when there were no white physicians within "several hundred miles." When his tribe was removed to a more western reserve he was retained at the agency, where the government built him a house and maintained him. For years he treated Indians and whites alike, "finally dying respected by both races."[28]

An account of a cure performed by an Indian woman doctor on the Canadian plains was reported in *The Lancet* of Great Britain early in the present century. A young Scotsman, before coming to Canada, had driven a nail into the palm of his left hand, and the wound had never satisfactorily healed. While he was crossing an ice-covered stream in Manitoba with a team of horses, the ice broke beneath him, and his immersion seemed to complicate the old injury. Next day the arm became very painful and began to swell; "possibly," the correspondent wrote, "there may have been blood poisoning." The nearest medical man was seventy miles away, and the young man set out on horseback to reach him, but his suffering became unendurable. Arriving at an Indian camp on the prairie, he showed the red men his plight, whereupon he was placed near the heat of the fire, and a pot of water was set to boiling. The account continued:

> The old squaw, having carefully rolled up the sleeve, took the wounded hand in hers and gently rubbed her other

27 "Report on the Indigenous Medical Botany of Massachusetts," *Transactions of the American Medical Association*, II, 810, 916.

28 Stone, *Medicine Among the American Indians*, 121–22.

hand to and fro over the swelling and up and down the whole arm, all the while chanting a weird song. At the same time all the other squaws . . . took up the chant and forming themselves into a circle walked round and round the two during the whole of the operation. The young fellow's mind was so acted upon by the effect of the mysterious chanting that his attention was entirely taken away from the pain he was suffering, which, of course, was the real object of the strange performance. He became so hot that he fell into a profuse perspiration, and when the squaw was satisfied with the results of her treatment she made a poultice from some particular leaves collected for such purposes and bound it over the hand. The Indians then lifted up the white man and carried him into the inner part of the tent, shut off from the rest, where he was laid down and covered with skins. Here he slept for 18 hours. When he awoke the pain and swelling had entirely gone from his arm and being now in a more fit state to complete the remainder of his journey he went on to the medical man and told him his experience. The medical man was so satisfied with what had been done that he said he should now be able to confine his attention to the wounded hand, but that if the patient had not undergone the treatment of the squaw he would have had to lose his arm. . . . The young Scotchman entirely recovered and is now hard at work with the contractors for the new railway through Saskatchewan territory.[29]

Richard Dunlop has told how a Cheyenne medicine man treated William Bent of Bent's Fort for a throat infection which threatened to choke him to death:

The medicine man strung a sinew with sandburs and dipped it into hot buffalo tallow. This he forced down Bent's throat with a peeled stick. When the tallow melted, he jerked

[29] "An Experience Among the Red Indians," from a correspondent, *The Lancet*, February 27, 1904, 611–12.

the string out, pulling the infected membrane with it. Bent survived.[30]

Frank Speck mentioned a Catawba medical practitioner named Tom Morrison who, in the late nineteenth century, doctored whites as well as Indians when they would accept his services. He practiced curing in "old Catawba style," which meant, according to Speck, no singing of formulas or recitation when administering to the afflicted, in contrast to the Cherokee method. Morrison treated Indians at no cost but charged others.[31]

"Many a white man owes his life to the medicinal knowledge of the Indians," wrote A. Hyatt Verrill, "and I can personally testify to the efficiency of Indians as physicians, for I was safely brought through an attack of yellow fever by Indians and Indian medicines."[32]

Mrs. Matilda Coxe Stevenson has told of her treatment by Zuñi "theurgists" who used a native medicine to cure rheumatism. It consisted of cakes made of the blossoms of *Eupatorium occidentale arizonicum* combined with other plants, including native squash blossoms, which are broken in water and rubbed on the affected parts while the practitioner prays. First a guest of Mrs. Stevenson was cured in this manner of a swelling on her cheek which attained the size of a hen's egg, the results being achieved after three daily treatments. Later Mrs. Stevenson suffered from rheumatism of the right shoulder, which a white physician was unable to relieve. The *Shu'maakwe* doctor brought about her complete recovery after six applications of the same medicine.[33]

Huron H. Smith's chief informant on Meskwaki ethnobotany during the 1920's, John McIntosh, was a medicine man of Potawatomi origin who also treated some white people in Iowa. McIntosh claimed that he used swamp milkweed (*Asclepias in-*

30 *Doctors of the American Frontier*, 14.

31 "Catawba Herbals and Curing Practices," *Journal of American Folk-Lore*, Vol. LVII, No. 223 (January–March, 1944), 38–39.

32 *The American Indian*, 121.

33 "Ethnobotany of the Zuni Indians," *Thirtieth Annual Report of the Bureau of American Ethnology, 1908–1909*, 50.

carnata L.) to recover four long worms from a Cedar Rapids woman. A root tea of this plant was said to expel worms in an hour. The same healer allegedly received a fee of $700 for curing a case of dropsy which "white physicians had pronounced incurable."[34]

The foregoing claims of Indian cures are scattered episodes, most frequently found in situations where no other medical help was available, and they do not indicate any marked preference on the part of white people for the services of Indian medical men. The relative isolation of Indians from settled white communities by itself was enough to keep to a minimum their opportunities to attempt cures among white people. The reported instances of Indian healing by some reputable reporters could perhaps be explained on several grounds—the natural tendency of most wounds or ills to cure themselves in time, the psychological effects of suggestion, the inspiration of confidence and hope, and finally, wrong diagnosis, resulting in "curing a disease that wasn't there," as Dr. Walter C. Alvarez put it in an article explaining why quacks sometimes cure.[35] It will be seen, however, that some of the Indian curative agents described above became official drugs and in a notable number of instances have been used for the same purposes that the Indians used them. Nearly ninety years ago Dr. Joseph Toner declared that the Indians "have always had practitioners, taught by experience how to administer medicines with more or less judgment."[36]

Although the number of people who were actually treated by Indian medicine men was small, the reputation of the aboriginal healers reached far beyond the frontier where it was made. It was the popular image of the Indian as a healer which created in the nineteenth century the great success of the white "Indian doctors," the patent medicines of alleged Indian origin, and the "Indian" medicine shows.

34 *Meskwaki Ethnobotany*, 191, 205.

35 "The Emergence of Modern Medicine from Ancient Folkways," *Annual Report of the Board of Regents of the Smithsonian Institution . . . 1938*, 412.

36 *Address Before the Rocky Mountain Medical Association, June 6, 1877*, 82.

V.

The Influence
of Indian Medicine
on Folk Medicine,
Irregular Practitioners,
and
Patent Medicines

American Folk Medicine

While American folk medicine had roots in Europe, it was also affected by the same circumstances which caused frontiersmen to resort occasionally to the services of Indian doctors, namely the scarcity of trained physicians, distrust of the profession and particularly of some of the current remedies, and poverty. Also important was the unavailability of conventional drugs and medicines. What has been said of the far West was true at an earlier time in the East:

There was a time, within the recollection of people still living, when between the Missouri River and the Pacific

Ocean there was no place where one could find medicines. Pharmacy was probably known and practiced at a fringe of places on the coast line of Western America; but in between, nothing. The redskin may have had emergency trifles tucked away in his belt or trappings, but he found his remedies on the spot when he wanted them. There were remedies everywhere; a fine field of botanic *materia medica* was ready for the aborigine or observing seeker.[1]

The earliest settlers who landed on the Atlantic shores had some knowledge of European remedies, but as they pushed westward they necessarily had to resort to the indigenous medicines, the properties of which could most readily be learned from the Indians. Thus, aboriginal herbals were often long used as folk remedies before they were accepted by official medicine. Many of the educated physicians of the time were slow to ascribe any virtue to savage medical knowledge:

The Indian remedies [wrote C. A. Browne] that came to the attention of the early colonists were slow in obtaining official recognition. *Hydrastis,* used as a remedy by the Cherokees and later by the early settlers, did not attract medical attention until 1798; it is now an important drug in all pharmacopeias; *Lobelia* was long known as a medicine among the North American Indians, before Dr. Cutler of Massachusetts introduced it to the medical profession. Ipecac, although for centuries in common use among natives of Brazil, was not employed in Europe until 1672. The popularity of some of the Indian remedies, when once physicians began to describe them, became so great in some cases as almost to cause extinction of the plant. Pinkroot, for example, which was used by the Indians as a vermifuge, was supplied to the drug markets by the Creek and Cherokee tribes of Georgia in large bales. The plants were pulled up

1 John T. Moore, "The Early Days of Pharmacy in the West," *Journal of the American Pharmaceutical Association,* Vol. XXV, No. 8 (August, 1936), 709.

by the roots and this ruthless destruction led to its complete extermination in many sections.[2]

The settlers not only used the Indian remedies, but they sometimes gathered and used them in accordance with the Indian customs. Thus, Joseph Doddridge, who was brought up on the Pennsylvania frontier, related that white walnut bark was peeled downward when intended to be used as a purge and upward for use as an emetic.[3]

The combination of charms, incantation, magic, and "laying on of hands" for avoiding or curing disease or injury, which survives to this day among the Pennsylvania Germans, is called "powwowing" by those who use it.[4] While "powwow" is an Indian word,[5] and the practices associated with the conjurations of the whites who use it closely parallel those of the Indians, much of it seems to be of Old World origin, with Indian adaptations. A. Monroe Aurand, himself a Pennsylvania German, claimed that the "strange practices and beliefs" of his people "come from the Fatherland." The custom of "pow-wowing," he wrote, "goes back ages and ages."[6] Indeed, a reading of his book and others dealing with these folk practices reveals much that is traceable to medieval witchcraft cults. Moreover, many of the formulas to be recited to ward off bad fortune or bring good luck, or to cure ailments, are simply prayers. So are the sacred formulas of the

2 "The Chemical Industries of the American Aborigines," *Isis*, Vol. XXIII (1935), 420.

3 *Notes on the Settlement and Indian Wars*, 169.

4 News item, *Chicago Tribune*, May 6, 1965: "*Folk Cures Practiced in Parts of 2 States*, University Park, Pa., May 5 (UP)—Pow-wowing—the practice of folk cures—continues to be practiced in parts of Pennsylvania and Missouri. Pennsylvania pow-wowers appear to be successful in taking away warts, stopping pain from burns, and healing almost any kind of skin ailment, according to Gary A. Noll, a graduate student in psychology at Pennsylvania State University."

5 Alexander F. Chamberlain reported that this word is of Algonquian origin, with the following several meanings: 1. A medicine-man. 2. The conjuring of a medicine-man over a patient. 3. A dance, feast, or noisy demonstration preceding a council, expedition, or hunt. 4. A council. 5. A conference. Frederick Webb Hodge (ed.), *Handbook of American Indians North of Mexico*, Bulletin 30, Bureau of American Ethnology, 303.

6 *The "Pow-Wow" Book*, 39.

Cherokees, with the only real difference being in the name of the deity to whom the prayers are addressed. The Indian influence on white "powwowing" is suggested by one of Aurand's correspondents, whose assertions he does not dispute:

> The first pow-wow doctors were Indian medicine men. It took the fancy of early settlers and they said "we can do that too." Instead of appealing to the demons and spirits in natural things, however, they appealed to religious superstition, perpetuating a sort of religious sorcery mixed with anything else that came in handy, and was available generally.[7]

Aurand reprinted some of the charms, remedies, and formulas first published in John George Hohman's original "pow-wow book" of 1820. To destroy warts, it declared, one should "roast chicken-feet and rub the warts with them; then bury them under the eaves." Toothache was cured by cutting out a piece of sod before sunrise, breathing upon it three times, and restoring it to the same place from which it was taken.[8] Some of the remedies Hohman listed may have been borrowed from the Indians, such as a tea made from the buds or inner bark of the birch tree for weakness of the limbs, the treatment of burns with the juice of male fern, the use of tree moss, boiled in red wine, for diarrhea or dysentery, and the manufacture of a salve for wounds from tobacco and elder leaves fried in butter.[9]

Another compilation of Pennsylvania German folk cures, published in 1935,[10] lists a large number of formulas in which old Indian remedies are combined with nonaboriginal substances. Sassafras, especially, is frequently prescribed; the berries were used to make a wine for colds, the blossoms were boiled to make a tea for fevers, and the leaves were chewed and laid on wounds to stop bleeding. Tobacco was chewed as a preventative and cure

[7] *Ibid.*, 22.

[8] *Ibid.*, Part III, "John George Hohman's 'Pow-Wow, or Long Lost Friend,'" 17, 19.

[9] Aurand, *The "Pow-Wow" Book*, 24, 28, 54.

[10] Thomas R. Brendle and Claude W. Unger, *Folk Medicine of the Pennsylvania Germans: The Non-Occult Cures.*

for toothache, and tobacco smoke was blown into the ear to kill the "woodland insect" which was believed to cause insanity by drying up the brain.[11] These herbal medicines were often combined with such substances as whisky, wine, cider, milk, or tallow.

An annual spring ritual among the Pennsylvania Germans was "thinning the blood," which was accomplished by such greens as dandelion, lettuce, watercress, plantain, and other herbs called *blutreinigungsmittel*. Among the blood-purifying roots were sassafras, sarsaparilla, burdock, and devil's bit. Some of these were chosen because of their red color and others for their bitter taste, which was believed to indicate strong medicinal powers.[12]

Another class of Pennsylvania German remedies was the *schwitzgegreider*, or sweat herbs, which included agrimony, wormwood, mugwort, feverfew, chamomile, and the mint family. For the same purpose, roots of Virginia snakeroot, dandelion, sanicle, or herbs like pipsissewa and sabbatia were put in whisky. Like the Aztecs, these people had a remedy for dandruff (*kopptetter*) consisting of the application of brewed sage or burdock leaves. Besides these household remedies, they employed sympathetic remedies and charm, or *brauch*, remedies.[13]

These treatments, on the surface, seem to reflect a combination of Old World superstitions with the use of both foreign and native remedies; many of the latter class are known to have been used by the Indians.

The home remedies used on the western Pennsylvania frontier in the eighteenth century, by those of Scotch-Irish and other ancestry as well as German, have been described by Joseph Doddridge. Some of the animal, mineral, and vegetable substances used were of foreign origin, but most of them were indigenous Indian remedies. Poultices of "Indian meal" or slippery-elm bark were used for burns. Sweating was the general remedy for fevers, induced by a strong decoction of Virginia snakeroot. Indian physic or bowman root and sometimes the

---

11 *Ibid.*, 40, 110, 116, 129.
12 *Ibid.*, 39, 91.
13 *Ibid.*, 42, 90, 101.

puccoon or bloodroot were used to provoke vomit. To treat venomous snakebites, the body of the offending reptile was cut up and the flesh applied to the wound.[14] Chestnut bark and white plantain were also among the numerous snakebite remedies, as were salt and gunpowder. Cupping or sucking the wound and making incisions were also common treatments. Gunshot wounds were treated with poultices of elm bark or flax seed. The oil of rattlesnakes, geese, wolves, bears, raccoons, groundhogs, and pole-cats was applied to joints swelled by rheumatism. Spikenard and elecampane were used to make cough syrup.

Doctors were unavailable on this frontier. Doddridge re-marked that "for many years in succession there was no person who bore even the name of a doctor within a considerable dis-tance of the residence of my father." It was his opinion that many people in that region "perished for want of medical skill and attention."[15] Perhaps others also survived for the lack of it, for he mentioned with regret, that bleeding was not employed as a curing device.

Folk curing mixed with medical and other superstitions has long flourished in that region known today as Appalachia. One writer viewed the phenomenon as "a middle age survival . . . the ensemble of a practical and speculative medievalism beneath the surface changes of modern times."[16] Indeed, not every practice which resembles that of the Indians was derived from them, for many of the beliefs and methods of primitive curing are found throughout the world.

---

[14] On Indian use of snake flesh as a remedy for bites, see Josselyn, *New Eng-land's Rarities*, 169; Loskiel, *History of the Mission of the United Brethren*, I, 114; and Hrdlička, *Physiological and Medical Observations*, 246. Cadwallader Colden was a strong believer in this treatment, *vide Letters and Papers*, II, 67–68. See also John Woods's account of treatment of a dog by this method in Woods, *Two Years Residence . . . in the Illinois Country*, in Vol. X in Thwaites (ed.), *Early Western Travels*, 342. Dr. Dan MacKenzie reported that the use of snake fat or oil for snakebite was still in vogue in rural parts of England in this century, and he traced the custom back to Pliny of Rome; *The Infancy of Medicine*, 117–18.

[15] *Notes on the Settlement and Indian Wars*, 168–73.

[16] J. Hampden Porter, "Folk-Lore of the Mountain Whites of the Alleghenies," *Journal of American Folk-Lore*, Vol. VII, No. 25 (April-June, 1894), 106.

The actual origin of the remedies employed, however, is more readily determined. Justice William O. Douglas has asserted that many of the herbal remedies of lower Appalachia were borrowed from the Cherokee Indians. Among the home remedies now or formerly used by the settlers in Cades Cove in the Great Smoky Mountains, he listed tea of spikenard roots for backache, wild cherry bark tea for measles and colds, poultices of cornmeal and peach leaves for boils and "risings," tea from yellow root (*Zanthorhiza apiifolia?*) for throat and stomach disorders, and several others of indefinite application, such as ginseng and sassafras.[17] In the Ohio valley, another writer declares, "some of the knowledge of the Indians was transmitted to and used by the early settlers. Even to this day in rural areas we find a surprising degree of dependence upon such simple native medicines."[18]

The White "Indian" Doctors

In the old Northwest, Pickard and Buley have written, "Indian influences were strong, and many early settlers relied upon the 'yarb and root' doctors who worked largely with remedies obtained from forest and garden."[19] In the Ohio valley, it is asserted, "the Indian doctor, not altogether a charlatan or fakir, could always get a following, and any quack might be certain to receive, at worst, a tolerant hearing."[20]

The frontier, as might be expected, was the land where self-styled "doctors" flourished, along with circuit-riding revival preachers and buckboard-riding peddlers. Variously known as "Indian" doctors, "botanic physicians," "herb doctors," "eclectics," "empirics," "Thomsonians," and plain "quacks," depending on who was describing them, they tried in their untrained

17 "The People of Cades Cove," *National Geographic Magazine*, Vol. CXXII, No. 1 (July, 1962), 84–85.

18 Emmet Field Horine, "Early Medicine in Kentucky and the Mississippi Valley: A Tribute to Daniel Drake, M.D.," *Journal of the History of Medicine*, Vol. III, No. 2 (Spring, 1948), 263.

19 *The Midwest Pioneer*, 36.

20 Works Progress Administration, *Medicine and Its Development in Kentucky*, 47.

way to fill the gap caused by the absence of physicians possessed of medical degrees. In those days no licensing laws or other legal impediments hindered them from plying their trade. Some of them were fakers and charlatans, while some others were doubtless honest men who imagined themselves to be human benefactors.

Many of the early botanic physicians professed to have absorbed their knowledge directly from contact with the Indians. Some of them had indeed, by reason of captivity, trade, or other occasion for proximity with the natives, found opportunities to learn the red man's procedure and remedies. Some claimed to be at least partly of Indian descent. It was through these men that some of the Indian medical remedies passed to the whites.

Though he never styled himself an "Indian" healer, one of the most famous of the so-called "empiric" practitioners was Samuel Thomson (1769–1843), a New Hampshire-born farmer with only a few months of formal education, who managed to become a *bête noire* to much of the medical profession of his time. His first interest in medicine was stimulated by trips into the field with an elderly female "root and herb" healer in his father's neighborhood. When, to avoid the hard labor of scratching a living from a Vermont homestead, he took to doctoring, he promoted the idea that herbs and natural remedies were superior to mineral and exotic drugs, and was much devoted to "steaming" or sweating patients in all kinds of ills. One of his favorite remedies was a species of lobelia, or Indian tobacco, with the use of which he became so closely identified that the hostility of the physicians was said to be directed at his panacea because of its identification with him. Although lobelia species had long been used by Indians and whites, Thomson claimed to have "discovered" it while looking for the cows at the age of four. Of it he wrote:

This plant is what I have called the Emetic Herb, and is the most important article I make use of in my practice. It is very common in most parts of this country, and may be prepared and used in almost any manner. It is a certain counter poison, having never been known to fail to counteract the effects of the most deadly poison, even when taken in large quantities for self-destruction. There is no danger to be apprehended from its use, as it is perfectly harmless in its operation, even when a large quantity is taken; it operates as an emetic, cleanses the stomach from all improper aliment, promotes an internal heat . . . and produces perspiration.[21]

At Jericho, Vermont, in the winter of 1807, Thomson claimed to have cured about twenty-eight persons who were suffering from dysentery with treatment consisting of "red pepper steeped in a tea of sumach leaves, sweetened, and sometimes the bark and cherries, to raise the heat and clear off the canker, which had the desired effect." Those who were strengthened by the tea were placed over steam and then put to bed.[22] Steam played such an important part in the Thomson treatment that he and his disciples were for years denominated as "steamers" by their critics.

While Thomson had no direct contact with the Indians, his remedies and methods of treatment, especially sweating, suggest primitive inspiration, and the old woman who tutored him may have had some earlier contact with the red men.

In the first half of the nineteenth century every muddy backwoods trail was trod by horseback-riding "Indian doctors" toting saddlebags of herb and root medicines to isolated cabins and frontier communities. Many of them published manuals outlining their philosophy of medicine, listing diseases and remedies and prefaced with "testimonials" from clergymen and former patients who claimed to have been cured of dread diseases by the author. Most of these white medicine men claimed to have learned their lore from the red men; so common was this claim that, whether true or not, it suggests that Indian medicine enjoyed a high reputation among the frontiersmen. One of these self-styled doctors, Peter Smith, informed his readers:

21 *New Guide to Health; or Botanic Family Physician*, 16–17.
22 *Ibid.*, 63–64.

I call myself an *Indian Doctor*, because I have incidentally obtained a knowledge of many of the simples used by the Indians; but chiefly because I have obtained my knowledge generally in the like manner that the Indians do. . . .

I have by continued observation come to be of the opinion, that our best medicines grow in the woods and gardens.[23]

In his *Indian Doctor's Dispensatory*, Peter Smith listed eighty-five medical prescriptions, many of which were well-known herbal remedies used by Indians and pioneers, but also including a number of proprietary medicines of uncertain composition. No Latin names are attached to the vegetable remedies, so that certain identification is not always possible. Among his potions and decoctions are listed such as "Abela, or Trumpet-weed root," which "the Africans give to make the wenches amorous and fruitful. It is supposed to excite venereal desire." Another intriguing substance, called devil's nip, was used as a charm:

It is said that any person carrying a root or two, need never fear that any snake will bite him. A little of it put into the mouth of a snake, is instant death to him. A German doctor used it to give to persons deranged and announced their cure by it.

A tea made from "star root" (also called devil's bit) "relieves from pains and distress which are peculiar to the fair sex." A proprietary medicine called "Dr. Reeder's chalybeate for female weakness" was said to include Virginia or Seneca snakeroot. "Doctor" Smith recommended "corn snake root" to cure rattlesnake bites, mountain mint as a diuretic and sudorific, boiled white pine bark as a poultice for sores, "squaw-root" or black snakeroot for snakebite, devil's-bit tea for backache and croup, spikenard for earache, pond-lily root for "king's evil" (scrofula), a sweat of Virginia snakeroot and sage tea for fevers, and a syrup of "squaw root" for catarrh.

[23] *The Indian Doctor's Dispensatory, being Father Smith's Advice Respecting Diseases and their Cure,* x–xi.

Contemporary with, but unrelated to "Father" Smith, was "Doctor" Daniel Smith, who stated that he was born in 1790 "in the then wilderness vicinity of Niagara Falls." In this environment, he claimed that he was "early initiated into the mode of treating diseases as practiced by the neighboring Aborigines." In his book, *The Reformed Botanic and Indian Physician*, he expounded his medical philosophy in the opening paragraph:

> Pause for a moment and view the Corner Stone of the Primitive Medical Edifice which is already laid, and no longer suffer yourselves to be cut to pieces by the lancet or the two-edge sword of the poisonous mineral drugs, which man's device has hatched up to pick your pockets and bear you to an untimely grave; for the God of Nature in early days supplied our ancient fathers with all the healing powers arising from the Vegetable Kingdom, to heal all the maladies they were afflicted with, when they broke Nature's unerring laws.[24]

Smith's materia medica included 867 vegetable remedies, nearly four times as many as the first *United States Pharmacopeia*. His list was not confined to Indian simples, or even indigenous plants, but included drugs from all parts of the world. In contrast to the scholarly references and descriptions of properties, usage, and dosage contained in the works of such men as Bigelow, Porcher, and Clapp, Smith devoted only a line or two to each remedy. For *Lobelia inflata*, for example, his entire comment was: "In Asthma, Colics, Spasms, and as an Emetic, it is very valuable." For mandrake root (*Podophyllum peltatum*), which is still an official cathartic, Smith mentioned only that it was "a substitute for mercury in Venereal, Scrofulous, and all other diseases."

Smith included a section on anatomy and, for the practical-minded farmer who wanted his money's worth, appendices on veterinary medicine, the raising and treatment of poultry, and

[24] *The Reformed Botanic and Indian Physician: A Complete Guide to Health*, 7.

"remarks on hunting, fishing, and catching game." The longest section contains his medical recipes, including such startling advice as the use of red onions as a poultice for cancer and the same substance admixed with oil of roasted almonds for deafness. Onions were pronounced useful for a variety of ailments; they could be rubbed on the head to cure baldness, and if fried and mixed with olive oil they could insure easy delivery. Lunacy could be treated with a decoction of agrimony or by rubbing the head with vinegar several times a day; if all else failed, his advice was: "be electrified."

Another botanic "Indian" physician, Robert D. Foster, is notable for the unusual length of his book's title,[25] if nothing else. In it he presented 204 "receipts," a list of 100 plants, and catechismlike questions and answers on anatomy, physiology, "practice of physic," obstetrics, and poisons. His recipe No. 25 prescribed the following for croup:

The best remedy for it is, equal parts of blood root, lobelia, garlic, skunks cabbage, elecampane, sage, and thorough wort, or Seneca snake root, or if the whole cannot be had, lobelia tincture, will do alone, or lobelia, and mullen roots, in decoction, give as much as possible as the stomach will immediately eject any of these articles in this disease.[26]

James W. Cooper, who described himself as an "Experienced Botanist, or Indian Physician," prefaced his manual with an extract from John Wesley's *Primitive Physic*, and pointed to Indian medicine as the proof that the practice of medicine need not be an exclusive profession:

Does it reflect honor on that kind Providence, who supplies the wants of all creatures, to suppose that the science of health, in which every child of Adam is so deeply concerned,

25 *The North American Indian Doctor, or Nature's Method of Curing and Preventing Disease According to the Indians . . . also, a treatise on Midwifery . . . also, A Materia Medica of Indian Remedies, or Vegetable Compounds, in the form of recipes for more than two hundred and fifty diseases, with a description of such plants as are not common.*

26 *Ibid.,* 83.

must necessarily be the exclusive privilege of a few? That it should be locked up in an unknown language, or merged in a mass of learned lumber, requiring an age of study to explore and apply its principles to useful purposes? A reference to the Aborigines of our country is sufficient to refute such doctrine. Is it credible that diseases, peculiar to our climate and country, can find no remedies nearer than foreign countries? Is it credible that the thousands of vegetables that beautify and perfume our fields and groves, have no valuable use in relation to the health and comfort of man?[27]

These polemics were followed by testimonials, including one bearing four signatures which stated: "We do hereby make known, that Dr. J. W. Cooper, by his Indian mode of practice, for the last seven months, lost but three patients out of seven or eight hundred cases.[28]

How many of Cooper's remedies were actually learned from the Indians is a moot question. Some of them, such as the following, have not yet been discovered in the prescriptions of any tribe:

Take fish worms, wash them, put them into a strong bottle, cork it tight; then put dough round the bottle and place it in the oven: when the dough has baked to a crust, take it out, strain and bottle for use. This oil is good for stiff joints and contracted sinews; used by rubbing on externally.[29]

One of the last of the "Indian" healers was John Goodale Briante, who claimed on the title page of his manual, published in 1870, that he was "for many years with the St. Francis Tribe of Indians, at Green Bay; also, for several years with the Pottowattamies and other Tribes." He announced that the book contained "directions for preparing and using their most valuable Remedies, as used by him, in his extensive practice throughout

27 *The Experienced Botanist or Indian Physician. Being a New System of Practice, Founded on Botany*, v.
28 *Ibid.*, xvi.
29 *Ibid.*, 87.

the Eastern and Middle States." One of Briante's recipes was a "Cancer Cure," prepared as follows:

Take "King of all Poison," pound up, pulverize it, bind it on the cancer, and it will take out the inflammation. Then use a wash made as follows: take hard-wood ashes, leach them, and boil down the liquor till it is very strong.

Apply this twice a day with a swab, to kill the cancer.[30]

In addition, the patient was to take a syrup, called "Was-a-mo-s" medicine, composed of the roots of spikenard, sweet fern, yellow dock, elecampane, and bloodroot, with the herb of white vervain, pigeon cherry and white-pine bark, and sweet cicely. This, he asserted, was also "an excellent medicine in all cases of Slow Fever, Bilious complaints, Costiveness &c."

The numerous ingredients of the foregoing composition stamp it as a white man's concoction. While Indians sometimes compounded simples, they seldom used more than two or three ingredients. Probably most of the "receipts" in the manuals of the white medicine men were the inventions of the authors, and many of the substances used were of foreign origin. Why then did they call themselves "Indian" doctors? From the readiness of quacks to identify themselves with Indian cures from early days down to the medicine shows of recent memory, it is evident that Indian medicine enjoyed such a high reputation in some parts of America that every charlatan felt that he could gain a hearing by claiming familiarity with aboriginal healing lore.

There were enough of these mountebanks plying their trade, in that day of no regulatory legislation, to incite complaining letters to medical journals. One of them published at Boston in 1846 protested against "quacks of low degree" who were designated as Blow-pipe, Mesmeric, Magnetic, Galvanic, Astrological, Botanical, Cayenne Pepper, Hydropathic, Indian, and Negro quacks. "Besides several hundreds of these of every shade and color, male and female, many of whom can neither read nor write," the writer complained, there were scores of respectable

---

30 *The Old Root and Herb Doctor or the Indian Method of Healing*, 30–31.

physicians "who for filthy lucre's sake lend themselves to these several impostures, and have reached the 'lowest deep' of degradation by becoming patrons of the most unprofessional delusions practiced by the tribe." Moreover, there were "advertising quacks" who were vendors of pills, panaceas, catholicos, lotions, syrups, cordials, bitters, sugar candy, etc., "all of which are vaunted as infallible cures for 'all incurable diseases' fortified by affidavits from clergymen! physicians! and other male and female witnesses, all of whom say or swear that they have been cured by these remedies, though since the date of the documents, which is prudently omitted, many of them are in their graves."[31]

The Patent Medicine Vendors

Some of the patent medicine promoters, like the "Indian" herb doctors, early saw the possibilities of gain through exploitation of the popular belief in aboriginal healing skill. The first American patent medicine, according to Bernard Jaffe, was "Tuscarora Rice," named for one of the Iroquois tribes, which was manufactured in 1711 and sold as a cure for tuberculosis; it was destined "to be followed by a flood which is still inundating the land." Physicians as well as charlatans "concocted strange medicines and elixirs of their own."[32]

Already in the eighteenth century, according to Wyndham Blanton, "Dr. Leroux's Patent Indian Vegetable Specific for the cure of Venereal Complaints" was being advertised in the *Virginia Gazette and Petersburg Intelligencer*.[33] It has been surmised by Stewart H. Holbrook that patent medicines flourished with the rise of newspapers.[34] If this is so, it is understandable that the heyday of patent medicines was in the nineteenth century, when newspapers experienced their most rapid multiplication. The decline of patent medicines in the present century is partly due

31 Unsigned letter, *Boston Medical and Surgical Journal*, Vol. XXXIV, No. 26 (July 29, 1846), 517–18.
32 *Men of Science in America*, 16.
33 *Medicine in Virginia in the Eighteenth Century*, 31–32.
34 *The Golden Age of Quackery*, 41.

to the stringent regulations of the federal government since the passage of the first pure food and drug act in 1906.

The patent medicine promoter often posed as a doctor or professor, a man of learning, while he peddled potions supposedly obtained from the unlettered aborigines. We are informed, for example, that "the noted Professor Silliman of Yale College was advertised as endorsing the curative powers of Old Sachem Bitters and Wigwam Tonic."[35] The learned pose, mentioned often by Holbrook and by James Harvey Young[36] was not the only one; others garbed themselves as "Quakers," "frontiersmen," and "cowboys."

The names of once-popular patent medicines frequently bore names suggestive of Indian origin. Some of those mentioned by Holbrook and Young are "Ka-ton-ka, the great Indian medicine," "Donald McKay's Indian Worm Eradicator," "Nez Perce Catarrh Snuff," "Modoc Oil," "Indian Cough Syrup," "War Paint Ointment," and "Sagwa," the last named being the principal panacea of the "Kickapoo Indian Medicine Company," famous for its medicine shows. The latter, according to Holbrook, also manufactured "the wonder-working Kickapoo Indian Prairie Plant" for female complaints, Kickapoo Indian Oil, Salve, Cough Cure, Pills, and Worm Killer, "all compounded [it was alleged] from ancient tribal formulas." Other nostrums of pretended Indian origin were Wright's Indian Vegetable Pills, Indian Balsam of Liverwort, Seminole Cough Balsam, and Osgood's Indian Cholalogue. One quack even operated an "Indian Medical Infirmary."[37]

In these years, Young wrote:

Pocahontas blessed a bitters and Hiawatha helped a hair restorer. Dr. Fall spent twelve years with the Creeks to discover why no Indian had ever perished of consumption. Another proprietor, knowing that Columbus's sailors had contracted syphilis in America [sic], had been persuaded that the cure must be lurking in the same hemisphere, and at

35 Bonner, *Medicine in Chicago: 1850–1950*, 206.
36 James Harvey Young, *The Toadstool Millionaires*.   37 *Ibid.*, 168.

length found it among "the remnant of the once powerful Cherokee." Edwin Eastman got a blood syrup from the Comanches, Texas Charlie a panacea from the Kickapoo, and Frank Cushing—a Smithsonian ethnologist, he—a stomach renovator from the Zuni.[38]

The Indian theme was heavily worked in labels and other advertising. Upon the wrapper of Wright's Indian Vegetable Pills, Young informs us, was engraved the figure of "a majestic Indian" sitting against a mighty tree gazing across a river, on which churned a side-wheeler, toward a thriving city on the opposite shore. Another remedy, Southern Balm, pictured an Indian handing a healing plant to Aesculapius. One patent medicine bottle was manufactured in the shape of an Indian maiden, while "Capon Springs Water" was touted as "a gift of the Cataubai Indians."[39] In the post-Civil War period, the Chattanooga Medicine Company sold a "Wine of Cardui for Women" and "Black Draught for All the Family" which featured on the carton a picture of a white woman standing beside a kneeling Indian maid who, pointing to a tall, leafy plant, said: "Take and Be Healed—The Great Spirit Planted It."[40]

Most of the patent "Indian" medicines contained few, if any, substances used by the Indians. Although they were often advertised as compounded by red men from the bounty of forest and field with the wisdom learned from their forefathers, these nostrums were always factory made with drugs purchased from pharmaceutical firms, usually with a generous admixture of alcohol. Stewart Holbrook said that his bottle of Kickapoo Oil, manufactured during or after 1919, bore a label which, in obedience to then-existing federal law, stated the ingredients to be "camphor, ether, capsicum, oil of cloves, oil of sassafras, and myrrh."[41] Of these components, only capsicum (from tropical

38 "Patent Medicines and Indians," *Emory University Quarterly*, Vol. XVII, No. 2 (1961), 89.

39 *Idem, The Toadstool Millionaires*, 133, 156–157, 176–77.

40 Holbrook, *Golden Age of Quackery*, 105.

41 *Ibid.*, 215.

America) and sassafras were used by the Indians; the remaining ingredients are of foreign origin. Kickapoo Cough Syrup, according to a former employee of the manufacturers, was composed of Jamaica rum and New Orleans molasses. "Ka-ton-ka" was reported by federal chemists to be a mixture of alcohol, sugar, aloes, and baking soda,[42] none of which (except certain aloes) is found in the materia medica of any American tribe.

The Medicine Shows

The most dramatic promotional stunt in the vending of alleged Indian remedies was the medicine show, which once ranked with the circus and the chautauqua as a seasonal relief to the monotony of small-town existence.[43] From the post-Civil War era until the beginning of World War I, these spectacles toured the country with bands of "real live Indians," pitching their tents in some mud flat and advertising their presence with a noisy and colorful parade down Main Street. Audiences were treated to an exhibition of "war dances" and other sights of the "wild west," followed by speeches of glib pitchmen offering for sale "genuine" native medicines guaranteed to be good for the cure of afflictions ranging from corns to cancer.

American medicine shows date back to the eighteenth century, for the Connecticut legislature saw fit in 1773 to meet the evil with a law prohibiting the sale of "any Physick, Drugs, or Medicines" by "any Mountebank" and all shows or exhibitions by them. The act was passed not only because "the Practice of Mountebanks, in dealing out and administering Physick and Medicine, of unknown composition . . . has a practice to destroy the Health, Constitution, and Lives of those who receive such Medicines," but also because "Plays, Tricks, Jugling, or unprofitable Feats of uncommon Dexterity and Agility of Body," which were featured in such shows, tended toward "Corruption of Man-

42 *Ibid.*, 207, 215.

43 An informative and entertaining illustrated article on this phenomenon, is Arrell M. Gibson's "Medicine Show," *The American West*, Vol. IV, No. 1 (February, 1967), 34 ff.

ners, promoting of Idleness, and the detriment of good Order and Religion." A year earlier, New Jersey had enacted a similar though less stringent law, which was re-enacted in 1783. Equivalent legislation is occasionally reported during the nineteenth century.[44]

The heyday of the *Indian* medicine show operators, however, belongs to the period of Barnum and Bailey and Buffalo Bill Cody. One of the large operators which flourished in the 1880's, according to Holbrook, was the Oregon Indian Medicine Company of Corry, Pennsylvania. It was never situated in Oregon, though its principal product, Ka-ton-ka, was allegedly manufactured from Indian herbs by Modoc and Nez Percé tribesmen in that state. This firm was outranked by the Kickapoo Indian Medicine Co., which was formed about 1881 by John E. Healy and Charles H. Bigelow, and headquartered in New Haven, Connecticut. These operators fielded as many as seventy-five road shows simultaneously, employing hundreds of Indians of assorted tribes, all portrayed as Kickapoos, and peddling a varied line of potions of which "Sagwa" was the best known. So profitable was the venture that other fortune hunters were issued charters to launch Kickapoo medicine shows, some of which made foreign tours. During thirty years the New Haven firm was reported to have had an average payroll of three hundred. When it was sold for $250,000 in 1912, an era was drawing to a close. Holbrook attributes the decline of the medicine show to the advent of automobiles and motion pictures.[45]

The one-time success of the medicine shows is explained by Young as the heritage of ancient folk beliefs which regarded disease as a curse from offended gods, for which cures "could not be found through human intelligence but in secret lore of an occult order, a kind of magical knowledge more dramatic and potent when possessed by the primitive and untutored." Faith in aboriginal therapeutic powers was also aided by the old belief

[44] David L. Cowen, "Colonial Laws Pertaining to Pharmacy," *Journal of the American Pharmaceutical Association,* Vol. XXIII (1934), 1241–42.

[45] *Golden Age of Quackery,* 212.

that providence had placed in each land the proper cures for its indigenous diseases and that the natives would therefore be acquainted with these remedies. It was also widely held that Indians were naturally more healthy and robust than whites, owing both to their way of life and their medicines. Lastly, Young attributed the early popularity of native medicines to the cultural nationalism of the post-Revolutionary period.[46]

Summary

In the present era of great progress in scientific medicine, with its spectacular achievements in surgery, "miracle drugs," and other conquests, folk and native medicine have lost their old halo, and the former exploitation of the image of the Indian as a healer by charlatans has served to obscure those discoveries and contributions of the aborigines which have won scientific favor. It is not generally understood that the worthless nostrums which passed as Indian medicine were in fact the inventions of white promoters and that some of the most valuable drugs in official use are of Indian origin.

Many of those who have investigated this field have exhibited a considerable respect for the attainments of primitive man. Frank Speck, whose field studies of Indian remedies reached from Canada to Louisiana, has declared:

Little doubt now remains among modern students of medical history of the possible discoveries to be made from the folklore and curative practices of less civilized natives in various parts of America. Medical experience acquired by processes of trial and error through a lengthy tribal career, has taught native medicine men, conjurers and priests some things which we are lately finding to possess interest and importance. The correction of human disorders has long been the object of endeavor among intelligent tribesfolk whose knowledge of floristic and animal sources as therapeutic aids

[46] Young, "Patent Medicines and Indians," *Emory University Quarterly*, Vol. XVII, No. 2 (1961), 89.

we can scarcely exhaust. . . . In many instances we owe the acknowledgment of disclosures proved to be of value when tested in laboratories to the modest "charlatans," as the healers are often termed, who have carried the traditions of plant properties and their applications through generations of practice.[47]

As an example of the benefits flowing from research into Indian curatives, Weston La Barre cited the struggle for the acceptance of quinine, the search for standardized curare, and Dr. Folker's research on the alkaloids of South American erythrina species, which has found practical use in metrazol therapy. "Primitive people are not ignorant children," he pointed out, "and the things they know are not automatically false."[48]

"The folk materia medica of any time or land," Rodney H. True has written, "need not altogther be despised when looked at from the practical standpoint . . . the medical lore of the people does contain, and has always contained, elements capable of adaptation and use in skilled hands. It is the crude stuff in which much of value lies hidden."[49] In the same vein, Professor E. H. Lucas advises that:

> . . . there exists a large number of drug plants recorded in folklore but consistently counted useless, apparently because casual administration has not shown the effects claimed for them. There are others which have never been tried out in modern times, either because the lore of them was not commonly known or because they have simply been overlooked.[50]

Not until the nineteenth century did the medical profession recognize the medical potentialities of the ancient Inca drug,

[47] "Catawba Herbals and Curing Practices," *Journal of American Folk-Lore,* Vol. LVII, No. 223 (January–March, 1944), 40–41.

[48] "Folk Medicine and Folk Science," *Journal of American Folk-Lore,* Vol. LV (October–December, 1942), 199–200.

[49] "Folk Materia Medica," *Journal of American Folk-Lore,* Vol. XIV (1901), 114.

[50] "Folk Lore and Plant Drugs," *Papers of the Michigan Academy of Sciences,* XLV, 130.

coca, and only then were its various principles isolated.[51] In the early eighteenth century, John Brickell told how an Indian doctor cured a planter's "ulcer" (leg sore) with "the rotten Grains of the *Maiz,* or *Indian Corn,* well dried and beaten to a Powder." Nearly two hundred years later corn smut, or ustilago, became official in the American pharmacopeia for its vasoconstrictor and antihemorrhagic properties. Many Indian tribes were cognizant of the properties of oak bark, which was widely used in maladies calling for an astringent or antiseptic remedy.[52] Indians, like ancient peoples of the Old World, knew how to make use of plants and trees, such as willow, which contain salicin.

The Decline of Folk Remedies

Several reasons have been given for the decline of folk cures, and of botanical medicines generally, including those which once enjoyed official acceptance. In the first category, the cause has been ascribed to advances in scientific medicine, the introduction of medical insurance plans, free services, and the general availability of medical care today.[53] The lesser use of medicines of botanical origin, which has been noticeable since the late nineteenth century, has been ascribed to the development of organic chemistry. In the laboratory it can be learned to what active principles plants owe their medical value, and what is the molecular nature of those active principles. The chemist is able to build the desired molecular structure synthetically and to produce substances having valuable medicinal properties.[54]

Other reasons for the decline of botanicals have been the difficulty of standardizing vegetable drugs, due to unequal strength of different samples, the natural obstacles to cultivation of some wild drug plants, the collection of wrong species by careless

[51] Leake, "Historical Notes on the Pharmacology of Anesthesia," *Journal of the History of Medicine,* Vol. I, No. 4 (October, 1946), 573–82.

[52] Edmund Andrews, "The Aboriginal Physicians of Michigan," *Contributions to Medical Research Dedicated to Victor Clarence Vaughan,* 45.

[53] Don James, *Folk and Modern Medicine,* 26.

[54] "Folk Materia Medica," *Journal of American Folk-Lore,* Vol. XIV (1901), 110.

collectors, the practice of adulteration, the fact that some drugs are at maximum strength only when collected in a certain brief season, that they often lose their strength in storage, that some wild plants become virtually unavailable due to overcollecting, and that some have undesirable side effects.

There have been a number of times in American history when the nation had to turn to native remedies. During the Revolutionary War the British blockade forced physicians to use drugs that could be grown and prepared in this country, and for that reason William Brown (1748–92) prepared the first American pharmacopeia.[55] A similar situation existed for the Confederacy during the Civil War, when Dr. Francis Porcher of Charleston was commissioned by the Confederate government to prepare a paper on indigenous medical and economic plants of the South which could be used as substitutes for those no longer available.[56] Several laboratories were established to process them, and Georgia druggists held a convention in 1863 to discuss how to obtain medicines.[57]

During each major war, Robert C. Wilson has pointed out, "we have been forced to seek for medicinal agents among the abundant plant life" to be found at home. As one example, he cited the shortage of quinine which developed after the Japanese conquered Java, which had become the main commercial source of cinchona bark after the industry was abandoned in South America.[58] Synthetic substitutes were developed, but in the current Viet Nam war it has been found that strains of malaria in that country are resistant to the laboratory products.

Several medical writers have deplored American dependence on foreign drugs; among them was the eighteenth-century German visitor, Dr. Schöpf, who declared:

[55] *Pharmacopoeia Simpliciorum* . . . (Philadelphia, Styner & Cist, 1778); see "The Lititz Pharmacopeia," *The Badger Pharmacist*, No. 22–25 (June–December, 1938), 1–70.

[56] Frances P. Porcher, *Resources of the Southern Fields and Forests . . . Being Also a Medical Botany of the Confederate States . . . .*

[57] Wilson, *Drugs and Pharmacy in the Life of Georgia*, 50.

[58] *Ibid.*, 51.

It is to be wished that the physicians of America ... may also have a patriotic eye to the completer knowledge of their native materia medica. It betrays an unpardonable indifference to their fatherland to see them making use almost wholly of foreign medicines, with which in large measure they might readily dispense, if they were willing to give their attention to home-products.[59]

Similar sentiments were echoed by Barton, Bigelow, Cutler, Rafinesque, and others. In time of need the plea was heeded, and in such a manner the value of many native plant medicines came to be recognized.

[59] Schöpf, *Travels in the Confederation, 1783–1784*, I, 289.

VI.

Indian
Health
and
Disease

Early European observers, in nearly unanimous accord, proclaimed the relative good health of American Indians, and their
freedom from deformity. Since Indians were not disease-free,
these accounts partly reflect the comparatively low state of European health in that period. Europe, with its urban centers and
higher population density, was more subject to the spread of
contagions which were unknown in America. The circumstances
of civilized living, poor as it was by present standards, also operated to preserve many infirm and defective individuals who
might have perished or left no progeny under the rigorous environment of America, where neolithic conditions still existed
in the greater part of the land.

148

Columbus was the first to remark upon the absence of deformity among the Indians.[1] A few years later, the French essayist, Michel de Montaigne, declared:

> . . . as my testimonies have told me, it is verie rare to see a sicke body amongst them; and they have further assured me, they never saw any man there either shaking with the palsie, toothlesse, with eies dropping, or crooked and stooping through age.[2]

In Panama, Lionel Wafer found the natives to be "streigt and clean-limb'd, big-bon'd, full-breasted and hansomly shap'd." Moreover, he "never saw among them a crooked and deformed person. They are very nimble and active, running very well." He was impressed by their "white even teeth."[3]

When Boston was still a village on the edge of the wilderness, William Wood remarked of the New England Indians:

> I have been in many places, yet did I never see one that was born either in defect or redundance a monster, or any that sickness had deformed, or casualty made decrepid [sic], save one that had a bleared eye, and another that had a wenne on his cheek.[4]

Most of them reached fifty, he declared, before "a wrinkled brow or gray hair bewray [sic] their age," a happy situation owing to the circumstance that "they are not brought down with suppressing labour, vexed with annoying cares, or drowned in the excessive abuse of overflowing plenty." Besides being possessed of "lusty and healthful bodies," they did not know:

> . . . those health-wasting diseases which are incident to other countries, as fevers, pleurisies, callentures, agues, obstructions, consumptions, subfumigations, convulsions, apoplex-

---

[1] *The Columbus Letter of March 14th, 1493* (Chicago, Newberry Library, 1953), 6.

[2] *Essays of Michael, Lord of Montaigne*, I, 192.

[3] *A New Voyage and Description of the Isthmus of Panama*, 131.

[4] *New England's Prospect*, 74.

ies, gouts, stones, tooth-aches, pox, measles, or the like; but spin out the thread of their days to a fair length, numbering threescore, fourscore, some a hundred years, before the worlds universal summoner cite them to the craving grave.[5]

In the same period, John Josselyn pronounced the New England Indians "tall and handsome timber'd people," who "live long, even to an hundred years of age, if they be not cut off by their Children,[6] war, and the plague, which together with the small pox hath taken away abundance of them." While he mistakenly thought that the "great pox" [syphilis] was a native disease caused by cannibalism, he declared "there are not so many Diseases raigning amongst them as our *Europeans*." Among their afflictions however, were "pestilent Feavers, Plague, Black-pox, Consumption of the Lungs, Falling sickness, King's evil, and . . . *Empyema*."[7]

The unanimity of opinion about the generally blissful health of the Indians was not confined to the English. A Dutch account from New York related that "it is somewhat strange that among these most barbarous people, there are few or none cross-eyed, blind, crippled, lame, hunch-backed, or limping men; all are well fashioned people, strong and sound of body, well fed, without blemish."[8] In French Canada, the Baron de Lahontan found that "the Savages are a robust and vigorous sort of People, of a Sanguine Temperament, and an admirable Complexion." They were "unacquainted with a great many Diseases that afflict the *Europeans*, such as the *Gout, Gravel, Dropsy*, &c. Their Health is firm, notwithstanding that they use no precaution to preserve it." As elsewhere reported wherever Indians were in contact with whites, Lahontan noted that the chief killer was smallpox.[9]

[5] *Ibid.*, 114.

[6] A reference to euthanasia, discussed below.

[7] *An Account of Two Voyages to New-England Made During the Years 1638, 1663*, 97, 102.

[8] Wassenaer's "Historisch Verhael" (1624), in Jameson (ed.), *Narratives of New Netherland*, 72.

[9] *New Voyages*, II, 465.

In North Carolina at the beginning of the eighteenth century, John Lawson declared that the Indians:

> . . . are never troubled with the Scurvey, Dropsy, nor Stone. The Phthisick, Ashma [sic], and Diabetes, they are wholly Strangers to. Neither do I remember I ever saw one Paralytick amongst them. The Gout, I cannot be certain whether they know what it is, nor not. Indeed, I never saw any Nodes or Swellings, which attend the Gout in Europe; yet they have a sort of Rheumatism or Burning of the Limbs, which tortures them grievously, at which time their Legs are so hot, that they employ the young People continually to pour Water down them. I never saw but one or two thus afflicted.[10]

Nevertheless, the ravages of the white man's gifts, smallpox and rum, were so devastating that Lawson believed that only one sixth as many Indians survived within two hundred miles of the white settlements as had lived in the same area a half century earlier.

Peter Kalm held that rheumatism and pleurisy were the chief afflictions of the Indians, which arose "from their being obliged frequently to lie in the wet parts of the woods at night, from the sudden changes of heat and cold . . . and from their being frequently loaded with too great a quantity of strong liquor." Kalm cited several newspaper accounts of Indians who were reputed to be over a hundred years old at the time of their deaths.[11]

It is difficult to draw conclusions concerning the life expectancy of early Indians, especially without figures on infant mortality and the death rate from accidents and disease in the early years. Reports of aged Indians, however, are not uncommon, even in recent times.[12] The brother and successor of Powhatan,

10 *History of North Carolina*, 237–38.

11 *Travels in North America*, II, 390, 647–48.

12 Hrdlička wrote in 1908: "The proportion of nonagenarians and especially centenarians among the Indians is far in excess of that among native white Americans . . . . The relative excess of aged persons (80 years and above) among the Indians can signify only that the infirmities and diseases known ordinarily as those of old age are less grave among them—a conclusion in harmony with general observation," *Physiological and Medical Observations*, 41.

Opechancanough, was said to be ninety-nine years of age when he was shot in 1644,[13] though some reports placed his age even higher. European beliefs that Indians were a short-lived people, Lawson wrote, were contrary to his observations, since they lived "to as great Ages as any of the Europeans, the Climate being free from Consumptions, which Distemper, fatal to England, they are Strangers to."[14] From skeletal remains, Wilton M. Krogman, a modern scholar and anthropologist, estimated that the life expectancy of aboriginal Americans was about thirty-seven years, plus or minus three years.[15] The life expectancy at birth for white Americans in the late eighteenth century was estimated at thirty-five years.[16]

During the last third of the eighteenth century, travelers continued to report favorably on the physical condition of the Indians. Robert Rogers commented that "you will rarely find among the Indians a person that is in any way deformed, or that is deprived of any sense." He found that Indians generally were "of a hale, robust, and firm constitution."[17] Jonathan Carver reported the Indians to be generally healthy and free from many of the diseases of "civilized nations," but subject to afflictions caused by their arduous way of life. Among these were "Pains and weaknesses in the stomach and breast," and above all, pleurisy, which they treated by sweating. Dropsy and paralytic complaints were "very seldom known among them." From the absence of venereal disease among the "Naudowessies" [Sioux or Dakota] and other western tribes, he concluded that "it had not its origin in America."[18]

The controversy over the place of origin of venereal diseases is discussed elsewhere (p. 77, 210–11). It is noteworthy that within the area which now comprises the United States, no explorer has

[13] Hodge (ed.), *Handbook of American Indians*, II, 139.

[14] *History of North Carolina*, 86.

[15] "Medical Practices and Diseases of the Aboriginal American Indians," *Ciba Symposia*, Vol. I, No. 1 (April, 1939), 16.

[16] Richard Shryock, *Medicine in America, Historical Essays*, 12.

[17] *A Concise Account of North America*, 210.

[18] *Travels Through the Interior*, 365–68.

reported from observation the presence of these diseases among Indians prior to their contact with whites. Diron d'Artaguette, governor-general of Louisiana, writing of the Illinois Indians in his journal of April 19, 1723, declared: "as for the other diseases which came from the corruption of the blood, they did not have them at all before seeing the French."[19] Dr. Colden was convinced that the yaws came from Africa but that the "Lues Venerea" (syphilis) originated in America.[20] This belief may have been rooted in Oviedo's dubious account, cited earlier. Dr. Barton claimed to have made an "extensive inquiry into the subject," and was satisfied that both syphilis and gonorrhea were unknown among North American Indians before white contact.[21] In the next century, Dr. Joseph M. Toner was convinced that syphilis was introduced to America from the Old World, where its presence had long been concealed from investigators by varying nomenclature.[22] In the present century, Dr. Aleš Hrdlička, a noted paleopathologist, insisted: "Notwithstanding some claims to the contrary, there is as yet not a single instance of thoroughly authenticated precolumbian syphilis."[23]

Philadelphia's imperious Dr. Rush flatly held that "the *small pox* and the *venereal disease* were communicated to the Indians of North America by the Europeans." So far as other diseases were concerned, he declared that gout was rare among them, and he knew of no evidence that they were ever subject to scurvy.[24] There were few instances of mental disorder. Incorrectly, he asserted that there were no accounts of "diseases from worms,"[25]

---

[19] Mereness (ed.), *Travels in the American Colonies*, 74.

[20] Letter to Gronovius (1745), in Colden, *Letters and Papers*, III, 98.

[21] *Essay Towards a Materia Medica*, I, 36.

[22] *Address Before the Rocky Mountain Medical Association*, 99–101.

[23] "Disease, Medicine and Surgery among the American Aborigines," *Journal of the American Medical Association*, Vol. XCIX, No. 20 (November 12, 1932), 1662.

[24] While scurvy was not common among the Indians, it was not unknown. *Cf.* account of Cartier's expedition, pp. 3–4, herein.

[25] *Cf.* Barton, *Essay Towards a Materia Medica*, II, 51, who reported that worms were common among them. Rush later added a footnote that they were not free of worms.

and that they "appear to be strangers to diseases and pains of the teeth."[26]

One eighteenth-century observer who maintained that Indians were "not less, rather more subject to disease than Europeans," was David Zeisberger (1780), who argued that their "rough manner of life and hardships of travel and the chase" were contributing causes. Rheumatism was common, "often leading to lameness, deafness, or blindness," and women suffered in the back and neck from carrying burdens on their heads. Moreover:

> They are subject to festering sores. Cured in one place, they break out in another. Chills and fever, dysentery, hemorrhage, and bloody flux in women are very common among them. Venereal diseases have, during the last years spread more and more, due, doubtless, to their disorderly life.[27]

It is relevant that the Indians of Zeisberger's experience (the Delawares), in contrast to those of earlier observers, had long been in contact with whites. Except for the venereal diseases, however, there is no doubt that the ills he mentioned had long been prevalent among Indians.

Zeisberger's fellow missionary, John Heckewelder, reported that the Indians were untouched by a scarlet fever epidemic that swept frontier Detroit in 1785. "However," he added, "a disorder called the Hooping-Cough, attended at length, with a sore-throat, I have known to prove destructive to the Indian children, in their settlements." He saw no cases of "the Itch" (scabies or eczema) and ascribed it "to their different mode of living; namely, their food, their well-aired houses, or huts, &c."[28]

As the above report indicates, the penetration of whites into the trans-Appalachian wilderness was altering the pleasant pic-

[26] *Medicine Among the Indians*, 114–17. Indians were not strangers to dental problems, though they were more favored than whites in this regard. See "Dentistry," herein.

[27] "History of the North American Indians," *Ohio Archaeological and Historical Quarterly*, Vol. XIX, Nos. 1–2 (January and April, 1910), 23–24.

[28] Letter of John Heckewelder, February 11, 1797, in *Philadelphia Medical and Physical Journal*, Vol. I, Pt. 1 (1805), 130.

ture painted by the earliest visitors. This escalation of disease continued to be reflected in the literature. In 1798 it was reported that Indians at Onondaga, New York, had been reduced from 133 to 105 in three years, and that most died of "phthisis pulmonalis" (tuberculosis).[29] As early as 1738, the Cherokees were reduced by one half in a year's time, Adair reported, from smallpox which was "conveyed into Charles-town by the Guinea-men [slaves], and soon after among them, by the infected goods."[30] Later they were swept by "intermittent fevers" (malaria) and "head-Pleurisy," which caused 350 to perish in one week of 1779.[31]

A French traveler among the Miamis in the early nineteenth century, Le Compte C. F. Volney, reported that the Indians were afflicted with "diseases of the stomach, intermittent and bilious fevers, consumption, and pleurisy," and above all, smallpox. The Quaker and Moravian missionaries maintained, according to Volney, that Indians under their influence were less subject to sickness than "the untamed savages." Volney held that many of the ills to which Indians were prey resulted from alternating hunger and gluttony, which "must necessarily impair the stomach and destroy the health." Deformed or infirm Indians were rare, he maintained, at least in the northern tribes, because defective babies and the helpless aged were put to death.[32] The last statement raises a large question, with strong witnesses on both sides.

Dr. Rush claimed that the weaker Indians were naturally eliminated by the rigorous environment:

> It is remarkable that there are no deformed Indians. Some have suspected, from this circumstance, that they put their deformed children to death, but nature here acts the part of an unnatural mother. The severity of the Indian manners destroys them.[33]

[29] Letter of James Geddes, November 16, 1798, in *Philadelphia Medical and Physical Journal*, Vol. I, Pt. 1 (1805), 129.

[30] *History of the American Indians*, 232.

[31] B. S. Barton, Ms. Journal for 1794, *Philadelphia Medical and Physical Journal*, Vol. I, Pt. 1, (1905), 132–33.

[32] *A View of the Soil and Climate of the United States of America*, 367–68.

[33] *Medicine Among the Indians*, 114.

Alexander von Humboldt, the versatile German who spent the years 1799–1804 in exploration of Central and South America, declared of the Indians on the Orinoco:

> I saw no person who had any natural deformity; and I may say the same of thousands of Caribs, Muyscas, and Mexican and Peruvian Indians, whom we observed during the course of five years.

He maintained that this circumstance was not due to deliberate destruction of handicapped persons, since the mission Indians were also well formed. He attributed it to the fact that deformed women in savage tribes did not find husbands, whereas in Europe they might, if they had a fortune.[34]

On the other hand, there are credible reports of mercy killing among some Indian tribes. As early as 1612–14, the Jesuit priest, Marc Lescarbot, reported that some Canadian Indians let the aged sick die, as a merciful act, and because their nomadic life did not allow for the care of the sick.[35] "In some countries," declared Charlevoix, "when the patient is despaired of, they dispatch him to keep him from languishing." He reported that the Onondagas even did away with infants who had lost their mothers.[36] Gabriel Sagard said that nomadic tribes, being "touched and moved by compassion," put to death those who were too old to follow the others.[37] Josselyn reported that Indians sometimes ended the lives of their aged parents "if they lived so long that they become a burden to them."[38] In the Missouri valley in 1850, Thaddeus Culbertson was told that "it was common for the Indians to leave the old to perish on the prairies." Instances were also cited of a blind Crow Indian being taken to

[34] Humboldt, *Personal Narrative of Travels to the Equinoctial Regions of America, During the Years 1799–1804,* I, 307. He later reported that among the Radaules, a deformed infant was killed by the father, while if twins were born, one of them would be dispatched by female relatives of the mother, for superstitious reasons. *Ibid.,* II, 248.

[35] Thwaites (ed.), *Jesuit Relations,* II, 151.

[36] *Journal of a Voyage to North America,* I, 165.

[37] *Long Journey to the Country of the Hurons,* 200.

[38] *Two Voyages to New-England,* 100.

battle in the hope that he might be killed, and of a small boy who was abandoned because of a severe leg injury. Culbertson affirmed, however, that these acts did "not necessarily arise from a cruel and unfeeling disposition," but from the belief that death would be preferable to their burdensome condition, and that they would be transferred "to a state of happiness and abundance."[39]

In the main, as Sagard pointed out, the sedentary tribes did not destroy the infirm. Moreover, no reports of the practice appear in the writings of such observers as De Liette, Lahontan, Beverley, Lawson, Carver, Hunter, and many others. The evidence we have seems insufficient to warrant the conclusion that mercy killing, or suicide,[40] fully explains the healthy condition of the Indians as it was described in the early years. It appears more likely that environmental factors, operating through the centuries, weeded out the weaker types in the process of natural selection, as Rush suspected. Dr. Erwin Ackerknecht, in a study of white captive children among the Indians, concluded that the disease resistance of the Indians "was the effect of continuous natural selection and nurture rather than of true racial heredity."[41] They were not prepared, of course, for the new diseases brought by the invaders.

Some years before the sprawling population of the young nation began to spill into the Great Plains, Dr. Edwin James observed (1820) that "few if any, instances of pulmonary consumption occur among the Indians of this region; the same remark is probably as true of the original native population of New York and New England."[42] Thirteen years later, at Fort Clark on the upper Missouri, Prince Maximilian reported that

[39] Culbertson, *Journal of an Expedition to the Mauvaises Terres and the Upper Missouri in 1850*, Bulletin 147, Bureau of American Ethnology, 93.

[40] Adair reported that Cherokee Indians disfigured by smallpox often committed suicide. *History of the Indians*, 233.

[41] Ackerknecht, "White Indians: Psychological and Physiological Peculiarities of White Children Abducted and Reared by North American Indians," *Bulletin of the History of Medicine*, Vol. XV, No. 1 (January, 1944), 15–36.

[42] *Account of an Expedition*, in Vol. XVI in Thwaites (ed.), *Early Western Travels*, 132. The fact that tuberculosis ("pulmonary consumption") is today a major affliction among Indians is another testimony of the adverse effects of white contact.

the Indians were troubled with bowel complaints, catarrh, and violent coughs.[43] Only a few years later, as the vanguard of trappers and traders increasingly penetrated this region, the Indians were decimated by epidemics of cholera and smallpox.[44] Early accounts are filled with depressing descriptions of the havoc wrought by introduced contagion. In 1842, Audubon heard much about the prevalence of smallpox "which destroyed such numbers of the Indians."

> Among the Mandans, Ricarees, [Arikara], and Gros Ventre [he wrote], hundreds died in 1837, only a few surviving, and the Assiniboines were nearly exterminated. Indeed, it is said that in the various attacks of this scourge, 52,000 Indians have perished.[45]

It was reported that in 1849 about two hundred Cheyenne lodges were wiped out by cholera.[46] Pestilence swept across the plains like a great grass fire. The Blackfeet, living near the "shining mountains," were hit by smallpox, which destroyed two-thirds of them in 1837, and the scourge returned in 1869–70.[47] Everywhere the dismal story was the same, as disease did more to clear the West for settlement than the cavalry.

It is readily seen that there are some discrepancies in the early accounts of Indian pathology. Some accounts, such as Rush's, were secondhand, others were of local application, and many failed to distinguish, or inaccurately distinguished, between indigenous and introduced diseases. Identification of some ills is confused by chaotic nomenclature. It is significant, however, that the greatest number of disorders is reported by the later observers (*e.g.*, Volney), who saw the Indians after they had long been in contact with whites.

[43] *Travels in the Interior of North America, 1832–1834* (Part III), Vol. XXIV in Thwaites (ed.), *Early Western Travels*, 18–19.

[44] Culbertson, *Journal of an Expedition*, 133.

[45] *Audubon Journals*, II, 23. See also *Travels in the Interior of North America, 1832–1834* (Part I), in Vol. XXII Thwaites (ed.), *Early Western Travels*, 33–36.

[46] Culbertson, *Journal of an Expedition*, 133.

There are methods other than the study of historical documents by which to determine the health and disease conditions of the early Indians. One of them is archaeology, and its branch, paleopathology, the study of primitive skeletal remains. A specialist in this field was the late Dr. Aleš Hrdlička, who also investigated the ills and medical practices of the Indians of his own time, particularly in the Southwest. His studies tend to confirm that the aboriginal Indian was generally healthy compared to Europeans of the colonial period:

> The skeletal remains of unquestionably precolumbian date [he concludes] are, barring few exceptions, remarkably free from disease. Whole important scourges were wholly unknown. There was no pathologic microcephaly, no hydrocephaly. There was no plague, cholera, typhus, smallpox or measles. Cancer was rare, and even fractures were infrequent. There was no lepra [leprosy]. . . . there is as yet not a single instance of . . . precolumbian syphilis. There were, apparently, no nevi [skin tumors]. There were no troubles with the feet, such as fallen arches. And, judging from later acquired knowledge, there was a much greater scarcity than in the white population of many diseases of the skin, of most mental disorders, and of other serious conditions.

The chief diseases to which the ancient Indians were subject, he added, were digestive disorders, particularly in children and older persons, pneumonia, arthritis, and localized maladies such as nutritional disorders.[48]

Indian graves yield more than bones. Frequently they contain works of art, including sculpture and pottery. One who has studied such artifacts with a view to learning something of Indian health is Dr. Abner I. Weisman, clinical professor of obstetrics and gynecology of the New York Medical College, who has collected some three thousand items obtained primarily from graves

47 John C. Ewers, *The Blackfeet*, 65–66, 250.

48 "Disease, Medicine and Surgery among the American Aborigines," *Journal of the American Medical Association*, Vol. XCIX, No. 20 (November 12, 1932), 1661–62.

in Mexico and Central and South America. In numerous statu-ettes in his collection, Dr. Weisman indicates that pre-Columbian sculptors depicted many of the diseases and physical states of their people and the knowledge and skill of their physicians and surgeons. According to his analysis, these figurines illustrate, among other things, the symptoms of malnutrition, deformity, physical and mental illness, the stages of pregnancy and child-birth, the techniques of amputation, trephining, and possibly Caesarian section. Some of the figures appear to represent indi-viduals suffering from headache, toothache, arthritis and spinal defects, neck pains, endemic goiter, obesity, phlebitis, leg de-formation—possibly due to calcium deficiency, eye diseases, skin ailments, angina, and perhaps hernia.[49] One pair of figures, male and female, made of terra cotta in the period A.D. 200–600 and found in the Mexican state of Nayarit, could be a source of controversy. They are said to exhibit "generalized skin lesions [which] resemble smallpox in its plague-like stage, but may rep-resent a form of treponematosis (yaws) found in the area."[50] The virtually unanimous opinion hitherto has been that neither of these diseases existed in pre-Columbian America. Since some of the other maladies listed above (*e.g.*, deformity, goiter, obesity), have seldom, if ever, been reported among the "wild" tribes, it is possible that the more sedentary Mexicans, from dietary or other causes, were subject to more disorders than the so-called savages.

A contemporary writer holds that in the last century "there developed an utterly false belief . . . that the Indian was a paragon of health. This was supposed to be so partly because of his medicines, more because of his mode of life."[51] The image of the robust aborigine may not be as mythical as some have be-lieved. Brickell reported that "these naked Indians will lye and sleep in the Woods without any Fire or covering, being inur'd

[49] *The Weisman Collection of Pre-Columbian Medical Miniatures*, an exhibit at the Field Museum of Chicago, May 15–June 20, 1967.

[50] Cover illustration, *Journal of the American Medical Association*, Vol. CXCVII, No. 5 (August 1, 1966).

[51] Young, "Patent Medicines and Indians," *Emory University Quarterly*, Vol. XVII, No. 2 (1961), 87.

thereto from Infancy."[52] Their feats of endurance could scarcely be performed by weaklings. "An Indian," wrote Loskiel, "makes nothing of dragging a deer of one hundred or one hundred and fifty pounds weight home, through a very considerable tract of forest."[53] Indeed, those who led this strenuous life were not immune from all ailments, but it appears that they were spared from most of the infectious and deficiency diseases.

A summary of the opinions of recent students of aboriginal health and healing[54] indicates that rheumatism and arthritis, dysentery and other digestive disorders, intestinal worms, and eye disorders were present. There were mastoid infections and respiratory ailments, but disorders caused by vitamin and mineral deficiencies were uncommon and were localized. Neurological and psychic disturbances, heart disease, arteriosclerosis, and cancer were rare.

Among the infectious diseases, it is generally held that scarlet fever, typhoid, cholera, diphtheria, smallpox, and measles were absent in pre-Columbian times. Malaria and yellow fever, according to an authority on tropical medicine, were introduced after the Spanish conquest.[55]

There is cause to believe, however, that disease patterns varied in different regions, and especially so between sedentary and nomadic peoples.

[52] *Natural History of North-Carolina*, 401.
[53] *Mission of the United Brethren*, I, 107.
[54] Ackerknecht, Adams, Brooks, Hrdlička, Krogman, and Scott.
[55] H. Harold Scott, *A History of Tropical Medicine*, I, 128–29, 452.

VII.

American Indian Therapeutic Methods

The American Indians made important achievements not only in the use of remedies but also in therapeutic procedures and hygienic practices. Although these have been partially dealt with by others, their studies have often been confined to the practices of particular tribes or regions or limited to special topics. Fragmentary accounts of such treatment methods, as distinguished from the medicines used, appear throughout this work, but a brief summary is in order to introduce illustrative information which did not logically fit into the preceding text. Space, of course, does not permit an extensive survey of all Indian treatments of every ill; those who wish more information may refer to the bibliography. The following is merely an abbreviated sketch of some of the more representative, significant, or interesting devices or methods used. Wherever relevant, those aspects of Indian practice which influenced the whites are emphasized but no judgment is passed on their validity.

Use of Specific Drugs

Anesthetics. It is astonishing that white medical science did not discover the properties of cocaine as a local anesthetic before Carl Koller's experiments of 1884.[1] The use of coca leaves as a stimulant by the Incas and by present-day South American Indians[2] is well known. It is highly probable also that coca was used as an anesthetic in their numerous trephinations, or skull surgery.[3] The aboriginal use of coca and other narcotic drugs, as well as hypnotism, for anesthetic effect has been mentioned by several writers.[4]

Narcotic and stimulant drugs. These substances arouse more than adequate interest nowadays, and it is a phenomenon of linguistic evolution that in popular parlance the term "drugs" has become narrowed to signify narcotics only. Since a vast literature already exists on this subject, this discussion will be brief. Mexican Indians used a number of hallucinogenic drugs, now popularly known as LSD (d-lysergic acid diethylamide), although the term properly belongs to ergot, a cereal fungus. The ancient

[1] Leake, "Historical Notes on the Pharmacology of Anesthesia," *Journal of the History of Medicine*, Vol. I, No. 4 (October, 1946), 573–82.

[2] Monardes, *Joyfull Newes*, II, 32; La Vega, *The Incas*, 87, 101; Safford, "Narcotic Plants and Stimulants of the Ancient Americans," *Annual Report of the Board of Regents of the Smithsonian Institution for the Year Ending June 30, 1926*, 388, 409; True, "Folk Materia Medica," *Journal of American Folk-Lore*, Vol. XIV (1901), 112; Margaret B. Kreig, *Green Medicine*, 72–73.

In the middle of the last century, Richard H. Spruce, the botanist, wrote: "With a chew, renewed at intervals of a few hours, an Indian will go for days without food or sleep." Spruce, *Notes of a Botanist on the Amazon and Andes* (2 vols.; London, Macmillan & Co., 1908), II, 447.

[3] Donald T. Atkinson, *Magic, Myth and Medicine*, 252.

[4] William R. Adams, "Aboriginal American Medicine and Surgery," *Proceedings of the Indiana Academy of Science*, Vol. LXI (1951), 52; Brooks, "The Medicine of the American Indian," *Journal of Laboratory and Clinical Medicine*, Vol. XIX, No. 1 (October, 1933), 7.

Mexican hallucinogens and other narcotics were obtained mainly from mushrooms and cacti.[5]

Fray Bernardino de Sahagún has furnished descriptions of the effects and uses of hundreds of Nahuatl medicines, including the narcotics. The *Teonanacatl*, a mushroom, was a bitter and caustic substance which:

> . . . makes one besotted; it deranges one. . . . It saddens, depresses, troubles one; it makes one hide. He who eats many of them sees many things which make him afraid, or make him laugh. He flees, hangs himself, hurls himself from a cliff, cries out, takes fright.

According to the priest, it was eaten in honey, and was used as a remedy for fever and gout.[6]

Of the important Aztec narcotic, *ololiuhqui*, derived from a wild morning glory,[7] Sahagún declared:

> It makes one besotted; it deranges one, troubles one, maddens one, makes one possessed. He who eats it, who drinks it,

[5] In the sixteenth century, Sahagún observed: "The first thing eaten at the party was certain black mushrooms, which they call nanacatl, which intoxicate and cause visions to be seen, and even provoke sensuousness." Safford, "Narcotic Plants and Stimulants of the Ancient Americans," *Annual Report of the Board of Regents of the Smithsonian Institution for the Year Ending June 30, 1916*, 405. See also Frank Barron, *et al.*, "The Hallucinogenic Drugs," *Scientific American*, Vol. CCX, No. 4 (April, 1964), 29–37; Robert F. Heizer, "The Use of Narcotic Mushrooms by Primitive Peoples," *Ciba Symposia*, Vol. V, No. 11 (February, 1944), 1713–16; R. Gordon Wasson, "The Hallucinogenic Fungi of Mexico," *Botanical Museum Leaflets, Harvard University*, Vol. XIX, No. 7 (February 17, 1961), 137–62.

[6] Fray Bernardino de Sahagún, *General History of the Things of New Spain* (Florentine Codex), tr. by Charles E. Dibble and Arthur J. O. Anderson, Book XI (No. 14, Pt. 12), 130.

[7] The origin of this drug was long in doubt, the *Ipomoea sidaefolia* and *Datura meteloides* being among the supposed sources. Dr. Richard E. Schultes of Harvard University identified it as from *Rivea corymbosa*, of the family *Convolvulaceae*. Kreig, *Green Medicine*, 81.

Bancroft wrote: "Acosta mentions that *oliliuhqui* was taken by persons who desired to see visions. This latter was a seed, which was also an ingredient of the *teopatli*, or divine medicine, composed besides of India rubber gum, ocotl-resin, tobacco, and sacred water. This medicine could only be obtained from the priests." Hubert H. Bancroft, *Works*, II, *The Native Races*, II, 601.

sees many things which greatly terrify him. He is really frightened. . . . He who hates people causes one to swallow it in drink [and] food to madden him. However, it smells sour; it burns the throat a little.

As a remedy for gout, it was spread on the surface of affected parts. An infusion of this plant was also drunk as a purge for fever, swollen abdomen, and nausea.[8]

Mixitl and *talapatl* were the Aztec names for medicines derived from species of *Datura*.[9] The first, wrote Sahagún, "paralyzes one, closes one's eyes, tightens the throat, stops off the voice, makes one thirsty, deadens the testicles, splits the tongue." The ground seeds were used externally as an application for gout. The *tlapatl*, he declared, "harms one, takes away one's appetite, maddens one, makes one besotted." An ointment made of it was used in treating gout.[10]

The *peyotl* (*Lophophora williamsii*, a cactus), had an effect like the narcotic mushrooms if eaten or drunk. The user saw "many things which frighten one, or make one laugh. It affects him perhaps one day, perhaps two days, but likewise it abates. However it harms one, troubles one, makes one besotted."[11]

There are reports from the early eighteenth century of the use of peyote by Indians in the American Southwest.[12] Its use was opposed by the early missionaries not so much for its physiological effects as for its connection with "superstitious rites."[13] Peyote began to spread to Indians throughout the United States in the late nineteenth and early twentieth centuries and became a

---

8 Sahagún, *General History*, 129–30.

9 See *Jimson weed*, herein. The plant has also been supposed to be *Datura meteloides*.

10 Sahagún, *General History*, 129–30.

11 *Ibid.*, 129.

12 J. S. Slotkin, "Early Eighteenth Century Documents on Peyotism North of the Rio Grande," *American Anthropologist*, N.S., Vol. LIII, No. 3 (July–September, 1951), 420–27.

13 Safford, "Narcotic Plants and Stimulants of the Ancient Americans," *Annual Report of the Board of Regents of the Smithsonian Institution for the Year Ending June 30, 1916*, 402–403.

central part of the ritual of the Native American Church.[14] In some states, legislation against its use has been enacted.[15]

While the main use of peyote among Indians has been ritualistic, it has also been used for healing purposes by Indians and whites. South Texas Mexicans used a decoction of the peyote "bulb" as a drink in fevers and as a lotion for the feet and head.[16] It was used by Indians as a pain killer,[17] and it is reported that U.S. Army surgeons used it for the same purpose.[18] Tribes of northern Mexico and southern Arizona chewed the root for application as a poultice to fractures, larger open wounds, and snakebite.[19] It was supposed to have had a beneficial effect on rheumatism and paralysis among the Kansas Potawatomis.[20] Psychotherapeutic effects have been attributed to it, and La Barre held that its ability to produce visions, in accordance with a preexisting cultural set, accounts for its popularity with Indians.[21]

About the last decade of the previous century, clinical investigators were moved to examine the properties of peyote after observing its use among Oklahoma Indians. True remarked that

[14] On the use of the drug in the Southwest, see Hrdlička, *Physiological and Medical Observations, passim*; on its introduction to Nebraska tribes, see Gilmore, "Uses of Plants by Indians of the Missouri River Region," *Thirty-third Annual Report of the Bureau of American Ethnology, 1911–12*, 104–106; on its use among the Winnebagos, see Paul Radin, *The Autobiography of a Winnebago Indian*, 48–57.

[15] In June, 1967, at Denver, Colorado, County Judge William Conley held that the Colorado law prohibiting the use of peyote was an abridgment of the religious freedom of an Apache Indian, Mana Pardeahtan, who was a member of the Native American Church.

[16] Bourke, "Popular Medicine, Customs, and Superstitions of the Rio Grande," *Journal of American Folk-Lore*, Vol. VII, No. 25 (April–June, 1894), 127.

[17] Brooks, "The Medicine of the American Indian," *Journal of Laboratory and Clinical Medicine*, Vol. XIX, No. 1 (October, 1933), 21.

[18] Andrews, "The Aboriginal Physicians of Michigan," *Contributions to Medical Research Dedicated to Victor Clarence Vaughan*, 45.

[19] Hrdlička, *Physiological and Medical Observations*, 250–51.

[20] Landes, "Potawatomi Medicine," *Transactions Kansas Academy of Sciences*, Vol. LXVI (1963), 593–96.

[21] Weston La Barre, "Primitive Psychotherapy in Native American Cultures: Peyotism and Confession," *Journal of Abnormal and Social Psychology*, Vol. XLII, No. 3 (July, 1947), 294–309.

"hospital tests showed that the alkaloidal principle contained in the cactus furnishes a valuable remedy for certain troubles of the nervous system."[22] Kluver believed that peyote offered a valuable instrument for clinical research in ophthalmology and psychiatry.[23] *Anhalonium* is the pharmaceutical name of the drug, containing several alkaloids, including mescaline, which is derived from this plant.[24]

Another Aztec remedy of narcotic effect was *yauhtli* (*Tagetes lucida*), which according to Sahagún made one feel "as if one were bitten by a scorpion." An infusion of the leaves was drunk for chills. The leaves were also used as an internal and external remedy for gout, and in external massage for paralysis.[25] Bancroft believed that this drug was used as an anesthetic in "painful operations."[26]

The seeds of *Sophora speciosa*, a shrub growing in Texas, contains a poisonous alkaloid which was used medicinally by the Tonkawas. It was occasionally used as an intoxicant, producing delirious exhilaration followed by a long sleep.[27]

Among other narcotic plants and stimulants of ancient America, Safford lists: tobacco, *cohoba* (*piptadenia* or *paricá*),[28] the red bean, *huacachcu* (a tree *datura*), *ayahuasca* (*caapi*), *yerba-maté*, *cassine*, *guaraná*, and cacao. Indians attributed divine powers to some of these and to other narcotic plants which they

[22] True, "Folk Materia Medica," *Journal of American Folk-Lore*, Vol. XIV (1901), 113.

[23] Heinrich Kluver, *Mescal—The Divine Plant and its Psychological Effects*.

[24] Claus, *Pharmacognosy*, 484.

[25] Sahagún, *General History*, 145–46.

[26] "For painful operations, it is possible that narcotics were administered, for at certain of the sacrifices it is related that the victims were sprinkled with yauhtli powder to render them less sensitive to pain. Mendieta states that a stupefying drink was given on similar occasions." Bancroft, *Native Races*, II, 601.

[27] Whitebread, "The Indian Medical Exhibit of the Division of Medicine in the United States National Museum," Pub. 2582, *Proceedings of the United States National Museum*, Vol. LXVII, art. x, 21.

[28] Spruce reported in the mid-nineteenth century that the snuff narcotic paricá was the "chief curative agent" among Indians on the upper tributaries of the Orinoco. Spruce, *Notes*, II, 430.

used in divination, medicine, and ceremonials. They were frequently carried as protective or good luck charms.[29]

An unidentified plant used by the Mohawks was reported to have effects similar to those of the Peruvian coca. Dr. Colden, in a letter to Gronovius, in December, 1744, gave the following information about it:

> I have not as yet been able to see the fruit of No 131 but I cannot doubt of its belonging to the Class of the Tetradynamia for besides its agreeing in all its parts of the Flower with the Characters of that Class it agrees likewise in Test having nearly the same with that of the Nasturtium. The Mohawk Indians told me that when they were quite faint with travel & fasting if they can come at the roots of this plant to eat they are restored & their spirits restored wonderfully.[30]

Stimulant beverages. Indian and African aborigines both contributed their stimulant medicaments to the earlier form of the popular beverage, Coca-Cola. The preparation was first made of coca leaves in 1885 by John S. Pemberton, an Atlanta pharmacist, and its name copyrighted as "French Wine of Cola, an Ideal Tonic." He later combined coca with the African kola nut, a caffeine-bearing substance, for a quick "pick-up" and remedy for headache.[31] After Coca Cola had become world famous, the government persuaded its proprietors to omit coca from its constituents, on the ground that it was a harmful drug.[32]

Root beer was brewed in colonial times from a variety of substances first used by Indians for healing purposes, including sassafras, oil of wintergreen, and birch oil. Methyl salicylate, the

[29] Safford, "Narcotic Plants and Stimulants of the Ancient Americas," *Annual Report of the Board of Regents of the Smithsonian Institution for the Year Ending June 30, 1916,* 424.

[30] Colden, *Letters and Papers,* III, 90.

[31] R. C. Wilson, *Drugs and Pharmacy in the Life of Georgia,* 217ff.

[32] Norman J. Taylor, *Plant Drugs that Changed the World,* 13.

active principle in wintergreen oil, has in the past been a legal ingredient of the concentrate, but sassafras was eliminated.[33]

Ginger ale, cream soda, and other popular drinks have included such aboriginal pharmaceuticals as capsicum, sarsaparilla, Jamaica ginger, vanilla, and allspice. Sarsaparilla once enjoyed an immense popularity in its own right.[34]

Guaraná, used by South American Indians,[35] has a high caffeine content and is a popular drink in Brazil. Maté, or Paraguay tea, is another aboriginal contribution to stimulant beverages. Several North American herbs used by Indians have been substituted for tea. Among them are *Ceanothus*, or New Jersey tea, widely used during the Revolutionary War as a substitute for East Indian tea;[36] Labrador tea (*Ledum* species), cassine or yaupon (*Ilex* species, holly), Oswego tea (*Monarda didyma* L.), goldenrod (*Solidago* species), sweet fern (*Myrica* or *Comptonia*), and wintergreen (*Gaultheria* species). [37] These have been used by Indians and whites for stimulant, diuretic, and emetic effects.

Intoxicating beverages. Peter Collinson observed in a letter to Dr. Colden in 1768 that Indians of Virginia and "other Nations to the Eastward" had no intoxicating liquors, "but when Wee come to Florida & all on to the Westward and Southward, they fermented Indian Corn and Sweet Potatoes & other things, & made Drinks that procured the highest Degree of Intoxication."[38]

Indians of Mexico and the American Southwest made fer-

[33] Brochure, "Root Beer," and letter from John R. Leitz, associate director of research, the Hires Company, Evanston, Ill., April 13, 1966.

[34] *American People's Encyclopedia* (1955), IV, 759.

[35] In the 1850's Spruce reported that Brazilians considered guaraná to be a preventative of every kind of sickness. Along the Orinoco it was considered a preservative against "the malignant bilious fevers which are the scourge of that region." It was also used for nervous affections and diarrhea. Spruce, *Notes*, I, 181; II, 448–49, 452.

[36] Schöpf, *Travels*, I, 415–20.

[37] Henry H. Rusby, "Beverages of Vegetable Origin," *Journal of the New York Botanical Garden*, Vol. V, No. 52 (April, 1904), 85.

[38] Colden, *Letters and Papers*, VII, 143.

mented liquors from maguey, nopal, mesquite beans, native grapes and other fruits, honey, pine bark, chenopodium, manzanita berries, and saguaro fruit.[39] The Apaches and other tribes fermented corn to make *tizwin*, described by Hrdlička as "ordinarily a weak alcoholic beverage with a slight nutritive value, and is not a strong intoxicant."[40]

Brooks remarked that alcoholic drinks were used by Mexican Indians for nervous conditions.[41] Two of their drinks remain popular today in the beverage trade: *pulque* and *tequila*, both made from the juice of the maguey or mescal plant (*Agave americana* and related species). [42]

There is disagreement as to whether Indians knew of distillation. Safford denied that they were familiar with this process,[43] while several others asserted the contrary.   Bourke maintained that "there seems . . . to be much to support the idea that the American Indian—at least the Aztec—had some acquaintance with rude processes of distillation not taught by the Europeans."[44] Bancroft stated that the Aztecs obtained balsam from the *huitiloxitl* by distillation.[45] Hrdlička reported that tribes of northern Mexico and southern Arizona made distilled liquors (mescal and tequila) from several species of agave, and another, called

---

[39] Browne, "The Chemical Industries of the American Aborigines," *Isis*, Vol. XXIII (1935), 410–11; Hrdlička, *Physiological and Medical Observations*, 126–29; Safford, "Narcotic Plants and Stimulants of the Ancient Americans," *Annual Report of the Board of Regents of the Smithsonian Institution for the Year Ending June 30, 1916*, 388.

[40] Hrdlička, *Physiological and Medical Observations*, 26.

[41] Brooks, "The Medicine of the American Indians," *Journal of Laboratory and Clinical Medicine*, Vol. XIX, No. 1 (October, 1933), 21.

[42] Rusby, "Beverages of Vegetable Origin," *Journal of the New York Botanical Garden*, Vol. V, No. 52 (April, 1904), 83; James M. Gavin, "Gringos Shout Ole for Tequila," *Chicago Tribune*, July 12, 1967. Of these, only *pulque*, a fermented drink, is definitely pre-Cortesian.

[43] Safford, "Narcotic Plants and Stimulants of the Ancient Americas," *Annual Report of the Board of Regents of the Smithsonian Institution for the Year Ending June 30, 1916*, 388.

[44] John G. Bourke, "Distillation by Early American Indians," *American Anthropologist*, O.S., Vol. VII (1894), 297.

[45] Bancroft, *Native Races*, II, 599.

sotol, from the *dasylirion.* All were "usually ardent and strongly alcoholic, particularly the tequila."[46]

Astringents. The native materia medica commonly included leaves, flowers, fruits, barks, seeds, or roots used for their astringent effect in diarrhea, hemorrhage, and other disorders requiring such a specific. Wild geranium, bayberry, sumach, hemlock, the oaks, persimmon, and other tannin-containing plants provided some of the substances so used. These drugs and the manner of their use in different tribes are described in the section on the remedies contributed by Indians to the pharmacopeia.

Cathartics. Some of the most widely used cathartic drugs were obtained from the Indians. *Cascara sagrada*[47] and *podophyllum* (may-apple root) are two of the better-known members of this group still in use. Some Indians used bear's oil for this purpose.[48] Most Indians used a variety of purgatives, but the Canadian Algonquins, according to Lahontan, "think all Purgatives inflame the Mass of the Blood, and weaken the Veins and Arteries by their Violent Shocks."[49]

Two once-popular drugs of this class were obtained from the Mexican Indians: mechoacan and jalap. Monardes called mechoacan the "rhubarb of the Indias" and reported that a Franciscan friar fell sick and was cured by mechoacan powder "in wine, drunk, given by an Indian Phisition sent by the Cacique."[50] This drug was admitted to the *Pharmacopoeia Londinensis* of 1618.[51]

[46] Hrdlička, *Physiological and Medical Observations,* 26, citing A. N. Rose.

[47] V. K. Chesnut, *Plants Used by the Indians of Mendocino County, California,* 298.

[48] "One of the favourite cathartics of our Indians, in cases of obstinate costiveness, is a large draught of Bear's-oil." B. S. Barton, *Philadelphia Medical and Physical Journal,* Vol. I, Pt. I (1805), 151.

[49] Lahontan, *New Voyages,* II, 468. There are several instances where the observations of Lahontan were not only critical of European medical practice, but were out of line with other reports of aboriginal practice. Whether this was owing to the fact that the Algonquins were an unusual tribe or that he fabricated make-believe customs in the manner of Jonathan Swift in order to attack the Old World we cannot know.

[50] Monardes, *Joyfull Newes,* I, 54–55.   [51] *Ibid.,* 95–96.

Jalap, obtained from a tuberous root,[52] is an ancient aboriginal remedy which was mentioned in the *Badianus Manuscript*.[53] It became a panacea among whites from Wesley to Rush and beyond. The evangelist recommended a tincture for king's evil, a decoction for a purge and to expel worms, as well as for "the whites" [venereal disease].[54] Francis Taylor took it with ipecac for fever,[55] and Rush provided the Lewis and Clark expedition with jalap and calomel pills for "bilious fever."[56] Jefferson was dosed with calomel and jalap for "spasmodic stricture of the ileum" and complained that his recovery was thereby delayed.[57]

The term jalap has also been applied to a root growing in the United States, *Ipomoea pandurata* (USP 1820–63).

Emetics. The vomit drugs are not the panaceas they once were, being used chiefly in cases where poisons or other foreign substances must be promptly expelled. The South American ipecac is still esteemed for this purpose.[58] The drug is derived from the bark of *Cephaelis ipecacuanha*, a tree of the Brazilian rain forest, and its use against amebic dysentery was learned from the natives

---

[52] The official jalap root (USP 1820–1936; NF 1936—) is that of *Exogonum purga*, which was introduced into Europe about 1565 by Spanish explorers who learned of it from the natives. Claus, *Pharmacognosy*, 373–74. *Ipomea*, or *Orizaba Jalap* (USP 1926–36; NF 1936—) is the dried root of *Ipomea orizabensis* Ledenois. *Ibid*., 375–76. See also John U. Lloyd, *Origin and History of All the Pharmacopeial Vegetable Drugs, Chemicals, and Preparations*, 176–177; Youngken, "Drugs of the North American Indians," *American Journal of Pharmacy*, Vol. XCVI, No. 96 (July, 1924), 493.

[53] Emmart (ed.), *Badianus Manuscript*, 253, note 1. It is here identified as *Ipomoea purga* Wend.

[54] Wesley, *Primitive Physic*, 102, 131, 132.

[55] Extract from Diary of Francis Taylor (April 2–3, 1796), in Blanton, *Medicine in Virginia, Eighteenth Century*, 416.

[56] Will, "The Medical and Surgical Practice of the Lewis and Clark Expedition," *Journal of the History of Medicine*, Vol. XIV, No. 3 (July, 1959), 291.

[57] Koch and Peden (eds.), *Life and Selected Writings of Thomas Jefferson*, 693.

[58] "The Children's Hospital medical center in Boston recently sent out a release recommending the inclusion of charcoal and ipecac in the home first-aid kit. These products are helpful antidotes in certain types of accidental poisoning . . . . Ipecac is an old time emetic; by making the child throw up, the poison comes with it." Dr. T. R. Van Dellen, *Chicago Tribune*, October 3, 1964.

by William Piso (1563–1636). Its alkaloid derivative, emetine, is still used for the same purpose.[59] Ipecac has been used as both an emetic and a laxative and was once used in the treatment of hepatitis.[60]

The idea that impurities in the body should be expelled from the mouth via emetics or from the rectum via cathartics was common enough among most Indians so that a large number of their drugs fall into these classes. The plant which Josselyn called white hellebore was used in New England for emetic purposes by both whites and Indians.[61] Father Paul Le Jeune spoke favorably of Huron emetics in 1637.[62] The Huron sorcerers, Brebeuf reported, sometimes prescribed an emetic "to make the charm, if there be any, come forth,—as I myself saw, when at La Rochelle, a poor woman who threw up a coal as large as one's thumb, after some doses of water."[63] Events did not always have such happy endings, if we may credit the Jesuit relation from Onondaga in 1655–56:

> A poor woman was less fortunate in her dream, running about day and night, and catching only an illness. They wished to cure her with the commonest remedies of the country, which are emetics compounded of certain roots steeped in water; but they gave her such a quantity that she

[59] Ackerknecht, *Short History*, 115. See also Lloyd, *History of the Vegetable Drugs of the Pharmacopeia of the United States*, Lloyd Library, Bulletin No. 18, Pharmacy Series No. 4, 49–51; Julian H. Steward (ed.), *Handbook of South American Indians*, Bureau of American Ethnology, Bulletin No. 143, V, 627; VI, 485–86; Castiglioni, "Herbs in the Medicine of Eastern Peoples and of the American Indians," *Ciba Symposia*, Vol. V, Nos. 5–6 (August–September, 1943), 1540.

[60] Scott, *History of Tropical Medicine*, II, 834–35. Cotton Mather considered ipecac a good vomit; Colden gave it for six days for both emetic and purge effects to a boy whose breath "smells like carrion" and cured him. Colden, *Letters and Papers*, V, 204. Wesley recommended it for both flux and as a sudorific. *Primitive Physic*, 76. Cullen, hostile to all American drugs, said other substances "are more effectual." *A Treatise of the Materia Medica, II, 333–34*. The name ipecac has also been applied to some U.S. plants of the *Euphorbia* and other species.

[61] Josselyn, *Two Voyages*, 49–50. The plant was probably green hellebore, *Veratrum viride (q.v.)*

[62] Thwaites (ed.), *Jesuit Relations*, XII, 25.

[63] *Ibid.*, X, 197.

died immediately, her stomach bursting to let out two kettle-fuls of water that she had been made to take.[64]

Emetics must have been something of a specialty among the Iroquois, if we may judge by these accounts and another by Barton:

> I have been assured, that the Six-Nations make use of at least twelve or fourteen different emetics. All of them, except the sulphat of Iron, are vegetables. It is probable that the Spiraea Ipecacuanha, Euphorbia Ipecacuanha, &c., are among the number of these vegetable emetics.[65]

Several Indian emetics acted as such only if taken in large doses. In moderate quantities, they often served other purposes, such as diuretic or stimulant, *e.g.*, the celebrated yaupon or cassine, the black drink of southern tribes.

Febrifuges. The greatest of all botanical febrifuges, the anti-malarial cinchona bark, from which quinine was extracted, was a discovery of South American Indians, though it does not appear to have been used by the advanced Incas. Because some of the early history of cinchona has been wrapped in myth or mystery, some writers have hesitated to grant the Indians credit for the discovery of it, but several authorities have marshaled imposing evidence of aboriginal use of this remedy for fevers.[66] Scott asserted that a Jesuit missionary at Loxa (Peru) was cured of an intermittent fever in 1600 by the cinchona bark he received from an Indian chief.[67]

North American tribes also had numerous febrifuges, many of them of acknowledged efficacy, although of lesser strength than

[64] *Ibid.*, XLII, 167.

[65] Barton, *Essay towards a Materia Medica*, I, 29.

[66] Maddox, *The Medicine Man*, 250–51; Castiglioni, "Herbs in the Medicine of Eastern Peoples and of the American Indians," *Ciba Symposia*, Vol. V, Nos. 5–6 (August–September, 1943), 1539–40; F. R. Fosberg, "Principal Economic Plants of Tropical America," in Frans Verdoorn (ed.), *Plants and Plant Science in Latin America*, 27.

[67] Scott, *History of Tropical Medicine*, I, 210.

cinchona. The dogwood bark, used by several tribes and containing properties similar to cinchona, was long used as a substitute for it, as was the bark of yellow poplar and wild cherry and the herbs of boneset and American centaury.[68]

The Cheyennes reduced fever with a tea of the leaves and stems of *Psoralea argophylla* Pursh.[69] The Meskwakis used the root of golden Alexander (*Zizia aurea* [L.] Koch).[70] The pounded root of *Verbesina virginica*, soaked in water, provided an extract which was taken during fever attacks by the Louisiana Choctaws.[71] A decoction of the root of the little rattlepod (*Astragalus caroliniana* L.) was used as a children's febrifuge by the Teton Dakotas.[72] Twentieth-century Rappahannocks investigated by Speck steeped the leaves of wild ginger (*Asarum* species) to reduce fever in typhoid, and an infusion of tea from sassafras roots to bring out the rash in measles and reduce fever. Plantain leaves (*Plantago major*) were bruised and bound to parts of the body to reduce fever.[73]

Vermifuges. For a century and a half the most widely used worm medicine in this country was probably the pulverized root of the pinkroot (*Spigelia marilandica* L.), a discovery of the Cherokee Indians.[74] Wormseed or Jerusalem oak (*Chenopodium ambrosioides* L.), which, despite its name, is an American plant, was used as a vermifuge by the Natchez,[75] and probably also by

[68] Drake, *Diseases of the Interior Valley*, 749–50.

[69] George Bird Grinnell, "Some Cheyenne Plant Medicines," *American Anthropologist*, N.S., Vol. VII, No. 1 (January–March, 1905), 40.

[70] Smith, *Meskwaki Ethnobotany*, 280.

[71] David I. Bushnell, Jr., *The Choctaw of Bayou Lacomb, St. Tammany Parish, Louisiana*, Bureau of American Ethnology Bulletin No. 48, 23.

[72] Gilmore, "Uses of Plants by the Indians of the Missouri River Region," *Thirty-third Annual Report of the Bureau of American Ethnology, 1911–12*, 91.

[73] Frank G. Speck, Royal B. Hassrick, and Edmund S. Carpenter, *Rappahannock Herbals, Folk-Lore and Science of Cures*, Proceedings of the Delaware County Institute of Science, Vol. X, No. 1, 25–26.

[74] John R. Beck, *Medicine in the American Colonies*, 54. See also pp. 57, 348 herein.

[75] Swanton, "Religious Beliefs and Medical Practices of the Chickasaw Indians," *Forty-second Annual Report of the Bureau of American Ethnology, 1924–25*, 668. See also pp. 325–26 herein.

the Mayas.[76] The Ojibwa vermifuges were the boiled or steeped roots of wild plum (*Prunus americana*), wild cherry (*Prunus serotina*), and horsemint (*Monarda mollis*).[77] Some western tribes used the turkey pea (*Tephrosia virginiana*) to destroy worms.[78]

Poisons. Indians in North, South, and Central America were familiar with the poisonous properties of certain plants. "Another destroyer of them," wrote Lawson, "is the Art they have, and often practice, of poisoning one another; which is done by a large white spongy Root, that grows in the Fresh-Marshes, which is one of their Poisons, not but that they have many other Drugs, which they poison one another withal."[79] Zeisberger declared that Indians were well versed in the use of poisonous roots and that there were "melancholy examples where they have by their use destroyed themselves or others."[80] The toxic effects of the raw root of the may apple (*Podophyllum peltatum*) were widely known, and it was occasionally used for suicide.[81] The Rappahannocks of Speck's acquaintance knew the poisonous properties of black nightshade (*Solanum nigrum*), but made a weak infusion of the dried leaves to be used as a sedative for sleepless persons.[82] Brickell reported that North Carolina Indians had:

> . . . a certain Method in poysoning their Arrows, and they will temper them so as to work slow or swift as they please; they can make it so strong, that no Art can save the Person

[76] Roys, *Ethno-Botany of the Maya*, 262. It was also used for gastric disturbances by Brazilian Indians. Levi-Strauss in Steward (ed.), *Handbook of South American Indians*, Bureau of American Ethnology Bulletin 143, VI, 405.

[77] Frances Densmore, "Uses of Plants by the Chippewa Indians," *Forty-fourth Annual Report of the Bureau of American Ethnology, 1926–27*, 346.

[78] Hunter, *Manners and Customs*, 393.

[79] Lawson, *History of North Carolina*, 239.

[80] Zeisberger, "History of the North American Indians," *Ohio Archaeological and Historical Quarterly*, Vol. XIX, Nos. 1–2 (January and April, 1910), 56.

[81] Lahontan, *New Voyages*, I, 368; Heckewelder, *History, Manners and Customs of the Indian Nations*, 224–25. The Menominees boiled the plant for an insecticide. Smith, *Menomini Ethnobotany*, 26. The Osages used it as an antidote for poisons. Hunter, *Manners and Customs*, 381.

[82] Speck, *Rappahannock Herbals*, 34.

or Beast that is wounded with them, except it be by their Kings and Conjurers, their young Men being ignorant of it.[83]

According to Sahagún, the Aztecs poisoned fish with the roots of the *Amolli* (*Sapindus saponarious*), which was also used as soap in washing clothes.[84] Humboldt in South America observed several plants, including *Galega piscatorium*, "of which the Indians make use . . . as a kind of *barbasco*, to intoxicate fish."[85] Plants of the *Erythrina* family, containing over a hundred species of herbs, shrubs, and trees, were used for toxic and medicinal purposes by Indians of Central and South America. Various parts were used for fish poison, hypnosis, diaphoresis, and emmenagogue. The insecticide *rotenone* is extracted from plants of this family.[86]

Perhaps the most famous of Indian poisons is the South American arrow poison, *curare*, prepared from an aqueous extract of *Strychnos toxifera* and related plants.[87] Though harmless when taken internally, it is fatal when it penetrates into the blood stream through a wound.[88] Humboldt, while at Esmeralda on the Orinoco, observed the preparation of this substance, which he said was "employed in war, in the chase, and, singularly enough, as a remedy for gastric derangements."[89]

An enormous literature has grown up about this substance.[90]

[83] Brickell, *Natural History*, 394.

[84] Sahagún, *General History*, 133.

[85] Humboldt, *Personal Narrative*, II, 366.

[86] George M. Hocking, *A Dictionary of Terms in Pharmacognosy*, 78, 194; Browne, "The Chemical Industries of the American Aborigines," *Isis*, Vol. XXIII (1935), 421; B. V. Christensen and Albert Voss, "The Histology of *Cracca Virginiana* Linne Root," *Journal of the American Pharmaceutical Association*, Vol. XXV, No. 6 (June, 1936), 519–23; Claus, *Pharmacognosy*, 672; La Barre, "Folk Medicine and Folk Science," *Journal of American Folk-Lore*, Vol. LV (October–December, 1942), 197–203; see *Devil's shoestring*, herein.

[87] The *erythrina* plants contain alkaloids with "curare-like action." Hocking, *Dictionary*, 78.

[88] Brown, "The Chemical Industries of the American Aborigines," *Isis*, Vol. XXIII (1935), 421.

[89] Humboldt, *Personal Narrative*, II, 438–39.

[90] A. R. McIntyre, *Curare—Its History, Nature and Clinical Use*, lists 1,330 references on curare.

During the nineteenth century, European physicians began to experiment with curare to cure muscle spasms or paralysis in cases of tetanus, epilepsy, chorea, or rabies. Many patients were lost because of the difficulty of standardizing the drug and determining a safe dosage that would not stop respiration. Since then, further progress has been made, so that curare and its by-products are used safely for several purposes. It became "the standard adjuvant in metrazol therapy of psychotics."[91] It has been used to stimulate the central nervous system in anesthesia, in abdominal surgery, in shock therapy, convulsive therapy, muscle spasm, and poliomyelitis, as well as Parkinson's disease and tetanus.[92] Dr. K. B. Thomas states that it "has achieved an established place in anaesthesia, from which it is not likely to be displaced for some time."[93] With the development of a standardized preparation, Dr. A. R. McIntyre reported, the clinical use of curare has rapidly increased. It provides more complete muscular relaxation without the use of excessively deep anesthesia. Its main use has been in abdominal surgery, including gall bladder, stomach, and hysterectomies, as well as thoracic surgery and tonsillectomy. Of three hundred patients ranging in age from 12 to 75 years, "curare proved perfectly safe in all age groups, including many that were poor surgical risks."[94] Curare has also been used in a patented taenicide.[95]

The effects of the drug on man, according to McIntyre, include ocular ptosis [paralytic eyelid drooping], change in voice, difficulty in swallowing, weakness of neck muscles, immobility of intestine, suppression of electrical activity of the brain, changes in cortical function, disturbance of the sensoria, and decrease of urine. Prolonged use or heavy dosage leads to a fall in blood pressure, blocking of automatic ganglia, immobility of the gut, and eventually, depression of the central nervous system, the stopping of respiration, and death.[96]

[91] La Barre, "Folk Medicine and Folk Science," *Journal of American Folk-Lore*, Vol. LV (October–December, 1942), 201.

[92] McIntyre, *Curare*, 182.

[93] K. Bryn Thomas, *Curare, Its History and Usage*, 125.

[94] McIntyre, *Curare*, 193–95.   [95] *Ibid.*, 164.   [96] *Ibid.*, 177, 179, 196, 212.

Curare, as reagent, was official in the USP, 1916–50. The composite drug, *tubocurarine chloride*, has been official since 1950.[97]

Drugless Therapy: Internal Ailments

Indian medical treatment was scarcely ever confined to the use of drugs only. The well-known ritualistic procedures have been discussed in Chapter II. However, there were other methods frequently used, especially in external ailments, but also in some ills of internal origin, which were found by white investigators to be sometimes useful and valid. The following survey of these curative devices, like the preceding review of Indian drugs, is not intended to be exhaustive.

Bleeding as therapy. Some, but not all, Indian tribes practiced the procedure of phlebotomy which remained popular with white physicians well into the nineteenth century. Bleeding or venesection was frequently employed in some tribes to relieve headache, fever, aches, and swellings.[98] It was much used for various ills by the Aztecs, the instruments used being *iztli* knives, porcupine quills, and maguey thorns.[99] The Incas bled to relieve pain, cutting the vein nearest to the supposed seat of the trouble.[100] The pirate surgeon, Lionel Wafer, observed that Panamanian natives practiced bleeding by shooting small arrows into the skin, which "penetrate no farther than we generally thrust our lancets."[101]

It is possible that some North American Indians learned the practice of bleeding from the whites, among whom it prevailed in folk medicine[102] as well as in official medicine. Of the Canadian Indians, Charlevoix noted that "they were formerly un-

[97] Claus, *Pharmacology*, 480–81.

[98] Walter Krickeberg, "Blood Letting and Bloody Castigation Among the American Indians," *Ciba Symposia*, Vol. I, No. 1 (April, 1939), 26–34.

[99] Bancroft, *Native Races*, II, 601.

[100] La Vega, *The Incas*, 38.

[101] Wafer, *A New Voyage*, 54.

[102] Douglas, "The People of Cades Cove," *National Geographic Magazine*, Vol. CXXII, No. 1 (July, 1962), 84.

acquainted with the method of bleeding,"[103] a report which is in accord with Lahontan's observation that the Algonquins were "astonish'd at our custom of Bleeding."[104] The attitude of these Indians anticipates that of the empiricist, Samuel Thomson, who maintained that "taking away the blood reduces the heat, and gives power to the cold they had taken, which increases the disorder."[105]

In the *Moravian Journals*, Zeisberger frequently mentioned his resort to bleeding of Indians to cure various ills, and Beauchamp maintained that it was more popular with the Indians than with the whites.[106] Peter Dougherty, a Presbyterian missionary to the Ottawas (1838–70), bled Indian patients.[107] These reports suggest that not all Indians practiced the method themselves, but Dr. Rush mentioned bleeding by Indians as one of the few signs of their advancement in therapeutics.[108]

Eighteenth-century Indians of Lower California, Father Jakob Baegert reported, let blood to relieve inflammation.[109] Hunter observed that Indians west of the Mississippi let blood for local pains, fevers, and inflammations, using a ligature, but said "they

---

[103] Charlevoix, *Journal*, I, 162.

[104] Lahontan, *New Voyages*, II, 469; see p. 88 herein.

[105] Thomson, *New Guide to Health*, 31.

[106] Beauchamp (ed.), *Moravian Journals*, 217. Zeisberger said bleeding was practiced among the Delawares. "History of the North American Indians," *Ohio Archaeological and Historical Quarterly*, Vol. XIX, Nos. 1–2 (January and April, 1910), 27.

[107] "Diaries of Peter Dougherty," *Journal of the Presbyterian Historical Society*, Vol. XXX, No. 4 (December, 1952), 243.

[108] Rush, *Medicine Among the Indians*, 123. Dr. Zina Pitcher declared: "I have never been able to settle the question in my own mind, as to whether this practice is original with the Indians, or has been borrowed from the whites." Schoolcraft, *Indian Tribes*, IV, 515. Dr. Clive M. McCay, professor of nutrition at Cornell University, has been quoted as saying: "If I had been sick 200 years ago, I would have been better off in the hands of a medicine man of the American Indian than I would have been in those of a European physician. The Indian would have given me mental therapy, food and herb remedies. The European physician would have drained away my blood!" Dr. H. E. Kirschner, "Remedial Properties of Herbs," *Let's Live*, May, 1967, 25.

[109] Jakob Baegert, "An Account of the Aboriginal Inhabitants of the Californian Peninsula," *Annual Report of the Smithsonian Institution, 1863–64*, 386.

seldom let blood in any considerable quantity, and never, that I know of, until fainting is induced."[110] In the 1830's, Josiah Gregg wrote that southern Plains tribes, such as the Comanches, "frequently let blood for disease, which is oftenest performed with the keen edge of a flint: and though they sometimes open a vein, they more commonly make their incisions indiscriminately."[111] The Maricopas resorted to bloodletting in persistent pains and paralysis of any limb. "They open veins," wrote Dr. Hrdlička, "distinguishing between veins and arteries, binding together the cut surfaces with rags when they think sufficient blood has been drawn."[112] The Montagnais relieved pain in the head by cutting the scalp with a knife so that it bled.[113]

Cautery and moxa. Localized burning of the skin to relieve rheumatic pains and other ills was widely practiced by the Indians. Josselyn wrote of *"Spunck,* an excrescence growing out of black birch," which was the "touchwood" of the Indians. "Therewith [he wrote] they help the sciatica, or gout of the hip, or any great ach;—burning the patient with it in two or three places upon the thigh, and upon certain veins."[114] A similar treatment with a different instrument was reported from North Carolina by Lawson:

> They cure the Spleen (which they are much addicted to) by burning with a Reed. They lay the Patient on his Back, so put a hollow Cane into the Fire, where they burn the End thereof till it is very hot, and on Fire at the end. Then

[110] Hunter, *Manners and Customs,* 396–97.

[111] Gregg, *Commerce of the Prairies,* Vol. XX in Thwaites (ed.), *Early Western Travels,* 334.

[112] Hrdlička, *Physiological and Medical Observations,* 248.

[113] Gladys Tantaquidgeon, "Notes on the Origin and Uses of Plants of the Lake St. John Montagnais," *Journal of American Folk-Lore,* Vol. XLV, No. 176 (April–June, 1932), 266.

[114] Josselyn, *New-England's Rarities,* 186. *Spunck* was identified by his editors as a species of *Polyporus.* The aboriginal term used here may be the origin of "spunk water," Huck Finn's cure for warts, which was found in the recesses of tree trunks.

they lay a Piece of thin Leather on the Patient's Belly, between the Pit of the Stomach and the Navel, so press the hot
Reed on the Leather, which burns the Patient so that you
may ever after see the Impression of the Reed where it was
laid on, which Mark never goes off so long as he lives. This
is used for the Belly-Ach sometimes.[115]

In the same period Robert Beverley described a similar practice among Virginia Indians:

But if the Humour happen to fix, and make a pain in any
particular Joynt, or Limb, their general cure then is by burning, if it be in any part that will bear it; their method of
doing this is by little sticks of Light-wood, the Coal of which
will burn like a hot Iron; the sharp point of this they run
into the Flesh, and having made a Sore, they keep it running
till the Humour be drawn off; Or else they take Punck,[116]
(which is a sort of soft Touchwood, cut out of the knots of
Oak or Hiccory Trees . . .) this they shape like a Cone . . . and
apply the Basis of it to the place affected. Then they set fire
to it, letting it burn out upon the part, which makes a running Sore effectually.

Sometimes, Beverley added, they used reeds for cauterizing,
heating them over the fire till they were about to burn, then
applying them upon a piece of thin wet leather.[117]
Of Indians on Manitoulin Island in the 1840's, Dr. Winder
reported: "That they are acquainted with the mode of relieving
inward pains by treatment similar to the moxa, is seen by their

[115] Lawson, *History of North Carolina*, 235.

[116] Benjamin Rush also spoke of a "a piece of rotten wood, called *punk*, which
they place upon the part affected, and afterward set it on fire: the fire gradually
consumes the wood, and its ashes burn a hole in the flesh." *Medicine Among the
Indians*, 123.

We have borrowed the aboriginal name "punk" for the stick used to light
fireworks. See also Webster's *New World Dictionary* (1954), 1181, which ascribes the
term to the Delawares.

[117] Beverley, *History and Present State of Virginia*, 217.

burning a piece of touchwood over the pained part, and suffering it to produce a blister."[118]

In the present century, Bushnell observed Choctaw use of a counterirritant as a remedy for severe pains in the stomach or rheumatic pains. Above the seat of the pain they pressed into the flesh a piece of cotton or similar substance, about the size of a small pea, which was burned in that position. Some Choctaws were scarred from the treatment.[119] Gilmore reported similar use of the stems of the lead or shoestring plant (*Amorpha canescens* Pursh) by the Omahas. The small stems were broken into short pieces and attached to the skin by moistening one end with the tongue. They were then ignited and allowed to burn down to the skin.[120] Procedures similar to those of the Choctaws and Omahas were observed among the Pimas and Maricopas by Hrdlička, the substance used being a small cottony ball of parasitic origin found on the *Lycium andersonii*. The Otomis of northern Mexico used as counterirritant a caustic herb which acted like cantharides.[121]

Cupping and Sucking. Lawson reported that during his stay among the Tuscaroras, then resident in North Carolina,

. . . there happened to be a Young Woman troubled with Fits. The Doctor who was sent for to assist her, laid her on her Belly and made a small Incision with Rattle-Snake-Teeth; then laying his Mouth to the Place, he sucked out near a Quart of black conglutinated Blood, and Serum.[122]

Virginia Indians, wrote Smith, treated swellings first by applying and burning pieces of touchwood, and "from thence draw the corruption with their mouth."[123] The Jesuit priest, Jacques Gravier, among the Houmas in 1700, scornfully remarked:

[118] Winder, "On Indian Diseases and Remedies," *Boston Medical and Surgical Journal*, Vol. XXXIV, No. 1 (February 4, 1846), 13.
[119] Bushnell, *Choctaw of Bayou Lacomb*, 24–25.
[120] Gilmore, "Uses of Plants by Indians of the Missouri River Region," *Thirty-third Annual Report of the Bureau of American Ethnology, 1911–12*, 93.
[121] Hrdlička, *Physiological and Medical Observations*, 246, 252–53.
[122] Lawson, *History of North Carolina*, 59.
[123] Tyler (ed.), *Narratives of Early Virginia*, 108.

... all they do for their sick is to suck them Until the Blood comes. I saw one in the hands of the old Medicine-men; one whistled and played on a gourd, another sucked; while the third sang the Song of the Crocodile [Alligator], whose skin served him as a drum.[124]

Alexander Ross, in the far Northwest, reported that Okanagan medicine men sucked affected parts and spit out the blood, though there was no mark on the patient's body.[125] Sucking was frequently done in various tribes with the aid of a hollow bone, horn, calabash, cylindrical stone, or stick.[126] The practice was still current among the Kansas Potawatomis in the 1930's,[127] and the Wisconsin Ojibwas in the 1940's.[128]

It has been held that these procedures, though linked with shamanistic applications in the case of foreign bodies, were logically used for snakebite and removal of pus from wounds and ulcers.[129] Modern cupping instruments used for snakebite and similar afflictions requiring the extraction of toxic substances have been called the legitimate heirs of the horns and hollow-tube bones used by the Indians for such purposes.[130]

Enemata. While instruments for the administration of the enema were of ancient usage in the Old World,[131] there is no question that the American Indians independently discovered the enema tube and bulbed syringe. Moreover, the central Ama-

---

124 Thwaites (ed.), *Jesuit Relations*, LXV, 149–51.

125 *Adventures of the First Settlers on the Oregon or Columbia River . . .* , Vol. VII in Thwaites (ed.), *Early Western Travels*, 289.

126 Bourke, "The Medicine-Men of the Apache," in *Ninth Annual Report of the Bureau of American Ethnology, 1887–88*, 472.

127 Landes, "Potawatomi Medicine," *Transactions Kansas Academy of Science*, Vol. LXVI (1963), 571.

128 Ritzenthaler, *Chippewa Preoccupation with Health*, 204ff.

129 Adams, "Aboriginal American Medicine and Surgery," *Proceedings Indiana Academy of Science*, Vol. LXI (1951), 51.

130 Maddox, *The Medicine Man*, 192, 225.

131 William Lieberman, "The History of the Enema," *Ciba Symposia*, Vol. V, No. 11 (February, 1944), 1694–1708.

zon tribes were the first to use rubber for this purpose.[132] The use of enemata was widespread among American Indians, with applications varying from treatment for constipation, diarrhea, and hemorrhoids, to administration of wine by Aztecs and the narcotic paricá by South American tribes.[133]

The injection of the enema has been depicted on ancient Peruvian pottery[134] and prescribed in the *Badianus Manuscript* of the Aztecs. Against dysentery, the latter used a clyster to inject into the anus various substances, including agave leaves, extracts of bladderwort, and fresh ground maize, dissolved in water.[135]

Guiana Indians still fashion an enema syringe from the bladder of a turtle, jaguar, or other mammal, which is attached to a reed nozzle.[136] In North America such syringes were commonly made of an animal or fish bladder and the hollow leg bone of a bird.[137] Some of the Ojibwas used a deer bladder and a hollow rush.[138] The Catawbas used a tubular type of syringe containing two telescoped sections.[139] Gilmore, who described enema devices among the Plains tribes, held the opinion that Indians had them prior to European contact.[140] Force is given to his view by the observation of Charlevoix in 1721 that the northern Indians

[132] Nordenskjöld, "The American Indian as an Inventor," in Kroeber and Waterman (eds.), *Sourcebook in Anthropology*, 494, 501.

[133] Safford, "Narcotic Plants and Stimulants of the Ancient Americans," *Annual Report of the Board of Regents of the Smithsonian Institution for the Year Ending June 30, 1916*, 396; Heizer, "The Use of the Enema among the Aboriginal American Indians," *Ciba Symposia*, Vol. V, No. 11 (February, 1944), 1686–93.

[134] La Vega, *The Incas*, 374, note.

[135] Emmart (ed.), *Badianus Manuscript*, 257, 264.

[136] Lowie, in Steward (ed.), *Handbook of South American Indians*, III, 51.

[137] Hallowell, "The Bulbed Enema Syringe in North America," *American Anthropologist*, N.S., Vol. XXXVII (1935), 708–10.

[138] Densmore, "Uses of Plants by the Chippewa Indians," *Forty-fourth Annual Report of the Bureau of American Ethnology, 1926–27*, 332.

[139] Speck, "Catawba Medicines and Curative Practices," *Publications of the Philadelphia Anthropological Society*, I, 192.

[140] Gilmore, "Uses of Plants by Indians of the Missouri River Region," *Thirty-third Annual Report of the Bureau of American Ethnology, 1911–12*, 90. He reported that the pulverized bark of the Kentucky coffee tree mixed with water was the enema substance and that it was watched for omens.

treated "bloody flux" by means of juice expressed from the boiled tips of cedar branches applied with "glisters" made from a bladder.[141]

Enema devices have been reported among the Creeks, Winnebagos, Menominees, Potawatomis,[142] Meskwakis, and many other tribes. Heizer published a map showing the location of thirty-one tribes which used enematic instruments.[143]

Fumigation or smoke treatment. Many western tribes treated respiratory, rheumatic, or other ills by fumigant substances such as cedar branches or sweet smelling herbs, which were heated or burned over live coals. Sometimes an infusion of herbs was poured over hot stones to form steam. Among the Navahos the latter treatment was used, with appropriate song and ritual, to treat headache, insomnia, eye trouble, and arthritis. Substances used included piñon, juniper, sage, and prickly pear cactus.[144]

The purple cone flower (*Echinacea angustifolia* DC), a universal panacea in the Plains area, was used in smoke treatment for headache. Red cedar was another widely used fumigant among Plains tribes. The Dakotas, Omahas, Poncas, and Pawnees burned the twigs and inhaled the smoke for head colds, while both patient and fumigant were enclosed in a blanket.[145] The Comanches attributed a "purifying effect" to juniper leaves.[146]

141 Charlevoix, *Journal*, I, 162. Toner seems to have been the only scholar who noted this testimony. *Address, Rocky Mountain Medical Association*, 88–89. Lahontan reported that the Algonquins affirmed "Glysters are only proper for the *Europeans*," although "they sometimes make use of them, when the *French* resort to their villages." Lahontan, *New Voyages*, II, 470.

142 Smith, *Potawatomi Ethnobotany*, 34.

143 Robert F. Heizer, "The Use of the Enema among the Aboriginal American Indians," *Ciba Symposia*, Vol. V, No. 11 (February, 1944), 1693.

144 Leland C. Wyman and Flora L. Bailey, "Two Examples of Navajo Physiotherapy," *American Anthropologist*, N.S., Vol. XLVI, No. 3 (July–September, 1944), 329–37.

145 Gilmore, "Uses of Plants by Indians of the Missouri River Region," *Thirty-third Annual Report of the Bureau of American Ethnology, 1911–12*, 63–64, 131.

146 G. A. Carlson and V. H. Jones, "Some Notes on Uses of Plants by the Comanche Indians," *Papers of the Michigan Academy of Sciences, Arts and Letters*, Vol. XXV (1939), 522.

The Creeks used cedar fumes for cramps in the neck muscles.[147]

To revive unconscious persons, the Meskwakis made smoke from several prairie plants, including a species of goldenrod (*Solidago ulmifolia* Muhl.). The Flambeaus spread pulverized flowers of pearly everlasting (*Anaphalis margaritacea* L.) over live coals to aid a patient stricken by paralysis. The Pillager Ojibwas inhaled the smoke from dried flowers of Philadelphia fleabane (*Erigeron philadelphicus*) to relieve a head cold.[148]

Massage. The ancient Incas massaged with ointments of sea algae and valerian leaves.[149] Spruce reported a century ago that in the Peruvian Andes massage was the first curative operation in all sickness. A gum resin was chewed and rubbed around the navel and the course of the colon. In his opinion the massage treatment sometimes had an excellent effect in lumbago and rheumatic ills.[150] Aztecs injured in falls entered the sweat bath, reported Sahagún, where "they manipulate him, they massage him."[151]

Massage was an important healing procedure among the Cherokees, who used it to relieve painful menstruation, sprains, and similar conditions, as well as for less valid purposes in swellings and snakebite. Before applying massage, the medicine man warmed his hands over live coals, then rubbed the affected part in circular motion with the right hand, most of the pressure being applied with the palm.[152]

The Pawnees treated colic by rubbing the abdomen with an ointment made from buffalo fat and the pulverized seeds of the black rattlepod (*Baptisia bracteata* Ell.).[153] Hrdlička reported that the Pimas and Maricopas frequently used massage on those

[147] Swanton, "Religious Beliefs and Medical Practices of the Creek Indians," *Forty-second Annual Report of the Bureau of American Ethnology, 1924–25,* 644.

[148] Smith, *Meskwaki Ethnobotany,* 217–18; *Ojibwe Ethnobotany,* 362–64.

[149] Helmuth Böttcher, *Wonder Drugs, A History of Antibiotics,* 84.

[150] *Notes of a Botanist,* II, 446.

[151] *Things of New Spain,* Book XI, 191.

[152] Mooney and Olbrechts, *Swimmer Manuscript,* 62.

[153] Gilmore, "Uses of Plants by Indians of the Missouri River Region," *Thirty-third Annual Report of the Bureau of American Ethnology, 1911–12,* 90.

who were sick, especially to alleviate localized pain. It was used in uterine pains, on the abdomen, together with a dry poultice of warm earth. He described an incident among the Pimas, in which a mixed-blood schoolgirl had a hysteric spell, whereupon other girls ran to her, rubbed her all over, and kneaded her stomach. Massage was also used by the Yumas and the Zuñis,[154] and was one of the means employed in the Navaho "repairing ceremony" for hysteric catalepsy.[155]

Massage was sometimes used with ointments to relieve pains of rheumatism and related afflictions.[156] It was also used in many tribes to relieve labor pains, to correct malposition of the fetus, and to aid in expulsion of the fetus.[157]

Psychic treatment. It is generally agreed that psychic disturbances were rare among Indians. Sagard, in the seventeenth century, was convinced that the Indian way of life was conducive to serenity and the avoidance of the tensions which plagued whites:

> But what also helps them much to keep in health [he wrote] is the harmony that prevails among them. They have no law-suits and take little pains to acquire the goods of this life, for which we Christians torment ourselves so much, and for our excessive and insatiable greed in acquiring them we are justly and with reason reproved by their quiet life and tranquil dispositions.[158]

Physical ills, however, were sometimes treated by methods which might today be called psychotherapeutic. The importance among the Iroquoian tribes (including the Huron and Cherokee

154 *Physiological and Medical Observations*, 241, 246, 248–49.

155 Wyman and Bailey, "Two Examples of Navajo Physiotherapy," *American Anthropologist*, N.S., Vol. XLVI, No. 3 (July–September, 1944), 336–37.

156 Lawson, *History of North Carolina*, 132; Zeisberger, "History of the North American Indians," *Ohio Archaeological and Historical Quarterly*, Vol. XIX, Nos. 1–2 (January and April, 1910), 53.

157 George J. Engelmann, *Labor Among Primitive Peoples*, 176ff.; Melvin R. Gilmore, "Notes on Gynecology and Obstetrics of the Arikara Tribe," *Papers Michigan Academy of Science, Arts and Letters*, Vol. XIV (1930), 73.

158 *Long Journey to the Country of the Hurons*, 192.

members of that linguistic group) of dream diagnosis and wish fulfillment has been touched upon.[159] According to their theory, disease could be caused by unfulfilled dreams or desires, and cure would follow the acting out of the dreams or the satisfaction of their desires.[160]

The opinions of some writers have also been cited that successful cures of the medicine men may have been partly the result of simple faith and community participation in the healing rites. "Whereas the shaman's methods may have little or negative virtue from the direct physiological standpoint," Spencer Rogers has declared, "they may be of some value on the patient's mind."[161] The symbolic value of the shaman's presence, his probing for dreams or taboo violations, leading to relief by confession, even the production of a tangible disease-causing object (see pp. 16–17), have all been thought to be aids in easing the patient's mind and creating the emotional basis for recovery. The involved curing ceremonial of the Navahos, it has been observed, "has a powerful appeal to the emotions. From the very moment the plan to have it is conceived, suggestion goes to work on the patient and gradually builds in force."[162] It was perhaps for this reason, as Driver has reported, that Dr. Thomas Noble, a white physician among the Navahos and Hopis in the 1940's:

> ... never took a case without first obtaining the approval of a local medicine man, who engaged in his curative "chants" both before and after the operation. This surgeon believed that the patient's chances of recovery were greater if Indian curing rites were retained. Since that time, physicians employed by our Federal Government in Indian health pro-

[159] See pp. 14, 20–22, 86–87, herein.

[160] Anthony F. C. Wallace, "Psychoanalysis among the Iroquois of New York State," in Harold E. Driver (ed.), *The Americas on the Eve of the Discovery*, 69–79.

[161] "The Methods, Results, and Values of Shamanistic Therapy," *Ciba Symposia*, Vol. IV, No. 1 (April, 1942), 1215–24.

[162] Wyman and Bailey, "Two Examples of Navajo Physiotherapy," *American Anthropologist*, N.S., Vol. XLVI, No. 3 (July–September, 1944), 334–35. citing A. H. and D. C. Leighton, "Elements of Psychotherapy in Navaho Religion," *Psychiatry*, Vol. IV (1941), 521.

grams have joined forces with the local medicine-men in the belief that treatment by the latter has psychotherapeutic value and can actually contribute to the saving of lives.[163]

In the eighteenth century, Charlevoix remarked: "what proves the power of imagination over men is, that these physicians with all their absurdities cure to the full as often as our own."[164] Snyderman relates that among the modern Senecas the belief in the power of the medicine to heal was and still is positively related to the actual cure, and he quotes an Indian as saying "people had faith in the medicine, and so the medicine worked." He provided an example in which this belief seemed to be verified in the case of an Indian apparently suffering from a severe neurotic disturbance.[165]

Speck mentioned that the Penobscots, in seeking to cure hiccough, would distract the sufferer's mind by a sudden question which would engage his attention.[166] Smith mentioned use of the "power of suggestion" in midwestern tribes. The Potawatomi medicine man, in treating a patient, would sing repeatedly that he was getting better and that the medicine man would see that he recovered. "He thus builds up faith in his patient," Smith commented, "and faith in the efficacy of his medicine. Confidence is half the battle with them as it is with the white patient." A similar procedure was reported by Smith among the Meskwakis.[167]

Weston LaBarre has examined the role of peyotism and confession in primitive psychotherapy. "The nearly pan-American distribution of the trait of confession," he writes, "leaves little doubt that it is a genuinely aboriginal psychotherapeutic technique." "The group ritual," he remarks, "aided by a narcotic, explains the growth of the peyote cult, which in the past seventy-

---

[163] Harold E. Driver, *Indians of North America*, 486.

[164] Charlevoix, *Journal*, I, 165.

[165] George P. Snyderman, "The Case of Daniel P.: An Example of Seneca Healing," *Journal of the Washington Academy of Sciences*, Vol. XXXIX, No. 7 (July 15, 1949), 217–20.

[166] "Medicine Practices of the Northeastern Algonquians," *Proceedings XIXth International Congress of Americanists*, 313.

[167] *Potawatomi Ethnobotany*, 36, 47; *Meskwaki Ethnobotany*, 192.

five years has spread to most tribes. Dreams or visions often result from the use of the peyote, and thus is continued an ancient Indian trait, the seeking of omens, cures, prognostications, and solutions to problems by these means."[168]

Surgery and anatomy. "What knowledge they have in Anatomy, I cannot tell," wrote Lawson, "neither did I ever see them employ themselves therein, unless as I told you before, when they make the Skeletons of their Kings and great Men's Bones."[169] Catesby held that *"Indians* are wholly ignorant in Anatomy, and their Knowledge of Surgery is very superficial."[170]

Dr. Major asserted that "we have no evidence of post mortem examinations among the Indians."[171] Dr. Toner maintained, however, that Indians learned much about the functions of vital organs from analogy with the animals they killed and thus understood that the lungs were organs of respiration, that the heart "is necessary for the circulation of the blood," and that a suppression of the action of the kidneys would be fatal to life.[172]

Zeisberger reported that Indian doctors sometimes felt the patient's pulse.[173] Hunter claimed that Indians were aware that respiration and the circulation of the blood were essential to life and that the first was performed by the lungs and the latter through the heart and blood vessels, though they did not understand the manner in which these organs functioned. From analogy with animals they knew which organs were vital and understood that the brain was the organ of thought and that it was essential to life.[174]

[168] "Primitive Psychotherapy in Native American Cultures: Peyotism and Confession," *Journal of Abnormal and Social Psychology*, Vol. XLII, No. 3 (July, 1947), 307.

[169] Lawson, *History of North Carolina*, 237.

[170] Catesby, *Natural History*, I, xv.

[171] "Aboriginal American Medicine North of Mexico," *Annals of Medical History*, N.S., Vol. X, No. 6 (November, 1938), 544.

[172] *Address, Rocky Mountain Medical Association*, 87.

[173] "History of the North American Indians," *Ohio Archaeological and Historical Quarterly*, Vol. XIX, Nos. 1–2 (January and April, 1910), 26.

[174] Hunter, *Manners and Customs*, 396.

One of the commonest kinds of minor surgery observed among the Indians was scarification; according to Lawson it was resorted to "almost in all Distempers." Their chief instruments for this purpose were rattlesnake fangs, from which the poison had been removed.[175] Hrdlička reported that scarification was performed by the San Carlos Apaches for any sharp or persistent pain. They would scarify any part of the body, even the temple, using a sharp object, such as a splinter of glass.[176] Speck reported scarification instruments in use among the northeastern Algonquians, being used to relieve pain, from the principle of counterirritant effect, and also from the idea of making an exit for the pain.[177]

Indians "are wholly strangers to Amputation," Lawson wrote, yet he described their amputation of a portion of the feet of captives, and the grafting of skin over the exposed end, which then healed.[178] An Ojibwa myth has been reported which involved grafting a detached scalp.[179] On the western Plains, fingers were sometimes amputated as punishment or to display grief,[180] and Bourke exhibited a Cheyenne necklace made of human fingers.[181]

John Long reported in 1788 the surgical repair of torn ears by the Ojibwas near Lake Nipigon. When ears were accidentally torn, "they cut them smooth with a knife, and sew the parts together with a needle and deer's sinews, and after sweating in a stove, resume their usual cheerfulness."[182] North American In-

---

175 Lawson, *History of North Carolina*, 237–38.

176 Hrdlička, *Physiological and Medical Observations*, 233. In early times, Indians incised the skin with sharp pieces of flint or obsidian. See *bleeding, supra.*

177 "Medicine Practices of the Northeastern Algonquians," *Proceedings XIXth International Congress of Americanists*, 306, 311-12.

178 Lawson, *History of North Carolina*, 210, 234.

179 Andrews, "The Aboriginal Physicians of Michigan," *Contributions to Medical Research Dedicated to Victor Clarence Vaughan*, 45–46.

180 Maximilian of Wied, *Travels in the Interior of North America, 1832–1834* (Part II), Vol. XXIII in Thwaites (ed.), *Early Western Travels*, 140; Edwin Thompson Denig, *Five Indian Tribes of the Upper Missouri*, 157.

181 "The Medicine-Men of the Apache," *Ninth Annual Report of the Bureau of American Ethnology, 1887–88*, illustration.

182 *John Long's Journal, 1768–1782.* Vol. II in Thwaites (ed.), *Early Western Travels*, 146.

dians used sutures of human hair,[183] deer tendons, and vegetable fibers, especially basswood.[184] South American Indians used a forerunner of modern skin clips by allowing leaf cutting ants to pinch the edges of a wound together, then twisting off their heads. Some Indians tried irrigated punctures on complicated wounds, others cauterized, some used wicks of twisted cloth or bark fibers as drains. Peruvians knew skin-flap techniques and used artificial limbs. Laced bark corsets were sometimes used for spinal and abdominal ailments.[185]

The most spectacular surgery performed in pre-Columbian America was trephination (skull surgery), of which the most abundant evidence has been found in Peru, though trephined skulls have been found in several parts of the United States and Canada.[186] Dr. Brooks believed that in the operation Indians of the Andes employed several anesthetic drugs, including cocaine and peyote.[187] Adams believed that the operation was performed in accordance with the surgical principle of fracture decompression, though perhaps with a view to releasing evil spirits.[188] The

[183] Aztecs sutured lip wounds with human hair. Bancroft, *The Native Races*, II, 599.

[184] Pitcher, in Henry Rowe Schoolcraft, *Historical and Statistical Information Respecting the History, Condition and Prospects of the Indian Tribes of the United States*, IV, 513.

[185] Adams, "Aboriginal American Medicine and Surgery," *Proceedings of the Indiana Academy of Science*, Vol. LXI (1951), 51–52.

[186] Aleš Hrdlička, "Trepanation Among Prehistoric People, Especially in America," *Ciba Symposia*, Vol. I, No. 6 (September, 1939), 166–69. It was formerly believed that the Indians were the first to practice trephination. When Oliver Wendell Holmes saw a painting of the seventeenth-century New England physician, John Clarke, in which that personage was holding a trephine in his hand, he snorted that no such instrument was known in white medicine until many years after Clarke's death. Holmes, *Collected Works*, IX, 326–27. Dr. Brooks maintained (*infra*) that Indians practiced this operation ages before the white man or even the Egyptians had advanced beyond the most primitive methods of medical or surgical procedure. According to Hrdlička, however, this operation was practiced in neolithic times in Europe, North Africa, and parts of Asia.

[187] "The Medicine of the American Indian," *Journal of Laboratory and Clinical Medicine*, Vol. XIX, No. 1 (October, 1933), 6–7.

[188] "Aboriginal American Medicine and Surgery," *Proceedings of the Indiana Academy of Science*, Vol. LXI (1952), 51–52.

reasons for trephination by primitive people have been suggested as (1) to permit the entry or projection of something into the body of the patient, (2) to permit the escape of, or to take from the body, something, or (3) to combat sorcery.[189]

Asepsis in surgery. Nordenskjöld held that "it is probable that the Indians, before it was known in the Old World, understood the application of aseptics, seeing that certain tribes dress their wounds with boiled water, without having learned this from the whites."[190] Bossu reported that the Choctaws used roots "in a solution with which the wound is bathed to help prevent gangrene."[191] When an Indian of the Illinois tribe was wounded by shot or arrow, an eighteenth-century report by Pierre de Liette declared, "they pour into him a quantity of warm water, in which they have diluted some of their drugs."[192]

The English trader, John Long, while with the Ojibwas near present Nipigon, Ontario, in 1778, described the use of aseptic techniques in tattooing operations:

[after a sweat bath, the candidate] Being extended on his back, the chief draws the figure he intends to make with a pointed stick, dipped in water in which gunpowder has been dissolved; after which, with ten needles dipped in vermilion, and fixed in a small wooden frame, he pricks the delineated parts, and where the bolder outlines appear, he incises the flesh with a gun flint; the vacant spaces, those not marked with vermilion, are rubbed with gunpowder, which

189 E. G. Wakefield and Samuel G. Dellinger, "Possible Reasons for Trephining the Skull in the Past," *Ciba Symposia*, Vol. I, No. 6 (September, 1939), 166–69. It has been suggested that these operations were performed to remove shattered bits of bone pressing against the brain as a result of head injuries, or to relieve paralytic conditions, epileptic fits, or unconsciousness. Jürgen Thorwald, *Science and Secrets of Early Medicine*, 302.

190 Nordenskjöld, in Kroeber and Waterman (eds.), *Source Book in Anthropology*, 494.

191 Bossu, *Travels*, 168.

192 Vernon W. Kinietz, *Indians of the Western Great Lakes*, 220.

produce the variety of red and blue; the wounds are then seared with punk wood, to prevent them from festering.

This operation, which is performed at intervals, lasts two or three days. Every morning the parts are washed with cold water, in which is infused a herb called Pockqueesegan.[193]

Maximilian of Wied, however, reported unhygienic methods among Blackfoot doctors. The practice of taking water into their mouths and spitting it over wounds, and the failure to wash or cleanse wounds, drew his criticism.[194] That such was not the prevailing practice, however, seems evident.

A once-important antiseptic drug obtained from the South American Indians is balsam of Peru (USP 1820——) which is obtained from *Myroxylon pereirae*, a tree of Central America and the west coast of South America. This substance has been used in medicine as a local irritant and parasiticide in certain skin diseases, and for its antiseptic and vulnerary properties has been used externally as an ointment on wounds.[195]

Six varieties of *Myroxylon* grow in Latin America, and several related species were mentioned by the Inca herbalist Ayala as means to combat fever and infections. According to his report, the balsam was prepared from the oil of the ground kernels of the fruit, which were said to possess the same curative value as the resin. Böttcher asserted that "it was capable of destroying the bacteria commonly encountered in wounds and thus protected the body from suppuration, scabies, eczema and inflammatory skin reactions."[196]

Before 1628, Father Espinosa mentioned the extraction of the resin of this tree by natives and declared that its fumes cured chills and colds in the head, while the resin mixed with oil, or the oil from the seeds, was used to cure wounds and sores. Bernard

---

[193] *John Long's Journal*, Vol. II in Thwaites (ed.), *Early Western Travels*, 84–85.

[194] *Travels in the Interior of North America, 1832–1834* (Part II), Vol. XXIII in Thwaites (ed.), *Early Western Travels*, 119–20.

[195] Claus, *Pharmacognosy*, 419–20; Lloyd, *Origin and History*, 26–27.

[196] Böttcher, *Wonder Drugs*, 84–85.

Cobo reported in 1653 that the pounded leaves were also used to heal fresh wounds.[197]

Surgical and medical inventions. A syringe was used by some tribes for cleansing wounds and injecting medicine into them. Sahagún reported that Aztecs used a syringe to inject remedies for dysuria or "venereal" disease.[198] Dr. Pitcher reported that Michigan Indians cleaned wounds with vegetable decoctions introduced by bladder and quill.[199] Such a syringe was reported among the Potawatomis by Smith and among the Ojibwas by Densmore.[200] Indians may have preceded Europeans in the use of this device.[201]

Stretchers or litters for carrying the sick or wounded have been described among the forest tribes by Pitcher,[202] and among the Lower California Indians by Baegert.[203]

Hospitals. According to Bancroft, hospitals were maintained in ancient Mexico:

> For severe cases, the expenses of treating which could not be borne except by the wealthy classes, hospitals were established by the government in all the larger cities, endowed with ample revenues, where patients from the surrounding country were cared for by experienced doctors, surgeons, and nurses well versed in all the native healing arts.[204]

197 Haggis, "Fundamental Errors in the Early History of Cinchona," *Bulletin of the History of Medicine*, Vol. X, No. 3 (October, 1941), 429, 431.

198 Sahagún, *Things of New Spain*, Book XI, 154.

199 Pitcher, in Schoolcraft, *Indian Tribes*, IV, 513.

200 Smith, *Potawatomi Ethnobotany*, 34; Densmore, "Uses of Plants by the Chippewa Indians," *Forty-fourth Annual Report of the Bureau of American Ethnology, 1926–27*, 332.

201 It is claimed that such syringes were not used in Europe before the eighteenth century. Leslie G. Mathews, *History of Pharmacy in Britain*, 305ff.

202 Pitcher, in Schoolcraft, *Indian Tribes*, IV, 513.

203 Baegert, "An Account of the Aboriginal Inhabitants of the California Peninsula," tr. by Charles Rau. *Annual Report of the Smithsonian Institution, 1863–64*, 386.

204 Bancroft, *Native Races*, II, 596–97.

Treatment of Internal Ailments,
Relying Principally on Drugs

Boils, tumors, abscesses.[205] Interestingly, the treatment for these conditions was remarkably similar in widely separated tribes. Hunter declared:

> The Indians are not very liable to swellings, tumors or boils; when they do occur they are generally suffered to come to a crisis without any application to them; when very much inflamed, they apply cooling plaisters of bruised herbs, or fomenting warm poultices. When the colour of the parts changes and the collection of matter is evident, they make an incision, and continue the poultices to promote a discharge.[206]

Zeisberger reported that Indians applied a warm poultice of Indian cornmeal to boils, which were lanced when ripe.[207] Dr. Winder found that Canadian Indians generally allowed "tumors and abscesses" to suppurate without any application, but if they became inflamed and painful, plasters of bruised herbs or warm, fomenting poultices were used. If matter formed, an incision was made for its escape, and the poultices continued to promote discharge.[208] Among the Crows, a doctor might lance parts of the body. Sometimes sores were washed and a poultice applied with a special mixture.[209] The Kwakiutls drew out boils and swellings by applying to them a soft and slimy fungus called "rotten on the ground."[210] This treatment is allied to that reported by Lawson in the seventeenth century, by which an Indian cured a white

---

[205] Here, as elsewhere, we use the terminology of the period, as it is not our province to evaluate the diagnoses or to translate them into modern terms.

[206] Hunter, *Manners and Customs*, 399.

[207] Zeisberger, "History of the North American Indians," *Ohio Archaeological and Historical Quarterly*, Vol. XIX, Nos. 1–2 (January and April, 1910), 149.

[208] Winder, "On Indian Diseases and Remedies," *Boston Medical and Surgical Journal*, Vol. XXIV, No. 1 (February 4, 1846), 13.

[209] Robert H. Lowie, *The Crow Indians*, 63.

[210] Boas, "Current Beliefs of the Kwakiutl Indians," *Journal of American Folk-Lore*, Vol. XLV, No. 176 (April–June, 1932), 187.

planter of a leg ulcer with "the rotten, doated Grains of Indian Corn, beaten to a Powder and the soft Down growing on a Turkey's Rump."[211]

The Chickasaws had an unusual remedy for what they called the "burning ghost disease," in which "the feet swell up and big blisters develop upon them." The prescription for this was to take dirt from the top of an old grave and heat it in a pan until dry, then apply it to the sores.[212] The three preceding remedies indicate that some Indians may have unknowingly stumbled upon the secrets of the healing qualities of antibiotic substances which civilized man finally discovered in the mid-twentieth century.

Diabetes. As previously indicated, the unacculturated Indians are believed to have been free of this disease, but it does exist among some modern Indians. Not until the 1940's did scientists stumble upon an oral drug for this disease, which avoided some of the disadvantages of insulin.[213] It is of interest that Indians of British Columbia are reported to have used orally a plant product which has been found to be efficient in the prevention and treatment of diabetes. This became known some thirty years ago when a patient[214] was brought to a hospital in Prince Rupert for an operation and showed signs of diabetes. For several years he had kept in apparent good health by taking a remedy consisting of a hot-water infusion of the root bark of a spiny, prickly shrub called devil's club (*Fatsia horrida*), which was in common use among Indians of British Columbia. Experiments performed on rabbits which were given the substance orally showed that it reduced the blood sugar substantially without toxic effects.[215]

211 Lawson, *History of North Carolina*, 231. Also reported by Brickell; see p. 118, 293, herein.

212 Swanton, "Social and Religious Beliefs and Practices of the Chickasaw Indians," *Forty-fourth Annual Report of the Bureau of American Ethnology, 1926–27,* 268.

213 Elliott P. Joslin, *Diabetic Manual* (Philadelphia, Lea & Febiger, 1959), 28–41, 149–52.

214 The patient was reported to be an Indian, in the account of the case given by Weston A. Price, *Nutrition and Physical Degeneration*, 266.

215 R. C. Large and H. N. Brocklesby, "A Hypoglycaemic Substance from the

Albert B. Reagan listed a devil's club (*Echinopanax horridum* Smith) as a medicine used by the Hoh and Quileute Indians of the Olympic peninsula but did not give any details regarding its purpose or the mode of use.[216]

Dr. Frederick Banting, the discoverer of insulin, so greatly admired Indians that when he heard a report that the Indians had used sumac leaves in the successful treatment of diabetes, he experimented with several bushels of the leaves in an unsuccessful attempt to learn the secret of their reputed cure.[217]

Digestive disorders. The term "flux" or "bloody flux" is frequently met in early accounts; such is the vague label of the disease which caused the death of Father Marquette in 1675. It is not always possible to determine the identity of these disorders, but they are frequently understood to be dysentery, which was a common disease among Indians, and still is in many tribes, due to polluted drinking water.

Numerous dysentery remedies are noted among the Aztecs, including agave leaves, extracts of bladderwort, and fresh ground maize (*atole*, a panacea among them), which were dissolved in warm water and injected into the anus by a clyster.[218] Among many remedies for diarrhea, they used *copal* (a tree sap), pulverized and dissolved in water.[219]

Among the Hurons, Father Paul Le Jeune reported in 1637, "dysentery is cured by drinking the juice of leaves or branches of the cedar, which have been boiled. Father Buteaux said he saw a child recover very soon, after having taken this medicine."[220]

While he was among the Congarees, Lawson reported that "the Queen . . . had a young child, which was much afflicted with

---

Roots of the Devil's Club (*Fatsia Horrida*)," *The Canadian Medical Association Journal*, Vol. XXX, No. 1 (July, 1938), 32–35.

[216] "Plants Used by the Hoh and Quileute Indians," *Transactions of the Kansas Academy of Science*, Vol. XXXVII (1934), 65.

[217] Seale Harris, *Banting's Miracle*, 179.

[218] Emmart (ed.), *Badianus Manuscript*, 257, 264.

[219] Sahagún, *Things of New Spain*, Book XI, 187.

[220] Thwaites (ed.), *Jesuit Relations*, XII, 25.

the Cholic; for which distemper she infused a root in Water, which was held in a Gourd; this she took into her Mouth and spurted in into the Infant's, which gave it ease."[221]

In these disorders, Indian remedies and therapeutic methods were not uncommonly used by whites in combination with other substances such as milk not possessed by the Indians. When William Byrd's slaves were affected with dysentery in 1732, he instructed his overseer:

> To let them Blood immediately about 8 Ounces; the next day to give them a Dose of Indian Physic, and to repeat the Vomit again the Day following, unless the Symptoms abated. In the mean time, they shou'd eat nothing but Chicken Broth, and Poacht Eggs, and drink nothing but a Quarter of a Pint of Milk boil'd with a Quart of Water, and Medicated with a little Mullein Root, or that of the Prickly Pear, to restore the Mucus of the Bowels, and heal the Excoriation.[222]

Broth or gruel was frequently used by Indians on restricted diets due to digestive trouble. (See *Diet*). Cholera morbus, Hunter declared, was treated with steam baths and cathartics followed by copious intake of a gruel of wild rice and wild licorice tea. Fomentations were applied to the stomach. For certain unidentified bowel complaints, ashes and wood soot were used. For diarrhea, Hunter reported, the Indians would:

> ... puke, sweat, and give astringents: when long continuance has induced great debility, they give frequent and large draughts of bitter infusions. I have frequently known them to cure it by chewing the inner bark of the burr oak.[223]

In several tribes, earth or clay was used to remedy bowel disturbances. Eighteenth-century Illinois and Miami Indians swallowed pills of "green earth for the flux of the abdomen and the blood." Clay was sometimes used instead and so was the root of an unidentified fern. For "looseness of the bowels" they used

221 Lawson, *History of North Carolina*, 26.
222 Byrd, *History of the Dividing Line*, II, 81.
223 Hunter, *Manners and Customs*, 369, 400–402.

sumach leaves or the boiled root of bean trefoil (*Menyanthes trifoliata*).[224]

The Indian turnip or Jack-in-the-pulpit (*Arisaema triphyllum*) was used for bowel complaints among the Delawares,[225] while the American ipecac, or Indian physic (*Euphorbia* species, *et al.*), has been used by other tribes and was a favorite of William Byrd.[226] Brickell recommended it as an effective remedy for the "Cholera-Morbus."[227] It was frequently used as an emetic.[228]

Rappahannocks in this century steeped blackberry runners for dyspepsia and the roots or berries for diarrhea. The root bark of dogwood was also a diarrhea remedy, while the dried bark of sweet gum, often mixed with red-oak bark, was used against dysentery.[229] Blackberry roots were used against dysentery by the Oneidas.[230]

For cramps in the bowels and bloody stool, the Cheyennes drank a tea of the leaves and stems of *Ambrosia psilostachya*. An infusion of the root of sweet flag (*Acorus calamus*) boiled in water was drunk for "pain in the bowels."[231] The sand puff (*Abronia fragrans*) was a Ute remedy for stomach and bowel trouble.[232] The Oglala Sioux used a decoction of the leaves of

224 Kinietz, *Indians of the Western Great Lakes*, 223–24.

225 Loskiel, *Mission of the United Brethren*, I, 116; Mahr, "Semantic Analysis of Eighteenth-Century Delaware Indian Names for Medicinal Plants," *Ethnohistory*, Vol. II, No. 1 (Winter, 1955), 13.

226 *History of the Dividing Line*, II, 81, 139. The terms ipecac and Indian physic have been applied to several different species, and Byrd's plant may have been *Gillenia trifoliata*. See pp. 319–21, 323–24, herein.

227 *Natural History*, 47.

228 Henkel, *American Root Drugs*, 42–43.

229 Speck, *Rappahannock Herbals*, 29.

230 Letter from James Anderson, August 4, 1804: "Last summer, when I was near the settlement of the Oneida-Indians (in the state of New-York), the dysentery prevailed much, and carried off some of the white inhabitants, who applied to the Indians for a remedy. They directed them to drink a decoction of the roots of Blackberry-bushes (Rubus occidentalis, Editor) which they did, after which not one died. All who used it agreed, that it is a safe, sure, and speedy cure." *Philadelphia Medical and Surgical Journal*, Vol. I, Pt. I (1805), 129–30.

231 Grinnell, "Some Cheyenne Plant Medicines," *American Anthropologist*, N.S., Vol. VII, No. 1 (January–March, 1905), 39, 42.

232 Chamberlin, "Some Plant Names of the Ute Indians," *American Anthropologist*, N.S., Vol. XI, No. 1 (January–March, 1909), 32.

Parosela aurea for colic and dysentery.[233] In acute indigestion the Papagos boiled red earth taken from beneath the fire, strained it, added a little salt, and gave it as a drink at mealtime, in lieu of food.[234]

Peruvian Indians used a type of clay against dysentery,[235] and another South American remedy, simaruba, which was later admitted to the pharmacopeia, was used by Bernard Romans in 1775 to cure "haemorrhoidal flux."[236]

Dropsy. Although early reports claim that dropsy was absent or rare among many tribes, there are scattered reports of remedies for it. The Illinois-Miamis swallowed a decoction made of sumach leaves, roots, and berries, together with roots of an unidentified plant. An observer remarked that "the dropsical ones find themselves very well from it."[237]

According to Hunter, the Indians were more subject to this disease following the introduction of "ardent spirits among them." Moreover, they had more remedies for it than for any other disease. Chief among these was an infusion of an unidentified "white flowering vine," but they also used a mixed decoction of wild cherry bark, sumach roots and leaves, black haw, sourwood leaves, and "a mineral substance collected from the banks of rivers." Several other remedies were also named.[238]

Earache. The ancient Mayas used Cayenne pepper (*Capsicum annuum* L.), often in combinations, for earache and other ills.[239]

Poplar or aspen buds stewed in bear fat yielded an aromatic salve used in earache and for other purposes among the Ojibwas.[240]

233 Gilmore, "Uses of Plants by Indians of the Missouri River Region," *Thirty-third Annual Report of the Bureau of American Ethnology, 1911–12*, 94.

234 Hrdlička, *Physiological and Medical Observations*, 241–42.

235 Böttcher, *Wonder Drugs*, 86.

236 Romans, *Concise Natural History*, 169.

237 Kinietz, *Indians of the Western Great Lakes*, 222.

238 Hunter, *Manners and Customs*, 401.

239 Roys, *Ethno-Botany of the Maya*, 229.

240 Smith, *Ojibwe Ethnobotany*, 352.

Rappahannock, Mohegan, and Malecite Indians blew tobacco smoke in the ear to stop earache,[241] a remedy which was once recommended by John Wesley.[242]

Epilepsy. This disease was not reported among early Indians, but there is a report of an Indian cure of a white patient suffering from it. According to Charlevoix:

A French soldier . . . in Acadia, was seized with the Epilepsy, and the fits were become almost daily and extremely violent: an Indian woman who happened to be present at one of his fits, made him two boluses of a pulverized root, the name of which she did not disclose, and desired that one might be given him at his next fit, told him that he would sweat much, and that he would have large evacuations both by vomiting and by stool, and added, that if the first bolus did not entirely cure him, the second certainly would: the thing happened as she had foretold; the patient had, indeed, a second fit, but this was his last. He from that day enjoyed a perfect state of health.[243]

For paralysis, of whatever origin, some South American Indians used the mild shock of the electric eel.[244]

Eye troubles. The Incas used a plant called *matecclu,* of the *Umbellifera* family, to treat eye diseases. The leaves were chewed and the paste applied. Garcilaso de la Vega maintained from personal observation that it was effective.[245] Some Brazilian Indians used the juice of red pepper (*Capsicum* species) for eye pains.[246]

---

241 Speck, *Rappahannock Herbals,* 29; Tantaquidgeon, "Mohegan Medicinal Practices, Weather-Lore, and Superstition," *Forty-third Annual Report of the Bureau of American Ethnology, 1925–26,* 264; Speck, "Medicine Practices of the Northeastern Algonquians," *Proceedings XIXth International Congress of Americanists,* 310.

242 *Primitive Physic,* 61.

243 *Journal,* I, 161.

244 Humboldt, *Personal Narrative,* II, 119.

245 *The Incas,* 143, 375, ed. note.

246 Levi–Strauss, in Steward (ed.), *Handbook of South American Indians,* VI, 485.

The Aztecs had numerous eye remedies. One was the chopped root of *Cicimatic* (*Canavalia villosa* Bent.) which was "required by one who suffers an eye ailment . . . has a fleshy growth over the eyes, who is about to become blind from flesh on the eyes. It is dropped in the eyes."[247] For ordinary inflammation, eye drops were made from several plants, including the *Bocconia arborea*.[248] One eye remedy was made of white incense and several animal substances.[249]

Lawson declared that he saw only one blind man among the Indians, but he could not learn the cause of the condition. Moreover, he asserted:

> No people have better Eyes, or see better in the Night or Day than the Indians. Some alledge that the Smoke of the Pitch-Pine which they chiefly burn, does both preserve and strengthen their Eyes.[250]

Elsewhere it has been written that Indians frequently suffered from ophthalmia, an inflammatory affliction precisely caused by their exposure to smoke from cooking fires in confined dwelling places.[251] The existence of a number of Indian eye remedies suggests that this is so. A French observer listed five eye remedies used by early Illinois-Miami Indians. The root of "wild chervil" (believed to be sweet cicely) was steeped in water and the liquid applied for "ills of the eyes." For "soreness of the eyes," they prescribed boiled "leaf of Litre" (unidentified) or boiled bark of white oak. For "films on the eyes," they devised "a shell of all sorts of river shell fish, burned and pulverized, blown in the eye."[252]

A remedy for sore eyes which was widely used by Indians and pioneers was a watery infusion of the roots of the goldenseal

247 Sahagún, *Things of New Spain*, Book XI, 184.

248 *Ibid.*, 148, 154.

249 Emmart (ed.), *Badianus Manuscript*, 217.

250 Lawson, *History of North Carolina*, 183.

251 W. M. Krogman wrote: "in the tipi-dwellers of the Plains area, conjunctival disorders were traceable to smoke-filled lodges." "Medical Practices and Diseases of the Aboriginal American Indians," *Ciba Symposia*, Vol. I, No. 1 (April, 1939), 16.

252 Kinietz, *Indians of the Western Great Lakes*, 223–24.

The coca plant (*Erythroxylon coca* Lamarck), USP 1882–1916. The divine plant of the Incas, used as a stimulant and anodyne, and possibly as an anesthetic in trephination. Sachets of coca leaves have been found in ancient Peruvian burials. The alkaloid cocaine (USP 1905–55, NF 1955——) was isolated from this plant in 1860, and first used for local anesthesia by Carl Koller in 1884.

Tlatoc Xochtli.

Corporis adustio.

Corporis nostri pars adusta adimitur succo ex Nochli. Teamoxtli, Amoxtli, Tehmill. hecapahtli, Texiyell huitzquihtl. quo perungenda erit & confricanda melle & ovi vitello.

Prickly pear, or nopal (*Opuntia tuna* Mill). From the *Badianus Manuscript*, an Aztec herbal of 1552. The prescription is in Latin, the plant names in Nahuatl. Nopal juice and the juice of several other plants, together with honey and egg yolk, are recommended as an ointment for burns.

Azticazth

Sanguinaria herba.

anguinis e naribus fluxum urticarum succus cum sale itarum in lotio & lacte infusus naribus supprimit.

Nettle, "Sanguinaria herba" (blood herb), *Urtica* species. From the *Badianus Manuscript*, an Aztec herbal of 1552. The **Latin** text asserts that blood flowing from the nose can be stopped by pouring the juice of nettles, ground with salt in urine and milk, into the nostrils.

"Jimson weed" (*Datura meteloides* D. C.). The seeds were used to induce visions, for poultices applied to burns and inflammations, and for other purposes. Seeds have been found in pre-Columbian caves.

Witch hazel (*Hamamelis virginiana* L.). Leaves official, USP, 1882–1916; distilled extract, NF since 1926. The bark and twigs have also been used for astringent and hemostatic purposes. Medicinal use of this plant by the Mohawks was mentioned by Dr. Cadwallader Colden in 1744.

Sweet gum (*Liquidambar styraciflua* L.), also called copal and American storax. The balsam from the trunk of this tree was used by Indians for a variety of ills, and became official in the USP in 1926. It has been used as a stimulant, expectorant, and antiseptic.

Flowering dogwood (*Cornus florida* L.), USP 1820–94, NF 1916–36, American Indian febrifuge.

May apple (*Podophyllum peltatum* L.), USP 1820–1942, 1955——; NF
1942–55. American Indian purgative.

Sassafras (*Sassafras albidum* [Nutt.] Nees), USP 1820–1926 (the root bark). An Indian remedy adopted by whites as a panacea, it became an important article of early colonial commerce. Generations of rural Americans took sassafras tea as a "spring tonic" to "purify the blood."

(*Hydrastic canadensis* L.).[253] The Comanches prescribed three plants for the treatment of "sore eyes." Eyes were sometimes bathed with a decoction of the boiled root of Osage orange (*Maclura pomifera*). Willow stems were burned and the ashes used, or the sap of prickly poppy (*Argemone intermedia*) was applied to the eyes.[254] Hunter, in the 1820's, reported an Indian eyewash made from young sassafras sprouts.[255] The Rappahannocks treated sore eyes in children by applying a wash of warm milk from a woman's breast. This was also used to cure granulated lids or running eyes.[256]

Fevers. Indian fever treatment commonly included rest, sweating, purgation, and a liquid diet or no food at all, in addition to the antifever medicines.[257] "In fevers," reported Charlevoix, "they use cooling lotions with decoctions of herbs, and by this means prevent inflammations and deliriousness."[258]

Of western tribes, Hunter observed:

In their treatment of fevers, they puke the patient at first and then while it is on, give him freely of sweating teas, and warm drinks; and when the fever is perfectly off and at no other time, they give bitters, and other tonic medicines in considerable quantities to prevent its return.[259]

Hunter appears to be describing malaria, once known as intermittent fever. The lack of precise differentiation between different types of fevers, a common shortcoming in early accounts, is a source of difficulty to a historian. For drugs used in fevers, see *febrifuges.*

253 See pp. 311–12, herein.

254 Carlson and Jones, "Some Notes on Uses of Plants by the Comanche Indians," *Papers of the Michigan Academy of Sciences, Arts and Letters,* Vol. XXV (1939), 533.

255 Hunter, *Manners and Customs,* 387.

256 Speck, *Rappahannock Herbals,* 40.

257 Major, "Aboriginal American Medicine North of Mexico," *Annals of Medical History,* N.S., Vol. X, No. 6 (November, 1938), 545.

258 *Journal,* I, 162.

259 Hunter, *Manners and Customs,* 400.

Gout. Dr. Edwin James declared that gout was unknown among western tribes.[260] Lahontan and other early writers said that it did not exist among eastern Indians. "I have heard of two or three cases of the GOUT among the Indians," Dr. Benjamin Rush told the American Philosophical Society, "but it was only among those who had learned the use of rum from the white people."[261] Nevertheless, some unknown eastern Indian was reported to have a remedy for the disease, which was communicated to Benjamin Franklin, a sufferer from gout, by Benjamin Kent of Boston:

> We have lately by an Indian discovered a small wilderness Root wch [*sic*] steeped in madira [Madeira] Wine has not fail'd on many tryals to carry off any fit of the Gout in a very few hours time [.] This information I have from those persons of the very best credit who have experienced it & what is very wonderfull a couple of Glasses of this wine will make the Part affected being well wraped [*sic*] up to sweat profusely while all other parts of the body are nowise affected.[262]

Gout must have been more prevalent among the sedentary and pulque-drinking Aztecs, since prescriptions for it are strewn through the writings of Sahagún and in the *Badianus Manuscript.* Tobacco leaves, pounded, ground, and mixed with lime, were applied to the affected parts. The leaves of *yauhtli* and *tecomaxochitl* were among the other remedies.[263]

Respiratory ailments. "They bleed in pleurisy," wrote Hunter, "fill skins with hot ashes and apply them over the pained parts, and sweat most violently. Whenever the patient begins to sweat freely, the hard breathing and pain in the side abate, and when the discharge of mucus from the mouth commences, they say he

260 *Account of an Expedition,* Vol. XV in Thwaites (ed.), *Early Western Travels,* 43.

261 *Medicine Among the Indians,* 118.

262 Letter dated January 19, 1766, MS, photoduplicate provided by the American Philosophical Society.

263 Sahagún, *Things of New Spain,* Book XI, 146.

is out of danger." Consumption (an old name for tuberculosis) was rare among the Indians, Hunter reported, but when it occurred cure was sought by warm infusions of Indian physic aided by large draughts of warm water and herb teas and by the sweat bath. "The cough root or Indian balsam" was also a valuable remedy to them. Local applications were used for breast pain, and the patient abstained from animal foods, cornmeal gruel being the main nourishment.[264]

In "consumption" the Winnebago and Dakota Indians used skunk cabbage (*q.v.*) as an expectorant.[265] The Rappahannocks treated asthma with a steeped infusion of red cedar berries (*Juniperus virginiana*) and wild ginger (*Asarum canadense*).[266]

The use of smoke smudges, or fumigation treatment (*q.v.*), through the burning of various herbs, evergreen branches, etc., for the relief of colds, catarrh, and various respiratory ills has been reported in numerous tribes, including the Fox, Potawatomis, and Ojibwas by Smith, and the Plains tribes by Gilmore.

Rheumatism, arthritis, and related disorders. Observers agree that these were common complaints among the Indians. Their treatment of such conditions was perhaps more rational than that in use among pioneer whites. John Wesley's prescription for rheumatism was to "wear washed wool of fine horse hair under the feet."[267] Iowa Germans some sixty years ago advised that in cases of rheumatism, "every evening, when you take off your shoes, place them upside down so that the heels and the soles will be up and the foot-opening down."[268]

The frequency of rheumatism, according to Hunter, had induced the Indians to seek a great variety of remedies, including "bleeding, steam bathing, warm infusions, fomentings, sweatings,

[264] Hunter, *Manners and Customs*, 400, 402.

[265] Andros, "The Medicine and Surgery of the Winnebago and Dakota Indians," *Journal of the American Medical Association*, Vol. I, No. 4 (August 4, 1883), 118.

[266] Speck, *Rappahannock Herbals*, 33.

[267] *Primitive Physic*, 104.

[268] Charles Bundy Wilson, "Notes on Folk-Medicine," *Journal of American Folk-Lore*, Vol. XXI (1908), 72.

frictions, unctions, &c." In his view, they were generally successful in relieving acute and even chronic cases, but they were "very
liable to return."[269] Zeisberger declared:

> I have witnessed where they have effected a thorough cure
> and not only once or twice. . . . If a simple remedy does not
> afford relief, they may use twenty or more kinds of roots.
> Even in such cases I know of cures having been effected. In
> treating rheumatism, bathing and sweating plays a great
> part.[270]

Plains tribes used the dried flowers of false lupine (*Thermopsis
rhombifolia*) in the smoke treatment for rheumatism. The flowers were mixed with hair and burned under the affected part,
the smoke and heat being confined under a close covering. "It
is said," Gilmore wrote, "that this remedy reduces swelling at
once and relieves pain."[271]

Mexican Indians used *ololiuhqui* in the treatment of rheumatism,[272] while the San Carlos Apaches made dry poultices of the
tops of greasewood (*Covillea tridentata*), which were heated over
the fire and applied to the affected parts.[273] The Senecas used
petroleum to rub rheumatic parts, and many tribes resorted to
sweat or vapor baths and fumigation.

Animal fats were used to rub on the skin for a variety of aches
and pains, as well as for protection from insects, sunburn, and
cold. (See *Massage, Skin conditions*). Josselyn pronounced bear's
grease "very good for aches and swellings. The Indians anoint
themselves therewith from top to toe; which hardens them against
the cold weather." Wildcat grease was "sovereign for all manner
of aches and shrunk sinews," while raccoon fat was "excellent
for bruises and aches."[274]

269 *Manners and Customs*, 401.

270 "History of the North American Indians," *Ohio Archaeological and Historical Quarterly*, Vol. XIX, Nos. 1–2 (January and April, 1910), 55.

271 "Uses of Plants by Indians of the Missouri River Region," *Thirty-third
Annual Report of the Bureau of American Ethnology, 1911–12*, 91.

272 Kreig, *Green Medicine*, 79–80.

273 Hrdlička, *Physiological and Medical Observations*, 233.

274 *New-England's Rarities*, 149–52.

Lawson noted that "the Fats of Animals are used by them to render their limbs pliable and when wearied to relieve their Joints," though the sweat house was the preferred treatment. Alligator flesh was "accounted proper for such as are troubled with the lame Distemper, (a sort of Rheumatism,) so is the Fat very prevailing to remove Aches and Pains, by Unction."[275]

Skunk oil was being used in this century by the Montagnais for a variety of internal and external ailments.[276] "Pole-cat grease" was also used by Kentucky mountaineers to treat rheumatism.[277]

Urinary complaints. Numerous herbal remedies were used by Indians to promote diuresis. Aztec remedies for dysuria included *atole*, a mixture of raw ground maize and water which was a panacea for myriad ills, the leaves of *Ixyayaual* or mountain balm, and the ground root of a gourd vine called *Oquichpatli*, which was mixed with grass and rubber for a suppository.[278]

Copaiba, a Brazilian native remedy, has been used in white medicine as a diuretic and genitourinary disinfectant.[279] Early accounts say, however, that Indians used it on wounds and bruises.[280] The Mayas used the seeds of red pepper (*Capsicum frutescens*) as a remedy for yellow urine.[281]

Within the area of the United States, sassafras, yaupon, and prickly pear were used, in the appropriate regions, as sources of diuretic decoctions. The Creeks drank a cold infusion of devil's shoestring (*Cracca virginiana*) for bladder trouble.[282] Ojibwa diuretic substances included hop hornbeam, nettle, female fern,

---

[275] *History of North Carolina*, 132, 236.

[276] Tantaquidgeon, "Notes on the Origin and Uses of Plants of the Lake St. John Montagnais," *Journal of American Folk-Lore*, Vol. XLV, No. 176 (April–June, 1932), 266.

[277] Sadie F. Price, "Kentucky Folk-Lore," *Journal of American Folk-Lore*, Vol. XIV (1901), 32.

[278] Sahagún, *Things of New Spain*, Book XI, 150, 173, 185.

[279] Claus, *Pharmacognosy*, 409–10; Lloyd, *Origin and History*, 112–16.

[280] Monardes, *Joyfull Newes*, I, 22–25.

[281] Roys, *Ethno-Botany of the Maya*, 129.

[282] Swanton, "Religious Beliefs and Medical Practices of the Creek Indians," *Forty-second Annual Report of the Bureau of American Ethnology, 1924–25*, 658.

bittersweet, goldenrod, wild currant, and goose grass.[283] Rappahannocks made small pills of hardened sap from spruce pine (*Pinus virginiana*), rolled in the fingers, and took them for "kidney trouble."[284] The Utes used a root decoction of *Lithospermum pilosum* as a diuretic.[285] The Papagos used ground and dried crickets as an internal remedy in case of painful urination.[286]

Venereal diseases. In 1526, Gonzalo Fernandez de Oviedo published at Toledo his *Natural History of the West Indies*, written to satisfy the curiosity of the young emperor, Charles V. In it he spoke of syphilis and of *guayacán (guaiacum)*,[287] a native remedy:

> Your Majesty may rest assured that this horrible disease came from the Indies. Although it is quite common among the natives, it is not so dangerous there as it is here in Europe. The Indians of the islands cure themselves very easily with this wood.

Splinters or filings of the wood were boiled in water, he reported, and the potion drunk early in the morning for several days on an empty stomach.[288] Oviedo's claim as to the place of origin of the disease has been disputed (see p. 77), and the

283 Densmore, "Uses of Plants by the Chippewa Indians," *Forty-fourth Annual Report of the Bureau of American Ethnology, 1926–27*, 346–48; Smith, *Ojibwe Ethnobotany*, 386.

284 Speck, *Rappahannock Herbals*, 27.

285 Chamberlin, "Some Plant Names of the Ute Indians," *American Anthropologist*, N.S., Vol. II, No. 1 (January–March, 1909), 35.

286 Hrdlička, *Physiological and Medical Observations*, 242.

287 *Guaiacum officinale* L. or *Guaiacum sanctum* L., also called *lignum vitae*, *lignum sanctum*, and *palo santo*.

288 Oviedo, *Natural History*, 88–89. Monardes likewise alleged that the disease was discovered in Santo Domingo, when a Spaniard "did suffer great paines of the Poxe, which he had by the companie of an Indian woman, but his servaunte beyng one of the Phisitions of that countrie, gave unto hym the water of Guaiacan, wherewith not onely his greevous paines were taken awaie that he did suffer: but healed verie well of the evill . . . ," *Joyfull Newes*, I, 28. Bossu claimed that "the Indian wife of a Castilian discovered a certain wood called guaiacum which can cure the disease," which he believed the Indians acquired from "sulphurous fumes" while working in Spanish mines. *Travels*, 14.

On the history of syphilis in Europe before the discovery of America, see

efficacy of the supposed remedy was a hoax, although it held its ground for nearly three centuries. Eventually, however, other uses, medical and otherwise, were found for it and its derivatives, so that guaiacum has been saved from the limbo of forgotten drugs.[289]

In the area comprising the United States and Canada, at least, the early writers agree that venereal afflictions were brought to the Indians by the whites, and their accounts are filled with allusions to various remedies for them which were used by Indians and whites. Syphilis, in these reports, is often called the "pox" or "great pox," not to be confused with smallpox. Carolina Indians, according to Lawson, cured the "pox" by a berry that salivated like mercury, combined with the use of sweating and decoctions. After being heated, they jumped into a river. Another disease "like the Pox" was treated with the juice of the tulip tree.[290] The yaws was treated, Brickell wrote, by a decoction which included Spanish oak bark, the middle bark of the pine tree, and sumach root.[291]

Peter Kalm maintained that the Indians had "an infallible

Holcomb, "The Antiquity of Congenital Syphilis," *Bulletin of the History of Medicine*, Vol. X, No. 2 (July, 1941), 148–77, and Munger, "Guaiacum, the Holy Wood from the New World," *Journal of the History of Medicine*, Vol. IV, No. 2 (Spring, 1949), 196–229.

[289] Boerhaave recommended a decoction of guaiacum for bone diseases. *Materia Medica*, 102. Wesley prescribed it for gout, "green sickness," and chronic rheumatism. *Primitive Physic*, 77, 79, 105. Samuel Stearns called it stimulant, diaphoretic, corroborant, while the resin was expectorant, aperient, and purgative. *American Herbal or Materia Medica . . .* , 168. In the Bahamas, Schöpf wrote, a decoction of the holy wood was a household remedy, being used largely as an emetic. It was also, because of its hardness, used for ship's gear. *Travels*, II, 275. A compound decoction of guaiacum was given in the first *Pharmacopoeia of the Massachusetts Medical Society* (1808), 101–102. In recent times, it has been used in acute and chronic sore throat and chronic constipation; the tincture is used for testing for presence of hemoglobin in urine. Castiglioni, "Herbs in the Medicine of Eastern Peoples and of the American Indians," *Ciba Symposia*, Vol. V, Nos. 5–6 (August–September, 1943), 1540. Guaiac resin is considered to be stimulant and diaphoretic, while guaicol, isolated in 1826, has been used in veterinary practice as an intestinal antiseptic. Claus, *Pharmacognosy*, 329, 378–79. On uses by tropical Indians, see Levi-Strauss in Steward (ed.), *Handbook of South American Indians*, V, 477.

[290] *History of North Carolina*, 231, 236–37.   [291] *Natural History*, 48.

art" of curing venereal disease, using substances which had perfectly cured both Indians and whites. He reported that he had learned later what plants were used as remedies and reported them to the Swedish Royal Academy of Sciences. His editors believed that these roots included *Stillingia sylvatica* and *Lobelia*.[292]

On two occasions Peter Collinson of London wrote to Governor Colden asking if he could supply information about a herb which the Indians called *Tautrittipang*, which was reputed to be a sovereign remedy for "the French disease."[293] In his travels in the American wilderness, the French botanist André Michaux was always on the lookout for venereal remedies. On August 18, 1795, he wrote that a decoction of "Sanicula marylandica" (thought by Thwaites to be *Spigelia*) roots were a sovereign remedy for long-continued venereal diseases. On December 11, 1795, at Kaskaskia, he was "confirmed once more in my opinion that the root of Veronica Virginiana . . . used as a decoction for a month, is effective for the cure of Venereal Diseases."[294]

Carver relates a story of the "cure" of gonorrhea by a decoction of prickly ash (*Zanthoxylum americana*):

> Soon after I set out on my travels, one of the traders whom I accompanied, complained of violent gonorrhoea with all its alarming symptoms: this increased to such a degree, that by the time we had reached the town of the Winnebagoes, he was unable to travel. Having made his complaint known to one of the chiefs of that tribe, he told him not to be uneasy, for he would engage that by following his advice, he should be able in a few days to pursue his journey, and in a little longer time to be entirely free from his disorder.
>
> The chief had no sooner said this than he prepared for him a decoction of the bark of the roots of the prickly ash

292 *Travels*, II, 290, and ed. note, 774. Blue lobelia (*Lobelia siphilitica* L.) was an Iroquois remedy which was in much demand by whites. See pp. 48–49, 330–32, herein.

293 Letters of April 6, June 5, 1757, Colden, *Letters and Papers*, V, 140, 149–50.

294 Michaux, *Journal of Travels into Kentucky*, in Vol. III of Thwaites (ed.), *Early Western Travels*, 68, 79.

... by the use of which, in a few days he was greatly recovered, and having received directions how to prepare it, in a fortnight after his departure from this place perceived that he was radically cured.[295]

When Dr. Edwin James was ascending the Missouri River with Stephen Long's expedition in 1819, two plants were called to his attention which were said to be used by the Indians and whites as a cure for venereal diseases; these he called *Liatris pychostachia*, used in gonorrhea, and *Syphoria racemosa*, used for syphilis.[296]

The Comanches treated gonorrhea with a drink made from boiled thistle roots (*Cirsium undulatum*). Syphilitic sores were treated with ashes from the stems of little bluestem grass (*Andropogon scoparius*).[297] For apparently venereal diseases, Crow medicine men put hot rocks under the genitalia and had the patient drink a powder in warm water, and also threw some of the mixture on him.[298]

The Pimas used the root of *Yerba mansa* (*Anemiopsis californica*) for syphilis, giving a tea of it to the patient and applying the powdered root externally to the sores. An infected mother was given the tea during pregnancy so that the child might be free of the disease. The White Mountain Apaches were reported to have at least six vegetable remedies for gonorrhea.[299]

The Penobscots treated gonorrhea patients with a decoction of wintergreen, wild indigo, cleaver's vine, spikenard root, Solomon's seal, moosewood, and boneset. This medicine was also a tonic used in kidney trouble and spitting up blood.[300]

[295] *Travels*, 368–69.

[296] *Account of an Expedition*, Vol. XIV in Thwaites (ed.), *Early Western Travels*, 129.

[297] Carlson and Jones, "Some Notes on the Uses of Plants by the Comanche Indians," *Papers of the Michigan Academy of Sciences, Arts and Letters*, Vol. XXV (1939), 533.

[298] Lowie, *The Crow Indians*, 63.

[299] Hrdlička, *Physiological and Medical Observations*, 232, 245.

[300] Speck, "Medicine Practices of the Northeastern Algonquians," *Proceedings XIXth International Congress of Americanists*, 311.

Treatment of Injuries and External Conditions

Burns and scalds. The Indian treatment of burns and scalds drew attention and praise from several early observers. "With a strong decoction of tobacco," wrote Josselyn, "they cure burns and scalds; boiling it in water from a quart to a pint, then wash the sore therewith, and strew on the powder of dried tobacco."[301] Lawson declared:

> They cure Scald-Heads infallibly, and never miss. Their chief Remedy, as I have seen them make use of, is, the Oil of Acorns, but from which sort of Oak I am not certain. They cure Burns beyond Credit.

Other remedies for scalds and burns mentioned by Lawson which were used by Indians were the seeds of Jimson weed (*Datura stramonium*) and an ointment made from the buds of the tulip tree (*Liriodendron tulipifera*). [302]

Forest Indians also boiled the bark of elm, young pines, and especially basswood for application to burns.[303] Because of its demulcent property, Dr. Stephen Williams in his 1849 report to the American Medical Association called basswood bark the best burn remedy he had ever used.[304] The Catawbas placed fresh leaves of prairie dock (*Parthenium integrifolium*) on burns.[305] Burn remedies used by the Kwakiutls included raw liver of the skate, seal blubber, kelp leaves, and chewed hemlock bark covered with shredded yellow cedar bark.[306] The Opatas of Mexico sometimes treated burns and scalds with dog excrement.[307]

301 *New-England's Rarities,* 189.

302 *History of North Carolina,* 79, 96, 231.

303 Kinietz, *Indians of the Western Great Lakes,* 223.

304 "Report on the Indigenous Medical Botany of Massachusetts," *Transactions of the American Medical Association,* Vol. II (1849), 880.

305 Speck, "Catawba Medicines and Curative Practices," *Publications of the Philadelphia Anthropological Society,* Vol. I (1937), 191, citing Swanton.

306 Boas, "Current Beliefs of the Kwakiutl Indians," *Journal of American Folk-Lore,* Vol. XLV, No. 176 (April–June, 1932), 188.

307 Hrdlička, *Physiological and Medical Observations,* 250.

Fractures, sprains, and dislocations. Early observers and modern writers alike have praised Indian skill in the treatment of bone injuries. Dr. Stone held that on the whole "their skill in the care of wounds, fractures and dislocations equalled and in some respects exceeded that of their white contemporary."[308] Volney testified, early in the last century, that "fractures and dislocations are not rare among them, but they are pretty dexterous in reducing them."[309]

An interesting native achievement in fracture treatment was the use of form-fitting splints. Padding of wet clay or rawhide was often used, as well as poultices.[310] The Ojibwas washed a fractured arm with warm water and greased it, applied a warm poultice of wild ginger and spikenard, covered with a cloth and bound the arm with thin cedar splints.[311] The Pimas used splints from the flat, elastic ribs of the giant cactus. The Mescalero Apaches rubbed dislocated parts until warm and then with a quick jerk forced the bone into place, rubbing medicine on afterward to allay the pain, and finally tied with a bandage. In fractures, rubbing and straightening as well as pain-allaying medicine was employed, and finally sticks were applied all around as splints, being bound tightly with rags.[312]

"If an Indian has dislocated his foot or knee, when hunting alone," wrote Zeisberger, "he creeps to the next tree and tying one end of his strap to it, fastens the other to the dislocated limb and, lying on his back, continued to pull until it is reduced."[313] In the West, Hunter reported:

[308] Stone, *Medicine among the American Indians,* 82–83.

[309] Volney, *View of the Soil and Climate of America,* 369. An unfavorable view of Indian fracture treatment came from Dr. Edwin James, who maintained that among the Omaha, healed fractures usually remained "more or less bent or crooked." *Account of an Expedition,* Vol. XV in Thwaites (ed.), *Early Western Travels,* 48.

[310] Adams, "Aboriginal American Medicine and Surgery," *Proceedings of the Indiana Academy of Science,* Vol. LXI (1951). 51.

[311] Densmore, "Uses of Plants by the Chippewa Indians," *Forty-fourth Annual Report of the Bureau of American Ethnology, 1926–27,* 334.

[312] Hrdlička, *Physiological and Medical Observations,* 238, 247.

[313] "History of the North American Indians," *Ohio Archaeological and Historical Quarterly,* Vol. XIX, Nos. 1–2 (January and April, 1910), 149.

They are acquainted with the advantage of relaxing the skeletal muscles in dislocations; for in cases where they do not readily succeed, they nauseate the patient to a most distressing degree, and then find very little difficulty in replacing a luxated bone.[314]

"For felons or sprains," goes an eighteenth-century report, the Illinois-Miamis used "some bark of hybrid ash, chewed, by putting on the injury."[315] The Cheyennes used bearberry *(Arctostaphylos uva ursi)* both internally and externally for sprained back. All parts of the above-ground plant were boiled and the infusion was drunk. Wet leaves were rubbed on the painful part.[316] Rappahannocks in Virginia used a red clay poultice on swellings and sprains.[317]

In the early eighteenth century John Lawson told an interesting story of the cure of "lameness" in a white member of his party by a local chieftain of the Esaws (Catawbas):

> In the morning, he desired to see the lame Man's affected Part, to the end that he might do something which (he believed) would give him his ease. After he had viewed it accordingly, he pulled out an Instrument, something like a Comb, which was made of a split Reed, with fifteen Teeth of a Rattle-Snakes, set at much the same distance as in a large Horn-Comb. With these he scratched the place where the Lameness chiefly lay till the Blood came, bathing it both before and after Incision, with warm Water, spurted out of his Mouth. This done, he ran into his Plantation and got some Sassafras Root . . . and dried it in the Embers, scraped off the outward Rind, and having beat it betwixt two Stones, applied it to the Part afflicted, binding it up well. Thus, in a day or two, the Patient became sound.[318]

314 *Manners and Customs*, 397.

315 Kinietz, *Indians of the Western Great Lakes*, 225.

316 Grinnell, "Some Cheyenne Plant Medicines," *American Anthropologist*, N.S., Vol. VII No. 1 (January–March, 1905), 41.

317 Speck, *Rappahannock Herbals*, 35.

318 *History of North Carolina*, 40.

Frostbite and freezing. Undoubtedly the custom of greasing the body with vegetable or animal oils helped to protect Indians from the cold. "This is begun in their Infancy," Lawson reported, "and continued for a long time, which fills the Pores and enables them better to endure, the Extremity of the Weather."[319]

Perhaps as a consequence of the foregoing preventative treatment, accounts of cold injuries and treatments are few. Hunter reported, however, that "Plaisters of the resin of the sap-pine are applied to frosted members, with decided advantage."[320] In the Great Lakes area, a decoction of the leaves of sumach and the root of an unidentified plant, possibly gold thread, was applied to frozen parts.[321]

Insect bites, etc. Plants of the mint family were commonly employed by Indians and whites for the prevention and relief of insect bites. The Rappahannock Indians of Virginia kept dried pennyroyal leaves in their homes to repel fleas.[322]

William Byrd mentioned two troublesome insect pests, deer tikes and horseflies. The juice of pennyroyal was used by him to prevent attacks of the first, and dittany for the second. Byrd reported that Indians also used bear's oil "as a General Defense, against every Species of Vermin." They maintained that "it keeps both bugs and Musquetoes from assaulting their Persons."[323]

In case of poisonous spider bites, according to Lederer's account (p. 117), sucking was employed to remove the venom.

The ancient Mayas applied tobacco leaves to insect bites and stings.[324] The Meskwakis made a lotion for bee stings from the flowers of stiff goldenrod (*Solidago rigida* L.)[325]

Skin conditions. William Wood was favorably impressed with

[319] *Ibid.*, 181.
[320] *Manners and Customs*, 398.
[321] Kinietz, *Indians of the Western Great Lakes*, 222.
[322] Speck, *Rappahannock Herbals*, 33.
[323] *History of the Dividing Line*, I, 162–63.
[324] Roys, *Ethno-Botany of the Maya*, 259.
[325] Smith, *Meskwaki Ethnobotany*, 217.

the manner in which New England Indians protected their skin with animal oils:

> Their smooth skins proceeded from the often anointing of their bodies with the oil of fishes, and the fat of eagles, with the fat of raccoons, which they hold in summer, the best antidote to keep the skin from blistering in the scorching sun; and it is their best armour against the musketoes, the surest expeller of the hairy excrement, and stops the pores of the body against the nipping winters cold.[326]

Robert Beverley of Virginia reported that Indians anointed their skin with puccoon and angelica juice mixed with bear's oil.[327] Hundreds of miles to the southwest and a century later, Hunter declared that the Indians mixed bear's oil with various herbs to form "excellent unctions for various cutaneous diseases."[328] Dr. Rush was informed that Indians greased themselves with bear's grease and clay, which "serves to lessen the sensibilities of the extremities of the nerves," and afforded protection against disease-causing "exhalations" in the air.[329]

Brickell reported that Indians "never miss curing most kinds of *Cutaneous Eruptions* by the Plants that are produced in this Country."[330] One of the skin annoyances to which Indians were subject was poison ivy infection,[331] for which they used several herbal remedies. *Grindelia robusta* (*q.v.*), used by Pacific coast Indians, came to white attention in this way. The Cheyennes used *Astragalus nitidus* for ivy poisoning.[332] The Menominees used a liquid wash or the freshly bruised plant of Virginia pepper-

---

326 *New England's Prospect*, 74–75.

327 *History and Present State of Virginia*, 220.

328 *Manners and Customs*, 371.

329 *Medicine Among the Indians*, 113.

330 *Natural History*, 394.

331 Zeisberger reported: "Some are affected with swelling of the face and body if they touch it, even when the wind blows it upon them. This is very painful until cure. Others do not suffer from the vine at all. This holds good of Indians as of others." "History of the North American Indians," *Ohio Archaeological and Historical Quarterly*, Vol. XIX, Nos. 1–2 (January and April, 1910), 56.

332 Grinnell, "Some Cheyenne Plant Medicines," *American Anthropologist*, N.S., Vol. VII, No. 1 (January–March, 1905), 40.

grass (*Lepidium virginicum*), while the Potawatomis and Meskwakis treated both poison ivy and nettle inflammation with the leaves of jewelweed (*Impatiens biflora*, touch-me-not). The last named has been used by whites for the same purpose, both in its natural form and in a commercial preparation.[333] Rappahannocks steeped a handful of beech tree bark (*Fagus grandifolia*) from the north side of the tree in a pint of water, to which a little salt was added. The wash was applied thrice daily to poison ivy sores. The same tribe treated nettle stings with applications of urine or salt and water.[334]

Early American Indians, according to Heckewelder, were generally free of skin diseases:

The Itch [scabies or eczema], I believe, is not common among the Indians; at least, I do not recollect of seeing one instance of an Indian that had it. I have wondered at this, and have ascribed it to their different mode of living; namely, their food, their well-aired houses, or huts, &c.[335]

Michaux reported in 1795 that a Frenchman who traded among the Cherokees had cured himself of the "Itch" by drinking for ten days a decoction of the copalm or *liquidambar* (sweet gum) tree.[336] Earlier, Lawson had declared that the gum from this tree "cures the Herpes and Inflamations, being applied to the Morphews and Tettars."[337]

In this century, Pillager Ojibwas made a medicinal tea for skin diseases from the small bedstraw plant (*Galium trifidum*).[338] For rash and eczema, the Omahas applied to the skin the crushed leaves and stems of the touch-me-not (*Impatiens biflora* or *I.*

[333] Smith, *Menomini Ethnobotany*, 33; *Potawatomi Ethnobotany*, 42; *Meskwaki Ethnobotany*, 205; *Ojibwe Ethnobotany*, 358; Douglas, "The People of Cades Cove," *National Geographic Magazine*, Vol. CXXII, No. 1 (July, 1962), 84.

[334] Speck, *Rappahannock Herbals*, 34, 38.

[335] Letter of February 11, 1797, in *Philadelphia Medical and Physical Journal*, I, Pt. I (1805), 130.

[336] *Journal of Travels into Kentucky*, in Vol. III, Thwaites (ed.), *Early Western Travels*, 77.

[337] *History of North Carolina*, 97.

[338] Smith, *Ojibwe Ethnobotany*, 387.

pallida).[339] To cure ringworm, the Rappahannocks rubbed the skin with the sap of red mulberry (*Morus rubra*) or the sap of fresh milkweed (*Asclepias syriaca*). The latter was also used to banish warts.[340]

The Aztecs had several remedies for dandruff, including the berries of *yiamolli* (*Phytolacca octandra* L.), or hot lye, wine dregs, various herbs, and faunal substances.[341]

Snakebite. In few, if any, ailments was the aboriginal reputation for skillful cures more celebrated (and perhaps, in many instances, less deserved) than in their treatment of snakebites. Since poisonous reptiles were numerous throughout the country, an important part of the Indian materia medica consists of supposed cures for snakebite. The white settlers, quite unused to this problem in Europe, and adhering to the doctrine that the Creator provided in each country the remedies for its own ills, at once assumed that the Indian remedies were valid. One early New England account says:

> . . . there are some Serpents called Rattle Snakes, that have Rattles in their Tayles that will not flye from a Man as others will, but will Flye upon him and sting him so mortally, that he will dye within a quarter of an houre after, except that the partie stinged have about him some of the root of an Hearbe called Snake weed to bite on.[342]

Lawson claimed that "the Indians are the best Physicians for the Bite of these and all other venomous Creatures of this Country. There are four sorts of Snake-Roots already discovered, which Knowledge came from the Indians, who have performed several great Cures."[343] William Byrd, who frequently encountered

---

[339] Gilmore, "Uses of Plants by Indians of the Missouri River Region," *Thirty-third Annual Report of the Bureau of American Ethnology, 1911–12*, 101.

[340] Speck, *Rappahannock Herbals*, 30, 32.

[341] Sahagún, *Things of New Spain*, Book XI, 133; Emmart (ed.), *Badianus Manuscript*, 212.

[342] "New England's Plantation," in Peter Force, *Tracts and Other Papers*, I, 12.

[343] *History of North Carolina*, 133.

poisonous reptiles during his travels, was always on the lookout for remedies for their bites. He mentioned a "Fern root" which was preferred by the southern Indians, and several other plants, including the Seneca snakeroot, as being useful for this purpose.[344]

Indians sometimes killed the offending snake, cut it up, and applied the flesh to the wound.[345] Dr. Colden was one of the ardent defenders of this procedure (which was of ancient European usage),[346] maintaining that "the snake himself carries the Antidote along with him in his Fat." If the snake should escape, he recommended as a substitute for its flesh, any sort of greasy substance, especially hog's lard.[347] John Woods, the English settler in Illinois, in 1820 reported the cure of a dog which had been bitten by a rattlesnake, through the application of the snake's own fat, sweet oil, and a purgative of castor oil.[348] Carver was also among those who believed in the efficacy of snakefat, though he also recommended salt brine, a decoction of buds or bark of the white ash, and above all, "the rattlesnake plantain," which he maintained was so effective that the taking of it internally and externally was a certain cure.[349]

James Adair, long a trader among southern Indians, listed several snakebite specifics used by the Creeks (see p. 101) and declared:

> When an Indian perceives he is struck by a snake, he immediately chews some of the root, and having swallowed a sufficient quantity of it, he applies some to the wound, which he repeats as occasion requires, and in proportion to the poison the snake has infused into the wound. For a short space of time, there is a terrible conflict through all the body, by the

[344] History of the Dividing Line, I, 88, 90.

[345] Josselyn, New-England's Rarities, 169; Loskiel, Mission of the United Brethren, I, 114.

[346] Snakefat as an application to serpent bites has been a practice that goes back to Pliny, and was still in vogue in rural England in the 1920's. McKenzie, The Infancy of Medicine, 117–18.

[347] Colden, Letters and Papers, III, 67–68.

[348] Two Years Residence, in Vol. X, Thwaites (ed.), Early Western Travels, 342.

[349] Carver, Travels, 450, 482–83.

jarring qualities of the burning poison, and the strong antidote; but the poison is soon repelled through the same chan-
nels it entered, and the patient is cured.[350]

In Pennsylvania in 1832, Prince Maximilian described a plant
called lion's heart, or *Prenanthes rubicunda,* which his host,
Dutot, had learned about from the Delaware Indians, and which
was held to be "a sovereign remedy against the bite of serpents."[351] This was probably the *Prenanthis serpentaria* or
"Lionsfoot" of Frederick Pursh, which the noted botanist asserted had cured a man who was bitten in the foot by a "Mocke-
son." The juice, boiled in milk, was taken inwardly, while the
steeped leaves were applied to the wound. It was an esteemed
remedy in Virginia.[352] Dr. Stephen Williams in 1849 called
Prenanthe alba "the famous Indian cure for the bite of venomous
serpents." He likewise listed the black ash (*Fraxinus samucifolia,*
now called *F. nigra*) as having a reputation for curing snakebites,
the leaves being held to be so poisonous to the reptiles that they
"would sooner run through a fire than over these leaves." A reputed Sioux remedy (*Gerardia quercifolia*) was also listed by
Williams as an alleged cure.[353]

Dr. Barton of Philadelphia listed about three dozen herbal
snakebite remedies, most of which were reputed to have been
learned from the Indians, and concluded that they were in themselves of no value, though the concomitant treatment often used,
such as sucking, and the application of a ligature, were deemed
rational and useful.[354]

350 *History of the Indians,* 235–36.

351 *Travels in the Interior of North America, 1832–1834* (Part I), Vol. XXII in
Thwaites (ed.), *Early Western Travels,* 95–96.

352 Richard Harlan, "Experiments Made on the Poison of the Rattlesnake
. . . ," and *Transactions of the American Philosophical Society,* N.S., Vol. III (1830),
301.

353 "Report on the Indigenous Medical Botany of Massachusetts," *Transactions
of the American Medical Association,* II (1849), 893, 922–23.

354 Benjamin S. Barton, "An Account of the Most Effectual Means of Prevention of the Deleterious Consequences of the Bite of the *Crotalus Horridus,* or *Rattle-
Snake," Transactions of the American Philosophical Society,* O.S., Vol. III (1793),
100–14; see p. 68, herein.

Dr. Richard Harlan in 1829 tested an alleged snakebite remedy, veiny hawkweed (*Hieracium venosum*) and found that there was no correlation between the use of this herb and the survival chances of the animals and poultry used in the test. Some creatures that were bitten survived with no treatment and others that were treated died anyway. He concluded that the amount of the poison, the location of the bites, and the size of the snake or the animal bitten were of greater importance.[355]

Dr. Hrdlička mentioned the cure of a Mescalero Apache Indian, bitten by a rattlesnake, through the use of an unidentified root, although it was not applied until more than two hours after the bite. No other treatment was mentioned, although the San Carlos Apaches practiced sucking of snakebites and scorpion stings.[356]   Bourke mentioned a plant called *huaco*, the root of which was used by Texas Mexicans as an internal and external snakebite remedy, with alleged efficacy. He believed the use of this plant to be of pre-Columbian origin.[357]

The Indians of Lower California in cases of snakebite applied a tight binding between the wound and the heart.[358] Mrs. Stevenson reported that the Zuñis practiced both sucking and the use of a plant called "turquoise flower" in snakebite cases. An Indian who was bitten on the foot by a rattlesnake had to walk fifteen miles before being treated by a native "theurgist," by which time the swelling extended to his thigh, and he died before nightfall. This was reported to be the first death in fifty years from snakebite at the pueblo of Zuñi.[359]

---

[355] "Experiments Made on the Poison of the Rattlesnake . . . ," and "Some Further Observations on the Poison of the Rattlesnake," *Transactions of the American Philosophical Society*, N.S., Vol. III (1830), 300–14, 400–21.

[356] Hrdlička, *Physiological and Medical Observations*, 234, 237.

[357] "Popular Medicine, Customs, and Superstitions of the Rio Grande," *Journal of American Folk-Lore*, Vol. VII, No. 25 (April–June, 1894), 140. One of the poison antidotes of the Aztecs has ahhuachcho as part of its name. Emmart (ed.), *Badianus Manuscript*, 255.

[358] Baegert, "An Account of the Aboriginal Inhabitants of the Californian Peninsula," *Annual Report of the Smithsonian Institution, 1863–64*, 386.

[359] "Ethnobotany of the Zuñi Indians," *Thirtieth Annual Report of the Bureau of American Ethnology, 1908–09*, 53, 54.

The Hopis hold live rattlesnakes in their mouths in the snake dance, a ritual practiced to bring rain. Dr. Brooks related that a trader at the Hopi village of Oraibi who had lived among these people for many years "had never seen a case of fatal snake bite among those tribes to whom the snake is sacred, and yet who handle them frequently and are often bitten by them, ill protected as they are by scanty clothing."[360] Robert F. Heizer reported that the Hopis are seldom bitten during the dance, but on the rare occasions when they are, no ill effects follow. Since their herbal remedy was tested and pronounced valueless, Dr. Heizer ascribed their apparent immunity from harmful effects to the fact that the snakes are rendered docile during nine days of captivity prior to the ceremony and the probability that their poison glands have been emptied in advance.[361]

Wounds and hemorrhage. "In any immoderate defluctions of Blood," observed Brickell, "or any other Humour from any part of the Body, they are never at a loss for a speedy Cure."[362] Herbal, animal, and mineral substances were all used as hemostatics by the Indians. Bleeding was arrested with spiderwebs in such widely scattered groups as the Mohegans, Kwakiutls, Mescalero Apaches, and white settlers from Tennessee to Oregon.[363] The spores or pulverized heads of various species of puffballs were used as hemostatics by the Kwakiutls (who used the spores),

[360] "The Medicine of the American Indian," *Journal of Laboratory and Clinical Medicine*, Vol. XIX, No. 1 (October, 1933), 18.

[361] Heizer, "The Hopi Snake Dance, Fact and Fancy," *Ciba Symposia*, V, No. 10 (January, 1944), 1681–84.

[362] Brickell, *Natural History*, 399; *Cf.* Lawson: "for what natural Issues of Blood happen immoderately, they are not to seek for a certain and speedy Cure." *History of North Carolina*, 234. Lawson's work was published twenty-three years earlier (1714) than Brickell's (1737).

[363] Tantaquidgeon, "Mohegan Medicinal Practices, Weather-Lore, and Superstition," *Forty-third Annual Report of the Bureau of American Ethnology, 1925–26*, 266; Boas, "Current Beliefs of the Kwakiutl Indians," *Journal of American Folk-Lore*, Vol. XLV, No. 176 (April–June, 1932), 189; Hrdlička, *Physiological and Medical Observations*, 237; Douglas, "The People of Cades Cove," *National Geographic Magazine*, Vol. CXXII, No. 1 (July, 1962), 85; Dunlop, *Doctors of the American Frontier*, 186.

Meskwakis, Mohegans, Ojibwas, various Plains tribes, and others.[364] The use of powdered puffballs to stop bleeding seems to have been practiced in old Europe. This remedy was recommended by such varied individuals as Hermann Boerhaave and John Wesley.[365] The same remedy (called *blutschwamm*) was used in this country by the Pennsylvania Germans.[366]

Some early Indians of the Great Lakes region arrested mouth bleeding by a decoction of pulverized sumach leaves and berries, mixed with an unidentified root which was probably an astringent.[367] The Cherokees controlled hemorrhage by a plaster of buzzard's down.[368] The Cheyennes prevented bleeding from the nose and lungs with an infusion of stems and berries of *Pterospora andromedea*.[369] An Ojibwa styptic was the root of tall cinquefoil (*Drymocallis arguta*) used dry or moistened and placed on soft duck down.[370] Although nosebleed was not a common complaint among them, the San Carlos Apaches arrested it by taking cold water into the nose or applying it by hand to the forehead, or by stuffing the nostrils with soft material such as calico or cotton.[371]

[364] Boas, "Current Beliefs of the Kwakiutl Indians," *Journal of American Folk-Lore*, Vol. XLV, No. 176 (April–June, 1932), 189; Smith, *Meskwaki Ethnobotany*, 200; Tantaquidgeon, "Mohegan Medicinal Practices, Weather-Lore, and Superstition," *Forty-third Annual Report of the Bureau of American Ethnology, 1925–26*, 266; Smith, *Ojibwe Ethnobotany*, 370; Gilmore, "Uses of Plants by Indians of the Missouri River Region," *Thirty-third Annual Report of the Bureau of American Ethnology, 1911–12*, 62.

[365] Boerhaave, *Materia Medica*, 97; Wesley, *Primitive Physic*, 35.

[366] Brendle and Unger, *Folk Medicine of Pennsylvania Germans*, 40.

[367] Kinietz, *Indians of the Western Great Lakes*, 222. The unidentified root was from "an herb very common in the woods, and which has on its leaves a kind of ball. They call this herb by the generic name of Pallaganghy, which is to say Ocre." The description given is insufficient for certain identification, but the clues given, and the use to which it was put, suggest gold thread (*Coptis trifolia*), widely used by northeastern tribes as a mouth astringent. Dr. Schöpf mentioned golden ragwort (*Senecio aureus*) as an Indian vulnerary (*Materia Medica Americana*, 123), but it is a prairie plant.

[368] Mooney and Olbrechts, *Swimmer Manuscript*, 72.

[369] Grinnell, "Some Cheyenne Plant Medicines," *American Anthropologist*, N.S., Vol. VII, No. 1 (January–March, 1905), 39.

[370] Densmore, "Uses of Plants by the Chippewa Indians," *Forty-fourth Annual Report of the Bureau of American Ethnology, 1926–27*, 332.

[371] Hrdlička, *Physiological and Medical Observations*, 234.

The Chickasaws in the eighteenth century combined herbs with alum in wound treatment.[372] Hunter echoed an opinion held by many when he said of the Indians: "I have known them to stop hemorrhagies [sic] which I am persuaded would otherwise have proved fatal."[373]

Shot and arrow wounds. Ambroise Paré (1510–90), celebrated for his treatment of gunshot wounds, found that the customary scalding oil aggravated the affliction, whereupon he used with more success a dressing of egg yolk, oil of roses, and turpentine.[374] The noted French surgeon was hardly ahead of the Indians in his wisdom, for the aborigines have been almost unanimously praised for their effective treatment of projectile wounds, as well as other traumata. Egg whites were much used by the Aztecs in mixing wound remedies, and so was agave juice.[375] Herb juices, honey, and egg yolk were used on burns in ancient Mexico,[376] while turpentine and other arboreal oleoresins were used in wound treatment from Peru to Canada.[377] Superstition, as Swanton pointed out, was superseded by practical treatment in conditions of obvious origin.[378]

"Some of them have been shot in at the mouth, and out of the ear," wrote William Wood in 1639, "some shot in the breast; some run through the flank with darts, and other desperate wounds, which either by their rare skill in the use of vegetatives, or diabolical charms, they cure in a short time."[379] From Bossu

---

[372] Swanton, "Social and Religious Beliefs and Practices of the Chickasaw Indians," *Forty-fourth Annual Report of the Bureau of American Ethnology, 1926–27*, 264, citing Adair.

[373] *Manners and Customs*, 396.

[374] Clendening, *Source Book of Medical History*, 192–93.

[375] Bancroft, *Native Races*, II, 599; Sahagún, *Things of New Spain*, Book XI, 179.

[376] Emmart (ed.), *Badianus Manuscript*, 301.

[377] See Balm of Gilead, Balsam Fir, Canada Turpentine, Pine, Turpentine, Balsam of Peru, etc.

[378] "Social and Religious Beliefs and Practices of the Chickasaw Indians," *Forty-fourth Annual Report of the Bureau of American Ethnology, 1926–27*, 264.

[379] *New England's Prospects*, 88–89.

we have an early description of Choctaw treatment of projectile wounds:

When an Indian is wounded with a bullet or an arrow, the medicine man first sucks the wound then spits out the blood. In France this is called "curing through secretion." In their dressings, they do not use lint or compresses. Instead, to make the wound suppurate, they blow into it powder made of a root. Another root powder is used to dry and heal the wound, and still other roots are used in a solution with which the wound is bathed to help prevent gangrene.[380]

Shot or arrow wounds, particularly if there was mouth bleeding, were treated among Illinois-Miami Indians by the crushed root of the crowfoot (*Ranunculus* species) dissolved in warm water.[381] Dr. Pitcher, reporting his observations among Michigan Indians in the mid-nineteenth century, said that gunshot wounds were cleansed with vegetable decoctions introduced with a bladder and quill syringe, and great care was taken to keep up the suppurating process. To guard against premature closing of the external orifice, they introduced a "tent" made of the bark of slippery elm, which was firm enough to permit its introduction to the required depth while its mucilaginous quality prevented irritation. "They exhibit great patience and assiduity," he wrote, "in the treatment of this description of wounds, to which their success may be attributed, possibly more than to the remedies applied."[382]

It is remarkable that the elm bark was similarly used by Indians a thousand miles away, according to Hunter's description of the methods used for treating shot wounds among Indians of the southwestern frontier:

When a ball simply lodges beneath the integuments, they extract it with the point of the scalping knife or the handle of their bullet moulds, which from its shape, is the better qualified of the two. When however the ball is lodged more

[380] *Travels*, 168.
[381] Kinietz, *Indians of the Western Great Lakes*, 223.
[382] Pitcher, in Schoolcraft, *Indian Tribes*, IV, 513.

deeply, or has penetrated in a circuitous direction, it is permitted to come out by the slower process of suppuration; or
to remain within a sac naturally formed by the surrounding
muscular integuments. When it is desirable to extract a ball,
they introduce a piece of the slippery elm bark as far into
the wound as is practicable, which is suffered to remain, till
the sought for object is obtained, or no danger is likely to
result by suffering it to remain. They also make incisions
with the knife on the surface, whenever it heals too fast for
the more deep seated parts in the wound. The slippery elm
bark beaten to a pulp and applied to the wounded part, is
the usual remedy among the Osages for the extraction of a
ball, thorn &c.; they sometimes apply the pounded roots of
the gall of the earth plant to wounds, inflammation generally
follows, and the foreign body is easily extracted.[383]

Dr. Edwin James, who found so little to praise in Omaha
medicine, called these Indians "very successful in the cure of
gunshot wounds."[384] Such comments abound in the literature of
the old West. Nathaniel Wyeth, in 1832, was impressed by the
wound treatment he observed among the Flatheads:

After the battle at Pierre's Valley, I had an opportunity of
seeing a specimen of Indian surgery in treating a wound. An
Indian squaw first sucked the wound perfectly dry, so that
it appeared white as chalk; and then she bound it up with a
piece of dry buck-skin as soft as woolen cloth, and by this
treatment the wound began to heal, and soon closed up, and
the part became sound again. The sucking of it so effectually
may have been from an apprehension of a poisoned arrow.
But who taught the savage Indian that a person may take
poison into his mouth without any risk, as the poison of a
rattlesnake without harm, provided there be no scratch or
wound in the mouth, so as to admit it into the blood?[385]

383 *Manners and Customs*, 98.
384 *Account of an Expedition*, Vol. XV in Thwaites (ed.), *Early Western
Travels*, 98.
385 *Wyeth's Oregon*, Vol. XXI in Thwaites (ed.), *Early Western Travels*, 78.

More recently, Bourke reported in 1892 that the Apaches met with "much success in their treatment of gunshot wounds, which they do not dress as often as white practitioners, alleging that the latter, by so frequently removing the bandages, unduly irritate the wounds."[386]

Other wounds. William Strachey conceded the dexterity of seventeenth-century Virginia natives in treating green wounds from axe or sword, but had less faith in their ability to cure complicated injuries, in which he included shot wounds.[387] Father Brebeuf thought that the ability of the Hurons to heal "ruptures" (skin breaks) was remarkably skillful.[388] Among the Ottawas, in 1688, Baron Lahontan observed that "the poor wounded Savages carefully purg'd with such Roots as the *Americans* are well vers'd in . . . and they wanted no good Restoratives of Jelly-broth."[389] Lawson claimed that he had never seen an Indian with a "foul Wound." He observed that the Indians took green elm bark, beat it into a pulp, then dried it over a fire. "This they use," he declared, "as a Sovereign Remedy to heal a Cut or green Wound, or any thing that is not corrupted. It is of a very glutinous Quality."[390]

Dr. Townsend, in Oregon in 1835, reported that among the Kalapooyahs, "wounds are treated with an application of green leaves, and bound with strips of pine bark."[391] One sour note must be reported, however. Prince Maximilian, when among the Blackfeet, noted that "these Indians are said to have successfully healed some severe wounds; but, as far as my observation goes, these cures were chiefly to be ascribed to the good constitution of the patients." Their constitutions were apparently good enough

---

386 "The Medicine-Men of the Apache," *Ninth Annual Report of the Bureau of American Ethnology, 1887–88*, 471.

387 *The Historie of Travaile into Virginia Britannia*, 108.

388 Thwaites (ed.), *Jesuit Relations*, X, 209.

389 *Voyages*, I, 161.

390 *History of North Carolina*, 95, 231–32.

391 *Wyeth's Oregon*, Vol. XXI in Thwaites (ed.), *Early Western Travels*, 322.

to enable many of them to survive scalping, for he reported that many wore caps over such cured wounds.[392]

Dr. Pitcher reported two cases of wounded lungs successfully treated by Indian doctors. A Canadian Indian, in 1827, was severely mauled by a grizzly bear, the wounds including two openings in the left half of the thorax from both of which came forth blood and air. When discovered, he was thought to be dead, but was removed to his lodge and placed in such a position that the blood and matter escaped from the chest. His wounds were assiduously washed with mucilaginous decoctions, and in a few months he was able to travel to Sault Ste. Marie.[393]

Hrdlička in 1908 alluded to certain roots which were dried and pounded to powder for application to open wounds and sores by the San Carlos Apaches.[394] Boas has described several herbs used as wound poultices by the Kwakiutls, including some for drawing blisters.[395] The Ojibwas applied the crushed root of sunflower (*Helianthus occidentalis*) to bruises and contusions.[396]

Several vulnerary drugs used by South American Indians found their way into pharmacopeias because whites were impressed by their uses among the natives. The balsam of Peru (*Myroxylon pereirae*) has been mentioned in our discussion of asepsis in surgery. Monardes declared that the Spaniards had learned also from the Indians the virtues of the balsam of Tolu (*Myroxylon balsamum*), which was "muche estemed amongest the Indians," because "it healeth all freashe woundes, comfortyng the partes, and joynyng theim without makyng any matter."[397] In 1625 a Portuguese monk learned of copaiba (*Copaifera officinalis*) from Brazilian Indians, and declared "it is

---

[392] *Travels in the Interior of North America, 1832–1834* (Part II), Vol. XXIII in Thwaites (ed.), *Early Western Travels*, 120.

[393] Pitcher, in Schoolcraft, *Indian Tribes*, IV, 514.

[394] Hrdlička, *Physiological and Medical Observations*, 234.

[395] "Current Beliefs of the Kwakiutl Indians," *Journal of American Folk-Lore*, Vol. XLV, No. 176 (April–June, 1932), 237.

[396] Hoffman, "The Mide'wiwin Or 'Grand Medicine Society' of the Ojibwa," *Seventh Annual Report of the Bureau of American Ethnology, 1885–86*, 199.

[397] Monardes, *Joyfull Newes*, II, 43–44.

much set by for wounds, and taketh away all the skarre."[398] The pounded leaves of jaborandi (*Pilocarpus jaborandi*) were also used as wound applications by Brazilian natives.[399] A styptic and astringent, matico (*Piper angustifolium*), was used by Andean tribes, but was not adopted in white medicine until 1839.[400]

Indian methods of wound treatment won both verbal plaudits from white physicians and the honor of imitation. Dr. Major, whose opinions of Indian medicine were generally critical, concluded that "the Indians treatment of traumatic states seem to have been, in the whole, admirable."[401] Dr. Harlow Brooks has declared that settlers bodily copied from the Indians most of their knowledge regarding the treatment of traumata.[402]

Obstetrics, Gynecology, and Pediatrics

Childbirth. The Indian practices associated with childbirth have been called more rational than those of Europeans of an earlier period. Christians long held that it was contrary to the will of God to ease the pain and discomfort of labor for it was the intended penalty of the Almighty for original sin. Persons were condemned to death by fire in the sixteenth century in Scotland and Germany for violating this injunction by the use of pain-relieving medicines. Even in the nineteenth century, Dr. Simpson was ostracized for using chloroform in obstetrics, Dr. Ignatz Semmelweis was ridiculed for his ideas on puerperal fever, and Carl Franz Credé was scorned for using nitrate of silver to prevent ophthalmia in babies born of gonorrheal mothers.[403]

Dr. Stone asserted that all Indians practiced Credé's method of

---

[398] Lloyd, *Origin and History*, 112.

[399] Steward (ed.), *Handbook of South American Indians*, I, 471, 537; VI, 485; True, "Folk Materia Medica," *Journal of American Folk-Lore*, Vol. XIV (1901), 112. It was also used to modify the solution of ipecac, an emetic, and was used in white medicine as a sialagogue. Lloyd, *Origin and History*, 243–45.

[400] *Ibid.*, 212–13.

[401] Major, *Annals of Medical History*, N.S., X (1938), 546.

[402] "The Medicine of the American Indian," *Bulletin of the New York Academy of Medicine*, 2d ser., Vol. V, No. 6 (June, 1929) 515. See p. 264, herein.

[403] Atkinson, *Magic, Myth, and Medicine*, 271–76.

expelling the placenta at least a century before publication of Credé's procedure.[404] Dr. George Engelmann, whose study of labor among primitive peoples was first published in 1883, regarded the obstetrical methods of primitive tribes as more reasonable than those used among civilized peoples. He described massage and manipulation techniques used in various tribes for the expulsion of the fetus and afterbirth which were in his own time just beginning to be adopted in white medicine. "Although constantly practiced by primitive people for thousands of years," he asserted, "these methods have been recently rediscovered by learned men, clothed in scientific principle, and given to the world as new." Referring to the third stage of labor, he wrote:

> The untutored, simple-minded savage, although crude in the method he pursues, obeys a correct, even if we should term it an animal, instinct, and approximates more closely to the techniques of science today . . . than does that of the semi-civilized, or of the ignorant of the enlightened communities of the present.
>
> Instinct has taught these peoples the necessity of expelling the placenta, and they attain this object by the correct means, by a *vis a tergo*, by expression—the Makah Indians even leaving this important duty to a specially skilled person.[405]

Although such techniques were advocated by Carl Franz Credé (1819–92), they were only slowly appreciated, but today (1883), Engelmann remarked, "the most illustrious masters look kindly upon a method of treatment as old as the world."[406]

Zeisberger's comments on the Indian knowledge of female medicine is typical of many others:

> In the matter of diseases peculiar to women, the women know a number of remedies, which usually act quickly and well, as in the case of hard labor, which sometimes occurs, though not frequently, and in other troubles. If

[404] *Medicine Among American Indians*, 74.
[405] *Labor Among Primitive Peoples*, 161, 171, 176, 197–98.
[406] *Ibid.*, 160.

mothers cannot suckle children for want of milk, they are able, by use of a drink, to increase the supply.[407]

The ease of childbirth among Indian women was long a cause of amazement to white observers. The Indian wives, wrote Josselyn, "have the easiest labours of any women in the world. . . . They are delivered in a trice, not so much as groaning for it."[408] Lawson held the same view, and thought that "their Remedies are a great Cause of this Easiness in that State."[409] In the same vein, Ezra Stiles wrote in 1761:

> I have often been told that a pregnant Squaw will turn aside & deliver herself, & take up the Infant and wash it in a Brook, & walk off. They do not lye by the Month; but make little more about Pregnancy and Lying in than the Cows.[410]

Protracted labor was, however, sometimes reported, and Carver mentioned that in such cases the Indians bound a handkerchief tightly over the mouth and nose of the woman, which brought on partial suffocation; from the struggles that ensued, "she was in a few seconds delivered." Of this, Dr. Toner remarked, "the insensibility and relaxation produced by this treatment may have relaxed the muscles, and in some respects resemble a state of anesthesia."[411]

To ease labor, medicines were given sometime before the expected birth or during it. A decoction of pulverized rattles from a rattlesnake's tail used by Sacajawea in 1804, was also mentioned as an aid to parturition by Bossu and by Lawson.[412] Herbal medicines were also commonly used. Among Illinois-Miamis, a de-

---

[407] "History of the North American Indians," *Ohio Archaeological and Historical Quarterly*, Vol. XIX, Nos., 1–2 (January and April, 1910), 56.

[408] Josselyn, *Two Voyages*, 99–100.

[409] *History of North Carolina*, 200. He further mentioned midwives well versed in remedies and doctors who specialized in delivery.

[410] *Extracts from the Itineraries and Miscellanies of Ezra Stiles, 1755–1794*, ed. by F. B. Dexter, 146, 411.

[411] Carver, *Travels*, 372, Toner, *Address, Rocky Mountain Medical Association*, 98–99.

[412] Lawson, *History of North Carolina*, 134, and p. 92, herein.

coction of sumach leaves and berries, and a root called "Palla-ganghy, which is to say Ocre," was given to confined women.[413] The Catawbas used an infusion of the bark of poplar, wild cherry, and dogwood, given the expectant mother to drink at frequent intervals.[414] Ruth Landes was told by her Kansas Potawatomi informant, Maquat, that his grandmother taught him "a secret childbirth remedy that I used on my [white] wife. It succeeded after all the white doctors in Nemaha County had despaired."[415]

Numerous other remedies were used by Indians during labor, either to promote contractions or to relieve pain. In cases of difficult birth, caused by a malpositioned fetus, the Aztecs used nopal (prickly pear, *Opuntia* species); the leaves were peeled, ground up, and given in water as a drink.[416] The Alabama-Koasatis used boiled roots of the cotton plant as an oxytocic agent (see p. 295) while the Zuñis used corn smut (*Ustilago zeae*) for easier labor. These two remedies have been recognized for the same uses in white medicine. To relieve labor pains, the Meskwakis used a decoction of the root of wild yam (*Dioscorea villosa* L.).[417] The trillium species have been called squaw root, birth root, and papoose root because of their widespread use by Indians as parturients.

Indian women did not always lie prone during delivery. Hrdlička's observations among southwestern tribes are in accord with those of Engelmann and others:

> Delivery takes place while the woman is squatting, or on her knees, or on hands and knees or elbows, or lying down;

413 Kinietz, *Indians of the Western Great Lakes*, 221–22.

414 Speck, "Catawba Medicines and Curative Practices," *Transactions of the Philadelphia Anthropological Society*, Vol. I, 190.

415 "Potawatomi Medicine," *Transactions Kansas Academy of Sciences*, Vol. LXVI (1963), 474. Dr. Z. Pitcher remarked in the 1850's: "I know of but one article having any just claim to the qualities imputed to it, used by them [the Indians] to facilitate parturition, and that is the *Sanguinaria canadensis* (blood root)." Schoolcraft, *Indian Tribes*, IV, 515.

416 Sahagún, *Things of New Spain*, Book XI, 180.

417 Smith, *Meskwaki Ethnobotany*, 200.

frequently she holds on to an attendant, or to a sash, rope, strap, or stick which is fastened somewhere for the purpose.

The assistance given by a midwife or female relative consisted "mainly of pressure or kneading with the hands or with a bandage about the abdomen, the object of which is to give direct aid in the expulsion of the child." Cedar decoctions or steam were also used to promote delivery.[418] In manipulation, the Arikaras placed a piece of fur over the hand to prevent wounding the vulva with the fingernails. For the same reason Arikara doctors never inserted the hand in the vagina for corrective manipulation. In case of malposition, Gilmore declared, "the helpers lift the woman and gently sway her from side to side while her abdomen is gently manipulated in order to change the child's position."

If there was postpartum hemorrhage, the Arikaras gave the juice of chokecherry (*Prunus melanocarpa*) to drink, and also combined the gum of that tree with the powdered root of the *Malva coccinea* (mallow) into an infusion given as a drink. In case of blood clot, or inflammation and abscess of the breast, the pulverized roots of red baneberry (*Actaea rubra*) were used, being combined, in the latter case, with the application of a poultice made from the spore mass of a puffball.[419]

Penobscot women tied a light bandage around their own and the infant's abdomen immediately after childbirth, believing it facilitated healing and prevented excessive bleeding.[420] This suggests the "squaw belt" that Sioux women attached to themselves immediately after the delivery of the child, which caused quick expulsion of the placenta and cessation of hemorrhage.[421] The Cherokees used herbal medicines to eliminate the afterbirth, including a decoction of mad dog skullcap (*Scutellaria lateriflora* L.), or leaf cup, saw briar, hemlock, and buttonwood.[422] For the

[418] Hrdlička, *Physiological and Medical Observations,* 55–56.

[419] Gilmore, "Notes on Gynecology and Obstetrics of the Arikara Tribe," *Papers of the Michigan Academy of Sciences, Arts and Letters,* Vol. XIV (1930), 74–76.

[420] Speck, "Medicine Practices of the Northeastern Algonquians," *Proceedings XIXth International Congress of Americanists,* 312.

[421] Engelmann, *Labor among Primitive Peoples,* 160.

[422] Mooney and Olbrechts, *Swimmer Manuscript,* 126.

same purpose, the Comanches used *Helenium microcephalum* (sneezeweed), which accomplished the object by inducing sneezing.[423] For afterbirth pains, the Rappahannocks put fowl feathers in a pot and burned them with yellow pine splints. The fumes from these were breathed by the confined woman.[424]

Infant care. As a prophylactic and therapeutic measure, the Cherokees placed a puffball on the navel of a newborn infant and left it there until the withered remains of the cord fell off.[425] Plains tribes followed a similar practice,[426] while the Pimas applied the pollen of the *Tylostoma* fungus to the cord of the newborn infant both as a preventative of inflammation and as a remedy when inflammation or suppuration developed.[427]

The Ojibwas bathed a newborn baby in water in which reindeer moss (*Cladonia rangiferina*) had been boiled.[428] Arikara babies were bathed in warm water, while the mouth, nostrils, and eyes were washed out with an infusion of the root of red baneberry.[429] Cherokee babies were bathed in a decoction of golden club (*Orontium aquaticum*) every new moon.[430] Several tribes used various powders as a baby talcum to prevent or relieve skin chafing. The Menominee remedy was pulverized gem puffballs (*Lycoperdon pyriforme*).[431] The Potawatomis used *Lycoperdon subincarnatum* for the same purpose.[432] Powdered puffballs and scorched cornmeal were used by the Rappahannocks.[433]

[423] Carlson and Jones, "Some Notes on Uses of Plants by the Comanche Indians," *Papers of the Michigan Academy of Sciences, Arts and Letters*, Vol. XXV (1939), 522.

[424] Speck, *Rappahannock Herbals*, 39.

[425] Mooney and Olbrechts, *Swimmer Manuscript*, 76.

[426] Gilmore, "Uses of Plants by Indians of the Missouri River Region," *Thirty-third Annual Report of the Bureau of American Ethnology, 1911–12*, 62.

[427] Hrdlička, *Physiological and Medical Observations*, 245.

[428] Smith, *Ojibwe Ethnobotany*, 373.

[429] Gilmore, "Notes on Gynecology and Obstetrics of the Arikara Tribe," *Papers Michigan Academy of Sciences, Arts and Letters*, Vol. XIV (1930), 77.

[430] Mooney and Olbrechts, *Swimmer Manuscript*, 76.

[431] Smith, *Menomini Ethnobotany*, 21.

[432] *Idem, Potawatomi Ethnobotany*, 64.

[433] Speck, *Rappahannock Herbals*, 33, 36.

Lawson remarked, over 250 years ago, that not even the youngest Indian women failed to be good nurses for their children, bringing them up free from rickets and "Disasters that proceed from the Teeth, with many other Distempers which attack our Infants in England, and other Parts of Europe. They let their children súck till they are well grown, unless they prove big with Child sooner. They always nurse their children themselves."[434]

If an Arikara mother had an insufficient flow of milk, an artificial baby food was made in the form of a broth of flint corn and buffalo meat. A wet nurse was used, if available.[435] Indians also had several remedies which were believed to increase the flow of milk.[436]

Menstruation. Menstruating women usually occupied a separate lodge, had a special diet, and were relieved of work during their periods. Lawson observed that "the Savage Women quit all Company, and dress not their own Victuals during their Purgations."[437] Among southwestern tribes, according to Hrdlička, "the menstruating woman is generally to some extent tabued."[438] Among the same tribes, he added, "scanty or very profuse menstruation, or habitually painful menstruation" was heard of much less than among American white women.

[434] Lawson, *History of North Carolina*, 200. Among southwestern tribes, Hrdlička reported: "The nursing of the infant presents one characteristic feature, found among all the tribes visited: It is generally prolonged much beyond the period customary among the whites. . . . unless a new pregnancy intervenes, the infant is not wholly weaned until 2, 3, or even 4 or more years old." From three to eight months after birth, he added, other food was added. *Physiological and Medical Observations*, 76.

[435] Gilmore, "Notes on Gynecology and Obstetrics of the Arikara Tribe," *Papers Michigan Academy of Sciences, Arts and Letters*, Vol. XIV (1930), 77.

[436] E.g., the Cheyenne, Omaha, and Ponca Indians used an infusion of the skeleton weed (*Lygodesmia juncea*), to increase milk flow. For the same purpose, baneberry (*Actaea arguta*), was used by the Cheyenne. Gilmore, "Uses of Plants by the Indians of the Missouri River Region," *Thirty-third Annual Report of the Bureau of American Ethnology, 1911–12*, 136; Grinnell, "Some Cheyenne Plant Medicines," *American Anthropologist*, N.S., Vol. VII, No. 1 January–March, 1905), 41.

[437] *History of North Carolina*, 201.

[438] *Physiological and Medical Observations*, 157.

Indians had several remedies to overcome delayed menstruation, to control profuse menstruation, or to relieve pain.[439] During their period, Arikara women took an infusion of the big wild sage (*Artemisia gnaphalodes*) or the roots of little wild sage (*Artemisia frigida*), a bitter tonic considered useful as an aid to the physiologic functions. For sanitary napkins, these women washed and cut into suitable pieces the soft and pliable buffalo-skin smoke flaps from their lodges. In this tribe it was also the custom for menstruating women to occupy a small lodge apart from their families.[440]

The Rappahannocks relieved menstrual pain with a tea of fresh or dried pennyroyal (*Hedeoma pulegioides*), or a tea made of split twigs of the spicebush (*Benzoin aestivale*). The last was also used to correct delayed menses.[441]

From the information presented in the next pages, it seems likely that Indian experimentation with emmenagogues led to the discovery in some tribes of the possibility of controlling the fertility cycle by these means.

Abortion and infanticide. In the eighteenth century, an informant told Ezra Stiles that New England Indians "abhorred Bastards & their Mothers." They were said to have had:

> . . . a sort of old Woman who procured Abortions by profession; that the Girls and their Parents & these old Squaws took especial precaution & care to force Abortions which was a general & customary Thing.

Sometimes the roots, powders, and decoctions failed to procure the desired result, in which case the young woman was delivered alone in the woods and killed the child as soon as it was born.[442]

---

[439] Emmart (ed.), *Badianus Manuscript*, 317, contains a formula for drying up of excessive menstrual fluid. *Cf.*, Bourke, "Popular Medicine, Customs, and Superstitions of the Rio Grande," *Journal of American Folk-Lore*, Vol. VII, No. 25 (April–June, 1894), 135, and remedies in this work.

[440] Gilmore, "Notes on Gynecology and Obstetrics of the Arikara Tribe," *Papers Michigan Academy of Sciences, Arts and Letters*, Vol. XIV (1930), 77.

[441] Speck, *Rappahannock Herbals*, 33.

[442] Stiles, *Itineraries*, 144–45.

Hrdlička declared that the desire for and love of children was universal among the Indians, but that artificial abortion was nevertheless practiced among all the tribes he visited. The causes were "shame or fear among the unmarried, and among married women inability through poverty to provide for the family, or a loss of previous children," as well as a desire in some cases to avoid the cares involved. Both physical means and herbal remedies were used. An infant was sometimes killed, especially if it was deformed, or the father was a non-Indian.[443]

Among the Cherokees, according to Mooney and Olbrechts, abortion was unknown.[444] Hunter, whose chief observations were among the Osages, reported that Indians sometimes used a "Black Root" as an abortive.[445]

Contraceptives. More than thirty years ago the late Norman Himes wrote that: "Judging by the paucity of reports, the primitive tribes of North America seem to have practiced contraception very little." He reported from the limited literature he had examined the use of several herbs, mostly unidentified, used as intended oral contraceptives among several tribes[446] and concluded, with respect to the Cherokee recipe:

It is highly probable that it was useless; *for no drug has yet been discovered which, when taken by mouth, will induce temporary sterility.*[447]

Himes concluded that "American tribes had no effective methods of preventing conception," and that they relied mainly on abortion, infanticide, and abstention to control family size.

[443] Hrdlička, *Physiological and Medical Observations*, 163–66.

[444] Mooney and Olbrechts, *Swimmer Manuscript*, 117.

[445] Hunter, *Manners and Customs*, 372.

[446] Shawnee: unidentified herb; Cherokee: roots of spotted cowbane (*Cicuta maculata*), chewed for four days; Neah Bay (Washington): unidentified herb decoction; Isleta: unidentified medicine; Canelos of Ecuador: *piripiri* roots.

Thomas Jefferson was informed that Virginia Indians "have learned the practice of procuring abortion by the use of some vegetable; and that it even extends to prevent conception for a considerable time after." Koch and Peden, *Selected Writings of Thomas Jefferson*, 211.

[447] Norman E. Himes, *Medical History of Contraception*, 12–17, my emphasis. This book was first published in 1936 and was never revised.

Events have since proved how wrong Himes was, for not only have oral contraceptives come into general use in advanced countries, but Indian herbs were finally subjected to laboratory tests in the search for an effective oral means of controlling fertility, and some of them were found to be effective. Just as America was considered to be undiscovered before the white men found it, so the Indian drugs were unreal or of no account until white men discovered them. This is one example among many of the ethnocentric attitude which has hurt the white men more than the Indian by delaying scientific inquiry into aboriginal herbal knowledge. The Cherokee drug *may* have been of no use, but what is striking here is the way it was rejected *a priori*, simply because white men knew of no oral contraceptive, and therefore, presumably, none existed. It is noteworthy that until recently it could not only be said that Indian recipes for controlling fertility had not been investigated, but that the very names of the drugs used were largely unknown.

In the early eighteenth century, Lawson reported that "the trading Girls" among the Indians "have an Art to destroy Conception."[448] Isaac de Rasieres wrote in 1628 of the New York Indians that "it is a wonder when a woman has three or four children."[449] At the beginning of the nineteenth century, Humboldt said that a leading cause of the depopulation of mission Indians on the Orinoco, who had not been reached by smallpox, was "the guilty practice of preventing pregnancy by the use of deleterious herbs."[450]

Hrdlička reported that among the southwestern tribes:

There is a very general belief among the Indians visited that sterility may be artificially induced. To produce this

[448] *History of North Carolina*, 198–99.

[449] Jameson (ed.), *Narratives of New Netherland*, 109. He did not, however, consider the possible effect of a high infant mortality. Hrdlička in 1908 reported an average of 5.5 living *persons* per family among the Hopi, 5.7 among the Zuñi, and seven children each among the Pima and San Carlos Apache. He held that, "It is not a deficient birth rate but great mortality which keeps the majority of the tribes from increasing rapidly." *Physiological and Medical Observations*, 42–43.

[450] Humboldt, *Personal Narrative*, II, 248–49.

result the women . . . take internally certain harmless substances . . . which to the Indian are representative of sterility.
The San Carlos Apache believe that artificial sterility can be
induced, but the means is not generally known. It is supposed to be some variety of root. . . .

Among the White Mountain Apache a woman desiring to
have no children, or to stop bearing, swallows now and then
a little of the red burned earth from beneath the fire. This
means, which is much believed in, is used mostly by the
dissolute unmarried, but also by sickly or very poor married
women. Some of the Huichol women drink a decoction of
a certain plant to prevent childbearing. Cora women, for the
same purpose, take internally the scrapings of the male
deer horn.[451]

The long periods of nursing infants, three years and more,
among the Indians, is one indication that they were spacing their
children. It is reported that if an Isleta (pueblo) woman did not
wish to conceive "she will not have intercourse for nine days
after menstruation . . . nor during pregnancy, nor for six months
after child birth."[452] Some Indians were aware of "safe periods"
for intercourse, and the Hopis believed that the time just before
menstruation offered the least likelihood of conception taking
place.[453]

Numerous herbal substances were used by Indians as oral contraceptives. The Cherokees believed that chewing the root of
spotted cowbane (*Cicuta maculata*) for four days would induce
permanent sterility. To use it, however, was considered "nothing
less than a crime."[454] One aboriginal oral contraceptive which

[451] Hrdlička, *Physiological and Medical Observations*, 165–66.

[452] Elsie Clews Parsons, "Isleta, New Mexico," *Forty-seventh Annual Report
of the Bureau of American Ethnology, 1929–30*, 213, cited in Himes, *Medical
History of Contraception*, 15.

[453] Clellan Ford, "Control of Conception in Cross Cultural Perspective,"
Annals of the New York Academy of Sciences, Vol. LIV (May 2, 1952), 764.

[454] Mooney and Olbrechts, *Swimmer Manuscript*, 117. This hostile attitude
toward birth control is also evidenced among the Navaho. The Bureau of Indian
Affairs has recently tried to introduce "family planning" services in this largest

has been tested in clinical experiments was the stoneseed (*Lithospermum ruderale,* fam. *Baraginaceae*) of the Nevada tribes. The Indian women drank an infusion of the roots for a period of six months. Of this drug Clellan Ford reports:

> Preliminary experimental work showed that feeding mice with alcoholic extracts of this plant abolished the normal estrous cycle, and decreased the weights of the sex organs, thymus, and pituitary. Noble, Plunkett, and Taylor carried on research by administering lyophylized aqueous extracts of both the tops and roots of the plants to rats and found that the number of estrous smears decreased. Subsequent work with rabbits led them to conclude that Lithosperma apparently inhibits the actions of gonadotrophins in the ovary. In view of the original uses of the plant, the authors suggest that the unit of activity in Lithosperma be expressed in terms of P.P.U.'s, *i.e.*, Papoose Preventative Units.[455]

De Laszlo and Henshaw listed several dozen fertility-affecting drugs used by primitive peoples, including Indians, some, but not all, of which had been tested. They were divided into three groups, as follows:

---

of American tribes. In the *Navajo Times* (Window Rock, Ariz.), July 29, 1965, acting editor Leslie Goodluck reviewed these efforts and retorted:

> We have yet to see a family in the hogan, no matter how poor they might be, who did not have one little extra piece of mutton or bread for another baby.
>
> We had Washington's STOCK REDUCTION program forced on us, now it would seem that they are trying to sell us a PEOPLE REDUCTION program.
>
> Washington has told us when and how to do a lot of things in the past— but we seriously doubt if they are going to be able to tell us either when not to, or how not to make babies. As long as there are big Navajos there are going to be little Navajos.

[455] Ford, "Control of Conception in Cross-Cultural Perspective," *Annals of the New York Academy of Sciences,* Vol. LIV (May 2, 1952), 766. It has been suggested that *Lithospermum* may also have been used by Comanche women. One writer declares that recently "a plague of sterility struck cattle on the mid-west ranges, resulting in worldwide research on an herb known to Indians as Desert Tea and to botanists as *Lithospermum.* . . . this herb is now believed to have been an Indian specific, especially with the *Shoshones.*" M. J. Atkinson, *Indians of the Southwest,* 303.

$Oc.$ So-called oral contraceptives thought to excite temporary sterility.

$Oc_1.$ Substances which in certain doses are believed to interfere with implantation or gestation but which might well prove to be in class Oc if used in smaller concentrations.

$Oc_2.$ Emmenagogues, plant materials believed to affect menstruation, many of which after investigation might be put in class $Oc.$ when their active principles have been isolated and their therapeutic activity determined.

In the first group they placed the following: Boiled roots of dogbane (*Apocynum androsaemifolium*) ["North America"]; powdered-root decoction of Indian turnip (*Arisaema triphyllum*) [Hopi ?]; decoction of boiled root and rhizome of wild ginger (*Asarum canadense*) ["North America"]; infusion of milkweed plant (*Asclepias halli*) drunk after childbirth [Navaho]; infusion of pulverized roots and rhizomes of milkweed (*Asclepias syriaca*), drunk to produce temporary sterility [Quebec]; "twisted medicine," *Bahia dissecta*, infusion of roots boiled and drunk by women during menstruation, and also used by men [Navaho]; poison arum (*Caladium seguinum*), "Heard of plants used by Indian women to render temporary or permanent sterility; on two occasions evidently Araceae"; stops spermatogenesis and follicle growth in rats [South America]; *Castilleja linariae folia*, Indian paint brush, "a decoction of this plant was sometimes used—as it dried up the menstrual flow" [Hopi]; *Cicuta maculata* [Cherokee]; antelope sage (*Eriogonum jamesii*), boiled root drunk by woman during menstruation to prevent conception; used by both sexes [Navaho]; deer's tongue (*Frasera speciosa*), "a half cupful taken once in a while" as a contraceptive [Nevada Shoshonean]; stoneseed, (*Lithospermum ruderale*), cold-water infusion of roots taken daily for six months to insure sterility [Nevada Shoshonean]; and rosemary (*Rosmarinus officinalis*), a tea of this plant and "ocean artemisia" taken for fertility control [Opata of Mexico].

In the second group they placed *Byrsonima crassifolia*, bark, leaves, and fruit used to expel placenta; roots used by Indians to produce expulsion [Oaxaca]; thistle (*Cnicus benedictus*), brewed and taken as tea [Quinault Indians]; squaw root (*Caulophyllum thalictroides*), powdered root taken to expedite parturition and menstruation [Chippewa]; *Cicuta maculata* [Cherokee]; rosemary [Opata]; *Montanoa tomentosa*, used for difficult parturition and postpartum uterine hemorrhage [Zapotec, Mexico]; rue (*Ruta graveolens*), decoction to promote menstruation, larger doses induce fetal expulsion [Europe and South America]; American mistletoe (*Pharadendron flavescens*), tea made from leaves [Indians of Mendocino County, Calif.]; *Leucaena glauca*, decoction of root and bark [West Indies and South America]; false solomonseal (*Smilacina stellata*), root infusion regulates menstrual disorders; conception prevented by tea of leaves [Nevada Indians].

In the third group they placed begonia (*Begonia balmisiana*) used to promote menstruation [Central America]; squaw root [Chippewa]; *Eupatorium odoratum*, root used, plant consecrated to goddess of pregnancy and childbirth [Zapotec, Mexico]; *Montanoa tomentosa* [Zapotec]; *Ruta graveolens* [South America]; *Leucaena glauca* [W. Indies and South America]; and *Smilacina stellata* [Nevada Indians].[456]

Taylor writes that the basic material for antifertility pills now in use is generally diosgenin from the Mexican wild yam (*Dioscorea*). "While a few of these steroid drugs are wholly synthetic," he adds, "the great bulk of them use diosgenin as the starting material for their manufacture."[457] The ancient Aztecs used *Dioscorea* for several medical purposes,[458] as do we (*e.g.*, cortisone), but there is no evidence that they used it to control fertility. Indian fertility drugs, however, helped to call attention to the

456 Henry de Laszlo and Paul S. Henshaw, "Plant Materials Used by Primitive Peoples to Affect Fertility," *Science*, Vol. CXIX, No. 3097 (May 7, 1954), 626–31. *A. triphyllum* reportedly is not native to Hopi country. DeLaszlo and Henshaw cited as their source a communication from William N. Fenton dated in 1952.

457 Taylor, *Plant Drugs That Changed the World*, 248.

458 Kreig, *Green Medicine*, 275.

possibilities and played a role in the research leading to recent discoveries in this field.[459]

Dentistry

Of the New England Indians, Josselyn remarked that "Their Teeth are very white, short and even, they account them the most necessary and best parts of man."[460] Skeletal remains indicate that ancient Indians, however, sometimes had problems with their teeth, including caries, abscesses, and worn molars.[461] It appears also that dental ills were more common among sedentary tribes who subsisted largely on corn than they were among the nomadic hunters.[462] It is further evident that the incidence of tooth decay was far less frequent among aboriginal Americans than among contemporary Americans.[463] Weston Price demonstrated in the 1930's that of 87 Indians living in remote parts of Yukon Territory who were examined by him, only four teeth out of 2,464 (0.16 per cent) had ever been attacked by dental caries. Indians living closer to white settlements had a rate of carious teeth ranging from 25.5 to 40 per cent, with the percentage increasing according to the degree of trading with the whites. Dr. Price, a dental surgeon, attributed the higher rate of tooth decay

[459] Other discoveries may also be in the making. Researchers at Indiana University have been exploring the effects on hormones of the drug *Lithospermum ruderale* (stoneseed), which is used by Shoshonean Indians of Nevada to suppress ovulation. Dr. William Breneman, an endocrinologist, tested chickens and mice with water extracts of substances from this plant and found that the liquid had "powerful inhibitory effects on such hormones as oxytocin, which controls contraction of the womb and suppresses blood pressure." *Science News Letter*, Vol. 87 (May 1, 1965), 281.

[460] *Two Voyages*, 97.

[461] Carl W. Beck and William P. Mulvaney, "Apatitic Urinary Calculi from Early American Indians," *Journal of the American Medical Association*, Vol. CXCV, No. 12 (March 21, 1966), 166–69.

[462] Krogman gave figures showing relatively higher rates of dental caries in Pueblo burials than among the hunting tribes. "Medical Practices and Diseases of the Aboriginal American Indians," *Ciba Symposia*, Vol. I, No. 1 (April, 1939), 15–16.

[463] Hrdlička, *Physiological and Medical Observations*, 190.

among certain Indians to their use of "the foods of modern commerce."[464]

The Aztecs attached some importance to cleaning the teeth, for the *Badianus Manuscript* directed that "unclean teeth are to be polished very diligently; when the tartar has been removed, they must be rubbed with a little cloth smeared with white ashes mixed with white honey so that their elegant brightness and proper gleam will last." It further prescribed that "pain in the teeth and gums is allayed by scarifying the gums and cleaning them of pus, if to the festering part be applied the seed and root of nettles, ground in the yolk of an egg and a little white honey." There were also involved directions for the treatment of decayed teeth.[465] According to Bernard Cobo in 1653, balsam of Peru was used by South American Indians to clean teeth, "tightening and soothing them."[466] Among the Incas a root like dandelion with caustic effects was applied for "invigorating the teeth and gums."[467]

The ancient Mayas knew how to make dental inlays and fillings, using hematite, jade, turquoise, and sometimes gold. The purpose, however, seems to have been ornamental rather than therapeutic.[468] Some Indians treated gum abscesses by lancing and cauterization, and removed aching teeth with a bone punch.[469]

Early accounts provide several descriptions of Indian ways of treating toothache and removing pain-causing teeth. According to Lawson:

They have several Remedies for the Tooth-ache, which often drive away the Pain: but if they fail, they have Recourse to

[464] Price, *Nutrition and Physical Degeneration*, 75–83.

[465] Emmart (ed.), *Badianus Manuscript*, 230–31.

[466] Haggis, "Fundamental Errors in the Early History of Cinchona," *Bulletin of the History of Medicine*, Vol. X, No. 3 (October, 1941), 431.

[467] La Vega, *The Incas*, 39.

[468] Samuel Fastlicht, "Dental Inlays and Fillings Among the Ancient Mayas," *Journal of the History of Medicine*, Vol. XVII, No. 2 (July, 1962), 393–401.

[469] Adams, "Aboriginal American Medicine and Surgery," *Proceedings of the Indiana Academy of Science*, Vol. LXI (1951), 52.

punching out the Tooth with a small Cane set against the same on a Bit of Leather. Then they strike the Reed and so drive out the Tooth; and howsoever it may seem to the Europeans, I prefer it before the common way of drawing Teeth by those Instruments that endanger the Jaw, and a Flux of Blood often follows which this Method of a Punch never is attended withal: neither is it half the Pain.[470]

Josselyn noted that upon the back of the dogfish grew a "thorn," two or three inches long, "that helps the toothach; scarifying the gums therewith."[471] Presumably this was an Indian device, for Josselyn's knowledge of the uses of New World flora and fauna came from them.

Some of the Iroquois toothache remedies were reported by Peter Kalm. An Indian woman on the Mohawk River, who had a violent toothache from "frequent drinking of tea," cured the same by boiling the sweet bay (*Myrica asplenifolia*) and tying it to her cheek as a hot poultice. The chief remedy for toothache among the Iroquois, which a white informant assured Kalm was effectual, consisted of the ripe seed capsules of the Virginia anemone, which were rubbed in pieces so that they resembled cotton. They were then dipped in brandy and the bitterness of the seeds, Kalm believed, was responsible for the effects.[472]

One of the most universal toothache remedies among Indians was the bark of the prickly ash (*Zanthoxylum* species; see pp. 352–54), which was soon adopted as a remedy by whites, who often called it the "toothache tree." The Choctaws chewed the bark of the buttonbush (*Cephalanthus occidentalis*) to relieve toothache.[473] Some of the other remedies used included the placing of a small wad of tobacco in the cavity, [474] or the applica-

---

[470] *History of North Carolina*, 234.

[471] Josselyn, *New-England's Rarities*, 164.

[472] Kalm, *Travels*, I, 227–28.

[473] Bushnell, *Choctaw of Bayou Lacomb*, 24.

[474] Speck, *Rappahannock Herbals*, 29; Mooney and Olbrechts, *Swimmer Manuscript*, 72.

tion of the root of purple coneflower (*Echinacea* species),[475] or bear spleen.[476] The Meskwakis used a tea made from the root bark of panicled dogwood (*Cornus paniculata*) to ease pain caused by sore teeth or neuralgia; it was held in the mouth.[477]

A toothache remedy in use among the Pennsylvania Germans is said to have been learned from the Indians. It consists of a decoction of the bark of the root of the "white poplar" (tulip tree, *Liriodendron tulipifera*) applied hot to the marrow of the infected tooth.[478]

Illinois-Miami Indians had two remedies for *"mal du Terre"* (trench mouth?), one of which was the decoction of sumach leaves and the root of "Pallaganghy," to be held in the mouth; the other was root bark of wild cherry "held a long time on the gum."[479]

In treating carious teeth, the Ojibwas heated an awl or other metal instrument (obtained from whites) almost red hot and inserted it into the hollow of the affected teeth. If extraction was necessary, they struck the tooth forcibly to loosen it. If the tooth was partly loosened, they tied a sinew around it, close to the root, attached it to something solid and pulled the tooth by jerking backward.[480] The Mescalero Apaches treated aching teeth by inserting a hot twig into the cavity, or on the surface if there was no cavity. Teeth were not pulled unless they were loose.[481]

Several substances were used to clean the teeth. Southern Indians and whites chewed a species of *Silphium*, containing a resinous substance.[482] Meskwakis cleaned the teeth with a white clay.[483] Teeth were also kept clean through the eating of raw fruits and vegetables.

[475] Carlson and Jones, "Some Notes on Uses of Plants by the Comanche Indians," *Papers Michigan Academy of Science*, Vol. XXV (1939), 525.

[476] Kinietz, *Indians of the Western Great Lakes*, 222.

[477] Smith, *Meskwaki Ethnobotany*, 219.

[478] Brendle and Unger, *Folk Medicine of the Pennsylvania Germans*, 116.

[479] Kinietz, *Indians of the Western Great Lakes*, 222.

[480] Densmore, "Uses of Plants by the Chippewa Indians," *Forty-fourth Annual Report of the Bureau of American Ethnology, 1926–27*, 335

[481] Hrdlička, *Physiological and Medical Observations*, 237.

[482] Bartram, *Travels*, 252–53; see p. 104, herein.

[483] Smith, *Meskwaki Ethnobotany*, 199.

Diet

Ackerknecht has declared that "primitive diets, though frugal, were as a rule better balanced than those of civilized peoples, and hence helped to lessen the incidence of deficiency diseases."[484] While Indians had no scientific knowledge of nutrition, many had arrived at an understanding that certain kinds of food were necessary for good health. Indians from one coast to the other seem to have understood which plant or animal substances could prevent or cure scurvy, and several examples have been previously cited. From the case of Cartier in 1535 to Prince Maximilian in 1834,[485] the records are strewn with reports of effective Indian scurvy cures. In the seventeenth century, Josselyn wrote that "the tops of Spruce-boughs, boiled in bear [beer] and drunk, is assuredly one of the best remedies for the scurvy; restoring the infected party in a short time. They [the Indians] also make a lotion of some of the decoction, adding honey and allum."[486] It is notable that "spruce beer" was one of the antiscorbutics used on Captain Cook's voyage of 1776–80,[487] and that spruce tea was drunk by the California gold-rushers of 1849 in order to prevent scurvy.[488]

Dr. Colden wrote to Peter Kalm in 1751 that the children of European migrants commonly lost their teeth from scurvy although the native Indians did not. "I have heard," he added, "that the Indians use the roots of one kind of Nymphaea" as a preventative."[489]

A recent instance of aboriginal wisdom in this area of health is reported by Dr. Weston Price, who asked an Indian of Yukon Territory why the Indians did not get scurvy and was promptly told that it was a white man's disease. When pressed as to whether it was possible for Indians to get scurvy, the Indian

---

484 Ackerknecht, "Primitive Medicine: A Contrast with Modern Practice," *The Merck Report* (July, 1946), 5.

485 See pp. 84–85, 108–109, herein.

486 *New-England's Rarities*, 200.

487 Scott, *History of Tropical Medicine*, I, 23.

488 Peter Decker, *The Diaries of Peter Decker*, 209.

489 Colden, *Letters and Papers*, IV, 259.

replied that it was, but that the Indians knew how to prevent it and the white man did not. Price then persuaded the Indian to reveal their means of prevention:

> He then described how when the Indian kills a moose he opens it up and at the back of the moose just above the kidney there are what he described as two small balls in the fat. These he said the Indian would take and cut up into as many pieces as there were . . . Indians in the family and each one would eat his piece. They would also eat the walls of the second stomach. By eating these parts of the animal the Indians would keep free from scurvy, which is due to the lack of vitamin C. The Indians were getting vitamin C from the adrenal glands and organs. Modern science has very recently discovered that the adrenal glands are the richest sources of vitamin C in all animal or plant tissues.[490]

Dr. Price also reported that Andean tribes ate dried fish eggs obtained from the sea in the belief that it maintained the fertility of their women. It provided them with essential iodine. These Indians also used dried kelp and in this instance gave the perfectly rational explanation that it was eaten "so they would not get 'big necks' [goiter] like the whites."[491] Another report involving the potato-eating Quechuas of Lake Titicaca revealed that before eating their potatoes they dipped them into an aqueous suspension of clay in order to prevent "souring of the stomach." The clay, upon examination, proved to consist mainly of kaolin with a trace of coumarin. "Such a practice," investigators remarked, "by a primitive people would appear rather remarkable in view of the comparatively recent introduction of kaolin into modern medicine as a protective agent for the gastric and intestinal mucosa and as a remedy for bacterial infections of the gut."[492]

Humboldt reported that the Ottomacs on the Orinoco, during

---

[490] *Nutrition and Physical Degeneration*, 75.

[491] *Ibid.*, 265.

[492] *Ibid.*, 267, quoting A. Lawson and H. P. Moon. Spruce saw Indians on the Alto Río Negro occasionally eat small roasted balls of white clay. Spruce, *Notes of a Botanist*, I, 345–46.

the season when floods prevented fishing, ate daily three quarters of a pound of clay slightly hardened by fire, which was moistened before swallowing. It was gathered from alluvial beds, was not mixed with organic matter, and contained 3 or 4 per cent of lime. In the Peruvian mountains, he saw pulverized lime sold in native markets. When eaten, it was mixed with coca leaves (*Erythroxylon peruvianum*). Elsewhere, the Guajiros swallowed lime alone and carried it with them in little boxes. Both products, Humboldt remarked, served to excite the secretion of saliva and gastric juice while suppressing appetite.[493]

Among Canadian Indians, Charlevoix reported that "they boast above all things of their skill in dieting, which according to them consists in abstaining from certain aliments which they reckon deterimental."[494] William Wood reported that New England Indians were healthy as long as they held to their native diet, but "when they change their bare Indian commons for the plenty of England's fuller diet, it is so contrary to their stomach, that death or a desperate sickness immediately accrues."[495] Indians held to certain beliefs concerning proper food. Food seasonings popular in Europe, even salt, were usually rejected.[496] "The Salts they mix with their Bred and Soup, to give them a Relish," said Lawson, "are Alkalis, viz.; Ashes, and calcined Bones of Deer, and other Animals. Sallads, they never eat any, as for Pepper and Mustard, they reckon us little better than Madmen, to make use of it amongst our Victuals."[497]

Some observers have remarked that because of the irregularity

[493] *Personal Narrative*, II, 495–96, 499.

[494] *Journal*, I, 162.

[495] *New England's Prospects*, 74.

[496] Although Indians knew of salt, and sometimes, as in Southern Illinois, obtained it by evaporation from salt springs, they seem to have seldom used it to season food. Such are the reports of many writers, including Josselyn, Charlevoix, and Zeisberger. The last named reported: "they use very little salt and seem not to require it. They often eat their food unsalted, even though they may have the salt, until they feel a longing for it." Zeisberger, "History of the North American Indians," *Ohio Archaeological and Historical Quarterly*, Vol. XIX, Nos. 1–2 (January and April, 1910), 53.

[497] *History of North Carolina*, 236.

of the food supply in hunting tribes, they alternated between fasting and overeating. "Sometimes," said Loskiel, "they fast from morning till late at night, and then, making a sudden transformation from hunger and want to the greatest plenty, they gratify their voracious appetites without restraint. The painful consequences of these irregularities are too visible in old age."[498] Zeisberger, his mentor,[499] reported that diarrhea was aggravated "because they [the Delawares] know nothing of dieting and continue to eat whatever they wish."[500] The Miami Indians, wrote Volney, "having no stores nor durable provision," were "liable to the most violent vicissitudes of scarcity and superfluity." When, following a long fast, they would bring down an animal, "they fall on it like vultures, and leave it not till they are gorged to the throat."[501] Indians received some plaudits, however, for the way they prepared their food. "They boil and roast their Meat extraordinarily much," wrote Lawson, "and eat abundance of Broth."[502] Dr. Rush noted that Indians took pains to preserve the juice of their meat while roasting it by turning it often. "The efficacy of this animal juice," he declared, "in dissolving meat in the stomach, has not been equalled by any of those sauces or liquors, which modern luxury has mixed with it for that purpose."[503]

Indians followed special dietary precautions during illness. "When they are sick, they only drink Broth, and eat sparingly," Baron Lahontan wrote of the Algonquins.[504] "In Wounds which penetrate deep and seem mortal," Lawson wrote, "they order a spare Diet, with drinking Fountain water."[505] During illness, Adair wrote, the Cherokees "always enjoin a most abstemious

---

[498] *Mission of the United Brethren*, I, 207.

[499] Many of the passages in Loskiel closely resemble earlier writings of Zeisberger.

[500] Zeisberger, "History of the North American Indians," *Ohio Archaeological and Historical Quarterly*, Vol. XIX, Nos. 1–2 (January and April, 1910), 149.

[501] *View of the Soil and Climate*, 368–69.

[502] *History of North Carolina*, 237.

[503] *Medicine Among the Indians*, 109.

[504] *New Voyages*, II, 467.

[505] *History of North Carolina*, 15.

life: they forbid them women, salt, and every kind of fresh-meat."[506] Hunter reported that Indians practiced the still popular maxim of "starving a fever." During fever and "consumption" they abstained from animal food, subsisting mainly on a gruel of parched corn meal.[507] Boas has reported on the dietary regimen of the Kwakiutls in diarrhea: hard food was eaten, but no clams or berries; only dog salmon or dry halibut. "Bark of fir was burned, and the coal pulverized and mixed with water in which water hemlock has been rubbed. This was taken internally."[508] Interestingly, charcoal has also been used in white medicine during digestive disturbances.

Among the Arikaras, Gilmore reported, pregnant and recently delivered women also followed special diets. The expectant mother was told to eat "good, wholesome, nourishing food, and, as her time of delivery approaches, to eat sparingly. She is warned that eating too much in the later stages of gestation will cause the baby to grow too large and fat, and that the pains of labor will be difficult and severe." During convalescence after delivery, she was to avoid heavy food. For the first three days, she was limited to a light soup or broth of the consistency of milk. Made of flint corn, this soup was considered easy to digest and an aid to the free flow of milk for the baby.[509]

Hygienic and Sanitary Practices

Bathing. Contrary to the assumptions of many whites, aboriginal Indians were a clean people and had a much higher regard for bathing than was common among their white neighbors. As late as 1850, Dr. Daniel Drake wrote that:

An overwhelming majority of our population seldom bathe at all. Of the efficacy of daily bathing, in the preservation of

---

[506] *History of the Indians,* 234.

[507] *Manners and Customs,* 402.

[508] "Current Beliefs of the Kwakiutl Indians," *Journal of American Folk-Lore,* Vol. XLV, No. 176 (April–June, 1932), 186.

[509] "Notes on Gynecology and Obstetrics of the Arikara Tribe," *Papers of the Michigan Academy of Sciences, Arts and Letters,* Vol. XIV (1930), 71, 74.

sound health and a hardy constitution, there can be no doubt; and it is much to be regretted, that the practice cannot be made more general.[510]

In contrast, more than a century earlier, John Brickell marveled that "when these *Savages* live near the Waters, they frequent the Rivers in Summer-time very much where both Men and Women often go in naked to wash themselves, not both Sexes together, yet this is not out of any point of modesty."[511] Among Indians west of the Mississippi, Hunter observed, bathing

. . . is much practiced, constitutes one of their greatest pleasures, and I am persuaded contributes very much to strengthen the body and invigorate the constitution. Men, women, and children, from early infancy, are in the daily habit of bathing, during the warm months, and not infrequently after cold weather has set in.[512]

Even the northern Indians, despite colder weather, practiced year round bathing.[513] Lewis H. Morgan, on his trip up the Missouri, was informed by a Potawatomi trader that "the northern Indians . . . particularly those who sleep entirely nude, usually in the coldest weather, roll up their clothes in their blanket and go to the river and plunge in and wash themselves before they dress daily."[514] Adair reported that southern Indians bathed in all seasons.[515]

Sweat bath. The sweat or vapor bath, according to Rivers, is an old Celtic and Teutonic practice found also in Africa, Melanesia, New Guinea, and Polynesia.[516] Except for its survival in the

[510] *Malaria in the Interior Valley,* 679.

[511] *Natural History,* 344.

[512] *Manners and Customs,* 370.

[513] Speaking of the Indian practice, Dr. Rush remarked: "The cold bath likewise fortifies the body and renders it less subject to those diseases which arise from the extremes and vicissitudes of heat and cold." *Medicine Among the Indians,* 113.

[514] *The Indian Journals, 1859–62,* 96.

[515] *History of the Indians,* 120.

[516] *Medicine, Magic and Religion,* 103. Wesley recommended "warm steams"

Finnish sauna, it seems to have nearly died out in Europe, at least, before the discovery of America.[517] It was in the New World, Rivers asserted, that the sweat bath reached its highest development.

Among the Aztecs, "the favorite remedy for almost every ill of the flesh was the vapor-bath, or temazcalli," wrote Bancroft.[518] In the *temazcalli*, wrote Sahagún, the sick "restore their bodies, their nerves. Those who are as if faint with sickness are there calmed, strengthened."[519] Sweat baths among the Virginia Indians were described by John Smith.[520] Lawson mentioned sweat baths among the Saponas and other tribes, "which they make much Use of; especially for any Pains in the Joints, got by Cold or Traveling."[521] De Vries saw sweat baths among Hudson River Indians, used "to cleanse themselves of their foulness."[522] The use of this device by Canadian Indians was reported by Father Jouvency, [523] while Bossu described it among the Choctaws, who used "steam cabinets in which are boiled all sorts of medicinal and sweet-smelling herbs. The vapor filled with the essence and salts of these herbs enters the patient's body through his pores and his nose and restores his strength." Bossu urged the white man to imitate the Indian custom at least three times a year, for it was a certain cure for many malfunctions, including the effects of overeating.[524]

In Canada, Sagard declared, "I have seen some of our Frenchmen in these sweat-baths along with the savages, and I was astonished that they wished and were able to endure it, and

for "indolent swellings" (*Primitive Physic*, 120), but the source of his idea is not known.

[517] Shortly before 1800, a Frenchman reported sweat houses in northwest Ireland. Dr. A. Martin, "Irish Sweat Huts," *Ciba Symposia*, Vol. I, No. 5 (August, 1939), 162.

[518] Bancroft, *Native Races*, II, 595.

[519] *Things of New Spain*, Book XI, 191.

[520] Tyler, *Narratives of Early Virginia*, 108.

[521] *History of North Carolina*, 39, 47, 236.

[522] Jameson, *Narratives of New Netherland*, 217–18.

[523] Thwaites (ed.), *Jesuit Relations*, I, 261.

[524] *Travels in the Interior*, 168, 219.

that a sense of propriety did not lead them to hold aloof from it."[525] Sweat lodges for a time came into general use among the colonists of the Canadian maritime provinces.[526]

Heckewelder told how in 1784 a man from Detroit came to the village of Christian Indians on the Huron River in order to utilize the sweat bath for an unstated ailment. The patient later reported that his use of the sweat oven "was the best thing he had ever done in his life for the benefit of his health."[527]

The sweat bath was more than a sanitary device; it was also a panacea for all diseases.[528] To the Indians, Loskiel asserted, the sweat bath was "their general remedy for all disorders, small or great . . . and in many cases the cure is complete."[529] It was one of the features of Indian therapeutics which was regarded as useful by the otherwise critical Benjamin Rush.[530] It was sometimes fraught with danger, because of their practice of following it up with a cold dip in a river or lake. Normally this led to no harm, but in smallpox epidemics, such as that of 1738 and in other years among the Cherokees, it was held responsible for a high fatality rate.[531]

A member of the Lewis and Clark expedition, William Bratton, became so crippled from rheumatic stiffness and back pains that he could neither ride nor walk. When other remedies failed, an Indian-type sweat bath was improvised, water being poured over hot stones in the Indian manner, to produce steam. The patient was also given a strong tea of horsemint, "having no

[525] Sagard, *Long Journey to the Country of the Hurons,* 198.

[526] Fenton, "Contacts between Iroquois Herbalism and Colonial Medicine," *Annual Report of the Board of Regents of the Smithsonian Institution for 1941,* 513, citing Bailey.

[527] *History, Manners and Customs of the Indian Nations,* 226–27.

[528] Walter Krickeberg, "The Indian Sweat Bath," *Ciba Symposia,* Vol. I, No. 1 (April, 1939), 23–24.

[529] *Mission of the United Brethren,* I, 109.

[530] *Medicine Among the Indians,* 122.

[531] Adair, *History of the Indians,* 234. A similar occurrence took place during a smallpox epidemic in 1865. Mooney and Olbrechts, *Swimmer Manuscript,* 61. In Carolina, Lawson wrote: "Their running into the Water, in the Extremity of this Disease, strikes it in, and kills all that use it." *History of North Carolina,* 237. See also Josselyn, *Two Voyages,* 103, for similar report of New England Indians.

snakeroot." It is reported that this procedure enabled Bratton to recover so completely that he could be active for the first time in four months.[532]

Sweat baths, accompanied by sudorific herbs, were so popular among the southern Plains Indians that Josiah Gregg called them the "primitive Thompsonians."[533] Bourke called the sweat bath "the main reliance for nearly all disorders" among the Apaches, and said the Zuñis used it for dyspepsia.[534] The San Carlos Apaches, according to Hrdlička, in one instance used sweat baths for children sick with measles, and they were taken occasionally for rheumatism or for other maladies when usual remedies failed.[535] The Kwakiutls used the sweat treatment when a disease could not be located and the symptoms were general weakness and localized pains.[536] The Penobscots were using the sweat bath when Speck was among them early in this century, and prepared for it by taking a "concoction" of seven sudorific herbs.[537]

Springs. Since colonial times the therapeutic value of bathing in and drinking the water of certain springs has been devoutly believed in by many Americans. Dr. John Morgan prescribed drinking from and bathing in mineral waters and his favorite was the "Yellow Springs" near Chester, Pennsylvania.[538] In the 1790's, Pacolet Springs, near Spartanburg, South Carolina, was being advertised as a health resort.[539] Jefferson believed that the hot baths of Virginia springs would cure herpes, a skin disease.[540]

[532] Drake Will, *Journal of the History of Medicine,* XIV (1959), 295.

[533] *Commerce of the Prairies,* Vol. XX in Thwaites (ed.), *Early Western Travels,* 334.

[534] "The Medicine-Men of the Apache," *Ninth Annual Report of the Bureau of American Ethnology, 1887–88,* 471.

[535] *Physiological and Medical Observations,* 234.

[536] Boas, "Current Beliefs of the Kwakiutl Indians," *Journal of American Folk-Lore,* Vol. XLV, No. 176 (April–June, 1932), 179.

[537] Speck, "Medicine Practices of the Northeastern Algonquians," *Proceedings XIXth International Congress of Americanists,* 312.

[538] Whitfield J. Bell, Jr., *John Morgan, Continental Doctor,* 152.

[539] Waring, *History of Medicine in South Carolina,* 109.

[540] Barton, *Essay Toward a Materia Medica,* II, 25.

Kalm reported that Canadians used sulphurous springs to cure the "itch."[541]

The Indians, too, used spring water internally and externally in the belief that it was healthful. "Hot Baths we have an account of from the Indians that frequent the Hill-Country," reported Lawson in North Carolina. Moreover, there were in that province "Chalybeate Waters of several Tastes and different Qualities, some purge, others work by the Enunctories. We have amongst the Inhabitants, a Water that is inwardly a great Aspersive, and outwardly, cures Ulcers, Tetters and Sores by washing therewith."[542] As we have seen, these Indians required that wounded patients drink "fountain water."[543]

A century later, Gregg reported that sulphurous warm springs at Ojo Caliente, New Mexico, were considered "highly efficacious in the cure of rheumatism and other chronic diseases."[544] These waters had been valued by Indians for medicinal purposes since before the Spanish conquest.[545] Huichol Indians of Sonora drank from and washed in the spring waters of certain caves, which were believed to have curative powers. The water was said to contain sulphurated hydrogen.[546]

Most of the popular spas in America today were used by the Indians in former times. For saline purgatives, Dr. Brooks declared, the Indians resorted to many mineral springs "now appropriated by us very largely, as, for example, those at Saratoga."[547] "*One Spring there is* at Black Point in the Province *of Main*," wrote Josselyn, "*coming out of muddy clay that will colour a spade, as if hatcht with silver, it is purgative and cures*

---

[541] *Travels*, II, 491.

[542] Lawson, *History of North Carolina*, 83–84.

[543] *Ibid.*, 15.

[544] *Commerce of the Prairies*, Vol. XIX in Thwaites (ed.), *Early Western Travels*, 311.

[545] Henry G. Alsberg, *The American Guide: A Source Book and Complete Travel Guide for the United States*, 1033.

[546] Hrdlička, *Physiological and Medical Observations*, 4, 251.

[547] Brooks, "The Medicine of the American Indian," *Bulletin of the New York Academy of Medicine*, 2d ser., Vol. V, No. 6 (June, 1929), 528.

scabs and Itch &c."[548] This may be the spring in the Penobscot tradition reported by Speck. These Indians declared that just previous to the coming of the white man a natural medicinal spring near Casco, Maine, believed to possess potent healing virtues, was visited by Indians from all parts of the country, a practice which continued after the arrival of the white man.[549]

Iuka Springs, Mississippi, was a former resort of the Chickasaw Indians.[550] Palm Springs, California, was a popular place to the Cahuila or "Agua Caliente" Indians, who still hold title to much valuable property at the posh resort.[551] Significantly, there are places called "Indian Springs" in Alabama, Arizona, California, Georgia, Indiana, Manitoba, Maryland, Mississippi, Nevada, and Tennessee.

See also *Water*, in the appendix on remedies.

Isolation. We have mentioned Sagard's observation of the Huron practice of isolating certain patients "who are infected with some unclean or dangerous disease" and his view that the practice was a laudable one which should be adopted in every country.[552] Such procedure was not in common use in Europe at the time, although the first use of quarantine or forty days' confinement, occurred in 1377 at Ragusa for the protection of Venice from diseases brought from the East by ships.[553] In 1647, when a "plague or pestilent fever" was raging in the West Indies, ships arriving at Boston and other New England ports were not permitted to land if they had come from the affected area.[554]

Isolation was the Indians' practice in other conditions which were thought to be either communicable or unclean. The segregation of menstruating women, as has been indicated, was a

[548] Josselyn, *Two Voyages*, 38.

[549] Speck, "Medicine Practices of the Northeastern Algonquians," *Proceedings XIXth International Congress of Americanists*, 313.

[550] Dunbar Rowland, *Encyclopedia of Mississippi History* (2 vols.; Madison, Selwyn A. Brant, 1907), I, 948.

[551] Federal Writers Project, *California, A Guide to the Golden State*, 628–29.

[552] *Long Journey to the Country of the Hurons*, 198. See p. 89, herein.

[553] Atkinson, *Magic, Myth, and Medicine*, 79–80.

[554] *Winthrop's Journal*, II, 329.

common practice. When smallpox raged, Indians not stricken would flee from their villages. Adair reported that wounded braves returning from war could not go immediately to their homes:

> The Indians . . . build a small hut at a considerable distance from the houses of the village for every one of their warriors wounded in war and confine them there . . . for the space of four moons . . . as in the case of their women after travail; and they keep them strictly separate, lest the impurity of one should prevent the cure of the other.[555]

Sanitation and Hygiene. "I never felt any ill, unsavory Smell in their Cabins," wrote Lawson, "whereas, should we live in our Houses, as they do, we should be poisoned with our own Nastiness, which confirms these Indians to be, as they really are, some of the Sweetest People in the World."[556] According to William Wood, the unconverted New England Indians would not adopt English clothing "because their women cannot wash them when they be soiled . . . therefore, they had rather go naked than be lousy."[557]

The foregoing observations are not exceptional, for most European visitors were impressed by the Indians' high regard for cleanliness in their persons and surroundings. William Bartram described sanitary measures taken by the Creek Indians during their busk ceremonials:

> . . . they collect all their worn out clothes and other despicable things, sweep and cleanse their houses, squares and the whole town, of their filth, which with all the remaining grain and other old provisions, they cast together in one common heap, and consume it with fire.[558]

Irving Leonard, editor of Bernal Díaz del Castillo's account of the conquest of Mexico, called attention to the Spaniard's

[555] *History of the Indians,* 124–25.
[556] *History of North Carolina,* 187.
[557] *New England's Prospect,* 77.
[558] *Travels,* 323.

description of the clean surroundings of the great temple, and added:

> ... it will be observed by any traveller in Mexico or Central America that the purely Indian villages of considerable size are almost always kept swept and tidy, while this is not the case in the towns and villages inhabited by the mixed race.[559]

Hrdlička, from his own observation, commented likewise on the general cleanliness in southwestern tribes:

> Except among the degraded, the old, or where the woman is indolent, the dwelling and its near surroundings are generally kept in fairly good order and reasonably clean. During the day there is a freedom from bad odors in and about the dwelling. Some of the brush houses are pleasantly fragrant.[560]

Indians realized the importance of preventing disease and had some notion of the bad effects of filth. Richard Spruce noted that "the domestic medicine of the South American Indian is chiefly hygienic, as such medicine ought to be, it being of greater daily importance to preserve health than to cure disease."[561]

The contagious and communicable diseases introduced from Europe brought new problems to the Indians, and yet they learned some rational means of dealing with them. Among the Jicarillas, all white men were believed to carry venereal infection, and so the women had nothing to do with them. Many tribes, especially in the far Southwest, followed the custom of incinerating everything connected with deceased persons, including their clothing, blankets, and lodges. "Whatever may have been the original reason for this custom," Hrdlička wrote, "today many of the tribes recognize clearly that the burning of everything with which the diseased came in contact hinders contagion."[562]

[559] Díaz del Castillo, *The Discovery and Conquest of Mexico*, 202.
[560] Hrdlička, *Physiological and Medical Observations*, 16.
[561] Spruce, *Notes of a Botanist*, II, 454.
[562] Hrdlička, *Physiological and Medical Observations*, 230–31.

VIII.

Conclusions

The Indians of North and South America used for medicinal purposes well over two hundred drugs which have been included in the official drug compendia of the United States. While the aboriginal uses of these drugs were frequently incorrect in the judgment of modern science, the examples of efficacious usage which have been cited constitute an imposing monument to the original Americans. There can be no doubt that by trial-and-error methods they arrived at an understanding of the properties and effects of many useful botanical medicines. Moreover, independently of Old World influence, they discovered some useful medical inventions and procedures. The surgical use of rubber and cotton, the bulbed syringe for enemata and medical injec-

262

tions, the Credé method of manipulation in parturition, tre-phination, and the use of anesthetics and antiseptics have all been credited to American Indians.[1]

The Indian influence on American medicine and pharmacology is of course not measured solely by the enumeration of officially recognized drugs borrowed from them. Millions of pioneer Americans never patronized a physician or pharmacist, yet they had their ills and their treatments. Almost any person born in rural America before the first World War, or even later, can recount memories of a variety of home remedies used for common ailments, sometimes listed in farmers' almanacs, and more often than not, these consisted of substances available in the immediate environment. Undoubtedly the earliest settlers in America sought plants resembling those familiar in the Old World and even introduced some of them to the new land, but many more were borrowed from the natives and handed down through generations so that American folk medicine became a blend of the herbal lore of two continents, or even three, for the Negro, too, had some influence on domestic remedies.

One of the significant aspects of American folk medicine is that it acted as an intermediate step on the road toward official acceptance of many native remedies. Few Indian simples were adopted by regular physicians before they had attracted attention through an apprenticeship in the hands of lay healers. Many drugs acquired a reputation during a long period of domestic use before they became official.

The scarcity of trained physicians and pharmacists on the frontier caused settlers to depend on native remedies, and even, at times, on the services of Indian medicine men. These circumstances, combined with a revulsion against some of the harsh drugs and objectionable practices, such as bleeding, of early physicians also gave rise to a numerous group of white lay healers

---

[1] E. Nordenskjöld, "The American Indian as an Inventor," *Sourcebook in Anthropology*, eds. A. L. Kroeber and T. T. Waterman, 493–94; Stone, *Medicine Among the American Indians*, 120–22.

who often claimed to have learned their healing art from the Indians, as in fact they sometimes had. The prevalence of such practitioners in the early nineteenth century and their appropriation of the name "Indian doctor," if not the paraphernalia of that functionary, is a testimonial of the former high repute of Indian therapeutics.

The esteem in which Indian curing skill was held by whites in an earlier day was also responsible for the success of traveling "Indian" medicine shows which vended miraculous potions allegedly composed of the red men's formerly secret remedies. Most of these products were mixtures of alcohol and flavoring agents of little or no therapeutic value, but their former popularity is another illustration of the image of the Indian as a healer of human ills.

However exaggerated, it is difficult to believe that such a reputation could be founded entirely on myth. Accounts of successful treatments or cures by Indian doctors of such external afflictions as snake and insect bites, burns and scalds, wounds of all sorts, fractures, dislocations, and bruises, have been frequent enough in early accounts of credible persons. They have earned for Indian healers varying degrees of approbation from medical men who either observed their practice personally or had learned of it by other means. Dr. Harlow Brooks, who for many years was closely associated with Indians, once stated that "in frontier medicine much, one may even say most, of the settlers' knowledge in regard to the treatment of traumata has been bodily copied from the Indians."[2]

There are also reports from qualified persons concerning successful Indian treatment of fevers, intestinal disorders, rheumatism, and the like. Indians were not so successful, however, in coping with infectious diseases which appear to have been introduced from abroad and for which the Indians had no resistance or experience in treatment. For native internal ailments they

2 Brooks, "The Medicine of the American Indian," *Bulletin of the New York Academy of Medicine,* 2d ser., Vol. V, No. 6 (June 1929), 519.

seem to have had some remedies of varying utility, although perhaps less successful than their external remedies. Dr. Erwin Ackerknecht has further suggested that Indians acquired through natural selection a considerable resistance to ordinary diseases.[3]

Indian medicine was closely allied to religious beliefs and mythology, and most internal diseases were attributed to supernatural causes. The means of treatment, therefore, were not entirely rational from the white viewpoint, although white medicine at the time of the discovery of America and later was also far from being scientific.

It has been suggested by some scholars that psychological factors played a role in some Indian cures, and in some tribes, particularly the Iroquois, dream analysis was a highly cultivated art. It should be emphasized, however, that psychic and occult beliefs and practices were applied in ailments for which there was no discernible physical cause and not to conditions of obviously external origin.

The degree of acceptance of Indian medicine was uneven, reflecting in a general way the quality of hostility between representatives of the two cultures, Amerind and European. Indian medicine was more acceptable to the white layman than to the priest or physician, with some notable exceptions, and aboriginal healing was more readily embraced by the trader and explorer than the settler; the settler in turn accepted it sooner than the inhabitants of old, established communities. Of the professional groups, the botanists seem to have been most favorably inclined toward native remedies. There were also regional and chronological differences. Indian medicine was more welcome in the rural and multifaith South than in urban and Puritan New England, and more favored in the French and Spanish possessions than in the English, a pattern which is repeated in attitudes toward such matters as intermarriage and the retention of aborig-

[3] "White Indians: Psychological and Physiological Peculiarities of White Children Abducted and Reared by North American Indians," *Bulletin of the History of Medicine*, Vol. XV, No. 1 (January, 1944), 29.

inal place names. In time of war, necessity forced attention to indigenous remedies. In times of growing nationalist feeling, patriotic or xenophobic sentiments have brought a like result; at other times, economic factors have brought renewed interest in native materia medica.

The resurrection of the forgotten story of American Indian contributions to medicine and other aspects of our culture has a certain practical importance. Ethnic arrogance is no longer fashionable in today's world where dark-skinned peoples have suddenly become politically important. A better understanding of what some of these people have given us can form the basis of a new and healthier attitude.

Appendix:
American Indian
Contributions
to
Pharmacology

NOTE: *The glossary in this section is in alphabetical order by common name. An index of common and scientific botanical names begins on page 519. Footnotes to this section begin on page 415.*

Introduction

About 170 drugs which have been or still are official in the *Pharmacopeia of the United States of America* or the *National Formulary* were used by North American Indians north of Mexico, and about fifty more were used by Indians of the West Indies, Mexico, and Central and South America. Hundreds more which have not become official drugs were used by both races.

These drugs were not always used in the same form by both races.

In the preparation of drugs, whites have used processes, such as distillation, which were not known to the Indians. Moreover, Indian usage of given remedies has not always corresponded with white usage. With these reservations in mind, it can still be said that the Indian acquaintance with the physiological effects of a large number of drugs is extensive. However, no systematic comparison of Indian and white uses of drugs is attempted here. The two official drug compendia named are reference works used primarily by pharmacists and do not state the uses of drugs, which remains the province of the physician. The *Dispensatory* lists the purposes for which drugs, whether official or not, have been or are used, without any implication of endorsement. The information on the uses of the drugs listed here is based mainly on the E. P. Claus revision of E. N. Gathercoal and E. H. Wirth's *Pharmacognosy* (1956).

For the dates during which the drugs were official, each decennial edition of the *Pharmacopeia* from 1820 through 1890 and the first edition of the *National Formulary* (1888) have been checked. For subsequent listings reliance has been placed primarily on E. N. Gathercoal's *Check List of Native and Introduced Drug Plants* as well as recent editions of the official compendia, and upon Claus. During the nineteenth century the *Pharmacopeia* maintained both a primary and a secondary list, in which the drugs of lesser choice were relegated to the latter. Drugs were often transferred from one list to another at each decennial revision. Most writers have chosen to ignore these changing classifications, and, to simplify the task, in most instances their example has been followed.

The facts of Indian usage of drugs have been obtained from three types of sources: (1) the accounts of early explorers, missionaries, travelers, traders, captives, etc., including the *Jesuit Relations* and Thwaites's *Early Western Travels*, and the writings of Hennepin, Lahontan, Charlevoix, Sagard, Lafitau, Lawson, Carver, Romans, Heckewelder, Zeisberger, Loskiel, Adair, Hawkins, Hunter, and others; (2) the reports of herbalists, botanists, or botanist-physicians, such as Josselyn, Brickell, Catesby, Kalm, Garden, Colden, Stearns, Cutler, Schöpf, Bartram, Barton, Pursh, Michaux, Nuttall, Bigelow, Rafinesque, Porcher, Williams, and Clapp; and (3) the later investigators and reporters on Indian ethnobotany and medical practice, who were mainly ethnologists and physicians: Palmer, Mooney, Hoffman, Bourke, Hrdlička, Boas, Bushnell, Gilmore, Speck, Smith, Densmore, Swanton, Brooks, Stone, Fenton, and others.

A small number of drugs listed here are adventive from Eurasia, or common to both hemispheres, or of uncertain origin. If used medicinally by the Indians we have listed them, although we cannot determine at this time whether each race learned the uses of these plants independently or if one taught the other.

In listing the indigenous drugs employed by Indians which became official in the white man's compendia, it is not contended in every case that the whites learned their uses from the Indians. It is indicated that all of them were used for therapeutic purposes by both races, how and for what purposes they were used, and, when the evidence is available, the circumstances of their adoption by whites.

Neither is there concern here with formulating any conclusions on the rational or efficacious use of remedies. That is beyond the competence of this study, but wherever observers have expressed opinions, they are quoted without evaluation.

Listed first are the botanical remedies, which are by far the most numerous, followed in turn by the nonbotanical remedies and the drugs of Latin-American origin, very briefly treated. An alphabetical listing by common names has been found most practicable, followed immediately by the preferred Latin name, with synonyms in some cases, and lastly, the alternate common names, if any. Botanists would prefer classification by genera, physicians might prefer to classify them according to properties and uses, and pharmacists might list them according to the Latin pharmaceutical name. Since this is not a work for specialists, and is written by one who is trained only in history, the chosen procedure seems most appropriate.

For space economy, the abbreviations USP (*Pharmacopeia of the United States of America*) and NF (*National Formulary*) are freely used.

Official Botanical Drugs Used by North American Indians

Adder's tongue, (*Erythronium americanum* L.), yellow adder's tongue, dog-tooth violet (Lily family). The bulbs were reported eaten as food by Winnebago children.[1] This plant was mentioned as an emetic and substitute for colchicum by Jacob Bigelow[2] and A. Clapp.[3] The root and herb were official in the USP, 1820–63, and were used like colchicum, a specific for gout.[4]

269

Alder (*Alnus* species). Josselyn reported in 1672 that "an Indian, bruising and cutting of his knee with a fall, used no other remedy than alder-bark, chewed fasting, and laid to it; which did soon heal it." He pronounced a decoction of alder "also excellent, to take the fire out of a burn or scald."[5] "Common alder" was an Onondaga remedy for ague and inflammation.[6] The Penobscots boiled the bark of alder species in water to make a drink to stop cramps and retching, while the Montagnais boiled the twigs and drank the brew for "impure blood."[7] The same tribe steeped red-alder bark for an infusion to stop cholera.[8] Speck also reported the use of alder by the Catawbas for children's constipation.[9] The Potawatomis scraped the inner bark of speckled alder (*Alnus incana* [L.] Moench) and used the juice to rub the body to cure itch. A bark tea was made for flushing the vagina and to make rectal application with a homemade syringe, to shrivel anal muscles, and to cure piles. Potions of bark tea were drunk to cure flux, and the powdered inner bark was used to sprinkle upon galled spots of ponies.[10] The Meskwakis boiled the bark of the same species and gave the decoction to children with bloody stools. The Menominees used the inner bark for poultices to reduce swellings, and an infusion of bark was given to solidify loose mucus in a cold and for a wash in sores. It was considered astringent and healing. An infusion of the inner bark of smooth alder (*A. rugosa*) was used in this tribe as an alterative.[11] The Delawares once chewed the bark of this species for a poultice.[12]

Brickell (1737) reported that the leaves and bark of black alder were cooling and binding and were used in "hot Swellings and Ulcers in the Body."[13] Barton, mentioning black alder under the names of Virginia winterberry (*Prinos verticillatus* L., and *Prinos Gronovii* Michx.), reported that the bark was astringent, bitter, and pungent; that the berries were bitter; that it was long a popular remedy, ordinarily employed as a decoction in intermittent fevers, dropsy, and gangrene, in the last of which it had "great efficacy." It was also given internally, and externally as a wash.[14]

Dr. Porcher held that the berries were tonic and astringent and were used in intermittent fever and diarrhea, while the leaves were a substitute for tea. He further remarked on the use of alder by the Indians.[15] Dr. Clapp added that it was useful, externally and internally, in decoction or infusion, for diseases of the skin, "especially those of the herpetic kind."[16] Wooster Beach found a decoction of black-alder bark good for worms and "to purify the blood." He claimed that a minister was cured by this remedy from a lung infection which rendered him unable to preach.[17]

Black alder, (*Prinos verticillatus* L.) was official in the USP, 1820–94, and was used as an astringent and tonic.[18]

Alum root (Heuchera americana L.). "This Heuchera, wrote Dr. Barton, "is one of the articles in the Materia Medica of our Indians. They apply the powdered root to wounds, ulcers, and cancers." He cautiously added that he did not believe that genuine cancer was cured by it, but he thought it certain "that it has proved very beneficial in some obstinate ulcers, which have been mistaken for cancer."[19]

This root, sometimes called American sanicle, was mentioned by Dr. Clapp as "a strong and pure astringent said to be used by the Indians as a styptic." An extract of it had been suggested as a substitute for rhatany and catechu by Dr. Griffith.[20] Dr. Porcher reported alum root in use by Indians for wounds and "cancerous ulcers." He called it a powerful astringent used in medicine as a substitute for colocynth.[21]

The foliage of this plant was used by the Meskwakis as an astringent in healing sores, while the Menominees used an infusion of the root of *H. hispida* Pursh, to stop diarrhea.[22]

This is one of the plants in which aboriginal use was identical with white usage. The dried rhizome and roots of *H. americana* were used as an internal and external astringent, although since largely replaced by tannic acid. The drug was official in the USP, 1820–82.[23]

Anemone (various *Anemone* species). The star anemone, (*Trientalis americana*), was used by the Tadoussacs of Quebec to brew a drink for any sickness and for consumption.[24] The root of Virginia anemone (*A. virginiana* L.) was used by the Menominees as a poultice for boils. The Meskwakis placed seeds of this plant on hot coals to produce smoke to be inhaled by patients with catarrh or to revive unconscious persons. The leaves of *A. cylindrica* Gray, were used by the same tribe as a poultice for bad burns, while the roots were used in a tea for headache and dizzy spells. The stem and fruit made a medicine for sore eyes. The *A. canadensis* L. was also used in a root tea used as a wash for eye ailments.[25] The same species was used by the Pillager Ojibwas as a throat lozenge, to clear the throat so they

271

could sing well. The Ojibwas used "thimbleweed" (*A. cylindrica*) root as a tea for lung congestion and tuberculosis.[26]

The root of "wind flower" (*A. canadensis*) was one of the most highly esteemed remedies of the Omahas and Poncas for many ills, especially wounds. It was applied externally and internally and used as a wash for sores affecting eyes or other parts. Another species, the pulsatilla, or pasque flower (*A. patens* L.) was used by the Omahas in the treatment of rheumatism and neuralgia; the fresh leaves were crushed and applied to the affected part. It was said to act as a counterirritant, causing a blister if left on the skin long enough.[27]

The last-named species was official in the USP, 1882–1905, and in the NF, 1916–47, together with two foreign species, under the name pulsatilla. Claus reported it used as a diuretic, expectorant, and emmenagogue.[28] Several species of anemone were listed as of medicinal value by Clapp, Porcher, Williams, Millspaugh, and others.

Angelica (herb), (*Angelica atropurpurea* L.), sometimes called masterwort, a name also applied to cow parsnip (*Heracleum lanatum* Michx.). William Byrd wrote on October 8, 1729: "The Root of this Plant, being very warm and Aromatick, is coveted by Woodsmen extremely as a dry Dram, that is, when Rum, that cordial for all Distresses, is wanting."[29] John D. Hunter in 1823 declared that angelica was held in high esteem by Indians in Arkansas, who always carried it in their medicine bags and mixed it with tobacco for smoking. It was often eaten when provisions were short on journeys. He reported that it was "liable to produce heartburn and other symptoms of indigestion," and had no great claim as a medicine, though it was sometimes given in children's diseases, and mixed with other medicines to make them more palatable.[30]

While William Bartram was on tour in South Carolina in 1788 he reported:

> The Angelica lucido or Nondo grows here in abundance; its aromatic carminative root is in taste much like that of the Ginseng (Panax) though more of the taste and scent of Anise seed; it is in high estimation with the Indians as well as white inhabitants, and sells at a great price to the Southern Indians of Florida, who dwell near the sea coast where it never grows spontaneously.[31]

Southern Indians, especially Creeks, used it for stomach disorders, dry bellyache, colic, hysterics, worms, and pains in the back.[32] Angelica was used by the Menominees to reduce swellings; they cooked the roots and pounded them to a pulp, and combined them with bruised leaves of *Artemisia canadensis* to make a poultice which was considered good for any pain in the chest or body.[33]

Dr. Clapp called angelica root a pleasant, aromatic carminative with a popular reputation in flatulent colic.[34] Dr. Millspaugh also ascribed diuretic, emmenagogue, and stimulant properties to it and reported its use with other diuretics in urinary diseases.[35] Additional uses reported by Alice Henkel were tonic and diaphoretic, and emetic in large doses.[36]

Angelica herb was official in the USP, 1820–63, while the root was official in the USP, 1863–73, and NF, 1916–36. The fruit was official in the USP, 1831–42, and NF, 1916–36. Claus reports that the official species was *Angelica archangelica* L., native to Europe.[37] He is mistaken, however, for the American species, *A. atropurpurea* L., is the only one named in the pharmacopeia from its first adoption on the secondary list in 1820 until its dismissal in 1863.

Angelica tree (*Aralia spinosa* L.; *Aralia villosa* Walt.), also called Hercules club, prickly ash, prickly elder, thorny ash, toothache bush. Loskiel reported that the Indians used a decoction of the bark and root of *A. spinosa* as a purifier of the blood, although he is never clear as to whether he meant the Onondagas or the Delawares, the two tribes with which he was most familiar.[38] The Iroquois, according to Fenton, used *A. villosa* for respiratory ailments.[39] In South Carolina, Dr. Porcher wrote, the Negroes considered *A. spinosa* "the rattlesnake's master, par excellence," for they relied on it almost exclusively for snakebite. The bark of the fresh root in substance was taken internally and also applied in powdered form to the wounded part.[40] It has moreover been reported used by Indians as a fever medicine, owing to its acrid taste.[41]

Aralia spinosa bark was official in the USP, 1820–82 and was used as a stimulant and diuretic.[42]

Arbor vitae (*Thuja occidentalis* L.), white cedar. Peter Kalm, the Swedish botanist and pupil of Linnaeus, reported in 1750 that in Canada and northern New York the arbor vitae:

is used for several medicinal purposes. The commandant of Ft. St. Frederic, M. de Lusignant, could never sufficiently praise its excellence for rheumatic pains. He told me he had often seen it tried with remarkably good success upon several persons. . . . An Iroquois Indian told me that a decoction of Thuya leaves was used as a remedy for cough. In the neighborhood of Saratoga, they use this decoction in intermittent fevers.[43]

While on a canoe trip in Maine, Thoreau wrote in his journal:

This night we had a dish of arbor-vitae, or cedar-tea, which the lumberer sometimes uses when other herbs fail,—

"A quart of arbor-vitae
To make him strong and mighty."

But I had no wish to repeat the experiment. It had too medicinal a taste for my palate.[44]

Although Thoreau reported that his Penobscot guide had no use for arbor vitae tea, various parts of this tree have been widely used by northern tribes. The Hurons believed that the odor of this tree was disliked by snakes and so they used branches of it for their beds while on journeys.[45] The Penobscots used the leaves in a poultice for swollen hands and feet, while the Montagnais bruised and steeped the twigs for a sweat drink.[46] The Flambeau Ojibwas used the leaves as a perfume, placing them on coals in purification rites, and brewed from them a tea for headache. The Pillager Ojibwas also used them for incense and with other evergreens as an ingredient in the sweat bath. They drank a decoction made from the boiled leaves as a blood purifier and cough remedy.[47] The Menominees used the leaves as a sudatory, as a smoke smudge to revive unconscious patients, and as a seasoner in other medicines. The inner bark was steeped for a tea used in suppressed menstruation. The Forest Potawatomis used the leaves for poultices and also in many medical combinations with other roots and leaves. The leaves served as a seasoner in compound medicines and as a smudge on coals for purification and for exorcism of evil spirits.[48] The Lake St. John Montagnais beat the twig ends into a mash which was steeped in boiling water and applied for one or two nights over the heart for pain there.[49]

Whites have used arbor vitae leaves for stimulant, diaphoretic, anthelmintic, febrifuge, and antispasmodic purposes. The plant yields an extract which was used in coughs, fevers, catarrh, rheum, and scurvy. Boiled in lard, the leaves yielded an oil used for salve. Most of these uses were in domestic or eclectic medicine.[50]

Arbor vitae twigs were official in the USP, 1882–94, and in the NF, 1916–36, being used for stimulant, diuretic, emmenagogue, and irritant purposes. The volatile, distilled leaf oil was official in the USP, 1942–50, and was used as a stimulant to heart and uterine muscle, and generally as a stimulant, irritant, and antiseptic. In overdose, Claus reported, it was abortifacient and convulsant. This oil entered the pharmacopeia as an aromatic substitute for lavender oil in soap liniment because of the wartime shortage of that product.[51]

Arnica (*Arnica fulgens, A. sororia, A. cordifolia, A. acaulis*, etc.). Verrill credited the Indians with the discovery of the medicinal value of the American species of arnica.[52] Speck reported that the *Arnica acaulis*, "water root, identity uncertain," was used by the Catawbas in a medicine which was drunk for a pain in the back.[53]

Dr. Porcher called *A. nudicaulis* Ell., a substitute for the European *A. montana*, and described it as a stimulant which also produced an emetic and cathartic effect, much used by the Germans in paralysis, amaurosis, and other nervous diseases.[54] Dr. Clapp held that *A. nudicaulis* and *A. mollis* Hook, were "supposed to have medical virtues similar to those of the leopard's bane" of Europe.[55]

It was the leopard's bane plant, *A. montana*, of Europe which was official in the USP, 1820–51. The flowers were official in the USP, 1851–1925, and in the NF, 1926 to 1960. The root was official in the USP, 1882–1905. Since 1947, the dried flower head of European arnica and the first three American species named at the beginning of this section were official in the *National Formulary*, 1947–60. Claus reports that this medicine has been used orally, intravenously, or locally as a stimulant, increasing temperature and secretions. Internally, it is reported to lead to transient depression and debility; externally, it is bactericidal and vesicant. It has been used mainly as a local irritant and vulnerary for bruises, sprains, abrasions, and slight wounds. The exigencies of World War II brought recognition to American arnica, now considered equal to that of Europe.[56]

Ash tree (*Fraxinus americana* L., and other species), white ash, and other species of ash. The missionary of the Moravian Brethren to the

275

Delawares, Loskiel, wrote in 1794: "A decoction of the buds or bark of the *white ash* (fraxinus Carolina) taken inwardly is said to be a certain remedy against the effects of this poison" of the rattlesnake.[57] Maximilian of Wied witnessed such a cure performed with white ash tea when he was visiting in the Pocono mountains of Pennsylvania in 1832.[58] Even more astonishing magic was reported accomplished by the white ash in a report by Samuel Stearns (1741–1809) in his *American Herbal*:

> A Mrs. *Lomis*, in Connecticut, informed me, that an Indian cured a cancer, by the internal and external use of the juice of *white-ash*, that issued out of the ends of the woods as it was burning.[59]

Moreover, he wrote, the bark of *Fraxinus albus*[60] was astringent and sudorific, yielding a resolvent and diuretic extract, while the seeds were aperient, diuretic, and aphrodisiac and often given with success in intermittent fevers.[61]

The Meskwaki Indians used an infusion of white-ash bark on sores and to cure the itch, including scalp itch caused by vermin. For old sores it was cooked in a syrup.[62] The Penobscots used the leaves of *F. americana* to make a strong, bitter decoction which was given to cleanse women after childbirth.[63] Mountain ash, black ash, and red ash have also been reported as used for various medicinal purposes by American tribes.

The bark of white ash (*Fraxinus americana* L.) and other species of ash, according to Dr. Clapp, was bitter, tonic, and astringent, and had been useful in fevers.[64] White ash bark was official in the NF, 1916–26, being used as a tonic and astringent.[65]

Balm of Gilead (*Populus candicans* Ait.), and *Balsam poplar* (*Populus balsamifera* L.), hackmatack, tacamahac. See also *Poplar*. The Menominees boiled the resinous buds of balm of Gilead in fat to make a salve for dressing wounds and to put up the nostrils for a cold in the head.[66] The balsam poplar was used by the Forest Potawatomis to make salve, the winter buds being melted with mutton or bear tallow, and the substance applied to persistent sores and eczema. They were similarly used by the Pillager Ojibwas, who also rubbed the ointment up the nostrils so that the balsamic odors could course through the respiratory passages and relieve congestion from colds, catarrh, and bronchitis.[67] Hoffman reported that the cotton down from buds of *Populus monolifera* Ait., were applied by the Ojibwas as an absorbent in open sores.[68]

Gerard called *tacmahac,* a name applied to the balsam poplar, an aboriginal name of West Indian origin.[69] Monardes reported in 1577 that "thei doe bryng out of the new Spain an other kinde of Gumme or Rosine, that the Indians doeth call Tacamahaca," which they used "chiefly in swellynges in any parte of the bodie," and which was furthermore useful to "taketh awaie any manner of greefe, that is come of a colde cause: as humours, and windinesse."[70] Samuel Stearns reported that "Tacamahaca" was used by North American Indians for "discussing and maturating tumours" and abating pains in the limbs. Among whites it was an ingredient in warm nervine plasters and was used to warm, irritate, and gently blister. It was sometimes employed in fumigation.[71] The Scottish physician, William Cullen, who took a negative attitude toward most American drugs, declared that the tacamahaca "of our shops should not have had a place here, not being employed as an internal medicine; and as an external I cannot perceive its virtues."[72]

Dr. Clapp in 1852 ascribed tonic and febrifuge properties to *P. candicans* and said it possessed medical qualities similar to the willows, yielding salicin and populin. He added that the bark of this species, as well as that of *P. balsamifera,* was covered with a fragrant, resinous matter which was said to be a stimulating diuretic. Rafinesque found the bark to be emetic and cathartic.[73] The Smoky mountain settlers used balm of Gilead buds like the Indians, to make a salve for muscular aches and soreness.[74]

Poplar buds, from both of the above-named species, were official in the *National Formulary,* 1916–65, and are used for their stimulant and expectorant properties.[75]

Balsam fir (Abies balsamea [L.] Mill.). John Josselyn in 1672 claimed that a tar made of the "firr-tree, or pitch tree" was "an excellent thing to take away those desperate stitches of the sides which perpetually afflicteth those poor people that are stricken with plague of the back. . . . You must make a large toast, or cake, slip or dip it in the tar, and bind it warm to the side."[76] Hunter called "Indian Balsam" one of the most valuable articles, among the aboriginal remedies. It was given for colds, coughs, asthma, consumptions, in substance or infusion, "with the most happy effects." He reported its use by white frontier doctors, who spoke well of it.[77]

Brickell, reporting in 1734 on the Indians of North Carolina, maintained that they "never make either *Pitch, Tar,* or Turpentine," and that "they are scarce ever known to make use of any *Gums* or *Rosins* in their Physick."[78] This was surely not true of the northern tribes. Penobscots smeared resin from the balsam fir over burns, sores, and cuts.[79] The Montagnais applied gum from this species or arbor vitae over the chest or back for pain in the heart or chest, and steeped balsam twigs for a strong laxative.[80] The Menominees used the liquid balsam pressed from the trunk blisters for colds and pulmonary troubles, while the inner bark was steeped for a tea given for pains in the chest. It was also used fresh for poultices, and as a seasoner for other medicines.[81] The Ojibwas, Hoffman reported, used the bark of balsam fir in decoction to induce diaphoresis, while the gum was taken internally as a remedy for gonorrhea and for sore chest. The same was externally applied for sores and cuts.[82] The Flambeau Ojibwas used the liquid balsam on sore eyes, the leaves as a reviver, and in combinations as a wash. The Pillagers used the needles in the sweat bath and also placed them on live coals and inhaled the fumes for colds. The Forest Potawatomis used the liquid from the bark blisters for colds, as a salve for sores, and in infusion to drink for consumption and internal affections.[83] Balsam-fir gum was used by the Kwakiutls as a constipation remedy. The root of the tree was held in the mouth to cure sores there.[84]

In medicine, the resinous exudation from the trunk and branches of *A. balsamea* has been called Canada balsam, which Dr. Clapp reported to be stimulant, diuretic, and possessed of properties similar to other liquid turpentines.[85] Given internally, Dr. Wooster Beach asserted, Canada balsam was stimulating and laxative; externally, it was called emollient and cooling and useful for application to sore nipples, cuts, and wounds. In cough drops, it was considered "equal or superior to copaiba."[86]

"Balsam traumatick," used in wound dressings, was part of the medicine chest of the Lewis and Clark expedition.[87] The root-and-herb doctor, John G. Briante, who claimed to have learned his lore from northern tribes, published a formula for "Indian healing balsam" in his recipe book.[88]

Canada turpentine, Canada balsam, or balsam of fir are official pharmaceutical names for the substance defined as the liquid oleo-resin obtained from *A. balsamea*. It was an official medicine in the USP, 1820–1916, but has been recognized in the USP since 1916 and the NF since 1926 as a medium for mounting microscopic specimens and as a cement for lenses. The buds of the balsam fir, which contain tannin and a bitter glycoside called picein, have been used as an adulterant or substitute for balm of Gilead.[89]

Bayberry (*Myrica cerifera* L.), sweet bay, wax myrtle, candleberry. "The *Bay* Tree," reported Brickell, not only yielded a wax for candle-making, but was:

> useful in Chirurgery, the Leaves are of a bitter astringent Nature, but grateful to the Stomach, and resists Vomiting; when made into a Pulse, helps all Inflamations, the stinging of Bees, and other venomous Beasts, the Bark of the Root in *Rhenish Wine* pro-vokes Urine, opens Obstructions, cures Dropsies and Jaundice, but kills the Foetus; the Berries expel Wind and ease all manner of Pains proceeding from Cold, therefore good in the Cholick, Palsies, Convulsions, Epilepsies, and many other Disorders; some have the Leaves turn'd up with Beer, which makes it pleasant and grateful to the stomach.

Elsewhere he wrote that a decoction of berries from the "Myrtle Tree" could "cure the falling out of the Womb, Tettars, and Scald Heads, by fomenting the Parts, and their Syrup is good in Coughs, and the like disorders in the Breast."[90]

Some might expect that a tree with such prodigious healing powers ascribed to it would be used extensively by Indians, but their applica-tions of bayberry, compared to Brickell's claims for it, were quite modest.[91] Louisiana Choctaws, wrote Bushnell, boiled the leaves and stems in water for a fever decoction.[92] Speck found the Houma Indians boiling the leaves for a tea used as a vermifuge.[93] The Creeks and Seminoles seem to have used bayberry only as a charm medicine to exorcise spirits of the dead and to prevent disease.[94] Some Indians, William Buchan reported, used "Myrica" as a mild emetic.[95]

Dr. Barton described wax myrtle as a powerful astringent which was used by country practitioners who gave decoctions of the root bark in "dropsical affections succeeding intermittents," as well as in treatment of uterine hemorrhage and as a gentle purgative.[96] Some empirics recommended it for jaundice and dysentery, as a poultice for "scrofulous swellings" and, in powder, as a snuff for sneezing.[97]

Physicians used the root bark as an astringent and errhine, emetic, narcotic, anodyne, and remedy for dysentery.[98] *Myrica cerifera* root bark was official in the *National Formulary*, 1916–36, and was employed as an astringent and tonic.[99]

Bearberry (Arctostaphylus uva ursi L.), a cranberry, received its name from the Indians because of the fondness of bears for the fruit. Previously we have mentioned Josselyn's comment on the astringent and anti-scorbutic properties of bearberry. Peter Kalm reported that Indians and colonists called this plant *Sagackhomi* and mixed the leaves with smoking tobacco.[100] *Uva ursi* was the subject of an "inaugural dissertation" at the University of Pennsylvania by Dr. John Mitchell in 1803.[101] His mentor, Dr. Barton, valued the plant as an astringent and recommended it for nephritis and kidney stones. He even claimed to "have used it, with advantage, in old gonorrhoea."[102] Dr. Clapp listed sixteen references to *uva ursi* in the medical literature, ascribed astringent and tonic properties to it, and called it useful in diseases of the urinary organs.[103] Huron H. Smith reported that the Menominees used the dried leaves of this plant as a seasoner in female remedies.[104]

Uva ursi has been official in the pharmacopeias of Dublin, Edinburgh, and London, as well as the USP, 1820–1936, and NF, 1936–50. The dried leaves were the official part, being used as an astringent, tonic, and diuretic. While the species is said to be native to both America and Europe, the commercial supply was largely American.[105]

Birch trees (Betula species). "The bark of birch," wrote Josselyn, "is used by the Indians for bruised wounds and cuts,—boyled very tender, and stamped betwixt two stones to a plaister, and the decoction thereof poured into the wound; and also to fetch the fire out of burns and scalds."[106] Birch leaves, Brickell reported, "are cleansing, disolve and purge watry Humours, help Dropsies and Stone in the Bladder, the Ashes of the Bark is effectual to heal sore Mouths, and take away Scabs."[107]

Throughout their natural range, birch trees were widely used as medicine by American Indians. A decoction of the inner bark of "Mountain birch," Hunter reported, was used by Indians west of the

Mississippi as a remedy in coughs, colds, and pulmonary ailments. Many of the frontier settlers, he observed, valued it highly as a table beverage.[108] Hoffman reported that the Ojibwas mixed the inner bark of "Yellow birch" (which he called *B. excelsa* Ait.) and mixed it with that of sugar maple for a diuretic decoction,[109] a usage considered rational and efficacious by Dr. Edmund Andrews.[110] Smith reported that the Ojibwas used the root of paper birch (*B. alba* L., var. *papyrifera*) in medicine as a seasoner to disguise unpleasant tastes; it was also cooked with maple sugar to make a syrup for stomach cramps. The cones of low birch (*B. pumila*) were heated over coals by the Pillagers to make an incense for catarrh patients. A tea was made from them for women in menses and as a post-parturition tonic. The Potawatomis used the twigs of yellow birch (*B. lutea* Michx.) and paper birch for an oil extract used as a medicinal seasoner.[111] Paper-birch bark has also been reported used by the Ojibwas in a medicinal enema.[112] Bark of paper birch and balsam fir was grated and eaten by the Montagnais as beneficial to diet.[113] The Catawbas, Speck reported, boiled the buds of *B. nigra* L., to a syrup and added sulphur to make a salve for ringworm and sores.[114] The Alabamas of Texas boiled the bark of the same tree for a remedy used in treating sore hooves in horses.[115] The Creeks used white birch as a tuberculosis remedy.[116]

Samuel Stearns called the "juice" of *Betula alba* ("White birch") antiscorbutic, deobstruent, diuretic, and laxative; the leaves and bark resolvent, detergent, and antiseptic. The leaves and bark applied externally, he claimed, "are said to resolve hard tumours, cleanse foul ulcers, and resist putrefaction." Moreover, "the fumigations of the bark have been employed for correcting contagious air."[117] When Dr. Clapp compiled his "Report on Medical Botany" (1852), the *B. nigra* L. ("red birch") and *B. lenta* L., ("cherry or sweet birch") were listed in the *United States Dispensatory*. The bark and small twigs were sometimes used in infusion as an aromatic diaphoretic. On distillation they yielded an oil identical to that of wintergreen.[118]

Sweet-birch oil was official in the USP, 1894–1916, and remains one of the officially recognized forms of methyl salicylate, in the USP since 1894. It is obtained by distillation from the twigs and bark of *B. lenta* L., ("Black birch"), an indigenous species, reported to be stimulant, diuretic, and astringent. Rectified birch-tar oil, listed in the *National Formulary*, 1916–55, was distilled from the dry bark of foreign species, and used externally as a counterirritant, parasiticide, and antiseptic in skin diseases.[119]

Blackberry (*Rubus villosus* Ait., and other species). Brickell found blackberry fruit cooling and astringent; the juice, with honey, alum, and red wine, he reported, "fastens loose Teeth."[120] The root bark of *R. villosus* and of the dewberry or low blackberry (*R. canadensis* L.) was quite generally praised for its astringent properties by nineteenth-century physicians, and its use was recommended for diarrhea, chronic dysentery, and cholera infantum.[121]

Wooster Beach reported that 500 Indians of the Oneida tribe were attacked by dysentery in one season, and all recovered by the use of blackberry root, while their white neighbors "fell before the disease."[122] The roots of both of the above-named species were boiled by the Catawbas for a remedy against diarrhea.[123] The Alabamas, according to Swanton, used blackberry for a toothache remedy and for a poultice against pneumonia, although he did not specify the part used. [124] The Kwakiutls boiled blackberry vines and roots with thimbleberry for a drink given to patients vomiting and spitting blood.[125] The Menominees and Prairie Potawatomis made an infusion of the steeped root of high-bush blackberry (*R. alleghriensis* Porter) for an eyewash to cure sore eyes, and also for a poultice. The Flambeau Ojibwas boiled the canes for a diuretic and used the roots for a tea to arrest flux. The Meskwakis used the root extract for stomach trouble and as a poison antidote.[126]

The dried bark of the rhizome and roots of the genus *Rubus* was official in the USP, 1820–1916, and the NF, 1916–36, being used for astringent and tonic purposes. The berries were official in the NF, 1916–26, for use in syrup as a flavoring agent.[127] A proprietary "blackberry balsam" is currently advertised as a diarrhea remedy "since 1846."

Blazing star (*Chamaelirium luteum* [L.] A. Gray), devil's bit. Each of these common names has been attached to other species, and the Latin names have also varied, so that the confused nomenclature makes it difficult to trace this plant's history. Two centuries ago Carver mentioned "devil's bit" as a universal remedy among the Indians "for every disorder that human nature is incident to, but some of the evil spirits envying mankind the possession of so efficacious a medicine, gave the root a bite, which deprived it of a great part of its virtues."[128] Loskiel attached the name "devil's bit" to *scabiosa succisa*, used as a medicine by the Indians of his acquaintance.[129] Hunter gave no Latin name to the "devil's bit" which he observed in use among tribes of Arkansas territory, who employed it in treating ulcers, as an escharotic, and for keeping tissues open, "the importance of which . . . the Indians very well understand."[130] The name "blazing star" has also been attached to *Liatris* (or *Lacinaria*) *scariosa*, used by the Meskwakis for urinary troubles,[131] and by the Pawnees for diarrhea.[132]

Dr. Benjamin Barton's "blazing star or devil's bit" was called *Veratrum luteum*; he reported that a tea or watery infusion of its roots was used as a tonic and anthelmintic.[133] Other physicians used it to check nausea and vomiting, for treatment of leucorrhea and "the uncomfortable sensations, such as pain in the head, side, loins, want of appetite, dejection of spirits, etc."[134] The name "blazing star" has been attached to *Chamaelirium luteum* L., a later name for Barton's plant, which Alice Henkel reported used as a "tonic in derangements of women."[135] The dried roots and rhizome of this species, listed as "Helonias, Blazing Star, or False Unicorn," were official in the *National Formulary*, 1916–47, being used as a diuretic and uterine tonic.[136]

Blue flag (*Iris versicolor* L.). This was one of the most widely used of all American aboriginal medicines. Josselyn, who called it "Blew Flower-de-luce," reported it excellent "to provoke vomiting, and for bruises on the feet and face."[137] Peter Kalm, visiting at Albany on October 30, 1749, received from his host, Colonel Lydius, a report on Indian use of iris root as a remedy for sores on the legs:

> They take the root, wash it clean, boil it a little, then crush it between a couple of stones. They spread this crushed root as a poultice over the sores and at the same time rub the leg with the water in which the root is boiled. Mr. Lydius said that he had seen great cures brought about by the use of this remedy.[138]

William Bartram reported that the Creeks cultivated this plant and used it as a cathartic.[139] Dr. Barton endorsed its cathartic properties,[140] and emetic and diuretic powers were ascribed to it by Dr. Clapp. He reported that the root decoction, in combination with other medicines, had been used by physicians in dropsy and in "removing soreness of the abdomen in remittent fever."[141]

Missouri valley Indians mixed the pulverized rootstock of blue flag with water or saliva for use as an earache remedy, for an eyewash, and as an application to sores and bruises.[142] The Meskwakis used the root in colds and lung trouble, and as a burn and sore poultice. Ojibwa Indians used it as an emetic and physic, while Potawatomis made of it a poultice for inflammation.[143] The Tadoussacs of Quebec crushed the entire plant and mixed it with flour for a poultice "put where there is pain."[144] Among the Penobscots, blue flag was a panacea, Speck considering it the most important article in their pharmacology. Strings of the root were preserved in every dwelling, and by steaming it they believed that disease could be kept away. The steeped root was a specific for cholera.[145]

The dried rhizome of *Iris versicolor* and *I. virginica* were official in the USP, 1820–95, and in the NF, 1916–42, under the name of blue flag. A mixture of resins from the drug has been named Irisin or Iridin. The medicine was employed as a cathartic, emetic, and diuretic.[146] Iris has also been used in domestic medicine as an alterative, diuretic, and purgative.[147]

Boneset (Eupatorium perfoliatum L.), thoroughwort, and other species of *Eupatoria*. Dr. Benjamin Barton devoted a half-dozen pages to boneset in his brief compendium of fifty-nine indigenous remedies. He mentioned its use by northern Indians as a fever remedy and said that their name for it signified "ague-weed"; so much was it identified with them that whites called it "Indian sage." He reported that it had been found useful in preventing recurrence of paroxysms in intermittent fever and also in combating the yellow fever epidemic of 1793 at Philadelphia. The "James River ringworm" or "herpes" in Virginia also was reported responsive to the magic of boneset. He listed its properties as astringent, emetic, sudorific, and tonic.[148]

Every writer on American materia medica in the late eighteenth and early nineteenth centuries extolled the powers of boneset.[149] David Schöpf called it emetic, purgative, and diaphoretic and recommended a decoction of it for intermittent fevers, arthritis, rheumatism, and gout.[150] It "deservedly holds a high rank among our indigenous medical plants," Dr. Clapp wrote in his report of 1852 to the American Medical Association.[151] Dr. Porcher said it was widely used by plantation Negroes as a tonic and diaphoretic in colds and fevers and in "the typhoid pneumonia prevalent among them" for which it was "convenient and useful."[152] During the Civil War, Dr. Porcher recommended boneset as a febrifuge medicine for Confederate troops, asserting that a drink made from it:

> drank hot during the cold stage of fever, and cold as a tonic and antiperiodic, is thought by many physicians to be even superior to the Dogwood, Willow, or Poplar, as a substitute for quinine. It is quite sufficient in the management of malarial fever that will prevail among our troops during the summer, and if it does not supply entirely the place of quinine, will certainly lessen the need for its use.[153]

Boneset was at one time a virtual panacea among both Indians and whites. An infusion or tea made from it, Lloyd reported, was very popular with white settlers, "being found in every well-regulated household." It became known to early American physicians as a bitter tonic.[154] "Cures effected by it," Jacob Bigelow reported, "appear to have been as speedy as those from any of the medicines in common use."[155] Dr. Stephen Williams asserted that "more virtues are ascribed to it, as a cathartic, emetic, diuretic, tonic, &c., than to almost any other plant in use."[156]

At least two noted botanists made use of *Eupatoria* species as a specific in their personal ills. Frederick Pursh, taken ill near Wilkes-Barre, Pennsylvania, in June, 1807, with "sickness of stomach and colical complaint," used an infusion of boneset, "which has done me good so often, very freely; but it would do no help this time." A few weeks later he was stricken with influenza, accompanied by a violent headache, and again took "Thoroughwort, set up with gin, which I used very freely." Again, however, his recovery was slow.[157] In 1819 the English botanist Thomas Nuttall, on tour in Arkansas, relieved a malarial attack with a decoction of "Eupatorium cuneifolium."[158]

The wide use of this plant among the Indians leaves little room to doubt that whites learned of it from them. Boneset was used for colds and fever by the Iroquois[159] and the Mohegans.[160] Creek women who complained of aches and pains in the hips were steamed in medicine made by boiling boneset; patients with epilepsy were likewise treated by steaming with a decoction of its roots.[161] The Alabamas used *Eupatorium serotinum* as a medicine for stomach pains.[162]

The Menominees made a tea from *E. perfoliatum* to dispel fever,[163] and the Meskwaki doctor, McIntosh, used a tea of boneset flowers and foliage as a vermifuge.[164] A related species, *Eupatorium purpureum*, "Joe Pye Weed" was also widely used by Indians and whites, but is separately treated here. *Eupatorium occidentale arizonicum* A. Gray, was one ingredient in a Zuñi remedy for rheumatism.[165]

Dr. Claus asserted that boneset "was a favorite remedy in the practice of American medicine at least a hundred years before there was a print in America materia medica." The dried leaves and flowering tops of *E. perfoliatum* were official in the USP for nearly a century, 1820–1916, and in the NF, 1926–50. The drug was used as a stimulant and diuretic, and in large doses was considered an emetic and cathartic.[166]

Eupatorium teucrifolium Willd., called wild horehound, was officially in the USP, 1820–42, the leaves and flowering tops being the parts used. The action of this plant has been described as similar to boneset. It has been called tonic, diaphoretic, and antiperiodic and was formerly used in malaria.[167]

Buckbean or *marsh trefoil (Menyanthes trifoliata* L.) Among the Kwakiutls the stems and roots of this plant were washed, broken in pieces, and boiled for a decoction given thrice daily for spitting blood and other internal diseases.[168] Smith said that the Menominees used the same plant for undisclosed medicinal purposes[169] and that whites used it as a tonic, purgative, emmenagogue, emetic, and vermifuge.[170] This species was official in the USP, 1820–42, and in the NF, 1916–26, being recommended as a tonic and febrifuge.[171]

Burdock (Arctium Lappa L.). This is an introduced Eurasian weed, but it has been used medicinally in many Indian tribes. Although John U. Lloyd says it was long used in Old World medicine,[172] it apparently received no official recognition, for it does not appear in the *Pharmacopoeia Londinensis* of 1618, in Hermann Boerhaave's *Materia Medica* of 1741, or William Cullen's *Treatise of the Materia Medica*, of 1789. John Wesley, however, recommended it for various ailments, including jaundice and King's evil.

Plains Indians adopted burdock for ceremonial use, and the Otos used a decoction of the root for pleurisy.[173] Burdock root was an ingredient of a medicine used by Meskwaki women in labor.[174] Flambeau Ojibwas used the root as part of a medicine for stomach pain, and supposed it to have a tonic effect. The Potawatomis made a burdock-root tea taken as a general tonic and blood purifier.[175] Whites have used the root as an alterative in blood and skin diseases.[176] Burdock was official in the USP, 1831–42, 1851–1916, and in the NF, 1916–47. It was employed as a diuretic and diaphoretic.[177]

Butterfly weed (*Asclepias tuberosa* L.), pleurisy root. Writers on materia medica credit Dr. Schöpf with bringing this plant to the attention of the medical profession. He called it a mild astringent and diuretic and recommended a decoction of the pulverized root for colic, hysteria, and hemorrhage, and a leaf decoction for dysentery.[178] Barton thought that this plant and the "Asclepias decumbens" which he praised so highly were the same species. He spoke of its virtues as a dysentery remedy, a purgative, sudorific, and escharotic, which was "useful in restraining fungous flesh in ulcers." He believed it was the plant used by southern Indians in treating chancre, and noted the use of the root by "practitioners of medicine," especially in Virginia, in treating certain forms of fever and pleurisy.[179]

All the early nineteenth-century writers on American materia medica extolled the virtues of this plant. To summarize all the claims made for it, Charles Millspaugh wrote:

The pleurisy-root has received more attention as a medicine than any other species of this genus, having been regarded, almost since the discovery of this country, as a subtonic, diaphoretic, alterative, expectorant, diuretic, laxative, escharotic, carminative, anti-spasmodic, anti-pleuritic, stomachic, astringent, anti-rheumatic, anti-syphilitic, and what not? It has been recommended in low typhoid states, pneumonia, catarrh, bronchitis, pleurisy, dyspepsia, indigestion, dysentery, helminthiasis, and obstinate eczemas.[180]

Dr. Millspaugh said that western United States and Canadian Indian tribes used the flowers, young seed pods, and young shoots as food. It was "much esteemed by the Indians," Alice Henkel wrote,[181] a statement verified by Gilmore, who found that the Omaha Indians ate the raw root for bronchial and pulmonary troubles. They also chewed it to put in wounds or pulverized the dry root for the same purpose. It was applied as a remedy for old obstinate sores.[182]

Smith called butterfly weed "one of the most important Menomini medicines." They pulverized the root and used it for cuts, wounds and bruises, as well as mixing it with other roots for other remedies. The Meskwakis used it as a dye rather than a medicine, but their doctor McIntosh, who was of Potawatomi origin, used it as an internal poison antidote.[183]

The Natchez believed this plant to be the best remedy for pneumonia and "winter fever." They boiled the roots and took a teacupful at a time. "If one sick with a hot dry fever," Swanton wrote, "drank this and wrapped himself up well in bed he would soon perspire freely."[184] The Catawbas made a decoction of the roots for dysentery.[185]

Asclepias tuberosa was official in the USP, 1820–1905, and the NF, 1916–36. The dried roots of this and other members of the milkweed family, (*q.v.*), were regarded officially as diaphoretic and expectorant, and in large doses emetic and purgative.[186]

Butternut (Juglans cinerea L.), white walnut. Loskiel reported that the Indians applied the bark of this tree for rheumatism, headache, and toothache and made a strong decoction of it to apply warm on fresh wounds. He called it "an excellent styptic."[187] Barton considered it possessed of purgative, anodyne, and blistering properties and claimed that it had been applied "with advantage, as a blister, to the bite of some of our venomous serpents." He recommended it in the treatment of dysentery, malignant fever in horses, and for the removal of maculae, or white spots on the skin.[188] Dr. Clapp called it a mild and certain cathartic, to which Dr. Porcher agreed, adding that an extract of it was a favorite remedy in General Marion's camp during the Revolutionary War.[189] Dr. Beach said physicians also used it during the Revolution, when medicines were scarce; he himself considered it useful in indigestion and "as an aperient in habitual costiveness."[190]

Smith found that the Menominees used sugar and syrup from this tree as a "standard Indian physic" and recalled that native whites in West Virginia had used butternut molasses for the same purpose early in this century. The Meskwakis boiled the twig bark for a cathartic. The Potawatomis used the bark as a physic and also drank infusions of the inner bark as a tonic.[191]

Hu Maxwell asserted that "butternut bark and bark of angelica have been used as medicine by regular physicians ever since the secret was learned from the Indian doctors."[192] The inner bark of the root of *Juglans cinerea* was official in the USP, 1820–1905, and NF, 1916–36. Dr. Claus called it a mild cathartic.[193]

Canada moonseed (Menispermum canadense L.), yellow parilla. This species was used medicinally for undisclosed purposes by the Pillager Ojibwas.[194] The dried rhizome was official in the USP, 1882–1905, and in the New York edition, 1831–42. It contains starch and three alkaloid principles and was used as a tonic and diuretic.[195]

Cascara sagrada (Rhamnus purshiana DC), and other species of the buckthorn family. This is a tree which is native to the northwest coast from northern California to British Columbia. From its bark has come a drug which has been called by Norman J. Taylor "the most widely used cathartic on earth." He believed that an unknown Spanish priest found the Indians using it and was so impressed with its mildness and efficacy that he christened it with its Spanish name, signifying "holy bark."[196] Whatever the details, no one disputes that this substance was first used by the aborigines, and then borrowed by the settlers, who passed it on to the medical profession. "Its journey from the aborigines," Lloyd wrote, "to scientific use and therapeutic study appears to parallel the course of such drugs as coca, jalap, benzoin, sassafras, croton tiglium, etc."[197] It was first brought to the attention of the medical profession by Dr. J. H. Bundy of Colusa, California, and marketed by Parke, Davis & Co. in 1877. It was not adopted into the pharmacopeia until the 1890 revision, published in 1894, and there it has remained ever since, no synthesized substitute having been found to replace it, although *Rhamnus californica* is sometimes substituted for it.[198] Pharmaceutical companies market cascara sagrada in pills, powders, and fluid extracts and in compounds with such substances as capsicum, podophyllum resin, and alcohol.[199]

Cedar, red (Juniperus virginiana L.). See also Juniper. John Brickell in 1734 reported that "the Wood of this Tree is profitable against the *French Pox* [syphilis], and an infusion in Vinegar helps Scabs and other cutaneous disorders."[200] Peter Kalm in 1749 was informed by the commander of Fort Frontenac that "red cedar and herbs, the medicinal value of which he praised most highly" grew abundantly near the fort.[201] A century later Dr. Clapp reported the properties of our indigenous red cedar to be equivalent to those of *Sabina* or *Savin*, a foreign drug used as a stimulant, diaphoretic, and remedy for amenorrhea. He warned, however, that the oil derived from it was a narcotic, irritant poison which had caused death in persons seeking by its use to induce abortion.[202] Dr. Beach held that the oil distilled from the leaves and berries was useful in inflammatory rheumatism.[203]

Aboriginal use of red cedar was widespread. The Teton-Dakotas used a decoction of the boiled fruit and leaves to fight the Asiatic cholera of 1849–50, reportedly with some effect.[204] The same medicine was used by Plains tribes for coughs in people and horses. The Dakotas, Omahas, Poncas, and Pawnees burned the twigs and inhaled the smoke for colds in the head, and also used them in their vapor baths.[205] On the Missouri River in 1833, Prince Maximilian reported that red cedar berries "as we were told, are eaten by the Indians for certain medicinal purposes."[206]

Swanton reported that the Chickasaws warmed the ends of cedar limbs in water with elder and placed them on the head for severe headache.[207] Cedar fumes were used by the Creeks to drive away cramps in the muscles of the neck. The Natchez used cedar for pains in the shoulders, breast, and back, for swellings in the legs and for mumps. The Alabamas boiled sprigs and leaves of cedar for warm applications to rheumatic pains.[208] The Ojibwas used the bruised leaves and berries of red cedar internally to remove headache.[209] The Meskwakis boiled the leaves for a drink used in weakness and for convalescent medicine. It was also mixed with other medicines and used as a seasoner.[210]

The young leafy twigs of our native juniper were official in the USP, 1820–94, and were used for a diuretic. Distilled cedar oil, as a reagent, has been official since 1916.[211]

Chestnut, American (*Castanea dentata* Marshall). Brickell reported that "the Leaves or Bark of the Tree boiled in Wine are good against the Bloody Flux, and all other kind of Fluxes."[212] The Mohegan

Indians used the leaves to make a tea for whooping cough.[213] It was similarly used in white medicine and was said to have a sedative action on the nerves of respiration.[214] The dried leaves of *Castanea* were official as a medicine in the USP, 1873–1905, and in the NF, 1916–47, being used as a tonic and astringent.[215]

Chinquapin or *Chinkapin* (*Castanea pumila* Mill.). This southerly-growing tree bears an Algonquian name signifying "great seed."[216] Brickell called it "a kind of Chestnut," having a nut of similar virtues, "but more binding, and are of excellent use to stop Fluxes."[217] Dr. Clapp called the bark astringent and tonic, and said it had been used in the cure of intermittents, though he felt it had "no peculiar virtues to recommend it."[218]

Chinquapin was a Cherokee remedy for feverish conditions in which the symptoms were headache, chills, and cold sweats, and for "fever blisters" prevalent in summer, especially in children. The brittle leaves were steeped warm and the patients blown with it.[219] The bark of this tree was official on the secondary list of the USP, 1820–51, and was used as an astringent because of its tannin content.[220]

Cohosh, blue (*Caulophyllum thalictroides* [L.] Michx.), papoose root, squaw root. Cohosh is an Algonquian name[221] which has been applied not only to this species but also to the black snakeroot (*Cimicifuga racemosa*) and white baneberry (*Actaea alba*). Of the blue, or "blueberry" cohosh, Rafinesque wrote: "This is a medical plant of the Indians, and although not yet introduced into our officinal books, deserves to be better known. I have found it often used in the country and by Indian doctors."[222] "Cohush," according to Stearns's *Herbal*, had been used in menstrual obstructions and to strengthen the stomach, although its medical powers were not fully ascertained.[223] Joseph Smith, the "practical physician," called blue cohosh an aperient and deobstruent and recommended it in the form of tea or decoction for exciting "the secretion of the glands" and in treating "venereal complaints."[224] Dr. Stephen Williams reported to the American Medical Association that the root was demulcent, antispasmodic, sudorific, and emmenagogue. Moreover:

The Indians and quacks recommended it in colic, sore throat, rheumatism, dropsies, &c. It partakes of the nature of ginseng and seneka. The Indian women use it successfully in cases of lingering parturition. It appears to be peculiarly suited to female complaints. It is a powerful emmenagogue, and promotes delivery, the menstrual flux, and dropsical discharges.[225]

Some of these uses may explain why this plant was commonly called squaw root and papoose root. Dr. Clapp reported that the plant was little used, if at all, in regular practice because its properties were not well ascertained.[226] Later investigations, however, led to its admission to the pharmacopeia in 1882, where it remained until 1905. It was also listed in the formulary, 1916–50, and was used for antispasmodic, emmenagogue, and diuretic purposes.[227]

Blue cohosh was considered the most effective fever remedy by the Omaha Indians, who used it in decoction and called it by a name which indicated its purpose.[228] It was used by the Menominees, Potawatomis, Ojibwas, and Meskwakis in a tea for suppression of profuse menstruation and for genitourinary troubles in both sexes. The Potawatomis also used it as an aid to parturition, while the Pillager Ojibwas made an emetic tea of it.[229]

Corn (*Zea mays* L.), and its pharmaceutical derivatives. Maize is the Haitian aboriginal name for the American Indian's greatest contribution to the world food supply.[230] Indians used it in a variety of food products, including hominy, succotash, samp, sagamite, pone, and pemmican, of which the preparation, C. A. Browne writes, "involved a rudimentary knowledge of certain chemical operations."[231] Indians also used corn for a variety of medicinal purposes, as we still do today. The Inca writer, Garcilaso de la Vega (1539–1616), remarked that the Spanish were particularly impressed:

> with the remarkable curative properties of corn, which is not only the principal article of food in America, but is also of great benefit in the treatment of affections of the kidney and bladder, among which are calculus and retention of the urine. And the best proof I can give of this is that the Indians, whose usual drink is made of corn, are afflicted with none of these diseases.[232]

The *Badianus Manuscript* of the Aztecs prescribed a decoction of ground corn in water for "heat in the heart," dysentery, and to produce lactation in women. They also made a poultice of it for infant inflammation.[233] Maya medicinal texts prescribed raw maize soaked in water for blood in the urine, and it was roasted or crushed with the leaves of a species of *Dioscorea* to poultice a sore or swelling.[234]

Josselyn in 1672 pronounced "Indian wheat" to be "excellent in cataplasms, to ripen any swelling or impostume. The decoction of the blew [blue] corn is good to wash sore mouths with. It is light of digestion; and the English make a kind of loblooy of it to eat with milk, which they call sampe."[235] Thomas Ashe of South Carolina called corn "a Grain of General Use to Man and Beast. . . . The American Physicians observe that it breeds good Blood, removes and opens Oppellations [constipation] and Obstructions. At Carolina they have lately invented a way of makeing with it good sound Beer."[236] Brickell related how an Indian doctor "took the rotten Grains of the *Maiz*, or *Indian Corn*, well dried and beaten to Powder," and cured an "ulcer" on a white man's leg.[237] Dr. Schöpf listed the farinaceous seeds and sweet stalk of *Zea mays* for dietetic use.[238] Samuel Stearns reported that "the country people boil it in milk, and apply it as a cataplasm, for the cure of burns, inflammations, and hard swellings."[239]

Lloyd said that a tea of corn silk was used in pioneer domestic medicine as a remedy for acute bladder infections and that he was informed by Dr. John Davis of Cincinnati that a decoction of corn silk, with a decoction of dried bean pods, was the most effective diuretic in his practice, as well as most satisfactory in acute cystitis.[240] Appalachian mountaineers used salted cornmeal as a poultice on sprains and a poultice of cornmeal and peach leaves, said to be a Cherokee remedy, for boils and risings.[241] In Pennsylvania cornmeal was used for a burn poultice.[242] John G. Briante, "the old root and herb doctor," recommended that Indian corn should be roasted like coffee and then boiled for a decoction used in dysentery.[243] With no miracle drugs to help him, Richard Dunlop reports, the saddlebag doctor of the frontier applied poultices of cornmeal and flaxseed to the side to cure lobar pneumonia.[244] The herbalist, Joseph E. Meyer, called cornsilk a diuretic and demulcent, useful as a mucilaginous drink or as an enema whenever a demulcent is indicated.[245] Corn oil has been recommended for numerous ailments by the exponent of Vermont folk medicine, Dr. D. C. Jarvis. He recommends it for hay fever, migraine, and asthma, saying that it aids in shifting the body chemistry from alkaline to acid. He also suggests corn-oil consumption if the margins of the eyelids are scaly or granulated, if the skin is affected with patches of dry, scaly eczema, for the control of angioneurotic edema, and for dandruff of the scalp.[246]

The Chickasaw Indians treated itching skin, followed by sores when scratched, by burning old corncobs and holding the affected part over the smoke.[247] Alabama Indians pounded up kernels of corn, mixed the meal with water, and poured the mixture through a sieve over the head of a patient sick with "slow fever." They also rubbed his body with it.[248] The Catawbas used corn grains as sympathetic magic objects in eliminating warts.[249] The Zuñi Indians used corn smut (*Ustilago zeae*, a fungus) for a medicine—

> given to women during parturition to hasten childbirth by increasing the severity of labor. It is given also to stop hemorrhage after childbirth, and for abnormal lochial discharge. The treatment is the same for all three ailments—a pinch of Ustilago is put into a small quantity of warm or cold water and the infusion is taken at intervals.[250]

The virtues attributed to ustilago by the Zuñis were accepted in medicine when that substance was made official in the USP, 1882–94, for the same purposes as the Indians used it. It served the same ends as the older drug, ergot,[251] although considered weaker and of lower toxicity. Other corn products which have been or are official drugs include cornsilk, USP, 1894–1906, and NF, 1916–46, used as a diuretic; corn oil, USP, 1936–42, and 1947 to date, described as a solvent for injections as well as for irradiated ergosterol; and corn starch, USP, 1894 to date. The properties of the last named are defined as nutrient, demulcent, protective, and absorbent. It is used externally to allay itching and as a dusting powder. Starch suspension is recommended as an antidote in iodine poisoning. Glycerite of starch is used as an emollient and base for suppositories and several pharmaceutical products, such as dextrose, dextrine, glucose (syrup), and the trademarked substance, Alomin, are derived wholly or partly from corn.[252]

Corydalus (Fumewort family), squirrel corn, turkey corn, colic weed, etc. The Pillager Ojibwas placed the root of golden corydalus (*Corydalus aurea*, Willd.) on coals and inhaled the smoke for clearing the head and relieving the patient.[253] The related species, *Dicentra canadensis* (called squirrel corn or colic weed) and *D. cucularia* (Dutchman's breeches) were supposed, Dr. Clapp reported, to be stimulant, diuretic, and diaphoretic. Physicians had used squirrel corn, he reported, as a remedy in cutaneous diseases and as a substitute for mercury in venereal diseases.[254]

The dried tubers of these two species were official in the NF, 1916–47, under the name of corydalus, turkey corn, or squirrel corn. They were said to be a tonic.[255]

Cotton (*Gossypium* species). Cotton has been called the only prominent example of a cultivated plant to be domesticated independently in prehistoric times in both hemispheres. It is, however, the American species, *G. hirsutum*, which is said to be most important economically. Cotton was cultivated in the West Indies and from Peru northward to the American Southwest. Columbus carried samples of American cotton home from his first voyage,[256] and Coronado found cotton in use among the Pueblo tribes.

Not only the cotton fiber but also the leaves, seeds, blossoms, and roots were used for a variety of medicinal purposes by the Mayas and Aztecs.[257] Cotton was used by the Pimas in fracture treatment,[258] and the Alabama and Koasati Indians boiled cotton-plant roots and gave the tea to women to ease labor in childbirth,[259] which is one of the uses to which it has been put by whites.

Dr. Schöpf recommended cottonseed oil for nephritis.[260] Much use of the roots was made in South Carolina for the treatment of asthma (one of the Maya uses), and Dr. Porcher said the decoction appeared to have emmenagogue properties and a specific action on the uterine organs. John U. Lloyd called cotton-root bark a stimulant and emmenagogue and said that in slave days a decoction of it was considered abortifacient.[261] Apparently unaware of the Indian uses of the cotton plant, he remarked that "the credit for the discovery of its uses must be given to the Negroes of the South," from whom it passed to southern physicians and in 1863 to the pharmacopeia, in which the root bark was official until 1916. From that date until 1950 it was listed in the *National Formulary*. According to Dr. Claus, it was credited with being emmenagogue and oxytocic (aiding contractions in parturition). Cotton fiber has been official in the pharmacopeia since 1851,[262] being used in wound dressings and for many other purposes.

Cranberry, high-bush, (Viburnum opulus L.), "cramp bark," and *Cranberry (Vaccinium oxycoccus* L.). Lloyd reported that Indians used a decoction of high-bush cranberry bark as a diuretic. Pills and plasters were devised from the plant and the bark was smoked by some western Indians in lieu of tobacco. The leaves of this and other species were used as tea by Indians and settlers in colonial days.[263] Dr. Millspaugh asserted (1887) that this species was "now proving valuable in many forms of uterine affections and puerperal diseases."[264]

Speck reported that the Penobscot and Malecite Indians steeped and drank *V. opulus* for swollen glands and mumps, although he did not name the part used.[265] The Pillager Ojibwas used the inner bark as a physic and drank a tea of it for stomach cramps. A decoction of it was used by the Meskwakis for cramps or "pain over the whole body." The *V. oxycoccus* was used as food by the Potawatomis and for a tea for a person slightly ill with nausea among the Ojibwas. Whites have used the bitter, astringent leaves of this species for diarrhea, diabetes, and "purifying the blood." The fruit has also been considered antiscorbutic.[266]

The dried bark of *V. opulus*, high-bush cranberry, or true cramp bark, was accepted in official medicine as a sedative and antispasmodic, being listed in the USP, 1894–1916, and NF, 1916–60. The commercial supply is reported to come from wild plants in northern states.[267]

Creosote bush (Larrea mexicana M.; syn.: *Covillea tridentata, Larrea tridentata*), greasewood. Dr. J. M. Bigelow, who was surgeon of the U.S.–Mexico boundary commission in 1848, is reported to have brought this plant to the attention of the medical profession. He announced that a liniment obtained by boiling its leaves and branches was useful as an application for bruises, rheumatism, and internally as a decoction with sarsaparilla for venereal nodes and chancre.[268]

This plant was quite generally used by southwestern tribes. Papago women boiled the leaves, added salt, and washed contusions with the hot decoction. The Pimas and Maricopas boiled the branches to extract the gum, which was drunk in hot decoction for stomach trouble and diarrhea. The leaves and smaller branches were heated and applied as a dry poultice for pain in the chest and other parts of the body. The Pimas relieved the pain of toothache by sharpening a young branch to a point, heating it in a fire, and inserting it into the cavity. The Maricopas used fresh twigs, heated, for applications in rheumatic pains.[269]

An exudate, called *Sonora gum*, is extracted from creosote bush. An infusion of the leaves has been used in throat, bronchial, and pulmonary complaints. The constituents of this product include resin, mucilage, a volatile oil, and cresols or phenols. *Creosote* was introduced into the USP in 1842, where it remained official for a hundred years. Since 1942 it has been included in the NF. The substance is defined as a distilled mixture of phenols from wood tar and is used as a disinfectant and internally as a stimulating expectorant. *Creosote carbonate*, USP, 1916–42, NF, 1942–55, is an expectorant and pulmonary antiseptic, preferred to creosote because it is borne more easily by the stomach and kidneys.[270]

Crowfoot (*Ranunculus* species), buttercup. This large family includes native species, species introduced from Europe, and species supposed to be indigenous to both continents. Several of the writers on materia medica have described the principal characteristic of the group as acridity and their juice has been mainly used in medicine as an external caustic or vesicant.[271]

The Montagnais Indians crushed the leaves of *R. acris* (an introduced species) and inhaled the odor from the hands to relieve headache.[272] The Potawatomis used the entire plant of bristly crowfoot (*R. pennsylvanicus*) as an astringent medicine for undisclosed ailments. McIntosh, the Meskwaki doctor, used the roots of abortive crowfoot (*R. abortivus*) as a styptic to stop nosebleed, though the tribe did not so use them. This tribe once used water yellow crowfoot (*R. delphinifolius*) flowers or stigmas for a snuff to cause sneezing and mixed the same with other herbs for catarrh and head cold.[273]

The fresh herb of *R. bulbosus* L., under the name of crowfoot or ranunculus, was official in the USP, 1820–82. Recognized as acrid, it was applied externally only as a counterirritant.[274] The species is of European origin.

Culver's root (*Veronica virginica* L.), Culver's physic, black root, Bowman's root, Brinton root, Leptandra. Cotton Mather in 1716 wrote to John Winthrop of New London, speaking of the fame of Culver's root as a cure for consumption and asking for some for his eldest daughter, who was ill. He received the drug and administered it to her, but she died the next month, "all the sooner, I have little doubt," remarked Oliver Wendell Holmes, "for this uncertain and violent drug, with which the meddlesome pedant tormented her."[275]

Culver's root was used as a cathartic by the Allegheny Senecas.[276] The Menominees used it as a strong physic, a reviver, and for purification when defiled by the touch of a bereaved person. The Meskwakis used the root for curing constipation and to dissolve kidney gravel, for ague tea, and medicine for women who were weak or in labor.[277]

Pioneers derived their knowledge of the cathartic properties of this root from the Indians, and early physicians used it for "bilious fevers" and pleurisy.[278] André Michaux, the French botanist, believed that the root of this plant was an effective cure for venereal diseases.[279] Dr. Clapp considered Culver's root to be a certain cathartic and a mild one in moderate doses. He reported that it had been used as a cholalogue and substitute for mercurial cathartics.[280]

This drug was included in the primary list of the first USP in 1820 under the name of veronica, and remained so listed until the 1840 revision, when it was dropped. It was restored in the 1860 revision, but under the name of *Leptandra* (because of its alternate Latin designation, *Leptandra virginica* Nutt.). The names represent the same plant, but there was a difference of opinion as to its correct genus.[281] *Leptandra* remained official in the USP, 1864–1916, and in the NF, 1916–55, the dried roots and rhizomes being the parts used, for cathartic and emetic purposes.[282] The drug was also reported used as an alterative and for liver disorders.[283]

Dandelion (Taraxacum officinale Weber). Called by some a naturalized European weed and by others a plant indigenous to most parts of the world, dandelion has long been used for medicinal purposes. According to Lloyd, it was an ingredient of many popular American "bitters" and "blood purifiers" and long enjoyed a high reputation as a home remedy.[284] The herb doctor, Joseph Smith, listed dandelion as an aperient and deobstruent and recommended it in the form of tea or syrup, which "opens the system in general."[285] Dr. Clapp reported that dandelion was mostly used (1852) in chronic diseases of the liver.[286]

Mohegan Indians steeped dandelion leaves for a physic.[287] Pillager Ojibwas made a tea of the roots for heartburn, while the Potawatomis used the roots for a bitter tonic. The Meskwakis considered dandelion root a strong medicine and took it for pain in the chest when other remedies failed.[288]

In the first issue of the *National Formulary* (1888), a "compound elixir of Taraxacum" appears in twelve of the 435 formulas listed.[289] The dried rhizome and root of dandelion was official in the USP, 1831–1926, and remained in the NF till 1965. Its uses have been diuretic, tonic, and aperient.[290]

Devil's shoestring (Tephrosia virginiana [L.] Pers.; syn.: *Cracca virginiana* L., *Galega virginiana, Galega officinalis*), catgut, goat's rue, rabbit's pea, turkey pea. This is an old Indian remedy which recently came into prominence following the discovery of its insecticidal properties and the isolation of rotenone and tephrosia from it. Rotenone was previously found in certain American trees and shrubs.[291]

Hunter reported that the Osage, Kansas, and Pawnee Indians used "turkey pea" in tea and in substance mainly to destroy worms.[292] Mooney reported that the Cherokees drank a decoction of this plant for lassitude. The women washed their hair in a decoction of its roots to prevent its falling out, because they believed the toughness of the roots would be transferred to their hair. For the same reason, ballplayers rubbed the decoction on their limbs to toughen them. At that time (1885) the *U.S. Dispensatory* described the plant as a cathartic and the roots as tonic and aperient.[293] The Creek Indians used a cold infusion of this plant for bladder trouble and a decoction of it for chronic coughing, sometimes combining it with sassafras.[294]

Dr. Porcher reported in 1849 that the roots "were used by Indians, and are now employed in popular practice, as a vermifuge." A decoction was said to act as powerfully and efficiently for this purpose as pinkroot (Spigelia).[295] The species has not, however, become an official drug.

Dogwood (Cornus species). The southern species, flowering dogwood (*Cornus florida* L.) is most frequently mentioned in early accounts. Lawson called its root bark "an infallible remedy against the worms."[296] Byrd used dogwood bark with "good Success" to cure malaria which afflicted members of his boundary survey party in 1729.[297] Peter Kalm described the use of *Cornus florida* root bark for malaria patients "who could not be cured by the Jesuit's bark, [but] recovered by the help of this." When the wife of his host, Colonel

299

Lydius, was afflicted with severe leg pains, an Indian woman "went out into the forest, cut twigs and cuttings of the dogwood, removed the bark, boiled them in water and rubbed the legs with the water. The pain disappeared within two or three days and she recovered her former health."[298]

David Zeisberger, the Moravian missionary, said the rind of dogwood root was sold in apothecary shops in place of cinchona.[299] "Many believe its virtues to be the same as those of Peruvian bark," wrote his coreligionist, George Loskiel.[300] *Cornus florida* was called astringent and carminative by Dr. Schöpf, who also recommended it for intermittent fever.[301] It was highly praised, together with *C. sericea*, by Dr. Barton as the most effective indigenous remedy for intermittents. The bark of the last-named species was also considered a useful astringent in diarrhea. He noted that Indians used an infusion of the flowers for intermittent fevers and that the same had been recommended for flatulent colic. He endorsed the opinions of Dr. John M. Walker on the tonic and stimulant powers of the two species.[302]

Dr. N. S. Davis, chairman of the committee on indigenous medical botany of the American Medical Association, declared in 1849 that because of the high price of cinchona and its frequent adulteration, no more acceptable service could be done for the profession than "to devise some concentrated and reliable preparation of the Cornus Florida bark." He cited several cases of the effective use of dogwood bark in curing malaria.[303] Dr. Porcher believed that the bark also had antiseptic properties, and during the Civil War he reported that it "has been employed with great advantage in place of quinine in fevers—particularly in cases of low forms of fever, and in dysentery, on the river courses, of a typhoid character. It is given as a substitute for Peruvian barks."[304] Several other physicians of that period extolled the value of dogwood bark as a substitute for quinine.[305]

Dogwood bark was a general fever remedy among the Pennsylvania Germans[306] and other rural folk. In pioneer days country doctors prescribed its use in the Indian manner, the flowers, fruit, and bark being steeped in water for a bitter drink given for "fever and ague."[307]

Dogwood was a remedy in numerous Indian tribes. In Arkansas, Hunter reported, the bark was given "with bitters of various kinds in fevers of the low type, and when there is great prostration of strength." It was also used as a poultice on sores.[308] The Alabama tribe boiled the inner bark for use in "the flux."[309] The Houmas of Louisiana took scrapings from the roots or bark of *C. florida* or *C. stricta* and boiled them in water for a decoction used in fever and malaria.[310] The Wisconsin Potawatomis used the root bark of redosier dogwood (*C. stolonifera* Michx.) as their most efficacious remedy for diarrhea and flux; the same species was described in the *U.S. Dispensatory* (1918 ed.) as a mild astringent, aromatic bitter, stomachic, and emetic. The Potawatomis also used the bark of alternate-leaved dogwood (*C. alternifolia* L.) in an eyewash to cure granulation of the eyelids. Whites have used it as a diaphoretic, febrifuge, and astringent. The Pillager Ojibwas used the inner bark of this species as an emetic. The Menominees used it as a diarrhea remedy, employing a rectal syringe made of an animal bladder and a hollow duck bone. The pulverized bark was used as a wet poultice. The bark of panicled dogwood (*C. paniculata* L'Her.) was made into a tea for flux by the Ojibwas, and an aggregate of the bark compressed into stopper shape was forced into the anus for piles. The Meskwakis used a bark tea of this species for flux, injecting it by an enema syringe fashioned like that of the Menominees. The same medicine was held in the mouth for aching teeth or neuralgia. The species was further used in this tribe as a smoke smudge to revive patients and in treating consumption. Whites once used it as a bitter, astringent, antiperiodic, and emetic.[311]

The dried bark of three species of dogwood have been official medicines in the USP and were used as bitter tonics and astringents: *Cornus circinata* or round-leaved dogwood, 1820–82; *Cornus florida* or flowering dogwood, 1820–94 (and NF, 1916–36); and *Cornus sericea* or swamp dogwood, 1820–82.[312]

Elder (*Sambucus canadensis* L.), and other species of elder. Peter Kalm mentioned the use of this shrub by Indians as a pain killer: "I have seen the Iroquois boil the inner bark of the *Sambucus Canadensis*, or Canada elder, and put it on that part of the cheek in which the pain was most violent. This, I am told, often diminishes the pain."[313] Of the same species, Loskiel declared that a "decoction of wood and buds is an excellent remedy in agues, and Indians use it likewise for inflammations."[314]

Choctaw Indians combined beaten elder leaves with salt for a headache poultice.[315] The Creeks pounded up the tender roots, stirred them in hot water, and bound them on women who suffered from swollen breasts. Scrapings from the stalks were used if roots could not be obtained.[316] Houma Indians boiled the bark of *S. canadensis* to make a liquid wash for application to painful and swollen parts and used the berries for a tonic wine.[317] The root bark of this species was used by the Meskwakis to free the lungs of phlegm. A bark tea was used in difficult parturition. The Menominees used the dried flowers in a febrifuge tea.[318]

Elder flowers and fruits were once a household remedy for diuretic and diaphoretic purposes, and for poultices and ointments in rheumatism, sores, and burns. The berries were used for cooling, aperient, and diuretic properties.[319] Dr. Clapp called elder "probably a valuable article . . . too long neglected." He called the inner bark of *Sambucus* a hydragogue cathartic, being emetic in large doses, and the leaves an excellent application to excoriations and chafed skin. The bark, simmered in lard, was a soothing ointment for irritable ulcers and burns.[320]

Sambucus berries were official in the USP, 1820–31; the expressed juice was used for wine and in a soft extract recognized in European pharmacy as the base of a refrigerant, diuretic drink. *Sambucus* flowers were official (together with those of the European *S. nigra* L.) in the USP, 1831–1905, and in the NF, 1916–47. They were used for distilling elder flower water, a perfume, and a flavoring. The properties of elder flowers have been given as mild stimulant, carminative, and diaphoretic.[321]

Elm, red or slippery (Ulmus fulva Michx.) and *American or White elm (Ulmus americana* L.). John Lawson reported that there were two elms, one growing on high ground and other on low ground; from the first kind:

> The Indians take the Bark of its Root and beat it, whilst green, to a Pulp, and then dry it in the Chimney, where it becomes of a reddish Colour. This they use as a Sovereign Remedy to heal a Cut or green Wound, or any thing that is not corrupted. It is of a very glutinous Quality.[322]

From the description, this appears to be the red elm. Brickell was of the opinion that the bark and leaves were "of a cleansing, drying, and binding Quality, and therefore good in Wounds and broken

Bones; the Liquor that issueth out of the Tree takes away Scruff, Pimples, Spots and Freckles from the Face; one Ounce of the inner-Bark in Wine, Purges Flegm."[323]

Samuel Stearns called the bark of slippery elm "good in various chronical, cutaneous eruptions and the leprosy of the Indians [syphilis?]; in a suppression of urine, dropsy, inflammation, and hard tumours."[324] The bark of American elm was reported used with good results for poultices on gunshot wounds by surgeons in the Revolutionary War, and by soldiers in Anthony Wayne's Indian campaign of 1794.[325] Dr. Porcher called slippery-elm bark an excellent demulcent and emollient application; a decoction of it was recommended by him in suppression of urine, bladder inflammation, dysentery, and diarrhea. Combined with sassafras root and guaiac, he called it a valuable drink to increase cutaneous transpiration and improve the tone of digestive organs.[326] Dr. Beach reported that slippery-elm tea was used by Indian women to procure easy labor; he listed numerous uses of the tree in white medicine and declared that "in point of utility, it is of far more value than its weight in gold."[327]

Long before there were drugstores in America, one writer remarked, "the red doctors understood the healing properties of the bark" of elm trees.[328] Indians taught the white man the use of the bark not only for poultices but as a medication in fevers and diarrhea.[329] Hunter observed that Indians of the Ozark region used the inner bark in colds and bowel complaints, valuing its demulcent properties; it was also much used as a cataplasm or emollient in ulcers and swellings. He found it nutritive, asserting that he had "subsisted for days on it." [330] Missouri valley Indians used a decoction of the inner bark as a laxative and a preservative of meat. They used the wood of American elm and other species to make mortars and pestles for grinding medicines and perfumes.[331] The Catawbas used slippery-elm bark for consumption and made a salve for rheumatism by peeling the fresh bark and mixing it with lard and "bear root."[332] The Houmas mixed American-elm bark with red oak for a dysentery remedy.[333] The Alabamas boiled slippery-elm bark in water along with gunpowder for a medicine used in delayed parturition. The Creeks used elm for a toothache remedy.[334] The Mohegans steeped the bark of American elm for a cough and cold medicine.[335] The bark of the same species was used by the Potawatomis, who also chewed the bark of slippery elm for an application to inflamed eyes. Splinters of this wood were used to lance boils, which were then poulticed, with "recovery complete and permanent." The Menominees used a tea of the inner bark for a physic and the same bark as a wound poultice. The Pillager Ojibwas used the inner bark for a sore throat medicine. The Meskwakis used it to poultice old sores, pounding it, wetting it, and combining it with other medicines. The root was boiled for a tea to promote easy childbirth and white-elm root bark was made into an eye lotion.[336] The Penobscots steeped and drank a decoction of American-elm bark for bleeding of the lungs, which Speck called "a trouble once common but now rare."[337]

The bark of *Ulmus fulva*, slippery elm, was official in the USP from 1820 until 1936, and was listed in the NF, 1936–60. It is used for protective, demulcent, and emollient purposes.[338]

Fern, male (*Dryopteris Filix-mas* [L.] Schott.). Under the pharmaceutical name of *Aspidium*, the rhizome and stipes of this European fern were official in the USP, 1831–1965. *American Aspidium* or marginal fern (*D. marginalis* [L.] A. Gray) was official in the USP, 1882–1916, and 1942–65. The extract of these species, called *Aspidium* oleoresin, extract of male fern, or male fern oleoresin, was official in the USP, 1870–1965. These substances have been used for anthelmintic and especially taenifuge purposes.[339]

Aspidium has been used since ancient times in the Old World. Dr. Barton believed that the anthelmintic powers of male fern had been exaggerated and urged more attention to native species.[340]

Several species of native ferns have been used for various medicinal purposes by the Indians, of which the most outstanding example is the maidenhair (*Adiantum pedatum* L.). While some of the ferns in the aboriginal materia medica have been used in white medicine, none became official drugs. The Delaware tribe used the exotic male fern as a tapeworm expellent, but August Mahr is doubtless correct in saying that they acquired their use of this plant from the whites.[341] The shield fern (*Aspidium cristatum* [L.] Sw., syn.: *Dryopteris spinulosa*) was used in a root tea for stomach trouble by the Flambeau Ojibwas.[342] This plant, Claus states, "appears to possess properties similar to the official drug." The rhizome of *Pteridium aquilinium*, the eastern brake or bracken, also contains several active principles.[343] It was used by the Delawares for a diuretic,[344] by the Menominees in a drink given to women with caked breast, and by the Ojibwas for stomach cramps in women.[345]

Fleabane (Erigeron species). Samuel Stearns said that "the chief use of the *flea banes* is for destroying fleas and gnats, by burning the herbs so as to waste away in smoke."[346] They have, however, been used for other purposes. Barton called the Philadelphia fleabane (*E. philadelphicus* L.) a powerful diuretic and sudorific, useful in gouty and gravelly complaints.[347] Houma Indians boiled the root of this species for a drink used in menstrual troubles. They also used the Canada fleabane (*E. canadensis* L.) in a tea given for leucorrhea.[348] Ojibwa Indians used the flowers of Philadelphia fleabane in a tea for fever, and the smoke from the burning of dried flowers was inhaled for a head cold. Both the Ojibwas and the Meskwakis snuffed the pulverized flowers up the nostrils to cause sneezing and loosen a head cold. The Meskwakis used *E. canadensis* (also called horseweed) as a steaming agent in the sweat bath. The daisy fleabane (*E. ramosus* Walt,. syn.: *E. strigosus* Muhl.) was used by the Flambeau Ojibwas as a perfume to cure sick headache.[349] The same species was taken by the Catawbas in a root drink for heart ailments.[350]

Three species of fleabane were accepted as official drugs for their stimulant and diuretic properties, and a volatile oil extracted from them has been used to quicken uterine contractions. The daisy fleabane (*E. heterophyllum* Muhl.)[351] was official in the USP, 1831–82, under the names of sweet scabious and *Erigeron*, successively; the Philadelphia fleabane was official for the same dates, and the Canada fleabane was official from 1820 to 1882. The leaves and flowering tops were the parts used. *Erigeron oil*, a volatile oil distilled from the herb of the last-named species, was official from 1863 to 1916.[352] Besides the official uses, the fleabanes have been widely used in domestic medicine.

Fringe tree (Chionanthus virginica L.), flowering ash, poison ash, snowdrop tree. This was the "Privet tree" of which John Brickell wrote: "The Leaves and Flowers are cooling and good in all Inflammations and soreness of the Eyes, Ulcers in the Mouth and Throat, looseness of the Gums, and to stop Fluxes."[353] The Louisiana Choctaws boiled the bark of this tree in water and used the extract to bathe wounds; a mash of the bark was made into a wet poultice for cuts and severe bruises.[354] The bark was used by the Alabamas and Koasatis for toothache, and by the Koasatis as an exterior plaster for internal pains, as well as a poultice for cuts and bruises.[355]

Dr. Millspaugh had much praise for the healing virtures of this bark:

> The previous use of the bark of this shrub as an astringent and vulnerary, and the bark of the root as a tonic after long and exhaustive diseases, is one that has great merit. The bark in infusion is a remedy that was too often neglected for foreign drugs in the treatment of typhoid forms of fever and intermittents, especially those of bilious character.

Dr. Millspaugh named other physicians who had found this bark to be diuretic, acronarcotic, and useful as a headache remedy. Rafinesque, the botanist, held that the root as a cataplasm caused the healing of wounds without suppuration.[356]

The dried bark of *Chionanthus* or *fringe tree* was listed in the *National Formulary*, 1916–47, and was used as a tonic.[357]

Garlic, Onions, and Leek (Allium and other species). The Indians were aware of wild garlic, for the name of the city of Chicago comes from their appellation for one of these plants. It has been previously mentioned that wild garlic gathered by Indian children saved Prince Maximilian from death by scurvy. Dr. F. Andros reported that the Winnebago and Dakota Indians used the bruised wild onion for the sting of bees and wasps, "which, from experience, [he wrote] I know almost instantly relieves the pain."[358] Wild onion (*A. sibiricum* L.) were used as food by Plains tribes.[359] The Cheyenne Indians used a species of wild garlic for treating carbuncles. They ground the bulb and stem fine and applied this as a poultice; when the carbuncle opened, they washed out the pus with a decoction of the same drug.[360] The Mohegans simmered cut-up onions into a syrup taken for colds.[361]

Onions have been used in American folk medicine. In eighteenth-century Pennsylvania, Doddridge reported, the juice of roasted onions or garlic was given to children for the croup.[362] Judge Douglas wrote that southern mountaineers used onion poultices for croup, pneumonia, and chest colds.[363]

The *Allium* or *garlic* which was official in the USP, 1820–1905, and in the NF, 1916–36, was the bulb of a European species, *A. sativum* L. It was considered carminative, expectorant, and diuretic.[364] It was the opinion of Dr. Clapp that the bulbs of the native meadow garlic, *A. canadense* Kalm, were equal to the official garlic and a good substitute for it. The indigenous wild onion, *A. cernuum* Roth, and wild leek, *A. tricoccum* Ait., had in his opinion medicinal properties similar to the garlic, "though said to be less powerful."[365]

Gentian (Gentiana family). Several species called "gentian"[366] were used by Indians for a variety of purposes, especially the horse gentian (*Triosteum perfoliatum* L.), or feverwort, and many of them were used in white medicine, but only one, or possibly two, have become official drugs. One of our early sources of information, J. D. Hunter, failed to name the species of "wild gentian" from which western Indians obtained the root for use in cases of debility, "especially when accompanied with affections of the stomach." It was used, sometimes in combination with dogwood or wild cherry bark, for malaria, palpitation of the heart, and dropsy.[367]

The Catawbas used the root of Sampson's snakeroot (*Gentiana Catesbaei* Walt.?)[368] to stop pains in the stomach. A hot or cold infusion was drunk or the roots were chewed. It was also applied to cure backache.[369] This plant and other gentians were used by Smoky mountain settlers in a tea for colic.[370] Under the name of American or blue gentian, *G. Catesbaei* was official in the USP, 1820–82, the rhizome and roots being used as a bitter tonic, the same as the European drug, *G. lutea* L., which was official in the USP, 1820–1955, and in the NF, 1955–65. American centaury (*Chironia angularis* L., or *Sabatia angularis* [L.] Pursh), used also as a bitter tonic, was official in the USP, 1820–82,[371] but information concerning aboriginal usage is not available. Formerly it was used in fevers, including malaria.[372]

Ginseng (Panax quinquefolius L.). The enormous popularity once held by this plant as a panacea is equaled by few. It would be difficult to find any plant with a reputation so disproportionate to its actual virtues. For this the Chinese, once an important market for it, and the Europeans, who were also convinced of its magic power, are more to be blamed than the Indians. Peter Kalm said that the French used ginseng root for curing asthma, as a stomachic, and for promoting fertility in women. Of the extraordinary activity it evoked, he reported:

> The trade which is carried on with it here [in Canada] is very brisk, for they gather great quantities of it and send them to France, whence they are brought to China and sold to great advantage. . . . During my stay in Canada all the merchants in Quebec and Montreal received orders from their correspondents in France to send over a quantity of ginseng, there being an uncommon demand for it this summer. . . . The Indians especially travelled about the country in order to collect as much as they could and sell it to the merchants at Montreal. The Indians . . . were likewise so taken up with this business that the French farmers were not able during that time to hire a single Indian, as they commonly do to help them in the harvest. [Ginseng] formerly grew in abundance round Montreal, but at present there is not a single plant of it to be found, so effectually have they been rooted out. This obliged the Indians this summer to go far within the English boundaries to collect these roots.[373]

The London market was also flooded with ginseng, to the extent that Peter Collinson complained in a letter to Colden: "Never Certainly was a more Impolitick thing done than to Send Such Quantities of Genseng Here—it has so Sunk the Markett—that there must be great Losses on it."[374] The *Moravian Journals* for 1752–54 abound with accounts of the effects of the ginseng craze on the activity of the Indians. At numerous Iroquois villages they found most of the inhabitants absent on ginseng-digging journeys. At Onondaga on August 31, 1752, it was reported that "a string of wampum had arrived from Mr. Johnson,[375] who sent word to the Indians to gather as many roots as they could, as he expected to be there in 10 days to purchase them." At length the missionaries themselves "went into the woods to gather roots, in order to buy several blankets, as the nights were growing cold."[376]

Ginseng was also shipped in quantities from South Carolina directly to China in the 1780's.[377] Loskiel reported that it once sold in Holland for twenty-five florins a pound, but the price later fell from an oversupply.[378] In Virginia in the late eighteenth century, the celebrated root once brought 67 cents to a dollar a pound.[379]

In America, too, ginseng was considered a cure-all. Kalm remarked that "the old surgeon, Mr. Rosbom, said that the root not only is invaluable for wounds but taken internally it also affects the urine and is fine for stones in the bladder."[380] In 1710, William Byrd used "drops of ginseng" in treating his daughter, who was ill with a fever.[381] Upon finding some ginseng plants in 1732, Byrd wrote:

> The Root of this is of wonderful Vertue in many Cases, particularly to raise the Spirits and promote Perspiration, which makes it a Specifick in Colds and Coughs. . . . I carry'd home this Treasure, with as much Joy, as if every Root had been the Graft of the Tree of Life, and washt and dry'd it carefully.[382]

Jonathan Carver maintained that "when chewed it certainly is a great strengthener of the stomach."[383] Samuel Stearns found it "beneficial in coughs, consumptions, and spasmodic disorders."[384] Manasseh Cutler thought that the demand for this drug in many countries would make it a valuable export, as "European physicians esteem it a good medicine in convulsions, vertigoes, and all nervous complaints."[385] Barton observed that the Indians made a tea from the leaves of ginseng, as well as from the root, but it did not appear that they "so highly esteem the Ginseng as their Tartar brethren in Asia do." His own belief was that "Ginseng is by no means a powerful stimulant."[386] Possibly his caution was influenced by the opinion of Dr. Cullen, who called ginseng nothing more than a very mild aromatic and denied that it had the aphrodisiac powers claimed for it by the Chinese.[387] Also cautious was the view of Jacob Bigelow, who held that the virtues of ginseng "do not appear, by any means, to justify the high estimation of it by the Chinese." It was not, he said, a very active substance and was properly classified as a demulcent, for which reason Dr. Fothergill had used a decoction of it in chronic coughs.[388]

By 1852, Dr. Clapp reported that ginseng was "seldom employed in this country."[389] For decades more, however, the plant was still dug, and even cultivated, for domestic use and foreign export. Alice Henkel reported in 1906 that the commercial price was five dollars a pound and upward, considered a good price for raw drugs. Exports for the year ending June 30, 1906, amounted to 160,940 pounds, valued at $1,175,844.[390] In World War II, when hygroscopic materials used for keeping cigarettes dry became scarce, one company turned to ginseng as a substitute.[391]

Ginseng was official in the USP from 1842 to 1882, but always on the secondary list. Dr. Claus called it a stimulant and stomachic, the active principles and constituents being a glycosidal substance called panaquilon, saponin, a bitter principle, a volatile oil containing a camphoraceous substance, resin, sugar, mucilage, and starch.[392]

There is cause to wonder if some Indian uses of ginseng might be partly due to white influence. It was one of the "ordinary remedies" of the Mohawks, but on the strength of Lafitau's account of the regard the Chinese had for it, a Mohawk woman "cured herself next day of an intermittent fever which had been plaguing her several months."[393] The Penobscots used it to increase the fertility of women, steeping a piece of the root, called "man root" from its shape, in water and drinking the liquid from time to time.[394] The Cherokees gathered the root for traders, but also used a decoction of it for headache, cramps, and female troubles; the chewed root was blown on the side for pains in that locality.[395] Swanton found ginseng to be a "highly esteemed remedy" among the Creeks, who drank an infusion of the roots for shortness of breath, croup in children, hoarse coughing, and fevers. For the last ailment, it was mixed with ginger and alcohol to produce sweat. Ginseng was also used to stem the flow of blood from cuts. The Alabama Indians broke the roots from the plants and rubbed the milky juice on sores.[396] The Houmas boiled the roots for a drink to stop vomiting and used the same infusion with whisky added to abate rheumatism.[397] Among the Menominees, Smith reported, ginseng was the special medicine of his informant's wife, but they were vague about its use; he supposed it to be a tonic and strengthener of mental powers. The Meskwakis gathered ginseng for a universal remedy, as well as for sale to traders. They used it as a seasoner to add power to other medicines and mixed it with other substances for a love potion. The Ojibwas made no use of ginseng, but gathered it for traders, always planting new seeds for what they pulled up. The Potawatomis pounded the root for a poultice to cure earache and soaked the pounded root to obtain a wash for sore eyes. It was also mixed with powdered medicines and used as a seasoner to mask unpleasant flavors.[398]

Gold thread (*Coptis trifolia* Salisb.). Carver declared that this plant was "greatly esteemed both by the Indians and the colonists as

a remedy for any soreness in the mouth, but the taste of it is exqui-
sitely bitter."[399] Samuel Stearns asserted:

> A watery decoction, infusion and gargle of the roots, have
> been used by the Indian and white people to advantage, when
> sweetened with honey, against the canker in the mouth and
> throat; and some have chewed the root for the same purpose.[400]

Dr. Clapp called a dose of the powdered root of gold thread a
"pure, simple, strong bitter," with a great popular reputation, especially in New England, being used as a remedy for "apthous sore
mouth of children." He pronounced it an excellent tonic in dyspepsia
and general debility.[401]

The Montagnais Indians called this herb "yellow plant" and boiled
it as a tea used as a wash for sore eyes, lips, and the interior of the
mouth.[402] Penobscots chewed the stems to allay canker on gums or
in the mouth and considered it good for mouths irritated by too much
tobacco smoking.[403] The Mohegans steeped gold thread for use as a
mouth wash for babies.[404] The Menominees used the roots for an
astringent mouth wash for sore throat in babies and to cure cankers
in the mouth. The Menominees and the Pillager Ojibwas used a
decoction to soothe and heal the gums of teething babies. Adults of
the last tribe also used it as a wash for sore mouth. The same uses
were reported among the Potawatomis. It appears that Indian uses
of this plant coincide with those of the whites, as Smith indicated.[405]

The entire plant of *Coptis* or gold thread was official in the USP,
1820–82, on the secondary list, and in the NF, 1916–36. Dr. Claus
classed it as a tonic and stomachic, with action similar to Hydrastis
(next listing).[406]

Golden seal (Hydrastis canadensis L.), yellow puccoon, yellow root,
etc. Alice Henkel has listed nineteen common names by which this
plant has been known. The name "yellow root" has led to much
confusion, for it is a name applied to *Zanthorhiza apiifolia* and other
plants.

Undoubtedly, *Hydrastis* was the "yellow root" described by Hunter,
which he said resembled puccoon. Indians west of the Mississippi
used a cold, watery infusion of the roots for sore eyes, which was said
to be a common ailment in the autumn. They also used a warm infu-

sion for dropsy and the powdered root as an escharotic. Hunter believed it had "some claims as a stimulant or tonic."[407]

Golden seal was used for many purposes by Indians, particularly the Cherokees. Mixed with bear's grease, it was used as an insect repellent. Some Indians used it as a diuretic, stimulant, and escharotic, using the powder as a blister and in cancer treatment and the infusion for dropsy. It was further regarded as a specific for sore and inflamed eyes and was popular with pioneers of the Ohio valley for this purpose, as well as for sore mouth. For the latter trouble, the root was chewed. Captain Meriwether Lewis considered it effective for both purposes. It was used by Indians and whites for skin diseases, indolent ulcers, gonorrhea, and as an internal tonic. In tincture or infusion, it was used for liver and stomach ailments. It has been reported to be slightly narcotic, as well as a laxative appropriate for dyspepsia.[408]

Hydrastis was overlooked by Kalm, Cutler, and Dr. Schöpf. Its use by Indians for a yellow dye was mentioned to the American Philosophical Society in 1782 by Hugh Martin, but it was Benjamin Barton who described its medical virtues in 1798.[409] The dried rhizome and roots of this plant were official in the USP, 1831–42 and 1863–1936, and in the NF, 1936–60. Three derivatives from it have also been official: *Hydrastine*, USP 1905–26, *Hydrastinine hydrochloride*, USP 1894–1926, and *Hydrastine hydrochloride*, USP 1916–26, NF 1926–50. Dr. Claus described Hydrastis as a bitter tonic and astringent used in inflammation of the mucous membrances. The official derivatives have been used as internal hemostatics. Berberine and L-Canadine are unofficial derivatives, the first being used as an antiperiodic, stomachic, and tonic; the second "paralyzes the central nervous system and causes severe peristalsis."[410]

Goldenrod (*Solidago* species). The Alabamas used the roots of an unidentified species of goldenrod for a tea drunk for a cold; a piece of the root was sometimes put into the cavity of an aching tooth.[411] The Houmas boiled a handful of roots from *S. nemoralis* for a tea to cure "yellow jaundice," a usage probably resulting from the doctrine of signatures.[412] Flowers or leaves of several species of goldenrod were used among the Menominees, Ojibwas, and Potawatomis for a tea used in fevers and pain in the chest. Roots were used for a poultice on boils. The Meskwakis used the flowers of one species for a lotion applied to bee stings and to cure swollen fauces. A root tea was used on burns and scalds, and plants were used in a fumigant to revive unconscious patients. Whites have used goldenrods for carminative, antispasmodic, and astringent purposes.[413]

The only species of goldenrod admitted to the *U. S. Pharmacopeia* was the American sweet-scented goldenrod (*S. odora* Ait.), which was on the secondary list from 1820 till 1882. It is not mentioned in Lloyd or Claus, and Gathercoal's check list gives the wrong date (1870) for its dismissal. Jacob Bigelow stated that the species contained a volatile oil on which the chief medicinal effects of the plant depended. Its properties were defined as stimulant, carminative, and diaphoretic.[414]

Grindelia (*Grindelia robusta*, Nutt. etc.) The grindelias are perennial herbs of western North America which have long been used by Indians for a variety of curing purposes. Their value was first brought to the attention of the medical profession about 1863 by Dr. C. A. Canfield of Monterey, California, who had noticed the aboriginal use of the plants as a poison ivy remedy. In 1875, Mr. James G. Steele of San Francisco recommended the use of grindelia for that purpose in a paper submitted to the American Pharmaceutical Association.[415] The dried leaf and flowering tops of *Grindelia* were official in the USP, 1882–1926, and have been in the NF, 1926–60. Several species have been official under this name, including *G. robusta* Nutt., *G. humilis* Hooker et Arnott, and *G. squarrosa* (Pursh) Dunal. Other species have been employed in medicine, including *G. hirsutala* and *G. glutinosa*. The grindelias have been used as a sedative, an antispasmodic, an expectorant, and remedy for poison ivy infection, a fluid extract being used for the latter case.[416]

California Indians used *G. robusta* not only for skin infections, but also for bronchial troubles.[417] Some western Indians are reported to have used a species of grindelia in decoction for venereal diseases.[418] *G. squarrosa* was taken in internal decoction by Indians and Mexicans of southern California to cure colds.[419] The Utes used it as a cough medicine.[420] The same species, called "sticky head" on the Great Plains, was used in decoction by the Teton Dakotas to cure colic in children. The Poncas believed it was good for consumption, and the Pawnees boiled the leaves and tops to make a wash for saddle galls and sores on horses' backs.[421]

Hardhack (Spiraea tomentosa L.), meadow sweet, steeple bush. Dr. Porcher reported that this plant had been used by the Indians and was brought to the attention of the medical profession by Dr. Cogswell of Connecticut. Porcher considered this plant to be a valuable tonic and astringent useful in diarrhea and cholera infantum. Dr. Clapp believed the same and added that the bark and leaves were more efficient and most employed, although the root was the official part.[422]

Mohegan Indians steeped the leaves of hardhack to make a medicine for dysentery.[423] The Flambeau Ojibwas made a tea from the leaves and flowers to drink for sickness of pregnancy and to aid parturition. Whites used the root and leaves as an astringent and tonic in diarrhea, hemorrhage, gonorrhea, and ulcers. The willow-leaved meadowsweet (*S. salicifolia* L.) was also used medicinally by the Potawatomis, the Meskwakis, and the whites. The Meskwakis used the seeds in a medicine to stop bloody flux.[424]

The root of hardhack, or *S. tomentosa*, was official in the pharmacopeia from 1820 to 1882, and is called an astringent by Dr. Claus.[425]

Haw, or *Hawthorn (Viburnum* and *Crataegus* species), black haw, etc. Brickell described the *"Black Thorn* or *Sloe* Tree," which may be our black haw (*V. prunifolium,* L.), and the *"Hawthorn* or *white Thorn* Tree." The bark of the first:

> being dryed and made into a fine Powder, and apply'd to inveterate old Sores (and especially in the Legs) very speedily cleanses and dries them up, and is one of the best Remedies on these occasions, I have ever met with.

Of the second species he declared that "the Leaves, Flowers, and Haws, are very binding, therefore good to stop all kinds of Fluxes; the Powder of the Stone drank in *Rhenish Wine,* is of very great service in the Stone, Gravel, and Dropsie."[426]

The bark of the black haw, according to Lloyd, was used in home medicine in the early nineteenth century, especially in the South. The drug was first described, he asserted, by Professor John King, who classed it as a uterine tonic, in his *American Family Physician* (1857). After it was commended by Dr. I. J. M. Goss in his *New Preparations* (1878), it grew rapidly in favor until it became official.[427] Dr. Clapp, however (not to mention Brickell), preceded these men in his description of the black haw, published in his report to the American Medical Association in 1852. He called a decoction of the bark of this species a popular remedy in uterine hemorrhage. A decoction of young twigs was astringent and used in domestic practice for diarrhea.[428] The black haw (*V. prunifolium*) was admitted to the USP in 1882 and dismissed in 1926, but it remained official in the NF, 1926–60. The *V. rufidulum* Raf., also called black haw, was accorded equal recognition. Black haw, Dr. Claus reported, is used as an astringent, tonic, nervine, uterine sedative, and diuretic.[429]

The two official species of black haw were both used by the Catawba Indians. The bark was beaten to a mash and mixed with wheat flour and water and drunk for dysentery. A tea made from the roots was used in stomach trouble.[430] The Menominees used the inner bark of maple-leaved viburnum (*V. acerifolium*) for a tea drunk for cramps or colic. The Pillager Ojibwas used nannyberry (*V. lentago* L.) for a diuretic tea, the inner bark being employed. The Flambeau Ojibwas used the fruit and bark of *Crataegus* species for a women's medicine. The Meskwakis used the unripe fruit of pear thorn (*C. tomentosa* L.) for bladder ailments. It was reputed to possess astringent and cardiac-tonic properties. The root bark was used for general debility. The fruit of Bicknell's thorn (*C. rotundifolia* Moench) was used by the Potawatomis for stomach complaints. All of these species were also used by whites, and some were listed in the *Dispensatory*, the last named being used for astringent and heart-tonic properties.[431] The Kwaki-utls chewed the leaves of a species of *Crataegus* for application to swellings.[432]

Hellebore, American (Veratrum viride Ait.), green hellebore, white hellebore, pokeweed, Indian poke. The Algonquian name *poke* has also been applied to *Phytolacca decandra* and the skunk cabbage, *Symplocarpus foetidus.*

The earliest mention of this plant was by Josselyn, who declared in 1672 that "the Indians cure their wounds with it," (p. 42). In 1750 Peter Kalm reported on its uses among the whites:

Some people boil the root for medicinal purposes, washing scorbutic parts with the water or decoction. This is said to cause some pain, and even a plentiful discharge of urine, but the patient is said to be cured thereby. When the children here are

315

plagued with vermin, the women boil this root, put the comb into the decoction, and comb the head with it, and this kills the lice most effectually.[433]

Green hellebore was used among the Iroquois as a catarrh remedy.[434] With the Cherokees it was an ingredient of an ointment containing several other herbs and roots used in rubbing rheumatism, etc.[435] Kwakiutl Indians drank the juice of blue hellebore, or devil's club, for internal pain.[436]

From the roots of this plant is extracted an active principle which was once used to reduce the heart rate and induce a fall in blood pressure, but some authorities have considered it too dangerous.[437] In the last century Dr. Porcher called *Veratrum* useful in gout, rheumatism, lung disease, and bowel complaints.[438] Some physicians of that period found the powdered root to be emetic, deobstruent, alterative, epispastic, and errhine. It was also called narcotic, and had been used in treating asthma, dyspepsia, and other ailments.[439]

The American or green hellebore, under the name *Veratrum*, was official in the USP, 1820–1942, and in the NF, 1942–60. The dried rhizome and roots are the official parts and are used as a hypotensive, cardiac depressant and sedative. Dr. Claus called it of value in the treatment of hypertension, the principal effect of small doses being upon the blood pressure, with no notable change in the respiratory or cardiac rate. Several pharmaceutical products are made from this drug.[440]

Hemlock (*Tsuga canadensis* Carr., and other species). It is thought by some that this may be the tree used by the Indians to cure Cartier's men of scurvy in 1535.[441] Of the "Hemlock-tree, a kind of spruce," Josselyn wrote in 1672:

> The Indians break and heal their swellings and sores with it; boyling the inner bark of young hemlock very well; then knocking of it betwixt two stones to a playster; and, annointing or soaking it in soyls' oyl, they apply it to the sore. It will break a sore swelling speedily.[442]

Most, if not all, of the northern forest tribes made use of this tree in medicine. The Ojibwas crushed and powdered the bark for internal use in diarrhea.[443] The Potawatomis mixed the inner bark with other medicines for the cure of flux, and brewed a tea from the leaves to induce copious perspiration to break up colds. Whites also used it for astringent and diaphoretic purposes. The Flambeau Ojibwas used this hemlock in medicinal teas to disguise unpleasant tastes; the bark was used for healing cuts, wounds, and stopping the flow of blood from wounds. The Menominees used the leaves in their sweat bath and the inner bark for a tea taken for colds and pains in the abdomen. The leaves of a related species, American yew or ground hemlock (*Taxus canadensis* Marsh) was used by the Potawatomis for a diuretic tea.[444] Micmac Indians used a tea of hemlock bark for coughs, colds, and grippe.[445] The twigs of ground hemlock were steeped for a tea in the treatment of colds by the Penobscots, while the Montagnais mixed this with *Lycopodium* or club moss (*q.v.*) for a brew used in weakness and fever.[446]

Canada or *Hemlock pitch*, from *T. canadensis*, an oleoresin, was official in the USP, 1831–94. It was employed externally in plasters as a counterirritant. The inner bark of this species was used to some extent in medicine as an astringent. It contains tannin, a small quantity of volatile oil, and resin.[447]

Hepatica (*Hepatica triloba* Chaix; *Hepatica acutiloba* DC), liver-leaf, liverwort. The Potawatomis used the roots and leaves of *H. triloba* for a sweet-tasting tea used in vertigo. *H. acutiloba* was used by the Meskwakis for deformities like twisted mouth or cross eyes. A root tea was taken internally and used externally as a wash. The Menominees used this species with maidenhair roots in various female disorders, especially leucorrhea.[448] The Cherokees used this plant for coughs either in tea or by chewing the root. The fourteenth edition of the *Dispensatory of the United States* (1877), which Mooney used for comparing aboriginal usage with that accepted in white medicine, called liverwort a very mild demulcent, tonic, and astringent, supposed by some to possess diuretic and deobstruent virtues. Formerly it was used in Europe for such complaints as chronic hepatitic affections (hence the name) but fell into complete neglect.[449] Clapp and Millspaugh reported substantially the same.[450]

The dried leaves of *H. triloba* were official in the USP, secondary list, under the name hepatica or liverwort, from 1831 to 1882. Claus reported that it could be given freely in infusion, and might have some tonic and stimulant properties.[451]

Hops (*Humulus Lupulus* L., syn.: *H. americanus* Nutt.). This plant is indigenous to both America and Europe.[452] Perhaps the earliest mention of it in America was by De Vries, who wrote in 1642 that "our Netherlanders can brew as good beer here as in our Fatherland, for good hops grow in the woods."[453]

Hop blossoms were used by the Mohegans for making a nerve medicine for sedation; a little bag of dried blossoms, heated, was also applied to toothache and earache.[454] The Teton Dakotas steeped the fruits to make a drink to allay fevers and intestinal pains. A part of the root was chewed and applied to wounds, alone or with other herbs.[455] The American hop was used by the Meskwaki doctor McIntosh to cure insomnia. The Pillager Ojibwas used it to make a tea which acted like a sodium bicarbonate on the system, increasing the excretion of urine and reducing acidity. The Menominees used the root bark of the three-leaved hop tree (*Ptelea trifoliata* L.), a plant brought to Wisconsin from Kansas, as a sacred medicine and panacea to season and render other medicines potent. The Meskwakis used it similarly and also in lung troubles, often in tea with other barks. Smith reported that this species had also been used by eclectics and as a home remedy.[456]

The dried strobile of *H. Lupulus* L., as *Humulus* or Hops, was official in the USP, 1820–1926, and in the NF to 1947, being used in medicine as a stomachic, sedative, and tonic. A derivative, lupulin used as a bitter tonic, sedative, and hypnotic, was also official in the USP, 1831–1916, and in the NF, 1916–47.[457]

Hydrangea (*Hydrangea arborescens* L.), seven-barks. This is an indigenous shrub with diuretic properties reported to have been used by the Cherokee Indians and early settlers in calculous complaints.[458] In 1756, Dr. Alexander Garden of Charleston wrote to Cadwallader Colden that he had recently been on a trip with Governor Glen to visit the Cherokee country, in "great hopes of returning rich with the Spoils of our Cherokee mountains," but because of their recall by a new governor after they had reached the lower Cherokee towns, his only "spoil" was "the *Hydrangea* of Gronovius."[459] Mooney found the late nineteenth-century eastern Cherokee using hydrangea roots in a decoction with other plants which was given to women who had strange dreams during their menstrual period.[460]

The dried rhizome and roots of this plant were official in the NF, 1916–26, and were used for diuretic and diaphoretic purposes.[461]

Indian hemp (*Apocynum cannabinum* L.), American hemp, black Indian hemp, etc., not to be confused with the Indian hemp of India, *Cannabis indica*, source of the narcotic *hashish*, or the Eurasian *Cannabis sativa*, the source of the narcotic *marijuana*.[462]

De Vries in 1642 and Peter Kalm in 1750, among others, have mentioned the use of fiber from this plant for weaving by Indians, who used it to make bags, pouches, ropes, quilts, etc.[463] Lloyd asserts *Apocynum* root has been used in decoction as an active hydragogue cathartic and diuretic in domestic medicine since the days of the earliest settlers, "who learned of its qualities from the Indians."[464] James Ewell called the powdered root bark of "Indian hemp" an emetic and cathartic; it also promoted perspiration and was regarded as beneficial in rheumatism, dropsies, asthmatic complaints, and whooping cough.[465] Dr. Clapp listed it as a diuretic and said many cases had been reported of its successful use in dropsy.[466]

The *A. cannabinum* and spreading dogbane (*A. androsaemifolium* L.) were used by the Iroquois for bloody flux.[467] The Penobscots called the former plant "worm root" and steeped it in water for a medicine to expel worms.[468] The dogbane has been used among the Forest Potawatomis as a diuretic and urinary medicine, and the green fruit was boiled for a heart and kidney medicine by the Prairie Potawatomis. The Flambeau Ojibwas steeped the stalk and root to make a tea for women, to keep the kidneys free in pregnancy. The Pillager Ojibwas ate the "sacred root" of this plant in the medicine-lodge ceremony and used it for throat trouble and headache; for the latter ailment the root was placed on live coals and the incense inhaled. The Meskwakis used the root for a dropsy remedy, and in a compound for an injured womb.[469]

The dried rhizome and roots of *A. cannabinum* L., Indian hemp, were official in the USP, 1831–1916, and in the NF, 1916–60. It is regarded as a cardiac stimulant. The same parts of *A. androsaemifolium*, dogbane, were official in the USP, 1820–82, and NF, 1942–50, and were used for diuretic, cathartic, diaphoretic, emetic, and expectorant purposes.[470]

Indian physic (*Gillenia trifoliata* Moench.). This plant has been

319

called American ipecac (q.v.), a name also applied to several other species. The name "Indian physic" has also been applied to a species of *Apocynum*, while the name "Bowman's root" has been applied to *Gillenia* as well as to other plants.[471]

Gillenia seems to be the "ipecac" which was so often used by William Byrd, rather than the *Euphorbia* species to which that name has also been applied. Of it he wrote in 1729:

> In the Stony Grounds we rode over we found great Quantity of the true Ipocoacanna, which in this part of the World is call'd Indian-Physick. This has Several Stalks growing up from the Same Root about a Foot high, bearing a Leaf resembling that of a Straw-Berry. It is not so strong as that from Brazil, but has the same happy Effects, If taken in Somewhat a larger Dose. It is an Excellent Vomit, and generally cures intermitting Fevers and Bloody Fluxes at once or twice taking.

He reported that a dose of this plant, in salty broth, was used with success to purge a member of his party who had "bloated bowels."[472] Several references to its use in a variety of complaints occur in Byrd's diary for 1710–11. It was employed for "distemper" among the Negroes, for a vomit in fevers suffered by his daughter as well as himself, and again by Byrd when he was afflicted by malaria.[473]

Brickell declared that "the *Cholera-Morbus* . . . is happily carried off by giving proper Doses of the *Ipecauacana* that grows plentifully in *Carolina*."[474] For lack of a description, it is not certain whether Brickell meant *Gillenia* or *Euphorbia*, both of which have been called by the name of the famous Brazilian *ipecacuanha*. The *Spiraea trifoliata* described by André Michaux is our plant, however. At Fort Massac on the Ohio in 1795 he mentioned it as "a purgative used by the Savages and the Illinois French. They call it Papiconah."[475] Barton used the same Latin name and reported that the root bark was used as an emetic and tonic and was thought beneficial in intermittent fever.[476]

Hunter found that the emetic and sudorific virtues of "Indian Physic" were well known to the Arkansas tribes, who used it in the cure of fevers and bowel complaints.[477] This plant was used as a purgative by the Delawares, whose name for it signified its purpose.[478] Mooney reported that two Cherokee "doctors" disagreed on the uses of this plant, one stating that it was good as a tea for bowel complaints, with fever and yellow vomit, while the other said that it was poisonous and no decoction was ever drunk, though the beaten root was a good poultice for swellings. The *Dispensatory* of 1877 reported it to be a mild and efficient emetic.[479] Porcher and Clapp so classified it, the latter reporting that "by the country people, a decoction of the roots, and sometimes of the whole plant, is given at intervals till it excites vomiting."[480]

Gillenia roots, variously called *American Ipecac* and *Indian Physic*, were official in the USP, 1820–82, but on the secondary list after 1842, and were used for their emetic action.[481]

Indian turnip (Arisaema triphyllum [L.] Schott., syn.: Arum tri-phyllum L.), Jack-in-the-pulpit, wake-robin, and related species, *Arisaema dracontium* (L.) Schott., dragon root or green dragon, *Arum maculatum* or cuckow point, and related plants.

This plant was the *wampee* ("it is white") of the Shawnees.[482] Kalm called it *Arum Virginicum*, wake-robin, and *Taw-ho* or *Tuckah*, the eastern aboriginal name. The Indians ate the spathe and berries, and the root, regarded as poisonous in the raw state, was prepared as food by placing it in a hole in the ground and building a fire over it. "How can men have learned," he remarked, "that plants so extremely opposite to our nature were eatable, and that their poison, which burns on the tongue, can be conquered by fire?"[483] Carver reported that the root of the "wake robin" resembled a small turnip, which would greatly inflame the tongue if tasted raw, "but when dried, it loses its astringent quality, and becomes beneficial to mankind, for if grated into cold water, and taken internally, it is very good for all complaints of the bowels."[484]

Loskiel mentioned that the "Cuckow pint" root inflamed the tongue when tasted, but if dried was good for bowel complaints.[485] The Delawares used it for a purgative, and it was recommended for constipation by Dr. Schöpf.[486] The root served as both food and medicine to the Iroquois.[487] The arum or cuckowpint, Cutler reported, had an acrid root, but the dried root, grated in water, was a carminative. The Indians, he added, used the root as a stimulant and boiled the shredded roots and berries with their meat.[488] Dr. Barton called *Arum triphyllum* a stimulant and reported that it was boiled in milk for consumption of the lungs, claiming that a Virginia Negro was thus cured. The allied plant, *Dracontium*, he further asserted, had been used by Indians in curing dropsy by means of covering the body with the leaves to induce "universal sweat, or rather vesication."[489]

The "Indian turnip," Hunter observed, was commonly used by the Osage and Shawnee Indians for coughs and intermittent fevers. For coughs it was given in decoction with spikenard and wild licorice. For malaria, when the fever was off, they gave it in substance combined with snakeroot and wild-cherry bark.[490] To Rafinesque, *Arum triphyllum* was a virtual panacea. He considered it efficacious for flatulence, stomach cramp, asthmatic and consumptive affections, quickening circulation, lingering atrophy, debilitated habits, prostration in typhoid fevers, deep-seated rheumatic pains, pains in the breast, and chronic catarrh.[491] John Briante, the "Indian doctor," prescribed the dried and pulverized root of Indian turnip in molasses for sore stomach.[492] Dr. Clapp called this root a stimulating expectorant, which had been found beneficial in chronic coughs, asthma, rheumatism, and flatulent colic.[493]

Pawnee Indians used *A. triphyllum* for treating headache by dusting the powdered root on top of the head and on the temples.[494] The Penobscots steeped it to make a liniment for general external use.[495] Some Ojibwa Indians used the root for treating sore eyes, as did the Menominees. The Meskwakis once used the chopped root to reduce swelling from snakebite and mixed it with plant gall for insomnia. The Menominees used dragon root (*A. dracontium*) in female disorders.[496] The Louisiana Choctaws used the root of *A. quinatum*, boiled in water, "to make blood."[497]

The corm of Indian Turnip (*A. triphyllum*) was official in the USP, 1820–73. It was reported to contain a volatile acrid principle, probably an alkaloid, mucilage, and calcium oxalate. It was used as a stimulant, expectorant, irritant, and diaphoretic.[498]

Indigoweed (Baptisia tinctoria [L.] R. Br.), wild indigo, and related species. Cutler believed that a fomentation of indigoweed would abate swelling and counteract the poison of rattlesnake bites.[499] Dr. Clapp reported that while the whole plant was active, the root was strongest. It was emetic and cathartic in large doses and affirmed to be an excellent antiseptic febrifuge; it had been used in *scarlatina anginosa*, typhus fever, putrid sore throat, and as a poultice on gangrenous ulcers.[500]

The Creek Indians boiled *Baptisia* roots in water and administered the decoction externally and internally to children who seemed drowsy and lifeless and on the point of becoming sick.[501] The Mohegans steeped the root and used it to bathe cuts and wounds.[502] The Meskwakis used false indigo (*Baptisia leucantha* T. & G.), in combinations for several purposes, including emetic, treatment of eczema, wounds, sores, snakebite, and catarrh. Smith reported that this species was also used by local whites in Iowa for several purposes, including emetic and cathartic.[503]

The indigoweed or *Baptisia tinctoria* has been used in white medicine as an emetic, cathartic, stimulant, astringent, and antiseptic. It was official in the USP, 1831–42, and the NF, 1916–36.[504]

Ipecac, wild (*Euphorbia ipecacuanha* L.), American ipecac, ipecac spurge, and other species of *Euphorbia*. The name "ipecac" properly belongs to certain *Cephaelis* species of South America, which have given to medicine a well-known emetic. The name in the United States has been applied not only to the *Euphorbia*, but to Indian physic or *Gillenia*, to the dogbane or *Apocynum androsaemifolium*, and the horse gentian or *Triosteum perfoliatum*.[505]

A native ipecacuanha was mentioned by Brickell, of which "the Root is so well known in every Apothecary's Shop, that it would be needless to trouble the Reader with a further description of it."[506] We cannot tell what plant he meant, and learned men of that day were often confused as to the identity of plants going by this name. Colden complained to Peter Collinson in 1742 because the London College of Physicians banned the use of a root from Maryland which was called "Ipecocuana" because it was believed to be a poisonous *Apocynum*. Some years later Colden identified "Virginian Ipecocuana" as the "Filipendula foliis ternis of Gronovius." [507]

Bernard Romans recommended "Ipecacuana" to induce vomiting in nervous or slow fever, without identifying the plant meant.[508] Loskiel mentioned that the Indians used "Ipecacuanha" not only as an emetic, but as an antidote for snakebite. Barton listed *E. ipecacuanha* as a strong emetic employed by country people.[509] Dr. Clapp evaluated this species and *E. corollata*, both on the USP secondary list (1852), as possessed of similar properties, the root or root bark being emetic, or cathartic in small amounts, as well as diaphoretic and expectorant. He considered both plants preferable to the true ipecac.[510]

Dr. Millspaugh reported that the emetic property of the root of
E. ipecacuanha "was well known to the aborigines."[511] The Creeks
used the roots of *Euphorbia* species in infusion to bring on bowel
action.[512] The Cherokees rubbed the juice of *E. hypericifolia* (*E.
maculata* L.) on skin eruptions; they also used it as a purgative and
drank a decoction for gonorrhea; the juice was used as an ointment
for sores and sore nipples and, in connection with other herbs, for
cancer. Mixed with large-flowering spurge (*E. corollata* L.) in infusion, the bruised root was a remedy for urinary and kidney ailments.[513] The *E. maculata* (*E. nutans* in Speck) was used for several
medicinal purposes by the Houmas.[514] Certain western *Euphorbia*
species were used for various curing purposes by the Omahas, the
Poncas, and the Pawnees.[515] Hrdlička reported that the San Carlos
Apaches used a species of *Euphorbia* (*E. pilulifera?*) to induce diarrhea and vomiting for a general cleaning out. For that purpose they
chewed the fresh raw roots.[516] The *E. polycarpa* was used by Indians
of Arizona and California as a snakebite remedy.[517] The Flambeau
Ojibwas used the root of *E. corollata* for a physic, pounding it and
steeping it in a cup of water. The Meskwakis used it for a laxative,
often combining it with a black root for a physic, drank it boiled in
water for rheumatism, mixed it with sumach berries to expel pinworms, and with may apple for a cathartic.[518]

The roots of *E. corollata* and *E. ipecacuanha* were both official in
the USP, 1820–82, being regarded as emetic in large doses, diaphoretic
and expectorant in small doses. Their use as cathartics was handicapped by a tendency to produce nausea, and they were supplanted by
other medicines. The *E. pilulifera* L., official in the NF, 1916–47, had
"some reputation as antiasthmatic."[519]

Jalap, wild (*Convolvulus pandurata*, syn.: *Ipomea pandurata* [L.]
G. F. W. Mey.), wild potato, morning glory family, and related
species. Not to be confused with Mexican jalap, *Exogonium purga*;
for its purgative properties, the name jalap has also been applied to
the *Podophyllum*, or may apple.[520]

William Bartram reported that "the dissolvent and diuretant
powers of the root of the convolvulus panduratus [*ipomea pandurata*] so much esteemed as a remedy for nephritic complaints, were
discovered by the Indians to the inhabitants of Carolina."[521] Doubtless this is also the "convolvulus jalappa" which Loskiel reported

"grows in abundance in the Indian country, and is prescribed as a purgative. In the rheumatism of the legs they roast the roots, then slit and apply them to the soles of the feet as hot as the patient can bear."[522]

The tuberous root of wild jalap or wild potato, *C. pandurata* or *I. pandurata*, was official in the USP, 1820–63. It was used as a powerful cathartic, but has since been replaced by other drugs. The serial stems of morning glory (*Ipomea purpurea* [L.] Roth.) have also been used in medicine.[523] The bush morning glory (*I. leptophylla* Torr.) was used as a nervine and anodyne by the Pawnees.[524] A species of morning glory, called *corihuela* by South Texas Mexicans, was used by them for dysentery and diarrhea.[525]

Jerusalem oak (*Chenopodium ambrosioides* L.), Mexican tea, wormseed. This is a plant of tropical America, though the same common name has been applied to the Old World species, *C. Botrys* L.[526] *Chenopodium* is native to the West Indies, Central America, and parts of South America and is believed to have been used by the Mayas as a vermifuge.[527] The plant has been naturalized in the United States since early times and grows wild from New England to Florida and west to California. It has been extensively cultivated in Maryland.[528]

Josselyn considered "oak of Hierusalem" a good remedy for "stuffing of the lungs upon colds, shortness of wind, and the ptisick,— maladies that the natives are often troubled with."[529] It was, however, more generally used as a vermifuge until recently. Peter Kalm reported in 1750 that the seeds were given to children for worms by the settlers in Pennsylvania and New Jersey, and he believed "for that purpose they are excellent."[530] Bernard Romans asserted that "the stincking weed which is known by the name of Jerusalem Oak" was "the most efficacious vermifuge, and safest medicine especially for children" to be found in the Floridas.[531] Dr. Clapp called it an "efficient vermifuge," though the expressed oil was preferred to the seeds.[532]

Wormseed was used as a spring tonic and febrifuge by the Creeks, while the Natchez employed it both to allay fever and to expel worms in children.[533] The Catawbas beat the whole plant to a mash and bound it as a poultice to draw out poison, especially in snakebite. They also applied it to sores.[534]

Oil of Chenopodium replaced male fern and thymol as an anthelmintic in medicine generally, because of the undesirable side effects of the latter. Experience indicated, however, that its active principle was not constant, while different preparations varied in strength and hence in toxicity and standardization, for which reasons it was replaced by carbon tetrachloride and later by still other chemical products.[535]

The fruit of *Chenopodium* was official in the USP, 1820–1905, while the oil from it was official in the USP, 1820–1947, and in the NF, 1947–60. This drug is classified as anthelmintic, especially for roundworms but also for hookworms and intestinal amebae.[536]

Jimson weed (Datura stramonium L.), angel's trumpet, apple of Peru, Jamestown lily, Jamestown weed, nightshade, stinkweed, thorn apple; also *Datura meteloides,* and other species of *Datura.* The name of Jimson or Jamestown weed was reputedly given to this plant because the soldiers sent against Nathaniel Bacon of Virginia in 1676 engaged in strange behavior after eating it.[537] Species of *Datura* are figured in the Aztec *Badianus Manuscript* and their use prescribed for many ailments.[538] Several authorities have held that *D. stramonium* is of Asiatic origin, although this may be one of the plants pictured in the Aztec herbal, and one writer maintained that Jimson weed reached England from the early colonies by way of pirate ships.[539]

The Aztecs used *Datura (stramonium* or *meteloides)* as a narcotic agent for "pain in the side," in the treatment of infected or abscessed ears, in a plaster applied after lancing of abscessed glands, for pain of the pubes, in an ointment to cure cracks in the soles of the feet, in a lotion for injured feet, in gout, and in a plaster for ulcers and pustules of the body.[540]

Lawson and Brickell called the seed of Jamestown weed a good application for inflammation and burns, the latter stating that the Indians so used it. Both alluded to the capacity of this substance to cause madness if taken internally.[541] William Byrd recommended the root and leaves for a burn poultice.[542] The narcotic effects of the plant were picturesquely described by Cotton Mather:

> In Virginia there is a plant called the Jamestown weed, where-
> of some having eaten plentifully became fools for several days;

one would blow up a feather in the air; a third sit naked, like a monkey, grinning at the rest; a fourth fondly kiss and paw his companions, and snear in their faces. In this frantic state they were confined, lest they kill themselves, though there appeared nothing but innocence in all their actions. After eleven days they returned to themselves, not remembering anything that had passed.[543]

In the middle of the eighteenth century, Peter Kalm remarked that "the *Datura* and *Phytolacca* are the worst weeds here, nobody knowing any particular use for them."[544] Benjamin Rush, called to treat a child who was ill from eating *Datura* seeds, brought relief with bleeding and emetics, prior to which, he reported, the child appeared stupid and blind, with much dilated pupils.[545] Cutler held that the leaves in cataplasms relieved external inflammations and that an ointment made from them eased hemorrhoids.[546] Cullen of Edinburgh reported that seeds and extract of *Stramonium*, including European varieties, were used in "mania," epilepsy, melancholy, rheumatism, ulcerous affections, and cancer.[547] Dr. Barton (one of whose students, Samuel Cooper, published a dissertation on this plant in 1797) approved the uses of this drug as mentioned by Cullen, but warned that it had the power to induce tetanus.[548] Samuel Stearns called attention to the experiments performed with this plant by Dr. Stoerk of Vienna, who used an extract of the juice for convulsions, epilepsy, and "madness."[549] Thomas Jefferson mentioned that the French in the time of Robespierre made a poison from Jimson weed which brought quick death whenever it was desired to rob the guillotine of a victim.[550]

Dr. Porcher called the weed an antispasmodic, useful in chorea and tetanus besides the ailments mentioned by Cullen and others.[551] Dr. Clapp further classified it as an anodyne with action similar to belladonna. All parts of the plant were considered active, but the seeds were most powerful.[552]

Seeds of *D. meteloides* Dunal, have been found in Utah Indian ruins. The plant was used as an intoxicant and hypnotic by Yokut medicine men in California, while Virginia Indians three thousand miles away used *D. stramonium* for the same effects in *huskinawing*, or puberty initiations.[553] In the present century, Robert R. Sollenberger reported that Rappahannock Indians of Virginia beat the seeds or leaves of Jimson weed and mixed them with grease or lard for a snakebite poultice. They also used the heated leaves as an application for itching feet and smoked them for shortness of breath.[554] The Catawbas applied the leaves to parts of the body affected with swellings, and an infusion of the leaves was used externally for allaying fever in bone fracture. It was held to be poisonous if taken internally.[555] The Zuñis used *D. meteloides* as a narcotic and made an application for wounds from the ground roots and flowers.[556] This species was used for narcotic effects by the Piutes[557] and the Walapais.[558]

Stramonium has been widely used in folk medicine.[559] A poultice or ointment made from the pulp of the bruised green leaves has been used to relieve the pain of insect bites and stings. The dried leaf has been smoked for asthma.[560] The plant is an important source of atropine, and in 1916 one American firm used one and half million pounds of it for the manufacture of this drug.[561]

The dried leaf and flowering or fruiting tops of *D. stramonium* were official in the USP, 1820–1950, and in the NF, 1950–65. The seed was official in the USP, 1820–1905, and the root from 1842 to 1863. The leaves of *Datura arborea* of South America, reported by Safford to have been used by natives there, have also been used medicinally. The action of all the *Daturas* is reported to be similar to that of belladonna: parasympatholytic, narcotic, anodyne, and mydriatic. They have been used in asthmatic troubles.[562] One pharmaceutical company markets a compound of *Stramonium*, witch hazel, and other ingredients for use as a "soothing, palliative ointment for temporary relief of pain from hemorrhoids."[563]

Joe Pye weed (*Eupatorium purpureum* L.), fever weed, Indian gravel-root, Jopi root, kidney root, purple boneset, queen of the meadow. This plant received its name from a New England Indian who is reported to have cured typhus with it by inducing powerful sweating.[564] One of the early notices of it is by Dr. Schöpf, who reported that the herb was considered antisyphilitic.[565] The herb doctor H. B. Skinner called it a powerful diuretic, which "removes strangury, gravel, and stone."[566] Dr. Williams said that it had been used by physicians as an internal infusion for catarrhal fevers, dyspepsia, and an auxiliary to other tonics and emetics. Its principal use, however, was as a diuretic, for which reason it was called gravel root.[567] Dr. Clapp reported its use in kidney and bladder troubles and that it was considered by most authorities to have properties similar to boneset.[568]

Joe Pye weed was used by the Iroquois and Cherokees as a diuretic.[569] The flowers of the closely related *E. serotinum*, Michx., also called Joe Pye weed, were boiled by the Houmas for a tea drunk in typhoid fever.[570] Wisconsin Potawatomis used the fresh leaves of *E. purpureum* for a burn poultice, while Smith's principal informant in that tribe used the root in a medicine to clear up afterbirth. Flambeau Ojibwas made a strong decoction of the root to wash a papoose until he was six years old, in the belief that this would strengthen him. The Menominees used Joe Pye weed and related plants for ailments of the genitourinary canal. To the Meskwakis it was a love medicine.[571]

The rhizome and roots of Joe Pye weed, *Eupatorium purpureum*, were official in the USP, 1820–42, and were used for their astringent and diuretic properties.[572]

Juniper (*Juniperus communis* L.), and its varieties, and other species of juniper. "*Oleum ex Baccis Juniperi*" (oil of juniper berries) was listed in the *Pharmacopoeia Londinensis* of 1618, and this substance was long used in European medicine as a diuretic.[573] *J. communis* is said to be indigenous to Europe but widely naturalized in North America, yet some maintain that it is native to both continents. In 1807, at Glens Falls, New York, Frederick Pursh wrote that "Juniperus comenunis [*sic*] or else a variety of it, grows on the rocks below the falls."[574]

Because some writers have applied the name "juniper" without distinction to various native species, and especially to the red cedar (*J. virginiana*), we cannot readily determine the species to which they refer. It is said that the Cree Indians used "juniper" berries for a diuretic. The leaves were dried and dusted over indolent sores, and the root was given in infusion for gravel.[575] The Kwakiutls, Boas reported, boiled "juniper" for a whole day, until the gum was given off, when the decoction was taken as medicine for shortness of breath. It was also believed to purify the blood.[576]

The dried berries of *J. communis* L., and its variety, *J. depressa*, Pursh, were official in the USP, 1820–73, and in the NF, 1916–60, being used as a diuretic. Juniper oil from the same species was official in the USP, 1820–1947, and the NF, 1947–55. It was used as a diuretic

329

and emmenagogue and genitourinary antiseptic.[577] See also *Cedar, red.*

Lady's slipper (Cypripedium parviflorum [Salisb.] Fern.; *C. pubescens* [Willd.] Corr.), and related species; American valerian, moccasin flower, whip-poor-will shoe. Once a favorite home remedy for nervous conditions of women and children, *Cypripedium* passed to the hands of the white "Indian doctors" and from them to the medical profession. "To give the references necessary to its American record," wrote John Lloyd, "would cite all the domestic writers on American medicine in the nineteenth century."[578]

Peter Kalm reported that a decoction of the root of *Cypripedium* was "said to be rather good for women in the throes of childbirth."[579] Dr. Porcher wrote that the yellow lady's slipper, *C. pubescens*, was employed by the Indians and held in high esteem in domestic practice as a sedative and antispasmodic, acting like valerian in alleviating nervous symptoms. It was said to have proved itself in hysteria and chorea.[580] Indians informed Dr. Williams that the principal use of *C. humile* was for women; it relieved them in difficult menstruation and facilitated parturition.[581] Dr. Clapp cited the case of a sleepless hypochondriac who obtained no benefit from opium but rested soundly after taking the powdered root of *C. pubescens*. He pronounced it beneficial in neuralgic affections.[582]

Cherokee Indians used a decoction of the root of *C. parviflorum* for worms in children.[583] Penobscots steeped *C. acaule* Ait. for a nerve medicine.[584] The Menominees used the root of the first-named species in female disorders and the second for male disorders. The Pillager Ojibwas used *C. pubescens* for female trouble.[585]

The various species and hybrids of *Cypripedium* are reported to contain similar properties and have been used in medicine as nerve stimulants and antispasmodics. The roots of *C. parviflorum* and *C. pubescens* were official in the USP, 1863–1916, and the NF, 1916–36.[586]

Lobelia (Lobelia cardinalis L.), cardinal flower; *(Lobelia inflata* L.), Indian tobacco; *(Lobelia siphilitica* L.), great lobelia, blue cardinal flower; *(Lobelia spicata* Lam.), "highbelia," pale-spike lobelia. The *L. siphilitica* received its specific name because of its reputation in the cure of syphilis. It was purchased from the Iroquois Indians for that purpose by Sir William Johnson,[587] and in 1758 Dr. Colden reported that the baronet had cured soldiers of this venereal affliction with less than an ounce of root per case in less than a week's time. Later that year Dr. Robert Whytt of Edinburgh wrote to Colden thanking him for his account of the antivenereal virtues of lobelia and requesting samples of the root for trial in the Royal Infirmary.[588]

Long before Samuel Thomson adopted lobelia as his special remedy, the various species of this plant were used in colonial times by Indians and whites for emetic, cathartic, and other purposes.[589] Samuel Stearns listed five species in his *American Herbal,* called the roots purgative, and reported that the Indians were credited with curing *lues venerea* with a decoction of them.[590] Dr. Schöpf listed three species in 1787, attributed purgative, emetic, and antisyphilitic properties to *L. siphilitica,* and the same, with a question mark, to *L. cardinalis.* The *L. inflata,* which later became official, was called astringent and useful in ophthalmia.[591]

Dr. Barton called *L. siphilitica* an effective diuretic, but held grave doubts of its power to cure syphilis, although he believed that it was useful for gonorrhea. This species, he observed, had been used in venereal diseases by the Cherokees and other southern tribes. He further stated that this tribe used a decoction of the root of *L. cardinalis* as a remedy against worms. *L. inflata,* for which he reported no Indian use, was called a stimulant and diuretic which had been found "very useful in the leucorrhoea, or whites."[592] Lloyd, citing a number of sources, was unable to find any definite reference to the use of *L. inflata* by Indians,[593] but Rafinesque definitely described this species as "one of their puke weeds, used by them to clear the stomach in their great councils." Its medicinal properties had since been confirmed and elucidated, he claimed, by numerous authorities. The root was then (1828) extensively used in medicine, although some physicians considered it a harmful narcotic. In his opinion, lobelia was never a proper emetic for common use, as milder ones were available. It was, however, the basis for many violent and dangerous quack medicines for consumption, which were erroneously called "Indian specifics." The Indians, Rafinesque asserted, had no specific for that disease, only palliatives.[594]

Dr. Porcher in 1849 reported that great use was made of *L. inflata* in South Carolina, especially by the "steam and vegetable practitioners." He granted, however, that "obstinate and violent cases of flatulent colic [were] immediately dissipated by preparations of this plant." The *L. cardinalis*, he added, was used by the Indians as an anthelmintic, and was reputedly as efficient for that purpose as pinkroot.[595]

Dr. Clapp published opinions on the four principal species of lobelia. *L. inflata*, or "emetic weed," which was then an official drug in London, Edinburgh, and the United States, was credited with expectorant, sedative, diaphoretic, and emetic properties, though in large doses it was "a dangerous narcotic sedative." He found it a "safe and efficacious medicine" in spasmodic asthma and other pulmonary infections. A dose of the powdered leaves was also recommended for dysentery and as an expectorant. The root of blue lobelia had not been confirmed as a syphilis remedy, although its diuretic power was recognized, and its successful use in dropsy had been reported. In large doses it was emetic and cathartic. The *L. cardinalis* was considered similar in its properties to *L. inflata*, although weaker. *L. spicata* was classified as a diuretic.[596]

The use of blue lobelia by the Iroquois Indians as a venereal remedy was the subject of a paper written by John Bartram in 1751.[597] The use of *L. inflata* for various purposes among the Penobscots has been indicated by Morris Mattson[598] and R. H. True[599] and among other Indians by Rafinesque. The common name of "Indian tobacco" has been applied to the lobelia species because the leaves were often smoked in lieu of tobacco or mixed with it. The Creeks used lobelia flowers in all kinds of cases, reported Swanton, "sometimes when a person was sick to delirium, and was used to ward off ghosts."[600] The Meskwakis used the red and blue lobelias for love medicines and other magic purposes.[601]

The dried leaves and tops of *L. inflata* were official in the USP, 1820–1936, and in the NF, 1936–60. Expectorant and emetic properties are ascribed to this drug. Lobelia or its alkaloids are contained in celmol, lobeline, lobelin, lobidine, and secremol.[602]

Magnolia (Magnolia species), beaver tree, cucumber tree, elk bark, Indian bark, sweet bay, tulip tree, umbrella tree. Magnolia was the *"Laurier à Tulippe"* which Du Pratz pictured and described as a useful febrifuge.[603] Dr. John Lining of Charleston, South Carolina (1708–60), used magnolia root bark in place of Peruvian bark for intermittent fevers.[604] The esteem in which the *Magnolia glauca* L.

(syn.: *M. virginiana* L.) was held in colonial times has been recorded by Peter Kalm:

> The virtues of this remedy are universally extolled, and even praised for their salutary effects in consumption. The bark being put into brandy, or boiled in any other liquor, is said not only to ease pectoral diseases, but likewise to be of some service against all internal pains and fever, and it was thought that a decoction of it could stop dysentery. Persons who had caught cold, boiled the branches of the beaver tree in water, and drank it to their great relief.[605]

Kalm related the case of an elderly Swedish settler afflicted with stubborn leg sores which were healed by an Indian who used the wood of this tree. The wood was burned to charcoal, reduced to powder, mixed with fresh pork fat, and rubbed on the open sores. "This dried up the holes," Kalm reported, "which before were continually open, and the legs of the old man remained sound to his death."[606]

Romans extolled the virtue of the root bark of "Magnolia major" mixed with various herbs in wine as a bitter infusion for intermittent fever. This was, he said, the remedy which was used by the French on the Mississippi.[607] Dr. Schöpf recommended a decoction of the bark of *M. glauca* or *M. acuminata* for diarrhea, coughs, phthisis, and fevers.[608] François André Michaux observed in 1802 that frontiersmen infused cones of *M. acuminata* in whisky for a bitter drink taken as a preventative against "intermittent fever," but announced his "doubts whether it would be so generally used if it had the same qualities mixed with water."[609]

Dr. Barton said that the bark of *M. glauca* was a celebrated remedy among "the Western Indians," who resorted to the Kanawha river where it was reported to grow in abundance and carried off large quantities of it for use in rheumatism and fevers. He ascribed aromatic, tonic, stimulant, bitter, gently cathartic, and sudorific powers to the bark and called it useful in intermittent fevers and inflammatory rheumatism. One of his students, Thomas D. Price, wrote his inaugural dissertation on the *M. glauca* in 1802. The *M. grandiflora*, combined with snakeroot, Barton declared, was used in Florida as a substitute for Peruvian bark in treating intermittent fevers.[610]

Hunter reported that the fruit and bark of the "cucumber tree" (*M. acuminata*) were used in decoction by western Indians as a vermifuge.[611] Louisiana Choctaws boiled the bark of *M. grandiflora* in water and used the liquid to bathe the body to lessen or prevent itching due to prickly heat.[612] Mississippi Choctaws, Speck reported, used the *M. virginiana australis* (syn.: *M. glauca*) for chills, as it produced sweat and "warms the blood." A tea for cramps was also made from it, because it "warms the body and blood."[613] The same species was used for similar purposes by the Houma Indians.[614]

The dried bark of *M. virginiana* L. (*M. glauca*) or "other species of *Magnolia*" was an official medicine in the USP, 1820–94. It was used in tincture or decoction as a bitter tonic, antimalarial, and diaphoretic.[615]

Masterwort (*Heracleum lanatum* Michx.), cow parsnip. Pillager Ojibwas pounded the fresh root and applied it as a poultice on sores. The Meskwakis used the root for colic and stomach cramps, the seed for head pains, and the stems as a wound poultice. To the Menominees this plant was an evil medicine used by sorcerers. White eclectics have used the plant in epilepsy and dyspepsia.[616] Joseph Smith, the quack doctor, recommended use of the roots in powder, decoction, or tincture, for flatulency, weakness of the stomach and bowels, dropsical complaints, and prevention of the fits in ague.[617]

The root was official in the USP, 1820–63, although the leaves and fruit were also used medicinally. The fresh leaves were used as a vesicant, counter-irritant, and gastrointestinal irritant.[618]

May apple (*Podophyllum peltatum* L.), mandrake, Indian apple, wild lemon, citron (Fr., 1700). Lahontan called the fruit wholesome, but said the poisonous root had been used by an Indian woman to commit suicide.[619] Brickell reported that "this Plant is of a very strong purging nature, and is frequently made use of in these Parts for several Disorders with good Success."[620] Mark Catesby called it an "excellent Emetic," for which reason it was known in the Carolinas as "Ipecacuana."[621] Zeisberger ate the juicy fruits, remarking on their thirst-quenching virtue.[622] Dr. Schöpf called the root emetic.[623] Barton found several grounds for valuing the may apple:

> The Podophyllym peltatum is a plant much esteemed by the Cheerake [Cherokee], and other tribes of North-American In-

dians. Its root is used as a purgative, emetic, and anthelmintic. . . . The advantages of this medicine over the Jalap I have often experienced in my practice. In the *first place*, being one of the most common vegetables in the United-States, it may always be had without fear of adulteration, or of injury from worms, &c. *secondly*: it operates in a smaller dose than either the Jalap or the Rhubarb: *thirdly*: it does not so frequently as the Jalap prove emetic: *fourthly*: it is not so liable to gripe as the last-mentioned vegetable, and *lastly*, it is not so nauseous as either the Jalap or the Rhubarb. I think, it is possessed of some degree of an anodyne, or narcotic quality.[624]

Later he pronounced the root "deleterious to worms," and said that the whites had learned the anthelmintic power of this plant from the Indians. It was also an "excellent cathartic."[625] The emetic and cathartic powers of may apple drew the attention of Bigelow, Porcher, Clapp, Beach, and others. Dr. Porcher said that the Shaker sect (once very active in the promotion of Indian remedies) prepared an extract from it which was much esteemed as a cathartic. To its previously announced uses, he added that the plant was diuretic, and that a few drops from the fruit poured into the ear were said to restore the power of hearing.[626]

The Delaware name for this plant indicated its purgative property.[627] Hunter reported that western Indians used the powdered root as a cathartic, as an antidote for poison, and at the commencement of fevers. The fruit was esteemed as a delicacy.[628] The Penobscots used it as a cure for warts.[629] The Menominees boiled the whole plant for an insecticide used on potato plants. The Meskwakis used may apple in mixtures, recognizing the root as a physic, emetic, and rheumatism remedy.[630]

Podophyllum was included in the first *Pharmacopoeia of the Massachusetts Medical Society* in 1808. The dried rhizome and roots were placed on the primary list of the first USP in 1820 and remain listed today, though they were dropped from 1942 to 1955. The drug was contained in several preparations of the first NF in 1888, and *Podophyllum* resin was included from 1942 to 1955. The resin was admitted to the USP in 1863, remained official to 1942, and was again listed in 1955 and since. *Podophyllum* has also been listed in the American Medical Association's compendium, *Useful Drugs*.[631] Both roots and resin (the latter product extracted from the powdered root) are considered drastic purgatives; the resin is also a hydragogue cathartic and is employed "as a caustic for certain papillomas."[632]

Mesquite (*Prosopis juliflora* [Swartz] DC, and *Prosopis glandulosa* Torr.). *P. juliflora* was the *mizquitl* of the Aztecs (hence, *mesquite*), who mixed the leaves with other substances for an eye lotion when the eyes were hot and painful from sickness.[633] Seventy years ago Bourke reported that this shrubby tree was used for the same purpose by Mexican Americans in Texas,[634] and Hrdlička found Indians of the American Southwest using it in a similar manner. The Mescalero Apaches ground the leaves to a powder, placed the substance in a thin cloth, added water, and squeezed the liquid on the eyes. The Pimas applied the sap to sore eyes. The Maricopas used the dried juice, ground fine, as a sore-eye remedy by applying the substance to the lids and later washing it off with warm water.

Other uses included a tea made by boiling the roots for a child in umbilical hernia. The boiled sap was used by the Pimas as an application to pemphigous and other sores which were common on the faces and head of children. For sore throat, they boiled the juice, together with the bark over which it flowed, into a tea which was drunk hot. In chronic indigestion the Papagos pounded the white inner bark very fine, boiled it with some salt, and gave a dose to the patient each morning before breakfast.[635] The Comanches used the leaves from *P. glandulosa* to neutralize stomach acidity. The meal from the pods was used as food.[636]

Mesquite gum was official in the NF, 1936–55, for use as a fermentative reagent in culture media.[637]

Milkweed (*Asclepias* species), silkweed. According to Dr. Porcher, the whorled or dwarf milkweed (*A. verticillata* L.) was a domestic remedy in repute for snakebite and was said to be "very deservedly celebrated."[638] The flesh-colored or swamp milkweed (*A. incarnata*, L.) was classified by Dr. Clapp as alterative, expectorant, diaphoretic, and, in large doses, laxative. It had been successfully used in asthma, catarrh, rheumatism, and secondary syphilis. The common milkweed (*A. cornuti* Decaisne, syn.: *A. syriaca* L.) was called anodyne and expectorant. He reported that it had been useful in asthma and catarrhal infections of the lungs in typhus fever.[639]

Hunter reported that *A. syriaca* and an unidentified milkweed peculiar to the western country were found on the Arkansas River. The Indians used their roots in decoction for the cure of dysentery, dropsy, and asthma. The same was also used as an emetic and "held in tolerably high estimation as a medicine in the above cases."[640] Tall-milkweed root (*A. exaltata* [L.] Muhl.) was eaten raw for stomach trouble by the Omaha and Ponca Indians.[641] The Natchez cut up the roots of *Asclepias* species for a tea used in kidney trouble including Bright's disease. During treatment, the patient was required to take nothing containing salt. Milkweed was also used by this tribe in the treatment of syphilis.[642] The Catawbas rubbed the juice of *Asclepias* on warts to make them disappear.[643] The root of *A. syriaca* was a female remedy among the Ojibwas, and was used by the Potawatomis for undisclosed purposes. The *A. incarnata* was used among the Meskwakis as a taenifuge or tapeworm remedy.[644]

Asclepias tuberosa (butterfly weed, *q.v.*), *A. incarnata*, and *A. syriaca* were official in the USP, under the name of *Asclepias*, 1820–63 and 1873–82. The roots have been used for diaphoretic and expectorant purposes, and in large doses are emetic and purgative.[645]

Mint family. Catnip (*Nepeta cataria* L.); Horse mint (*Monarda punctata* L.); Pennyroyal (*Hedeoma pulegioides* [L.] Pers.); Wild bergamot (*Monarda fistulosa* L.), Wild mint (*Mentha arvensis* L.), and other species of mint.

Catnip. Reported to be naturalized from Europe, catnip has been an Indian remedy. Carver said "it has nearly the virtues of common mint."[646] The Menominees used this and other mints for pneumonia. The Flambeau Ojibwas steeped the herb in lukewarm water and bathed patients with it to raise body temperature, besides brewing a tea of it for a blood purifier.[647]

Smoky mountain people made catnip tea for colds.[648] Dr. Wooster Beach, who believed this species to be indigenous, classified it as diaphoretic, carminative, diluent, and refrigerant, recommending an infusion of the leaves and flowers for fever and colds, and a poultice of the same for painful swellings.[649]

The dried leaves and flowering tops of catnip were official in the USP, 1842–82, and NF, 1916–50. Carminative, stimulant, diaphoretic, and tonic properties have been ascribed to this plant.[650]

Horse mint. Dr. Clapp ascribed similar medicinal properties to the

337

three species of *Monarda* considered here. The *M. punctata*, horse mint, an indigenous plant, was held to be the most powerful and yielded in distillation the largest proportion of fragrant and pungent oil. In his opinion, the plants might be used in infusion as diaphoretics and carminatives, in colds, flatulent colic, and to relieve nausea and vomiting, as with other mints. The oil of horse mint was a powerful rubefacient which, applied to the skin, produced redness and vesication. One doctor was reported to have found it useful as an external application in typhus fever, rheumatism, deafness, and *cholera infantum*.[651]

The Winnebagos and Dakotas used horse mint as a stimulant, and a hot decoction was used both internally and externally for Asiatic cholera; Dr. Andros commented cryptically, "I think they were as successful as I was in the treatment."[652] The Catawbas mashed up the green leaves of this plant and let them stand in cold water to be drunk for relief of backache.[653] The Creeks used an infusion of the entire plant to induce sweating. Boiled together with everlasting (*Gnaphalium*), it was administered internally for delirium. For dropsy and swelling in the legs, horse mint was boiled with red willow and administered internally and externally.[654] The Meskwakis used the tops of this plant to cure chills and agues. It was also used in several combinations; in powdered form with Philadelphia fleabane and golden Alexander, it was sniffed up the nose for sick headache.[655]

The leaves and tops of *M. punctata* were official in the USP, 1820–82. Dr. Jacob Bigelow described it as a warm diaphoretic, antiemetic, and carminative, used in flatulent colic, rheumatism, etc.[656] Monarda oil, the principal active constituent of this plant, was official during the same period. It was used internally as a carminative and diaphoretic, and externally in liniments as a stimulant, counterirritant, and vesicant. Another derivative, thymol, obtained from several plants, including *M. punctata, M. fistulosa* (wild bergamont), and *M. didyma* (Oswego tea), was official in the USP, 1882–1950, and in the NF since 1950. It has been used as an antifungal, antibacterial, and anthelmintic, especially for hookworm.[657]

Pennyroyal, "squaw mint." In Pennsylvania in 1698, Gabriel Thomas mentioned pennyroyal as one of the "wild herbs which are there very common."[658] It was used by the Indians and was introduced by them to the settlers, from whom it reached the attention of the medical profession.[659] The Onondagas called it the "smelling weed" and a tea made from it was "headache medicine."[660] William Byrd found pennyroyal to be an effective repellent and remedy against "tikes" [chiggers] which "insinuate themselves into the Flesh."[661] John Wesley advised that pennyroyal be drunk for obstructed menses.[662] Peter Kalm reported that an extract from it was considered a wholesome tea to drink in colds for it promoted perspiration. He was informed that the application of this plant to pains in any limb would bring immediate relief.[663] Dr. Schöpf called pennyroyal (under the name *Cunila pulegioides*) antispasmodic and diaphoretic and useful for fevers and arthritis.[664]

In cases of itching and watering eyes, the Chickasaws soaked this plant in water and placed it on the forehead.[665] The Mohegans made it into a tea to warm the stomach.[666] The Catawbas boiled it for a cold remedy.[667] In the far West, the Mescalero and Lipan Indians used *H. reverchoni* for prolonged headache by rubbing the aromatic twigs and inhaling the odor.[668] An infusion of the leaves of rough pennyroyal (*H. hispida* Pursh.) was used by some Plains tribes as a cold remedy; they also used it as a flavor and tonic appetizer in diet for the sick.[669]

The dried leaves and flowering tops of *Hedeoma* or American pennyroyal were official in the USP, 1831–1916, being used for their stimulant, carminative, and emmenagogue properties. Pennyroyal oil was official from 1916 to 1931. It has been called a powerful but dangerous ecbolic and intestinal irritant, which caused abortion and sometimes death when eaten by cattle.[670]

Wild bergamot. Among the Koasatis, a patient sick with a chill is bathed in a decoction of the leaves of this plant.[671] The Ojibwas drank a decoction of the root for pain in the stomach and intestines.[672] The Flambeau Ojibwas dried the whole plant and boiled it to get the volatile oil to inhale for catarrh and bronchial affections. The Menominees used the leaves and flowers, alone or with other herbs, in a tea which was the universal remedy for catarrh. The Meskwakis used it in combinations to cure colds.[673] The Teton Dakotas boiled the flowers and leaves together to make a medicine taken internally for abdominal pains. The Winnebagos boiled the leaves for a lotion applied to pimples and other dermal eruptions.[674]

The Bergamot oil which was official in the USP, 1842–1905, and NF since 1916, is derived from a European tree. The American

339

bergamot is, however, a source of *thymol*, which is official, although *M. punctata* and *M. didyma* are the main sources. Wild bergamot has been used in domestic medicine as a carminative and stimulant, and to combat nausea, vomiting, and diarrhea.[675]

Wild mint. This is the only indigenous species of *Mentha*. Dr. Clapp reported in 1852 that it was little used in medicine but would be a tolerable substitute for the European species when they could not be obtained.[676]

The Cheyennes ground the leaves and stems of this species and boiled them for a medicine to prevent vomiting.[677] Wild mint was used by all the Missouri valley tribes as a carminative, being steeped in water and sweetened with sugar for a drink. Because of its aromatic flavor, it was also used as a beverage.[678] Among the Menominees it was combined with catnip and peppermint for a pneumonia remedy, being drunk as a tea and also used as a chest poultice. The Flambeau Ojibwas brewed a tea from the entire plant for use as a blood remedy. It was also used in the sweat bath, and the Pillagers made a tea of it to break fevers. The Potawatomis used the leaves or tops for fevers and as a stimulating tea for pleurisy. Whites have used the whole plant for its bitter, pungent, antispasmodic, antirheumatic, stimulant, and anodyne properties.[679]

Wild mint (*Mentha arvensis*, var. *canadensis* L.) has not been official, but it contains a volatile oil from which pulegone and thymol (USP 1882–1950, NF 1950—) or carvacrol have been isolated.[680]

Moss, club (*Lycopodium* species), ground pine. The Potawatomis used the spores of fruiting spikes of *L. clavatum* L., var. *monstachyon* G. & H., as a medicine for its styptic and coagulant properties. The tree club moss (*L. obscurum*, var. *dendroideum* Michx. [DC] Eaton) was used by them for the same purpose and also gathered for sale to whites. The Flambeau Ojibwas used the dried leaves of ground pine (*L. complanatum* L.) as a reviver.[681] The *L. dendroideum* was boiled and drunk as a purgative by the Montagnais in case of biliousness and was said to be very effective. The same species was thought to have some medicinal value to the Penobscots.[682]

Lycopodium spores, from *L. clavatum* L., were official in the USP, 1863–1947, and in the NF, 1947–60. They are used for dusting powder to protect tender surfaces and as an absorbent. In pharmacy this substance is used to prevent adhering of pills and suppositories.

Other species are sometimes used, including ground pine, *L. complanatum*. From this species an alkaloid, *lycopodine*, has been isolated.[683]

Mullen, or Mullein (Verbascum thapsus L.). This common pasture weed, easily identified by its furry leaves, was introduced from Europe, although Brickell thought it was indigenous. F. A. Michaux in 1802 said he saw none of it west of the Alleghenies.[684] It must have spread rapidly, for Edwin James saw it along the Missouri west of St. Charles in 1819 and remarked that it "follows closely the footsteps of the whites."[685] Peter Kalm said that Swedish settlers called it wild tobacco and tied the leaves around their feet and arms when they had the ague. Some prepared a tea for dysentery from the leaves. A decoction of the roots was injected into the wounds of cattle when afflicted with worms, which caused them to die and fall out.[686]

Some Indians smoked mullein leaves as tobacco.[687] The Mohegans smoked them to relieve asthma and sore throat,[688] and the Penobscots smoked the dried and powdered leaves for asthma.[689] The Catawbas boiled the root and sweetened it to make a syrup for croup in children. The leaves were mashed and applied as a poultice for pain and swelling, sprains, bruises, and wounds.[690] The Choctaws put the leaves on the head as a headache poultice.[691] The Creeks boiled the roots with those of button willow for a drink used internally for coughs. The leaves were also boiled and the patient bathed in the infusion while it was hot.[692] The Forest Potawatomis smoked the dried leaves for asthma, but Smith was uncertain whether they learned the practice from the whites or vice versa. A smoke smudge was made of the leaves and the fumes inhaled for catarrh and to revive an unconscious patient. The Menominees smoked the root for pulmonary diseases. Smith said he had often seen whites smoke the leaves for asthma and bronchitis, and that the flowers were believed to be diuretic and had been used for tuberculosis.[693]

Mullein leaves and flowers were official in the NF, 1916–36, and were classified as demulcent; the leaves were also emollient and the flowers pectoral.[694]

Mustard (Brassica species). The black and white mustards which were official in the USP until recently are of European derivation. A native species, *Brassica arvensis*, according to Dr. Claus, might be admixed with black mustard.[695]

The European black mustard, *B. nigra*, has been naturalized in the United States and its leaves were used by the Mohegans to relieve toothache or headache by binding them on the skin.[696] The Meskwakis ground up the seeds of the same species and used the substance as a snuff to cure a head cold.[697] The Utes made some medicinal use of hedge mustard, *Sisymbrium canescens* Nutt.[698]

The principal use of the mustards in white medicine has been the employment of the seeds as plasters and poultices and internally for emetic and laxative purposes.[699]

Nightshade (Solanum species). The Comanches used a species of *Solanum* as a general tonic and tuberculosis remedy.[700] The Houmas boiled the roots of black nightshade (*S. nigrum*, L.) for an infusion given to babies with worms. The green leaves were crushed and mixed with grease to produce a poultice used on sores.[701] The Rappahannocks used a weak infusion of the leaves to cure insomnia.[702]

The black nightshade, which according to *Gray's Manual* is naturalized from Europe, is related to the plants providing belladonna, the leaf of which has been official in the USP since 1820. It is used as a stimulant for the central nervous system and for several other purposes. Leaves of *S. nigrum* are sometimes used as an adulterant or substitute.[703] The fruit of *S. carolinense* L., called horse nettle, was official in the NF, 1916–36, being used as a sedative and antispasmodic.[704]

Oak (Quercus species). Oak bark, containing tannin, was an aboriginal astringent and antiseptic. It was used in infusion for diarrhea and in washes for wounds and ulcers.[705] According to Hunter, several varieties of oaks were used by Indians for such purposes.[706]

Black oak (Q. velutina Lam.). The Meskwakis mixed the inner bark with other roots for use in lung troubles. The Menominees crushed and boiled the bark to furnish a watery infusion for sore eyes.[707] The inner bark of this species was official in the USP from 1820 to 1873. Its only recent use, according to Dr. Claus, has been for yellow pigment,[708] but in earlier years it was used for the same purposes as white oak, namely, astringent and antiseptic.[709] Dr. Clapp preferred it as an external application to "foul ulcers."[710]

White oak (Quercus alba L.) has been by far the most important of the oaks in the medicine of both the red and the white man.

Josselyn reported that the Indians boiled white-oak acorns in a lye of maple ashes until the oil floated on top. This was stored in bladders and used "to annoint their naked limbs; which corroborates them exceedingly." From a moss that grew at the roots of the white oak, the Indian women made a decoction for children's "scall'd heads."[711] Peter Kalm called white-oak bark the best remedy which had yet been found against dysentery.[712] Dr. Schöpf considered the pulverized bark of white oak a substitute for Peruvian bark.[713]

White-oak bark was an Iroquois astringent.[714] The Penobscots recognized the same property, steeping the bark and drinking it for bleeding piles. They also ate the acorns to induce thirst, believing it beneficial to drink plenty of water.[715] Houma Indians crushed the roots and mixed them with whisky for a liniment to rub on rheumatic parts.[716] The Ojibwas scraped the root bark and inner bark and boiled it for a decoction used internally for diarrhea.[717] The Meskwakis boiled the inner bark and drank the tea to cause expulsion of phlegm from the lungs and when the chest was bound up.[718] The Menominees used an infusion of the bark for an enema to relieve piles.[719]

The inner bark of white oak was official in the USP, 1820–1916, and in the NF, 1916–36. It was used for astringent and tonic purposes.[720]

Oregon grape (Berberis aquifolium, or Mahonia), and other species of barberry. Oregon grape was a favorite with the California Indians, who made a decoction of the roots with water or steeped them in liquor and took the medicine internally for general debility or to create an appetite. Palmer considered it equal to sarsaparilla in medicinal virtues.[721] This may be the species mentioned by Boas as in use among the Kwakiutls, who boiled the dried bark and drank the decoction for biliousness.[722]

Oregon-grape root was long used in western domestic medicine as a tonic and blood purifier.[723] Introduced to American medicine in 1877 by Dr. J. H. Bundy, *B. aquifolium* was official in the USP, 1905–16, and in the NF, 1916–47. The dried rhizome and roots were used for a bitter tonic.[724]

An eastern "Barberry-Tree or Bush" was described by John Brickell. "The Bark and Leaves," he claimed, "open *Obstructions*, and are of singular use in *Jaundice*. The Fruit is very cooling in Fevers, grateful to the Stomach, and causeth a good Appetite."[725] This was probably the American barberry (*B. canadensis* Mill), which was official in the USP, New York edition, 1831–42, and was used in an acidulous drink as a febrifuge.[726] The introduced barberry, *B. vulgaris* L., was used by the Catawbas, who boiled the stems and roots in a tea for ulcerated stomach.[727] The Penobscots pounded the roots or bark in a mash and applied it to ulcerated gums or sore throat.[728] The bark of this species, considered similar to *B. aquifolium* in properties, was official in the USP, 1863–82.[729]

Partridge berry (*Mitchella repens* L.), squaw berry, squaw plum, squaw vine. The names which have been applied to this plant suggest its use in female medicine by Indians. Most investigators have found Indians reluctant to give details of such remedies, as is indicated by Speck's cryptic note on the use of this plant by the Penobscots: "somewhat non-specific—to be steeped."[730] The Menominees informed Smith that they steeped the leaves to make a tea for insomnia.[731] H. B. Skinner (1844) claimed that "a tea of this plant gives much relief to women in labour."[732] Dr. Clapp wrote that it was said to be a mild diuretic, and a tea made from it was formerly used in dropsy.[733]

Dr. Claus reported that this plant was "said to have been employed by the American Indians as a parturient." The plant contains a bitter principle and tannin, while the fruit contains a saponin. *Mitchella* or *Squaw Vine* was official in the NF, 1926–47, and was used as an astringent, tonic, and diuretic.[734]

Passion flower (*Passiflora incarnata* L.), apricot vine. The fruit is called by the aboriginal name, *maypop*. The Mayas used the crushed plant of *Passiflora* species as a poultice for swellings, and in internal decoction for ringworm. The juice of one variety was applied with cotton to sore eyes.[735] Other species were reported used by the Aztecs for emetic and purgative effects.[736] The Houma Indians of Louisiana crushed the root of *P. incarnata* and placed it in their drinking water for a "blood tonic."[737]

P. incarnata has been called antispasmodic and sedative.[738] Dr. Schöpf reported that it was used in epilepsy.[739] Presently it is an ingredient in a proprietary sleeping pill. The dried flowering and fruiting tops of *P. incarnata* were official in the NF, 1916–36, although the

344

rhizome and roots have also been used in medicine. Dr. Claus reported that *Passiflora* may contain an alkaloid in small percentage but stated no uses for this drug.[740] The *Dispensatory* of 1950 stated:

> The passion flower was formerly used as a nerve sedative to allay general restlessness, to relieve insomnia, and in the relief of certain types of convulsions and spasmodic disorders. It was also attributed with anodyne properties and used in the treatment of various neuralgias. I. Ott . . . found that it is a depressant to the motor side of the spinal cord, but increases the rate of respiration, and that it has very little effect upon the circulation, only temporarily reducing the arterial pressure.[741]

Persimmon (Diospyros virginiana L.). The range of this tree is mainly south of U.S. Highway 40, the old National Road, and west to Kansas. Generations of rural folk have feasted on its fruits, which are considered edible only after the first frost. They were also an important food and medicine to the Indians, to whom we owe the name.

Jean Bossu considered the persimmon an excellent astringent and superb remedy for dysentery and bloody flux. The powdered seeds mixed with water and strained through a cloth made a drink which he recommended for kidney stones.[742] Lawson called the persimmon fruit "the greatest Astringent I ever met withal" and asserted that it was good for cleansing foul wounds. He further thought that the bark could be used as a substitute for Peruvian bark.[743] Peter Kalm remarked on the astringent quality of the unripe fruit but called it one of the most palatable fruits of the land after the frost had removed its bitterness.[744] Isaac Bartram called attention to the distilled liquor which was made from it in the southern states and recommended the cultivation of the tree to free the colonies from dependence on the West Indies for rum.[745] James Woodhouse, with Barton's commendation, published his inaugural dissertation on the chemical and medical properties of the persimmon.[746] Dr. Schöpf had recommended persimmon as a styptic in hemorrhage,[747] while Barton called the bark useful in intermittent fevers and ulcerous sore throat. He reported that the root bark had been used for a tonic medicine in dropsy and that it had a gentle purgative effect. In Virginia the ripe fruit had been found useful for expelling worms in children.[748] Styptic, astringent, and antimalarial powers were credited to the persimmon inner bark by Dr. Porcher, while Dr. Clapp called it a bitter tonic and said

345

the unripe fruit had been used successfully in bowel complaints and hemorrhage.[749]

The Cherokee Indians boiled the persimmon fruit for a medicine taken in bloody bowel discharges,[750] while the Alabamas boiled the roots for a tea used in "bowel flux."[751] The Catawbas boiled the bark for an infusion used to wash a baby's mouth to cure thrush.[752]

The unripe persimmon fruit was official in the USP, 1820–82. Because of its tannin content, it was used medicinally as an astringent.[753]

Pine (Pinus species). Cadwallader Colden wrote to Gronovius in December, 1744:

> The Indians likewise cure all sort of wounds without digestion by the Inner bark of the Pinus No 192 of the collection I sent you They soak it so long in Water as to make it soft & then apply it If I be not misinform'd it is effectual even in Gun shot wounds The Wound keeps of a fresh & ruddy colour till it unites without digesting.[754]

Hunter reported that "Sap pine" was a Sauk, Fox, and Chippewa remedy which was the healing gum of the traders, held in high esteem for the treatment of breast complaints and coughs, as well as a favorite remedy in gonorrhea and languid ulcers. "It relieves pain," he wrote, "arrests inflammation, reduces swelling, and disposes the parts to heal." He mentioned that a friend in Minnesota got excruciating pains in the limbs and in the small of the back from exposure, when a Chippewa Indian prescribed this medicine and applied a plaster to his loins, which relieved him in a short time. Applied externally, it was considered an excellent remedy for rheumatism.[755]

The Louisiana Choctaws treated boils and ulcers with applications of salve made of pine pitch mixed with grease and tallow. This salve was likewise applied to wounds caused by splinters and thorns.[756] The Alabamas boiled the inside bark of pine saplings in water and drank the liquid for flux.[757]

White Pine (P. strobus L.). This was the "board-pine" which, according to Josselyn, "yields a very sovereign turpentine for the curing of desperate wounds." The Indians used the boiled bark as a plaster for burns and scalds, and a moss from the pine, boiled in spring water, was used on stab wounds.[758]

Dr. Williams reported (1849) that the Indians used the bark of white pine in a poultice for piles and ulcerations and made a drawing plaster by boiling the roots. The buds were used in decoction as a purgative and the cones or strobiles for rheumatism. The tar was dissolved in spirits as a wash in burns, tetter, and the itch. The bark combined with spikenard furnished a syrup for coughs and a resin for fresh wounds.[759]

The Ojibwas crushed white pine needles for an application to headache; for the same purpose and for backache they inhaled the fumes of the heated needles.[760] The Mohegans steeped the bark and drank the liquid for colds.[761] The Tadoussacs boiled the leaves for a sorethroat remedy,[762] while the Montagnais boiled the gum for a decoction taken for sore throat, colds, and consumption.[763] The Menominees steeped the inner bark of the young trees for a drink used for pain in the chest, or pounded it to shreds and used the same as a poultice on wounds, sores, and ulcers. It was one of their most important medicines. The Potawatomis used the pitch or resin of the wood and bark as the base of a salve.[764]

The dried inner bark of *White Pine* was official in the NF, 1916–65, under the name *Pinus Alba*. According to Dr. Claus, the drug contains tannic acid and an oleoresin; the bark contains considerable mucilage and a small quantity of coniferin. It has expectorant properties and is an ingredient in several trademarked pharmaceutical products used in pulmonary ailments.[765]

Yellow pine (Pinus echinata Mill.) and *Long-leaved pine (P. palustris* Mill.), etc. The Creeks used yellow pine resin for tuberculosis.[766] Resin from both species was chewed by the Catawbas as a "tastie" or for special benefit to the stomach.[767]

Dr. Beach called *P. palustris* and the pitch pine (*P. rigida* Mill.) stimulant, laxative, diuretic, pectoral, vermifuge, discutient, antiherpetic, detergent, balsamic, and vulnerary. He held that the bark and gum were useful in rheumatism and consumption, increasing the menstrual flow, treating kidney ailments, and as plasters for ulcers.[768]

The following products of *P. palustris* and other species of pine have been or are official medicines:

Pine oil, NF 1947—; disinfectant, deodorant, insecticide, carrier of pyrethrins and rotenone.

Pine tar, USP 1820–1950, NF 1950—; antibacterial, irritant, parasiticide, expectorant; *Oil of tar*, USP 1882–1916; *Rectified tar oil*, USP 1916–47, NF, 1947–60; used for the same purposes as pine tar.

347

Resin, rosin, or *colophony,* USP, 1820–1947, NF 1947—; used in cerates, plasters, ointments; slightly antiseptic and stimulant, used in veterinary medicine as a diuretic.

Turpentine, gum turpentine, USP 1820–1916, NF 1916–55; an oleoresin used externally in plasters as a counterirritant.[769] Gum turpentine was used by New England Indians.[770] Dr. Benjamin Barton was informed by his friend, Colonel Winthrop Sargent, governor of Mississippi Territory, that certain Indians cured the gleets by eating turpentine[771] derived mainly from southern yellow pine.

Pinkroot (Spigelia marilandica L.), Carolina pink, Indian pink, wormroot. For almost two centuries this was the most celebrated vermifuge on the American continent. Dr. Alexander Garden of Charleston, who learned of the use of pinkroot among the Cherokees, in 1768 sent a specimen of it to Dr. Colden with the comment that it was "an Excellent anthelmintic Given either in powder or Decoction."[772]

Dr. Benjamin Rush considered Carolina pinkroot and the *Anthelmia* or worm grass of Jamaica to be "two of the most powerful vermifuge medicines we are acquainted with."[773] Bernard Romans, who was a physician, recommended an infusion of the entire plant to expel worms and to treat intermittent fever, but suggested caution because of a strong narcotic quality.[774] Dr. Barton recommended it for the same purposes, but considered the powdered root more efficacious. He considered it "doubtful whether there is, in the whole series of anthelmintics yet known, a more efficacious medicine against worms, especially the common round worm."[775] *Spigelia* became official in the pharmacopeias of London, Edinburgh, and Dublin, as well as the United States. It was extolled by Porcher, Clapp, Beach, and many other writers on materia medica. Lloyd stated that it was mainly used in domestic medicine, being purchased at drug stores in powdered form and prepared at home.[776] Indians gathered it in large quantities for the drug trade, so that in some areas the plant became scarce.[777]

During Mooney's field study among the Cherokees (late nineteenth century) pinkroot was still being used in decoction as a vermifuge, alone or with other substances.[778] It has been reported used by the Osages for sudorific and sedative effects.[779]

Spigelia or pinkroot was official in the USP from 1820 to 1926. Dr. Claus called it an excellent and useful anthelmintic drug, but said it had fallen into disrepute because inferior substances had been substituted for or admixed with it.[780]

Pipsissewa (*Chimaphila umbellata* [L.] Nutt., formerly *Pyrola umbellata*), prince's pine, wintergreen. (See also *Wintergreen: Pyrola* and *Gaultheria* species). John R. Bartlett in 1860 called this "a popular domestic remedy much used by the Indians and now of the U. S. Pharmacopoeia."[781] The curiosity aroused by that remark was part of the impetus which led to the writing of this book. As might be expected from its quaint Algonquian name, this plant has been a time-honored aboriginal remedy. It is reported that Indians used hot infusions of the plant to induce profuse perspiration in the treatment of typhus.[782] Loskiel reported that Indians ate the berries as a stomachic,[783] and the Ojibwas were using a tea of it for the same purpose 150 years later.[784]

Dr. Barton's student, John S. Mitchell, devoted part of his inaugural essay to this plant,[785] reporting that it was used with beneficial effect in intermittent fever and as a diuretic. Barton classed it with *uva ursi*, having considerable astringency; he also called it a topical stimulant and said that the bruised leaves when externally applied induced vesication of the skin.[786] Samuel Thomson used pipsissewa in treating a cancer patient,[787] and one of his disciples, J. W. Comfort, recommended a decoction of it for scrofulous eruptions, rheumatism, dropsy, and urinary complaints.[788] Dr. Clapp later reported that it was esteemed for the same purposes.[789] During the Civil War, Dr. Porcher recommended pipsissewa to the Confederacy as an emergency substitute for mercury and further described it as an aromatic tonic and diuretic, useful in convalescence from low fevers followed by dropsical symptoms.[790]

Pipsissewa has had a prominent place in folk medicine. It provided one of the sweat herbs and antiscorbutic drinks of the Pennsylvania Germans and was also prescribed for an external tumor.[791] In domestic medicine, Lloyd wrote, pipsissewa was in favor as a tea in the regions where it grew and was used especially for rheumatic and nephritic conditions. "In those directions," he declared, "it crept into some favor with the medical profession, and thus anticipated the uses of salicylic acid and the salicylates, which in structural form are the constituents of this plant."[792]

Hunter reported that pipsissewa was "held in considerable esteem by the Indians, and is used as an anodyne and sudorific, especially in diseases of the breast, colds, etc."[793] Among the Mohegans the plant was steeped for application to blisters.[794] The Penobscots used it in the same way, while the Montagnais boiled it for a drink to induce sweating.[795] The Menominees considered the plant a valuable remedy in female ailments and also used it as a seasoner in other medicines.[796] The Catawbas called it "fire-flower" and used a medicine made from it for backache.[797]

Chimaphila or *pipsissewa*, the dried leaf of *C. umbellata*, was official in the USP, 1820–1916, and in the NF, 1916–47. It was used as an astringent, tonic, and diuretic.[798]

Poison ivy (*Rhus toxicodendron* L., syn.: *Rhus radicans* L.), "poison oak." Indians used the juice of this plant for a black dye, and white settlers made ink from it.[799] Samuel Stearns said that it had been given in decoction to consumptive patients, but "with no good success."[800] Dr. Bigelow reported that the plant had been used in England and France for the treatment of paralysis and cutaneous eruptions. He maintained that there was no advantage to be derived from this plant which could justify the hazard of keeping it in apothecary shops.[801]

The leaflets of the plant were, however, official in the USP from 1820 to 1905. Dr. Claus said that the plant contains a phenolic oily resin called toxicodendrol, and was believed to possess narcotic and antirheumatic powers, but in his opinion the dried leaves were of questionable medicinal value.[802]

Indians of Lower California were reported to have used a poultice of mashed poison ivy leaves as a remedy for ringworm.[803] The Potawatomis and Meskwakis pounded the root into a poultice to induce swellings to open.[804] The Houmas boiled the leaves for a tea used as a tonic and rejuvenator to keep the body "fresh at all times."[805]

The allergic skin rash produced on most people from contact with any part of this plant also gave rise to some remedies. Grindelia came to the notice of medicine in this way. The Potawatomis relieved the itch caused by poison ivy or nettle by applying the juice of the jewel weed (*Impatiens biflora* Walt.).[806] Gilmore, however, found no antidote for ivy poisoning among the Plains Indians.

Poke (*Phytolacca decandra* L., syn.: *P. americana* L.), American nightshade, coakum, garget, Indian poke, inkberry, pigeonberry, pocan, pokeweed, scoke. The name *poke* has also been applied to the American or green hellebore (*Veratrum viride*), wild tobacco (*Nicotiana rustica*), and skunk cabbage (*Symplocarpus foetidus*).

Lloyd reports that American Indians used the powdered root as a poultice, a practice which was followed by early settlers for application to an inflammatory condition of cow's udders called garget.[807] John Bartram and Cadwallader Colden were convinced that poultices of the root would cure cancer.[808] Peter Kalm was informed by John Bartram that he had eliminated a violent pain in his foot caused by a stone through the application of a leaf of *Phytolacca*.[809] Carver and Loskiel reported that Indians applied the roots to the hands and feet of a person afflicted with fever.[810] Cutler attributed emetic and cathartic properties to the roots.[811] Dr. Schöpf listed the root as an anodyne, among other things, and recommended a tincture for carcinoma.[812] Benjamin Schultz wrote a dissertation on this plant for his medical degree at the University of Pennsylvania in 1795,[813] and his mentor, Dr. Barton, called the berries a popular rheumatic remedy. Barton had used the juice of the berries in scrofula and "cancerous ulcers."[814]

Dr. Clapp found *Phytolacca* to be emetic and cathartic, but slow and attended with nervous symptoms. In small doses it was alterative and had been used "with advantage" in rheumatism, cutaneous diseases, and secondary syphilis. A decoction or ointment of the root was used externally as a remedy for the "itch."[815]

Speck reported that Pamunkey Indians of Virginia boiled poke berries to make a remedy for rheumatism.[816] Fenton listed pokeweed in the Iroquois materia medica.[817] The berries have also been used by several tribes for a dye.[818]

The dried root of *Phytolacca* was official in the USP, 1820–1916, and in the NF, 1916–47. Dr. Claus ascribed emetic and purgative properties to this drug. The berries were also official in the USP, 1820–1905.[819] These and other parts of the plant have been used in medicine as an alterative, for treating skin and blood diseases, and in the relief of pain and inflammation.[820]

Poplar (*Populus* species). Bushnell reported that the leaves and bark of "Carolina poplar" (*P. angulata* Mich., syn.: *P. balsamifera* L., cottonwood) were boiled in water by Louisiana Choctaws to create a steam for treating snakebite.[821] The Chickasaws boiled cottonwood and willow root together for a drink taken internally for dysentery. Unstated parts of the cottonwood were also used by them, in a manner not described, for fevers.[822] The Creeks used a species of cottonwood in treating fractures and sprains. The bark was boiled and the resulting liquid poured over the injured part; splints were made from the inner bark, and it was asserted that the bone would then knit very soon.[823]

Poplar bark, official in the USP, 1895–1936, as a source of salicin, is the bark of *Populus alba*, the white or silver poplar; it was used as a tonic and febrifuge.[824] See also *Balm of Gilead*.

Prickly ash (Zanthoxylum americanum Mill., syn.: *Z. fraxineum* Willd., and *Zanthoxylum clava-herculis* L., syns.: *Z. carolinianum* Lam., *Fagara clava-herculis* [L.] Small.), hercules club, toothache tree; the first species ranges in the north, the second in the southern states.

"The Root of this Tree," Lawson wrote, "is Cathartick and Emetick, used in Cachexies."[825] Prickly-ash bark was reported used by the Illinois-Miamis to draw off pus.[826] Mark Catesby called the seeds and bark aromatic, hot, and astringent, and said they were used for toothache by people inhabiting the seacoasts of Virginia and the Carolinas.[827] Carver reported that the prickly ash was highly esteemed by the Indians for its medicinal qualities and held that it would "radically remove all impurities of the blood." He claimed that a trader who traveled with him was cured of gonorrhea by a decoction of prickly-ash bark prepared by a Winnebago chief.[828] Loskiel asserted that the wood of *Z. clava-herculis* was used by the Indians for toothache.[829]

Dr. Schöpf called this species a toothache remedy, and further ascribed sialagogue and astringent powers to it.[830] André Michaux reported from Illinois in 1795 that he had no doubt that the root of this tree could be used "for obstructions of the liver and Spleen."[831] Dr. Barton believed that the southern species was the "Pelletory" which Lawson reported relieved toothache by inducing the flow of saliva.[832] He held that the bark of both species of prickly ash promised to be a very useful medicine "in cases of paralytic infections of the tongue, or of the muscles concerned in deglutition." He reported that the berries of *Z. fraxinifolium* (*fraxineum*) were used in Virginia as a remedy in "violent cholicky affections" and called attention to London notices concerning use of the bark in rheumatic affections and ulcers.[833] Thomas Nuttall, in Arkansas in 1819, remarked that the bark of the prickly ash was "efficacious for allaying the toothache."[834] Lloyd reported that it was used as a remedy against Asiatic cholera at Cincinnati in 1849.[835]

The bark of these two species was used in several ways by a number of tribes. Hunter said that the Indians valued prickly ash for a rheumatism remedy and took decoctions of the boiled roots as a sudorific and internal remedy. The inner bark, seethed in bear's grease, was used externally as an embrocation and poultice and in powdered form was applied to ulcers by Indians and settlers.[836] The Houmas applied the pulp of grated roots and bark to aching teeth, and mixed grated roots with whisky to rub on limbs to reduce and relieve swelling.[837] The Alabamas used the scraped roots for a toothache remedy and the inner bark for both toothache and (boiled in water) for the "itch."[838] The Comanches used the bark of Z. americanum as a medicine for fever, sore throat, and toothache.[839] The Meskwakis used the trunk bark, root bark, berries, and the leaves of this species. The bark and berries were regarded as a strong expectorant and were used in cough syrup and medicines for stopping hemorrhage and tuberculosis. The Menominees also used all parts of the tree; the ripe berries, thrown in hot water, made a medicine used in the mouth to spray on chest and throat in bronchial diseases and sores. It was also a seasoner in mixtures. The root bark was used in poultices and, combined with other medicines, was often put on swellings. The teeth of garfish moistened with medicine were used to open swellings so that pulverized or liquid medicine might enter, then the poultice was applied. The liquid of the berries was often drunk for minor maladies. The Flambeau and Pillager Ojibwas made trips farther south to get this bark, which does not grow near them. They used it to treat quinsy and sore throat, while the berries were used for sore throat and bronchitis.[840]

At one time prickly-ash bark was collected in large quantities by Southern Negroes and used for toothache and rheumatism.[841] It was an old domestic remedy among whites since the earliest settlers learned its uses from the Indians for the treatment of rheumatism, toothache, and colic. Diaphoretic and antirheumatic powers have been ascribed to both species of prickly ash, and the dried bark from them was official in the USP, 1820–1926, and in the NF, 1926–47. The berries were official in the NF, 1916–47, and were used for tonic, mild stimulant, diaphoretic, antirheumatic, carminative, and antispasmodic purposes.[842]

Puccoon (Sanguinaria canadensis L.), bloodroot. "*Pocones,*" wrote John Smith in 1612, "is a small roote that groweth in the mountaines, which being dryed and beate in powder turneth red: and this they use for swellings, aches, annointing their joints, painting their heads and garments." It had still other uses: ". . . and at night where his lodging is appointed, they set a woman fresh painted red with Pocones and oile, to be his bedfellow."[843] Such doings annoyed the chaplain of Byrd's survey party in 1729, who "observ'd with concern, that the Ruffles of Some of our Fellow Travellers were a little discolour'd with pochoon, wherewith the good Man had been told those Ladies us'd to improve their invisible charms."[844]

Early Indians are reported to have used this root as a dye and insect repellent, but its principal use was as an emetic.[845] Carver called it "a strong emetic, but a very dangerous one."[846] Loskiel regarded it the same way,[847] while Cutler called it both emetic and cathartic, though it "must be given with caution."[848]

Puccoon was the subject of several experiments performed in 1803 by William Downey, the results of which were published as his inaugural dissertation for a medical degree at the University of Pennsylvania.[849] Downey performed nine experiments with the roots, four with the leaves, and two with the seed vessel and seeds, in order to determine medical properties, and seven more to determine the coloring properties. His eighth experiment with the roots was performed with the aid of William Bartram, who served as "guinea pig." Downey dissolved powdered puccoon root in water and gave eight grains of the "gummous matter" to Bartram four hours after he had eaten breakfast. Downey reported:

> In fifteen minutes a slight nausea came on with a burning at the stomach; forty, he complained of a head-ach [*sic*], the nausea, at intervals, much more violent; sixty, he was vomited twice, the motions were pretty strong.

In his conclusions Downey stated that as an emetic puccoon was but little inferior to the ipecacuanha, either in the certainty or speed-

354

iness of its operation, but he recommended use of the roots as a decoction or extract because there were less irritating than the powder or paste. The seeds were judged to be slightly narcotic, and the leaves produced "tremours, headaches, torpor," which were effects induced by substances "deleterious to the human system." Concerning the "properties of puccoon as a medicine," Downey asserted that it was a stimulating tonic in small doses, the leaves and seeds were "incitants" and sometimes acted as diaphoretics and diuretics. The pulverized root was called an errhine (sneeze powder) inferior to none.

He was informed by Bartram that some southern people used bloodroot as a preventative of intermittent fever and agreed that "from its general properties, very probably it might be a very useful medicine in this disease." Under certain conditions, Downey thought that puccoon might be useful in dysentery, jaundice (said to be so recommended by Colden), ulcerous sore throat, amenorrhea, gonorrhea, and "ulcers of long standing." He reported that the root juice had been mentioned as a cure for warts and some snakebites but avoided a commitment as to its efficacy in those cases.[850]

Sanguinaria continued to receive attention from medical men in the next half century. Dr. Clapp listed twenty-nine references to it in the medical literature to "show the attention the Sanguinaria has received . . . and the high estimation in which it is held as a remedial agent." Though authorities were not in agreement on its mode of operation, Clapp said that he had used it for more than thirty years and found that "it frequently cures or relieves pneumonic inflammation, while it checks or suppresses expectoration. I have employed it with much advantage in incipient phthisis, pneumonia, vesicular emphysema, and spasmodic asthma."[851]

Indians west of the Mississippi, Hunter reported, held puccoon "in high esteem as a remedy in several of their diseases; but most particularly in rheumatism, for which it is taken in the same manner as the prickly ash. I have known them to use the dry powdered root as an escharotic."[852] The Onondagas used bloodroot as an emetic,[853] while the Tuscaroras used it both for divination and as an internal infusion in illness.[854] The Rappahannocks made a tea of bloodroot for a purge in fevers and rheumatism[855] The Mohegans steeped the root for use as a blood medicine and emetic.[856] The Menominees added it to other medicines to strengthen their effect. The Meskwakis chewed the root and placed the spittle on burns. The Pillager Ojibwas and the Potawatomis squeezed the root juice on a lump of maple sugar and held it in the mouth for sore throat; the latter tribe also steeped the root for an infusion used in diphtheria.[857]

The dried rhizome of bloodroot (*S. canadensis* L.) was official in the USP, 1820–1926, and remained in the NF from 1926 to 1965. It has been used in medicine as a stimulating expectorant, emetic, tonic, and alterative.[858]

Pumpkin (*Cucurbita pepo* L.) Indians used several species of the gourd family, in widely separated places, for food, medicine, and utensils. The only one of them to become an official drug was the pumpkin, the dried ripe seed of which was official in the USP, 1863–1936, being used for anthelmintic and taenifuge purposes.

The Mayas used pumpkin sap as an application to burns.[859] Pumpkin was the *maycock* of the Virginia Algonquians,[860] and Peter Kalm was convinced of its American origin, being informed by the Indians that they had pumpkins "long before the Europeans discovered America, which seems to be confirmed by the accounts of the first Europeans that came into these parts who mentioned pumpkins as common food among the Indians."[861]

Mrs. Stevenson reported that *C. pepo*, called "squash," was used by the Zuñis for both food and medicine. The seeds and blossoms made an external application used to bring relief from the effects of cactus needles.[862] Yuma medicine men administered an emulsion of pumpkin and watermelon seeds to wounds.[863] The Menominees used the seeds of squash and pumpkin to facilitate the passage of urine. The seeds were pulverized in a mortar and the powder mixed with water.[864] Catawba Indians chewed pumpkin seeds fresh or dried and swallowed them as a kidney medicine.[865]

Dr. Porcher declared in 1849 that pumpkin seeds yielded an essential oil which when triturated with water furnished a cooling and nutritive milk; when boiled to a jelly they were said to be a useful diuretic.[866] Pumpkin seed, in the form of an infusion as well as in a pulpy mass, was long a favorite home remedy among whites for intestinal parasites, which use introduced it to the medical profession.[867]

Purple coneflower (*Echinacea angustifolia* DC). This is a plant of the western plains, where, according to Gilmore, Indians used it as a "remedy for more ailments than any other plant." It was a universal antidote for snakebite and other venomous bites, stings, and poisonous conditions. It was used in smoke treatment for headache as well as for distemper in horses. Pieces of the root were used to relieve toothache and treat enlarged glands, as in mumps. Jugglers bathed their hands in the juice so they could put them in scalding water, and a Winnebago informed Gilmore that he used this plant to make his mouth insensible to heat, so that for show he could take a live coal in the mouth. Burns were bathed with the juice, and the plant was used in the steam bath to make the heat endurable.[868] The Comanches used the roots for toothache and sore throat.[869] The Sioux regarded the scraped root as a remedy for hydrophobia, snakebite, and septic conditions. The Meskwakis used it to cure fits and stomach cramps. Among whites the root has been used to treat eczema and ulcerous conditions not respondent to iodide or other alteratives.[870]

Dr. Clapp in 1852 described the properties of the pungent root of purple coneflower as aromatic and carminative and said it was much used in popular medicine.[871] The dried rhizome and roots of *Echinacea* or *cone flower* (*E. angustifolia* DC, or *E. pallida* Nutt.) were official in the NF, 1916–50. They have been used to induce saliva and for alterative and diaphoretic purposes.[872]

Raspberries: *Black raspberry* (*Rubus occidentalis* L.), and *Red raspberry*, (*R. strigosus* Michx., or *R. idaeus* L.). The Ojibwas took a decoction of the crushed roots of black raspberry for pain in the stomach.[873] The Flambeau Ojibwas used red raspberries as a seasoner for medicines, and they, as well as the Potawatomis, used the root bark to make a tea applied to sore eyes. Red raspberries were also used by the Meskwakis and Menominees to season medicines. The Menominees used the root of black raspberry with St. John's wort (*Hypericum ascyron*) in treating early stages of consumption.[874] The Omaha Indians scraped and boiled the roots of red and black raspberry and gave the tea to children for bowel trouble.[875]

The leaves, roots, and fruit of the raspberry species have been considered astringent and therefore have been used as specifics in dysentery.[876] The fruits have also been used for their refrigerant and laxative properties.[877] In official medicine, red raspberry has not been used for remedial purposes but as a flavoring agent. The fruit was official in the USP, 1882–1905, and NF, 1916–42, while the juice was official in the NF, 1942–50, and in the USP since 1950. It is used in the preparation of raspberry syrup, (USP 1882–1905, 1950—; and NF, 1916–50) which serves "as a pleasant disguising agent in pharmaceutical mixtures, especially those of an acidulous nature."[878] Black raspberry has never been official.

Rhubarb. The properties of American "wild rhubarb" were one of the questions which engaged the attention of Dr. Lawrence Bohun before illness forced him to leave Jamestown in 1611.[879] Dr. Barton mentioned a wild rhubarb in use among the Indians, called *Mechameck*, and supposed it to be a species of *Convolvulus*, or bindweed.[880] Prince Maximilian of Wied reported in the 1830s:

> These Indians have some efficacious remedies derived from the vegetable Kingdom, one of which is a whitish root from the Rocky Mountains, which is called, by the Canadians, rhubarb, which is said to resemble our rhubarb in its effect and taste, and likewise to act as an emetic.[881]

It is not possible to determine which species of plants engaged the attention of these men. Certain plants related to rhubarb were used by western Indians, including the round-leaved sorrel (*Oxyria digynia* Campd.) and the *yerba Colorado*, a species of *Rumex*. The water smartweed (*Polygonum* species) also belongs to this group.[882] The official rhubarb (USP 1820–1950, NF 1950–65) is the root of Eurasian species, used for cathartic, stomachic, astringent, and tonic purposes.[883]

Rock rose (Helianthemum canadense [L.] Michx.), frostweed, frostwort. The overground plant was official in the USP, 1851–82, and NF, 1916–26. It was used as a tonic and astringent, but herbalists and eclectics have attributed several other powers to it.[884] Joseph E. Meyer, in an account called "Red Man's Medicinals," lists this plant among many used by whites since colonial times, but does not clearly assert that it was borrowed from the Indians.[885] Research for this book has failed to uncover evidence of aboriginal usage of this plant, but it is listed here as an item for future investigation.

Saffron or *Safflower, American* or *Indian (Carthamus tinctorius).* The tubular florets of this indigenous species were official in the USP, 1820–82. Dr. Claus reported that they were used for the same purpose as crocus, now employed principally as a coloring agent although formerly used as a diaphoretic, emmenagogue, and promoter of eruption in measles.[886] Despite the name "Indian safflower" the only Indian use of it found in this survey is Loskiel's report that Indians drank saffron tea as part of the treatment for relief of the effects of poison ash.[887]

Sage (Salvia species). Various species of *Salvia* were used by Lower California Indians. The seeds were ground and stirred in water; the mucilaginous substance prevented evaporation in the mouth and throat.[888] The Catawbas on the other side of the continent made a salve of the roots of wild sage (*S. lyrata*) for application to sores.[889] In the nineteenth century the leaves of this species were used by whites to destroy warts.[890]

S. officinalis, reported indigenous to Europe and the United States, was the official sage (USP 1842–1916, NF 1936–50), used as a stimulant, carminative, condiment, and astringent gargle.[891] Indian use of this species has not been reported in sources used for this work. See also *Wormwood (Artemisia)*.

Sarsaparilla, wild (Aralia nudicaulis L.). Not to be confused with the South American variety; the name *sarsaparilla* has been loosely applied to a number of plants, including the *Passiflora incarnata* and *Cocculus carolinus* (by Speck), to the "Prickley Bind-weed," (by Brickell), and to the Canada moonseed (*Menispermum canadense* L.).

The earliest notice of the American sarsaparilla occurs in the account of the voyage of Captain Davies to Sagadahoc, on the Kennebec River of Maine, in 1608:

when Capt. Davies arrived there . . . he found . . . good store of sarsaparilla gathered, and the new pynnace all finished.[892]

The younger John Winthrop is said to have prescribed "Sassaparilla" in a case of "palsy" in 1652.[893] Josselyn mentioned two "Sarsaparilla" plants growing in New England, the effects of one of them being "answerable to that we have from other parts of the world."[894] Du Pratz observed sarsaparilla, "so well known it is useless to mention," growing in Louisiana.[895] Carver was not restrained in his description of the utility of this plant:

359

The bark of the roots, which alone should be used in medicine, is of a bitterish flavour, but aromatic. It is deservedly esteemed for its medicinal virtues, being a gentle sudorific, and very powerful in attenuating the blood when impeded by gross humours.[896]

Cutler called *Aralia* roots aromatic and nutritious and beneficial in debilitated habits. "It is said," he reported, "the Indians would subsist upon them for a long time, in their war and hunting excursions." Whites used them as an ingredient in "diet drinks."[897] Loskiel found this plant (which he called *Smilax sarsaparilla*) growing in great abundance in the Iroquois country, declaring that "the root is used in medicine, and its virtues are well known." One of its uses was the application of a decoction of the roots to wounds.[898] Rafinesque asserted that the class of plants to which sarsaparilla belonged was popular in medicine and that the *Aralias* and Spikenards "made part of the Materia Medica of the native tribes, and are extensively used by country practitioners." They were held to be endowed with vulnerary, pectoral, sudorific, stimulant, diaphoretic, cordial, and depurative properties, the roots being most efficacious.[899]

Dr. Clapp called *A. nudicaulis* a mild and somewhat stimulating diaphoretic and alterative, which might be used for the same purpose as the sarsaparilla of the shops.[900] In the middle of the nineteenth century, proprietary medicines alleged to contain sarsaparilla were so popular that an irate physician protested:

> Such . . . is the furor for swallowing it, that the manufacturers employ steam engines in its preparation, and these syrups and extracts of sarsaparilla are becoming among the chief exports from the commercial emporium and [a sufficient quantity] will soon be made here to supply all creation with physic for a century to come. Some of the "regular faculty" have been carried away by this speculation, and are now installed as superintendents of these sarsaparilla factories, and making their fortunes.[901]

Stewart Holbrook relates that "Ayer's Sarsaparilla," manufactured at Lowell, Massachusetts, contained fluid extract of sarsaparilla, stillingia, yellow dock, may apple, sugar, iodide potassium, and iodide of iron. In 1911 the Connecticut State Agricultural Station analyzed nine proprietary sarsaparillas:

> to find they were of a most complex composition, containing

not only sarsaparilla but yellow dock, stillingia, burdock, licorice, sassafras, mandrake, buckthorn, senna, black cohosh, pokeroot, wintergreen, cascara sagrada, cinchona bark, prickly ash, glycerin, iodide of potassium and iron, and alcohol.[902]

With few exceptions, Indians did not compound sarsaparilla with other herbs. Montagnais and Penobscot women cut up the roots, tied the pieces on a string, and kept them in their lodges until needed. Montagnais Indians fermented the berries in water for a wine used as a tonic. The Penobscots dried the roots, crushed them to powder, and steeped the substance together with roots of sweet flag for a cough medicine.[903] Some tribes made a decoction of the root for a sore-eye lotion.[904] The Kwakiutls mixed the beaten root with an oil for a medicine used for coughing and spitting blood.[905] Speck's Houma informants asserted that there were seven kinds of sarsaparilla for use through the "four seasons." The roots were boiled for a tea taken for "feelings of high blood pressure" and as a "blood purifier."[906] The Catawbas boiled the root for a tea which was sweetened with sugar and taken as a tonic and health beverage.[907] Creeks used the root for difficulty in passing urine, when blood was passed, and for pain about the lower part of the abdomen and in the back. It was also used for pleurisy.[908] Meskwaki Indians pounded the root to make a poultice for burns and sores. It was mixed with the inner bark of prickly ash and another root to give strength to "one who is weak." Flambeau Ojibwas pounded the root for a poultice for boils and carbuncles. Pillager Ojibwa women used it for "purification" in pregnancy; it was also pounded and boiled for a cough remedy. The Potawatomis used the pounded root for a poultice on swellings and infections. They believed the *Aralia hispida* to have similar powers, and employed it as an alterative and tonic.[909]

The rhizome of American wild sarsaparilla, *A. nudicaulis*, was official in the USP, 1820–82. It was used as a stimulant, alterative, and diaphoretic.[910]

Sassafras (Sassafras officinalis Nees & Ebermaier, and var. *albidum* Blake). Lloyd did not exaggerate when he wrote that "this tree at one time created greater interest in the old world than any other American product, not excepting tobacco." Ships were dispatched to America to collect sassafras before any other North American product had made an impression on European medicine.[911] At Roanoke Island, Hariot said it was found by experience "to bee farre better and of more uses than the wood which is called *Guaiacum*, or *Lignum Vitae*."[912] Ralph Lane predicted that once the country was settled, "will Sassafras, and many other rootes and gummes there found make good marchandise and lading for shipping."[913] The bark of sassafras was listed in the *Pharmacopoeia Londinensis* of 1618 and at that time ranked with tobacco as a principal export from Virginia. On November 17, 1619, the Virginia Company in London complained of the excessive emphasis on tobacco and sassafras in the colony and demanded attention to a greater variety of products, to avoid starvation. A year later, the company took notice of a drastic fall in the price of sassafras due to oversupply and resolved to offer the colony more munitions in return for reducing their sassafras exports. In 1622, however, the colonists received an order from the Earl of Southampton "for the sending home of threescore thousand weight of Sasafras," whereupon every man was given a quota to bring in, with a fine of tobacco provided for noncompliance. The demand for sassafras was brisk enough in 1625 to cause the complaint that the London adventurers "bestowe their moneyes . . . upon two comodities onely, Tobacco and Sassafras matters of present profitt, but no wayes foundacons of a future state."[914]

Early Pennsylvania settlers, according to William Penn, infused sassafras or pine into their molasses beer.[915] Josselyn in New England found the root chips, boiled in beer, "excellent to allay the hot rage of feavers." The leaves provided an ointment for bruises and dry blows; the root bark was used in place of cinnamon and was sold in Barbados for two shillings a pound. "And why," Josselyn inquired, "may not this be the bark the Jesuit's powder was made of, that was so famous, not long since, in England, for agues?"[916] Lawson called the sassafras blossom "very cleansing to the Blood." The oily berries were:

> Carminative and extremely prevalent in Clysters for the Colick. The Bark of the Root is a Specific to those afflicted with the Gripes. The same in Powder and a Lotion made thereof, is much used by the Savages to mundify old Ulcers, and for several other Uses, being highly esteemed among them.[917]

Byrd called the sassafras flower, eaten in the spring with other salad, "a splendid blood purifier." Moreover, "the fruit or berries, as also the rind, are useful in many sicknesses."[918] The Dutch physician Hermann Boerhaave called the sassafras tea "a drink to be taken in the Fit."[919]

Sassafras was of medical and economic importance in French Louisiana. "There are entire forests of sassafras trees, used for medicine and dyes," wrote Bossu.[920] Du Pratz yielded nothing to Monardes or Lawson in his appraisal of the virtues of the "great tree" in medicine.[921] When Louisiana passed to American control, sassafras continued to be one of the products extracted from the forests by plantation slaves. It was used "with success in the critical diseases so common to New Orleans," according to one writer.[922]

Peter Kalm was informed by John Bartram that a woman in Virginia had cured herself of severe pain in the foot, which for three years "almost hindered her from walking," by rubbing the affected parts with sassafras oil extracted by boiling the berries. Kalm was impressed by the aromatic wood and remarked that some Pennsylvanians put sassafras chips in chests with their woolens in the belief that the odor would repel moths. An old Swedish colonist related to him that his mother had cured many people of dropsy by a decoction of sassafras root. Colonel Lydius told him that the natives considered sassafras valuable in treatment of diseased eyes.[923]

Carver admired the medicinal qualities of sassafras and reported that the berries were used in the colonies as a substitute for pimento. Much of his traveling was beyond the northern range of this tree, and he regretted that it was so seldom met with.[924] Cutler claimed that bedsteads made of sassafras wood would never be infested with bugs. He reported that it was:

> Said to be an excellent diuretic and diaphoretic, and therefore efficacious in obstructions of the viscera, cachexies, scorbutic complaints and in the venereal disease. An infusion of the bark of the roots makes a grateful drink. A very pungent, hot oil is extracted from it, which is said to possess most of the virtues of the wood. It has been exported in considerable quantities to *Europe*.[925]

Dr. Barton believed that sassafras bark was useful in intermittent fevers, and the oil of sassafras, "when externally applied to the body in rheumatic and gouty affections, is remarkable for its power of shifting the pain from its original seat," although, he prudently added, it "ought to be used with caution."[926] Stearns called the wood, root, and bark stimulant, aperient, diuretic, diaphoretic, and corroborant, and claimed that sassafras "sweetens and purifies the blood and juices; and is good in scorbutic, venereal, cachectic, and catarrhal disorders."[927] Coxe's *Dispensatory* reported that sassafras root, because of its volatile oil, "is a gently stimulating, heating, sudorific, and diuretic remedy."[928]

Dr. Bigelow thought that the virtues of sassafras had been overrated and asserted that its reputation in the cure of such diseases as rheumatism, dropsy, and especially syphilis, "has fallen into deserved oblivion, while it is now recognized only with regard to its general properties, which are those of a warm stimulant and diaphoretic."[929] Numerous virtues were still attributed to sassafras, however, by Dr. Williams and Dr. Clapp in their reports to the American Medical Association on indigenous medical plants,[930] and Porcher, in his report prepared for the Confederate government, commented:

> whenever a soldier suffered from measles, pneumonia, bronchitis, or cold, his companion or nurse was directed to procure the roots and leaves of Sassafras, and a tea made with this supplied that of Flax Seed or Gum Arabic. Each leaf of Sassafras contains a great amount of mucilage.[931]

Sassafras has always been important in folk medicine, being regarded by rural people as a "spring tonic" and "purifier of the blood." Smoky mountain people used it as a beverage in place of milk when the latter was not available.[932] Pennsylvania Germans called the tree *fiewerbaum* because the fresh or dried blossoms were used for fevers. The berries were used to make wine for colds. They also chewed the leaves to lay on wounds to stop bleeding.[933]

Sassafras became an ingredient in popular beverages such as root beer[934] and in proprietary medicines. To supply the demand, oil of sassafras was commercially manufactured on a considerable scale in several eastern states in the late nineteenth century. Lloyd reported that in 1883 in Buckingham County, Virginia, forty distillers were manufacturing sassafras oil, consuming daily 80,000 pounds of the root, yielding about fifty gallons of oil, weighing about 450 pounds. It was shipped to the New York market in five-gallon cans.[935] In Louisiana, Choctaw Indians prepared from the leaves a powder called gumbo filet, used to give flavor and consistency to gumbo soup.[936]

Sassafras was used in some way by virtually all Indians living in its range, which is mainly south of 42 degrees latitude. Loskiel reported that the Delawares and Iroquois used the flowers for tea and the berries for medicine.[937] Lafitau said that the Iroquois used sassafras as a venereal remedy.[938] Hunter found that Arkansas tribes in spring made a drink of the young blossoms and the root bark. The bruised leaves were applied as poultices, the pith of young sprouts were steeped for an eyewash, and the dried root bark was smoked like tobacco.[939] The Houma Indians boiled the fresh or dried roots for an infusion drunk for measles and scarlet fever.[940] The Louisiana Choctaws boiled the roots and drank the extract "to thin the blood."[941] The Creeks boiled the roots with certain grass for a warm drink given to patients with pains in the bowels and stomach accompanied by vomiting.[942] Seminole Indians formerly used sassafras for coughing, gallstones, and pain in the bladder.[943]

The dried root bark of sassafras (*S. albidum* [Nutt.] Nees) was official in the USP, 1820–1926, and remained official in the NF, 1926–65. This product has been described by Dr. Claus as aromatic and carminative. Sassafras oil (USP 1820–1955, NF 1955–65) is the volatile oil distilled from the root, and safrole (USP 1905–16) is a phenolic ether, obtained from sassafras oil or camphor oil. Both of these products have been described as carminative and stimulant and are used as flavoring in confections, pharmaceutical preparations, and in perfumery and soaps.[944]

Saw palmetto (*Serenoa serrulata* [Michx.] Hook. f., syn.: *Sabal serrulatum* Roem & Schult.; *Serenoa repens* [Bartram] Small) and other species of palmetto. The Mayas made an infusion of the leaves or roots and a decoction from the interior of the trunk of *Sabal japa* as remedies for dysentery and abdominal pains. From the interior of the trunk they obtained a remedy for snake and insect bites and a poultice for ulcers. The crushed root was applied to sores on a man's breast.[945]

Benjamin Hawkins reported in 1799 that the berries of the dwarf saw palmetto (*S. repens?*) were eaten by bear, deer, turkeys, and Indians.[946] Early settlers in North Carolina used the branches to make brooms, while hats and baskets were made from them in Bermuda.[947]

Dr. Porcher ascribed purgative properties to the sweet pulp of saw palmetto.[948] Lloyd related that southern settlers saw that animals feeding on the fruit grew sleek and fat, and so they attributed therapeutic qualities to the berries and prepared a decoction of them for domestic medication. The plant has a volatile oil, and several articles about it which appeared in medical literature in the 1870's led to the admission of saw-palmetto berries to the USP, in which they were official from 1906 to 1916. The NF listed this drug from 1926 to 1950. Its properties are given as diuretic, sedative, and anticatarrhal.[949] The berries are also credited with the power to improve digestion and allay neuralgic troubles and irritation of the mucous membranes.[950]

Houma Indians used the juice of the crushed roots of dwarf palmetto (*Sabal adamsonii*) as a lotion for sore eyes, the burning sensation being considered a counterirritant. The same decoction was boiled and drunk for kidney troubles. The dried root was used for "swimming in head" or "high blood pressure."[951] The Alabamas used the beaten roots of *Sabal* species boiled with bramble brier (*Smilax glauca*) for stomach trouble. The substance was applied externally for a broken or injured back.[952]

Senna, American (Cassia marilandica L.). Barton held that the American senna, used as a purgative, was virtually equivalent to European senna, an opinion later expressed by other authorities.[953] Dr. Porcher said that southern Negroes applied *Cassia* leaves smeared with grease as a dressing for sores.[954] The bruised root moistened with water was used by the Cherokees for the same purpose. They also drank a decoction of it for fever and for an unspecified disease in which symptoms included black spots on the body and partial paralysis.[955] Meskwaki Indians soaked the seeds in water until they became mucilaginous and then ate them for sore throat.[956] Houma Indians boiled the roots of *Cassia* species with wild beans to make a tea for typhoid fever.[957]

The dried leaflets of *American Senna* were official in the USP, 1820–82, and were described as a mild laxative.[958]

Skullcap (Scutellaria lateriflora L.), mad dog skullcap. Dr. Schöpf listed the *Scutellaria* species as tertian fever remedies,[959] but his contemporary, Dr. Lawrence Van Derveer of New Jersey, used this plant in treating hydrophobia, from whence came its popular name. Other physicians of the period employed it either as a preventative or cure in the same disease, but it fell into disrepute when it was adopted by quacks who promoted it by advertising. It later was accepted in official medicine for other purposes, but Lloyd, who has written much on the history of this drug, asserted that the earlier claims for it were never adequately tested.[960]

As late as 1844, "Doctor" H. B. Skinner was calling this herb "a sovereign remedy for the hydrophobia or canine madness."[961] Dr. Clapp reported that few if any physicians had any confidence in its prophylactic powers, although he felt that from its bitterness it might be found useful as a tonic.[962] Dr. Beach considered it nervine and antispasmodic.[963]

The Cherokees combined skullcap with three other herbs for a decoction drunk to promote menstruation; it was drunk also for diarrhea, and with other herbs in a decoction for breast pains and in "purification" following violation of certain menstrual taboos.[964] The marsh skullcap (S. galericulata L.) was used by the Flambeau Ojibwas as a heart medicine. Small skullcap (S. parvula Michx.) was used by the Meskwakis for flux.[965]

The dried overground plant of S. lateriflora was official in the USP, 1863–1916, and in the NF, 1916–47. Uses of this plant are given as tonic, nervine, and antispasmodic.[966]

Skunk cabbage (Symplocarpus foetidus [L.] Nutt., syn.: *Spathyema foetida* [L.] Raf., *Dracontium foetidum* L., *Ictodes foetida* [by Dr. Beach], *Arum americanum* [by Cutler], etc.), *Tabac du Diable* or *Chou Puant* (in Quebec), skunkweed, poke.

As some of the names indicate, this plant, which is native to moist, rich woodlands, is most noted for its odor. It was sketched and described by Josselyn, but no medicinal powers were ascribed to it.[967] Kalm reported that the English called it polecat-root and that he found its scent so nauseous that his head ached. Dr. Colden informed him that he used the root in all cases where the root of arum was used, especially against scurvy.[968] Carver asserted that the colonists cured the itch with a lotion made from the roots.[969] Cutler said that Indians taught the white man the uses of this plant. He held that the dried and powdered roots were excellent for asthma, often giving relief when other means were ineffectual.[970] Dr. Clapp, following

Bigelow, described its properties as antispasmodic and narcotic, and emetic in large doses. He reported that it had been used with much success in asthma, catarrh of aged persons, and hysteria.[971] Beach reported its use for obstructed menses, worms, and rheumatism.[972]

Winnebago and Dakota Indians used the skunk cabbage as an expectorant in asthma.[973] Kwakiutl Indians used the roots or leaves for a poultice on sores and swellings and to draw out splinters and thorns.[974] Menominee Indians also made a poultice for wounds from the powdered root. It was further used by them as a remedy for cramps and a seasoner with other medicines. The root hairs alone were used to stop hemorrhage. The Meskwakis used the root hairs or fine rootlets for toothache and the leaf bases as a poultice for swellings. The seeds were also used for undisclosed purposes.[975] The Micmac Indians treated headache by tying skunk cabbage in a bundle and smelling it.[976]

The dried rhizome and roots of skunk cabbage were an official drug in the USP, 1820–82. They were used as an antispasmodic, emetic, and diuretic,[977] and in affections of the respiratory organs, nervous disorders, rheumatism, and dropsy.[978]

Snakeroot. The term "snakeroot" has been applied to a wide range of plants. The *Eupatorium urticaefolium* Reich., as well as the *Aristolochia serpentaria* L., and American valerian have all been called "white snakeroot." Although the *A. serpentaria* is usually called thus, Whitebread called it "black snakeroot," a term which has been applied to black cohosh (*Cimicifuga racemosa* [L.] Nutt.) and to the American sanicle (*Sanicula marilandica* L.). The name Sampson's (or *Samson's*) snakeroot has been applied to both *Psoralea psorilioides* (Walt.) Cory, and to *Gentiana catesbaei* Walt. The term button snakeroot has been applied to several species of *Liatris*, as well as to *Eryngium* species. The term snakeroot has also been applied to *Senecio aureus* L., and other plants. In early reports the term snakeroot is often used with no other identifying information. This does not exhaust the account of the chaos in the nomenclature of these plants, but it indicates the difficulty of tracing their history. Early references to undifferentiated varieties of "snakeroot" will be discussed first, followed by the official species.

An early writer in New Netherland asserted that anyone bitten by a rattlesnake was in great danger of his life, but "fortunately . . . there grows spontaneously in the country the true snakeroot, which is very highly esteemed by the Indians as an unfailing cure."[979] In North Carolina, Lawson found "four sorts of Snake-Root, besides the common Species, which are great Antidotes against the Serpent's Bite, and are easily raised in the Garden."[980] Byrd frequently mentioned unidentified varieties of snakeroot, which he used mainly to promote sweating in various ills. For example, on July 8, 1711, his diary records:

> I went to bed and had a very severe fit [from malaria]. I took more snakeroot and sweated very much with it, but it made my hot fit the worse and last the longer.[981]

On September 24, 1729, Byrd relates:

> I found near our Camp some Plants of that kind of Rattle-Snake Root, called Star-grass. . . . The Root . . . is very bitter, and where it meets with any Poison, works by Violent Sweats, but where it meets with none, has no Sensible Operation but that of putting the Spirits into a great Hurry, and so of promoting Perspiration.[982]

Byrd was convinced that snakes had such an aversion to this plant that a person who rubbed his hands with the juice of it could handle the vipers safely. The next day he wrote that because the "Vipers remain in Vigour generally till towards the End of September," his party was equipped with "three Several Sorts of Rattle-Snake-Root, made up into proper Doses, and ready for immediate use, in case any of the Men or their Horses had been bitten."[983]

Bishop Spangenberg's journal of a trip to Onondaga in 1745 mentions a plant having blossoms like "geese flowers" which with its root was used for snakebites.[984] Romans wrote that "Snakeroot" was used in the South for malaria, and in 1808 Cuming used "snake root" with other herbs to treat a case of ague in Ohio.[985] John Redman used "Snakeroot" in the yellow fever epidemic at Philadelphia in 1792.[986] The Onondaga Indians are reported to have used the bruised leaves of "snake-root" externally and internally, and it was supposed to have a high reputation for curing rattlesnake bites.[987] In 1944, Greenlee wrote that Florida Seminoles sometimes boiled "Snakeroot" in a pot and took it internally for stomachache.[988]

Black snakeroot (Cimicifuga racemosa [L.] Nutt., syn.: *Actaea racemosa*), black cohosh, squaw-root. Lloyd reports that the Indians introduced this drug to early American domestic medicine, and it was described by early writers on materia medica, none of whom "added anything not given by the Indians as far as the field of action of the drug is concerned," except for some nineteenth-century instances of the use of this plant for treating smallpox. As the name squaw-root suggests, Indians used this plant for a female remedy, as well as for debility, to promote perspiration, as a gargle for sore throat, and for rheumatism.[989]

Dr. Barton considered *cimicifuga* a valuable medicine, and acknowledged a debt to the Indians for knowledge of its uses while describing their way of steaming it for relief of rheumatism. He called the root astringent and held that a decoction of it was beneficial in putrid sore throat and would also cure the itch.[990] Peter Smith claimed that Indians cured the ague with black snakeroot, and he recommended it as a diuretic, antiscorbutic, and cure for yellow fever and snakebite.[991]

Dr. Porcher said the root was used in medicine for uterine disorders and rheumatism, while Dr. Clapp called it "unquestionably one of the most valuable of our indigenous medicinal plants." He cited seven physicians who had found it useful in various ills and stated that for years he had prescribed *cimicifuga* in bronchitis, phthisis, chorea, and other nervous affections, "generally with very satisfactory results."[992]

Dr. Andros reported that "Black cohosh" was used by the Winnebagos and Dakotas as a decoction in rheumatism.[993] The Penobscots drank a decoction of it for kidney trouble or when "feeling all played out."[994]

Black snakeroot, under the various names *Cimicifuga, Black cohosh,* and *Macrotys,* was official in the USP, 1820–1936, and in the NF, 1936–50. The dried rhizome and roots were the parts used. A mixture of the resinous constituents of this plant, called *macrotin* or *cimicifugin,* has also been used in medicine. The *cimicifuga* drugs have been used for sedative, emmenagogue, and alterative purposes, though Dr. Claus asserts their use is empirical.[995] *Blackiston's Dictionary* said of this drug: "There is no evidence of therapeutic usefulness, but the drug is occasionally used in chronic rheumatism, chorea, and tinnitus."[996]

370

Button snakeroot (*Eryngium aquaticum* L., and *E. yuccifolium* Michx.). These are distinguished as two species in *Gray's Manual*, although some of the early writers failed to differentiate them. Dr. Garden of Charleston discovered the *E. yuccifolium* on a trip to the Cherokee country and in 1755 sent seeds of it to Dr. Colden, reporting that the plant was called "Button Snakeroot" and that the root was used "as a very powerfull attenuant & Diaphoretic."[997] Hawkins reported that the Creeks made an emetic drink called *possau* from button snakeroot and used it in the *Boos-ke-tau* ceremonies.[998] Thomas Nuttall found inhabitants of Arkansas using *E. aquaticum* as a medicine "acting as a diuretic, and in larger doses proving almost emetic."[999] Swanton reported that the Creeks used button snakeroot pounded up, mixed with water, and drunk cold for neuralgia, kidney trouble, snakebite, rheumatism, and as a "blood purifier." The Natchez used the chewed stem and leaves as a nosebleed remedy, and made a tea of the parched plants for the flux.[1000] The Meskwakis used the root of *E. yuccifolium* as a medicine for bladder trouble and poisons other than rattlesnake.[1001]

Dr. Porcher attributed diaphoretic, escharotic, expectorant, and sometimes emetic properties to *E. aquaticum*. It was used in dropsy, pleurisy, colds, and inflammatory discharges of the mucous passages.[1002] The rhizome of *E. yuccifolium*, under the name of *Eryngo* or *Button Snakeroot*, was official in the USP, 1820–73, being used for diaphoretic, expectorant, and emetic purposes.[1003]

Seneca snakeroot (*Polygala senega* L.), Senega, Seneca, milkwort. The name of this plant is said to be derived from its use by Seneca Indians as a snakebite remedy, although it has been used for other purposes by Indians and whites. Byrd was convinced that it would cure gout, reporting that it had "enabled Cripples to throw away their Crutches and walk several Miles, and what is Stranger Still, it takes away the Pain in half an hour."[1004]

The promotion of this plant as a cure for pleurisy in 1736 by John Tennent of Virginia has been previously mentioned. Dr. Garden was convinced that the root was endowed with the power to cure several other ailments. In 1768 he shipped a bundle of it to Dr. Colden with these remarks:

The Seneka is the most powerfull & efficacious Antiphlogistic attenuant among the Galenical Medicines—It is possibly Equal-

371

ly efficacious as any of the Most noted Antimonials . . . & I am sure it is much safer—I give it with and without Nitre in all inflammatory disorders whatever & with the greatest success—It is likewise very powerfull in Lentors of Every kind even of the Leucophlegmatic & Oedematous sort as well as the inflammatory Lentors or even in Lentors of the nervous juices or relaxation of their fibrillae.[1005]

Dr. Barton felt that Seneca was helpful as a diuretic in dropsy and as a diaphoretic in rheumatism and declared that he had "sometimes treated my patients almost entirely with Seneca." Besides the virtues already mentioned, he attributed emetic, expectorant, and salivating powers to it and reported its use by himself and others in the treatment of hives, croup, and hydrothorax. He had no faith, however, in its ability to cure snakebite or pneumonia.[1006] By the middle of the nineteenth century, Dr. Porcher was more restrained than his predecessors, remarking of Seneca, "if beneficial, it only acts as a diffusable stimulant." Dr. Clapp preferred not to commit himself but referred to accounts of others.[1007]

Loskiel verified that Seneca root was chewed and applied to snakebite by the Indians,[1008] but many other uses are reported. Hunter said that western Indians used it in cold infusions during the remission of (malarial) fevers and in pulmonary diseases. It was given warm in combination with other drugs to promote sweat or to discharge collections of mucus from the trachea and lungs. It was esteemed in female complaints and in diseases of children which involved difficulty in breathing.[1009] In the late nineteenth century, the Menominees almost exterminated the plant in their district by collecting it for the drug trade.[1010] The Ojibwas used a decoction of the roots for coughs and colds and gave an infusion of the leaves for sore throat and to destroy water bugs that had been swallowed.[1011] Seneca snakeroot was the chief remedy for heart trouble among the Potawatomis and Meskwakis.[1012] Two related species of the *Polygala* or milkwort family are reported used by other tribes. The Montagnais boiled bitter milkwort (*P. polygama*) for a cough medicine,[1013] while the Louisiana Choctaws dried the blossoms of orange milkwort (*P. lutea*) and mixed them with hot water to make a poultice for swellings.[1014]

Seneca snakeroot, *Polygala senega* L., was official in the USP, 1820–

1936, and in the NF, 1936–60. It has been used in medicine as an expectorant and cough remedy, a stimulant, irritant, emetic, and diuretic. *P. rubella* (USP 1820–82) was reported to "have some value as a bitter tonic."[1015]

Virginia snakeroot (Aristolochia serpentaria L.). Dr. Schöpf wrote that the roots of this plant were used not only for snakebite, but also for diaphoretic, anthelmintic, and diuretic purposes and the treatment of intermittent fevers.[1016] Dr. Barton called Virginia snakeroot "one of the more stimulating tonic bitters," and considered it a valuable medicine in various fevers.[1017] Stearns said it would raise the pulse and correct "the putrid disposition of the humours."[1018] This is one of the more favored drugs of the cautious Dr. Cullen, who seldom endorsed the virtues claimed for American simples. He thought it possessed of some merit for its antiseptic, stimulant, and tonic powers.[1019] Coxe's *Dispensatory* recommended it to supplement Peruvian bark in intermittent fevers, to excite sweating in typhus and "putrid diseases," for "exanthemous diseases, when the fever is of the typhoid type, to support the action of the skin, and keep out eruption," for gangrene, and as a gargle in "putrid sore throat."[1020] Dr. Bigelow declared that *serpentaria* was a tonic and diaphoretic and in certain cases an antispasmodic and anodyne.[1021]

Prince Maximilian of Wied, while staying at Delaware Water Gap, Pennsylvania, in 1832, was shown several plants "to the roots of which the inhabitants of the country ascribe medicinal virtues; for instance, the snake root, perhaps *Aristolochia serpentaria*, which is said immediately to stanch the most violent bleeding of any wound."[1022]

In the eighteenth century, Loskiel reported that Indians applied the chewed root of this plant to snakebite, and from its excessive bitterness it was in much use by them as a sudorific and stomachic.[1023] This was also one of the *schwitzgegreider,* or sweat herbs, of the Pennsylvania Germans.[1024] Hunter reported that Arkansas Indians used this root in warm infusion to procure sweating and in a cold infusion for a tonic in cases of debility.[1025] The Cherokees blew a decoction of the root upon a patient for fever and feverish headaches and drank it for coughs. The root was chewed and spit upon snakebites, and the bruised root was placed in the hollow tooth for toothache. It was also held against the nose to relieve soreness caused by constant blowing in colds.[1026] The Louisiana Choctaws drank an extract of the root to relieve stomach pains.[1027] The Alabamas mashed the leaves for a snakebite poultice and drank a tea of the leaves to assist the cure.[1028] The Natchez boiled the whole plant for a warm infusion taken internally for fevers.[1029] The Penobscots steeped this plant "for fits,"[1030] and the Mohegans applied a mash of the roots to snakebites.[1031]

Virginia snakeroot was included in the pharmacopeia of the Massachusetts Medical Society in 1808, the pharmacopeia of the New York Hospital in 1816, and the USP in 1820. In the middle of the nineteenth century, it had a place in the pharmacopeias of London, Edinburgh, and Dublin. It was mentioned in all the works on materia medica and, according to Dr. Clapp, had been used as a medicine since 1633.[1032] The dried rhizome and roots continued to be an official drug in the USP until 1942 and in the NF until 1955. *Texas snakeroot (A. reticulata* Nutt.) was also official in the USP, 1851–1942, and NF, 1942–55. Later writers have described the properties of these species as diaphoretic, tonic, aromatic bitter, and stimulant.[1033]

Spikenard (Aralia racemosa L.). Carver found spikenard berries "of such a balsamic nature, that when infused in spirits, they make a most palatable and reviving cordial."[1034] This plant has been used by mountaineers and in domestic practice generally for a cough syrup, rheumatic remedy, sweat herb, and poultice for sores.[1035] Settlers at Cades Cove, Tennessee, borrowing from the Cherokees, made a root tea of this plant for backaches.[1036] Peter Smith, the "Indian doctor," used spikenard for a salve and the root juice to cure earache, declaring that "this is likely to help a deaf ear, if anything will, and is a real Indian cure."[1037]

Hunter reported that spikenard was valued by the Shawnees for expelling wind from the stomach, stopping coughs, and relieving asthma and pain in the breast.[1038] Micmac Indians made a salve of spikenard for use on cuts and wounds.[1039] The Ojibwas used the roots with wild ginger for a poultice on fractures.[1040] The Menominees used the root in blood poisoning, as a poultice on sores, and for a tea given in stomachache. Potawatomis pounded the root to a pulp for a hot poultice in inflammations. Meskwaki mothers had a spikenard medicine sprayed on their heads in childbirth. It was also used to season other medicines.[1041] False spikenard (*Smilacina racemosa*

L.) was used medicinally by the Mohegans, Flambeau Ojibwas, and Forest Potawatomis.

American Spikenard, Aralia racemosa L., has been official in the *National Formulary*, 1916–65. The powdered rhizome and roots are used for stimulant and diaphoretic purposes.[1042]

Squaw weed (Senecio aureus L.), golden ragwort, groundsel, life root, senecio. This plant was mentioned by Dr. Schöpf as a vulnerary among the Indians.[1043] The juice of the plant in honey or the seeds in substance were the parts employed.[1044] Dr. T. Gundrum published an article in 1898 advocating the use of a fluid extract of this plant as a hemostatic in capillary hemorrhage and stating that no physician seemed to be aware of its value for that purpose.[1045] The dried overground plant of *S. aureus* was official, under the name *Senecio*, in the *National Formulary*, 1916–36. Dr. Claus reported that it was "said" to be stimulant, diuretic, and an emmenagogue, but that the claims were not substantiated.[1046]

As suggested by the name "squaw weed," this plant was used among the Indians as a female remedy. The Catawbas made a tea of all parts of the plant to check the pains of childbirth, to hasten the birth of the child, and for female troubles in general. Speck doubtfully identified as *Senecio smallii* a plant which this tribe used as a consumption remedy.[1047] *Senecio* species were used for undetermined medicinal purposes by the Utes[1048] and being rich in tannin have served some tribes as an astringent.[1049]

Stargrass (Aletris farinosa L.), ague root, blazing star, colic root, unicorn root. Brickell of North Carolina wrote that stargrass was "used with good Success in most Fevers in this Country."[1050] This plant may be the "Star root" which John Bartram told Dr. Colden was called breast root from its use as a poultice for sore breasts. He told of a man who was cured of a "grievous pain of his back & brest" with the powdered leaves of the herb. He added that "ye star root is chiefly used by several for ye pain of ye stomach thay boil ye root in water & drink ye decoction after ye method of our Indians from whome they learned ye use of it."[1051]

Rafinesque reported that *Aletris* was used by many country physicians and Indian doctors and was highly valued by them and the

Indians for its tonic, stomachic, narcotic, and repercussive virtues.[1052] Dr. Bigelow called the root of stargrass a most intense bitter used in small doses as a tonic but producing narcotic symptoms in large doses. Its chief use was as a stomachic.[1053]

Speck reported in 1937 that the Catawba Indians placed stargrass leaves in water for dysentery, and for any form of colic or stomach disorder.[1054]

The dried rhizome and roots of *Aletris* were official in the USP, 1820–73, and in the NF, 1916–47. The drug is reported to contain saponin and a bitter principle and has been used as a uterine tonic and diuretic.[1055] In 1907, however, it was chiefly valued for use in digestive troubles.[1056]

Stillingia (*Stillingia sylvatica* L.), queen's root. This is a plant native to the pine barrens of the South and was reported by Barton to be used in that region as a cathartic and by southern Indians as a venereal remedy.[1057] Lloyd reported that it was widely used in popular medicines sold as "blood purifiers." It was also used in domestic medicine as a purgative and alterative, and for cutaneous diseases.[1058]

Swanton said that the Creek Indians mashed *Stillingia* roots and boiled them, and a woman who had just borne a child drank the liquid and was bathed in it. A woman suffering from irregular periods bathed in this liquid with devil's shoestring (*Tephrosia* [or *Cracca*] *virginiana* L.) added.[1059]

The dried root of *Stillingia* was official in the USP, 1831–1926, and in the NF, 1926–47. Dr. Claus described it as a tonic, usually combined with other drugs and reported that since 1860 it was used both empirically and by the medical profession.[1060]

Sumach (*Rhus glabra* L., and other *Rhus* species). Some of the early writers did not distinguish between the sumach species, which are generally similar in appearance and properties. "The English use to boyl it in beer," wrote Josselyn, "and drink it for colds; and so do the Indians, from whom the English had the medicine."[1061] Brickell declared that sumach berries were used in the cure of yaws, while "the Leaves and Seeds stop all kind of *Haemorrhoides*, all Issues of Blood and weakness of the Stomach and Intestines; outwardly they resist putrefaction; drie up running *Sores*, heal old *Ulcers*, *Gangrens*, &c. the Gum put into the Teeth eases the Pains thereof."[1062] Romans called sumach good medicine for "hard dry and bloody stools" and said it was used by the French of lower Louisiana for medicine, tanning, and making vinegar.[1063]

Barton reported that the bark of R. glabrum was said to be useful in intermittents and for removing warts and tetters. The species was called "Indian salt" in some areas because the Indians used a saline powder from the berries as a condiment with meat and a "fixer" in red dyes.[1064] Meriwether Lewis was convinced that sumach and lobelia, which he had seen used by Ojibwa Indians for venereal disease, were both "effecatious and sovereign" for lues venerea and gonorrhea.[1065]

Dr. Porcher reported that the root bark of R. glabra had been used in burn cataplasms and in a gargle for sore throat. The excrescences were considered by some doctors to be astringent.[1066] Dr. Clapp called the leaves astringent and ascribed the same properties to staghorn sumach, R. typhina L.[1067] The berries of these species, placed in vinegar, were used as a sore-throat gargle by the Pennsylvania Germans.[1068]

Sumach leaves, often mixed with willow bark, were smoked as tobacco by Indians. Hunter reported that the roots and leaves were used by Indians in several diseases but especially as an ingredient in their favorite composition for dropsy.[1069] The Pawnees boiled the fruits of R. glabra to make a remedy for dysmenorrhea and bloody flux. The Omahas boiled the fruits for a styptic wash to stop hemorrhage in women after parturition and made a decoction of the root for urinary ailments. A wet poultice of the leaves or berries was used by this tribe as an application for skin poisoning, apparently from poison ivy.[1070] The Comanches used the bark of R. trilobata Nutt., in treating colds.[1071] The Natchez used the roots of the same species for a poultice on boils. The Creeks boiled the roots of R. glabra or R. copallina for an infusion taken for dysentery. Mixed with tobacco it was considered a sovereign remedy for all cephalic and pectoral complaints.[1072] The Catawbas made a tea of staghorn-sumach berries for relief of gravel in the bladder.[1073]

The Potawatomis used the root bark of this species as a hemostatic, the leaves for a sore throat gargle, and the berries for a medicinal tea. They were also mixed with other plant medicines to expel worms. The Flambeau Ojibwas used a tea of R. glabra root bark for a hemostatic, the trunk and twig inner bark admixed with other medicines for astringent purposes, and the steeped blossoms for sore eyes. The leaves were used in poultices and the fruit for a throat cleanser as

well as the basis of a beverage. The Meskwakis mixed the berries of
R. typhina with spurge root and bur-oak bark to expel pinworms.
The root of *R. glabra* served them for a rubefacient. The Menominees
used *R. typhina* extensively; from the root bark was made a tea for
"inward" troubles; the inner bark of the trunk was recognized as an
astringent and used as a remedy for piles; the hairy twigs were used
in female diseases, and the acidulous berries were combined with other
botanicals for consumption and pulmonary troubles.[1074] The Micmacs
used *R. typhina* for sore throat, and a tea made from it was poured into
the ear for earache.[1075]

The berries of smooth sumach, *Rhus glabra*, were an official medicine in the USP, 1820–1916, 1926–36, and in the NF, 1916–26. They
have been used as a sore-throat gargle, and for astringent and tonic
purposes. The fruits of *R. typhina*, which are more acid, have often
been used in place of the official drug, and so has the bark of both
species.[1076]

Sweet flag (Acorus calamus L.), calamus. This marsh plant is said
to be common to both hemispheres and has been used for medicine
since ancient times.[1077] Dr. Clapp called it a pleasant aromatic carminative used in flatulent colic and debility of the stomach and bowels.[1078]

Gilmore asserted that sweet flag was "held in high esteem by all
tribes" of the Plains region. It was used by them as a carminative; a
decoction was drunk for fever, and the rootstock was chewed to relieve
toothache and stop coughing. An infusion of the pounded root was
drunk for colic. For a cold remedy, Indians chewed the rootstock,
drank a decoction, or used it in the smoke treatment.[1079] Winnebago
and Dakota Indians used a drink made from calamus as a diaphoretic
in fevers.[1080] The Menominees used small doses of medicine made from
the root for stomach cramps and as a physic. Besides these uses, the
Pillager Ojibwas employed calamus for "cold in the throat." Potawatomis sniffed the powdered root up the nose for catarrh and used it as
an ingredient of a remedy to stop hemorrhage. Meskwaki Indians used
the boiled root for similar purposes as well as for burn treatment.[1081]

Calamus or *sweet flag* was official in the USP, 1820–1916, and in the
NF, 1936–50. It was considered effective as a carminative, stimulant,
and aromatic bitter tonic, besides being used as a flavoring agent.[1082]

Sweet gum (Liquidambar styraciflua L.), copal, American storax.

Monardes mentioned copal as the Aztec incense which was also used in medicine. He also described "Liquid Ambar" as:

> A Rosine taken out by incision of certaine trees . . . and the Indians do call it Ococal. . . . It is used in Medicine for manye diseases, and it is of greater vertue for to heal colde diseases, for it healeth excellently well, all partes wheresoever it be applied.[1083]

A gum extract identified as the product of *L. styraciflua* was applied hot to the cheek for toothache by the Aztecs.[1084]

English settlers in the southern colonies took early notice of this tree, perhaps because they had heard of it from the Spanish. Hariot mentioned "*Sweet Gummes*" among the commodities of "*Virginia*" (North Carolina) in 1588.[1085] Lawson declared that the fragrant gum yielded by incisions of the sweet-gum tree in the spring "cures the Herpes and Inflamations, being applied to the Morphew and Tettars."[1086] Such a remedy could hardly escape the notice of William Byrd, who wrote in 1729:

> One of the Men, by an Overstrain, had unhappily got a Running of the Reins, for which I gave him every Morning a Little Sweet Gumm dissolv'd in Water, with good success. This gumm . . . is as healing in its Virtue as Balm of Gilead, or the Balsams of Tolu and Peru. It is likewise a most Agreeable parfume, very little inferior to Ambergris.[1087]

Mark Catesby also compared sweet gum to the balsam of Peru, and reported that it was chewed by the Indians, "esteeming it a preservative of their teeth." He mentioned a "Gum Elimy" which was a good vulnerary much used for horses.[1088] Peter Kalm said that sweet-gum resin was "much praised in medicine, but flows best in the south."[1089]

Sweet gum was the "copal" or "copalm" of the French and Spanish. Bossu related that "some trees contain copal, a gummy substance which is a balm as good as that made in Peru. Animals wounded by hunters cure themselves by rubbing against a tree from which this balm flows."[1090] "Copalm," boasted Du Pratz, was a common tree in Louisiana, having "un baume dont les vertus son infinies." He held it to be valuable against fevers, wounds and ulcers, pulmonary ailments, obstructions, colic, and internal maladies.[1091]

Stearns reported that Indians used liquidambar resin to cure fevers and heal wounds.[1092] In 1795, André Michaux told how:

379

A Frenchman who traded among the Cheroquis Savages cured himself of the Itch by drinking for ten days a decoction of Chips of that tree he called Copalm and which is the true Liquidambar.[1093]

Dr. Barton called liquidambar a stimulant, and said that it was used with advantage in diarrhea.[1094] Dr. Porcher reported that the resin was formerly used in scabies and that the oil called copalm which was extracted from this species in Mexico was used as an excitant in the mucous system and was given in the treatment of chronic catarrhs, as well as affections of the lungs, intestines, and urinary passages. He considered both the bark and leaves to be excellent astringents and recommended the bark boiled in milk or water for diarrhea and dysentery.[1095]

Settlers in southern Appalachia once used sweet-gum bark and melted mutton tallow for diarrhea and "flux."[1096] The Mississippi Choctaws boiled the leaves to apply to cuts and for bathing sore feet.[1097] Choctaws of Bayou Lacomb boiled the roots and combined the substance with water in which roots of pennywort (*Obolaria virginica*) had been boiled and used the mixture for a dressing on cuts and wounds.[1098] The Houmas boiled the roots for a tea applied to sore spots on the skin.[1099] Sweet gum was also a Catawba remedy, for undisclosed purposes.[1100]

The balsam from the trunk of *L. styraciflua* was admitted to the USP in 1926, under the name *American Storax*, and is still official. It is used for stimulant, expectorant, and antiseptic purposes. It should not be confused with Levant storax, which has been official since 1831.[1101]

Tansy (Tanacetum vulgare L.). This flower was introduced from Europe, and was official in the USP, 1820–1905, being employed as a stimulant, emmenagogue, and anthelmintic.[1102] Catawba Indians used it in a steam bath for sore or swollen feet or ankles. A tea made from it was taken internally for colds, female troubles, and as an abortifacient. For headache, the plant was beaten and bound on the head.[1103]

Tobacco (Nicotiana species). Since the sixteenth century, tobacco was widely celebrated in Europe as a panacea for an amazing variety of human ailments, but there is no reason to suppose that these alleged

therapeutic virtues were learned from the Indians, who first cultivated the plant. Arturo Castiglioni pointed out that in pre-Columbian
times "no special value was attributed to tobacco as a medicament,"
although he added that this affords no proof that therapeutic value
was not ascribed to tobacco.[1104] Herbert Spinden asserted that the
use of tobacco as "medicine" among the Indians was mainly shamanistic or as a charm.[1105] Such uses are widely reported for the historic
period.

The *Badianus Manuscript* lists only two medicinal uses for tobacco among the Aztecs: 1) in combination with other herbs and
substances as a diarrhea remedy, and 2) combined with salt and pepper
as an abdominal purge in "recurrent disease."[1106] It was more extensively used by the Mayas, being prescribed for asthma, bites and stings,
bowel complaints, chills and fever, convulsions, nervous complaints,
sore eyes, skin diseases, and urinary ailments.[1107] Dr. Ackerknecht
stated that tobacco was cultivated by South American tribes exclusively as a medicant against a certain fly larva which is parasitic to
the skin, but Claude Levi-Strauss reported that tobacco juice was
used as an emetic in the Guianas.[1108] Lionel Wafer, the pirate surgeon,
reported that Panamanian Indians grew tobacco only for cigars.[1109]

Monardes wrote that Spaniards were taught by the Indians to use
tobacco juice on wounds and reported that it was also used as an
antidote for arrow poison. He alleged that the plant was also good
for headaches, cold humours, expelling worms, and reducing swellings, while the leaf extract was called antiseptic and the smoke was
inhaled for breast congestion.[1110] He was not clear, however, as to
whether the Indians used tobacco for these purposes.

Hariot believed that the Carolina Indians were spared from the
"greevous diseases" of Englishmen because they smoked tobacco, but
the Indian uses of tobacco as he reported them seemed to have been
ritualistic rather than therapeutic. It was thrown into fires as an offering, cast into the wind and water to abate storms, scattered about a
fish weir to improve the catch, and offered to the air in thanksgiving
for escape from danger.[1111]

Before the sixteenth century had ended, the bulky tobacco literature
had already begun to take shape. The ease and speed with which this
plant acquired a reputation as a cure for such a wide range of ills is
astonishing when we reflect that some valuable Indian remedies were
adopted in white medicine much later. Some of the tobacco tracts

sound as if they were written as promotional literature. One, published at London in 1595 under the name of "A. C.," may be taken as representative. A decoction of tobacco, it said, could be drunk as a remedy for bad breath. It was good for headache, and, it continued, "Who hath ever found a more sovraign remedy against coughs, rheume in the stomacke, head, and eyes?" Moreover:

> It hath cured the disease called the Wolfe, the Canker, the King's evill, all old sores, wounds, tetters, broad biles, Apostumes, pricking of the fish called Vives . . . and diverse other diseases, which experience has not yet brought to light.

The brochure further recommended the application of warm leaves of tobacco for gout and in syrup "to dissolve grosse humours, to ease the hard drawing of the breath, breake an old cough or fleume, and . . . dissolution of hard swellings in the body."[1112]

Not all the literature was favorable. The "Counterblaste to Tobacco" of James I has been widely quoted for its quaint condemnation of smoking as "a custome lothsome to the eye, hatefull to the Nose, harmefull to the braine, dangerous to the Lungs, and in the blacke stinking fume thereof, nearest resembling the horrible Stigian smoke of the pit that is bottomlesse."[1113] Cotton Mather spoke with unaccustomed moderation in allowing that the plant might have some virtues, although warning that "the smoke of this plant, conveyed by the salival juice into the blood, and also the vellication which the continued use of it in snuff gives to the nerves, may lay foundations for disease in millions of unadvised people."[1114]

It is not surprising that a commodity which offered such eminent promise of quick profit would triumph over all opposition. John Rolfe found the Virginia Indians growing *N. rustica* and soon introduced (1612) the *N. tabacum* from the West Indies. From that day Virginia's economic future was made and tobacco became the basis of plantation life from Maryland to North Carolina. "Tobacco, a stinking, nauseous, and unpalatable weed," wrote an early president of William and Mary College, "is certainly an odd Commodity to make the Staple and Riches of a Country." Yet he felt compelled to add that if the effort of James I to suppress it had succeeded, the crown would have been robbed of "one of its noblest Jewels and most considerable Revenues, and the Nation of a very advantageous and important Branch of Trade."[1115] *Unguentum Nicotianae* was included in the *Pharma-*

copoeia Londinensis of 1618 and retained a prominent place in works on materia medica until recent times, although the principal use of tobacco, even at that early date, was for smoking.

Among the reports of remedial uses of tobacco by Indians in the territory now composing the United States, there is Josselyn's account that New England natives cured burns and scalds by washing with a boiled decoction of the leaves followed by application of a powder of the dried leaves. In another instance he reported that "an Indian dissolv'd a scirrhous tumour of the arm and hip with a fomentation of tobacco; applying afterwards the herb, stamp'd betwixt two stones."[1116]

In general, however, reports of the therapeutic uses of tobacco by North American Indians in the early historic period are rather sparse compared to the numerous applications of the plant by whites and suggests that white uses of tobacco did not all arise from aboriginal tutelage. The more frequent reports of curative uses of tobacco in a later period are subject to the suspicion that they may be due to the example of whites.

The medicinal use of tobacco was endorsed by Hermann Boerhaave, by several colonial almanacs, [1117] and by John Wesley. The latter recommended tobacco smoke for earache, toothache, and convulsions.[1118] Peter Kalm reported that among the numerous toothache cures used in the colonies was one which involved placing a wad of cotton in the bowl of a pipe, placing tobacco over it, and smoking it until some of the tobacco "oil" was absorbed by the cotton, which was then applied to the cavity.[1119] Romans recommended that plantation Negroes should be encouraged to chew and smoke tobacco as a protection against malaria.[1120] Nicholas R. von Rosenstein of Stockholm, in 1765, called a clyster of tobacco smoke the most efficacious remedy for worms in children.[1121] Dr. Barton sought to discharge worms by an external poultice of the pounded leaves of tobacco mixed with vinegar applied to the stomach. He used the same method to induce vomiting in persons who attempted suicide by swallowing opium.[1122]

Dr. Bigelow considered tobacco to be an active diuretic in dropsy, a palliative in dysury, and reported it used as an enema for relaxing and cathartic effects in "strangulated hernia." He reported that tobacco had been used successfully against lockjaw in the West Indies, and he claimed that a cataplasm of it applied to the stomach promoted vomiting. He cautioned, however, that "the practice of attempting to resuscitate drowned persons by injections of tobacco smoke, is undoubtedly useless and pernicious."[1123]

Tobacco has been widely used as a folk remedy in the United States and elsewhere. It was used for several therapeutic purposes by the Pennsylvania Germans.[1124] An old folk remedy which moved west from the Alleghenies to the Rockies consisted of the insertion of tobacco snuff into the nose of an expectant mother in order to induce sneezing and hasten labor.[1125] In a section of rural Ontario, snuff was sniffed into the nose to cure allergies affecting the nasal passages, such as rose fever and hay fever.[1126] In some areas, wet tobacco was applied to bee stings.[1127]

Hunter reported that Indians west of the Mississippi used tobacco in three ways. Combined with chips of water oak as a discutient, it was applied to abscesses, "gatherings," and other local inflammations. The leaves were laid warm over the affected part and kept moist by continual addition of the infusion to them. The dried leaf was applied to old ulcers, and the leaves were also steeped in bear's grease for use as an embrocation on swellings and cutaneous and eruptive diseases. This method was frequently used externally for dropsy, and an application to the abdomen was thought to act as a vermifuge.[1128]

The Menominees inhaled tobacco smoke to induce a narcotic state.[1129] The blowing of tobacco smoke into the ear for earache was reported in this century among the Chickahominys, the Mohegans, and the Malecites.[1130] Creek Indians cut up tobacco and placed it in water to make a weak tea drunk by the patient and used as a wash in cases of stomach cramps.[1131] Louisiana Choctaws blew tobacco smoke on snakebites.[1132] The Catawbas boiled a strong decoction of tobacco for sick horses.[1133] Modern Seminoles were reported using tobacco in magical practices to ward off danger and sickness, but it was also smoked for undisclosed medicinal purposes.[1134]

The dried leaves of Virginia tobacco, *Nicotiana tabacum*, were official in the USP, 1820–1905. The properties of the drug are listed as narcotic, sedative, diaphoretic, and emetic, but it is no longer used for therapeutic purposes. As a dust, it is used as an insecticide on vegetable crops, a purpose already in use before the isolation of nicotine in 1828. The latter product, a poisonous local irritant and paralyzant, is also used as an insecticide. Nicotinic acid and nicotinamide, however, are used in several pharmaceutical preparations.[1135]

Trillium (*Trillium erectum* L.), and other species of *Trillium*; bath root, beth root (corrupted from birth root), Indian balm, squaw flower, wake-robin; the last name was applied in early times to the Jack-in-the-pulpit, *Arum triphyllum* L.

The visiting botanist Frederick Pursh wrote in his journal, June 22, 1807, of the *Trillium erythrocarpum* "which flowers white and red here, & is called Bathroot, & thought to possess great power in diseases of the lungs and liver."[1136] Rafinesque reported the use of trillium by the Indians to facilitate parturition; a Dr. Lee reported it used for this purpose and for other female disorders by Indians on the shores of Lake Superior. Dr. Clapp listed six species, ascribing similar properties to all of them: sedative, astringent, somewhat tonic and alterative. They were used in hemorrhage, leucorrhea, and cutaneous affections. "I have known," he added, "a case of palpitation of the heart that was more relieved by chewing and swallowing a piece of the root than by an other means."[1137]

The Potawatomis used an infusion of the root of the large white trillium (*T. grandiflorum* Michx.) for sore nipples. The Menominees grated the raw root for a poultice to reduce eye swelling; for cramps it was grated, steeped, and drunk as a tea. For irregular menses it was similarly prepared. The drink was also taken to remove defilement entailed by intercourse during the menstrual period.[1138]

The dried rhizome and roots of *T. erectum* and other species of *Trillium* were official in the *National Formulary*, 1916–47. The drug is reported to contain saponin, starch, and a small amount of volatile oil. It was once used for astringent, tonic, alterative, and expectorant purposes, and more recently, as a uterine stimulant.[1139]

Tulip tree (Liriodendron tulipifera L.), yellow poplar. Lawson declared that an ointment made from the buds of this tree would cure scalds, inflammations, and burns, while the juice was used to cure yaws.[1140] Kalm reported that the crushed leaves were poulticed on the forehead to cure headache, and the pounded bark in dry form was fed to horses to expel worms. "Many people believe," he observed, "its roots are as efficacious against the fever as Jesuit's bark."[1141] Dr. Schöpf called the roots a febrifuge, being infused in wine for intermittents, as well as for rheumatism and arthritis. Anthelmintic powers were ascribed to the bark, while the seed was called aperient.[1142] Dr. Barton said that tulip bark was frequently used in intermittents, although he questioned the validity of its reputation as a remedy for gout and rheumatism.[1143]

Fortescue Cuming, an English visitor, was informed in 1808 that an inward decoction of the root of this tree was an infallible remedy for the bite of any snake and was moreover "a most powerful alterative, and purifier of the blood."[1144] Dr. Bigelow described the bark as a stimulating tonic and diaphoretic, which had been used successfully in intermittent fevers. In chronic rheumatism it acted as a warm sudorific.[1145] Dr. Porcher considered the leaves to be diuretic and cited Rafinesque's opinion that the seeds were laxative. During the Civil War, Porcher recommended the bark of this tree and the willow in cold infusion for the fevers of Confederate soldiers.[1146]

Loskiel reported that the fruit and root bark of this tree were "a powerful Indian specific against agues."[1147] Western Indians, according to Hunter, used an infusion of the root bark as a preventative of intermittent fevers, while the seed balls were given to children to destroy worms.[1148] The root scrapings were used as a vermifuge by modern Catawbas.[1149]

Tulip bark from *L. tulipifera* was official in the USP, 1820–82, and was used as a bitter tonic, antiperiodic, and diuretic.[1150]

Vervain (Verbena hastata L.), American blue vervain, verbena. The plant was described by Josselyn as a wound herb not inferior to the English species.[1151] Cutler said that during the Revolutionary War, when certain drugs were unobtainable, army surgeons substituted a species of verbena for an emetic and expectorant and found its operation "kind and beneficial."[1152]

The Teton Dakotas boiled the leaves of this plant to make a drink for stomachache, while the Omahas steeped the leaves for a beverage.[1153] The Menominees made a tea of the roots to clear up cloudy urine.[1154]

The dried overground plant of verbena, *V. hastata*, was official in the *National Formulary*, 1916–26, and was used as a diaphoretic and expectorant.[1155]

Violet (Viola pedata L., *V. odorata* L., and other species of *Viola*). In colonial times Indians applied the bruised leaves of an unidentified species of yellow violet to boils and painful swellings to ease pain and promote suppuration.[1156] Concerning the various violets, Bigelow wrote:

The violets are generally mucilaginous plants, and employed as demulcents in catarrh and strangury. Some of them are allied to ipecacuanha, and contain *emetin* in their substance. The *Viola pedata*, a native species retained in the Pharmacopoeia, is considered a useful expectorant and lubricating medicine in pulmonary complaints, and is given in syrup or decoction.[1157]

Two species of violet (*V. cucullata* Ait. and *V. beckwithii*) were used medicinally by the Ute Indians.[1158] The Ojibwas used a decoction of the roots of tall white violet (*V. canadensis* L.) for pains in the region of the bladder, and downy yellow violet (*V. pubescens* Ait.) for sore throat.[1159] The root of the last-named species has been used by the Potawatomis for a heart medicine. It has been the source of an extract used by whites as an emetic and alterative. The Flambeau Ojibwas used the whole plant of *V. conspersa* Reich., for a tea used in heart trouble.[1160]

The rhizome of the sweet or English violet, naturalized from Europe, contains an emetic principle and has been cultivated as a drug plant, although it has not been official. The herb of the indigenous pansy-violet, *V. pedata*, was official in the USP, 1820–70, while the introduced species, *V. tricolor*, was official only in the edition of 1883.[1161]

Wahoo (*Euonymus atropurpureus* Jacq., or *E. americanus* L.), burning bush, Indian arrowroot, spindle tree. The aboriginal name *wahoo*, attributed to both the Sioux and the Creeks, has also been applied to the winged elm (*Ulmus alata* Michx.).

The *Euonymus* was said by Lloyd to have been a long-time favorite remedy in domestic medicine. In the late nineteenth century there was a craze for it in England.[1162] Dr. Clapp ascribed laxative, diuretic, and tonic powers to this drug and reported it used with advantage in dropsy and liver affections. He added that "a quack medicine of some repute was made from it."[1163] Dr. Porcher reported similar properties in both species: emetic, discutient, and antisyphilitic. They were believed to be narcotic and the seeds were "said to be nauseous, purgative, and emetic, and are used in some places to destroy vermin in the hair."[1164]

Winnebago women drank a decoction of the inner bark of *E. atropurpureus* for uterine trouble.[1165] The Meskwakis steeped the inner bark of the trunk for an eye lotion. The fresh trunk bark was pounded into a poultice for old facial sores. Whites used it as a liver stimulant and laxative.[1166] The Mohegans made a tea of wahoo bark for use as a physic.[1167]

Dr. Claus credited the Indians with introducing this drug to the early settlers. The dried root bark of *wahoo* or *E. atropurpureus* was official in the USP, 1863–1916, and in the NF, 1916–47. It is classed as a mild purgative with a mild effect on the heart, similar to digitalis.[1168]

Water avens (Geum rivale L., and other *Geum* species). Cutler recommended a root decoction as a gargle for sore throat, and said that Canadians used the powdered root for tertian agues.[1169] Stearns was informed that South American Indians used *Geum* for intermittent fevers, esteeming it equal to Peruvian bark.[1170] The Ojibwa Indians boiled the roots of *G. strictum* Ait., for a weak decoction taken internally for soreness in the chest and for coughs.[1171] The Flambeau Ojibwas used *G. macrophyllum* Willd., as a female remedy.[1172]

The dried root of *Geum rivale* was official in the USP, 1820–82, and was used as an astringent.[1173]

Wild carrot (Daucus carota L.), Queen Anne's lace. This may be the "Beaver root" described by Hunter as resembling garden carrot, which western Indians used as a tonic.[1174] Crow Indians used a species of wild carrot for a multitude of healing and ceremonial purposes.[1175] Carrot fruit or wild carrotseed, from *D. carota*, was official in the USP, 1820–82, and was used as a diuretic, stimulant, and menstrual excitant.[1176] According to *Gray's Manual*, the species is naturalized from Europe.

Wild cherry (Prunus virginiana L., choke cherry, and *P. serotina* Ehr., wild black cherry). "No more popular bark of a native tree, excepting sassafras, is known to home medication," wrote John Lloyd of wild cherry.[1177] The above two species, though distinct, are treated as synonymous in some editions of the pharmacopeia (*e.g.*, USP, VI rev., 271).

Josselyn considered the fruit of wild cherry a good remedy for fluxes.[1178] Cutler recommended an infusion or tincture of the inner bark for jaundice.[1179] Barton ascribed bitter, astringent, narcotic, and stimulant powers to the bark, especially the root bark, and called it useful for intermittent fevers, worms, dyspepsia, consumption, "and in lumbar abscess, attended with hectic fever, and colliquative sweats."[1180] One of Barton's students, Charles Morris, wrote his dissertation on this tree.[1181] Dr. Bigelow called the bark of *P. virginiana* "undoubtedly a useful tonic, [which] appears to possess, in some degree, a narcotic and antispasmodic property."[1182]

When Captain Meriwether Lewis (whose mother was reported to be a "yarb [herb] doctor") was ill with abdominal cramps and fever on the upper Missouri, he took a mixture of choke cherry twigs boiled in water and was well the next day.[1183] For colds, the Pennsylvania Germans frequently used a tea of the outer bark of the young branches, or the inner bark, sometimes combined with the fruit, soaked in whisky. A wine made from the syrup of wild cherries was also widely used among them as a medicinal.[1184] Southern mountaineers used a tea of wild-cherry bark for measles and colds.[1185]

A warm infusion of the bark of *P. serotina* was given to Cherokee women in the first pains of childbirth.[1186] The Ojibwas used the inner bark of this species, boiled, bruised, or chewed, as an application to external sores. An infusion of the inner bark was sometimes given to relieve pains and soreness in the chest.[1187] Formerly the pounded bark was used as a poultice after amputation of frozen members.[1188] The Poncas treated diarrhea with either a decoction of the bark or an infusion of the dried and pulverized fruit.[1189] The Penobscots steeped the bark of *P. virginiana* for diarrhea and the bark of *P. serotina* for coughs. The steeped fruit of the last species was used for a bitter tonic.[1190] The Menominees used the steeped inner bark or the boiled berries of this tree for diarrhea and the pounded inner bark for a poultice on wounds. The Flambeau Ojibwas used the bark for a tea taken for coughs and colds, while the Pillagers used *P. virginiana* for lung trouble. The Potawatomis used the bark of this species for an eyewash and made a tonic drink from the berries. The same tribe used the inner bark of *P. serotina* as a seasoner in other medicines. The Meskwakis made a tea of the root bark as a sedative and stomach remedy. For its astringent quality, the bark was boiled for a rectal-douche fluid used in treating piles.[1191] The Mohegans placed the ripe fruit of *P. serotina* in a bottle and allowed it to ferment in its own juice for about a year, after which it was thought to be an excellent remedy for dysentery. For colds, the leaves were steeped together with boneset.[1192]

Wild cherry, or wild black cherry bark, from the dried stems, has been official in the USP from 1820 to the present date. It has been listed under the names of both species, *P. virginiana* and *P. serotina*. In the 1882 edition, the first was the official name, but the drug was defined as the bark of the second species. Wild cherry has appeared in several preparations of the NF since the first edition in 1888. The bark has been used as a sedative and pectoral, but wild cherry syrup has also been used as a flavoring agent.[1193]

Wild geranium (Geranium maculatum L.), alum root, crane's bill. Josselyn considered it "admirable for agues."[1194] Cutler called the root an astringent and said it was frequently used in gargles for cankerous sores in the mouth and throat.[1195] Dr. Schöpf described it as a mild astringent and vulnerary and recommended it for dysentery.[1196] In the vicinity of Fort Massac on the Ohio, André Michaux wrote in 1795, was found "the Geranium called herbe or rather Racine à Becquet which is given for Chronic Diseases during several weeks."[1197] Dr. Colden was quoted by Barton as saying that a root decoction of this plant was used in New York for dysentery. Barton emphasized its astringency and said that western Indians used it as a venereal remedy. He recommended it for gonorrhea, gleets, cholera in children, diarrhea, and "perhaps in nephritis."[1198] Dr. Bigelow considered geranium one of the best astringents.[1199] Dr. Clapp declared that "the medical references attest the high estimation in which it is held by many of the most experienced physicians."[1200] According to Dr. William Winder of Montreal, geranium was one of the favorite remedies among the Indians of Great Manitoulin Island in Lake Huron in the 1840's:

> With the Indians it is a favorite external styptic, the dried root being powdered and placed on the mouth of the bleeding vessel. It is also much used by them as a wash in leucorrhea. Internally . . . they consider it very efficacious in haemotopsis, and in this opinion they are fully sustained by Thatcher, Mease, Bigelow, and others.[1201]

The Cherokees used geranium root in decoction with wild grape (*Vitis cordifolia*) to wash the mouths of children for thrush; it was also used alone for the same purpose by blowing the chewed fiber in the mouth.[1202] The Menominees regarded geranium root as binding and used it in flux and similar intestinal ailments. The Pillager Ojibwas used it both for flux and for treating sore mouth. The Meskwakis used an infusion of the root for sore gums and pyorrhea, toothache, neuralgia, piles, and hemorrhoids. For piles a poultice of the pounded root was used. It was further used as a burn poultice and in combination with other substances, for diarrhea.[1203]

The dried rhizome of wild geranium, G. *maculatum*, was official in the USP, 1820–1916, and in the NF, 1916–36. It was used as a tonic and astringent.[1204]

Wild ginger (*Asarum canadense* L.), Canada snakeroot, colic root, colt's foot, Indian ginger. The root and leaves of wild ginger were classified by Dr. Barton as powerful emetics.[1205] Dr. Williams called the root a warm stimulant, similar to Virginia snakeroot, and believed it to be useful in low stages of fevers, nervous affections and palpitations; one doctor claimed to have cured tetanus with a decoction of this root, he reported. Williams said that a snuff made from the powdered root was useful in disorders of the head and eyes and was used for many complaints by Canadian Indians. When a party of them visited Dr. Williams at Deerfield in 1837, they were offended when he declined to accept from them a preparation of ginger root for the palpitation of the heart with which he was then afflicted.[1206] Dr. Clapp considered wild-ginger root to be diaphoretic and carminative.[1207]

Hunter reported several uses of ginger root among Indians west of the Mississippi:

> The Indian women esteem it as emmenagogue; it is also sometimes taken as an abortive. Taken into the stomach it is apt to produce pyrosis, or the water brash, and nausea. The Indians apply it externally to recent wounds to prevent their bleeding.[1208]

Wild ginger was used by the Montagnais for general medicinal purposes, while the Catawbas used the related *A. arifolium* for heart pains.[1209] The Pillagers considered it a "potato" for sick people; if they chewed the root, they could eat anything desired. The Menominis, Potawatomis, and Meskwakis all held similar beliefs, each tribe regarding the root as a seasoner to make food palatable and safe to eat. The Meskwakis also used it for throat trouble, for earache and sore ears, and in combination for lung trouble as well as stomach cramps.[1210]

The dried rhizome and roots of *Asarum canadense* were official in the USP, 1820–73, and in the NF, 1916–47. They have been used as an aromatic stimulant, carminative, tonic, and diaphoretic. Dr. Claus reported that two antibiotic substances have been isolated from this drug, one of which is "very active against Gram-positive pus-forming bacteria."[1211]

Wild lettuce (*Lactuca* species). The Menominees rubbed the milk juice from the fresh plant of *L. canadensis* L. on poison ivy eruptions. The Flambeau Ojibwas made a tea of *L. spicata* to ease lactation in women with caked breasts; the Potawatomis would not reveal their use for this plant, a common reticence among some Indians where female remedies are concerned. The Meskwakis brewed a tea from the leaves of *L. scariola* L. (syn.: *L. virosa* Ryd.), or prickly lettuce, which was given in convalescence after childbirth to hasten the flow of milk from the breasts. Whites formerly used the milk juice of this plant as a soporific and sedative, and gave it in syrup to babies for certain infant diseases.[1212]

The flowering herb of *L. virosa* (an adventive plant), under the pharmaceutical name of *Lactuca elongata*, was official in the USP, 1820–51. *Lactucarium*, the dried milk juice of *L. virosa* and other species of *Lactuca* naturalized from Europe was official from 1820–1926. These drugs were used for sedative, diuretic, and expectorant purposes.[1213]

Wild yam (*Dioscorea villosa* L.), colic root, rheumatism root. This root has been reputed to possess expectorant, diaphoretic, and, in large doses, emetic properties. It was once used in colic and by southern Negroes for muscular rheumatism.[1214] Meskwaki Indian women used this root to relieve the pains of childbirth.[1215] Mexican species of *Dioscorea* were used medicinally by the Mayas and Aztecs.[1216] The dried rhizome of *D. villosa* was official in the NF, 1916–42, and was used as a diaphoretic and expectorant.[1217]

Willow (*Salix* species). The anodyne properties of the salicin in willow have been recognized in the Old World since ancient times, as well as by the American Indians. During the eighteenth and nineteenth centuries in America, willow bark was commonly recommended as a febrifuge.[1218]

Hunter described a "green twig very common on banks of rivers and water courses" (doubtless some species of willow) which was used by western Indians in infusion for colds and asthma in order to induce perspiration. The roots were used for anthelmintic purposes and the inner bark as a febrifuge and sudorific.[1219] California Indians used willow bark tea for lumbago.[1220] Pima Indians of Arizona gave a decoction of willow leaves for fever.[1221] The Houma Indians used a decoction of the roots and bark of black willow (*S. nigra* Marsh) or *S. longipes* for fever and for feebleness attributed to "thinness of blood."[1222] The Catawbas made a root tea of water willow for swellings on the back,[1223] Chickasaw Indians used the roots of red willow for headache and sometimes for nosebleed. It was also used as an emetic "to make one feel strong and healthy." Creeks bathed in a boiled infusion of the roots to ward off fevers. The Alabamas drank and bathed in an infusion of willow roots to cure fevers. Red willow provided a fever remedy for the Natchez.[1224] The Mohegans steeped the bark of red willow (*S. lucida*) and drank the infusion to cure vomiting and remove bile from the stomach.[1225] The Penobscots smoked the bark scrapings from the same species to relieve asthma and steeped willow bark for a cold remedy. The Montagnais made a mash of red-willow bark which was bandaged to the head to relieve headache; the leaves were steeped and drunk for the same purpose.[1226] The Menominees used the roots from gall-bearing shrubs of dwarf willow (*S. humilis* Marsh) for spasmodic colic, dysentery, and diarrhea. The Pillager Ojibwas used the bark of bog willow (*S. pedicellaris* Pursh) for stomach trouble. The bark of *S. lucida* was used by the same band as an external remedy for sores and by the Flambeau band as a styptic. *S. fragilis* L. was used for similar purposes. The Potawatomis boiled the root bark of pussy willow (*S. discolor* Muhl.) and other willows for a tea used to stop bleeding. The Meskwakis used a root tea of *S. humilis* in an enema for flux.[1227]

The bark of *S. alba* L., indigenous to Europe but naturalized in North America, and of *S. nigra* Marsh, a native tree, has been used in medicine as an astringent. *Salicin*, the well-known pain killer, which is present in all willows, was official in the USP, 1882–1926, and NF, 1936–55.[1228] Aspirin and other synthetic substitutes have become popular since the late years of the previous century.

Wintergreen (Chimaphila, Gaultheria, Moneses, and *Pyrola* species;

see also *Pipsissewa*). "They are excellent wound herbs," wrote Josselyn of the *Pyrola* species, some of which were known in Europe.[1229] The Indians ate wintergreen berries, reported Carver, "esteeming them very balsamic, and invigorating to the stomach." Moreover, the people inhabiting the interior of the colonies made a diet drink of the sprigs and berries "for cleansing the blood from scorbutick disorders."[1230] *Pyrola floribus* was called rheumatism weed by Cutler because it is said to have been considered by the Indians as an effective remedy in rheumatism."[1231] Dr. Barton said that he had used strong infusions of "mountain tea" (*Gaultheria procumbens*) which was "evidently possessed of a stimulant and anodyne quality." It was reported useful in asthma and was a principal article in the materia medica of the Indian tribes.[1232] This species, also known as checkerberry, was used for tea by Thoreau's Indian guide.[1233] Samuel Thomson combined it with hemlock in a decoction used for dropsy.[1234]

The spotted wintergreen (*C. maculata* Pursh, or *P. maculata* L.), according to Porcher, was considered by the Indians to be of universal efficacy, but was used especially in nephritic, scrofulous, and rheumatic disorders. It had been recommended for obstinate ulcers and cutaneous eruptions. *G. procumbens* was considered stimulant, aromatic, astringent, and anodyne and was used for dysentery, ammenorrhea, the promotion of mammary secretions, toothache, and as a flavoring agent. During the Revolutionary War, it had been a substitute for tea.[1235] The shin-leaf (*P. rotundifolia*), Dr. Clapp declared, was used with other *Pyrola* species by Indians and empirics as sudorifics, astringents, and nervines in coughs and diseases of the breast.[1236]

Wintergreens were used as a stomachic by the Onondagas.[1237] Mohegans steeped the leaves of *P. elliptica* and used the liquid as a gargle for sores and cankers in the mouth. The Montagnais boiled the roots of this species for a drink taken for weakness and "back sickness." Leaves of *P. uliginosa* were boiled in water to be taken for any kind of ailment. This tribe also steeped *Moneses uniflora* (L.) Gray, to make a medicine for paralysis.[1238] Rheumatism was treated with the tea from the leaves of *G. procumbens* by the Potawatomis, Menominees, and Ojibwas. The Potawatomis also took this tea for fevers and lumbago.[1239]

The wintergreens were once important folk remedies. "The aspirin which is so popular today," wrote Dr. Alvarez, "is first cousin to the smelly oil of wintergreen which our grandmothers used to put on flannel and tie around our aching joints." [1240] Gaultheria oil was once an important ingredient in proprietary medicines[1241] and has been used to flavor soft drinks.

The dried leaves of *G. procumbens* L. (wintergreen, teaberry, or checkerberry), were official in the USP, 1820–94. *Spotted wintergreen* was official from 1831–42. Gaultheria oil, wintergreen oil, or methyl salicylate, obtained by distillation from *Gaultheria* plants, has been official from 1820 to the present time. *Gaultheria* and its products are considered to be stimulant, diuretic, and astringent. A methyl salicylate which is produced either synthetically or by maceration and distillation of either *Gaultheria* or *Betula* (birch) leaves has been official since 1894. It is called a local irritant, antiseptic, antirheumatic, and a flavor.[1242]

Witch hazel (*Hamamelis virginiana* L.). The white man's debt to the American aborigines for the medicine derived from this shrub was acknowledged by Dr. Colden in a letter to John Frederick Gronovius of Leyden in 1744:

> I shall tell you what I learn'd of the use of the Hamamelis from a Minister of the Church of England who officiats among the Mohawk Indians. He saw an allmost total blindness occasioned by a blow cur'd by receiving the Warm Stream of a Decortion [*sic*] of the Bark of this Shrub through a Funnel upon the place this was don by direction of a Mohawk Indian after other means had for a considerable time prov'd ineffectual. I have since experienc'd the benefit of it used in the same manner in an Inflammation of the eye from a blow.[1243]

The Reverend Cutler declared that "the Indians considered this tree as a valuable article in their *materia medica*," and listed its several uses by them:

> They applied the bark, which is sedative and discutient, to painful tumors and external inflammations. A cataplasm of the inner rind of the bark, is found to be very efficacious in removing painful inflammations of the eyes. The bark chewed in the mouth is, at first, somewhat bitter, very sensibly astringent, and then leaves a pungent, sweetish, taste, which will remain for a considerable time.[1244]

Porcher, Williams, and Clapp confirmed Indian usage of this drug in their reports on indigenous medical plants to the American Medical Association, 1849–52. They credited it with anodyne, sedative, astringent, tonic, and discutient properties and reported its use in the control of internal hemorrhage, piles, suppressed menses, pains in the side, and eye inflammation.[1245]

Smith reported that the Menominee Indians of Wisconsin learned the uses of witch hazel from their neighbors, the Stockbridge Indians, an immigrant Mohican group from Massachusetts. A decoction of it was rubbed on the legs of participants in games to keep them limbered up. The twigs were steeped for a decoction to cure lame back. The Potawatomis used witch hazel in sweat baths, placing the twigs in water and creating steam with hot rocks, to relieve sore muscles.[1246]

Hamamelis leaves were official in the USP, 1882–1916, and in the NF, 1916–55. The bark and twigs were official in the USP, 1906–16. These parts were used for astringent and hemostatic purposes. Distilled witch hazel extract (USP 1905–26; NF 1888–1905, 1926—) has been used as an astringent and is rubbed on the body to relieve congestions, bruises, hemorrhoids, etc.[1247] A compound medicine of witch hazel, stramonium leaves, and other ingredients is sold by one pharmaceutical company as a "soothing, palliative ointment for temporary relief of pain from hemorrhoids."[1248]

Wormwood (*Artemisia* species), sagebrush. (See also *Sage*). When Maximilian of Wied was on the upper Missouri in 1833, he reported that a Gros Ventre woman, who had cut off one joint of her little finger as a sign of mourning, held the bleeding stump wrapped in a handful of wormwood leaves.[1249] Several species of *Artemisia* and related plants have been used by western Indians for a variety of medicinal purposes.[1250] The Potawatomis of Forest County, Wisconsin, introduced the *Artemisia frigida* Willd., into their area from the west for use as a medicinal. The foliage and flowers were used as a fumigant to revive a comatose patient, the fumes being directed into the nostrils by a paper cone.[1251]

Although the native species of *Artemisia* have not been official drugs, *A. frigida* is used as a source of camphor (USP 1820 to date). The official *A. absinthium* (USP 1831–1905; NF 1916–26) was obtained from Europe.[1252]

Yarrow (*Achillea millefolium* L.), milfoil. This plant belongs to a family native to the northern hemisphere, but botanists say that this species is naturalized from Europe. It was considered indigenous to this continent, however, by Josselyn and Brickell.[1253] It has been widely used by Indians since early times. A report dating from 1724 relates that yarrow was used on cuts by the Illinois and Miami tribes.[1254]

Piute Indians made a tea of yarrow to be taken internally for weak and disordered stomachs, and their white neighbors used it as a bitter.[1255] The Ute name of this plant signifies "wound medicine" and they applied it externally on bruises, etc., and used it as a tea in sickness.[1256] The Winnebagos used an infusion of yarrow to bathe swellings and treat earache.[1257] Among the Chickasaws it was a remedy for cramp in the neck.[1258] The Meskwakis boiled yarrow to bathe "some place on the body that is ailing" and used the leaves and flowers of the indigenous *A. lanulosa* Nutt., for fevers and ague. The leaves were also used as a poultice for rash in children, and the fresh tops were rubbed on eczema sores. Pillager Ojibwas used the florets for ceremonial smoking and as a fumigant to break fever. The Potawatomis used them for a fumigant to ward off evil spirits and to revive a comatose patient. The Flambeau Ojibwas used the leaves of *A. lanulosa* for a poultice on spider bites.[1259] The Montagnais steeped *A. millefolium* for a fever medicine,[1260] and the Micmacs used it as a sweat herb to cure colds.[1261]

Dr. Clapp called yarrow a mild aromatic astringent, the leaves being superior to the flowers, and the American plant more active than the European. It was used in diarrhea, leucorrhea, passive hemorrhages, and dyspepsia.[1262] The dried leaves and flowering tops of yarrow, *A. millefolium*, were official in the USP, 1863–82. They were used for tonic, stimulant, and emmenagogue purposes.[1263]

Yellow dock (*Rumex crispus* L., and other species of *Rumex*). This plant, and its relative, bitter dock (*R. obtusifolius* L.), are naturalized European weeds. They are among the few adventive plants adopted by some of the Indians and used along with native species of *Rumex*.

Cutler declared that the Indians used the root of water dock (*R. floribus*, now *R. verticillatus* L.) with great success in cleansing foul ulcers, and that they endeavored to keep it a secret from the Europeans.[1264] Choctaws sought to ward off smallpox by bathing in a decoction of leaves of this species.[1265] The "common dock" was a jaundice remedy among the Chickasaws, probably because of its yellow flowers.[1266] The Teton Dakotas bound the crushed green leaves of *R. crispus* to boils to bring suppuration.[1267] The roots, which contain tannin, were used by the Flambeau Ojibwas for closing and healing cuts.[1268] The Pimas used canaigre root (*R. hymenosepalus* Torr.) as a remedy for sore lips and sore throat.[1269] The same root was used as a diarrhea remedy by the Wichitas and Pawnees.[1270] The Houmas used the roots of the native *R. mexicana*, according to varying colors, for liver trouble, intestinal disorders, jaundice, and regulation of menstruation.[1271] The Meskwaskis boiled the root of *R. brittanica* L., for a poison antidote, while the Potawatomis used the same article for a blood purifier.[1272]

R. obtusifolius was official in the USP, 1820–1905, while *R. crispus* was listed in the USP, from 1863–1905, and in the NF, 1916–36. At one time they were used for treatment of skin diseases and for alterative and depurative purposes; later they were used as laxatives and tonics.[1273]

Yellow jasmine or *jessamine* (*Gelsemium sempervirens* of several authors), evening trumpet flower. Some writers declared that the properties of this plant were discovered by accident in 1821 when the servant of a southern planter gave the wrong medicine to his master who was suffering from fever.[1274] John Brickell, however, had much to say about the virtues of "Yellow-Jessamine" nearly a century earlier:

> The Flowers are an excellent perfume, an Oil made of them with Oil of Olive is of excellent use in Convulsions, Cramps, and Stitches in the side. The Flowers are of the nature of *Camomile*, and are good in all hard and cold swellings, in Clysters, help the Collick and pains of the Womb, and cure the Schirrus thereof, help delivery, Coughs, shortness of breath, Pleurisies, pain of the Stomach and Bowels.[1275]

Although Brickell frequently acknowledged that he obtained knowledge of various simples from the Indians, he did not indicate whether they used this plant.

398

This remedy was first employed extensively by eclectics, but was official in the USP, 1863–1926, and in the NF, 1926–55. The drug, used in powdered form, was said to have a depressant effect on the central nervous system. Its properties are described as antispasmodic, nervine, sedative, and mydriatic.[1276]

Yellow root (*Zanthorhiza apiifolia* L'Her.). The name yellow root has also been given to the more northerly golden seal (*Hydrastis canadensis, q.v.*). *Zanthorhiza* is a shrub of the southern states and Mexico. Dr. Barton described it as a bitter-tasting root bark and tonic.[1277] Dr. Porcher called it a bitter tonic similar to quassia and colombo and reported its use as a dye by the Indians.[1278]

A decoction of the root of this plant was used in childbirth by the Cherokee.[1279] Their white neighbors made a tea of the roots for sore throat and stomach disorders, a remedy said to be borrowed from the Indians.[1280] The Catawbas boiled the root for jaundice, ulcerated stomach, colds, and sore mouth. A piece of the green or dried root was chewed to "relieve the stomach." Its virtue was thought to reside in its bitterness.[1281]

The rhizome and roots of yellow root, *Z. apiifolia*, were official in the USP, 1820–82, and were used as a tonic.[1282]

Yerba santa (*Eriodictyon californicum* [Hooker et Arnott] Torrey, syn.: *E. glutinosum*), holy herb, mountain balm. This plant, an evergreen shrub indigenous to the mountains of California and northern Mexico, was long used by Indians. Edward Palmer wrote in 1878 that it was "a great medicine among the Indians of Southern Utah, Arizona, and California." A decoction of it was taken internally for rheumatism and partial paralysis or applied externally. For lung affections the dry leaves were chewed or smoked, or a tea made from them was taken internally.[1283] Others have reported the use of this plant by Indians for bronchitis, stomach troubles, and, by Mexican tribes, for syphilis.[1284]

Yerba santa, Lloyd wrote, was brought to the attention of the medical profession in 1875 by Dr. J. H. Bundy of Colusa, California, who published an article about it in the *Eclectic Medical Journal*. Soon thereafter a pharmaceutical preparation of the plant was marketed by Parke-Davis & Co., and it eventually became an official drug[1285] in the USP, 1894–1905, 1916–47, and in the NF from 1947.

The dried leaf in powdered form has been used as a stimulating expectorant and, for its aromatic and balsamic taste, has been used to disguise the bitterness of medicines such as quinine.[1286]

American Indian Nonbotanical Remedies

This class of remedies is small, and only those which have also been used in white medicine are listed here. In each instance, it appears that the uses of these substances were discovered independently by each race. They are listed here not as a demonstration of cultural borrowing but as examples of aboriginal discovery.

Alum. A mineral substance which was listed in early foreign pharmacopeias and in the USP during the nineteenth century, alum has been used mainly as an astringent. In large doses it has been considered cathartic.[1287] In modern times it has been used in preparing a diphtheria toxoid.[1288] In popular medicine it has been used with honey as a sore-throat remedy, [1289] and combined with copperas to cure sore mouth in horses.[1290] William Byrd believed that spring water impregnated with alum "dos wonders for those that are afflicted with Dropsy."[1291]

The *Wapeih* (Alg., "white") mentioned by Hariot in 1588 as "a kinde of earth so called by the naturall inhabitants" was probably alum. He compared it to *"terra Sigillata,"* and reported that after refinement "it hath beene found by some of our Phisitions and Chirurgeons to bee of the same kinde of vertue and more effectuall. The inhabitants use it very much for the cure of sores and woundes: there is in divers places great plentie, and in some places of a blewe sort."[1292] William Strachey mentioned Indian reports of "allam mines and copper" in Virginia.[1293]

Alum combined with herbs was used in wound treatment by the Chickasaws.[1294] Houma Indians added it to the roots of trumpet vine to make a gargle for diphtheria.[1295] California Indians used alum "in the form of a crude native salt leached or shaken from the roots of several plants" as a condiment.[1296]

Castoreum (USP 1820–82) is the pharmaceutical name for "the dried preputial follicles of the beaver, *Castor fiber,* collected in Canada, the United States, and Siberia. It contains a musklike secretion used as a fixative in perfumery."[1297] In an earlier day it was used as an emmenagogue and antispasmodic to "hysteric females."[1298] *Castoreum* was listed in the *Pharmacopoeia Londinensis* of 1618.

"From this beast," Brickell wrote of the beaver, "comes the *Castoreum*, which is it's *Stones*, the Virtues whereof are so well known that it would be needless to insert them."[1299] Josselyn reported that the "solid cods" of the beaver were "much used in physick." English women in America used the grated powder in a drought of wine "for wind in the stomach and belly; and venture many times, in such cases, to give it to women with child."[1300]

For wounds and cuts the Mohegan Indians bandaged on a piece of beaver castor and left it on overnight.[1301] Among the Penobscots beaver testicles were a panacea for female troubles. The scraped castor was often added to other medicines. Half-dried castor was placed in the nostril, on the end of a needle, to relieve congestion in measles.[1302]

Charcoal (wood charcoal, USP, 1820–1936; activated charcoal, USP, 1936–50; NF, 1950—). Dr. Bigelow called charcoal a powerful antiseptic which also counteracted offensive odors of putrescent animal and vegetable substances. It was used to purify liquids by filtration, in poultices for offensive ulcers, especially gangrene, and in bowel troubles and dysentery.[1303]

Charcoal, mainly of animal origin, was used for several therapeutic purposes by the Aztecs.[1304] Josselyn mentioned the use of "Coals of birch, pulverized and wrought with the white of an Egg to a Salve," as "a gallant Remedy for dry Scurfy-sores upon the Shins, and for bruised Wounds and Cuts."[1305] Some Indian tribes inserted finely pulverized and heated charcoal into the nostrils to check nosebleed.[1306] Hunter reported that wood soot, "fine black dust," was often given in infusion or tea to Indian children in cases of griping and bowel complaints. Sourness of the stomach was treated by a "ley from water and the ashes obtained from sound wood." Ashes from tobacco and mountain laurel were "applied with considerable advantage to ill-conditioned ulcers."[1307]

Tewa Indians of Santa Clara Pueblo poured hot water over charcoal, stirred the mixture, let it settle, then drank the water for cough and sore throat. Charcoal in water was taken for biliousness. For laryngitis, piñon charcoal was wrapped in a wet cloth which was then tied about the throat as a compress.[1308]

Iron (*Ferri sulphas*, sulphate of iron, "copperas.") This substance was official in the USP through the nineteenth century. "Ferrous Sulphate" still appears in pharmaceutical preparations. Dr. Bigelow called the official drug a tonic and astringent, and one of the most useful medicines in menorrhagia and leucorrhea.[1309]

Dr. Barton mentioned sulphate of iron as an emetic among New York Indians.[1310] Hunter reported other uses of this substance by Indians west of the Mississippi:

> From the cliffs of rocks bordering on some streams, mineralized waters much resembling a dilute solution of copperas (sulphate of iron) exude and especially in very dry weather deposit a substance which I now believe to be oxide of iron. The Indians collect it, and place much reliance on its vermifuge powers. They give it as such by simply mixing it with cold water.

It was also an ingredient in their remedy for dropsy, in which case it was combined with sourwood leaves and wild cherry bark. This mineral substance, he added, was found in considerable quantities on the Grand Saline, Vermillion, and Blue Earth rivers.[1311]

Petroleum. This product was listed in the *Pharmacopoeia Londinensis* of 1618. No fossil-oil product was included in the American pharmacopeia until 1882, when the sixth decennial revision declared:

> In accordance with the general demand of the medical profession, a new base for ointments, derived from petroleum, has been added under the title Petrolatum.[1312]

It was still listed in the sixteenth revision (1960) as white petrolatum, described as an "oleaginous ointment base."

The Seneca Indians discovered oil in America, and it is appropriate that Edwin Drake's firm which drilled the first well in western Pennsylvania in 1859 was called the "Seneca Oil Company." Charlevoix mentioned the oil springs of western New York in 1721, reporting that "the Indians make use of its water to mitigate all kinds of pains."[1313] Zeisberger wrote that Indians scooped the oil from the top of pools and used it "as a medicine in all sorts of cases for external application, thus for tooth-ache, head-ache, swelling, rheumatism, strained joints. Some also take it internally and it appears to have hurt no one in this way."[1314] In 1750, Peter Kalm was sufficiently interested in reports of oil obtained from the Seneca Indians to visit a white man who possessed some of it, and related that "the gentleman who had it in a bottle related that nothing was better for wounds than this. If a little were applied to the sore, it would heal within a short time, which he had experienced on many journeys."[1315] Dr. Colden reported that thirty-seven casks and thirty barrels of oil were shipped from the port of New York between November of 1761 and February of 1762.[1316]

Loskiel classed "Fossil oil" as one of the favorite medicines of the Indians. Besides its use in external complaints of all sorts, he reported that it would burn in a lamp and that the Indians sold it to white people at four guineas a quart.[1317] In 1792 Tobias Hirte published a short leaflet on the medicinal uses of Seneca oil. [1318]

Thaddeus Mason Harris, a New England clergyman, traveling in western Pennsylvania in 1803, reported that "Seneca Indian Oil" was held in high repute in that vicinity as a medicine, being regarded as an "infallible specific" for chilblains and rheumatism.[1319] In 1807, "Seneca Oil" collected from Oil Creek, a tributary of the Allegheny, was being sold at $1.50 to $2.00 a gallon.[1320]

The well-known American writers on materia medica during this period were silent concerning the medical value of petroleum. However, the Scottish physician, William Cullen, declared petroleum "in every form ... a very disagreeable remedy, and I have never found its powers to be so considerable as to compensate that inconveniency."[1321]

Water (USP 1820—). Water has been included in the pharmacopeia as a solvent for some drugs. In former times Wesley and others prescribed cold water as a therapeutic agent for many ailments. The Indians have done likewise.

Carolina tribes are reported to have used cold water as a rheumatism remedy.[1322] Montagnais Indians applied it to burns.[1323] Ritualistic use of water to ward off disease has been reported among tribes from Mexico to New York.[1324]

Indians also used spring water as a remedy for such ills as rheumatism, fevers, backache, headache, pains in the breast or stomach, and weak or sore eyes.[1325] Many springs which later became popular spas for whites, such as at Saratoga, New York, were once used by Indians for health purposes.[1326]

Indians were also prodigious bathers at a time when the practice was not customary among the whites.[1327] They always immersed themselves in a stream or lake after taking the sweat bath. Of this practice Harold Driver remarked:

> The shock experienced by plunging into cold water after the sweat bath is parallel to hydrotherapy treatments commonly used today for patients suffering from nervous tension. Therefore it was probably effective for ailments of a psychosomatic nature.[1328]

Summary

The foregoing section on botanical remedies contains 145 headings, followed by six nonbotanical entries. To my knowledge, the first list includes every plant indigenous to North America north of Mexico which has been an official drug. A minimum number of 161 species under these headings have been or are official drugs. Three others which are not official are listed because official drugs are obtained from them as by-products, and one non-official species is listed because of its importance as the source of an insecticide. Sixteen species are adventive plants which were used by the Indians, and a few more are indigenous to both hemispheres. Of six indigenous species listed, there is no positive proof of Indian usage, although it would be incorrect to conclude that Indians did not use them, because the evidence is not complete.

A considerable number of plants are incidentally mentioned because they are related to official drugs. Many more in this group could be named, and the entire list of Indian botanical remedies assembled during this study is well in excess of five hundred. It could well be expanded, and one writer has claimed that the Cherokees alone used eight hundred species.[1329]

It is difficult to give the precise number of official drugs which have been used by Indians. The pharmacopeia once said, for example, that the official drug *Trillium* consisted of the roots of *T. erectum* "or other species of trillium." Twelve species are listed in *Gray's Manual*. Likewise, *Magnolia virginiana* "or other species of magnolia" were once recognized. Ten species of magnolia are listed in Sargent's *Manual*, not counting varieties. Corn has provided four official drugs, of which Indians used three: corn smut, corn silk, corn starch, and corn oil. Both the root bark and the fiber of cotton have been official. How shall they be counted? I have credited Indians north of Mexico with the discovery of a minimum number of about 170 official drugs, but this figure is subject to revision.

Other plants used by Indians, many of them not listed here, are sources of substances which are official drugs. There are also official by-products obtained from official plants. Some of these by-products are obtained by processes not used by the Indians, but the same properties, in varying degrees, exist in the raw drug, and wherever Indian usage of a drug corresponds with what scientific research has found to be efficacious, the aborigines must be credited with the wisdom necessary to discover these uses. In many instances they do not correspond, and yet this is surely less cause for wonder than is the number which were correctly used.

Official Drugs Used by Latin-American Indians

Approximately four dozen drugs which have been or are official in the *Pharmacopeia of the United States* or the *National Formulary* were borrowed from Indian tribes occupying the West Indies and the American continents from the Rio Grande to Tierra del Fuego. We are fortunate in that many details of Aztec therapeutics are preserved in the *Badianus Manuscript* and that much of the Maya practice was preserved in texts which have been drawn upon by Ralph Roys in his *Ethno-Botany of the Maya*. An Inca codex on medicine was written about 1613 by Filepe Guáman de Ayala, and a lesser amount of information has been given by La Vega. Monardes, Hernandez, Sahagún, Oviedo, and other early writers recorded much that is of interest concerning the curative procedures of Indians in these regions. Some of the most valuable drugs were obtained, however, from the so-called "uncivilized" tribes who were not in the orbit of the three great Indian civilizations extant at the time of the discovery. To complete the list of American Indian contributions to pharmacology, it seems necessary to mention briefly those from this region, although their importance far overrides the space given to them here.

It has been said that native Mexican physicians communicated knowledge to the Spanish concerning twelve hunded plants.[1330] Hrdlička mentions the anonymously written *Rudo Ensayo* which contained accounts of native medicinal herbs and their uses among tribes of northern Mexico.[1331] Sigerist remarks that the Aztecs had

405

physicians of great experience and that the Spanish conquerors were much impressed with the medical lore of the Indians, mentioning it with much praise in all their early reports.[1332] Roys declared that Maya medicine was unhampered by theories of humors and distempers which long served as the basis of European medicine. In the Maya medical texts, he relates, are found many plants which have become official drugs, and he asserts that the Mayas anticipated modern gland therapy in cases where a nerve stimulant was required.[1333]

Of the medical discoveries of the South American Indians, Dr. Ackerknecht has written:

> Ipecac, Curare (which has made possible some of the basic discoveries in physiology) Cascara sagrada, Chenopodium, Lobelia, and Peruvian and Tolu balsam still hold an eminently honorable place in our own pharmacopeia in spite of the dominant fashion in synthetic drugs. The abundance of new drugs is commensurate with the other treasures which our culture has borrowed with important consequences from South American Indian ethnobotany—the wealth of new nutritive plants, poisons, and narcotics.[1334]

Dr. Ackerknecht further maintained that the quantity and quality of our information on South American Indian drug and herb lore has steadily decreased since the Conquest, and he charged that "the responsibility lies with our civilization itself, which unjustly underestimates the value of such studies."

Claude Levi-Strauss has declared that "few primitive people have acquired as complete a knowledge of the physical and chemical properties of their botanical environment as the South American Indian. With the exception perhaps of Cinchona bark . . .[1335] there is no species used in modern pharmacopoeia which was not familiar to the natives in pre-Columbian days. Furthermore, it is probable that only a fraction of the herbs used by modern Indians are presently known and exploited."[1336]

Some of the medicinal substances used by South American, Central American, and Caribbean Indians, such as cotton and chenopodium, were also used by Indians in the United States, and so they will not be repeated in the following list. The drugs listed below are exclusively those which have been official in the United States, and which were used by Indians for medicine, food, or economic purposes in America.

Drug List

Angostura bark or *Cusparia bark* (*Galipea officinalis*), USP 1820–1882. Aromatic bitter, stimulant, tonic, and stomachic. Angostura bark of *Cusparia trifoliata* was used by Venezuelan Indians as a fish poison. By whites it was formerly used as a febrifuge and substitute for cinchona.

Arrowroot or *Maranta* (*Maranta arundinacea* L.), USP 1820–82; as reagent, USP and NF, 1936–60. Formerly used as a convalescent nutrient, especially for children, now as a reagent. Maranta was grown as food by Arawak and Taino tribes, and the root was once used as an antidote to arrow poison. The Mayas used the root as a poultice for smallpox, and an infusion was drunk for pus in the urine.

Balsam of Copaiba, or *Copaiba.* USP 1820–1942, NF 1942–55. Derivatives: *Copaiba oil,* USP 1851–1916, *Copaiba resin,* USP 1882–1905. Genitourinary disinfectant, diuretic, stimulant, expectorant, and laxative. Copaiba was first described in 1625 by a Portuguese monk, Manoel Tristaon, as a native remedy for wounds.

Balsam of Peru, or *Peruvian balsam,* from *Myroxylon pereirae,* USP 1820–60, NF, 1960—. Local irritant and parasiticide in certain skin diseases; external antiseptic and vulnerary. Several related species of *Myroxylon* were mentioned by the Inca herbalist Ayala as remedies for fevers and infections. Other uses have been mentioned by Cobo and Böttcher.

Balsam of Tolu, from *Myroxylon balsamum,* USP 1820—. Expectorant, flavoring. In 1822 Dr. Bigelow called it useful in chronic bronchitis, asthma, and catarrh. The Spanish found the drug in use by Colombian Indians, and Monardes asserted that "it healeth all freashe woundes, comfortyng the partes, and joynyng theim without makyng any matter."

Boldo or *Boldus,* from *Boldu boldus* Molina, NF 1916–36. Aromatic stimulant, mild diuretic. The plant is an evergreen, native to Chile. Fruits and berries of related species have been used as food by certain Araucanian tribes.

Brazil wood, from *Caesalpinia echinata* Lamarck, USP 1894–1916. An extract, brazilin, is used as an indicator, like litmus. Brazil wood was used for a red dye by the Tupinamba and other South American tribes.

Capsicum or *Cayenne pepper,* from *Capsicum frutescens* L., or *C. annuum* L., USP 1820–1942, NF 1942–65. Irritant, carminative. Both species are native to tropical America. *Capsicum* was mentioned by the physician accompanying Columbus on his second voyage to America, and its medicinal virtues were praised by Monardes. It was prescribed for a variety of ailments among the Mayas, as well as by Peruvian Indians. It was grown as a condiment in pre-Columbian times by Araucanian tribes, and red pepper juice was used by Brazilian Indians to cure eye pains.

Cascarilla bark, from *Croton eluteria,* USP 1820–1905. Aromatic bitter and tonic; used in fumigating mixtures; flavoring liquors, scenting tobacco. Crushed leaves of some *Croton* species were used by the Mayas for erysipelas; other species were used for malaria, wounds, and as a diaphoretic.

Cinchona or *Peruvian bark* (from several species) , USP 1820–1942; NF 1942–55. The evidence indicates that this bark was used as a febrifuge by non-Inca tribes of Peru, and that it came into use by whites after 1630. Until derivatives and synthetics became popular, it was the chief antimalarial drug, best known for its extract, miscalled *quinine,* a name taken from a different tree.

Cinchona flava, Yellow cinchona, Calisaya bark, or *Yellow bark,* from *Cinchona calisaya* Weddell, USP 1820–94; as Cinchona, 1894–1948.
Cinchona pallida, Pale cinchona, Pale Peruvian bark, Loxa bark, or *Crown bark,* from *Cinchona officinalis* Hooker, USP 1820–82; as Cinchona 1882–1916.
Cinchona rubra, Red cinchona, Red Peruvian bark, or *Red bark,* USP 1820–1926; as Cinchona 1926–42. From *C. succiruba* Pavon.
(Twenty-seven other antimalarial official drugs, of which twenty-three are cinchona derivatives, and four synthetics, are listed in Claus, 464–67).

Coca Leaves, from *Erythroxylon coca* Lamarck, USP 1882–1916.

Derivatives: Cocaine, USP 1905–55, NF 1955—; Cocaine hydrochloride, USP 1894—. Coca was the "divine plant" of the Incas, and its leaves are chewed by South American Indians to this day. It was and is taken to give strength and endurance on journeys, to overcome hunger, and also to conquer pain. Some believe it was used as an anesthetic in pre-Columbian trephination (skull surgery). This drug was largely ignored by scientific medicine until the nineteenth century. Its active alkaloid, cocaine, was isolated in 1860, and in 1884 Carl Koller first discovered its value as a local anesthetic. Because of its powerful narcotic effects, the drug is subject to tight legal restrictions.

Cochineal or *Coccineal,* the red juice from *Coccus cacti,* an insect of tropical America, mainly used by Indians for a dye. USP 1831–1955, NF 1955—. Used as a coloring agent officially, but had wider uses in folk medicine.

Cocillana or *Guapi bark,* from *Guarea rusbyi* Britton, NF 1916–26. Cocillana is an ingredient of Cosanyl and Celmol. *Guarea* is the native name, and the species is named for Dr. H. H. Rusby, who introduced the drug to medicine. Used by South American natives as an emetic, it has been used as both an emetic and expectorant in white medicine. As an expectorant it is said to resemble ipecac in its action on the respiratory organs.

Cocoa or *Cacao butter, Theobroma oil,* from *Theobroma cacao,* USP 1863—. *Cacao* or *Powdered cocoa,* USP 1960—, NF 1916–60. Cocoa was a favorite beverage and medicinal among the Aztecs, and the name is from their language. Cacao products have nervine and stimulant properties, but are used chiefly as beverages and flavoring agents.

Condurango bark, from *Marsdenia condurango* Richenbach *filius,* NF 1916–47. A shrub of the mountainous regions of Ecuador and Peru, condurango was long used as a remedy by the Indians of that region, but was not introduced into European and North American medicine until about 1871. It is called a stomachic bitter and astringent, especially useful for diseases of the gastric mucosa.

Contrayerva, the root of *Dorstenia contrayerva* W., USP 1820–64. This plant was used in both Maya and Aztec medicine, the former using the crushed leaves as a poultice. Dr. Bigelow (1822) called the official drug a stimulant and sudorific tonic, recommended by some writers as useful in low stages of typhoid and malignant fevers.

Curare, or *South American arrow poison,* from several species of *Strychnos,* etc. USP reagent, 1916–50. Derivative: Tubocurarine chloride, USP 1950—. Von Humboldt reported that Indians on the Orinoco used curare not only as an arrow poison, but as an internal remedy for gastric derangements. Its present uses, principally as an antiparalytic drug, are described in Chapter VII, under poisons.

Damiana or *Turnera,* leaf of *Turnera diffusa* or *T. aphrodisiaca,* NF 1916–42. A shrub native of Brazil, Bolivia, Mexico, the West Indies, and California. The drug has been called stimulant and laxative, with some reputation as an aphrodisiac. Mentioned in Maya texts.

Guaiac wood or *Lignum vitae,* from *Guajacum officinale* L., or *G. sanctum* L., USP 1820–1905, NF 1916–26. *Guaiac* or *Guaiac resin,* USP 1820–1926, NF 1926–60. Derivatives: *Guaicol,* USP 1905–42, NF 1942–60; *G. carbonate,* USP 1916–36, NF 1936–46. "Guayacán" was mentioned by Oviedo in 1526 as a drug used by West Indian natives to cure syphilis. For its history in that connection see Chapter VII, under venereal disease. Wood chips and resin from guaiac wood are classed as diagnostic agents, with stimulant and diaphoretic properties. The two derivatives have been used in veterinary practice as intestinal antiseptics.

Guaraná, from the seed of *Paullina cupana* Kunth., USP–1926, NF 1926–47. Rich in caffeine, guaraná is a popular beverage among both Indians and Europeans in South America. Spruce reported in the 1850's that Brazilians considered it to be a preventative of every kind of sickness. It was also used as a remedy for fevers, nervous affections, and diarrhea. Its official use has been as a nervine, stimulant, astringent, and tonic.

Honey, USP 1820–1947, NF 1947—. (Pharmaceutical name: *Mel*). Honey was used from ancient times in both hemispheres. Honey bees were domesticated by the Aztecs and honey was prescribed for several ills in the *Badianus Manuscript.* Classed as a nutrient and demulcent, honey has been used as a vehicle similar to syrup, although it possesses more laxative action. It has also been used as a pill excipient.

Ipecac, from roots of *Cephaelis* species, USP 1820—. *Panama ipecac*, USP 1905—. The uses of this celebrated emetic were learned from Brazilian Indians by William Piso (1563–1636). Natives used it in amebic dysentery, and its alkaloid derivative, emetine, is still used for that purpose. Ipecac has also been used in treating hepatitis and as a laxative, but it is most famous for its use as an emetic.

Ipomea, Orizaba Jalap, or *Mexican Scammony*, dried root of *I. orizabensis* Led., USP 1926–36, NF 1936–65. Derivative: *Ipomea resin*, USP 1926–36, NF 1936–65. Several varieties of *Ipomea* appear in the *Badianus Manuscript*. The official drug is classed as a hydragogue cathartic.

Jaborandi or *Pilocarpus*, from several species of Brazilian shrubs, USP 1882–1916. Three additional varieties and two derivatives have been official. An aboriginal vulnerary with multiple uses in white medicine.

Jalap or *Jalap root*, from *Exogonium purga*, USP 1820–1936, NF 1936–65. *Jalap resin*, USP 1860–1936, NF 1936–65. *Compound Jalap powder*, USP 1820–1936, NF 1936–50. The Spanish colonizers learned the uses of jalap from Mexican natives and introduced it to Europe about 1565. It is classed as a hydragogue cathartic and purgative.

Krameria or *Rhatany*, root of *K. trianda* and other species, USP 1831–1916, 1926–36, NF 1916–26. The Spanish botanist Hipolita Ruiz (1784) observed native women of Lima using this drug as a tooth preservative and astringent. He introduced it to Spain. It is classed as an astringent and tonic.

Latex products: Elastica, Caoutchouc, or "India" rubber, from *Hevea* species, USP 1894–1916. Brazilian Indians were the first to use rubber and from it they fashioned the enema tube and syringe. Used pharmaceutically as a basis for plasters, and also in the manufacture of many surgical implements, syringes, and catheters.

Logwood or *Hematoxylon, H. campechianum* L., USP 1820–1916, NF 1916–36; Hematoxylin, as reagent, USP 1905–26, 1936—; NF, 1926–60. Used as an astringent and dye by Aztecs and Central American Indians. Presently used as an astringent, indicator, and stain.

Manaca, dried root of *Brunfelsia hopeana*, NF 1926–36. A Brazilian shrub. A related species, *B. grandiflora*, has been used by native

Indians for aphrodisiac and shamanistic purposes. In white medicine it has been used for rheumatism and syphilis.

Matico, the leaves of *Piper angustifolium,* USP 1863–1916, NF 1916–36. A shrub indigenous to Peru and Bolivia. Lloyd believed that the Spanish learned from the Indians its value as a styptic and astringent. It has been used in medicine for these purposes, and also as a vulnerary, stimulant, and antiseptic to the urinary tract.

Nectandra or *Bebeeru bark,* from dry bark of *N. rodiaei,* of Guyana, USP 1863–82. South American Indians used the seeds to make flour, while a bark decoction was used as a febrifuge. In white medicine the bark was used for astringent purposes.

Papain, the dried and purified latex of the fruit of *Carica papaya* L., NF 1947–50; official as reagent, USP 1955–60. The papaya, indigenous to tropical America but cultivated in Florida, was mentioned as a native food by Oviedo in 1526. Claus reports that the official drug is used as a digestant for proteins, having an action similar to pepsin. In the meat industry it is used for tenderizing ham. Papaya products are widely touted in "health food" stores. Papaya juice, sap, and shoots were used in Maya medicine.

Pareira, the root of *Chondrodendron tomentosum,* USP 1842–1916, NF 1916–36. Portuguese missionaries in Brazil learned the uses of this drug from the Indians in the seventeenth century. It was especially extolled for its value "in suppressions of urine and in nephritic and calculous complaints." (Lloyd, 1921). Claus described it as a bitter tonic, antipyretic, and diuretic.

Peanut oil, from *Arachis hypogea,* USP 1947 to date. Peanuts are native to South America and are still widely used as food by the Indians of the Andean region. In the pharmaceutical industry peanut oil is used as a vehicle in liniments, ointments, plasters, and soaps in place of olive oil. It is also used as a lubricant but its principal use is as a food oil.

Pimenta or *Allspice,* fruit of *P. officinalis,* USP 1820–1916, NF 1916–36. *Pimenta oil* or *Allspice oil,* USP 1820–1926, NF 1820–1926. A variety of this plant yields Tabasco, or Mexican allspice. Early explorers found pimenta in use as a spice in the West Indies. The fruit and oil have been used for stimulant and carminative purposes and as aromatic flavoring agents.

Quassia or *Bitterwood*, from *Quassia amara* L., and other species, USP 1820–1936, NF 1936–60. This drug is said to be named Quassia for a Negro slave in Surinam who discovered its properties as a febrifuge. There is some reason to believe he may have learned of it from the Indians. Roys was convinced that Quassia was used by the Mayas. The wood yields quassin, a tonic and stomachic which is used in dyspepsia, atonic diarrhea, and as an enema in the irritation caused by pinworms. (Dorland, 1940). Claus attributed insecticidal properties to it.

Quillaja, or *Soap bark*, USP 1882–1916, NF 1916–55. A species of *Saponaria* used by Indians of Chile and Peru as a substitute for soap. Infusions of the drug were also used as a wash. It is classed as an emulsifying agent, irritant, and expectorant.

Rue, the leaves of *Ruta graveolens* L., USP 1831–82; *Rutin*, a derivative, NF 1950–65. Although this plant is called Eurasian in *Gray's Manual*, it has been placed in the materia medica of the Aztecs (Emmart) and the Mayas (Roys). Rue and Rutin are described by Claus as capillary antihemorrhagics and vitamin P factors.

Sarsaparilla, from several species of *Smilax*, USP 1820–1955, NF 1955–65. Not to be confused with the U.S. plant, *Aralia nudicaulis*, which has also been called sarsaparilla. The root is the official part. Monardes asserted that "the Indians did use it for a great Medicine, with the whiche they did heale many and divers diseases." He further held that it healed "the Poxe." In official medicine it has been a tonic and flavoring agent.

Simaruba bark, from the root of *S. officinalis* and *S. amara*, USP 1820–73. Related species were used by the Mayas for numerous ills. In official medicine it was a bitter tonic.

Tapioca, USP 1820–82, formed by heating cassava starch. An important food of Brazilian Indians from earliest times to the present, it has been chiefly used as a nutrient for convalescents.

Tonka bean, used as adulterant of powdered vanilla; it is the source of *Coumarin*, NF 1916–60, a flavoring agent and ingredient of aromatic castor oil. A native of the Guianas, long cultivated by Indians.

Vanilla or *Vanilla bean*, fruit of *V. planifolia*, and other species native to Mexico, USP 1863–1916, 1950–60, NF 1916–50, 1960—. An element of the pharmaceutical product kaomin. Vanilla was used by the Aztecs as a flavoring for chocolate, and the plant also appears in one of the medical formulas of the *Badianus Manuscript*.[1337]

Footnotes
to
Appendix

[1] Merritt L. Fernald and Alfred C. Kinsey, *Edible Wild Plants of Eastern North America,* 132–33.

[2] *Treatise on the Materia Medica,* 135.

[3] "Report on Medical Botany," *Transactions of the American Medical Association,* V, 888–89.

[4] Claus, *Pharmacognosy,* 526.

[5] *New-England's Rarities,* 183.

[6] Beauchamp, "Onondaga Plant Names," *Journal of American Folk-Lore,* Vol. XV, No. 17 (April–June, 1902), 94.

[7] Speck, "Medicine Practices of the Northeastern Algonquians," *Proceedings XIXth International Congress of Americanists,* 309, 315.

[8] Gladys Tantaquidgeon, "Notes on the Origin and Uses of Plants of the Lake St. John Montagnais," *Journal of American Folk-Lore,* Vol. XLV, No. 176 (April–June, 1932), 266.

9 "Catawba Medicines and Curative Practices," *Publications of the Philadelphia Anthropological Society*, I, 188.

10 Huron H. Smith, *Potawatomi Ethnobotany*, 1–230.

11 *Idem, Meskwaki Ethnobotany*, 206; *Menomini Ethnobotany*, 26.

12 Mahr, "Semantic Analysis of Eighteenth-Century Delaware Indian Names for Medicinal Plants," *Ethnohistory*, Vol. II, No. 1 (Winter, 1955), 20–21.

13 *Natural History of North-Carolina*, 72.

14 *Essay Towards a Materia Medica*, Pt. II, 6.

15 "Report on the Indigenous Medical Plants of South Carolina," *Transactions of the American Medical Association*, II, 781.

16 "Report on Medical Botany," *Transactions of the American Medical Association*, V, 818–19.

17 Wooster Beach, *The American Practice Condensed*, 664.

18 Claus, *Pharmacognosy*, 235.

19 Barton, *Essay Towards a Materia Medica*, I, 9; II, 2.

20 "Report on Medical Botany," *Transactions of the American Medical Association*, V, 773–74.

21 "Report on the Indigenous Medical Plants of South Carolina," *Transactions of the American Medical Association*, II, 746.

22 Smith, *Meskwaki Ethnobotany*, 246; *Menomini Ethnobotany*, 53.

23 Claus, *Pharmacognosy*, 236.

24 Frank G. Speck, "Tadoussac-Escoumains Field Notes," MS, 1915, American Philosophical Society.

25 Smith, *Menomini Ethnobotany*, 48; *Meskwaki Ethnobotany*, 238.

26 *Idem, Ojibwe Ethnobotany*, 382–83.

27 Gilmore, "Uses of Plants by Indians of the Missouri River Region," *Thirty-third Annual Report of the Bureau of American Ethnology*, 80–82.

28 *Pharmacognosy*, 217–18.

29 *History of the Dividing Line*, I, 99.

30 *Manners and Customs*, 369.

31 *Travels*, 207.

32 Swanton, "Religious Beliefs and Medical Practices of the Creek Indians," *Forty-second Annual Report of the Bureau of American Ethnology, 1924–25*, 657.

33 Smith, *Menomini Ethnobotany*, 55.

34 "Report on Medical Botany," *Transactions of the American Medical Association*, V, 777–78.

35 *American Medicinal Plants*, I, 64.

[36] *American Root Drugs,* 51.

[37] *Pharmacognosy,* 361.

[38] *Mission of the United Brethren,* I, 114.

[39] "Contacts between Iroquois Herbalism and Colonial Medicine," *Annual Report of the Board of Regents of the Smithsonian Institution for 1941,* 524.

[40] "Report on the Indigenous Medical Plants of South Carolina," *Transactions of the American Medical Association,* II, 703.

[41] Hu Maxwell, "Indian Medicines Made from Trees," *American Forestry,* Vol. XXIV, No. 292 (April, 1918), 207.

[42] Claus, *Pharmacognosy,* 358. In 1808, this drug was the subject of an unpublished medical doctorate dissertation at the University of Pennsylvania, by Thomas G. Prioleau, of Charleston, S.C.

[43] *Travels,* II, 467–69.

[44] *The Maine Woods,* 125.

[45] Maxwell, *American Forestry,* XXIV, 209.

[46] Speck, "Medicine Practices of the Northeastern Algonquians," *Proceedings XIXth International Congress of Americanists,* 309, 315.

[47] Smith, *Ojibwe Ethnobotany,* 380.

[48] Smith, *Menomini Ethnobotany,* 46; *Potawatomi Ethnobotany,* 71.

[49] Tantaquidgeon, "Notes on the Origin and Uses of Plants of the Lake St. John Montagnais," *Journal of American Folk-Lore,* Vol. XLV, No. 176 (April–June, 1932), 266.

[50] Clapp, "Report on Medical Botany," *Transactions of the American Medical Association,* V, 875; Smith, *Potawatomi Ethnobotany,* 71.

[51] *Pharmacognosy,* 316.

[52] *The American Indian,* 120.

[53] "Catawba Medicines and Curative Practices," *Publications of the Philadelphia Anthropological Society,* I, 189.

[54] "Report on the Indigenous Medical Plants of South Carolina," *Transactions of the American Medical Association,* II, 798.

[55] "Report on Medical Botany," *Transactions of the American Medical Association,* V, 803–804.

[56] Claus, *Pharmacognosy,* 213–15.

[57] *Mission of the United Brethren,* I, 114.

[58] *Travels in the Interior of North America, 1832–1834* (Part I), Vol. XXII in Thwaites (ed.), *Early Western Travels,* 101.

[59] The various "cancer" cures reported in the eighteenth century evidently result from the fact that external, non-malignant sores were called by this name.

[60] As the text indicates, the species has been known by several different Latin names.

[61] Samuel Stearns, *American Herbal, or Materia Medica*, 51.

[62] Smith, *Meskwaki Ethnobotany*, 233.

[63] Speck, "Medicine Practices of the Northeastern Algonquians," *Proceedings XIXth International Congress of Americanists*, 310.

[64] "Report on Medical Botany," *Transactions of the American Medical Association*, V, 849.

[65] Claus, *Pharmacognosy*, 221.

[66] Smith, *Menomini Ethnobotany*, 52.

[67] *Idem, Potawatomi Ethnobotany*, 81; *Ojibwe Ethnobotany*, 387.

[68] Hoffman, "The Midē'wiwin Or 'Grand Medicine Society' of the Ojibwa," *Seventh Annual Report of the Bureau of American Ethnology, 1885–85*, 199.

[69] "Plant Names of Indian Origin," *Garden and Forest*, Vol. IX, No. 439 (July 22, 1896),293.

[70] *Joyfull Newes*, I, 13–14. The West Indian species is not *P. balsamifera.*

[71] *American Herbal*, 322.

[72] Benjamin S. Barton (ed.), *Professor Cullen's Treatise of the Materia Medica* .... 4th American ed. 2 vols. (Philadelphia. Edward Parker, 1812), II, 261.

[73] "Report on Medical Botany," *Transactions of the American Medical Association*, V, 871.

[74] Douglas, "The People of Cades Cove," *National Geographic Magazine*, CXXII, 84.

[75] Claus, *Pharmacognosy*, 172–73.

[76] *New-England's Rarities*, 199.

[77] *Manners and Customs*, 378–80.

[78] Brickell, *Natural History of North-Carolina*, 267, 399.

[79] Speck, "Medicine Practices of the Northeastern Algonquians," *Proceedings XIXth International Congress of Americanists*, 309.

[80] Tantaquidgeon, "Notes on the Origin and Uses of Plants of the Lake St. John Montagnais," *Journal of American Folk-Lore*, Vol. XLV, No. 176 (April–June, 1932), 266.

[81] Smith, *Menomini Ethnobotany*, 45.

[82] "The Midē'wiwin Or 'Grand Medicine Society' of the Ojibwa," *Seventh Annual Report of the Bureau of American Ethnology, 1885–86*, 198.

[83] Smith *Ojibwe Ethnobotany*, 378; *Potawatomi Ethnobotany*, 68–69.

[84] Boas, "Current Beliefs of the Kwakiutl Indians," *Journal of American Folk-Lore*, Vol. XLV, No. 176 (April–June, 1932), 185–87.

[85] "Report on Medical Botany," *Transactions of the American Medical Association*, V, 874.

[86] *American Practice Condensed*, 665.

[87] Will, "The Medical and Surgical Practice of the Lewis and Clark Expedition," *Journal of the History of Medicine*, Vol. XIV, No. 3 (July, 1959), 280.

[88] *The Old Root and Herb Doctor*, 43.

[89] Claus, *Pharmacognosy*, 173, 397.

[90] *Natural History of North-Carolina*, 73, 82.

[91] It will be frequently noticed that white men's claims concerning the powers of native simples were more extravagant than claims by the Indians.

[92] *The Choctaw of Bayou Lacomb*, 23.

[93] "A List of Plant Curatives Obtained from the Houma Indians of Louisiana," *Primitive Man*, Vol. XIV, No. 4 (October, 1941), 56.

[94] Swanton, "Religious Beliefs and Medical Practices of the Creek Indians," *Forty-second Annual Report of the Bureau of American Ethnology, 1924–25*, 664; Greenlee, "Medicine and Curing Practices of the Modern Florida Seminoles," *American Anthropologist*, N.S., Vol. XLVI, No. 3 (July–September, 1944), 323.

[95] *Every Man His Own Doctor, or, a Treatise on the Prevention and Cure of Diseases . . .* , 445.

[96] *Essay Towards a Materia Medica*, II, 4.

[97] Buchan, *Every Man His Own Doctor*, 445; Joseph Smith, *The Dogmaticus, or Family Physician*, 63.

[98] Clapp, "Report on Medical Botany," *Transactions of the American Medical Association*, V, 868.

[99] Claus, *Pharmacognosy*, 392.

[100] *Travels in North America*, II, 488–89.

[101] *An Essay on the Arbutus uva ursi, and Pyrola umbellata & maculata, of Linnaeus* (Philadelphia. Eaken and Mecum, 1803).

[102] *Essay Toward a Materia Medica*, I, 10; II, 49.

[103] "Report on Medical Botany," *Transactions of the American Medical Association*, V, 810–11.

[104] *Menomini Ethnobotany*, 35.

[105] Claus, *Pharmacognosy*, 190–93.

[106] *New-England's Rarities*, 185.

[107] *Natural History of North-Carolina*, 72.

[108] *Manners and Customs*, 382. "Birch beer" is still a popular southern beverage.

[109] "The Midē'wiwin Or 'Grand Medicine Society' of the Ojibwa," *Seventh Annual Report of the Bureau of American Ethnology, 1885–86*, 199.

[110] "The Aboriginal Physicians of Michigan," *Contributions to Medical Research Dedicated to Victor Clarence Vaughan*, 45.

[111] Smith, *Ojibwe Ethnobotany*, 358–59; *Potawatomi Ethnobotany*, 43–44.

[112] Robert F. Heizer, "The Use of the Enema among the Aboriginal Indian Americans," *Ciba Symposia*, Vol. V, No. 11 (February, 1944), 1686.

[113] Speck, "Medicine Practices of the Northeastern Algonquians," *Proceedings XIXth International Congress of Americanists*, 313.

[114] "Catawba Herbals and Curing Practices," *Journal of American Folk-Lore*, Vol. LVII, No. 23 (January–March, 1944), 43. He called the species "yellow birch," a name given also to other species; there is much confusion in nomenclature here.

[115] W. E. S. Folsom-Dickerson, *The White Path*, 64.

[116] Swanton, "Social and Religious Beliefs and Practices of the Chickasaw Indians," *Forty-second Annual Report of the Bureau of American Ethnology, 1924–25*, 659.

[117] *American Herbal*, 68–69.

[118] "Report on Medical Botany," *Transactions of the American Medical Association*, V, 869.

[119] Claus, *Pharmacognosy*, 328, 351.

[120] *Natural History of North-Carolina*, 91.

[121] Bigelow, *Treatise on Materia Medica*, 320; Clapp, "Report on Medical Botany," *Transactions of the American Medical Association*, V, 768–69; Porcher, "Report on the Indigenous Medical Plants of South Carolina," *Transactions of the American Medical Association*, II, 732–33.

[122] Beach, *American Practice Condensed*, 670. See also 201, note 230.

[123] Speck, "Catawba Herbals and Curing Practices," *Journal of American Folk-Lore*, Vol. LVII, No. 23 (January–March, 1944), 45.

[124] "Social and Religious Beliefs and Practices of the Chickasaw Indians," *Forty-second Annual Report of the Bureau of American Ethnology, 1924–25*, 664.

[125] Boas, "Current Beliefs of the Kwakiutl Indians," *Journal of American Folk-Lore*, Vol. XLV, No. 176 (April–June, 1932), 185.

[126] Smith, *Menomini Ethnobotany*, 50; *Potawatomi Ethnobotany*, 79; *Ojibwe Ethnobotany*, 386; *Meskwaki Ethnobotany*, 243.

[127] Claus, *Pharmacognosy*, 64, 235.

[128] *Travels Through the Interior Parts*, 480–81.

[129] *Mission of the United Brethren*, II, 116.

[130] *Manners and Customs*, 375–76.

[131] Smith, *Meskwaki Ethnobotany*, 216.

[132] Gilmore, "Uses of Plants by Indians of the Missouri River Region," *Thirty-third Annual Report of the Bureau of American Ethnology, 1911–12*, 134.

[133] *Essay Towards a Materia Medica*, II, 52.

[134] Clapp, "Report on Medical Botany," *Transactions of the American Medical Association*, V, 891.

[135] *American Root Drugs*, 17–18.

[136] Claus, *Pharmacognosy*, 157.

[137] *New-England's Rarities*, 171.

[138] *Travels in North America*, II, 606.

[139] *Travels*, 288.

[140] *Essay*, I, 32.

[141] "Report on Medical Botany," *Transactions of the American Medical Association*, V, 883.

[142] Gilmore, "Uses of Plants by Indians of the Missouri River Region," *Thirty-third Annual Report of the Bureau of American Ethnology, 1911–12*, 72.

[143] Smith, *Meskwaki Ethnobotany*, 224; *Ojibwe Ethnobotany*, 371; *Potawatomi Ethnobotany*, 60.

[144] Speck, "Tadoussac-Escoumains Field Notes," MS, 1915.

[145] *Idem*, "Medicine Practices of the Northeastern Algonquians," *Proceedings XIXth International Congress of Americanists*, 309, 311, 315.

[146] Claus, *Pharmacognosy*, 383.

[147] Henkel, *American Root Drugs*, 23.

[148] Barton, *Essay*, I, 28; II, 22–26, 55.

[149] A candidate for a medical degree at New York University declared after experiments, that "intermitting and remitting fevers . . . may as effectually be cured by this indigenous product of our own country as by the bark of Peru." Andrew Anderson, *An Inaugural Dissertation on the Eupatorium Perfoliatum of Linnaeus*, 53.

[150] Schöpf, *Materia Medica Americana*, 121.

[151] "Report on Medical Botany," *Transactions of the American Medical Association*, V, 791–92.

[152] "Report on the Indigenous Medical Plants of South Carolina," *Transactions of the American Medical Association*, II, 791–92.

[153] *Resources of the Southern Fields and Forests*, 9.

[154] John U. Lloyd, *Origin and History of all the Pharmacopeial Vegetable Drugs, Chemicals and Preparations*, 137.

[155] *Treatise on Materia Medica*, 175.

[156] "Report on the Indigenous Medical Botany of Massachusetts," *Transactions of the American Medical Association*, II, 894.

[157] Frederick Pursh, *Journal of a Botanical Excursion in the Northeastern Parts of the States of Pennsylvania and New York during the Year 1807*, 23, 53.

[158] *Journal of Travels*, Vol. XIII in Thwaites (ed.), *Early Western Travels*, 244.

[159] Fenton, "Contacts between Iroquois Herbalism and Colonial Medicine," *Annual Report of the Board of Regents of the Smithsonian Institution for 1941*, 524.

[160] Tantaquidgeon, "Mohegan Medicinal Practices, Weather-Lore, and Superstition," *Forty-third Annual Report of the Bureau of American Ethnology, 1925–26*, 265.

[161] Swanton, "Religious Beliefs and Medical Practices of the Creek Indians," *Forty-second Annual Report of the Bureau of American Ethnology, 1924–25*, 658.

[162] Folsom-Dickerson, *The White Path*, 64.

[163] Huron H. Smith's informant thought that its use was acquired from the white man. Smith himself erroneously believed that "Eupatorium is nowhere official in the white man's medicine." *Menomini Ethnobotany*, 30.

[164] *Idem, Meskwaki Ethnobotany*, 214.

[165] Stevenson, "Ethnobotany of the Zuñi Indians," *Thirtieth Annual Report of the Bureau of American Ethnology, 1908–1909*, 50; see also p. 122, herein.

[166] Claus, *Pharmacognosy*, 216–17.

[167] *Ibid.*, 217; Clapp, "Report on Medical Botany," *Transactions of the American Medical Association*, V, 791; Millspaugh, *American Medicinal Plants*, I, 78–2.

[168] Boas, "Current Beliefs of the Kwakiutl Indians," *Journal of American Folk-Lore*, Vol. XLV, No. 176 (April–June, 1932), 185.

[169] From the literature it frequently appears that when Indians are reluctant to give details about a medicine, it is a gynecological remedy.

[170] Smith, *Menomini Ethnobotany*, 36.

[171] Claus, *Pharmacognosy*, 196.

[172] *Origin and History*, 179–80.

[173] Gilmore, "Uses of Plants by Indians of the Missouri River Region," *Thirty-third Annual Report of the Bureau of American Ethnology, 1911–12*, 135.

[174] Smith, *Meskwaki Ethnobotany*, 211.

[175] *Idem, Ojibwe Ethnobotany*, 363; *Potawatomi Ethnobotany*, 49.

[176] Henkel, *American Root Drugs*, 64–65.

[177] Claus, *Pharmacognosy*, 77.

[178] Schöpf, *Materia Medica Americana*, 30.

[179] *Essay*, I, 30; II, 41–43, 56.

[180] *American Medicinal Plants*, II, 135ff.

[181] *American Root Drugs*, 56–57.

[182] Gilmore, "Uses of Plants by Indians of the Missouri River Region," *Thirty-third Annual Report of the Bureau of American Ethnology, 1911–12*, 109.

[183] *Menomini Ethnobotany*, 25; *Meskwaki Ethnobotany*, 205.

[184] "Religious Beliefs and Medical Practices of the Creek Indians," *Forty-second Annual Report of the Bureau of American Ethnology, 1924–25*, 668.

[185] Speck, "Catawba Herbals and Curing Practices," *Journal of American Folk-Lore*, Vol. LVII, No. 223 (January–March, 1944), 44.

[186] Claus, *Pharmacognosy*, 220.

[187] *Mission of the United Brethren*, II, 113.

[188] *Essay*, I, 23, 32; II, 43–44.

[189] "Report on Medical Botany," *Transactions of the American Medical Association*, V, 864; Porcher, "Report on the Indigenous Medical Plants of South Carolina," *Transactions of the American Medical Association*, II, 760.

[190] *American Practice Condensed*, 658–59.

[191] *Menomini Ethnobotany*, 38–39; *Meskwaki Ethnobotany*, 224; *Potawatomi Ethnobotany*, 60–61.

[192] "Indian Medicine Made from Trees," *American Forestry*, Vol. XXIV, No. 292 (April, 1918), 208.

[193] *Pharmacognosy*, 221.

[194] Smith, *Ojibwe Ethnobotany*, 375.

[195] Claus, *Pharmacognosy*, 483.

[196] *Plant Drugs that Changed the World*, 167.

[197] *Origin and History*, 264–65.

[198] Maddox, *The Medicine Man*, 244–45; Claus, *Pharmacognosy*, 127–28.

[199] Eli Lilly & Co., *Catalog* (Indianapolis. January 4, 1965), 26, 59.

[200] *Natural History of North-Carolina*, 64.

[201] Kalm, *Travels in North America*, II, 544.

[202] "Report on Medical Botany," *Transactions of the American Medical Association*, V, 876; see also Bigelow, *Treatise on Materia Medica*, 322.

[203] *American Practice Condensed*, 659.

[204] Corlett, *The Medicine Man*, 322.

[205] Gilmore, "Uses of Plants by Indians of the Missouri River Region," *Thirty-third Annual Report of the Bureau of American Ethnology, 1911–12*, 63–64.

[206] *Travels in the Interior of North America, 1832–1834* (Part I), Vol. XXII in Thwaites (ed.), *Early Western Travels*, 292–93.

[207] "Social and Religious Beliefs and Practices of the Chickasaw Indians," *Forty-fourth Annual Report of the Bureau of American Ethnology, 1926–27*, 267.

[208] *Idem*, "Religious Beliefs and Medical Practices of the Creek Indians," *Forty-second Annual Report of the Bureau of American Ethnology, 1924–25*, 644, 657, 668.

[209] Hoffman, "The Midē'wiwin Or 'Grand Medicine Society' of the Ojibwa," *Seventh Annual Report of the Bureau of American Ethnology, 1885–86*, 198.

[210] Smith, *Meskwaki Ethnobotany*, 234.

[211] Claus, *Pharmacognosy*, 305.

[212] *Natural History of North-Carolina*, 70.

[213] Tantaquidgeon, "Mohegan Medicinal Practices, Weather-Lore, and Superstition," *Forty-third Annual Report of the Bureau of American Ethnology, 1925–26*, 265.

[214] Millspaugh, *American Medicinal Plants*, II, 158–2.

[215] Claus, *Pharmacognosy*, 228.

[216] A. F. Chamberlain, in Hodge (ed.), *Handbook of American Indians*, I, 275.

[217] *Natural History of North-Carolina*, 76.

[218] "Report on Medical Botany," *Transactions of the American Medical Association*, V, 867.

[219] Mooney and Olbrechts, *Swimmer Manuscript*, 200, 211.

[220] Claus, *Pharmacognosy*, 228.

[221] Gerard, *Garden and Forest*, Vol. IX, No. 236, 262.

[222] *Medical Flora*, I, 99.

[223] *American Herbal*, 110.

[224] *The Dogmaticus*, 62.

[225] "Report on the Indigenous Medical Botany of Massachusetts," *Transactions of the American Medical Association*, II, 914, citing Rafinesque.

[226] "Report on Medical Botany, *Transactions of the American Medical Association*, V, 729.

[227] Claus, *Pharmacognosy*, 153; Henkel, *American Root Drugs*, 37–38.

[228] Gilmore, "Uses of Plants by Indians of the Missouri River

Region," *Thirty-third Annual Report of the Bureau of American Ethnology, 1911–12,* 83.

[229] Smith, *Menomini Ethnobotany,* 25; *Meskwaki Ethnobotany,* 205; *Potawatomi Ethnobotany,* 43; *Ojibwe Ethnobotany,* 358.

[230] Gerard, *Garden and Forest,* Vol. IX, No. 437, 282.

[231] "The Chemical Industries of the American Aborigines," *Isis,* XXIII, 407.

[232] La Vega, *Royal Commentaries,* 43.

[233] Emmart (ed.), *Badianus Manuscript,* 252, 257, 320–21.

[234] Roys, *Ethno-Botany of the Maya,* 249.

[235] *New-England's Rarities,* 188.

[236] Alexander S. Salley, Jr., *Narratives of Early Carolina, 1650–1708,* 146.

[237] *Natural History of North-Carolina,* 396.

[238] *Materia Medica Americana,* 134.

[239] *American Herbal,* 187.

[240] *Origin and History,* 355.

[241] Douglas, "The People of Cades Cove," *National Geographic Magazine,* Vol. CXXII, No. 1 (July, 1962), 84–85.

[242] Doddridge, *Notes on the Settlement and Indian Wars,* 168.

[243] *The Old Root and Herb Doctor,* 43.

[244] *Doctors of the American Frontier,* 193.

[245] *The Herbalist,* 147.

[246] *Folk Medicine,* 151.

[247] Swanton, "Social and Religious Beliefs and Practices of the Chickasaw Indians," *Forty-fourth Annual Report of the Bureau of American Ethnology, 1926–27,* 268.

[248] *Idem,* "Religious Beliefs and Medical Practices of the Creek Indians," *Forty-second Annual Report of the Bureau of American Ethnology, 1924–25,* 665.

[249] Speck, "Catawba Herbals and Curing Practices," *Journal of American Folk-Lore,* Vol. LVII, No. 223 (January–March, 1944), 46.

[250] Stevenson, "Ethnobotany of the Zuñi Indians," *Thirtieth Annual Report of the Bureau of American Ethnology, 1908–1909,* 61–62.

[251] Ergot, a parasitic growth on the rye plant, is described by Dr. Claus as oxytocic, stimulating uterine contractions during parturition; vasoconstrictor and antihemorrhagic properties are ascribed to it. *Pharmacognosy,* 508.

[252] Claus, *Pharmacognosy,* 72, 251, 508–10, 533; Eli Lilly & Co., *Catalog,* January 4, 1965, 3, 40.

[253] Smith, *Ojibwe Ethnobotany,* 369–70.

[254] "Report on Medical Botany," *Transactions of the American Medical Association,* V, 736.

[255] Claus, *Pharmacognosy*, 479.

[256] Emily C. Davis, *Ancient Americans; The Archaeological Story of Two Continents*, 276.

[257] Roys, *Maya Ethno-Botany*, 282; Emmart (ed.), *Badianus Manuscript*, 213, note; 231.

[258] Hrdlička, *Physiological and Medical Observations*, 247.

[259] Folsom-Dickerson, *The White Path*, 65.

[260] *Materia Medica Americana*, 108.

[261] *History of the Vegetable Drugs of the Pharmacopeia of the United States*, 43–44.

[262] Claus, *Pharmacognosy*, 99, 387.

[263] *History*, 91–92, citing Rafinesque.

[264] *American Medicinal Plants*, I, 74–2.

[265] "Medicine Practices of the Northeastern Algonquians," *Proceedings XIXth International Congress of Americanists*, 310.

[266] Smith, *Ojibwe Ethnobotany*, 361, 369; *Meskwaki Ethnobotany*, 308; *Potawatomi Ethnobotany*, 58.

[267] Claus, *Pharmacognosy*, 176–78.

[268] Clapp, "Report on Medical Botany," *Transactions of the American Medical Association*, V, 750–51.

[269] Hrdlička, *Physiological and Medical Observations*, 242, 244–45; Maxwell, "Indian Medicines Made from Trees," *American Forestry*, Vol. XXIV, No. 292 (April, 1918), 208.

[270] Claus, *Pharmacognosy*, 328–29, 379.

[271] Barton, *Essay*, I, 23; Millspaugh, *American Medicinal Plants*, I, 3–6; Clapp, "Report on Medical Botany," *Transactions of the American Medical Association*, V, 718–20.

[272] Speck, "Medicine Practices of the Northeastern Algonquians," *Proceedings XIXth International Congress of Americanists*, 315.

[273] Smith, *Potawatomi Ethnobotany*, 75; *Meskwaki Ethnobotany*, 239–40.

[274] Claus, *Pharmacognosy*, 218.

[275] Holmes, *Collected Works*, IX, 341–42.

[276] Fenton, "Contacts between Iroquois Herbalism and Colonial Medicine," *Annual Report of the Board of Regents of the Smithsonian Institution for 1941*, 524.

[277] Smith, *Menomini Ethnobotany*, 54; *Meskwaki Ethnobotany*, 247.

[278] Lloyd, *Origin and History*, 180–81.

[279] *Journal of Travels into Kentucky*, Vol. III in Thwaites (ed.), *Early Western Travels*, 79.

[280] "Report on Medical Botany," *Transactions of the American Medical Association,* V, 827.

[281] Perhaps because of the changing nomenclature of this drug, there are errors in the historical sketches of it in the works of Lloyd and Claus concerning the dates of its official acceptance. The information given here is obtained from the pharmacopeias.

[282] Claus, *Pharmacognosy,* 383.

[283] Henkel, *American Root Drugs,* 59–60.

[284] *Origin and History,* 334–35.

[285] *The Dogmaticus,* 62.

[286] "Report on Medical Botany," *Transactions of the American Medical Association,* V, 806.

[287] Tantaquidgeon, "Mohegan Medicinal Practices, Weather-Lore, and Superstition," *Forty-third Annual Report of the Bureau of American Ethnology, 1925–26,* 266.

[288] Smith, *Ojibwe Ethnobotany,* 366; *Potawatomi Ethnobotany,* 54; *Meskwaki Ethnobotany,* 218.

[289] *The National Formulary of Unofficial Preparations,* 1st issue, n.p. (American Pharmaceutical Association, 1888), formulas #40, 54, 56–58, 72, 74, 81, 88, 105, 151, 430.

[290] Claus, *Pharmacognosy,* 75–76; Henkel, *American Root Drugs,* 60–61.

[291] Claus, *Pharmacognosy,* 672; Christensen and Voss, "The Histology of *Cracca Virginiana* Linné Root," *Journal of the American Pharmaceutical Association,* Vol. XXV, No. 6 (June, 1936), 519–23.

[292] *Manners and Customs,* 393.

[293] Mooney, "The Sacred Formulas of the Cherokees," *Seventh Annual Report of the Bureau of American Ethnology, 1885–86,* 325.

[294] Swanton, "Religious Beliefs and Medical Practices of the Creek Indians," *Forty-second Annual Report of the Bureau of American Ethnology, 1924–25,* 647, 658.

[295] "Report on the Indigenous Medical Plants of South Carolina," *Transactions of the American Medical Association,* II, 741. Dr. Porcher seems to be the only early writer on materia medica who commented upon the properties of this plant.

[296] *History of North Carolina,* 96.

[297] *History of the Dividing Line,* I, 80.

[298] *Travels,* I, 196; II, 606.

[299] "History of the North American Indians," *Ohio Archaeological and Historical Quarterly,* Vol. XIX, Nos. 1–2 (January and April, 1910), 51.

[300] *Mission of the United Brethren,* II, 115.

[301] *Materia Medica Americana,* 14.

302 *Essay*, I, 12; II, 19–20.

303 N. S. Davis, "Report of the Committee on Indigenous Medical Botany," *Transactions of the American Medical Association*, II, 673–74.

304 "Report on the Indigenous Medical Plants of South Carolina," *Transactions of the American Medical Association*, II, 709; *Resources of the Southern Fields and Forests*, 9.

305 Clapp, "Report on Medical Botany," *Transactions of the American Medical Association*, V, 783–84; Drake, *Systematic Treatise*, 750; Beach, *American Practice Condensed*, 652–53.

306 Brendle and Unger, *Folk Medicine of the Pennsylvania Germans*, 91.

307 Maxwell, "Indian Medicines Made from Trees," *American Forestry*, Vol. XXIV, No. 292 (April, 1918), 207.

308 *Manners and Customs*, 376.

309 Swanton, "Religious Beliefs and Medical Practices of the Creek Indians," *Forty-second Annual Report of the Bureau of American Ethnology, 1924–25*, 660.

310 Speck, "A List of Plant Curatives Obtained from the Houma Indians of Louisiana," *Primitive Man*, Vol. XIV, No. 4 (October, 1941), 55.

311 Smith, *Potawatomi Ethnobotany*, 54–55; *Ojibwe Ethnobotany*, 366–67; *Menomini Ethnobotany*, 32–33; *Meskwaki Ethnobotany*, 219.

312 Claus, *Pharmacognosy*, 222.

313 *Travels*, I, 228.

314 *Mission of the United Brethren*, II, 115.

315 Speck, "Choctaw-Creek Medicines," MS, 1904, American Philosophical Society.

316 Swanton, "Religious Beliefs and Medical Practices of the Creek Indians," *Forty-second Annual Report of the Bureau of American Ethnology, 1924–25*, 661.

317 Speck, "A List of Plant Curatives Obtained from the Houma Indians of Louisiana," *Primitive Man*, Vol. XIV, No. 4 (October, 1941), 60.

318 Smith, *Meskwaki Ethnobotany*, 207; *Menomini Ethnobotany*, 27–28.

319 Alice Henkel, *American Medicinal Flowers, Fruit, and Seeds*, 15–16; Maxwell, "Indian Medicines Made from Trees," *American Forestry*, Vol. XXIV, No. 292 (April, 1918), 208.

320 "Report on Medical Botany," *Transactions of the American Medical Association*, V, 785–86.

[321] Claus, *Pharmacognosy*, 358–60.

[322] *History of North Carolina*, 95.

[323] *Natural History of North-Carolina*, 66–67.

[324] *American Herbal*, 739.

[325] Buchan, *Every Man His Own Doctor*, 463.

[326] "Report on the Indigenous Medical Plants of South Carolina," *Transactions of the American Medical Association*, II, 758.

[327] *American Practice Condensed*, 676.

[328] Maxwell, "Indian Medicines Made from Trees," *American Forestry*, Vol. XXIV, No. 292 (April, 1918), 210.

[329] Lloyd, *Origin and History*, 338–39.

[330] *Manners and Customs*, 388.

[331] Gilmore, "Uses of Plants by Indians of the Missouri River Region," *Thirty-third Annual Report of the Bureau of American Ethnology, 1911–12*, 75–76.

[332] Speck, "Catawba Medicines and Curative Practices," *Publications of the Philadelphia Anthropological Society*, I, 191; "Catawba Herbals and Curing Practices," *Journal of American Folk-Lore*, Vol. LVII, No. 223 (January–March, 1944), 43.

[333] *Idem*, "A List of Plant Curatives Obtained from the Houma Indians of Louisiana," *Primitive Man*, Vol. XIV, No. 4 (October, 1941), 56.

[334] Swanton, "Religious Beliefs and Medical Practices of the Creek Indians," *Forty-second Annual Report of the Bureau of American Ethnology, 1924–25*, 660, 665.

[335] Tantaquidgeon, "Mohegan Medicinal Practices, Weather-Lore, and Superstition," *Forty-third Annual Report of the Bureau of American Ethnology, 1925–26*, 266.

[336] Smith, *Potawatomi Ethnobotany*, 86–87; *Menomini Ethnobotany*, 56; *Ojibwe Ethnobotany*, 392; *Meskwaki Ethnobotany*, 251.

[337] "Medicine Practices of the Northeastern Algonquians," *Proceedings XIXth International Congress of Americanists*, 311.

[338] Claus, *Pharmacognosy*, 93–94.

[339] *Ibid.*, 398; Henkel, *American Root Drugs*, 12; Lloyd, *Origin and History*, 23–24.

[340] Barton, *Essay*, I, 41.

[341] Mahr, "Semantic Analysis of Eighteenth-Century Delaware Indian Names for Medicinal Plants," *Ethnohistory*, Vol. II, No. 1 (Winter, 1955), 15.

[342] Smith, *Ojibwe Ethnobotany*, 381–82.

[343] *Pharmacognosy*, 400.

[344] Mahr, "Semantic Analysis of Eighteenth-Century Delaware In-

dian Names for Medicinal Plants," *Ethnohistory*, Vol. II, No. 1 (Winter, 1955), 14.

[345] Smith, *Ojibwe Ethnobotany*, 381–82.

[346] *American Herbal*, 148.

[347] *Essay*, II, 46.

[348] Speck, "A List of Plant Curatives Obtained from the Houma Indians of Louisiana," *Primitive Man*, Vol. XIV, No. 4 (October, 1941), 62, 64.

[349] Smith, *Ojibwe Ethnobotany*, 364; *Meskwaki Ethnobotany*, 213–14.

[350] Speck, "Catawba Medicines and Curative Practices," *Publications of the Philadelphia Anthropological Society*, I, 191.

[351] The use of three separate Latin names for daisy fleabane herein, taken from various authors, indicates the confusing nomenclature of the fleabanes. *Erigeron annuus* (L.) Pers., is also called daisy fleabane.

[352] Claus, *Pharmacognosy*, 317.

[353] *Natural History of North-Carolina*, 85.

[354] Bushnell, *The Choctaw of Bayou Lacomb*, 23.

[355] Folsom-Dickerson, *The White Path*, 63.

[356] *American Medicinal Plants*, II, 136–2.

[357] Claus, *Pharmacognosy*, 153.

[358] F. Andros, "The Medicine and Surgery of the Winnebago and Dakota Indians," *Journal of the American Medical Association*, Vol. I, No. 4 (August 4, 1883), 117.

[359] Gifford S. Nickerson, "Some Data on Plains and Great Basin Uses of Certain Native Plants," *Tebiwa*, Vol. IX, No. 1 (1966), 46.

[360] Youngken, "Drugs of the North American Indian," *American Journal of Pharmacy*, Vol. XCVII, No. 97 (March, 1925), 160. The species indicated was *Allium brevistylum* S. Wats.

[361] Tantaquidgeon, "Mohegan Medicinal Practices, Weather-Lore, and Superstition," *Forty-third Annual Report of the Bureau of American Ethnology, 1925–26*, 269.

[362] Doddridge, *Early Settlement and Indian Wars*, 168–69.

[363] Douglas, "The People of Cades Cove," *National Geographic Magazine*, Vol. CXXII, No. 1 (July, 1962), 84.

[364] Claus, *Pharmacognosy*, 353.

[365] "Report on Medical Botany," *Transactions of the American Medical Association*, V, 888.

[366] Several plants called "gentian" belong to other genera.

[367] *Manners and Customs*, 378. The Arapahos used the root of *Frasera speciosa* Dougl. (green gentian) for medicinal purposes.

Nickerson, "Some Data on Plains and Great Basin Indian Uses of Certain Native Plants," *Tebiwa*, Vol. IX, No. 1 (1966), 49.

[368] The name "Sampson's snakeroot" has been given both to *G. Catesbaei* and to *Psoralea psoralioides* (Walt.) Cory.

[369] Speck, "Catawba Medicines and Curative Practices," *Publications of the Philadelphia Anthropological Society*, I, 191.

[370] Douglas, "The People of Cades Cove," *National Geographic Magazine*, Vol. CXXII, No. 1 (July, 1962), 84.

[371] Claus, *Pharmacognosy*, 194–96.

[372] Millspaugh, *American Medicinal Plants*, II, 129–2.

[373] *Travels*, II, 436–37.

[374] *Letters and Papers*, IV, 405.

[375] Sir William Johnson (1715–74), fur trader among the Mohawks who was later made a baronet and appointed superintendent of Indian affairs for the northern colonies in 1756.

[376] Beauchamp (ed.), *Moravian Journals*, 113, 122–27, 132, 134, 138 153–54, 201–203, 216.

[377] Waring, *History of Medicine in South Carolina*, 109.

[378] *Mission of the United Brethren*, II, 117.

[379] Blanton, *Medicine in Virginia in the Eighteenth Century*, 31.

[380] *Travels*, II, 611.

[381] *The Secret Diary of William Byrd of Westover, 1709–12*, ed. Louis B. Wright and Marion Tinling, 275, 287.

[382] *History of the Dividing Line*, II, 65.

[383] *Travels*, 479.

[384] *American Herbal*, 155.

[385] *Some of the Vegetable Productions*, 492–93.

[386] *Essay*, I, 20.

[387] *Treatise of the Materia Medica*, II, 115.

[388] *American Medical Botany*, II, 90–95.

[389] "Report on Medical Botany," *Transactions of the American Medical Association*, V, 781.

[390] *American Root Drugs*, 49–50.

[391] Joseph C. Robert, *The Story of Tobacco in America*, 271.

[392] *Pharmacognosy*, 153–54.

[393] Fenton, "Contacts between Iroquois Herbalism and Colonial Medicine," *Annual Report of the Board of Regents of the Smithsonian Institution for 1941*, 519.

[394] Speck, "Medicine Practices of the Northeastern Algonquians," *Proceedings XIXth International Congress of Americanists*, 310.

[395] Mooney, "The Sacred Formulas of the Cherokees," *Seventh Annual Report of the Bureau of American Ethnology, 1885–86*, 326.

396 "Religious Beliefs and Medical Practices of the Creek Indians," *Forty-second Annual Report of the Bureau of American Ethnology, 1924–25*, 648, 656, 665.

397 Speck, "A List of Plant Curatives Obtained from the Houma Indians of Louisiana," *Primitive Man*, Vol. XIV, No. 4 (October, 1941), 61.

398 Smith, *Menomini Ethnobotany*, 24; *Meskwaki Ethnobotany*, 204; *Ojibwe Ethnobotany*, 356–57; *Potawatomi Ethnobotany*, 41.

399 *Travels*, 480.

400 *American Herbal*, 160.

401 "Report on Medical Botany," *Transactions of the American Medical Association*, V, 720.

402 Tantaquidgeon, "Notes on the Origin and Uses of Plants of the Lake St. John Montagnais," *Journal of American Folk-Lore*, Vol. XLV, No. 176 (April–June, 1932), 266.

403 Speck, "Medicine Practices of the Northeastern Algonquians," *Proceedings XIXth International Congress of Americanists*, 309.

404 Tantaquidgeon, "Mohegan Medicinal Practices, Weather-Lore, and Superstition," *Forty-third Annual Report of the Bureau of American Ethnology, 1925–26*, 265.

405 *Menomini Ethnobotany*, 48; *Ojibwe Ethnobotany*, 383; *Potawatomi Ethnobotany*, 74.

406 Henkel, *American Root Drugs*, 34; Claus, *Pharmacognosy*, 475–77.

407 *Manners and Customs*, 394–95.

408 Alice Henkel and G. Fred Klugh, *Golden Seal*, U.S. Department of Agriculture Bulletin No. 51, miscellaneous papers, Part VI, *passim;* Henkel, *American Root Drugs*, 31–32; Buchan, *Every Man His Own Doctor*, 437; Williams, "Report on the Indigenous Medical Botany of Massachusetts," *Transactions of the American Medical Association*, II, 872; Clapp, "Report on Medical Botany," *Transactions of the American Medical Association*, V, 722–23; Beach, *American Practice Condensed*, 657–58; Lloyd, *Origin and History*, 164–66.

409 Barton, *Essay*, II, 13–14.

410 *Pharmacognosy*, 473–75.

411 Swanton, "Religious Beliefs and Medical Practices of the Creek Indians," *Forty-second Annual Report of the Bureau of American Ethnology, 1924–25*, 664.

412 Speck, "A List of Plant Curatives Obtained from the Houma Indians," *Primitive Man*, Vol. XIV, No. 4 (October, 1941), 66.

413 Smith, *Menomini Ethnobotany*, 31; *Ojibwe Ethnobotany*, 366; *Potawatomi Ethnobotany*, 53–54; *Meskwaki Ethnobotany*, 217–18.

414 *Treatise on Materia Medica*, 346.

415 Lloyd, *Origin and History*, 158–59.

416 Claus, *Pharmacognosy*, 370–72.

417 Culley, "The California Indians: Their Medical Practices and Their Drugs," *Journal of the American Pharmaceutical Association*, Vol. XXV, No. 4 (April, 1936), 338; Shuman, "Southern California Medicine," *Annals of Medical History*, Vol. X, No. 3 (May, 1928), 221.

418 Whitebread, "The Indian Medical Exhibit of the Division of Medicine in the United States National Museum," Pub. 2582, *Proceedings of the United States National Museum*, Vol. LXVII, art. x, 21.

419 Palmer, "Plants Used by the Indians of the United States," *American Naturalist*, Vol. XII (September, 1878), 652.

420 Chamberlin, "Some Plant Names of the Ute Indians," *American Anthropologist*, N.S., Vol. XI, No. 1 (January–March, 1909), 34.

421 Gilmore, "Uses of Plants by Indians of the Missouri River Region," *Thirty-third Annual Report of the Bureau of American Ethnology, 1911–12*, 133.

422 Porcher, "Report on the Indigenous Medical Plants of South Carolina," *Transactions of the American Medical Association*, II, 735; Clapp, "Report on Medical Botany," *Transactions of the American Medical Association*, V, 765.

423 Tantaquidgeon, "Mohegan Medicinal Practices, Weather-Lore, and Superstition," *Forty-third Annual Report of the Bureau of American Ethnology, 1925–26*, 266.

424 Smith, *Ojibwe Ethnobotany*, 386; *Potawatomi Ethnobotany*, 79–80; *Meskwaki Ethnobotany*, 243.

425 *Pharmacognosy*, 235.

426 *Natural History of North-Carolina*, 78–79.

427 *Origin and History*, 353.

428 Clapp, "Report on Medical Botany," *Transactions of the American Medical Association*, V, 786.

429 *Pharmacognosy*, 175–76.

430 Speck, "Catawba Herbals and Curing Practices," *Journal of American Folk-Lore*, Vol. LVII, No. 223 (January–March, 1944), 45.

431 Smith, *Menomini Ethnobotany*, 28; *Ojibwe Ethnobotany*, 361, 384; *Meskwaki Ethnobotany*, 241; *Potawatomi Ethnobotany*, 76.

432 Boas, "Current Beliefs of the Kwakiutl Indians," *Journal of American Folk-Lore*, Vol. XLV, No. 176 (April–June, 1932), 187.

433 *Travels*, I, 257–58.

434 Fenton, "Contacts between Iroquois Herbalism and Colonial Medicine," *Annual Report of the Board of Regents of the Smithsonian Institution for 1941*, 523.

[435] Mooney and Olbrechts, *Swimmer Manuscript*, 203–204.

[436] Boas, "Current Beliefs of the Kwakiutl Indians," *Journal of American Folk-Lore*, Vol. XLV, No. 176 (April–June, 1932), 183.

[437] Taylor, *Plant Drugs that Changed the World*, 43.

[438] "Report on the Indigenous Medical Plants of South Carolina," *Transactions of the American Medical Association*, II, 837.

[439] "Report on Medical Botany," *Transactions of the American Medical Association*, V, 890; Henkel, *American Root Drugs*, 18–19; Millspaugh, *American Medicinal Plants*, II, 176ff.

[440] Claus, *Pharmacognosy*, 512–13.

[441] See pp. 84–85, herein.

[442] *New-England's Rarities*, 200–201.

[443] Hoffman, "The Midē'wiwin Or 'Grand Medicine Society' of the Ojibwa," *Seventh Annual Report of the Bureau of American Ethnology*, 1885–86, 198.

[444] Smith, *Potawatomi Ethnobotany*, 71, 84–85; *Ojibwe Ethnobotany*, 380; *Menomini Ethnobotany*, 46.

[445] Wilson D. Wallis, "Medicines Used by the Micmac Indians," *American Anthropologist*, N.S., Vol. XXIV (1922), 25.

[446] Speck, "Medicine Practices of the Northeastern Algonquians," *Proceedings XIXth International Congress of Americanists*, 309, 315.

[447] Claus, *Pharmacognosy*, 237, 397–98.

[448] Smith, *Potawatomi Ethnobotany*, 75; *Meskwaki Ethnobotany*, 239; *Menomini Ethnobotany*, 49.

[449] Mooney, "The Sacred Formulas of the Cherokees," *Seventh Annual Report of the Bureau of American Ethnology, 1885–86*, 326.

[450] Clapp, "Report on Medical Botany," *Transactions of the American Medical Association*, V, 717–18; Millspaugh, *American Medicinal Plants*, I, 2–2.

[451] Claus, *Pharmacognosy*, 218.

[452] Bigelow, *American Medical Botany*, III, 22.

[453] Jameson (ed.), *Narratives of New Netherland*, 219.

[454] Tantaquidgeon, "Mohegan Medicinal Practices, Weather-Lore, and Superstition," *Forty-third Annual Report of the Bureau of American Ethnology, 1925–26*, 266.

[455] Gilmore, "Uses of Plants by the Indians of the Missouri River Region," *Thirty-third Annual Report of the Bureau of American Ethnology, 1911–12*, 77.

[456] Smith, *Meskwaki Ethnobotany*, 244, 250; *Ojibwe Ethnobotany*, 391; *Menomini Ethnobotany*, 51.

[457] Claus, *Pharmacognosy*, 274–75.

[458] Henkel, *American Root Drugs*, 41–42.

[459] Colden, *Letters and Papers*, V, 90.

[460] Mooney and Olbrechts, *Swimmer Manuscript*, 246.

[461] Claus, *Pharmacognosy*, 223.

[462] Norman Taylor, *Narcotics: Nature's Dangerous Gifts*, 7–28. There is much confusion in the nomenclature of hemp plants. Cutler (*Vegetable Productions*, 424) calls *Asclepias foliis* by the name of Indian hemp. The same common name has been applied locally to *Abutilon avicennae* G. (Fannie Bergen, "Popular American Plant Names," *Journal of American Folk-Lore*, Vol. IX, No. 34 [July–September, 1896], 183). Beach called *A. cannabinum* Indian physic and American ipecacuanha (*American Practice Condensed*, 646). Bourke called *Cannabis indica* by the name *marijuana*, and "loco" weed, though the latter name, he said, was also given to other plants. ("Popular Medicine, Customs, and Superstitions of the Rio Grande," *Journal of American Folk-Lore*, Vol. VII, No. 25 [April–June, 1894], 120, 125, 134.)

[463] Jameson (ed.), *Narratives of New Netherland*, 219.

[464] *Origin and History*, 17–18.

[465] *The Medical Companion . . .*, 515.

[466] "Report on Medical Botany," *Transactions of the American Medical Association*, V, 846.

[467] Fenton, "Contacts between Iroquois Herbalism and Colonial Medicine," *Annual Report of the Board of Regents of the Smithsonian Institution for 1941*, 846.

[468] Speck, "Medicine Practices of the Northeastern Algonquians," *Proceedings XIXth International Congress of Americanists*, 310.

[469] Smith, *Potawatomi Ethnobotany*, 38; *Ojibwe Ethnobotany*, 355; *Meskwaki Ethnobotany*, 201.

[470] Claus, *Pharmacognosy*, 380–82. "*Cannabis Americana*," Dr. Claus wrote, was recognized in a separate USP monograph in 1870 and 1880, then dropped, and again restored, 1916–42.

[471] Millspaugh, *American Medicinal Plants*, II, 148–50.

[472] *History of the Dividing Line*, I, 85, 139.

[473] *Secret Diary*, 132–33, 196, 385.

[474] *Natural History of North-Carolina*, 47.

[475] *Journal of Travels into Kentucky*, in Vol. III, Thwaites (ed.), *Early Western Travels*, 77.

[476] *Essay*, I, 27.

[477] *Manners and Customs*, 380.

[478] Mahr, *Ethnohistory*, II, 13.

[479] Mooney, "The Sacred Formulas of the Cherokees," *Seventh Annual Report of the Bureau of American Ethnology, 1885–86*, 326.

[480] Porcher, "Report on the Indigenous Medical Plants of South Carolina," *Transactions of the American Medical Association,* II, 735–36; Clapp, "Report on Medical Botany," *Transactions of the American Medical Association,* V, 765–66.

[481] Claus, *Pharmacognosy,* 472; Henkel, *American Root Drugs,* 42–43.

[482] Gerard, *Garden and Forest,* IX, 303.

[483] *Travels,* I, 67, 260–61.

[484] *Travels,* 484–85.

[485] *Mission of the United Brethren,* I, 116.

[486] Mahr, *Ethnohistory,* II, 13–14.

[487] Beauchamp, "Onondaga Plant Names," *Journal of American Folk-Lore,* Vol. XV, No. 17 (April–June 1902), 102.

[488] *Some of the Vegetable Productions,* 407.

[489] *Essay,* I, 21; II, 29–30.

[490] *Manners and Customs,* 380.

[491] *Medical Flora,* I, 69.

[492] *The Old Root and Herb Doctor,* 44.

[493] "Report on Medical Botany," *Transactions of the American Medical Association,* V, 877.

[494] Gilmore, "Uses of Plants by Indians of the Missouri River Region," *Thirty-third Annual Report of the Bureau of American Ethnology, 1911–12,* 69.

[495] Speck, "Medicine Practices of the Northeastern Algonquians," *Proceedings XIXth International Congress of Americanists,* 310.

[496] Smith, *Ojibwe Ethnobotany,* 356; *Menomini Ethnobotany,* 23; *Meskwaki Ethnobotany,* 202.

[497] Bushnell, *The Choctaw of Bayou Lacomb,* 23.

[498] Claus, *Pharmacognosy,* 534; Henkel, *American Root Drugs,* 13–14.

[499] *Some of the Vegetable Productions,* 473.

[500] "Report on Medical Botany," *Transactions of the American Medical Association,* V, 761–62.

[501] Swanton, "Religious Beliefs and Medical Practices of the Creek Indians," *Forty-second Annual Report of the Bureau of American Ethnology, 1924–25,* 658.

[502] Tantaquidgeon, "Mohegan Medicinal Practices, Weather-Lore, and Superstition," *Forty-second Annual Report of the Bureau of American Ethnology, 1925–26,* 266.

[503] *Meskwaki Ethnobotany,* 228.

[504] Henkel, *American Root Drugs,* 43–44; Claus, *Pharmacognosy,* 222.

[505] Clapp, "Report on Medical Botany," *Transactions of the American Medical Association*, V, 845–46; Bergen, "Popular American Plant Names," *Journal of American Folk-Lore*, Vol. IX, No. 34 (July–September, 1896), 190.

[506] *Natural History*, 21.

[507] *Letters and Papers*, II, 282–83; V, 217.

[508] *East and West Florida*, 162.

[509] *Essay*, I, 27.

[510] "Report on Medical Botany," *Transactions of the American Medical Association*, V, 861–62.

[511] *American Medicinal Plants*, II, 149.

[512] Swanton, "Religious Beliefs and Medical Practices of the Creek Indians," *Forty-second Annual Report of the Bureau of American Ethnology, 1924–25*, 661.

[513] Mooney, "The Sacred Formulas of the Cherokees," *Seventh Annual Report of the Bureau of American Ethnology, 1885–86*, 325; Mooney and Olbrechts, *Swimmer Manuscript*, 179–80.

[514] Speck, "A List of Plant Curatives Obtained from the Houma Indians of Louisiana," *Primitive Man*, Vol. XIV, No. 4 (October, 1941), 66.

[515] Gilmore, "Uses of Plants by Indians of the Missouri River Region," *Thirty-third Annual Report of the Bureau of American Ethnology, 1911–12*, 99.

[516] *Physiological and Medical Observations*, 232.

[517] Palmer, "Plants Used by the Indians of the United States," *American Naturalist*, Vol. XII (October, 1878), 651.

[518] Smith, *Ojibwe Ethnobotany*, 369; *Meskwaki Ethnobotany*, 221.

[519] Claus, *Pharmacognosy*, 384–85, 472–73.

[520] Fernald (ed.), *Gray's Manual of Botany*, 673. *I. pandurata* has also been called wild sweet potato and *mechoacanna*, the name of another Mexican drug. Fanny Bergen, "Popular American Plant Names," *Journal of American Folk-Lore*, Vol. VII, No. 25 (April–June, 1894), 95.

[521] Quoted in Swanton, "Religious Beliefs and Medical Practices of the Creek Indians," *Forty-second Annual Report of the Bureau of American Ethnology, 1924–25*, 670.

[522] *Mission of the United Brethren*, I, 116.

[523] Claus, *Pharmacognosy*, 374–75.

[524] Gilmore, "Uses of Plants by Indians of the Missouri River Region," *Thirty-third Annual Report of the Bureau of American Ethnology, 1911–12*, 110.

[525] Bourke, "Popular Medicine, Customs, and Superstitions of the Rio Grande," *Journal of American Folk-Lore*, Vol. VII, No. 25 (April–June, 1894), 125.

[526] Clapp, "Report on Medical Botany," *Transactions of the American Medical Association*, V, 851.

[527] Roys, *Ethno-Botany of the Maya*, 262.

[528] Henkel, *American Medicinal Flowers*, 4–5.

[529] *New-England's Rarities*, 178–79.

[530] *Travels*, I, 86.

[531] *East and West Florida*, 170.

[532] "Report on Medical Botany," *Transactions of the American Medical Association*, V, 852, under name of *Aristolochia anthelmintica* Spach.

[533] Swanton, "Religious Beliefs and Medical Practices of the Creek Indians," *Forty-second Annual Report of the Bureau of American Ethnology, 1924–25*, 657.

[534] Speck, "Catawba Herbals and Curing Practices," *Journal of American Folk-Lore*, Vol. LVII, No. 223 (January–March, 1944), 45.

[535] Scott, *A History of Tropical Medicine*, II, 851–52.

[536] Claus, *Pharmacognosy*, 344–45.

[537] Safford, "Narcotic Plants and Stimulants of the Ancient Americans," *Annual Report of the Board of Regents of the Smithsonian Institution for the Year Ending June 30, 1916*, 408, citing Robert Beverley.

[538] Emmart (ed.), *Badianus Manuscript*, 253, note 1.

[539] Donald T. Atkinson, *Magic, Myth, and Medicine*, 95.

[540] Emmart (ed.), *Badianus Manuscript*, 253, note 1, Safford, *op cit.*, 406.

[541] Lawson, *History of North Carolina*, 79; Brickell, *Natural History*, 21.

[542] Blanton, *Medicine in Virginia in the Eighteenth Century*, 184.

[543] *The Christian Philosopher*, 148.

[544] *Travels*, I, 81.

[545] Benjamin Rush, "An Account of the Effects of Strammonium, or Thorn Apple," *Transactions American Philosophical Society*, I, 2d ed. corrected (1789), 385–86.

[546] *Some of the Vegetable Productions*, 419.

[547] *Treatise of the Materia Medica*, II, 200–201.

[548] *Essay*, I, 17; II, 27–28, 48–49, 51.

[549] *American Herbal*, 47.

[550] Koch and Peden, *Writings of Thomas Jefferson*, 629.

[551] "Report on the Indigenous Medical Plants of South Carolina," *Transactions of the American Medical Association*, II, 820–22.

[552] "Report on Medical Botany," *Transactions of the American Medical Association*, V, 840.

438

553 Safford, "Narcotic Plants and Stimulants of the Ancient Americans," *Annual Report of the Board of Regents of the Smithsonian Institution for the Year Ending June 30, 1916*, 387–88, 405–407. See also Arturo Castiglioni, "Magic Plants in Primitive Medicine," *Ciba Symposia*, V, Nos. 5–6 (August–September, 1943), 1538–39.

554 "Rappahannock Field Notes," MS, 1940, American Philosophical Society,

555 Speck, "Catawba Herbals and Curing Practices," *Journal of American Folk-Lore*, Vol. LVII, No. 223 (January–March, 1944), 47.

556 Stevenson, "Ethnobotany of the Zuñi Indians," *Thirtieth Annual Report of the Bureau of American Ethnology, 1908–1909*, 46–47.

557 Palmer, "Plants Used by the Indians of the United States," *American Naturalist*, Vol. XII (September, 1878), 650.

558 Bourke, "The Medicine-Men of the Apache," *Ninth Annual Report of the Bureau of American Ethnology, 1887–88*, 455. Bourke called the plant *D. Stramonium*, probably in error. See also Corlett, *The Medicine Man*, 320.

559 Margaret B. Kreig, *Green Medicine*, 93, 96.

560 Lloyd, *Origin and History*, 324.

561 Safford, "Narcotic Plants and Stimulants of the Ancient Americans," *Annual Report of the Board of Regents of the Smithsonian Institution for the Year Ending June 30, 1916*, 408.

562 *Ibid.*, 388; Claus, *Pharmacognosy*, 450–52; Henkel, *American Medicinal Flowers*, 13.

563 Eli Lilly & Co., *Catalog*, January 4, 1965, 63.

564 Williams, "Report on the Indigenous Medical Botany of Massachusetts," *Transactions of the American Medical Association*, II, 894.

565 *Materia Medica Americana*, 120.

566 *The Family Doctor, or Guide to Health*, 115.

567 "Report on the Indigenous Medical Botany of Massachusetts," *Transactions of the American Medical Association*, II, 894.

568 "Report on Medical Botany," *Transactions of the American Medical Association*, V, 790–91.

569 Fenton, "Contacts between Iroquois Herbalism and Colonial Medicine," *Annual Report of the Board of Regents of the Smithsonian Institution for 1941*, 524; Mooney, "The Sacred Formulas of the Cherokees," *Seventh Annual Report of the Bureau of American Ethnology, 1885–86*, 327.

570 Speck, "A List of Plant Curatives Obtained from the Houma Indians of Louisiana," *Primitive Man*, Vol. XIV, No. 4 (October, 1941), 64. Fernald, in *Gray's Manual of Botany* (1950), applies the name of Joe Pye weed to four of the twenty-six species of *Eupatoria* listed therein.

[571] Smith, *Potawatomi Ethnobotany*, 52; *Ojibwe Ethnobotany*, 364; *Menomini Ethnobotany*, 30; *Meskwaki Ethnobotany*, 214.

[572] Claus, *Pharmacognosy*, 217; Henkel, *American Root Drugs*, 61–62.

[573] Clapp, "Report on Medical Botany," *Transactions of the American Medical Association*, V, 876.

[574] *Journal of a Botanical Excursion*, 56.

[575] Corlett, *The Medicine Man*, 320.

[576] "Current Beliefs of the Kwakiutl Indians," *Journal of American Folk-Lore*, Vol. XLV, No. 176 (April–June, 1932), 185.

[577] Claus, *Pharmacognosy*, 290–91; Henkel, *American Medicinal Flowers*, 2–3.

[578] *History of the Vegetable Drugs*, Lloyd Library Bulletin No. 18, 34.

[579] *Travels*, II, 611.

[580] "Report on the Indigenous Medical Plants of South Carolina," *Transactions of the American Medical Association*, II, 835–36.

[581] "Report on the Indigenous Medical Botany of Massachusetts," *Transactions of the American Medical Association*, II, 907.

[582] "Report on Medical Botany," *Transactions of the American Medical Association*, II, 880–81.

[583] Mooney, "The Sacred Formulas of the Cherokees," *Seventh Annual Report of the Bureau of American Ethnology, 1885–86*, 327.

[584] Speck, "Medicine Practices of the Northeastern Algonquians," *Proceedings XIXth International Congress of Americanists*, 310.

[585] Smith, *Menomini Ethnobotany*, 44; *Ojibwe Ethnobotany*, 377.

[586] Claus, *Pharmacognosy*, 218–19; Henkel, *American Root Drugs*, 23–24.

[587] Barton, *Essay*, I, 36.

[588] *Letters and Papers*, V, 215–17, 262.

[589] Lloyd, *Origin and History*, 185.

[590] *American Herbal*, 108.

[591] *Materia Medica Americana*, 128.

[592] *Essay*, I, 36–40; II, 56, 59; see also Bigelow, *Treatise on Materia Medica*, 248–49. Bigelow added rheumatism to the list of ailments relieved by lobelia.

[593] *Origin and History*, 184–85. One source said there was traditionary evidence of its use by Penobscots.

[594] *Medical Flora*, II, 23–25.

[595] "Report on the Indigenous Medical Plants of South Carolina," *Transactions of the American Medical Association*, II, 786.

[596] Clapp, "Report on Medical Botany," *Transactions of the American Medical Association*, V, 807–809.

[597] Fenton, "Contacts between Iroquois Herbalism and Colonial Medicine," *Annual Report of the Board of Regents of the Smithsonian Institution for 1941*, 522.

[598] Morris Mattson, *American Vegetable Practice* (Boston, 1841), cited in Lloyd, *Origin and History*, 184–85.

[599] "Folk Materia Medica," *Journal of American Folk-Lore*, Vol. XIV (1901), 113–14.

[600] "Religious Beliefs and Medical Practices of the Creek Indians," *Forty-second Annual Report of the Bureau of American Ethnology, 1924–25*, 662.

[601] Smith, *Meskwaki Ethnobotany*, 231–32.

[602] Claus, *Pharmacognosy*, 433–34.

[603] *Histoire de la Louisiane*, II, 36.

[604] Waring, *Medicine in South Carolina*, 259.

[605] *Travels*, I, 109–10.

[606] *Ibid.*, 110.

[607] *East and West Florida*, 160.

[608] *Materia Medica Americana*, 91.

[609] *Journal of Travels into Kentucky*, in Vol. III, Thwaites (ed.), *Early Western Travels*, 143.

[610] *Essay*, I, 13–14; II, 20–21.

[611] *Manners and Customs*, 394.

[612] Bushnell, *Choctaw of Bayou Lacomb*, 23.

[613] "Choctaw-Creek Medicines," MS, 1904.

[614] *Idem*, "A List of Plant Curatives Obtained from the Houma Indians of Louisiana," *Primitive Man*, Vol. XIV, No. 4 (October, 1941), 56.

[615] Claus, *Pharmacognosy*, 222.

[616] Smith, *Ojibwe Ethnobotany*, 390; *Meskwaki Ethnobotany*, 249; *Menomini Ethnobotany*, 55.

[617] *The Dogmaticus*, 61.

[618] Claus, *Pharmacognosy*, 360.

[619] *New Voyages*, I, 368.

[620] Brickell, *The Natural History of North Carolina*, 23.

[621] Catesby, *The National History of Carolina, Florida and the Bahama Islands*, I, 24.

[622] Beauchamp (ed.), *Moravian Journals*, 38, 109n.

[623] *Materia Medica Americana*, 86.

[624] "A Botanical Description of the Podophyllum Diphyllum, of Linnaeus . . . ," *Transactions of the American Philosophical Society*, O.S., III, 344–45.

625 *Essay,* I, 31, 39–40.

626 "Report on the Indigenous Medical Plants of South Carolina," *Transactions of the American Medical Association,* II, 687–88; see also Bigelow, *Treatise on Materia Medica,* 295–96.

627 Mahr, *Ethnohistory,* II, 21–23.

628 *Manners and Customs,* 381.

629 Kreig, *Green Medicine,* 299.

630 Smith, *Menomini Ethnobotany,* 26; *Meskwaki Ethnobotany,* 206.

631 Robert A. Hatcher, *Useful Drugs,* 170.

632 Claus, *Pharmacognosy,* 365–67; *U. S. Pharmacopeia,* XVI (1969), 551–53; Lloyd, *Origin and History,* 248–56; Henkel, *American Root Drugs,* 39–40.

633 Emmart (ed.), *Badianus Manuscript,* plate 15, 218; Gerard, "Plant Names of Indian Origin," *Garden and Forest,* Vol. IX, Nos. 435–36, 438–40 (1896), 283.

634 "Popular Medicine, Customs, and Superstitions of the Rio Grande," *Journal of American Folk-Lore,* Vol. VII, No. 25 (April–June, 1894), 125– 26.

635 Hrdlička, *Physiological and Medical Observations,* 237, 242, 245, 247–48; Maxwell, "Indian Medicines Made from Trees," *American Forestry,* Vol. XXIV, No. 292 (April, 1918), 210–11.

636 Carlson and Jones, "Some Notes on Uses of Plants by the Comanche Indians," *Papers of the Michigan Academy of Sciences, Arts and Letters,* Vol. XXV (1939), 523.

637 Claus, *Pharmacognosy,* 55–56.

638 "Report on the Indigenous Medical Plants of South Carolina," *Transactions of the American Medical Association,* II, 829.

639 "Report on Medical Botany," *Transactions of the American Medical Association,* V, 847.

640 *Manners and Customs,* 381.

641 Gilmore, "Uses of Plants by Indians of the Missouri River Region," *Thirty-third Annual Report of the Bureau of American Ethnology, 1911–12,* 110.

642 Swanton, "Religious Beliefs and Medical Practices of the Creek Indians," *Forty-second Annual Report of the Bureau of American Ethnology, 1924–25,* 667–68.

643 Speck, "Catawba Herbals and Curing Practices," *Journal of American Folk-Lore,* Vol. LVII, No. 223 (January–March, 1944), 44.

644 Smith, *Ojibwe Ethnobotany,* 357; *Potawatomi Ethnobotany,* 42; *Meskwaki Ethnobotany,* 205.

645 Claus, *Pharmacognosy,* 220.

[646] *Travels*, 486.

[647] Smith, *Menomini Ethnobotany*, 39; *Ojibwe Ethnobotany*, 372.

[648] Douglas, "The People of Cades Cove," *National Geographic Magazine*, Vol. CXXII, No. 1 (July, 1962), 85.

[649] *American Practice Condensed*, 663.

[650] Claus, *Pharmacognosy*, 358.

[651] Clapp, "Report on Medical Botany," *Transactions of the American Medical Association*, V, 833.

[652] "The Medicine and Surgery of the Winnebago and Dakota Indians," *Journal of the American Medical Association*, Vol. I, No. 4 (August 4, 1883), 118.

[653] Speck, "Catawba Herbals and Curing Practices," *Journal of American Folk-Lore*, Vol. LVII, No. 223 (January–March, 1944), 45.

[654] Swanton, "Religious Beliefs and Medical Practices of the Creek Indians," *Forty-second Annual Report of the Bureau of American Ethnology, 1924–25*, 657.

[655] Smith, *Meskwaki Ethnobotany*, 226–27.

[656] *Treatise on Materia Medica*, 261–62.

[657] Claus, *Pharmacognosy*, 320–21.

[658] Myers, *Narratives of Early Pennsylvania*, 348.

[659] Lloyd, *Origin and History*, 162–63.

[660] Beauchamp, "Onondaga Plant Names," *Journal of American Folk-Lore*, Vol. XV, No. 17 (April–June, 1902), 97.

[661] *History of the Dividing Line*, I, 162–63.

[662] *Primitive Physic*, 92.

[663] *Travels*, I, 103.

[664] *Materia Medica Americana*, 6.

[665] Swanton, "Social and Religious Beliefs and Practices of the Chickasaw Indians," *Forty-fourth Annual Report of the Bureau of American Ethnology, 1926–27*, 268.

[666] Tantaquidgeon, "Mohegan Medicinal Practices, Weather-Lore, and Superstition," *Forty-third Annual Report of the Bureau of American Ethnology, 1925–26*, 265.

[667] Speck, "Catawba Medicines and Curative Practices," *Publications of the Philadelphia Anthropological Society*, I, 188.

[668] Hrdlička, *Physiological and Medical Observations*, 235.

[669] Gilmore, "Uses of Plants by the Indians of the Missouri River Region," *Thirty-third Annual Report of the Bureau of American Ethnology, 1911–12*, 112.

[670] Claus, *Pharmacognosy*, 315.

[671] Folsom-Dickerson, *The White Path*, 64.

[672] Hoffman, "The Midē'wiwin Or 'Grand Medicine Society' of

the Ojibwa," *Seventh Annual Report of the Bureau of American Ethnology, 1885–86,* 201.

673 Smith, *Ojibwe Ethnobotany,* 372; *Menomini Ethnobotany,* 39; *Meskwaki Ethnobotany,* 225.

674 Gilmore, "Uses of Plants by the Indians of the Missouri River Region," *Thirty-third Annual Report of the Bureau of American Ethnology, 1911–12,* 111.

675 Claus, *Pharmacognosy,* 321, 352; Smith, *Meskwaki Ethnobotany,* 225.

676 "Report on Medical Botany," *Transactions of the American Medical Association,* V, 829.

677 Grinnell, "Some Cheyenne Plant Medicines," *American Anthropologist,* N.S., Vol. VII, No. 1 (January–March, 1905), 39.

678 Gilmore, "Uses of Plants by the Indians of the Missouri River Region," *Thirty-third Annual Report of the Bureau of American Ethnology, 1911–12,* 112.

679 Smith, *Menomini Ethnobotany,* 39; *Ojibwe Ethnobotany,* 371–72; *Potawatomi Ethnobotany,* 61.

680 Claus, *Pharmacognosy,* 315.

681 Smith, *Potawatomi Ethnobotany,* 64; *Ojibwe Ethnobotany,* 375.

682 Speck, "Medicine Practices of the Northeastern Algonquians," *Proceedings XIXth International Congress of Americanists,* 309, 316.

683 Claus, *Pharmacognosy,* 252–53.

684 *Journal of Travels into Kentucky,* in Vol. III, Thwaites (ed.), *Early Western Travels,* 187.

685 *Account of an Expedition,* Vol. XIV in Thwaites (ed.), *Early Western Travels,* 128–29.

686 Kalm, *Travels,* I, 69.

687 Corlett, *The Medicine Man,* 320.

688 Tantaquidgeon, "Mohegan Medicinal Practices, Weather-Lore, and Superstition," *Forty-third Annual Report of the Bureau of American Ethnology, 1925–26,* 265.

689 Speck, "Medicine Practices of the Northeastern Algonquians," *Proceedings XIXth International Congress of Americanists,* 310.

690 *Idem,* "Catawba Medicines and Curative Practices," *Publications of the Philadelphia Anthropological Society,* I, 190.

691 *Idem,* "Choctaw-Creek Medicines," MS, 1904.

692 Swanton, "Religious Beliefs and Medical Practices of the Creek Indians," *Forty-second Annual Report of the Bureau of American Ethnology, 1924–25,* 660–61.

693 *Potawatomi Ethnobotany,* 84; *Menomini Ethnobotany,* 53.

694 Claus, *Pharmacognosy*, 98; Henkel, *American Medicinal Flowers*, 14–15.

695 *Pharmacognosy*, 166, 168.

696 Tantaquidgeon, "Mohegan Medicinal Practices, Weather-Lore, and Superstition," *Forty-third Annual Report of the Bureau of American Ethnology, 1925–26*, 264.

697 Smith, *Meskwaki Ethnobotany*, 319.

698 Chamberlin, "Some Plant Names of the Ute Indians," *American Anthropologist*, N.S., Vol. XI, No. 1 (January–March, 1909), 36.

699 Henkel, *American Medicinal Flowers*, 6–7.

700 Carlson and Jones, "Some Notes on Uses of Plants by the Comanche Indians," *Papers of the Michigan Academy of Sciences, Arts and Letters*, XXV, 524.

701 Speck, "A List of Plant Curatives Obtained from the Houma Indians of Louisiana, *Primitive Man*, Vol XIV, No. 4 (October, 1941), 65.

702 Speck, et al., *Rappahannock Herbals*, 34.

703 Claus, *Pharmacognosy*, 438, 440, 442.

704 *Ibid.*, 454.

705 Andrews, "The Aboriginal Physicians of Michigan," *Contributions to Medical Research Dedicated to Victor Clarence Vaughan*, 45.

706 *Manners and Customs*, 382.

707 Smith, *Meskwaki Ethnobotany*, 222; *Menomini Ethnobotany*, 36.

708 *Pharmacognosy*, 234.

709 Bigelow, *Treatise on Materia Medica*, 312.

710 "Report on Medical Botany," *Transactions of the American Medical Association*, V, 847.

711 *New-England's Rarities*, 182.

712 *Travels*, I, 128.

713 *Materia Medica Americana*, 138.

714 Fenton, "Contacts between Iroquois Herbalism and Colonial Medicine," *Annual Report of the Board of Regents of the Smithsonian Institution for 1941*, 523.

715 Speck, "Medicine Practices of the Northeastern Algonquians," *Proceedings XIXth International Congress of Americanists*, 309–10.

716 *Idem*, "A List of Plant Curatives Obtained from the Houma Indians of Louisiana,"*Primitive Man*, Vol. XIV, No. 4 (October, 1941), 56.

717 Hoffman, "The Midē'wiwin Or 'Grand Medicine Society' of the Ojibwa," *Seventh Annual Report of the Bureau of American Ethnology, 1885–86*, 198.

445

[718] Smith, *Meskwaki Ethnobotany*, 221.

[719] Heizer, "The Use of the Enema among the Aboriginal American Indians," *Ciba Symposia*, Vol. V, No. 11 (February, 1944), 1686.

[720] Claus, *Pharmacognosy*, 234.

[721] "Plants Used by the Indians of the United States," *American Naturalist*, Vol. XII (October, 1878), 650.

[722] "Current Beliefs of the Kwakiutl Indians," *Journal of American Folk-Lore*, Vol. XLV, No. 176 (April–June, 1932), 186.

[723] Henkel, *American Root Drugs*, 37.

[724] Lloyd, *Origin and History*, 31; Claus, *Pharmacognosy*, 483–84.

[725] *Natural History*, 106.

[726] Claus, *Pharmacognosy*, 484. The fruit was the official part.

[727] Speck, "Catawba Herbals and Curing Practices," *Journal of American Folk-Lore*, Vol. LVII, No. 223 (January–March, 1944), 44.

[728] *Idem*, "Medicine Practices of the Northeastern Algonquians," *Proceedings XIXth International Congress of Americanists*, 309.

[729] Claus, *Pharmacognosy*, 484.

[730] Speck, "Medicine Practices of the Northeastern Algonquians," *Proceedings XIXth International Congress of Americanists*, 309.

[731] *Menomini Ethnobotany*, 51.

[732] *The Family Doctor*, 115.

[733] "Report on Medical Botany," *Transactions of the American Medical Association*, V, 788.

[734] Claus, *Pharmacognosy*, 231.

[735] Roys, *Ethno-Botany of the Maya*, 287, 295.

[736] Emmart (ed.), *The Badianus Manuscript*, 264, citing Sahagún.

[737] Speck, "A List of Plant Curatives Obtained from the Houma Indians of Louisiana," *Primitive Man*, Vol. XIV, No. 4 (October, 1941), 63.

[738] Meyers, *The Herbalist*, 92.

[739] *Materia Medica Americana*, 131.

[740] *Pharmacognosy*, 532.

[741] Arthur Osol and George E. Farrar, Jr., *The Dispensatory of the United States of America*, 1950 Edition, 1544.

[742] *Travels in the Interior*, 194.

[743] *History of North Carolina*, 105.

[744] *Travels*, I, 69.

[745] "A Memoir on the Distillation of Persimons," *Transactions of the American Philosophical Society*, O.S., Vol. I, 2d ed. corrected, 301–304.

[746] *An Inaugural Dissertation, on the Chemical Properties of the Persimmon Tree* ... (Philadelphia, William Woodhouse, 1792).

[747] *Materia Medica Americana,* 154–55.

[748] *Essay,* I, 11; II, 53; appendix, 47.

[749] Porcher, "Report on the Indigenous Medical Plants of South Carolina," *Transactions of the American Medical Association,* II, 780–81; Clapp, "Report on Medical Botany," *Transactions of the American Medical Association,* V, 819; see also Bigelow, *Treatise on Materia Medica,* 166.

[750] Mooney and Olbrechts, *Swimmer Manuscript,* 275.

[751] Folsom-Dickerson, *The White Path,* 72.

[752] Speck, "Catawba Herbals and Curing Practices," *Journal of American Folk-Lore,* Vol. LVII, No. 223 (January–March, 1944), 46.

[753] Claus, *Pharmacognosy,* 235.

[754] *Letters and Papers,* III, 89–90.

[755] *Manners and Customs,* 385–86.

[756] Bushnell, *Choctaw of Bayou Lacomb,* 24.

[757] Swanton, "Religious Beliefs and Medical Practices of the Creek Indians," *Forty-second Annual Report of the Bureau of American Ethnology, 1924–25,* 664.

[758] *New-England's Rarities,* 198.

[759] "Report on the Indigenous Medical Botany of Massachusetts," *Transactions of the American Medical Association,* II, 921.

[760] Hoffman, "The Midē'wiwin Or 'Grand Medicine Society' of the Ojibwa," *Seventh Annual Report of the Bureau of American Ethnology, 1885–86,* 198.

[761] Tantaquidgeon, "Mohegan Medicinal Practices, Weather-Lore, and Superstition," *Forty-third Annual Report of the Bureau of American Ethnology, 1925–26,* 264.

[762] Speck, "Tadoussac-Escoumains Field Notes," MS, 1915, American Philosophical Society.

[763] Speck, "Medicine Practices of the Northeastern Algonquians," *Proceedings XIXth International Congress of Americanists,* 315.

[764] Smith, *Menomini Ethnobotany,* 46; *Potawatomi Ethnobotany,* 70; see also Maxwell, "Indian Medicines Made from Trees," *American Forestry,* Vol. XXIV, No. 292 (April, 1918), 210.

[765] Claus, *Pharmacognosy,* 410.

[766] Swanton, "Religious Beliefs and Medical Practices of the Creek Indians," *Forty-second Annual Report of the Bureau of American Ethnology, 1924–25,* 659.

[767] Speck, "Catawba Herbals and Curing Practices," *Journal of American Folk-Lore,* Vol. LVII, No. 223 (January–March, 1944), 46.

[768] *American Practice Condensed,* 665.

[769] Claus, *Pharmacognosy,* 291, 320, 329, 365, 393–95.

· 770 Bradley, "Medical Practices of the New England Aborigines," *Journal of the American Pharmaceutical Association*, Vol. XXV, No. 2 (February, 1936), 146.

771 Barton, *Essay*, I, 36–37, n.

772 *Letters and Papers*, VII, 141.

773 "An Account of the Effects of Strammonium Or Thorn Apple," *Transactions of the American Philosophical Society*, O.S., Vol. I, 2d ed. corrected, 385.

774 *East and West Florida*, 156, 160.

775 Barton, *Essay*, I, 38–39; appendix, 61–63; *Cullen's Materia Medica*, II, 413.

776 *Origin and History*, 321.

777 Henkel, *American Root Drugs*, 52–53.

778 Mooney and Olbrechts, *Swimmer Manuscript*, 214, 249.

779 Millspaugh, *American Medicinal Plants*, II, 131–2.

780 Claus, *Pharmacognosy*, 532.

781 *Dictionary of Americanisms*, 323.

782 Gerard, "Plant Names of Indian Origin," *Garden and Forest*, Vol. IX, Nos. 435–36, 438–40 (1896), 292.

783 Loskiel, *Mission of the United Brethren*, I, 116.

784 Smith, *Ojibwe Ethnobotany*, 368.

785 See p. 419, note 101, herein.

786 *Essay*, II, 2–3, 31.

787 *New Guide to Health*, 142.

788 J. W. Comfort, *The Practice of Medicine on Thomsonian Principles . . .* , 482.

789 "Report on Medical Botany," *Transactions of the American Medical Association*, V, 815–16.

790 *Southern Fields and Forests*, 10.

791 Brendle and Unger, *Folk Medicine of the Pennsylvania Germans*, 90, 155.

792 *History of the Vegetable Drugs of the Pharmacopeia of the United States*, 16.

793 *Manners and Customs*, 384.

794 Tantaquidgeon, "Mohegan Medicinal Practices, Weather-Lore, and Superstition," *Forty-third Annual Report of the Bureau of American Ethnology, 1925–26*, 265.

795 Speck, "Medicine Practices of the Northeastern Algonquians," *Proceedings XIXth International Congress of Americanists*, 316.

796 Smith, *Menomini Ethnobotany*, 35.

797 Speck, "Catawba Medicines and Curative Practices," *Publications of the Philadelphia Anthropological Society*, I, 190.

[798] Claus, *Pharmacognosy*, 193.

[799] Cutler, *Vegetable Productions*, 422–23; Brickell, *Natural History*, 96.

[800] *American Herbal*, 193.

[801] *Treatise on Materia Medica*, 377–78.

[802] *Pharmacognosy*, 655–56.

[803] Bourke, "The Medicine-Men of the Apache," *Ninth Annual Report of the Bureau of American Ethnology, 1887–88*, 472, citing Bancroft, *Native Races*, I.

[804] Smith, *Potawatomi Ethnobotany*, 38; *Meskwaki Ethnobotany*, 201.

[805] Speck, "A List of Plant Curatives Obtained from the Houma Indians of Louisiana," *Primitive Man*, Vol. XIV, No. 4 (October, 1941), 59.

[806] Smith, *Potawatomi Ethnobotany*, 42; called *I. capensis* Meerb. by Gray.

[807] *Origin and History*, 240.

[808] See p. 49, herein.

[809] Kalm, *Travels*, I, 104.

[810] Carver, *Travels*, 484; Loskiel, *Mission of the United Brethren*, I, 116.

[811] *Some of the Vegetable Productions*, 447.

[812] *Materia Medica Americana*, 71.

[813] Benjamin Shultz, *An Inaugural Botanico-Medical Dissertation on the Phytolacca Decandra of Linnaeus* . . . (Philadelphia, Thomas Dobson, 1795). He reported that the Cherokees used the powdered root for chancres, without much effect. He pronounced it an escharotic in ulcers and tumors, also emetic, cathartic, anodyne, narcotic, diaphoretic, diuretic, and "a medicine superior to any yet discovered for curing [intermittent fever]," p. 43.

[814] *Essay*, II, 27–28.

[815] "Report on Medical Botany," *Transactions of the American Medical Association*, V, 853.

[816] "Virginia Indian Folk Lore Plants," MS, *circa* 1941, American Philosophical Society.

[817] "Contacts between Iroquois Herbalism and Colonial Medicine,"*Annual Report of the Board of Regents of the Smithsonian Institution for 1941*, 523.

[818] Beauchamp, "Onondaga Plant Names," *Journal of American Folk-Lore*, Vol. XV, No. 17 (April–June, 1902), 96; Gilmore, "Uses of Plants by Indians of the Missouri River Region," *Thirty-third Annual Report of the Bureau of American Ethnology, 1911–12*, 78.

[819] Claus, *Pharmacognosy*, 155.

[820] Henkel, *American Root Drugs*, 29–30; *American Medicinal Flowers*, 5–6.

[821] *The Choctaw of Bayou Lacomb*, 24.

[822] Swanton, "Social and Religious Beliefs and Practices of the Chickasaw Indians," *Forty-fourth Annual Report of the Bureau of American Ethnology, 1926–27*, 267.

[823] *Idem*, "Religious Beliefs and Medical Practices of the Creek Indians," *Forty-second Annual Report of the Bureau of American Ethnology, 1924–25*, 660.

[824] Claus, *Pharmacognosy*, 171.

[825] *History of North Carolina*, 103.

[826] Kinietz, *Indians of the Western Great Lakes*, 225.

[827] *Natural History*, I, 26.

[828] *Travels*, 368–69, 473.

[829] *Mission of the United Brethren*, I, 115.

[830] *Materia Medica Americana*, 148.

[831] *Journal of Travels into Kentucky*, in Vol. III, Thwaites (ed.), *Early Western Travels*, 79.

[832] *History of North Carolina*, 102.

[833] Barton, *Essay*, II, 38–39; appendix, 54–55.

[834] *Journal of Travels into the Arkansa Territory*, Vol. XIII in Thwaites (ed.), *Early Western Travels*, 110.

[835] *Origin and History*, 354.

[836] *Manners and Customs*, 384.

[837] Speck, "A List of Plant Curatives Obtained from the Houma Indians of Louisiana," *Primitive Man*, Vol. XIV, No. 4 (October, 1941), 61.

[838] Swanton, "Religious Beliefs and Medical Practices of the Creek Indians," *Forty-second Annual Report of the Bureau of American Ethnology, 1924–25*, 663; Folsom-Dickerson, *The White Path*, 63.

[839] Carlson and Jones, "Some Notes on Uses of Plants by the Comanche Indians," *Papers of the Michigan Academy of Sciences, Arts and Letters*, Vol. XXV (1939), 524.

[840] Smith, *Meskwaki Ethnobotany*, 244–45; *Menomini Ethnobotany*, 51–52; *Ojibwe Ethnobotany*, 387.

[841] Charles Sprague Sargent, *Manual of the Trees of North America*, II, 636.

[842] Claus, *Pharmacognosy*, 387–88; Henkel, *American Medicinal Flowers*, 8–9; Lloyd, *Origin and History*, 354.

[843] Tyler (ed.), *Narratives of Early Virginia*, 93, 108.

[844] Byrd, *History of the Dividing Line*, I, 77.

845 Lloyd, *Origin and History*, 282–83.

846 *Travels*, 481.

847 *Mission of the United Brethren*, I, 116.

848 *Some of the Vegetable Productions*, 455.

849 William Downey, *An Investigation of the Properties of the Sanguinaria Canadensis; or Puccoon*.

850 *Properties of the Sanguinaria, passim*; see also Barton, *Essay*, I, 28; II, 39–41, 52; appendix, 55. Barton reported that bloodroot was also used as a vermifuge.

851 "Report on Medical Botany," *Transactions of the American Medical Association*, V, 735; see also Porcher, "Report on the Indigenous Medical Plants of South Carolina," *Transactions of the American Medical Association*, II, 689–92; Williams, "Report on the Indigenous Medical Botany of Massachusetts," *Transactions of the American Medical Association*, II, 876.

852 *Manners and Customs*, 384.

853 Beauchamp, "Onondaga Plant Names," *Journal of American Folk-Lore*, Vol. XV, No. 17 (April–June, 1902), 102.

854 Frans M. Olbrechts, "Tuscarora Indian Prescriptions for Medicines," MS, n.d., American Philosophical Society.

855 Robert R. Sollenberger, "Rappahannock Field Notes," MS, 1940, American Philosophical Society.

856 Tantaquidgeon, "Mohegan Medicinal Practices, Weather-Lore, and Superstition," *Forty-third Annual Report of the Bureau of American Ethnology, 1925–26*, 264.

857 Smith, *Menomini Ethnobotany*, 44; *Meskwaki Ethnobotany*, 234; *Ojibwe Ethnobotany*, 377; *Potawatomi Ethnobotany*, 68.

858 Claus, *Pharmacognosy*, 477–79; Henkel, *American Root Drugs*, 40–41.

859 Roys, *Ethno-Botany of the Maya*, 258.

860 Gerard, "Plant Names of Indian Origin," *Garden and Forest*, Vol. IX, Nos. 435–36, 438–40 (1896), 282.

861 *Travels*, II, 517.

862 "Ethnobotany of the Zuñi Indians," *Thirtieth Annual Report of the Bureau of American Ethnology, 1908–09*, 597.

863 Hrdlička, *Physiological and Medical Observations*, 249.

864 Smith, *Menomini Ethnobotany*, 33.

865 Speck, "Catawba Herbals and Curing Practices," *Journal of American Folk-Lore*, Vol. LVII, No. 223 (January–March, 1941), 45.

866 "Report on the Indigenous Medical Plants of South Carolina," *Transactions of the American Medical Association*, II, 711.

867 Lloyd, *Origin and History*, 236.

868 "Uses of Plants by Indians of the Missouri River Region," *Thirty-third Annual Report of the Bureau of American Ethnology, 1911–12*, 131.

869 Carlson and Jones, "Some Notes on Uses of Plants by the Comanche Indians," *Papers of the Michigan Academy of Sciences, Arts and Letters*, XXV, 521.

870 Smith, *Meskwaki Ethnobotany*, 212.

871 "Report on Medical Botany," *Transactions of the American Medical Association*, V, 798.

872 Claus, *Pharmacognosy*, 77–78; Henkel, *American Root Drugs*, 63.

873 Hoffman, "The Midē'wiwin Or 'Grand Medicine Society' of the Ojibwa," *Seventh Annual Report of the Bureau of American Ethnology, 1885–86*, 199.

874 Smith, *Ojibwe Ethnobotany*, 386; *Potawatomi Ethnobotany*, 79; *Meskwaki Ethnobotany*, 243; *Menomini Ethnobotany*, 50.

875 Gilmore, "Uses of Plants by Indians of the Missouri River Region," *Thirty-third Annual Report of the Bureau of American Ethnology, 1911–12*, 84–85.

876 Clapp, "Report on Medical Botany," *Transactions of the American Medical Association*, V, 769.

877 Henkel, *American Medicinal Flowers*, 8.

878 Claus, *Pharmacognosy*, 64.

879 Seward, "Pioneer Medicine in Virginia," *Annals of Medical History*, N.S., Vol. X, No. 1 (January, 1938), 62.

880 *Essay*, I, 30.

881 *Travels in the Interior of North America, 1832–1834* (Part II), Vol. XXIII in Thwaites (ed.), *Early Western Travels*, 120.

882 Millspaugh, *American Medicinal Plants*, II, 141–2.

883 Claus, *Pharmacognosy*, 135.

884 *Ibid.*, 236–37; Millspaugh, I, 28; Meyer, *The Herbalist*, 107.

885 *Nature's Remedies*, 13.

886 *Pharmacognosy*, 207–209.

887 *Mission of the United Brethren*, I, 116.

888 Rusby, "Beverages of Vegetable Origin," *Journal of the New York Botanical Garden*, Vol. V, No. 52 (April, 1904), 82.

889 Speck, "Catawba Medicines and Curing Practices," *Publications of the Philadelphia Anthropological Society*, I, 191, citing Swanton.

890 Clapp, "Report on Medical Botany," *Transactions of the American Medical Association*, V, 833.

891 Claus, *Pharmacognosy*, 280–82; *cf.* Schöpf, *Materia Medica*, 7.

892 Burrage (ed.), *Early English and French Voyages*, 419.

893 Viets, *Medicine in Massachusetts*, 25.

894 *New-England's Rarities*, 196.

895 *Histoire de la Louisiane*, II, 56.

896 *Travels*, 479.

897 *Vegetable Productions*, 432.

898 *Mission of the United Brethren*, I, 113, 116.

899 *Medical Flora*, I, 55.

900 "Report on Medical Botany," *Transactions of the American Medical Association*, V, 780.

901 *Boston Medical and Surgical Journal*, Vol. XXXIV, No. 26 (July 29, 1846), 518–19.

902 Holbrook, *Golden Age of Quackery*, 49.

903 Speck, "Medicine Practices of the Northeastern Algonquians," *Proceedings XIXth International Congress of Americanists*, 310, 315.

904 Whitebread, "The Indian Medical Exhibit of the Division of Medicine in the United States National Museum," Pub. 2582, *Proceedings of the United States National Museum*, Vol. LXVII, art, X, 22.

905 Boas, "Current Beliefs of the Kwakiutl Indians," *Journal of American Folk-Lore*, Vol. XLV, No. 176 (April–June, 1932), 184.

906 "A List of Plant Curatives Obtained from the Houma Indians of Louisiana," *Primitive Man*, Vol. XIV, No. 4 (October, 1941), 58.

907 Speck, "Catawba Herbals and Curing Practices," *Journal of American Folk-Lore*, Vol. LVII, No. 223 (January–March, 1944), 44.

908 Swanton, "Religious Beliefs and Medical Practices of the Creek Indians," *Forty-second Annual Report of the Bureau of American Ethnology, 1924–25*, 658.

909 Smith, *Meskwaki Ethnobotany*, 203; *Ojibwa Ethnobotany*, 356; *Potawatomi Ethnobotany*, 40–41.

910 Claus, *Pharmacognosy*, 147–48, 357; Henkel, *American Root Drugs*, 48.

911 John U. Lloyd, "Historical Story of Sassafras," *The Western Druggist*, Vol. XX, No. 11 (November, 1898), 484.

912 *New Found Land of Virginia*, n.p. Guaiacum was then a syphilis remedy, and sassafras was believed to be endowed with similar powers.

913 Burrage (ed.), *Early English and French Voyages*, 257.

914 Robinson (ed.), *Proceedings of the Virginia Company*, II, 20–21, 31–32, 100; Blanton, *Medicine in Virginia in the Seventeenth Century*, 102; Tyler (ed.), *Narratives of Early Virginia*, 434.

915 Myers (ed.), *Narratives of Early Pennsylvania*, 267.

916 *New-England's Rarities*, 201.

917 *History of North Carolina*, 96.

918 *Natural History of Virginia, or the Newly Discovered Eden*, 26. The belief in the virtue of sassafras as a "Spring tonic" and "blood purifier" has long been firmly rooted in the folklore of rural America. The root bark, used for a tea, was the more common application. See Lloyd, *Origin and History*, 295–96, for that author's personal recollections.

919 *Materia Medica*, 109.

920 Bossu, *Travels in the Interior*, 196.

921 *Histoire de la Louisiane*, II, 36.

922 Robertson, *Louisiana under the Rule of Spain*, I, 101, citing Paul Aliot's *Historical and Political Reflections on Louisiana*.

923 *Travels*, I, 78–79, 179–80; II, 606.

924 *Travels*, 472.

925 *Vegetable Productions*, 441.

926 *Essay*, I, 11, 20; II, 27.

927 *American Herbal*, 292.

928 *The American Dispensatory*, 322.

929 *American Medical Botany*, II, 145. Earlier, Cullen found no merit in sassafras. *Materia Medica*, II, 142–43.

930 Williams, "Report on the Indigenous Medical Botany of Massachusetts," *Transactions of the American Medical Association*, II, 879; Clapp, "Report on Medical Botany," *Transactions of the American Medical Association*, V, 857–58.

931 Porcher, *Southern Fields and Forests*, 8.

932 Douglas, "The People of Cades Cove," *National Geographic Magazine*, Vol. CXXII, No. 1 (July, 1962), 84.

933 Brendle and Unger, *Folk Medicine of the Pennsylvania Germans*, 40, 90, 129.

934 Brochure, "Root Beer," and letter from John R. Leitz, Associate Director of Research, The Hires Company, Evanston, Ill., April 13, 1966.

935 "Historical Story of Sassafras," *The Western Druggist*, Vol. XX, No. 11 (November, 1898), 487.

936 Sargent, *Trees of North America*, I, 363–64.

937 *Mission of the United Brethren*, I, 115.

938 *Moeurs des Sauvages Ameriquains*, II, 368.

939 *Manners and Customs*, 387.

940 Speck, "A List of Plant Curatives Obtained from the Houma Indians of Louisiana," *Primitive Man*, Vol. XIV, No. 4 (October, 1941), 60.

941 Bushnell, *Choctaw of Bayou Lacomb*, 23.

[942] Swanton, "Religious Beliefs and Medical Practices of the Creek Indians," *Forty-second Annual Report of the Bureau of American Ethnology, 1924–25,* 641.

[943] Greenlee, "Medicine and Curing Practices of the Modern Florida Seminoles," *American Anthropologist,* N.S., Vol. XLVI, No. 3 (July–September, 1944), 323.

[944] Claus, *Pharmacognosy,* 341–42; Lloyd, *Origin and History,* 289–97.

[945] Roys, *Ethno-Botany of the Maya,* 293.

[946] *Collections Georgia Historical Society,* III, 21.

[947] Brickell, *Natural History,* 84.

[948] "Report on the Indigenous Medical Plants of South Carolina," *Transactions of the American Medical Association,* II, 836. His Latin designation for saw palmetto was *Chamaerops serrulata* L.

[949] Lloyd, *Origin and History,* 277–78; Claus, *Pharmacognosy,* 360.

[950] Henkel, *American Medicinal Flowers,* 304.

[951] Speck, "A List of Plant Curatives Obtained from the Houma Indians of Louisiana," *Primitive Man,* Vol. XIV, No. 4 (October, 1941), 55.

[952] Folsom-Dickerson, *The White Path,* 72.

[953] Barton, *Essay,* I, 31; this view was also held by Dr. Clapp, "Report on Medical Botany," *Transactions of the American Medical Association,* V, 762–63.

[954] "Report on the Indigenous Medical Plants of South Carolina," *Transactions of the American Medical Association,* II, 744.

[955] Mooney, "The Sacred Formulas of the Cherokees," *Seventh Annual Report of the Bureau of American Ethnology, 1885–86,* 325.

[956] Smith, *Meskwaki Ethnobotany,* 228.

[957] Speck, "A List of Plant Curatives Obtained from the Houma Indians of Louisiana," *Primitive Man,* Vol. XIV, No. 4 (October, 1941), 65.

[958] Claus, *Pharmacognosy,* 143.

[959] *Materia Medica Americana,* 98.

[960] *Origin and History,* 301–17.

[961] *The Family Doctor,* 116.

[962] "Report on Medical Botany," *Transactions of the American Medical Association,* V, 834–35.

[963] *American Practice Condensed,* 679.

[964] Mooney, "The Sacred Formulas of the Cherokees," *Seventh Annual Report of the Bureau of American Ethnology, 1885–86,* 325.

[965] Smith, *Ojibwe Ethnobotany,* 372; *Meskwaki Ethnobotany,* 227.

[966] Claus, *Pharmacognosy,* 219–20.

967 *New-England's Rarities*, 206–207.

968 Kalm, *Travels*, I, 257.

969 *Travels*, 484.

970 *Vegetable Productions*, 407–409.

971 "Report on Medical Botany," *Transactions of the American Medical Association*, V, 878.

972 *American Practice Condensed*, 660.

973 Andros, "The Medicine and Surgery of the Winnebago and Dakota Indians," *Journal of the American Medical Association*, Vol. I, No. 4 (August 4, 1883), 118.

974 Boas, "Current Beliefs of the Kwakiutl Indians," *Journal of American Folk-Lore*, Vol. XLV, No. 176 (April–June, 1932), 186, 188.

975 Smith, *Menomini Ethnobotany*, 23; *Meskwaki Ethnobotany*, 203.

976 Wallis, "Medicines Used by the Micmac Indians," *American Anthropologist*, N.S., Vol. XXIV (1922), 27.

977 Claus, *Pharmacognosy*, 534.

978 Henkel, *American Root Drugs*, 15.

979 Jameson (ed.), *Narratives of New Netherland*, 298.

980 *History of North Carolina*, 79.

981 *Secret Diary*, 371; see also 19, 392.

982 *History of the Dividing Line*, I, 83.

983 *Ibid.*

984 Beauchamp (ed.), *Moravian Journals*, 6.

985 Romans, *East and West Florida*, 160; Cuming, *Sketches of a Tour*, Vol. IV in Thwaites (ed.), *Early Western Travels*, 122–23.

986 Richard H. Shryock, *Medicine and Society in America, 1660–1860*, 66–67, citing Redman's *Account of the Yellow Fever*, 16–18.

987 Beauchamp, "Onondaga Plant Names," *Journal of American Folk-Lore*, Vol. XV, No. 17 (April–June, 1902), 98.

988 "Medicine and Curing Practices of the Modern Florida Seminoles," *American Anthropologist*, N.S., Vol. XLVI, No. 3 (July–September, 1944), 323.

989 *Origin and History*, 54–62.

990 *Essay*, I, 9; appendix, 46.

991 *Indian Doctor's Dispensatory*, 33.

992 Porcher, "Report on the Indigenous Medical Plants of South Carolina," *Transactions of the American Medical Association*, II, 686–87; Clapp, "Report on Medical Botany," *Transactions of the American Medical Association*, II, 686–87; Clapp, "Report on Medical Botany," *Transactions of the American Medical Association*, V, 723–25.

[993] "The Medicine and Surgery of the Winnebago and Dakota Indians," *Journal of the American Medical Association*, Vol. I, No. 4 (August 4, 1883), 117.

[994] Speck, "Medicine Practices of the Northeastern Algonquians," *Proceedings XIXth International Congress of Americanists*, 310–11.

[995] Claus, *Pharmacognosy*, 392; Henkel, *American Root Drugs*, 35–36.

[996] Normand L. Hoerr and Arthur Osol (eds.), *Blackiston's New Gould Medical Dictionary*, 2d ed. (McGraw-Hill Book Co., Inc., 1956).

[997] *Letters and Papers*, V, 1; Waring, *Medicine in South Carolina*, 222.

[998] *Collections Georgia Historical Society*, III, 70, 76.

[999] *Journal of Travels*, Vol. XIII in Thwaites (ed.), *Early Western Travels*, 110.

[1000] Swanton, "Religious Beliefs and Medical Practices of the Creek Indians," *Forty-second Annual Report of the Bureau of American Ethnology, 1924–25*, 655–56, 668.

[1001] Smith, *Meskwaki Ethnobotany*, 248.

[1002] "Report on the Indigenous Medical Plants of South Carolina," *Transactions of the American Medical Association*, II, 699.

[1003] Claus, *Pharmacognosy*, 361; Henkel, *American Root Drugs*, 50–51.

[1004] *History of the Dividing Line*, I, 139.

[1005] *Letters and Papers*, VII, 141–42.

[1006] Barton, *Essay*, I, 26, 32–33; appendix, 56–58.

[1007] Porcher, "Report on the Indigenous Medical Plants of South Carolina," *Transactions of the American Medical Association*, II, 718; Clapp, "Report on Medical Botany," *Transactions of the American Medical Association*, V, 760.

[1008] *Mission of the United Brethren*, I, 114.

[1009] *Manners and Customs*, 387.

[1010] Walter James Hoffman, "The Menomini Indians," *Fourteenth Annual Report of the Bureau of American Ethnology, 1892–93*, I, 292.

[1011] *Idem*, "The Midē'wiwin Or 'Grand Medicine Society' of the Ojibwa," *Seventh Annual Report of the Bureau of American Ethnology, 1885–86*, 199.

[1012] Smith, *Meskwaki Ethnobotany*, 236.

[1013] Speck, "Medicine Practices of the Northeastern Algonquians," *Proceedings XIXth International Congress of Americanists*, 314.

[1014] Bushnell, *Choctaw of Bayou Lacomb*, 24.

[1015] Claus, *Pharmacognosy*, 150–51; Henkel, *American Root Drugs*, 46–47; Lloyd, *Origin and History*, 317–18.

[1016] *Materia Medica Americana*, 131.

[1017] *Essay*, I, 15–16.

[1018] *American Herbal*, 303.

[1019] *Materia Medica*, II, 61.

[1020] *American Dispensatory*, 103–104.

[1021] *Treatise on Materia Medica*, 337.

[1022] *Travels in the Interior of North America, 1832–1834* (Part I), Vol. XXII in Thwaites (ed.), *Early Western Travels*, 95.

[1023] *Mission of the United Brethren*, 114, 117.

[1024] Brendle and Unger, *Folk Medicine of the Pennsylvania Germans*, 90.

[1025] *Manners and Customs*, 393.

[1026] Mooney, "The Sacred Formulas of the Cherokees," *Seventh Annual Report of the Bureau of American Ethnology, 1885–86*, 324.

[1027] Bushnell, *Choctaw of Bayou Lacomb*, 24.

[1028] Folsom-Dickerson, *The White Path*, 74.

[1029] Swanton, "Religious Beliefs and Medical Practices of the Creek Indians," *Forty-second Annual Report of the Bureau of American Ethnology, 1924–25*, 667.

[1030] Speck, "Medicine Practices of the Northeastern Algonquians," *Proceedings XIXth International Congress of Americanists*, 310.

[1031] Tantaquidgeon, "Mohegan Medicinal Practices, Weather-Lore and Superstition," *Forty-third Annual Report of the Bureau of American Ethnology, 1925–26*, 266.

[1032] "Report on Medical Botany," *Transactions of the American Medical Association*, V, 850.

[1033] Claus, *Pharmacognosy*, 286; Henkel, *American Root Drugs*, 26–27.

[1034] *Travels*, 478.

[1035] Clapp, "Report on Medical Botany," *Transactions of the American Medical Association*, V, 779–80; Porcher, "Report on the Indigenous Medical Plants of South Carolina," *Transactions of the American Medical Association*, II, 703; Beach, *American Practice Condensed*, 647.

[1036] Douglas, "The People of Cades Cove," *National Geographic Magazine*, Vol. CXXII, No. 1 (July, 1962), 85.

[1037] *Indian Doctor's Dispensatory*, 53.

[1038] *Manners and Customs*, 389.

[1039] Wallis, "Medicines Used by the Micmac Indians," *American Anthropologist*, N.S., Vol. XXIV (1922), 26.

[1040] Densmore, "Uses of Plants by the Chippewa Indians," *Forty-*

fourth Annual Report of the Bureau of American Ethnology, 1926–27, 334.

1041 Smith, *Menomini Ethnobotany*, 24; *Potawatomi Ethnobotany*, 41; *Meskwaki Ethnobotany*, 203.

1042 Claus, *Pharmacognosy*, 357; Henkel, *American Root Drugs*, 48–49.

1043 *Materia Medica Americana*, 123.

1044 Porcher, "Report on the Indigenous Medical Plants of South Carolina," *Transactions of the American Medical Association*, II, 798.

1045 T. Gundrum, "*Senecio Aureus* as a Hemostatic," *Western Druggist*, Vol. XX, No. 6 (June, 1898), 307–308.

1046 Claus, *Pharmacognosy*, 531.

1047 Speck, "Catawba Herbals and Curing Practices," *Journal of American Folk-Lore*, Vol. LVII, No. 223 (January–March, 1944), 44; *idem*, "Catawba Medicines and Curative Practices," *Publications of the Philadelphia Anthropological Society*, I, 191, citing Swanton.

1048 Chamberlin, "Some Plant Names of the Ute Indians," *American Anthropologist*, N.S., Vol. XI, No. 1 (January- March, 1909), 36.

1049 Smith, *Menomini Ethnobotany*, 31. It was not so used, however, by this tribe.

1050 *Natural History*, 22.

1051 *Letters and Papers*, III, 130.

1052 *Medical Flora*, I, 40.

1053 *Treatise on Materia Medica*, 57.

1054 "Catawba Medicines and Curing Practices," *Publications of the Philadelphia Anthropological Society*, I, 188.

1055 Claus, *Pharmacognosy*, 156.

1056 Henkel, *American Root Drugs*, 20.

1057 *Essay*, I, 33; appendix, 56.

1058 Lloyd, *Origin and History*, 322–23; Porcher, "Report on the Indigenous Medical Plants of South Carolina," *Transactions of the American Medical Association*, II, 725; Clapp, "Report on Medical Botany," *Transactions of the American Medical Association*, V, 863–64.

1059 "Religious Beliefs and Medical Practices of the Creek Indians," *Forty-second Annual Report of the Bureau of American Ethnology, 1924–25,* 662.

1060 *Pharmacognosy*, 384; see also Henkel, *American Root Drugs*, 47–48.

1061 *New-England's Rarities*, 197.

[1062] *Natural History*, 82.

[1063] *East and West Florida*, 109, 162.

[1064] *Essay*, I, 24; appendix, 53–54.

[1065] Will, "The Medical and Surgical Practice of the Lewis and Clark Expedition," *Journal of the History of Medicine*, Vol. XIV, No. 3 (July, 1959), 293. Porcher said the species seen by Lewis was mountain sumach, *R. copallina*. "Report on the Indigenous Medical Plants of South Carolina," *Transactions of the American Medical Association*, II, 749.

[1066] "Report of the Indigenous Medical Plants of South Carolina," *Transactions of the American Medical Association*, II, 747–48.

[1067] "Report on Medical Botany," *Transactions of the American Medical Association*, V, 753–54.

[1068] Brendle and Unger, *Folk Medicine of the Pennsylvania Germans*, 129.

[1069] *Manners and Customs*, 389–90.

[1070] Gilmore, "Uses of Plants by Indians of the Missouri River Region," *Thirty-third Annual Report of the Bureau of American Ethnology, 1911–12*, 99–100.

[1071] Carlson and Jones, "Some Notes on the Uses of Plants by the Comanche Indians," *Papers of the Michigan Academy of Sciences, Arts and Letters*, XXV, 524.

[1072] Swanton, "Religious Beliefs and Medical Practices of the Creek Indians," *Forty-second Annual Report of the Bureau of American Ethnology, 1924–25*, 659, 667.

[1073] Speck, "Catawba Herbals and Curing Practices," *Journal of American Folk-Lore*, Vol. LVII, No. 223 (January–March, 1944), 43.

[1074] Smith, *Potawatomi Ethnobotany*, 38; *Ojibwe Ethnobotany*, 354; *Meskwaki Ethnobotany*, 201; *Menomini Ethnobotany*, 22.

[1075] Wallis, "Medicines Used by the Micmac Indians," *American Anthropologist*, N.S. Vol. XXIV (1922), 25, 27.

[1076] Claus, *Pharmacognosy*, 236; Henkel, *American Medicinal Flowers*, 9–10; Lloyd, *Origin and History*, 271–72.

[1077] Lloyd, *Origin and History*, 33.

[1078] "Report on Medical Botany," *Transactions of the American Medical Association*, V, 879.

[1079] "Uses of Plants by Indians of the Missouri River Region," *Thirty-third Annual Report of the Bureau of American Ethnology, 1911–12*, 70.

[1080] Andros, "The Medicine and Surgery of the Winnebago and Dakota Indians," *Journal of the American Medical Association*, Vol. I, No. 4 (August 4, 1883), 117.

[1081] Smith, *Menomini Ethnobotany*, 23; *Ojibwe Ethnobotany*, 355; *Potawatomi Ethnobotany*, 40; *Meskwaki Ethnobotany*, 202.

[1082] Claus, *Pharmacognosy*, 215–16.

[1083] *Joyfull Newes*, I, 11–12, 20–21.

[1084] Emmart (ed.), *Badianus Manuscript*, 231.

[1085] *New Found Land of Virginia*, n.p.

[1086] *History of North Carolina*, 97.

[1087] *History of the Dividing Line*, I, 165.

[1088] *Natural History*, I, 30; II, 65.

[1089] *Travels*, I, 292.

[1090] *Travels*, 196.

[1091] *Histoire de la Louisiane*, II, 27–29.

[1092] *American Herbal*, 207.

[1093] *Journal of Travels into Kentucky*, in Vol. III, Thwaites (ed.), *Early Western Travels*, 77.

[1094] *Essay*, I, 17.

[1095] Porcher, "Report on the Indigenous Medical Plants of South Carolina," *Transactions of the American Medical Association*, II, 763; *idem*, *Southern Fields and Forests*, 9.

[1096] Douglas, "The People of Cades Cove," *National Geographic Magazine*, Vol. CXXII, No. 1 (July, 1962), 84.

[1097] Speck, "Choctaw-Creek Medicines," MS, 1904.

[1098] Bushnell, *Choctaw of Bayou Lacomb*, 23.

[1099] Speck, "A List of Plant Curatives Obtained from the Houma Indians of Louisiana," *Primitive Man*, Vol. XIV, No. 4 (October, 1941), 61–62.

[1100] *Idem*, "Catawba Herbals and Curing Practices," *Journal of American Folk-Lore*, Vol. LVII, No. 223 (January–March, 1944), 44.

[1101] Claus, *Pharmacognosy*, 418–19.

[1102] *Ibid.*, 316.

[1103] Speck, "Catawba Herbals and Curing Practices," *Journal of American Folk-Lore*, Vol. LVII, No. 223 (January–March, 1944), 45–46.

[1104] "The Use of Tobacco Among the American Indians," *Ciba Symposia*, Vol. IV, Nos. 11–12 (February–March, 1943), 1431.

[1105] *Tobacco is American*, 49.

[1106] Emmart (ed.), *Badianus Manuscript*, 359–60, 294–95.

[1107] Roys, *Ethno-Botany of the Maya*, 259.

[1108] Steward (ed.), *Handbook of South American Indians*, V, 629; VI, 485.

[1109] *A New Voyage*, 109.

[1110] *Joyfull Newes*, I, 75–81.

[1111] *New Found Land of Virginia*, n.p.

461

[1112] A. C., *Tabaco, The Distinct and Severall Opinions of the Late and Best Phisitions That Have Written of the Divers Natures and Qualities Thereof, passim.*

[1113] Berthold Laufer, *Introduction of Tobacco into Europe,* 135.

[1114] Mather, *The Christian Philosopher,* 145–46.

[1115] William Stith, *The History of the First Discovery and Settlement of Virginia,* 21, 182–83.

[1116] *New-England's Rarities,* 189, 230.

[1117] Francisco Guerra, "Medical Almanacs of the American Colonial Period," *Journal of the History of Medicine,* Vol. XVI, No. 3 (July, 1961), 247.

[1118] *Primitive Physic,* 61, 68, 121.

[1119] *Travels,* I, 227.

[1120] *East and West Florida,* 161.

[1121] Clendening, *Source Book of Medical History,* 256.

[1122] *Essay,* I, 40; appendix, 63–64.

[1123] *Treatise on Materia Medica,* 359–60.

[1124] See pp. 127–28, herein.

[1125] Dunlop, *Doctors of the American Frontier,* 182.

[1126] J. Frederick Doering, "Folk Remedies for Diverse Allergies," *Journal of American Folk-Lore,* Vol. LVII, No. 224 (April–June, 1944), 141.

[1127] Douglas, "The People of Cades Cove," *National Geographic Magazine,* Vol. CXXII, No. 1 (July, 1962), 85.

[1128] Hunter, *Manners and Customs,* 391–92.

[1129] Hoffman, "The Menomini Indians," *Fourteenth Annual Report of the Bureau of American Ethnology, 1892–93,* I, 252.

[1130] Speck, "Virginia Indian Folk Lore Plants,"MS, *circa* 1941, American Philosophical Society; Tantaquidgeon, "Mohegan Medicinal Practices, Weather-Lore, and Superstition," *Forty-third Annual Report of the Bureau of American Ethnology, 1926–27,* 264; Speck, "Medicine Practices of the Northeastern Algonquians," *Proceedings XIXth International Congress of Americanists,* 310.

[1131] Swanton, "Religious Beliefs and Medical Practices of the Creek Indians," *Forty-second Annual Report of the Bureau of American Ethnology, 1926–27,* 641.

[1132] Bushnell, *Choctaw of Bayou Lacomb,* 24.

[1133] Speck, "Catawba Medicines and Curative Practices," *Publications of the Philadelphia Anthropological Society,* I, 190.

[1134] Greenlee, "Medicine and Curing Practices of the Modern Florida Seminoles," *American Anthropologist,* N.S., Vol. XLVI, No. 3 (July–September, 1944), 323–24.

[1135] Claus, *Pharmacognosy*, 668–69; Eli Lilly & Co., *Catalog*, January 4, 1965.

[1136] *Journal*, 27.

[1137] "Report on Medical Botany," *Transactions of the American Medical Association*, V, 885–86; see also Beach, *American Practice Condensed*, 879–80.

[1138] Smith, *Potawatomi Ethnobotany*, 63; *Menomini Ethnobotany*, 41.

[1139] Claus, *Pharmacognosy*, 157; Henkel, *American Root Drugs*, 20–21.

[1140] *History of North Carolina*, 96, 237.

[1141] *Travels*, I, 108–109, 196.

[1142] *Materia Medica Americana*, 90.

[1143] *Essay*, I, 14; appendix, 48.

[1144] *Sketches of a Tour*, Vol. IV in Thwaites (ed.), *Early Western Travels*, 154–55.

[1145] Bigelow, *Treatise on Materia Medica*, 248; see also Clapp, "Report on Medical Botany," *Transactions of the American Medical Association*, V, 727.

[1146] Porcher, "Report on the Indigenous Medical Botany of South Carolina," *Transactions of the American Medical Association*, II, 896; idem, *Southern Fields and Forests*, 9.

[1147] *Mission of the United Brethren*, I, 115.

[1148] *Manners and Customs*, 392.

[1149] Speck, "Catawba Herbals and Curing Practices," *Journal of American Folk-Lore*, Vol. LVII, No. 223 (January–March, 1944), 43.

[1150] Claus, *Pharmacognosy*, 221–22.

[1151] *New-England's Rarities*, 205.

[1152] *Vegetable Productions*, 405.

[1153] Gilmore, "Uses of Plants by Indians of the Missouri River Region," *Thirty-third Annual Report of the Bureau of American Ethnology, 1911–12*, 111.

[1154] Smith, *Menomini Ethnobotany*, 58.

[1155] Claus, *Pharmacognosy*, 221.

[1156] Stearns, *American Herbal*, 336, citing Cutler.

[1157] Bigelow, *Treatise on Materia Medica*, 399; see also Porcher, "Report on the Indigenous Medical Plants of South Carolina," *Transactions of the American Medical Association*, II, 714, wherein expectorant and demulcent properties are also ascribed to *V. pedata*.

A recent writer called the common blue violet (*V. papilionacea*) "nature's vitamin pill," because it is said to be rich in vitamins A and

C. He gave several recipes for preparing the leaves and flowers as food. Euell Gibbons, *Stalking the Useful Herbs*, 65–69.

[1158] Chamberlin, "Some Plant Names of the Ute Indians," *American Anthropologist*, N.S., Vol. XI, No. 1 (January–March, 1909), 37.

[1159] Hoffman, "The Midē'wiwin Or 'Grand Medicine Society' of the Ojibwa," *Seventh Annual Report of the Bureau of American Ethnology, 1885–86*, 201.

[1160] Smith, *Potawatomi Ethnobotany*, 88; *Ojibwe Ethnobotany*, 392.

[1161] Claus, *Pharmacognosy*, 473; Gathercoal, *Checklist of Native and Introduced Drug Plants*, n.p.; *Pharmacopoeia of the United States*, 6th decennial revision, 379.

[1162] *Origin and History*, 135.

[1163] "Report on Medical Botany," *Transactions of the American Medical Association*, V, 757–58. The species mentioned was *E. atropurpureus*.

[1164] "Report on the Indigenous Medical Plants of South Carolina," *Transactions of the American Medical Association*, II, 728.

[1165] Gilmore, "Uses of Plants by Indians of the Missouri River Region, *Thirty-third Annual Report of the Bureau of American Ethnology, 1911–12*, 102.

[1166] Smith, *Meskwaki Ethnobotany*, 209.

[1167] Tantaquidgeon, "Mohegan Medicinal Practices, Weather-Lore, and Superstition," *Forty-third Annual Report of the Bureau of American Ethnology, 1925–26*, 265.

[1168] Claus, *Pharmacognosy*, 220–21.

[1169] *Some of the Vegetable Productions*, 454.

[1170] *American Herbal*, 53.

[1171] Hoffman, "The Midē'wiwin Or 'Grand Medicine Society' of the Ojibwa," *Seventh Annual Report of the Bureau of American Ethnology, 1885–86*, 200.

[1172] Smith, *Ojibwe Ethnobotany*, 384.

[1173] Claus, *Pharmacognosy*, 235.

[1174] Hunter, *Manners and Customs*, 371–72.

[1175] Lowie, *The Crow Indians*, 63. The species named was *Leptotaenia multifida*, Nutt., which is not listed in *Gray's Manual*.

[1176] Claus, *Pharmacognosy*, 360.

[1177] *Origin and History*, 257–58.

[1178] *New-England's Rarities*, 197.

[1179] *Vegetable Productions*, 449.

[1180] *Essay*, I, 11; II, 21–22, 51.

[1181] *An Inaugural Dissertation on the Prunus Virginiana. . .* (Philadelphia, John Geyer, 1802).

[1182] *Treatise on Materia Medica,* 307–308.

[1183] Will, *Journal of the History of Medicine,* XIV, 289.

[1184] Brendle and Unger, *Folk Medicine of the Pennsylvania Germans,* 129.

[1185] Douglas, "The People of Cades Cove," *National Geographic Magazine,* Vol. CXXII, No. 1 (July, 1962), 85.

[1186] Mooney, "The Sacred Formulas of the Cherokees," *Seventh Annual Report of the Bureau of American Ethnology, 1885–86,* 123.

[1187] Hoffman, "The Midē'wiwin Or 'Grand Medicine Society' of the Ojibwa," *Seventh Annual Report of the Bureau of American Ethnology, 1885–86,* 199.

[1188] Densmore, "Uses of Plants by the Chippewa Indians," *Forty-fourth Annual Report of the Bureau of American Ethnology, 1925–26,* 333–34.

[1189] Gilmore, "Uses of Plants by Indians of the Missouri River Region," *Thirty-third Annual Report of the Bureau of American Ethnology, 1911–12,* 89.

[1190] Speck, "Medicine Practices of the Northeastern Algonquians," *Proceedings XIXth International Congress of Americanists,* 310.

[1191] Smith, *Menomini Ethnobotany,* 49–50; *Ojibwe Ethnobotany,* 385; *Potawatomi Ethnobotany,* 77–78; *Meskwaki Ethnobotany,* 242.

[1192] Tantaquidgeon, "Mohegan Medicinal Practices, Weather-Lore, and Superstition," *Forty-third Annual Report of the Bureau of Amercian Ethnology, 1925–26,* 264.

[1193] Bernard Fantus and H. A. Dyniewicz, "The Vehicle Value of Syrup of Cherry NF VI," *Journal of the American Pharmaceutical Association,* Vol. XXV, No. 8 (August, 1936), 701–705; Claus, *Pharmacognosy,* 159–61; Eli Lilly & Co., *Catalog,* January, 4, 1965, 163.

[1194] *New-England's Rarities,* 177.

[1195] *Vegetable Productions,* 469.

[1196] *Materia Medica Americana,* 107.

[1197] *Journal of Travels into Kentucky,* in Vol. III, Thwaites (ed.), *Early Western Travels,* 77.

[1198] Barton, *Essay,* I, 7; II, 1; appendix, 45.

[1199] *Treatise on Materia Medica,* 196.

[1200] "Report on Medical Botany," *Transactions of the American Medical Association,* V, 748–49.

[1201] William Winder, [untitled remarks on Indian remedies], *Boston Medical and Surgical Journal,* Vol. XXXIV, No. 1 (February 4, 1846), 11.

1202 Mooney, "The Sacred Formulas of the Cherokees," *Seventh Annual Report of the Bureau of American Ethnology, 1885–86*, 326.

1203 Smith, *Menomini Ethnobotany*, 37; *Ojibwe Ethnobotany*, 370–71; *Meskwaki Ethnobotany*, 222–23.

1204 Lloyd, *Origin and History*, 153; Henkel, *American Root Drugs*, 44–45; Claus, *Pharmacognosy*, 235.

1205 *Essay*, I, 28.

1206 "Report on the Indigenous Medical Botany of Massachusetts," *Transactions of the American Medical Association*, II, 883.

1207 "Report on Medical Botany," *Transactions of the American Medical Association*, V, 849–50.

1208 *Manners and Customs*, 394.

1209 Speck, "Medicine Practices of the Northeastern Algonquians," *Proceedings XIXth International Congress of Americanists*, 314; *idem*, "Catawba Medicines and Curative Practices," *Publications of the Philadelphia Anthropological Society*, I, 188.

1210 Smith, *Ojibwe Ethnobotany*, 357; *Menomini Ethnobotany*, 25; *Potawatomi Ethnobotany*, 42; *Meskwaki Ethnobotany*, 204.

1211 Henkel, *American Root Drugs*, 25–26; Claus, *Pharmacognosy*, 327–28.

1212 Smith, *Menomini Ethnobotany*, 31; *Ojibwe Ethnobotany*, 365; *Potawatomi Ethnobotany*, 52; *Meskwaki Ethnobotany*, 216.

1213 Claus, *Pharmacognosy*, 223.

1214 Clapp, "Report on Medical Botany," *Transactions of the American Medical Association*, V, 884; Henkel, *American Root Drugs*, 21–22.

1215 Smith, *Meskwaki Ethnobotany*, 220.

1216 Roys, *Ethno-Botany of the Maya*, 262; Emmart (ed.), *Badianus Manuscript*, 211, 214.

1217 Claus, *Pharmacognosy*, 152.

1218 Cutler, *Vegetable Productions*, 491; Williams, "Report on the Indigenous Medical Botany of Massachusetts," *Transactions of the American Medical Association*, II, 919; Porcher, *Southern Fields and Forests*, 9.

1219 *Manners and Customs*, 378.

1220 Shuman, "Southern California Medicine," *Annals of Medical History*, N.S. Vol. X, No. 3 (May, 1938), 218.

1221 Hrdlička, *Physiological and Medical Observations*, 245.

1222 Speck, "A List of Plant Curatives Obtained from the Houma Indians of Louisiana," *Primitive Man*, Vol. XIV, No. 4 (October, 1941), 60.

1223 Speck, "Catawba Herbals and Curing Practices," *Journal of American Folk-Lore*, Vol. LVII, No. 223 (January–March, 1944), 44.

1224 Swanton, "Social and Religious Beliefs and Practices of the Chickasaw Indians," *Forty-fourth Annual Report of the Bureau of American Ethnology, 1926–27*, 266, 268; *idem*, "Religious Beliefs and Medical Practices of the Creek Indians," *Forty-second Annual Report of the Bureau of American Ethnology, 1924–25*, 659, 668.

1225 Tantaquidgeon, "Mohegan Medicinal Practices, Weather-Lore, and Superstition," *Forty-third Annual Report of the Bureau of American Ethnology, 1925–26*, 266.

1226 Speck, "Medicine Practices of the Northeastern Algonquians," *Proceedings XIXth International Congress of Americanists*, 309, 315.

1227 Smith, *Menomini Ethnobotany*, 52; *Ojibwe Ethnobotany*, 388–89; *Potawatomi Ethnobotany*, 81–82; *Meskwaki Ethnobotany*, 245.

1228 Claus, *Pharmacognosy*, 170–71.

1229 *New-England's Rarities*, 203–204.

1230 *Travels*, 476.

1231 *Vegetable Productions*, 444.

1232 *Essay*, I, 19.

1233 Thoreau, *The Maine Woods*, 201.

1234 *New Guide to Health*, 48.

1235 Porcher, "Report on the Indigenous Medical Plants of South Carolina," *Transactions of the American Medical Association*, II, 776–77.

1236 "Report on Medical Botany," *Transactions of the American Medical Association*, V, 815.

1237 Beauchamp, "Onondaga Plant Names," *Journal of American Folk-Lore*, Vol. XV, No. 17 (April–June, 1902), 102.

1238 Speck, "Medicine Practices of the Northeastern Algonquians," *Proceedings XIXth International Congress of Americanists*, 314–15.

1239 Smith, *Potawatomi Ethnobotany*, 56–57; *Ojibwe Ethnobotany*, 369; *Menomini Ethnobotany*, 35.

1240 "Emergence of Modern Medicine," *Annual Report of the Board of Regents of the Smithsonian Institution for the Year Ending June 30, 1938*, 426.

1241 *Origin and History*, 144–50.

1242 Claus, *Pharmacognosy*, 193, 350–51.

1243 *Letters and Papers*, III, 89.

1244 *Vegetable Productions*, 412.

1245 Porcher, "Report on the Indigenous Medical Plants of South Carolina," *Transactions of the American Medical Association*, II, 708; Williams, "Report on the Indigenous Medical Botany of Massachusetts," *Transactions of the American Medical Association*, II, 882; Clapp, "Report on Medical Botany," *Transactions of the American Medical Association*, V, 775.

[1246] Smith, *Menomini Ethnobotany*, 37; *Potawatomi Ethnobotany*, 59.

[1247] Lloyd, *Origin and History*, 162; Claus, *Pharmacognosy*, 226.

[1248] Eli Lilly & Co., *Catalog*, January 4, 1965, 63.

[1249] *Travels in the Interior of North America, 1832–1834* (Part II), Vol. XXIII in Thwaites (ed.), *Early Western Travels*, 140.

[1250] Palmer, "Plants Used by the Indians of the United States," *American Naturalist*, Vol. XII (September, 1878), 651–52; Chamberlin, "Some Plant Names of the Ute Indians," *American Anthropologist*, N.S. Vol. XI, No. 1 (January–March, 1909), 32; Gilmore, "Uses of Plants by Indians of the Missouri River Region," *Thirty-third Annual Report of the Bureau of American Ethnology, 1911–12*, 135; Whitebread, "The Indian Medical Exhibit of the Division of Medicine in the United States National Museum," Pub. 2582, *Proceedings of the United States National Museum*, Vol. LXVII, art. x, 21; Smith, *Meskwaki Ethnobotany*, 211.

[1251] Smith, *Potawatomi Ethnobotany*, 49.

[1252] Claus, *Pharmacognosy*, 306, 308, 316.

[1253] Josselyn, *New-England's Rarities*, 178; Brickell, *Natural History*, 22.

[1254] Kinietz, *Indians of the Western Great Lakes*, 224.

[1255] Palmer, "Plants Used by the Indians of the United States," *American Naturalist*, Vol. XII (September, 1878), 651.

[1256] Chamberlin, "Some Plant Names of the Ute Indians," *American Anthropologist*, N.S., Vol. XI, No. 1 (January–March, 1908), 32.

[1257] Gilmore, "Uses of Plants by Indians of the Missouri River Region," *Thirty-third Annual Report of the Bureau of American Ethnology, 1911–12*, 134.

[1258] Swanton, "Social and Religious Beliefs and Practices of the Chickasaw Indians," *Forty-fourth Annual Report of the Bureau of American Ethnology, 1926–27*, 267.

[1259] Smith, *Meskwaki Ethnobotany*, 210; *Menomini Ethnobotany*, 29; *Ojibwe Ethnobotany*, 362; *Potawatomi Ethnobotany*, 47.

[1260] Speck, "Medicine Practices of the Northeastern Algonquians," *Proceedings XIXth International Congress of Americanists*, 315.

[1261] Wallis, "Medicines Used by the Micmac Indians," *American Anthropologist*, N.S., Vol. XXIV (1922), 25.

[1262] "Report on Medical Botany," *Transactions of the American Medical Association*, V, 800, citing Griffith.

¹²⁶³ Claus, *Pharmacognosy*, 354.

¹²⁶⁴ *Vegetable Productions*, 436.

¹²⁶⁵ Bushnell, *Choctaw of Bayou Lacomb*, 23.

¹²⁶⁶ Swanton, "Social and Religious Beliefs and Practices of the Chickasaw Indians," *Forty-fourth Annual Report of the Bureau of American Ethnology, 1926–27*, 267.

¹²⁶⁷ Gilmore, "Uses of Plants by Indians of the Missouri River Region," *Thirty-third Annual Report of the Bureau of American Ethnology, 1911–12*, 77.

¹²⁶⁸ Smith, *Ojibwe Ethnobotany*, 381.

¹²⁶⁹ Hrdlička, *Physiological and Medical Observations*, 245.

¹²⁷⁰ Gilmore, "Uses of Plants by Indians of the Missouri River Region," *Thirty-third Annual Report of the Bureau of American Ethnology, 1911–12*, 77.

¹²⁷¹ Speck, "A List of Plant Curatives Obtained from the Houma Indians of Louisiana," *Primitive Man*, Vol. XIV, No. 4 (October, 1941), 56–57.

¹²⁷² Smith, *Meskwaki Ethnobotany*, 237; *Potawatomi Ethnobotany*, 73.

¹²⁷³ Henkel, *American Root Drugs*, 27–29; Clapp, "Report on Medical Botany," *Transactions of the American Medical Association*, V, 855–56; Claus, *Pharmacognosy*, 139.

¹²⁷⁴ Lloyd, *Origin and History*, 150–52; Millspaugh, *American Medicinal Plants*, II, 130 ff.; Claus, *Pharmacognosy*, 503.

¹²⁷⁵ Brickell, *Natural History*, 92.

¹²⁷⁶ Henkel, *American Root Drugs*, 51–52; Claus, *Pharmacognosy*, 503.

¹²⁷⁷ *Essay*, II, 11–13.

¹²⁷⁸ "Report on the Indigenous Medical Plants of South Carolina," *Transactions of the American Medical Association*, II, 687.

¹²⁷⁹ Mooney and Olbrechts, *Swimmer Manuscript*, 274.

¹²⁸⁰ Douglas, "The People of Cades Cove," *National Geographic Magazine*, Vol. CXXII, No. 1 (July, 1962), 85.

¹²⁸¹ Speck, "Catawba Medicines and Curative Practices," *Publications of the Philadelphia Anthropological Society*, I, 188; *idem*, "Catawba Herbals and Curing Practices," *Journal of American Folk-Lore*, Vol. LVII, No. 223 (January–March, 1944), 46.

¹²⁸² Claus, *Pharmacognosy*, 477.

¹²⁸³ Palmer, "Plants Used by the Indians of the United States," *American Naturalist*, Vol. XII (September, 1878), 651.

¹²⁸⁴ Shuman, "Southern California Medicine," *Annals of Medical History*, N.S., Vol. X, No. 3 (May, 1938), 221; Culley, "The California

Indians: Their Medical Practices and Their Drugs," *Journal of the American Pharmaceutical Association*, Vol. XXV, No. 4 (April, 1936), 338; Brooks, "The Medicine of the American Indians," *Journal of Laboratory and Clinical Medicine*, Vol. XIX, No. 1 (October, 1933), 21.

[1285] Lloyd, *Origin and History*, 132–34.

[1286] Claus, *Pharmacognosy*, 372–73. Joseph E. Meyer claimed that *yerba santa* was also valuable in spasms of asthma, throat and bronchial irritations, and as a tonic. *The Herbalist*, 146–47.

[1287] Bigelow, *Treatise on Materia Medica*, 60.

[1288] Claus, *Pharmacognosy*, 628.

[1289] Douglas, "The People of Cades Cove," *National Geographic Magazine*, Vol. CXXII, No. 1 (July, 1962), 84.

[1290] Thwaites (ed.), *Early Western Travels*, X, 286.

[1291] *History of the Dividing Line*, II, 72.

[1292] *New Found Land of Virginia*, n.p.

[1293] Strachey, *The Historie of Travaile into Virginia Britannia*, 33.

[1294] Swanton, "Social and Religious Beliefs and Practices of the Chickasaw Indians," *Forty-fourth Annual Report of the Bureau of American Ethnology, 1926–27*, 264, citing Adair.

[1295] Speck, "A List of Plant Curatives Obtained from the Houma Indians of Louisiana," *Primitive Man*, Vol. XIV, No. 4 (October, 1941), 65.

[1296] Culley, "The California Indians: Their Medical Practices and Their Drugs," *Journal of the American Pharmaceutical Association*, Vol. XXV, No. 4 (April, 1936), 338.

[1297] Claus, *Pharmacognosy*, 318.

[1298] Bigelow, *Treatise on Materia Medica*, 120.

[1299] *Natural History*, 122.

[1300] *New-England's Rarities*, 153.

[1301] Tantaquidgeon, "Mohegan Medicinal Practices, Weather-Lore, and Superstition," *Forty-third Annual Report of the Bureau of American Ethnology, 1925–26*, 266.

[1302] Speck, "Medicine Practices of the Northeastern Algonquians," *Proceedings XIXth International Congress of Americanists*, 312.

[1303] *Treatise on Materia Medica*, 114. For a definition of the pharmaceutical charcoals see Claus, *Pharmacognosy*, 174–75.

[1304] Emmart (ed.), *Badianus Manuscript*, 224, 304–305, 316–17, 322.

[1305] *New-England's Rarities*, 185.

[1306] Pitcher in Schoolcraft, *Indian Tribes*, IV, 513.

[1307] *Manners and Customs*, 369, 394.

[1308] Wilfred W. Robbins, John P. Harrington, and Barbara Freire-

Marreco, *Ethnobotany of the Tewa Indians*, Bulletin 55, BAE (Washington, Government Printing Office, 1916), 28.

[1309] *Treatise on Materia Medica*, 126.

[1310] *Essay*, II, xiv.

[1311] *Manners and Customs*, 380–81.

[1312] *Pharmacopeia of the United States*, 6th decennial revision, XXXII.

[1313] *Journal of a Voyage to North America*, I, 323.

[1314] "History of the North American Indians," *Ohio Archaeological and Historical Quarterly*, Vol. XIX, Nos. 1–2 (January and April, 1910), 52–53.

[1315] Travels, II, 608.

[1316] *Letters and Papers*, VI, 210–11.

[1317] *Mission of the United Brethren*, I, 117–18.

[1318] *Indianisch-French-Crieck-Seneca-Spring Oel* . . . (Chestnut Hill, Pa., Samuel Saur, 1792).

[1319] *Journal of a Tour*, in Vol. III, Thwaites (ed.), *Early Western Travels*, 346.

[1320] Cuming, *Sketches of a Tour*, Vol. IV in Thwaites (ed.), *Early Western Travels*, 101–102, printer's note no. 60.

[1321] *Treatise of the Materia Medica*, II, 256.

[1322] Toner, *Address*, 97, citing Brickell.

[1323] Tantaquidgeon, "Notes on the Origin and Uses of Plants of the Lake St. John Montagnais," *Journal of American Folk-Lore*, Vol. XLV, No. 176 (April–June, 1932), 265.

[1324] Hrdlička, *Physiological and Medical Observations*, 251; Parker, "Secret Medicine Societies of the Seneca," *American Anthropologist*, N.S., Vol. XI, No. 2 (April–June, 1909), 172–73.

[1325] Swanton, "Religious Beliefs and Medical Practices of the Creek Indians," *Forty-second Annual Report of the Bureau of American Ethnology, 1924–25*, 669.

[1326] Brooks, "The Medicine of the American Indians," *Bulletin of the New York Academy of Medicine*, 2d ser., Vol. V, No. 6 (June, 1929), 528.

[1327] Hunter, *Manners and Customs*, 370.

[1328] *Indians of North America*, 504.

[1329] Marie B. Mellinger, "Medicine Plants of the Cherokees," *Tile and Till*, Vol. LI, No. 4 (July–August, 1965), 51.

[1330] W. I. Thomas, *The Relation of the Medicine-Man to the Origin of the Professional Occupations*, 6.

[1331] *Physiological and Medical Observations*, 250.

[1332] Henry E. Sigerist, in foreword to Emmart (ed.), *Badianus Manuscript*, ix.

[1333] *Ethno-Botany of the Maya*, xxi-xxii.

[1334] Ackerknecht, in Steward (ed.), *Handbook of South American Indians*, V, 628.

[1335] Cinchona bark is no exception. The fact that the Incas did not seem to use it obscures the evidence that it was used by others. Maddox quotes Wellcome and cites other evidence that cinchona bark was used in ancient times, and is still used, by some tribes, as a febrifuge. (Maddox, *The Medicine Man*, 250–51.) Castiglioni was convinced that the bark was used by Indians at Loxa, where the Jesuits obtained it. "Herbs in the Medicine of the Eastern Peoples and of the American Indians," *Ciba Symposia*, Vol. V, Nos. 5–6 (August–September, 1943), 1539–40. See also A. A. Moll, *Aesculapius in Latin America*, 187.

[1336] Steward (ed.), *Handbook of South American Indians*, VI, 484.

[1337] The principal sources used in compiling this list are, in addition to those cited at the beginning of this section, Lloyd's *Origin and History of the Pharmacopeial Vegetable Drugs* and Paul C. Standley's *Flora of Yucatan*. The present uses of the drugs are taken mainly from Claus, *Pharmacognosy*.

Bibliography

Unpublished Material

Harper, Francis Lee. Letter to author, February 3, 1966.

Kent, Benjamin. Letter to Benjamin Franklin, January 19, 1766. American Philosophical Library.

Klink, Jane Seymour. "Relation of the Medicine Man to the Educational System of the Early Races of North America." Unpublished Master's thesis, Department of Sociology, University of Chicago, 1902.

Maguire, Edward Francis, S. J. "Frequent Diseases and Intended Remedies of the Frontier (1780–1850)." Unpublished Master's thesis, Department of Education, St. Louis University, 1953.

Olbrechts, Frans M. "Tuscarora Indian Prescriptions for Medicines." MS, n.d. American Philosophical Society.

Phelps, J. W. "Diary, Kept While at Mackinac, Chicago, and Western Posts, 1840–41." New York Public Library, item No. 825.

Sollenberger, Robert R. "Rappahannock Field Notes." MS, 1940. American Philosophical Society.

Speck, Frank G. "An Addendum to Catawba Indian Herbals and Curative Practices." MS, 1943. American Philosophical Society.

———. "Choctaw-Creek Medicines." MS, 1904. American Philosophical Society.

———. "A List of Plant Curatives Obtained from the Houma Indians of Louisiana." MS, 1941. American Philosophical Society.

———. "Tadoussac-Escoumains Field Notes." MS, 1915. American Philosophical Society.

———. "Virginia Indian Folk Lore Plants." MS, circa 1941. American Philosophical Society.

Stimson, Anna Katharine. "Contributions toward a Bibliography of the Medicinal Use of Plants by the Indians of the United States of America." Master's thesis, Department of Anthropology, University of Pennsylvania, 1946. (Xerox copy.)

White, Leslie A. "Medicine Societies of the Southwest." Ph.D. dissertation, Department of Anthropology, University of Chicago, 1927.

Books and Pamphlets

A. C. Tabaco. The Distinct and Severall Opinions of the Late and Best Phisitions That Haue Written of the Diuers Natures and and Qualities Thereof. London, printed by Adam Islip, 1595.

Ackerknecht, Erwin H. A Short History of Medicine. New York, The Ronald Press Co., 1955.

Adair, James. The History of the American Indians; Particularly Those Nations Adjoining to the Mississippi . . . . London, printed for Edward and Charles Dilly, 1775.

Alsberg, Henry G. The American Guide: A Source Book and Complete Travel Guide for the United States. New York, Hastings House, 1949.

American Medical Association. Transactions of the American Medical Association. Vol. II: 1849. Philadelphia, printed for the Association by T. K. and P. G. Collins, 1849.

———. Transactions of the American Medical Association. Vol. V:

1852. Philadelphia, printed for the Association by T. K. and P. G. Collins, 1852.

American Philosophical Society. *Transactions of the American Philosophical Society, Held at Philadelphia, for Promoting Useful Knowledge*. Vol. I. 2d ed., corrected. Philadelphia, printed by Aitken and Son, 1789.

———. *Transactions of the American Philosophical Society, Held at Philadelphia, for Promoting Useful Knowledge*. Vol. II. Philadelphia, printed and sold by Robert Aitken, 1786.

———. *Transactions of the American Philosophical Society, Held at Philadelphia, for Promoting Useful Knowledge*. Vol. III. Philadelphia, printed and sold by Robert Aitken & Son, 1793.

Anderson, Andrew. *An Inaugural Dissertation on the Eupatorium Perfoliatum of Linnaeus*. New York, C. S. Van Winkle, 1813.

Ashburn, Colonel P. M. *The Ranks of Death: A Medical History of the Conquest of America*. Ed. by Frank D. Ashburn. New York, Coward McCann, Inc., 1947.

Atkinson, Donald T. *Magic, Myth and Medicine*. Cleveland, World Publishing Co., 1956.

Atkinson, M. J. *Indians of the Southwest*. San Antonio, The Naylor Co., 1963.

Audubon, John James. *Audubon and His Journals*. Ed. by Maria R. Audubon. 2 vols. New York, Dover Publications, 1960.

Aurand, A. Monroe, Jr. *The "Pow-Wow" Book*. Harrisburg, Pa., privately printed by the Aurand Press, 1929.

Bailey, Libert H. *How Plants Got Their Names*. New York, Dover Publications, 1963.

Bancroft, Hubert Howe. *The Works of Hubert Howe Bancroft*: Vol. II, *The Native Races*. San Francisco, The History Co., 1886.

Bartlett, John Russell. *Dictionary of Americanisms, A Glossary of Words and Phrases Usually Regarded as Peculiar to the United States*. 3d ed. Boston, Little Brown & Co., 1860.

Barton, Benjamin Smith. *Collections for an Essay towards a Materia Medica of the United States*. 3d ed., with additions. Philadelphia, printed for Edward Earle and Co., 1810.

———. *Elements of Botany Or Outlines of the Natural History of Vegetables*. 2d ed. 2 vols. Philadelphia, printed for the author, 1812.

Bartram, John. *Observations on the Inhabitants, Climate, Soil,*

475

Rivers, Productions, Animals and Other Matters Worthy of of Notice . . . . London, printed for J. Whiston & B. White, 1751.

Bartram, William. *The Travels of William Bartram.* Ed. by Francis Harper. New Haven, Yale University Press, 1958.

Beach, W. W. (ed.). *The Indian Miscellany, Containing Papers on the History, Antiquities, Arts, Languages, Traditions, and Superstitions of the American Aborigines* . . . . Albany, J. Munsell, 1877.

Beach, W[ooster]. *The American Practice Condensed, Or the Family Physician: Being the Scientific System of Medicine: on Vegetable Principles, Designed for All Classes.* 17th ed., revised. New York, Clark, Austin and Smith, 1857.

Beall, Otho T., Jr., and Richard H. Shryock. *Cotton Mather, First Significant Figure in American Medicine.* Baltimore, The Johns Hopkins Press, 1954.

Beauchamp, William M. (ed.). *Moravian Journals Relating to Central New York, 1745–1766.* Syracuse, N.Y., Onondaga Historical Association, The Dehler Press, 1916.

Beck, John R. *Medicine in the American Colonies.* Albuquerque, Horn & Wallace, 1966.

Bell, Whitfield J., Jr. *John Morgan, Continental Doctor.* Philadelphia, University of Pennsylvania Press, 1965.

Beverley, Robert. *The History and Present State of Virginia.* Ed. by Louis B. Wright. Chapel Hill, University of North Carolina Press, 1947.

Bigelow, Jacob. *American Medical Botany, Being a Collection of the Native Medicinal Plants of the United States* . . . . 3 vols. in 1. Boston, Cummings & Hilliard, 1817–1820.

———. *A Treatise on the Materia Medica.* Boston, Charles Ewer, 1822.

Blair, Emma Helen (ed.). *The Indian Tribes of the Upper Mississippi Valley and Region of the Great Lakes* . . . . 2 vols. Cleveland, Arthur H. Clark Co., 1912.

Blanton, Wyndham B. *Medicine in Virginia in the Eighteenth Century.* Richmond, Garrett & Massie, Inc., 1931.

———. *Medicine in Virginia in the Seventeenth Century.* Richmond, The William Byrd Press, Inc., 1930

Blochman, Lawrence G. *Doctor Squibb: The Life and Times of a Rugged Idealist.* New York, Simon & Schuster, 1958.

Boerhaave, Herman. *Herman Boerhaave's Materia Medica* . . . . London, printed for W. Innys & R. Manby, 1741.

Bolton, Herbert E. (ed.). *Spanish Exploration in the Southwest 1542– 1706.* New York, Barnes and Noble. 1963.

Bonner, Thomas Neville. *Medicine in Chicago: 1850–1950.* Madison, American History Research Center, 1957.

Boorstin, Daniel J. *The Americans: The Colonial Experience.* New York, Vintage Books, 1964.

Bossu, Jean-Bernard. *Travels in the Interior of North America, 1751–1762.* Tr. and ed. by Seymour Feiler. Norman, University of Oklahoma Press, 1962.

Böttcher, Helmuth. *Wonder Drugs, A History of Antibiotics.* Philadelphia, J. B. Lippincott Co., 1964.

Bradford, William. *Of Plymouth Plantation.* Ed. by Harvey Wish. New York, Capricorn Books, 1962.

Brendle, Thomas R., and Claude W. Unger. *Folk Medicine of the Pennsylvania Germans: The Non-Occult Cures.* (In *Proceedings of the Pennsylvania German Society,* Vol. XLV, Pt. II, 1–303.) Norristown, Pennsylvania German Society, 1935.

Briante, John Goodale. *The Old Root and Herb Doctor Or the Indian Method of Healing.* Claremont, N.H., Granite Book Co., 1870.

Brickell, John. *The Natural History of North-Carolina, With an Account of the Trade, Manners, and Customs of the Christian and Indian Inhabitants.* Dublin, James Carson, 1737. (Reprint, ed. by J. Bryan Grimes, by authority of the Trustees of Public Libraries, Raleigh, 1911.)

Brinton, Daniel G. *The Myths of the New World.* 2d ed. revised. New York, Henry Holt & Co., 1876.

Buchan, William. *Every Man His Own Doctor, Or A Treatise on the Prevention and Cure of Diseases* . . . . New Haven, pub. by Nathan Whiting, 1816.

Bullock, W[illiam]. *Sketch of a Journey through the Western States of North America* . . . [1827]. in Vol. XIX in Reuben Gold Thwaites (ed.), *Early Western Travels (q.v.).* Cleveland, Arthur H. Clark Co., 1905.

Burrage, Henry S. (ed.). *Early English and French Voyages (Hakluyt)*. New York, Charles Scribner's Sons, 1906.

Bushnell, David I., Jr. *The Choctaw of Bayou Lacomb, St. Tammany Parish, Louisiana*. Bureau of American Ethnology Bulletin No. 48. Washington, D.C., Government Printing Office, 1909.

Byrd, William. *History of the Dividing Line and Other Tracts*. 2 vols. Ed. by Thomas H. Wynne. Richmond, 1866.

——. *Natural History of Virginia, Or the Newly Discovered Eden*. Ed. and tran. from a German version by Richmond Croom Beatty and William J. Mulley. Richmond, The Dietz Press, 1940.

——. *The Secret Diary of William Byrd of Westover, 1709–12*. Ed. by Louis B. Wright and Marion Tinling. Richmond, The Dietz Press, 1941.

Candler, Allen D. (comp.). *The Colonial Records of the State of Georgia*. Vol. II: *1732–52*. Atlanta, Franklin Printing & Publishing Co., 1904.

Candolle, Alphonse de. *Origin of Cultivated Plants*. New York, D. Appleton & Co., 1892.

Carver, J[onathan], Esq. *Travels through the Interior Parts of North America in the Years 1766, 1767, and 1768*. Dublin, printed for S. Price, *et al.*, 1779.

Castañeda, Pedro. *The Journey of Coronado*. Ed. by G. P. Winship. Ann Arbor, University Micofilms, 1966.

Catesby, Mark. *The Natural History of Carolina, Florida, and the Bahama Islands*. 2 vols. London, printed for C. Marsh, 1754.

Charlevoix, Pierre François Xavier de. *Journal of a Voyage to North America*. Ed. by Louis Phelps Kellogg. 2 vols. Chicago, The Caxton Club, 1923.

Chesnut, V. K. *Plants Used by the Indians of Mendocino County, California*. Contributions U.S. National Herbarium, Vol. VII, No. 3. Washington, D.C., Government Printing Office, 1902.

Clarke, Adam. *A Dissertation on the Use and Abuse of Tobacco . . . .* Newburyport, Mass., Thomas & Whipple, 1812.

Claus, Edward P. *Gathercoal* [Edmund Norris] *and Wirth* [Elmer Hauser] *Pharmacognosy*. 3d ed., revised. Philadelphia, Lea & Febiger, 1956; 4th ed., 1961.

Clendening, Logan. *Source Book of Medical History*. New York, Paul B. Hoeber, Inc., 1942.

Colden, Cadwallader. *Letter Book.* Vol. I. (In *Collections of the New-York Historical Society,* Vol. IX) New York, printed for the Society, 1876.

———. *Letters and Papers.* Vols. I–VIII, 1711–1775. (In *Collections of the New-York Historical Society,* Vols. L–LVI.) New York, printed for the Society, 1918–1923.

Collections of the Virginia Historical Society, Miscellaneous Papers, 1672–1865. Richmond, 1887.

Comfort, J. W. *The Practice of Medicine on Thomsonian Principles ... and a Materia Medica Adapted to the Work.* Philadelphia, A. Comfort, 1843.

Connor, Jeanette Thurber (tr. and ed.). *Colonial Records of Spanish Florida.* Vols. I–II. Deland, Florida State Historical Society, 1925–1930.

Coon, Nelson. *An American Herbal: Using Plants for Healing.* N.p., Hearthside Press, Inc., 1963.

Cooper, J[ames] W. *The Experienced Botanist Or Indian Physician. Being a New System of Practice, Founded on Botany.* Lancaster, Pa., printed for the author and publishers, John Beer, printer, 1840.

Corlett, William Thomas. *The Medicine Man of the American Indian and His Cultural Background.* Springfield, Ill., Charles C. Thomas, 1935.

Cowen, David L. *Medicine and Health in New Jersey: A History.* Princeton, D. Van Nostrand Co., Inc., 1964.

Crèvecoeur, J. Hector St. John de. *Letters from an American Farmer.* New York, E. P. Dutton, 1957.

Culbertson, Thaddeus A. *Journal of an Expedition to the Mauvaises Terres and the Upper Missouri in 1850.* Ed. by John Francis McDermott. Bureau of American Ethnology Bulletin No. 147. Washington, D.C., Government Printing Office, 1952.

Cullen, Thomas S. *Early Medicine in Maryland.* N.p., 1927.

Cullen, William. *Professor Cullen's Treatise of the Materia Medica.* Ed. by Benjamin Smith Barton. 2 vols. 4th American ed. Philadelphia, Edward Parker, 1812.

Cuming, Fortescue. *Sketches of a Tour of the Western Country ... Concluded in 1809.* Vol. IV in Reuben Gold Thwaites (ed.), *Early Western Travels* (q.v.). Cleveland, Arthur H. Clark Co., 1905.

Curtin, L. S. M. *Healing Herbs of the Upper Rio Grande.* Los Angeles, Southwest Museum, 1965.

————. *Some Plants Used by the Yuki Indians of Round Valley, Northern California.* Los Angeles, Southwest Museum, 1957.

Cutler, Rev. Manasseh. *An Account of Some of the Vegetable Productions, Naturally Growing in This Part of America.* Boston, 1785. Reprinted as Bulletin of the Lloyd Library of Botany, Pharmacy and Materia Medica, No. 7, Reproduction Series, No. 4. Cincinnati, 1903.

Dahlgren, B. E. *Cacao.* Chicago, Field Museum of Natural History, 1923.

Davis, Emily Cleveland. *Ancient Americans: The Archaeological Story of Two Continents.* New York; Henry Holt & Co., 1931.

Decker, Peter. *The Diaries of Peter Decker, Overland to California in 1849.* Ed. by Helen S. Giffen. Georgetown, Calif., The Talisman Press, 1966.

Denig, Edward Thompson. *Five Indian Tribes of the Upper Missouri.* Norman, University of Oklahoma Press, 1961.

DeVoto, Bernard (ed.). *The Journals of Lewis and Clark.* Boston, Houghton Mifflin & Co., 1953.

Díaz del Castillo, Bernal. *The Discovery and Conquest of Mexico.* New York, Grove Press, n.d.

Diller, Theodore. *Pioneer Medicine in Western Pennsylvania.* New York, Paul B. Hoeber, Inc., 1927.

Doddridge, Joseph. *Notes on the Settlement and Indian Wars of the Western Half of Virginia and Pennsylvania.* Albany, Joel Munsell, 1876.

Downey, William. *An Investigation of the Properties of the Sanguinaria Canadensis; Or Puccoon.* Philadelphia: Eaken and Mecum, 1803. Reprinted as Bulletin of the Lloyd Library of Botany, Pharmacy and Materia Medica, No. 9, Reproduction Series, No. 5. Cincinnati, 1907.

Drake, Daniel. *Natural and Statistical View, Or Picture of Cincinnati and the Miami Country.* Cincinnati, printed by Looker and Wallace, 1815.

————. *A Systematic Treatise, Historical, Etiological, and Practical, on the Principal Diseases of the Interior Valley of North America....* Cincinnati, Winthrop B. Smith & Co., 1850.

Driver, Harold E. *The Americas on the Eve of the Discovery*. Englewood Cliffs, N.J., Prentice-Hall, 1964.

———. *Indians of North America*. Chicago, University of Chicago Press, 1961.

Duffy, John (ed.). *The Rudolph Matas History of Medicine in Louisiana*. Vol. I of 2 vols. Baton Rouge, Louisiana State University Press, 1958.

Dunlop, Richard. *Doctors of the American Frontier*. Garden City, N.Y., Doubleday & Co., 1965.

Du Pratz. See Le Page du Pratz.

Duran-Reynolds, M. L. *The Fever Bark Tree*. Garden City, N.Y., Doubleday & Co., 1946.

Emmart, Emily Walcott (ed.). *The Badianus Manuscript, an Aztec Herbal of 1552, by Martin de la Cruz and Juannes Badianus*. Baltimore, Johns Hopkins Press, 1940.

Engelmann, George J., M.D. *Labor among Primitive Peoples, Showing the Development of the Obstetric Science of Today, from the Natural and Instinctive Customs of All Races* . . . . 3d ed., revised, enlarged, and rearranged. St. Louis, J. H. Chambers & Co., 1884.

Ewell, James. *The Medical Companion* . . . . Philadelphia, Anderson & Meehan, 1816.

Ewers, John C. *The Blackfeet, Raiders of the Northwestern Plains*. Norman, University of Oklahoma Press, 1958.

Faux, W[illiam]. *Memorable Days in America* . . . [1818–19]. Vol. XI in Reuben Gold Thwaites (ed.), *Early Western Travels (q.v.)*. Cleveland, Arthur H. Clark Co., 1904.

Federal Writers' Project. *California, A Guide to the Golden State*. New York, Hastings House, 1954.

Felter, Harvey Wickes. *The Genesis of the America Materia Medica*. Bulletin of the Lloyd Library of Botany, Pharmacy and Materia Medica, No. 20, Reproduction Series, No. 8. Cincinnati, 1927.

Fenton, William N. *American Indian and White Relations to 1830: Needs and Opportunities for Study*. Chapel Hill, University of North Carolina Press, 1957.

Fernald, Merritt Lyndon, and Alfred Charles Kinsey. *Edible Wild Plants of Eastern North America*. Cornwall-on-the-Hudson, N.Y., Idlewild Press, 1943.

Field Museum. *The Weisman Collection of Pre-Columbian Medical Exhibits.* Chicago, Field Museum, 1967.

Flower's Letters from Lexington & the Illinois, 1819. In Vol. X in Reuben Gold Thwaites (ed.), *Early Western Travels (q.v.).* Cleveland, Arthur H. Clark Co., 1904.

Flower's Letters from the Illinois, 1820–21. In Vol. X in Reuben Gold Thwaites (ed.), *Early Western Travels (q.v.)* Cleveland, Arthur H. Clark Co., 1904.

Folsom-Dickerson, W. E. S. *The White Path.* San Antonio, The Naylor Co., 1965.

Forbes, Jack D. (ed.). *The Indian in America's Past.* Englewood Cliffs, N.J., Prentice-Hall, 1964.

Force, Peter. *Tracts and Other Papers, Relating Principally to the Origin, Settlement, and Progress of the Colonies in North America . . . .* Vol. I. New York, Peter Smith, 1947.

Foster, Robert D. *The North American Indian Doctor, Or Nature's Method of Curing and Preventing Diseases According to the Indians . . . .* Canton, Ohio, printed for the author by Smith and Bevin, 1838.

Franchère, Gabriel. *Narrative of a Voyage to the Northwest Coast . . .* [1811–14]. Vol. VI in Reuben Gold Thwaites (ed.), *Early Western Travels (q.v.).* Cleveland, Arthur H. Clark, Co., 1904.

Garland, Joseph, M.D. *The Story of Medicine.* Boston, Houghton-Mifflin Co., 1949.

Gayarré, Charles. *History of Louisiana.* 4 vols. 3d ed. New Orleans, Armand Hawkins, 1885.

Gibbons, Euell. *Stalking the Healthful Herbs.* New York, David McKay Co., 1966.

Gipson, Lawrence Henry (ed.). *The Moravian Indian Mission on White River: Diaries and Letters, May 5, 1799 to November 12, 1806.* Indianapolis, Indiana Historical Bureau, 1938.

Gordon, Maurice Bear. *Aesculapius Comes to the Colonies.* Ventnor, N.J., Ventnor Publishers, Inc., 1949.

Gregg, Josiah. *Commerce of the Prairies, Or the Journal of a Santa Fe Trader . . .* [1845]. Vols. XIX–XX in Reuben Gold Thwaites (ed.), *Early Western Travels (q.v.).* Cleveland, Arthur H. Clark Co., 1905.

Grinnell, George Bird. *The Story of the Indian.* New York, D. Appleton-Century Co., 1935.

Haggard, Howard W. *Devils, Drugs, and Doctors*. New York, Blue Ribbon Books, Inc., 1929.

Hakluyt, Richard. See Burrage.

Hall, C. C. (ed.) *Narratives of Early Maryland, 1633–1684*. New York, Charles Scribner's Sons, 1910.

Hariot [Harriott], Thomas. *A Briefe and True Report of the New Found Land of Virginia*. Reproduced in facsimile from the 1st London ed. of 1588, with an introductory note by Luther S. Livingston. New York, Dodd, Mead, & Co., 1903.

Harris, Seale. *Banting's Miracle*. Philadelphia, J. B. Lippincott, 1946.

Harris, Thaddeus Mason. *The Journal of a Tour into the Territory Northwest of the Alleghany Mountains . . . 1803*. In Vol. III in Reuben Gold Thwaites (ed.), *Early Western Travels (q.v.)*. Cleveland, Arthur H. Clark Co., 1904.

Harshberger, John W. *The Botanists of Philadelphia, and Their Work*. Philadelphia, Press of T. C. Davis & Sons, 1899.

Hart, Albert Bushnell (ed.). *American History Told by Contemporaries*. Vol. I: *Era of Colonization, 1492–1689*. New York; The Macmillan Co., 1922.

Hatcher, Robert A. *Useful Drugs*. 12th ed. Chicago, American Medical Association, 1940.

Hawkins, Benjamin. *A Sketch of the Creek Country in the Years 1798 and 1799*. In *Collections of the Georgia Historical Society*. Vol. III, Pt. I. Savannah, printed for the Society, 1848.

Heckewelder, John Gottlieb Ernestus. *History, Manners and Customs of the Indian Nations Who Once Inhabited Pennsylvania, and the Neighboring States*. Philadelphia, The Historical Society of Pennsylvania, 1876.

———. *A Narrative of the Mission of the United Brethren among the Delaware and Mohegan Indians . . . .* Philadelphia, published by McCarty & Davis, 1820.

Henkel, Alice. *American Medicinal Flowers, Fruits, and Seeds*. U.S. Department of Agriculture, Bureau of Plant Industry Bulletin No. 26. Washington, D.C., Government Printing Office, 1913.

———. *American Root Drugs*. U.S. Department of Agriculture, Bureau of Plant Industry Bulletin No. 107. Washington, D.C., Government Printing Office, 1907.

———. *Weeds Used in Medicine*. U.S. Department of Agriculture,

Farmer's Bulletin No. 188. Washington, D.C., Government Printing Office, 1904.

———. *Wild Medicinal Plants of the United States*. U.S. Department of Agriculture, Bulletin No. 89. Washington, D.C., Government Printing Office, 1906.

———. and Fred G. Klugh. *Golden Seal*. U.S. Department of Agriculture, Bulletin No. 51, Miscellaneous Papers, Pt. VI. Washington, D.C., Government Printing Office, 1905.

Hennepin, Louis. *A New Discovery of a Vast Country in America*. Reprinted from the 2d London ed. of 1698. Ed. by Reuben Gold Thwaites. 2 vols. Chicago, A. C. McClurg Co., 1903.

Himes, Norman E. *Medical History of Contraception*. New York, Gamut Press, 1963.

Hindle, Brooke. *The Pursuit of Science in Revolutionary America, 1735–1789*. Chapel Hill, University of North Carolina Press, 1956.

The Hires Company, Division of Beverages International, Evanston, Ill. *Root Beer*. A brochure furnished by John R. Leitz, associate director of research, April 13, 1966.

Hodge, Frederick Webb (ed.). *Handbook of American Indians North of Mexico*. Bureau of American Ethnology Bulletin No. 30, 2 vols. Washington, D.C., Government Printing Office, 1907–1910.

———. and T. H. Lewis (eds.). *The Spanish Explorers in the Southern United States, 1528–1543*. New York, Barnes and Noble, 1959.

Hodgson, Adam. *Remarks During a Journey through North America, in the Years 1819, 1820, and 1821* . . . .New York, collected, arranged, and published by Samuel Whiting, 1823.

Holbrook, Stewart H. *The Golden Age of Quackery*. New York, The Macmillan Co., 1959.

Holmes, Oliver Wendell. *Medical Essays, 1842–1882*. In *Collected Works of Oliver Wendell Holmes*, Vol. IX. Boston, Houghton-Mifflin Co., 1892.

Hosmer, James K. (ed.). *Winthrop's Journal, "History of New England," 1630–1649*. 2 vols. New York, Charles Scribner's Sons, 1908.

Howard, James H. *The Ponca Tribe*. Bureau of American Ethnology

Bulletin No. 195. Washington, D.C., Government Printing Office, 1965.

Hrdlička, Aleš. *Physiological and Medical Observations among the Indians of Southwestern United States and Northern Mexico.* Bureau of American Ethnology Bulletin No. 34. Washington, D.C., Government Printing Office, 1908.

Hughes, Thomas. *Medicine in Virginia, 1607–1699.* Williamsburg, Va., 350th Anniversary Celebration Corporation, 1957.

Hulme's Journal, 1818–19. In Vol. X in Reuben Gold Thwaites (ed.), *Early Western Travels (q.v.),* Cleveland, Arthur H. Clark Co., 1904.

Humboldt, Alexander von. *Personal Narrative of Travels to the Equinoctial Regions of America, During the Years 1799–1804.* 3 vols. London, George Bell & Sons, 1877.

Hunter, John D. *Manners and Customs of Several Indian Tribes Located West of the Mississippi . . . .* Reprint of Philadelphia, 1823. Minneapolis, Ross & Haines, 1957.

Jaffe, Bernard. *Men of Science in America.* New York, Simon and Schuster, 1944.

James, Don. *Folk and Modern Medicine.* Derby, Conn., Monarch Books, 1961.

James, Edwin. *Account of an Expedition, from Pittsburgh to the Rocky Mountains . . . under the Command of Maj. Stephen H. Long . . . .* Vols. XIV–XVII in Reuben Gold Thwaites (ed.), *Early Western Travels (q.v.).* Cleveland, Arthur H. Clark Co., 1905.

———. *A Narrative of the Captivity and Adventures of John Tanner During Thirty Years Residence among the Indians in the Interior of North America* [1830]. Reprint. Minneapolis, Ross and Haines, 1956.

Jameson, J. Franklin (ed.). *Narratives of New Netherland, 1609–1664.* New York, Charles Scribner's Sons, 1909.

Jarvis, D. C., M.D. *Folk Medicine.* Greenwich, Conn., Fawcett Publications, 1961.

Joslin, Elliott P. *Diabetic Manual.* Philadelphia, Lea & Febiger, 1959.

Josselyn, John. *An Account of Two Voyages to New-England Made During the Years 1638, 1663.* Boston, William Veazie, 1865.

————. *New-England's Rarities Discovered* . . . . In *Archaeologica Americana, Transactions and Collections of the American Antiquarian Society.* Boston, 1860, Vol. IV, 105–238.

Jung, Carl. *Contributions to Analytical Psychology.* New York, Harcourt Brace & Co., 1928.

Kalm, Peter. *Peter Kalm's Travels in North America.* English version of 1770, 2 vols., revised from original Swedish and ed. by Adolph B. Benson. New York, Wilson-Erickson, Inc., 1937.

Kellogg, Louise Phelps. *The British Regime in Wisconsin and the Northwest.* Madison, The State Historical Society of Wisconsin, 1935.

———— (ed.). *Early Narratives of the Northwest, 1634–1699.* New York, Charles Scribner's Sons, 1917.

————. *The French Regime in Wisconsin and the Northwest.* Madison, The State Historical Society of Wisconsin, 1925.

Kenton, Edna (ed.). *Black Gown and Redskins, Adventures and Travels of the Early Jesuit Missionaries in North America, 1610–1797.* London, Longmans, Green & Co., 1956.

King, Lester S. *The Medical World of the Eighteenth Century.* Chicago, University of Chicago Press, 1958.

King, W. F. *One Hundred Years of Public Health in Indiana.* Indiana Historical Society Publications, Vol. VII, No. 6. Indianapolis, 1921.

Kinietz, W. Vernon. *Indians of the Western Great Lakes.* Ann Arbor, Ann Arbor Paperbacks, 1965.

Kluver, Heinrich. *Mescal—the Divine Plant and Its Psychological Effects.* London, Kegan Paul, Trench, Trubner & Co., Ltd., 1928.

Koch, Adrienne, and William Pedens. *The Life and Selected Writings of Thomas Jefferson.* New York, Modern Library, 1944.

Kreig, Margaret B. *Green Medicine.* Chicago, Rand McNally & Co., 1964.

Kremers, Dr. Edward. *Documents Pertaining to the Medicinal Supplies within the North American Colonies from 1643 to 1780.* Introduction and supplement by Dr. George Urdang. Madison, American Institute of History of Pharmacy, 1944.

————. and George Urdang. *History of Pharmacy.* 3d ed., revised by Glenn Sonnedecker. Philadelphia, J. B. Lippincott Co., 1963.

Kroeber, Alfred L. *Cultural and Natural Areas of Native North America*. Berkeley, University of California Press, 1963.

Lafitau, Jean-François. *Moeurs des Sauvages Ameriquains Comparées aux Moeurs des Premiers Temps*. 2 vols. Paris, Charles Estienne Hochereau, 1774.

Lahontan, Baron de. *New Voyages to North-America*. Ed. by Reuben Gold Thwaites. 2 vols. Chicago, A. C. McClurg Co., 1905.

Langdon, William Chauncy. *Everyday Things in American Life, 1607–1776*. New York, Charles Scribner's Sons, 1937.

Laufer, Berthold. *Introduction of Tobacco into Europe*. Chicago, Field Museum of Natural History, 1924.

La Vega, Garcilaso de. *The Royal Commentaries of the Inca Garcilaso de la Vega, 1539–1616*. Ed. by Alain Gheerbrant. New York, The Orion Press, 1962.

Lawson, John. *History of North Carolina* [1714]. Reprint. Richmond, Garrett & Massie, 1937.

Lederer, John. *The Discoveries of John Lederer . . . .* Ed. by William P. Cumming. Charlottesville, Va., University of Virginia Press, 1958.

Le Page du Pratz. *Histoire de la Louisiane*. 3 vols. Paris, l'Aîné de Bure, La Veuve Delaquette, Lambert, 1758.

Lewis, Meriwether, and William Clark. *The Journals of Lewis and Clark*. Ed. by Bernard DeVoto (*q.v.*). Boston, Houghton Mifflin & Co., 1953.

Leyel, Mrs. C. F. *The Magic of Herbs, a Modern Book of Secrets*. New York, Harcourt, Brace & Co., 1926.

Lincoln, Charles H. (ed.). *Narratives of the Indian Wars, 1675–1699*. New York, Barnes & Noble, 1952.

Linton, Ralph. *Annual Ceremony of the Pawnee Medicine Men*. Chicago, Field Museum of Natural History, 1923.

Lloyd, John U. *History of the Vegetable Drugs of the Pharmacopeia of the United States*. Lloyd Library, Bulletin No. 18, Pharmacy Series No. 4. Cincinnati, 1911.

———. *Origin and History of All the Pharmacopeial Vegetable Drugs, Chemicals, and Preparations*. Cincinnati, The Caxton Press, 1921.

———. and C. G. Lloyd. *Drugs and Medicines of North America*. Lloyd Library, Bulletins No. 29, 30, 31, Reproduction Series, No. 9. Cincinnati, 1930–31.

Long, John. *John Long's Journal, 1768–1782*. Vol. II in Reuben Gold Thwaites (ed.), *Early Western Travels (q.v.)*. Cleveland, Arthur H. Clark Co., 1904.

Loskiel, George Henry. *History of the Mission of the United Brethren among the Indians in North America*. 3 pts. Tr. from the German by Christian Ignatius LaTrobe. London, printed for the Brethren's Society for the Furtherance of the Gospel, 1794.

Lowery, Woodbury. *The Spanish Settlements within the Present Limits of the United States, 1513–1561*. New York, Russell & Russell, Inc., 1959.

Lowie, Robert H. *The Crow Indians*. New York, Rinehart & Co., 1956.

McCary, Ben C. *Indians in Seventeenth-Century Virginia*. Williamsburg, Va., 350th Anniversary Celebration Corporation, 1957.

McDowell, William L., Jr. *Colonial Records of South Carolina: Documents Relating to Indian Affairs, May 21, 1750–August 7, 1754*. Columbia, South Carolina Archives Dept., 1958.

McIlwaine, H. R. *Minutes of the Council and General Court of Colonial Virginia . . . .* Richmond, 1924.

McIntyre, A. R. *Curare—Its History, Nature and Clinical Use*. Chicago, The University of Chicago Press, 1947.

McKenzie, Dan. *The Infancy of Medicine*. London, Macmillan & Co., 1927.

Maddox, John Lee. *The Medicine Man: A Sociological Study of the Character and Evolution of Shamanism*. New York, The Macmillan Co., 1923.

[Martyn, Benjamin]. *An Impartial Enquiry into the State and Utility of the Province of Georgia*. London, printed for W. Meadows, 1741.

Mather, Cotton. *The Christian Philosopher: A Collection of the Best Discoveries in Nature with Religious Improvements* [1720]. Charlestown, published at the Middlesex Bookstore, J. McKown, Printer, 1815.

Matthews, Leslie G. *History of Pharmacy in Britain*. Edinburgh & London, E. & S. Livingstone, Ltd., 1962.

Mereness, Newton D. (ed.). *Travels in the American Colonies*. New York, Antiquarian Press, Ltd., 1961.

Meyer, Joseph Ernest. *Nature's Remedies*. Hammond, Ind.; Indiana Botanic Gardens, 1934.

———. *The Herbalist.* N.p., published by the author, 1960.

Michaux, André. *Journal of Travels into Kentucky: July 15, 1793– April 11, 1796.* In Vol. III in Reuben Gold Thwaites (ed.), *Early Western Travels (q.v.).* Cleveland, Arthur H. Clark Co., 1904.

Millspaugh, Charles F[rederick]. *American Medicinal Plants, an Illustrated and Descriptive Guide to the American Plants Used as Homoeopathic Remedies.* 2 vols. New York, Boericke & Tafel, 1887.

Minutes of the Provincial Council of Pennsylvania . . . . Vol. I. Philadelphia, published by the state, printed by Jo. Severns & Co., 1852.

Moll, A. A. *Aesculapius in Latin America.* Philadelphia, W. B. Saunders Co., 1944.

Monardes, Nicholas. *Joyfull Newes out of the Newe Founde Worlde.* Written in Spanish by Nicholas Monardes, Physician of Seville, and Englished by John Frampton, Merchant, anno 1577, an introduction by Stephen Gasalee. 2 vols. New York, Alfred A. Knopf, 1925.

Montaigne, Michael, Lord of. *Essays of Michael, Lord of Montaigne.* 3 vols. Boston, Houghton Mifflin & Co., 1902.

Mooney, James, and Frans M. Olbrechts. *Swimmer Manuscript— Cherokee Sacred Formulas and Medicinal Prescriptions.* Bureau of American Ethnology Bulletin No. 99. Washington, D.C., Government Printing Office, 1932.

Moorhead, John J., M.D. *Harlow Brooks, Man and Doctor.* New York, Harper & Bros., 1937.

Morgan, Lewis Henry. *The Indian Journals, 1859–62.* Ed. with introduction by Leslie A. White. Ann Arbor, University of Michigan Press, 1959.

———. *League of the Ho-de-no-sau-nee or Iroquois.* 2 vols. New Haven, Human Relations Area Files, 1954.

Myers, A. C. *Narratives of Early Pennsylvania, West New Jersey, and Delaware, 1630–1707.* New York Charles Scribner's Sons, 1912.

Nuttall, Thomas. *A Journal of Travels into the Arkansa Territory During the Year 1819. . . . .* Vol. XIII in Reuben Gold Thwaites (ed.), *Early Western Travels (q.v.).* Cleveland, Arthur H. Clark Co., 1905.

Ogden, George W. *Letters from the West . . .* [1823]. In Vol. XIX in Reuben Gold Thwaites (ed.), *Early Western Travels (q.v.).* Cleveland, Arthur H. Clark Co., 1905.

Oviedo, Gonzales Fernández de. *Natural History of the West Indies.* Tr. and ed. by Sterling A. Stoudemire. Chapel Hill, University of North Carolina Press, 1959.

Packard, Francis R., M.D. *History of Medicine in the United States.* Vol. I of 2 vols. New York, Paul B. Hoeber, Inc., 1931.

Palmer, William P. (ed.). *Calendar of Virginia State Papers and Other Manuscripts, 1652–1781.* Vol. I. Richmond, R. F. Walker, Supt. of Public Printing, 1875.

Pattie, James O. *Personal Narrative During an Expedition from St. Louis . . . .* Vol. XVIII in Reuben Gold Thwaites (ed.), *Early Western Travels (q.v.).* Cleveland, Arthur H. Clark Co., 1905.

Peithman, Irvin M. *The Unconquered Seminole Indians.* St. Petersburg, Fla., The Great Outdoors Publishing Co., 1957.

Pickard, Madge E., and R. Carlyle Buley. *The Midwest Pioneer: His Ills, Cures, and Doctors.* Crawfordsville, Ind., R. E. Banta, 1945.

Pickering, Charles. *Chronological History of Plants: Man's Record of His Own Existence Illustrated through Their Names, Uses, and Companionship.* Boston, Little, Brown, & Co., 1879.

Porcher, Francis Peyre. *Resources of the Southern Fields and Forests, Medical, Economical, and Agricultural, Being Also a Medical Botany of the Confederate States . . . .* Prepared and published by the order of the Surgeon-general, Richmond, Va. Charleston, Evans and Cogswell, 1863.

Price, Weston A. *Nutrition and Physical Degeneration: A Comparison of Primitive and Modern Diets and their Effects.* Fourth printing enlarged. New York, Paul B. Hoeber, 1945.

Priestley, Herbert Ingram. *The Coming of the White Man, 1492–1848. A History of American Life.* Vol. I. New York, The Macmillan Co., 1929.

Pursh, Frederick, *Journal of a Botanical Excursion in the Northeastern Parts of the States of Pennsylvania and New York During the Year 1807.* Ed. by William M. Beauchamp. Syracuse, N.Y., Onondaga Historical Association, reprinted by the Dehler Press, 1923.

Quaife, Milo M. (ed.). *The Western Country in the Seventeenth Cen-*

tury: The Memoirs of Antoine Lamothe Cadillac and Pierre Liette. New York, The Citadel Press, 1962.

Radin, Paul. *The Story of the American Indian.* New York, Liveright Publishing Corporation, 1927.

——. *Autobiography of a Winnebago Indian.* New York, Dover Publications, 1963.

Rafinesque, C[onstantine] S[amuel]. *Medical Flora, Or Manual of the Medical Botany of the United States of North America.* 2 vols. Philadelphia, Atkinson and Alexander, 1828–30.

Rand, James Hall. *The North Carolina Indians.* Chapel Hill, University of North Carolina, 1913.

Rapport, Samuel, and Helen Wright. *Great Adventures in Medicine.* 2d revised ed. New York, Dial Press, 1961.

Rishel, Jonas. *The Indian Physician, Containing a New System of Practice Founded on Medical Plants . . . .* New Berlin, N.H., printed for the author and proprietor by Joseph Miller, 1828.

Ritzenthaler, Robert E. *Chippewa Preoccupation with Health.* Public Museum Bulletin, Vol. XIX, No. 4. Milwaukee, 1953.

Rivers, W. H. R. *Medicine, Magic, and Religion.* New York, Harcourt Brace & Co., 1924.

Robbins, Wilford W., John P. Harrington, and Barbara Freire Marreco. *Ethnobotany of the Tewa Indians.* Bureau of American Ethnology Bulletin No. 55. Washington, D.C., Government Printing Office, 1908.

Robert, Joseph C. *The Story of Tobacco in America.* New York, Alfred A. Knopf, 1949.

Robertson, James Alexander. *Louisiana under the Rule of Spain, France, and the United States, 1785–1807.* 2 vols. Cleveland, Arthur H. Clark Co., 1911.

Robinson, Conway. *Abstract of the Proceedings of the Virginia Company of London, 1619–1624.* Prepared from the records in the Library of Congress and ed. with an introduction and notes by R. A. Brock. Vol. I. Richmond, Virginia Historical Society, 1888.

Rogers, Robert. *Journals of Major Robert Rogers.* London, printed for the author and sold by J. Millan, 1765.

——. *A Concise Account of North America.* London, printed for the author and sold by J. Millan, 1765.

Romans, Bernard. *A Concise Natural History of East and West Florida*. New Orleans, Pelican Publishing Co., 1962. (Reprint of New York ed., 1775.)

Ross, Alexander. *Adventures of the First Settlers on the Oregon or Columbia River* .... Vol. VII in Reuben Gold Thwaites (ed.), *Early Western Travels* (*q.v.*). Cleveland, Arthur H. Clark Co., 1904.

Roys, Ralph L. *The Ethno-Botany of the Maya*. Publication No. 2, Department of Middle American Research. New Orleans, Tulane University, 1931.

Rush, Benjamin. *The Autobiography of Benjamin Rush*. Princeton, published for the American Philosophical Society by Princeton University Press, 1948.

———. *An Inquiry into the Natural History of Medicine among the Indians of North America, and a Comparative View of Their Diseases and Remedies With Those of Civilized Nations*. Read before the American Philosophical Society, Philadelphia, February 4, 1774. N.p., n.d.

———. *Letters of Benjamin Rush*. Ed. by L. H. Butterfield. 2 vols. Princeton, published for the American Philosophical Society by Princeton University Press, 1951.

Sagard, Father Gabriel. *The Long Journey to the Country of the Hurons*. Ed. by George M. Wrong. Toronto, The Champlain Society, 1939.

Sahagún, Fray Bernardino de. *General History of the Things of New Spain* (Florentine Codex), Book XI. Tr. by Charles E. Dibble and Arthur J. O. Anderson. Santa Fe, The School of American Research and the University of Utah, Monographs of the School of American Research and the Museum of New Mexico, 1963.

Salley, Alexander S., Jr., (ed.), *Journal of the Commissioners of Indian Trade of South Carolina, 1710–1715*. Columbia, printed for the Historical Commission of South Carolina by the State Company, 1926.

———. *Narratives of Early Carolina, 1650–1708*. New York, Charles Scribner's Sons, 1911.

Schoolcraft, Henry Rowe. *Historical and Statistical Information Respecting the History, Condition and Prospects of the Indian*

Tribes of the United States. 6 vols. Philadelphia, Lippincott, Grambo & Co., 1851.

Schöpf, Johann David. *Materia Medica Americana Potissimum Regni Vegetabilis.* Reprint of Erlangen, Germany, 1787. Lloyd Library Bulletin No. 6, Reproduction Series No. 3. Cincinnati, 1903.

————. *Travels in the Confederation, 1783–1784.* Ed. by Alfred J. Morrison. 2 vols. Philadelphia, William J. Campbell, 1911.

Scott, H[enry] Harold. *A History of Tropical Medicine.* 2 vols. London, Edward Arnold & Co., 1939.

Shryock, Richard H. *Medicine in America: Historical Essays.* Baltimore, The Johns Hopkins Press, 1966.

————. *Medicine and Society in America, 1660–1860.* New York, New York University Press, 1960.

Shultz, Benjamin. *An Inaugural Botanico-Medical Dissertation, on the Phytolacca Decandra of Linnaeus.* Philadelphia, Thomas Dobson, 1795.

Sigerist, Henry E. *American Medicine.* New York, W. W. Norton & Co., Inc., 1934.

Skinner, H. B. *The Family Doctor, Or Guide to Health* . . . . Boston, published for the author, 1844.

Sloan, George W. *Fifty Years in Pharmacy.* Indiana Historical Society Publications, Vol. III, No. 5. Indianapolis, The Bobbs-Merrill Co., 1903.

Slotkin, J[ames] S[ydney]. *The Peyote Religion: A Study in Indian-White Relations.* Glencoe, Ill., The Free Press, 1956.

Smith, Daniel. *The Reformed Botanic and Indian Physician, a Complete Guide to Health.* Utica, N.Y., Curtiss & White, Printers, 1855.

Smith, Elias. *The American Physician and Family Assistant.* 3d ed. Boston, H. Bowen's Print Shop, 1832.

Smith, Huron H. *Ethnobotany of the Forest Potawatomi Indians.* Bulletin of the Public Museum, Vol. VII, No. 1. Milwaukee, 1933.

————. *Ethnobotany of the Menomini Indians.* Bulletin of the Public Museum, Vol. IV, No. 1. Milwaukee, 1923.

————. *Ethnobotany of the Meskwaki Indians.* Bulletin of the Public Museum, Vol. IV, No. 2. Milwaukee, 1928.

————. *Ethnobotany of the Ojibwe Indians.* Bulletin of the Public Museum, Vol. IV, No. 3. Milwaukee, 1932.

Smith, Joseph. *The Dogmaticus, Or Family Physician.* Rochester, N.Y., printed for the author by Marshall & Dean, 1829.

Smith, Peter. *The Indian Doctor's Dispensatory, Being Father Smith's Advice Respecting Diseases and Their Cure.* Reprint of Cincinnati ed., 1812. Lloyd Library Bulletin No. 2, Reproduction Series No. 2. Cincinnati, 1901.

Speck, Frank G., Royal B. Hassrick, and Edmund S. Carpenter. *Rappahannock Herbals, Folk-Lore and Science of Cures.* Proceedings of the Delaware County Institute of Science, Vol. X, No. 1. Media, Pa., November 1, 1942.

Spinden, Herbert J. *Tobacco Is American: The Story of Tobacco before the Coming of the White Man.* New York, New York Public Library, 1950.

Spruce, Richard. *Notes of a Botanist on the Amazon and Andes.* 2 vols. London, Macmillan & Co., Ltd., 1908.

Standley, Paul C. *Flora of Yucatan.* Publication No. 279, Botanical Series, Vol. III, No. 3. Chicago, Field Museum of Natural History, 1930.

Stearns, Samuel. *American Herbal Or Materia Medica* . . . . Walpole, N.H., printed by Dr. Carlisle, for Thomas and Thomas, and the author, 1801.

Steward, Julian H. (ed.). *Handbook of South American Indians.* Bureau of American Ethnology Bulletin No. 143. 7 vols. Washington, D.C., Government Printing Office, 1946–59.

Stiles, Ezra. *Extracts from the Itineraries and Other Miscellanies of Ezra Stiles, 1755–1794* . . . . Ed. by Franklin Bowditch Dexter. New Haven, Yale University Press, 1916.

Stith, William. *The History of the First Discovery and Settlement of Virginia.* London, reprinted for S. Birt, 1753.

Stone, Eric. *Medicine among the American Indians.* Clio Medica, Vol. VII. New York, Hafner Publishing Co., 1962.

Strachey, William, Gent. *The Historie of Travaile into Virginia Britannia.* London, printed for the Hakluyt Society, 1849.

Tax, Sol, (ed.). *Indian Tribes of Aboriginal America. Selected papers of the XXIXth International Congress of Americanists.* 3 vols. Chicago, University of Chicago Press, 1952.

Taylor, Norman. *Narcotics: Nature's Dangerous Gifts.* New York, Delta Books, 1963.

———. *Plant Drugs That Changed the World.* New York, Dodd Mead & Co., 1965.

Thomas, K. Bryn. *Curare: Its History and Usage.* Philadelphia, J. B. Lippincott Co., 1963.

Thomas, W. I. *The Relation of the Medicine-Man to the Origin of the Professional Occupations.* Chicago, University of Chicago Press, 1903.

Thomson, Samuel. *New Guide to Health; Or Botanic Family Physician . . .* Boston, printed for the author, J. Q. Adams, Printer, 1835.

Thoreau, Henry David. *The Maine Woods.* New York, W. W. Norton & Co., 1950.

Thorwald, Jürgen. *Science and Secrets of Early Medicine.* New York, Harcourt Brace & World, 1963.

Thwaites, Reuben Gold (ed.). *Early Western Travels, 1748–1846.* 32 vols. Cleveland: Arthur H. Clark Co., 1904–1907.

———. *The Jesuit Relations and Allied Documents: Travels and Explorations of the Jesuit Missionaries in New France, 1610–1791.* 75 vols. Cleveland, The Burrows Bros. Co., 1896–1901.

Tolmie, William Fraser. *The Journals of William Fraser Tolmie.* Vancouver, B.C., Mitchell Press, Ltd., 1963.

Toner, Joseph Meredith. *Address before the Rocky Mountain Medical Association, June 6, 1877.* Washington, D.C., published for the Association, 1877.

Tooker, Elizabeth. *Ethnography of the Huron Indians, 1615–1649.* Bureau of American Ethnology Bulletin No. 190. Washington, D.C., Government Printing Office, 1964.

Tracy, W. W., Jr. *List of American Varieties of Peppers.* U.S. Department of Agriculture, Bulletin No. 6. Washington, D.C., Government Printing Office, 1902.

Trease, George Edward. *Pharmacy in History.* London, Ballière, Tindall, and Coxe, 1964.

Tyler, Lyon Gardner (ed.). *Narratives of Early Virginia, 1606–1625.* New York, Barnes and Noble, 1959.

Underhill, Ruth. *Red Man's America.* Chicago, University of Chicago Press, 1953.

Venegas, Miguel. *A Natural and Civil History of California*. 2 vols. Ann Arbor, University Microfilms, 1966.

Verrill, A Hyatt. *The American Indian: North, South and Central America*. New York, The New Home Library, 1943.

Viets, Henry R., M.D. *A Brief History of Medicine in Massachusetts*. Boston, Houghton Mifflin Co., 1930.

Volney, C. F. *A View of the Soil and Climate of the United States of America*. Tr. by C. B. Brown. Philadelphia, J. Conrad & Co., 1804.

Wafer, Lionel. *A New Voyage and Description of the Isthmus of America*. Ed. by George Parker Winship. Reprinted from the original edition of 1699. Cleveland, The Burrows Brothers Co., 1903.

Waring, Joseph Ioor. *A History of Medicine in South Carolina, 1670–1825*. Charleston, South Carolina Medical Association, 1964.

Warshaw, Leon J. *Malaria: The Biography of a Killer*. New York, Rinehart & Co., 1949.

Wertenbaker, Thomas Jefferson. *The First Americans, 1607–1690*. New York, The Macmillan Co., 1927.

Wesley, Rev. John. *Primitive Physic; Or, an Easy and Natural Method of Curing Most Diseases*. 34th ed. London, published by John Mason, 1836.

Wied, Maximilian, Prince of. *Travels in the Interior of North America, 1832–1834*. Vol. XXII–XXIV in Reuben Gold Thwaites (ed.), *Early Western Travels (q.v.)*. Cleveland, Arthur H. Clark Co., 1906.

Wilson, Edmund. *Apologies to the Iroquois . . . .* New York, Farrar, Straus, & Cudahy, 1960.

Wilson, Robert Cumming. *Drugs and Pharmacy in the Life of Georgia, 1733–1959*. Atlanta, Foote & Davies, 1959.

Winthrop, John. *Winthrop's Journal, "History of New England," 1630–1649*. 2 vols. Ed. by James K. Hosmer (q.v.). New York, Charles Scribner's Sons, 1908.

Wissler, Clark. *Indians of the United States*. Garden City, N.Y., Doubleday & Co., 1949.

Wood, William. *New England's Prospect*. 3d ed. Boston, Thomas & John Fleet, 1764.

Woods, John. *Two Years Residence . . . in the Illinois Country . . .*

June 5, 1820–July 3, 1821. In Vol. X in Reuben Gold Thwaites (ed.), *Early Western Travels* (*q.v.*). Cleveland, Arthur H. Clark Co., 1904.

Works Progress Administration. *Medicine and Its Development in Kentucky.* Louisville, The Standard Printing Co., 1940.

Wyeth's Oregon, Or a Short History of a Long Journey, 1832; and Townsend's Narrative of a Journey across the Rocky Mountains, 1834. Vol. XXI in Reuben Gold Thwaites (ed.), *Early Western Travels* (*q.v.*). Cleveland, Arthur H. Clark Co., 1905.

Wyman, Leland C., and Stuart K. Harris. *Navajo Indian Medical Ethnobotany.* University of New Mexico Bulletin No. 366. Albuquerque, University of New Mexico Press, 1941.

Young, James Harvey. *The Toadstool Millionaires: A Social History of Patent Medicines in America before Federal Regulation.* Princeton, Princeton University Press, 1961.

Zeisberger, David. *Diary of David Zeisberger, a Moravian Missionary among the Indians of Ohio.* Ed. by Eugene F. Bliss. 2 vols. Cincinnati, Robert Clarke & Co., for the Historical and Philosophical Society of Ohio, 1885.

Articles

Ackerknecht, Erwin H. "Origin and Distribution of Skull Cults," and "Head Trophies in America," *Ciba Symposia*, Vol. V, No. 10 (January, 1944), 1654–61, 1670–76.

———. "Paleopathology," in Sol Tax, (ed.), *Anthropology Today: Selections.* (International Symposium on Anthropology, New York, 1952.) Chicago, University of Chicago Press, 1962.

———. "Primitive Autopsies and the History of Anatomy." Reprint from *Bulletin of the History of Medicine*, Vol. XIII, No. 3 (March, 1943), 334–39.

———. "Primitive Medicine: A Contrast with Modern Practice," *The Merck Report*, July, 1946, 4–8.

———. "Primitive Medicine and Culture Pattern." Reprint from *Bulletin of the History of Medicine*, Vol. XII, No. 4 (November, 1942), 545–74.

———. "Problems of Primitive Medicine." Reprint from *Bulletin of the History of Medicine*, Vol. XI, No. 5 (May, 1942), 503–521.

———. "White Indians: Psychological and Physiological Peculiarities of White Children Abducted and Reared by North American Indians," *Bulletin of the History of Medicine,* Vol. XV, No. 1 (January, 1944), 15–36.

Adams, William R. "Aboriginal American Medicine and Surgery," *Proceedings of the Indiana Academy of Science,* Vol. LXI (1951), 49–53.

Alvarez, Walter C. "The Emergence of Modern Medicine from Ancient Folkways," *Annual Report of the Board of Regents of the Smithsonian Institution for the Year Ending June 30, 1938.* Washington, D.C., Government Printing Office, 1938, 409–30.

Anderson, Fanny J. "Medicine at Fort Detroit in the Colony of New France, 1701–1760," *Journal of the History of Medicine,* Vol. I, No. 2 (April, 1946), 208–28.

Andrews, Edmund. "The Aboriginal Physicians of Michigan," *Contributions to Medical Research Dedicated to Victor Clarence Vaughan.* Ann Arbor, George Wahr, 1903, 42–50.

Andros, F. "The Medicine and Surgery of the Winnebago and Dakota Indians," *Journal of the American Medical Association,* Vol. I, No. 4 (August 4, 1883), 116–18; No. 13 (October 6, 1883), 402.

Baegert, Jakob. "An Account of the Aboriginal Inhabitants of the Californian Peninsula," Tr. by Charles Rau. *Annual Report, Smithsonian Institution, 1863–64.* Washington, Government Printing Office, 1864–65. (Reprint, 1869.)

Barkley, W. W. "Drug Collecting and Cultivation in Mississippi," *Journal of the American Pharmaceutical Association,* Vol. XXV, No. 12 (December, 1936), 1156–59.

Barron, Frank, *et al.* "The Hallucinogenic Drugs," *Scientific American,* Vol. CCX, No. 4 (April, 1964), 29–37.

Barton, Benjamin Smith. "An Account of the Most Effectual Means of Preventing the Deleterious Consequences of the Bite of the *Crotalus Horridus,* Or Rattle-Snake," *Transactions of the American Philosophical Society,* O.S., Vol III (1793), 100–14.

———. "A Botanical Description of the *Podophyllum Diphyllum* of Linnaeus . . . ," *Transactions of the American Philosophical Society,* O.S., Vol. III (1793), 334–47.

Bartram, Isaac. "A Memoir of the Distillation of Persimons," *Trans-*

actions of the American Philosophical Society, O.S., Vol. I, 2d ed. corrected (1789), 301–304.

Battle, Herbert. "The Domestic Use of Oil among the Southern Aborigines," *American Anthropologist*, N.S., Vol. XXIV (1922), 171–82.

Beauchamp, W[illiam] M. "The Good Hunter and Iroquois Medicine," *Journal of American Folk-Lore*, Vol. XIV (1901), 153–59.

———. "The Onondaga Flora," in Frederick Pursh, *Journal of a Botanical Excursion* . . . . Syracuse, Dehler Press, 1923, 81–110.

———. "Onondaga Plant Names," *Journal of American Folk-Lore*, Vol. XV, No. 17 (April–June, 1902), 91–103.

Beck, Carl W., and William P. Mulvaney. "Apatitic Urinary Calculi from Early American Indians," *Journal of the American Medical Association*, Vol. CXCV, No. 12, (March 21, 1966), 168–69.

Bergen, Fanny D. "Popular American Plant Names." Pt. I: *Journal of American Folk-Lore*, Vol. VII, No. 25 (April–June, 1894), 89–104; Pt. IV: *Journal of American Folk-Lore*, Vol. IX, No. 34 (July–September, 1896), 179–93.

———. "Some Customs and Beliefs of the Winnebago Indians," *Journal of American Folk-Lore*, Vol. IX, No. 32 (January–March, 1896), 51–54.

Boas, Franz. "Current Beliefs of the Kwakiutl Indians," *Journal of American Folk-Lore*, Vol. XLV, No. 176 (April–June, 1932), 177–260.

Bourke, John G. "Distillation by Early American Indians," *American Anthropologist*, O.S., Vol. VII (1894), 297–302.

———. "The Medicine-Men of the Apache," *Ninth Annual Report of the Bureau of American Ethnology, 1887–88*. Washington, D.C., Government Printing Office, 1892, 451–603.

———. "Popular Medicine, Customs, and Superstitions of the Rio Grande," *Journal of American Folk-Lore*, Vol. VII, No. 25 (April–June, 1894), 119–46.

Bradley, Will T. "Medical Practices of the New England Aborigines," *Journal of the American Pharmaceutical Association*, Vol. XXV, No. 2 (February, 1936), 138–47.

Brooks, Harlow. "The Medicine of the American Indian," *Bulletin of the New York Academy of Medicine*, 2d ser., Vol. V, No. 6 (June, 1929), 509–37.

———. "The Medicine of the American Indian," *Journal of Labora-*

tory and Clinical Medicine, Vol. XIX, No. 1 (October, 1933), 1–23.

Browne, C. A. "The Chemical Industries of the American Aborigines," *Isis*, Vol. XXIII (1935), 406–24.

Browne, John Mason. "Indian Medicine." Reprint from *Atlantic Monthly*, July, 1866, in W. W. Beach, *Indian Miscellany*. Albany, J. Munsell, 1877, 74–85.

Carlson, G. A., and V. H. Jones. "Some Notes on Uses of Plants by the Comanche Indians," *Papers of the Michigan Academy of Sciences, Arts and Letters*, Vol. XXV, 1939. Ann Arbor, University of Michigan Press, 1940.

Castiglioni, Arturo, M.D. "Herbs from Antiquity to the Renaissance,"*Ciba Symposia*, Vol. V, Nos. 5–6 (August–September, 1943), 1541–52.

———. "Herbs in the Medicine of Eastern Peoples and of the American Indians," *Ciba Symposia*, Vol. V, Nos. 5–6 (August–September, 1943), 1536–40.

———. "Magic Plants in Primitive Medicine," *Ciba Symposia*, Vol. V, Nos. 5–6 (August–September, 1943), 1522–35.

———. "Tobacco in Europe," *Ciba Symposia*, Vol. IV, Nos. 11–12 (February–March, 1943), 1436–56.

———. "The Use of Tobacco among the American Indians," *Ciba Symposia*, Vol. IV, Nos. 11–12 (February–March, 1943), 1426–35.

Chamberlain, Alexander F. "Algonkian Words in American English . . . ," *Journal of American Folk-Lore*, Vol. XV, No. 19 (October–December, 1902), 240–67.

———. "Contributions of the American Indian to Civilization," *Proceedings, American Antiquarian Society*, N.S., Vol. XVI (October, 1903–October, 1904). Worcester, Mass., 1905. 91 ff.

———. "Kootenay Medicine Men," *Journal of American Folk-Lore*, Vol. XIV (1901), 95–99.

———. "Memorials of the Indian," *Journal of American Folk-Lore*, Vol. XV, No. 17 (April–June, 1902), 107–16.

Chamberlain, Lucy Sarah. "Plants Used by the Indians of Eastern North America," *American Naturalist*, Vol. XXXV, No. 409 (January, 1901), 1–10.

Chamberlin, Ralph V. "Some Plant Names of the Ute Indians,"

American Anthropologist, N.S., Vol. XI, No. 1 (January–March, 1909), 27–40.

Christensen, B. V., and Elbert Voss. "The Histology of *Cracca Virginiana* Linné Root," *Journal of the American Pharmaceutical Association*, Vol. XXV, No. 6 (June, 1936), 519–23.

Clapp, A. "Report on Medical Botany . . . . A Synopsis, Or Systematic Catalogue of the Indigenous and Naturalized, Flowering and Filicoid . . . Medicinal Plants of the United States . . . ," *Transactions of the American Medical Association*, Vol. V (1852). Philadelphia, printed for the Association by T. K. and P. B. Collins, 1852, 689–906.

Clements, Forrest E. "Primitive Concepts of Disease," *University of California Publications in American Archaeology and Ethnology*, Vol. XXXII (1932), 185–252. (Abstract of Ph.D. dissertation.)

Cobb, Carolus M. "Some Medical Practices among the New England Indians and Early Settlers," reprinted from the *Boston Medical and Surgical Journal*, Vol. CLXXVII, No. 4 (July 26, 1917), 97–105.

Cohen, Felix. "Americanizing the White Man," *The American Scholar*, Vol. XXI, No. 2 (Spring, 1952), 177–91.

Collin, Nicholas. "An Essay on Those Inquiries in Natural Philosophy, Which at Present Are Most Beneficial to the United States of North America," *Transactions of the American Philosophical Society*, O.S., Vol. III (1793), iii–xxvii.

Cook, E. Fullerton. "National and International Standards for Medicines," in *Annual Report of the Board of Regents of the Smithsonian Institution for the Year Ending June 30, 1937.* Washington, D.C., Government Printing Office, 1938, 431–50.

Cowen, David L. "Colonial Laws Pertaining to Pharmacy," *Journal of the American Pharmaceutical Association*, Vol. XXIII (1934), 1236–42.

Culley, John. "The California Indians: Their Medical Practices and Their Drugs," *Journal of the American Pharmaceutical Association*, Vol. XXV, No. 4 (April, 1936), 332–39.

Darling, Dr. ———. "Indian Diseases and Remedies," *Boston Medical and Surgical Journal*, Vol. XXXIV, No. 1 (February 4, 1846), 9–11.

Davis, N. S. "Report of the Committee on Indigenous Medical Botany," *Transactions of the American Medical Association*, Vol. II (1849). Philadelphia, printed for the Association by T. K. and P. G. Collins, 1849, 663–75.

De Laszlo, Henry, and Paul Henshaw. "Plant Materials Used by Primitive Peoples to Affect Fertility," *Science*, Vol. CXIX, No. 3097 (May 7, 1954), 626–31.

Densmore, Frances. "Uses of Plants by the Chippewa Indians," *Forty-fourth Annual Report of the Bureau of American Ethnology, 1926–27*. Washington, D.C., Government Printing Office, 1928, 275–397.

Dixon, Roland B. "Some Aspects of the American Shaman," *Journal of American Folk-Lore*, Vol. XXI (1908), 1–12.

Doering, J. Frederick. "Folk Remedies for Diverse Allergies," *Journal of American Folk-Lore*, Vol. LVII, No. 224 (April–June, 1944), 140–41.

Dougherty, Peter. "Diaries of Peter Dougherty," *Journal of the Presbyterian Historical Society*, Vol. XXX, No. 4 (December, 1952), 236–53.

Douglas, William O. "The People of Cades Cove," *National Geographic Magazine*, Vol. CXXII, No. 1 (July, 1962), 60–95.

Edwards, Everett E. "American Indian Contributions to Civilization," *Minnesota History*, Vol. XV, No. 3 (September, 1934), 255–72.

Elmendorf, William W. "Soul Loss Illness in Western North America," in Sol Tax (ed.), *Indian Tribes of Aboriginal America, Selected Papers of XXIXth International Congress of Americanists*, Vol. II. Chicago, University of Chicago Press, 1952, 104–14.

"An Experience among the Red Indians," from a correspondent, *The Lancet* (London), February 27, 1904, 611–12.

Fastlicht, Samuel. "Dental Inlays and Fillings Among the Ancient Mayas," *Journal of the History of Medicine*, Vol. XVII, No. 2 (July, 1962), 393–401.

Fenton, William N. "Contacts between Iroquois Herbalism and Colonial Medicine," *Annual Report of the Board of Regents of the Smithsonian Institution for 1941*. Washington, D.C., Government Printing Office, 1942, 503–26.

Ford, Clellan S. "Control of Conception in Cross-Cultural Perspective," *Annals of the New York Academy of Sciences*, Vol. LIV (May 2, 1952), 763–68.

Fosberg, F. R. "Principal Economic Plants of Tropical America," in Frans Verdoorn, *Plants and Plant Science in Latin America*. Waltham, Mass., Chronica Botanica Co., 1945, 18–35.

G. R. "Early Observations on Indian Baths," *Ciba Symposia*, Vol. I, No. 5 (August, 1939), 163.

Gathercoal, E. N. "Proposed Changes in Monographs of Some Vegetable Drugs for the New U.S. Pharmacopoeia," *Journal of the American Pharmaceutical Association*, Vol. IX, No. 7 (July, 1920), 700–702.

Gerard, W. R. "Plant Names of Indian Origin," *Garden and Forest*, Vol. IX, Nos. 435–36, 438–40 (1896), 252–53; 262–63; 282–83; 292–93; 302–303.

Gibson, Arrell M. "Medicine Show," *The American West*, Vol. IV, No. 1 (February, 1967), 34–39, 74–79.

Gilmore, Melvin R. "Notes on Gynecology and Obstetrics of the Arikara Tribe," *Papers of the Michigan Academy of Sciences, Arts and Letters*, Vol. XIV (1930), 71–81.

———. "Uses of Plants by Indians of the Missouri River Region," *Thirty-third Annual Report of the Bureau of American Ethnology, 1911–12*. Washington, D.C., Government Printing Office, 1919, 43–154.

———. "Vegetal Remains of the Ozark Bluff-Dweller Culture," *Papers Michigan Academy of Sciences, Arts and Letters*, Vol. XIV (1930), 83–102.

Greenlee, Robert F. "Medicine and Curing Practices of the Modern Florida Seminoles," *American Anthropologist*, N.S., Vol. XLVI, No. 3 (July–September, 1944), 317–28.

Grinnell, George Bird. "Some Cheyenne Plant Medicines," *American Anthropologist*, N.S., Vol. VII, No. 1 (January–March, 1905), 37–43.

Guerra, Francisco. "Medical Almanacs of the American Colonial Period," *Journal of the History of Medicine*, Vol. XVI, No. 3 (July, 1961), 234–55.

———. "Some Bibliographers of Early Medical Americana," *Journal of the History of Medicine*, Vol. XVII, No. 1 (January, 1962), 94–115.

Gundrum, T. "*Senecio Aureus* as a Hemostatic," *Western Druggist*, Vol. XX, No. 6 (June, 1898), 307–308.

Hagar, Stansbury. "Micmac Magic and Medicine," *Journal of American Folk-Lore*, Vol. IX, No. 34 (July–September, 1896), 170–77.

Haggis, A. W. "Fundamental Errors in the Early History of Cinchona," *Bulletin of the History of Medicine*, Vol. X, No. 3 (October, 1941), 417–59; Vol. X, No. 4 (November, 1941), 568–92.

Hallowell, A. I. "The Bulbed Enema Syringe in North America," *American Anthropologist*, N.S., Vol. XXXVII (1935), 708–10.

———. "The Impact of the American Indian on American Culture," *American Anthropologist*, N.S., Vol. LIX, No. 2 (April, 1957), 201–17.

Halstead, Frank G. "A First Hand Account of a Treatment by Thomsonian Medicine in the 1830s," *Bulletin of the History of Medicine*, Vol. X (1941), 680–87.

Harlan, Richard, M.D. "Experiments Made on the Poison of the Rattle-snake; in Which the Powers of the Hieracium Venosum, As a Specific, Were Tested . . . ," in *Transactions of the American Philosophical Society*, N.S., Vol. III. Philadelphia, 1830, 300–14.

———. "Some Further Observations on the Poison of the Rattle-snake," in *Transactions of the American Philosophical Society*, N.S., Vol. III. Philadelphia, 1830, 400–402.

Heaton, Claud E., M. D. "Obstetrics in Colonial America," *Ciba Symposia*, Vol. I, No. 12 (March, 1940), 389–94.

Heizer, Robert F. "The Hopi Snake Dance, Fact and Fancy," *Ciba Symposia*, Vol. V, No. 10 (January, 1944), 1681–84.

———. "The Use of the Enema among the Aboriginal American Indians," *Ciba Symposia*, Vol. V, No. 11 (February, 1944), 1686–93.

———. "The Use of Narcotic Mushrooms by Primitive Peoples," *Ciba Symposia*, Vol. V, No. 11 (February, 1944), 1713–16.

Henshaw, Henry W. "Fallacies Respecting the Indians," *American Anthropologist*, N.S., Vol. VII, No. 1 (January–March, 1905), 104–13.

Herbert, Lester G. "What Did the Indians Know About Medicines and Healing Treatment?" *Medical Journal and Record*, Vol. CXXIII, No. 1 (January 6, 1926), 22–24; No. 2 (January 20, 1926), 117–19.

Hoffman, W[alter] J[ames]. "The Menomini Indians," in *Fourteenth Annual Report of the Bureau of American Ethnology, 1892–93*, Pt. I. Washington, D.C., Government Printing Office, 1896, 11–328.

———. "The Midē'wiwin Or 'Grand Medicine Society' of the Ojibwa," *Seventh Annual Report of the Bureau of American Ethnology, 1885–86*. Washington, D.C., Government Printing Office, 1891, 149–300.

Holcomb, R. C. "The Antiquity of Congenital Syphilis," *Bulletin of the History of Medicine*, Vol. X, No. 2 (July, 1941), 148–77.

Horine, Emmet F. "Early Medicine in Kentucky and the Mississippi Valley: A Tribute to Daniel Drake, M.D.," *Journal of the History of Medicine*, Vol. III, No. 2 (Spring, 1948), 263–78.

———. "Episodes in the History of Anesthesia," *Journal of the History of Medicine*, Vol. I, No. 4 (October, 1946), 521–26.

Hrdlička, Aleš. "Disease, Medicine and Surgery among the American Aborigines," *Journal of the American Medical Association*, Vol. XCIX, No. 20 (November 12, 1932), 1661–66.

———. "Trepanation among Prehistoric People, Especially in America," *Ciba Symposia*, Vol. I, No. 6 (September, 1939), 170–77.

Johnson, Frederick. "Notes on Micmac Shamanism," *Primitive Man*, Vol. XVI, Nos. 3–4 (July and October, 1943), 53–80.

Kempton, J. H. "Maize, Our Heritage from the Indian," *Annual Report of the Board of Regents of the Smithsonian Institution for the Year Ending June 30, 1937*. Washington, D.C., Government Printing Office, 1938, 385–408.

Krickeberg, Walter. "Blood Letting and Bloody Castigation among the American Indians," *Ciba Symposia*, Vol. I, No. 1 (April, 1939), 26–34.

———. "The Indian Sweat Bath," *Ciba Symposia*, Vol. I, No. 1 (April, 1939), 19–25.

Krogman, Wilton Marion. "Medical Practices and Diseases of the Aboriginal American Indians," *Ciba Symposia*, Vol. I, No. 1 (April, 1939), 11–18.

La Barre, Weston. "Folk Medicine and Folk Science," *Journal of American Folk-Lore*, Vol. LV (October–December, 1942), 197–203.

———. "Primitive Psychotherapy in Native American Cultures:

Peyotism and Confession," *Journal of Abnormal and Social Psychology*, Vol. XLIII, No. 3 (July, 1947), 294–309.

———. "Twenty Years of Peyote Studies," *Current Anthropology* (January, 1960), 45–60.

Landes, Ruth. "Potawatomi Medicine," *Transactions, Kansas Academy of Science*, Vol. LXVI, No. 4 (Winter, 1963), 553–99.

Large, R. G., and H. N. Brocklesby. "A Hypoglycaemic Substance from the Roots of the Devil's Club (*Fatsia Horrida*)," *Canadian Medical Association Journal*, Vol. XXX, No. 1 (July, 1938), 32–35.

Leake, Chauncey D. "Historical Notes on the Pharmacology of Anesthesia," *Journal of the History of Medicine*, Vol. I, No. 4 (October, 1946), 573–82.

Leinind, Morris C. "Colonial Epidemic Diseases," *Ciba Symposia*, Vol. I, No. 12 (March, 1940), 372–78.

Lloyd, John Uri. "Concerning Indian Medication," *Eclectic Medical Journal* (September, 1935), not paginated. (Reprint from *Eclectic Medical Journal*, September, 1908.)

———. "Copaifera Officinalis," *The Western Druggist*, Vol XX, No. 2 (February, 1898), 54–57.

———. "Historical Story of Sassafras," *The Western Druggist*, Vol. XX, No. 11 (November, 1898), 484–89.

Locke, William. "A Drug List of King Philip's War," *Badger Pharmacist*, No. 25 (February, 1939), 1–18.

Lorimer, J. Letter to Hugh Williamson, from Pensacola, West Florida, January 7, 1769, read before the American Philosophical Society, April 21, 1769. *Transactions of the American Philosophical Society*, O.S., Vol. I, the 2d ed. corrected (1789), 320–25.

Lucas, Prof. E. H. "Folk Lore and Plant Drugs," *Papers of the Michigan Academy of Sciences, Arts & Letters*, Vol. XLV (1959), Ann Arbor, University of Michigan Press, 1960, 127–36.

Mahr, August C. "Materia Medica and Therapy among the North American Forest Indians," *Ohio State Archaeological and Historical Quarterly*, Vol. LX, No. 4 (1951), 331–54.

———. "Semantic Analysis of Eighteenth-Century Delaware Indian Names for Medicinal Plants," *Ethnohistory*, Vol. II, No. 1 (Winter, 1955), 11–28.

Major, Robert Carlisle, M.D. "Aboriginal American Medicine North of Mexico," *Annals of Medical History*, N.S., Vol. X, No. 6 (November, 1938), 534–49.

Maxwell, Hu. "Indian Medicines Made from Trees," *American Forestry*, Vol. XXIV, No. 292 (April, 1918), 205–11.

Mellinger, Marie B. "Medicine Plants of the Cherokees," *Tile and Till*, Vol. LI, No. 4 (July–August, 1965), 51–53.

Mooney, James. "Indian Doctors," *Am ur-Quell* [also called *Der Urquell*] *Monatschrift Für Volkkunde*, Vol. IV, B II Hft. (Lunden, Germany, 1893), 37–39.

———. "The Sacred Formulas of the Cherokees," *Seventh Annual Report of the Bureau of American Ethnology, 1885–86*. Washington, D.C., Government Printing Office, 1891, 301–397.

Moore, John T. "The Early Days of Pharmacy in the West," *Journal of the American Pharmaceutical Association*, Vol. XXV, No. 8 (August, 1936), 705–15.

Morgan, Dr. J[ohn]. "An Essay on the Expression of Oil from Sunflower Seed," *Transactions of the American Philosophical Society*, O.S., Vol. I, 2d ed., corrected. Philadelphia, 1789, 305–309.

Mullett, Charles F. "Medical History: Some Problems and Opportunities," *Journal of the History of Medicine*, Vol. I, No. 1 (January, 1946), 189–207.

Munger, Robert S. "Guaiacum, the Holy Wood from the New World," *Journal of the History of Medicine*, Vol. IV, No. 2 (Spring, 1949), 196–229.

Nickerson, Gifford S. "Some Data on Plains and Great Basin Indian Uses of Certain Native Plants," *Tebiwa, The Journal of the Idaho State University Museum*, Vol. IX, No. 1 (1966), 45–51.

Nordenskjöld, E. "The American Indian As an Inventor," in *Sourcebook in Anthropology*. A. L. Kroeber, and T. T. Waterman, (eds.). Revised ed. New York, Harcourt Brace & Co., 1931, 489–505.

Palmer, Edward. "Plants Used by the Indians of the United States," *American Naturalist*, Vol. XII (September, 1878), 593–606; Vol. XII (October, 1878), 646–55.

Parker, Arthur C. "Secret Medicine Societies of the Seneca," *American Anthropologist*, N.S., Vol. XI, No. 2 (April–June, 1909), 161–85.

Pitcher, Zina. "Medical Knowledge of the Indians," in Henry R. Schoolcraft, . . . *Indian Tribes of the United States*, IV, 502–19.

Porcher, Francis P[eyre]. "Report on the Indigenous Medical Plants of South Carolina," *Transactions of the American Medical Association*, Vol. II (1849). Philadelphia, printed for the Association by T. K. and P. G. Collins, 1849, 677–862.

Porter, J. Hampden. "Folk-Lore of the Mountain Whites of the Alleghanies," *Journal of American Folk-Lore*, Vol. VII, No. 25 (April–June, 1894), 105–17.

Prentiss, D. W., and Francis P. Morgan. "Therapeutic Uses of Mescal Buttons (Anhalonium Lewinii)," reprint from *Therapeutic Gazette*, January, 1896.

Price, Sadie F. "Kentucky Folk-Lore," *Journal of American Folk-Lore*, Vol. XIV (1901), 30–38.

Quinan, Clarence. "The American Medicine-Man and the Asiatic Shaman: A Comparison," *Annals of Medical History*, Vol. X, No. 6 (November, 1938), 508–33.

Reagan, Albert B. "Plants Used by the Hoh and Quileute Indians," *Transactions of the Kansas Academy of Science*, Vol. XXXVII (1934), 55–70.

Richtman, W. O. "A History of the Cultivation of Medicinal Plants in the United States," *Journal of the American Pharmaceutical Association*, Vol. IX (1920), 816–18.

Rogers, Spencer L. "The Methods, Results, and Values of Shamanistic Therapy," *Ciba Symposia*, Vol. IV, No. 1 (April, 1942), 1215–24.

———. "Primitive Theories of Disease," *Ciba Symposia*, Vol. IV, No. 1 (April, 1942), 1190–1201.

———. "Shamans and Medicine Men," *Ciba Symposia*, Vol. IV, No. 1 (April, 1942), 1202–14.

Rusby, Henry H. "Beverages of Vegetable Origin," *Journal of the New York Botanical Garden*, Vol. V, No. 52 (April, 1904), 79–85.

Rush, Benjamin. "An Account of the Effects of Strammonium, Or Thorn Apple," *Transactions of the American Philosophical Society*, O.S., Vol. I, 2d ed. corrected, Philadelphia, 1789, 384–87.

———. "An Account of the late Dr. Hugh Martin's Cancer Powder, With Brief Observations on Cancers," *Transactions of the*

American Philosophical Society, O.S., Vol. II, Philadelphia, 1786, 212–17.

———. "An Account of the Sugar Maple Tree of the United States ... in a Letter to Thomas Jefferson, Esq. ... ," *Transactions of the American Philosophical Society*, O.S., Vol. III, Philadelphia, 1793, 64–81.

———. "An Enquiry into the Cause of the Increase of Bilious and Intermitting Fevers in Pennsylvania, With Hints on Preventing Them," *Transactions of the American Philosophical Society*, O.S., Vol. II, Philadelphia, 1786, 206–212.

Rydberg, P. A. "Plants Used by Ancient American Indians," *Journal of the New York Botanical Garden*, Vol. XXV, No. 295 (July, 1924), 204–205.

Safford, W. E. "Narcotic Plants and Stimulants of the Ancient Americans," *Annual Report of the Board of Regents of the Smithsonian Institution for the Year Ending June 30, 1916.* Washington, D.C., Government Printing Office, 1917. 387–424.

———. "Our Heritage from the American Indians," *Annual Report of the Board of Regents of the Smithsonian Institution for the Year Ending June 30, 1926.* Washington, D.C., Government Printing Office, 1927, 405–10.

Seward, Blanton P. "Pioneer Medicine in Virginia," *Annals of Medical History*, N.S., Vol. X, No. 1 (January, 1938), 61–70; Vol. X, No. 2 (March, 1938), 169–88.

Shuman, John W., M.D. "Southern California Medicine," *Annals of Medical History*, N.S., Vol. X, No. 3 (May, 1938), 215–36; Vol. X, No. 4 (July, 1938), 336–68.

Slotkin, J. S. "Early Eighteenth Century Documents on Peyotism North of the Rio Grande," *American Anthropologist*, N.S., Vol. LIII, No. 3 (July–September, 1951), 420–27.

Snyderman, George S. "The Case of Daniel P.: An Example of Seneca Healing," *Journal of the Washington Academy of Sciences*, Vol. XXXIX, No. 7 (July 15, 1949), 217–20.

Speck, Frank G. "Catawba Herbals and Curing Practices," *Journal of American Folk-Lore*, Vol. LVII, No. 223 (January–March, 1944), 37–50.

———. "Catawba Medicines and Curative Practices," *Publications of the Philadelphia Anthropological Society*, Vol. I. (Twenty-

Fifth Anniversary Studies, ed. by D. S. Davidson.) Philadelphia, University of Pennsylvania Press, 1937, 179–98.

———. "A List of Plant Curatives Obtained from the Houma Indians of Louisiana," *Primitive Man*, Vol. XIV, No. 4 (October, 1941), 49–73.

———. "Medicine Practices of the Northeastern Algonquians," *Proceedings of the XIXth International Congress of Americanists*. Washington, D.C., 1915 (published 1917), 303–32.

———. "Reptile Lore of the Northern Indians," *Journal of American Folk-Lore*, Vol. XXXVI (1924), 273–80.

Stevenson, Matilda Coxe. "Ethnobotany of the Zuni Indians," *Thirtieth Annual Report of the Bureau of American Ethnology, 1908–1909*. Washington, D.C., Government Printing Office, 1915, 31–102.

Stockberger, W. W. "Production of Drug-Plant Crops in the United States," *Yearbook of the United States Department of Agriculture, 1917*. Washington, D.C., Government Printing Office, 1918, 169–76.

Stone, Eric, M.D. "Medicine among the Iroquois," *Annals of Medical History*, N.S., Vol. VI, No. 6 (November, 1934), 529–39.

Swanton, John R. "Religious Beliefs and Medical Practices of the Creek Indians...," *Forty-second Annual Report of the Bureau of American Ethnology, 1924–25*. Washington, D.C., Government Printing Office, 1928, 472–672.

———. "Social and Religious Beliefs and Practices of the Chickasaw Indians," *Forty-fourth Annual Report of the Bureau of American Ethnology, 1926–27*. Washington, D.C., Government Printing Office, 1928, 169–274.

Tantaquidgeon, Gladys. "Mohegan Medicinal Practices, Weather-Lore, and Superstition," *Forty-third Annual Report of the Bureau of American Ethnology, 1925–26*. Washington, D.C., Government Printing Office, 1928, 264–79.

———. "Notes on the Origin and Uses of Plants of the Lake St. John Montagnais," *Journal of American Folk-Lore*, Vol. XLV, No. 176 (April–June, 1932), 265–67.

Toner, Joseph M. "Some Points in the Practice of Medicine Among the North American Indians, with Incidental Reference to the Antiquity of the Office of Physician," *Virginia Medical Monthly*, Vol. IV, No. 5 (August, 1877), 334–50.

True, Rodney H. "Folk Materia Medica," *Journal of American Folk-Lore*, Vol. XIV (1901), 105–14.

Urdang, George. "The American Institute of the History of Pharmacy," *Bulletin of the History of Medicine*, Vol. X, No. 5 (December, 1941), 690–700.

———. "Pharmacopoeias As Witnesses of World History," *Journal of the History of Medicine*, Vol. I, No. 1 (January, 1946), 46–70.

Viets, Henry R. "Some Features of the History of Medicine in Massachusetts During the Colonial Period, 1620–1770," *Isis*, Vol. XXIII (1935), 389–405.

Wakefield, E. G., and Samuel C. Dellinger. "Possible Reasons for Trephining the Skull in the Past," *Ciba Symposia*, Vol. I, No. 6 (September, 1939), 166–69.

Walker, Edwin F. "America's Indian Background," *Masterkey*, Vol. XIX (1945), 7–13, 83–88, 119–25.

Wallace, Anthony F. C. "Dreams and Wishes of the Soul: A Type of Psychoanalytic Theory among the Seventeenth Century Iroquois," *American Anthropologist*, N.S., Vol. LX, No. 2 (April, 1958), 234–48.

Wallis, Wilson D. "Medicines Used by the Micmac Indians," *American Anthropologist*, N.S., Vol. XXIV (1922), 24–30.

Warfield, J. Ogle. "Materia Medica of the Algonquian Indians of Virginia" (a brief summary of a paper), *American Anthropologist*, N.S., Vol. XIII (1911), 119.

Wasson, R. Gordon. "The Hallucinogenic Fungi of Mexico: An Inquiry into the Origins of the Religious Idea Among Primitive Peoples," *Botanical Museum Leaflets, Harvard University*, Vol. XIX, No. 7 (February 17, 1961), 137–62.

Weinland, J. L. "Some U.S.P. Drugs Used by Early Central American Indians," *The Purdue Pharmacist* (December 6, 1933), 6–8; (January 23, 1934), 3–8.

Whitebread, Charles. "The Indian Medical Exhibit of the Division of Medicine in the United States National Museum," Pub. 2582, *Proceedings of the United States National Museum*, Vol. LXVII, art. x. Washington, D.C., Government Printing Office, 1925, 1–26.

Will, Drake W. "The Medical and Surgical Practice of the Lewis and Clark Expedition," *Journal of the History of Medicine*, Vol. XIV, No. 3 (July, 1959), 273–97.

Williams, Stephen W. "Report on the Indigenous Medical Botany of Massachusetts," *Transactions of the American Medical Association*, Vol. II (1849). Philadelphia, printed for the Association by T. K. and P. G. Collins, 1849, 863–927.

Wilson, Charles Bundy. "Notes on Folk-Medicine," *Journal of American Folk-Lore*, Vol. XXI (1908), 68–73.

Winder, Dr. William. "On Indian Diseases and Remedies," *Boston Medical and Surgical Journal*, Vol. XXXIV, No. 1 (February 4, 1846), 10–13. Reprinted from *British-American Journal of Medical and Physical Science* (Montreal), Vol. I (1845–46), 255–57.

Wisdom, Charles. "The Supernatural World and Curing," in Sol Tax (ed.), *Heritage of Conquest*. Glencoe, Ill., The Free Press, 1952, 119–41.

Woodhouse, Henry. "Colonial Medical Practice," *Ciba Symposia*, Vol. I, No. 12 (March, 1940), 379–88.

Wrenshall, Letitia Humphreys. "Incantations and Popular Healing in Maryland and Pennsylvania," *Journal of American Folk-Lore*, Vol. XV, No. 19 (October–December, 1902), 268–74.

Wright, John S. "Indian Medicine," *School Science and Mathematics*, Vol. XLV, No. 393 (April, 1945), 329–35.

Wyman, Leland C., and Flora L. Bailey. "Two Examples of Navajo Physiotherapy," *American Anthropologist*, N.S., Vol. XLVI, No. 3 (July–September, 1944), 329–37.

Young, James Harvey. "Patent Medicines and Indians," *Emory University Quarterly*, Vol. XVII, No. 2 (1961), 86–92.

Youngken, Heber W. "Drugs of the North American Indians," *American Journal of Pharmacy*, Vol. XCVI, (July, 1924), 485–502; Vol. XCVII, (March, 1925), 158–85; (April, 1925), 257–71.

Zeisberger, David. "History of the North American Indians," Archer B. Hulbert and William N. Schwarze, eds., in *Ohio Archaeological and Historical Quarterly*, Vol. XIX, Nos. 1–2 (January and April, 1910), 12–153.

Dispensatories, Formularies, Pharmacopeias,

and Related Sources

Bache, Dr. Franklin, and Dr. George Bacon Wood. *Dispensatory of the United States*. 1st ed. Philadelphia, 1833.

[Brown, William]. *Pharmacopoeia Simpliciorum et Efficaciorum in Usum Nosocomii Militaris* . . . . Philadelphia, Styner & Cist, 1778. (Published as "The Lititz Pharmacopoeia," in *The Badger Pharmacist.* Nos. 22–25 [June–December, 1938], 1–70. Latter used.)

Coxe, John Redman. *The American Dispensatory, Containing the Operations of Pharmacy, Together With the Natural, Chemical, Pharmaceutical and Medical History of the Different Substances Employed in Medicine* . . . . 4th ed. Philadelphia, Thomas Dobson & Son, 1818.

Jackson, James, and John C. Warren. *Pharmacopoeia of the Massachusetts Medical Society.* Boston, 1808.

The National Formulary of Unofficinal Preparations. 1st issue. N.p., published by the American Pharmaceutical Association, 1888.

The National Formulary of Unofficinal Preparations. 9th ed. Washington, D.C., American Parmaceutical Association, 1950.

Osol, Arthur, and George E. Farrar, Jr. *The Dispensatory of the United States of America, 1950 Edition.* Philadelphia, J. B. Lippincott Co., 1947–50.

Pharmacopoeia Londinensis of 1618. Reproduced in facsimile with a historical introduction by George Urdang. Madison, State Historical Society of Wisconsin, 1944.

Pharmacopoeia of the New York Hospital. Published under the authority of the physicians and surgeons of that institution. New York, published by Collins & Co., 1816.

The Pharmacopoeia of the United States of America, 1820. 1st ed. By the authority of the Medical Societies and Colleges. Boston, printed by Wells and Lilly, for Charles Ewer, December, 1820.

The Pharmacopoeia of the United States of America. By the authority of the Medical Societies and Colleges. 2d ed. Boston, Charles Ewer, December, 1828.

The Pharmacopoeia of the United States of America. By authority of the National Medical Convention held at Washington, A.D. 1830. 1st ed., revised. Philadelphia, John Grigg, 1831.

The Pharmacopoeia of the United States of America. 2d decennial revision. 1st ed. revised. Philadelphia, Grigg & Elliott, 1842.

The Pharmacopoeia of the United States of America. 3d decennial revision. Officially called "1st edition revised." Philadelphia, Lippincott, Grambo, & Co., 1851.

The Pharmacopoeia of the United States of America. 4th decennial revision. By authority of the National Convention for revising the Pharmacopoeia, held at Washington, A.D. 1860. Philadelphia, J. B. Lippincott & Co., 1864.

The Pharmacopoeia of the United States of America. 5th decennial revision. By authority of the National Convention for Revising the Pharmacopoeia, held at Washington, A.D. 1870. Philadelphia, J. B. Lippincott & Co., 1873.

The Pharmacopoeia of the United States of America. 6th decennial revision. By authority of the National Convention for Revising the Pharmacopoeia, held at Washington, A.D. 1880. New York, William Wood & Co., 1883.

The Pharmacopeia of the United States of America. 14th revision. By authority of the U.S. Pharmacopoeial Convention, Inc. Easton, Pa., Mack Publishing Co., 1950.

The Pharmacopeia of the United States of America. 16th revision. Easton, Pa., Mack Publishing Co., 1960.

McGeachy, Beth. *Handbook of Florida Palms.* St. Petersburg, Fla., The Great Outdoors Publishing Co., 1955.

Muenscher, Walter Conrad. *Poisonous Plants of the United States.* New York, The Macmillan Co., 1939.

Pearsall, Gordon S. *List of the Flora and Fauna of the Forest Preserve District of Cook County.* N.p., The Forest Preserve District of Cook County, Illinois, n.d.

Peattie, Donald Culross. *Flora of the Indiana Dunes.* Chicago, Field Museum of Natural History, 1930.

Sargent, Charles Sprague. *Manual of the Trees of North America.* 2d corrected ed. 2 vols. New York, Dover Publications, 1961.

Smith, A. W. *A Gardener's Book of Plant Names.* New York, Harper and Row, 1963.

Spencer, Edwin Rollin. *Just Weeds.* New York, Charles Scribner's Sons, 1940.

Taylor, Norman J. *A Guide to the Wild Flowers East of the Mississippi and North of Virginia.* Cleveland, The World Publishing Co., 1941.

Wherry, Edgar T. *Wild Flower Guide, Northeastern and Midland United States.* New York, Doubleday & Co., Inc., & The American Garden Guild, Inc., 1948.

Bibliographical Aids

American Anthropologist, General Index, Current Anthropological Literature and Memoirs of the American Anthropological Association, 1888–1928. Compiled by Alfred Vincent Kidder *et al.* N.p., 1930.

American Philosophical Society. *List of Papers and Books in the Society's Publications Classified According to Subject.* Philadelphia, The American Philosophical Society, 1940.

Current Work in the History of Medicine, an International Bibliography. Vols. XXX–XL. London, The Wellcome Historical Medical Library, 1962–63.

Dockstader, Frederick J. *The American Indian in Graduate Studies.* New York, Museum of the American Indian, Heye Foundation, 1957.

Edwards, Everett E., and Wayne D. Rasmussen. *A Bibliography of the Agriculture of the American Indians.* U.S. Department of Agriculture, Miscellaneous Publication No. 447. Washington, D.C., Government Printing Office, 1942. (Medicinal plants, 89–96.)

Gibson, G. D. "A Bibliography of Anthropological Bibliographies: The Americas," *Current Anthropology,* Vol. I (1960), 61–75.

Index Catalogue, Library of the Surgeon-General's Office. (Surgeon-General's Catalogue.)

King, Nydia M. *A Bibliography of Paperback Books on the History of the Sciences and Health Professions, and Methods and Philosophy of History, As a Contribution to the 25th Anniversary Colloquiam on Historiography of the American Institute of the History of Pharmacy.* Madison, Wis., 1966.

Koudelka, Janet B. (ed.). "Bibliography of the History of Medicine in the United States and Canada, 1964." Reprint from *Bulletin of the History of Medicine,* Vol. XXXIX, No. 6 (November–December, 1965), 542–79.

Library of Congress. *Guide to the Study of the United States of America.* Washington, D.C., Government Printing Office, 1960.

"List of Publications of the Museum of the American Indian, Heye Foundation." 9th ed. *Indian Notes and Monographs,* No. 49. New York, Museum of the American Indian, Heye Foundation, August, 1957.

Lloyd, John Uri, Theodor Just, and Corinne Miller Simons. *Catalogue of the Pharmacopoeias, Dispensatories, Formularies and Allied Publications* [1493–1957]. Reprinted from *Lloydia*, Vol. XX, No. 1 (March, 1957), for the Lloyd Library and Museum. Cincinnati, 1957.

Meisel, Max. *A Bibliography of American Natural History, the Pioneer Century: 1769–1865.* Vol. I. New York, The Premier Publishing Co., 1924.

Murdock, George Peter. *Ethnographic Bibliography of North America.* 3d ed. New Haven, Conn., Human Relations Area Files, 1960.

National Library of Medicine. *Early American Medical Imprints, a Guide to Works Printed in the United States, 1668–1820.* By Robert B. Austin. Washington, D.C., U.S. Department of Health, Education and Welfare, Public Health Service, 1961.

Quarterly Cumulative Index Medicus. (Index Medicus.)

Rouse, Irving, and John M. Goggin. *An Anthropological Bibliography of the Eastern Seaboard.* (Eastern States Archaeological Federation, Research Publication I.) New Haven, Conn., published by the Federation at the Yale Peabody Museum, 1947.

Sonnedecker, Glenn, *et al. Some Bibliographic Aids for Historical Writers in Pharmacy.* Madison, American Institute of the History of Pharmacy, 1958. (Mimeographed.)

Sonnedecker, Glenn, J. Hampton Hoch, and Wolfgang Schneider. *Some Pharmaco-Historical Guidelines to the Literature.* Madison, American Institute of the History of Pharmacy, 1959.

Stimson, Anna Katharine. "Contributions toward a Bibliography of the Medicinal Use of Plants by the Indians of the United States of America." Unpublished Master's thesis, Department of Anthropology, University of Pennsylvania, 1946.

Sturtevant, William C. *Bibliography on American Indian Medicine and Health.* Washington, D.C., Bureau of American Ethnology, March, 1962. (Mimeographed.)

Thwaites, Reuben Gold (ed.). *Jesuit Relations and Allied Documents.* Vol. LXXI: *Bibliography.* 75 vols.; Cleveland, The Burrows Bros. Co., 1896–1901.

Wycoff, Edith. "Bibliography Relating to Botany, Exclusive of Floras," *Bibliographical Contributions from the Lloyd Li-*

brary, Vol. II, Nos. 1–12. Cincinnati, Lloyd Library of Botany, Pharmacy and Materia Medica, 1911–17.

———. "Floras of North America and the West Indies," *Bibliographical Contributions from the Lloyd Library*, Vol. I, No. 9, Sec. R, 355–47. Cincinnati, Lloyd Library of Botany, Pharmacy and Materia Medica, 1911–17.

Reference Books and Guides to

Information Sources

Blackiston's New Gould Medical Dictionary. Ed. by Normand L. Hoerr and Arthur Osol. 2d ed. New York, Blackiston Division, McGraw Hill Book Co., Inc., 1956.

Dorland, W. A. Newman. *The American Illustrated Medical Dictionary*. 18th ed. Philadelphia, W. B. Saunders Co., 1940.

Eli Lilly & Company. *Catalog*. January 4, 1965. And supplement, "Botanical Synonyms."

Fernald, Merritt L. *Gray's Manual of Botany*. 8th edn., New York, American Book Co., 1950.

Gathercoal, E. N. *Check List of Native and Introduced Drug Plants in the United States*. With the collaboration of H. W. Youngken. Prepared under the auspices of the Committee on Pharmaceutical Botany and Pharmacognosy of the Division of Biology and Agriculture of the National Research Council. Chicago, 1942.

Hocking, George MacDonald. *A Dictionary of Terms in Pharmacognosy, and Other Divisions of Economic Botany*. Springfield, Ill., Charles C. Thomas, publisher, 1955.

Library of Congress, National Referral Center for Science and Technology. *A Directory of Information Resources in the United States: Social Sciences*. Washington, D.C., October, 1965.

Library of Congress, Reference Division. *The Rare Book Division: A Guide to Its Collections and Services*. Washington, D.C., 1965.

Mathews, Mitford M. (ed.). *A Dictionary of Americanisms*. 2 vols. Chicago, University of Chicago Press, 1951.

Index of
Botanical
Names

NOTE

Some of the sources used for this book were written more than three hundred years ago, before scientific plant classification began, and others were written very recently. For this reason, and also because pharmaceutical names frequently differ from botanical names, the text reflects the involved evolution of plant nomenclature. In citing sources, we necessarily render their botanical names as given, whether still current or not. In listing USP or NF drugs, we ordinarily give the name recognized at the time of official listing. In many instances, the changes in particular names have been traced in the text, but it was not our purpose or within our competence to pursue this task exhaustively. Moreover, it was considered unwise to clutter the text with lengthy synonymy. However, the index is designed to match, wherever possible, the current names with those given in the text.

Where two or more scientific names are given for the same species, the one which is preferred in the latest standard references is marked with an asterisk (*), and older synonyms and names no longer current are marked with a dagger (†). A dagger following an unpaired scientific name signifies that the name is not listed in the references used—which are primarily the manuals of Gray and Sargent, with supplements for certain regions and classes of plants. A dagger following a generic name indicates either that several species are described under the listing or that the specific name is not known. A dagger following a common name signifies that the species cannot be identified, either because several species bear the same common name—and too little distinguishing information was given in the source—or because the term is no longer used and is not readily traceable.

Since this book is intended for the general reader, the preferred listing in the index is by common name, but the scientific name is cross-referenced for the benefit of specialists. Italic page numbers indicate where the principal treatment, if any, may be found for each plant.

Rhus copallina L. (Dwarf or Mountain
sumach): 377, 460n.
Rhus glabra L. (Smooth sumach): 376–
78
Rhus radicans L.: see Poison ivy
Rhus toxicodendron L.: see Poison oak
Rhus trilobata Nutt.† (R. aromatica Ait.
var. serotina*), Fragrant sumach: 377
Rhus typhina L. (Staghorn sumach):
376–78
Robinia: see Black locust
Rock rose (Helianthemum canadense
[L.] Michx.): 358
Rosemary (Rosmarinus officinalis†): 243
Rubber: see Hevea spp.
Rubus allegheniensis Porter (High bush
blackberry): 282
Rubus canadensis L. (Low blackberry or
Dewberry): 282
Rubus idaeus L. (Red raspberry):
357–58
Rubus occidentalis L. (Black raspberry):
357
Rubus parviflorus Nutt. (Thimble-
berry): 282
Rubus strigosus Michx.† (var. of R.
idaeus L.*), Red raspberry: 357–58
Rubus villosus Ait.† (R. flagellaris
Willd.*), Blackberry: 282
Rudbeckia fulgida Ait. (Coneflower):
102n.
Rue†: 59
Rue (Ruta graveolens L.): 244, 413
Rumex brittanica L.† (R. orbiculatus
Gray*), Water dock: 398
Rumex crispus L.: see Yellow dock
Rumex hymenosepalus Torr.†
(Canaigre root): 398
Rumex mexicana† (R. mexicanus
Meisn.*): 398
Rumex obtusifolius L. (Bitter dock):
397–98
Rumex spp.: 397–98; see also Yellow
dock and Yerba Colorado
Rumex verticillatus L.* (R. floribus†),
Swamp or Water dock: 397–98
Rushes†: 107
Ruta graveolens L.: 244, 413

Sabal spp.: see Saw palmetto
Sabbatia†: 128; see also American
centaury

Sabina, Savin (Cedar, or Juniper): 290
Saffron or Safflower, American or Indian
(Carthamus tinctorius L.): 358–59
Sagackhomi (Indian name for Bear-
berry): 280
Sage or Sagebrush†: 59, 128, 133, 135,
186, 359, 396; see also under Artemisia
and Salvia spp.
Saguaro or Sahuaro (Cereus giganteus?),
Giant cactus: 170, 215
Saint Andrew's cross (Ascyrum hyperi-
coides L.): 101
Saint John's wort† (Hypericum spp.):
91, 357
Salix alba L. (White willow): 393
Salix discolor Muhl. (Large pussy
willow): 393
Salix fragilis L. (Crack willow): 393
Salix humilis L.† (S. humilis Marsh.*),
Small pussy willow: 393
Salix longipes Sh.† (S. caroliniana
Michx.*): 393
Salix lucida Muhl. (Red or Shining
willow): 393
Salix nigra Marsh. (Black willow): 393
Salix pedicellaris Pursh (Bog willow):
393
Salix spp. (Willows): 393; see also
Willow
Salix tristis† (Red root): 55n.
Salvia lyrata L. (Sage, Cancer weed): 359
Salvia officinalis L. (Sage): 359
Sambucus canadensis L. (Elder): 50,
301–302
Sambucus nigra L. (Elderberry, Eur.):
302
Sand puff (Abronia fragrans†): 201
Sanguinaria canadensis L.: see Puccoon
Sanicle†: 128
Sanicle, American, or Black snakeroot
(Sanicula marilandica L.): 368; see
also cohosh, black, and Snakeroot,
black
Sanicle, Canadian†: 62
Sanicula marilandica L.: 212
Sap pine†: 107, 216, 346; see also Pine
Saponaria: 413
Sarracenia purpurea L. (Pitcher plant):
95
Sarsaparilla, of Latin America (Smilax
spp.): 76, 359, 413

Sarsaparilla (unspecified): 11, 44, 59, 62, 72, 169, 296, *359–61*
Sarsaparilla, Wild or American (*Aralia nudicaulis* L.): 91–92, 128, *359–61*, 413
"Sarvas tree" (Serviceberry, *Amelanchier* spp.?): 107
Sassafras (*Sassafras officinalis* Nees & Ebermaier, and var. *albidum* Blake): 7, 37–39, 42, 44, 48, 52–53, 57–59, 62, 73, 76, 85, 92, 97–98, 107, 127–28, 130, 140–41, 168–69, 175, 205, 209, 216, 289, 299, *361–65*, 388
Saw palmetto (*Serenoa repens* [Bart.] Small†, *S. serrulata* [Michx.] Hook f.†, *Sabal serrulatum* [Roem & Schult.]†): 103n., *365–66*
Scabiosa succisa† (Devil's bit [Loskiel]): 283
Scammony†: 91
Scarlet root†: 55
Scutellaria galericulata L.† (*S. epilobiifolia* Hamilton*): 367
Scutellaria lateriflora L. (Mad dog skullcap): 102n., 235, *366–67*
Scutellaria parvula Michx. (Small skullcap): 367
Sea algae†: 187
Sea-rod†: 73
Seneca snakeroot: *see* Snakeroot, Seneca
Senecio aureus L.: *see* Squaw weed
Senecio smallii Britt.: 375
Senna, adventive (*Cassia angustifolia* Vahl.): 91, 366
Senna, American (*Cassia marilandica* L.): 102n., 361, 366
Serenoa spp.: *see* Saw palmetto
Seven-barks (*Hydrangea*): 103n., *318–19*
Shellbark walnut (Hickory): 107
Shinleaf: 394
Silphium†: 104, 248
Simaruba amara, S. officinalis: 202, 413
Sisymbrium canescens Nutt.† (*Descurainia pinnata* [Walt.] Britt.*), Hedge mustard, Tansy mustard: 342
Skullcap, mad dog: *see Scutellaria lateriflora*
Skullcap, small: *see Scutellaria parvula*
Skunk cabbage (*Symplocarpus foetidus* [L.] Nutt.): 135, 207, 315, 351, *367–68*
Small bedstraw (*Galium trifidum* L.): 219

Smilacina racemosa (L.) Desf. (False spikenard): *374–75*
Smilacina stellata (L.) Desf. (False Solomon's seal): 244
Smilax†: 91
Smilax aristolochiaefolia Miller, *et al.* spp. (Sarsaparilla, Latin American): 413
Smilax bona-nox L.: *see* China brier
Smilax glauca Walt. (Bramble brier, Saw brier, Wild sarsaparilla): 235, 366
Smilax tamnoides L.: *see* China root
Snakeroot, general: 38, 51, 56–57, 59, 73, 87, 91, 97–99, 117, 220, 322, 333; confused nomenclature, 368–69; species of, *368–74*
Snakeroot, black (*Cimicifuga racemosa* [L.] Nutt.): 59, 133, 291, 368, 370; *see also Sanicula marilandica*
Snakeroot, button (*Eryngium yuccifolium* Michx. and *E. aquaticum* L.): 103, 368, 371; *see also Liatris pycnostachya*
Snakeroot, Canada: *see* Wild ginger
Snakeroot, corn, unidentified: 133
Snakeroot, fern, unidentified: 101, 221
Snakeroot, Sampson's (*Psoralea psoralioides* [Walt.] Cory, or *Gentiana catesbaei* Walt.): 307, 368, 431n.
Snakeroot, Seneca (*Polygala senega* L.): 38, 48–50, 69–70, 101, 107, 133, 135, 221, 292, *371–73*
Snakeroot, Texas (*Aristolochia reticulata* Nutt.): 374
Snakeroot, Virginia, or White (*Aristolochia serpentaria* L.): 33, 57, 62, 102n., 107, 128, 133, 368, *373–74*, 391
Snakeroot, white, unidentified: 368
Snakeweed†: 220
Sneezeweed (*Helenium microcephalum*†): 236
Soap bark: 413
Solanum carolinense L. (Horse nettle): 103n., *342*
Solanum nigrum L. (Black nightshade): 342
Solidago nemoralis Ait. (Goldenrod): *312–13*
Solidago odora Ait. (Sweet scented goldenrod): 313
Solidago rigida L. (Stiff goldenrod): 217

Index

571